200 Best Jobs for Renewing America

Part of JIST's Best Jobs® Series

Laurence Shatkin, Ph.D., and The Editors @ JIST

Also in JIST's **Best Jobs** Series

- Best Jobs for the 21st Century
- 50 Best Jobs for Your Personality
- 50 Best College Majors for a Secure Future
- 200 Best Jobs for College Graduates
- 300 Best Jobs Without a Four-Year Degree
- 200 Best Jobs Through Apprenticeships
- 40 Best Fields for Your Career
- 225 Best Jobs for Baby Boomers
- 250 Best-Paying Jobs

- 150 Best Jobs for Your Skills
- 150 Best Jobs Through Military Training
- 175 Best Jobs Not Behind a Desk
- 150 Best Jobs for a Better World
- 10 Best College Majors for Your Personality
- 200 Best Jobs for Introverts
- 150 Best Low-Stress Jobs
- 150 Best Recession-Proof Jobs

JIST Works
America's Career Publisher®

200 Best Jobs for Renewing America

© 2010 by JIST Publishing

Published by JIST Works, an imprint of JIST Publishing
7321 Shadeland Station, Suite 200
Indianapolis, Indiana 46256-3923

Phone: 800-648-JIST   Fax: 877-454-7839
E-mail: info@jist.com   Web site: www.jist.com

Some Other Books by the Authors

Laurence Shatkin

Great Jobs in the President's Stimulus Plan
Quick Guide to College Majors and Careers
90-Minute College Major Matcher
Your $100,000 Career Plan
New Guide for Occupational Exploration
150 Best Recession-Proof Jobs

The Editors at JIST

EZ Occupational Outlook Handbook
Salary Facts Handbook
Enhanced Occupational Outlook Handbook
Guide to America's Federal Jobs
Health-Care CareerVision Book and DVD

Quantity discounts are available for JIST products. Please call 800-648-JIST or visit www.jist.com for a free catalog and more information.

Visit www.jist.com for information on JIST, free job search information, tables of contents and sample pages, and ordering information on our many products.

Acquisitions Editor: Susan Pines
Development Editor: Stephanie Koutek
Cover and Interior Designer: Aleata Halbig
Cover Illustration: Design Pics, Fotosearch
Interior Layout: Aleata Halbig
Proofreaders: Linda Seifert, Jeanne Clark
Indexer: Cheryl Lenser

Printed in the United States of America

14 13 12 11 10 09   9 8 7 6 5 4 3 2 1

Library of Congress Cataloging-in-Publication Data
Shatkin, Laurence.
  200 best jobs for renewing America / Laurence Shatkin and the editors at JIST.
     p. cm. -- (JIST's best jobs series)
  ISBN 978-1-59357-727-8 (alk. paper)
  Includes index.
  1. Occupations--United States. 2. Vocational guidance--United States. 3. Sustainable development--United
States. 4. Manpower policy--United States. I. JIST Works, Inc. II. Title. III. Title: Two hundred best jobs for
renewing America.
  HF5382.5.U5S4635 2009
  331.7020973--dc22
                              2009029868

ISBN 978-1-59357-727-8

This Is a Big Book, But It Is Very Easy to Use

America is reinventing itself. In order to succeed in the 21st century, we're working to improve education, expand health care, fix the infrastructure, overhaul our manufacturing industries, adopt green technologies, and continue our leadership in high-tech innovation.

All of these exciting developments will create job openings. Why shouldn't one of them be yours? Whether you're starting your career or planning a career change, you'll want to learn how the national renewal can mean a rewarding job for you.

The 200 jobs in this book are expected to grow as the economy shifts toward industries that will be competitive in the decades ahead. The jobs are selected for and ordered on 200 lists that emphasize those with the highest earnings and the highest demand for workers. Specialized lists arrange these jobs by the level of education required, by personality types, and by characteristics of the people who work in them.

Every job on the lists is described in detail later in the book, so you can explore the jobs that interest you most. For each job, you'll learn the earnings, important work tasks, skills, educational and training programs, fastest-growing industries, personality types, and many other informative facts.

You'll also find an analysis of how America is reshaping its economy and why this will affect certain industries and jobs more than others.

Using this book, you'll be surprised how quickly you'll get new ideas for careers that are good bets in the evolving economy and can suit you in many other ways.

When you are done with this book, pass it along or tell someone else about it. We wish you well in your career and in your life.

Credits and Acknowledgments: While the authors created this book, it is based on the work of many others. The occupational information is based on data obtained from the U.S. Department of Labor and the U.S. Census Bureau. These sources provide the most authoritative occupational information available. The job titles and their related descriptions are from the O*NET database, which was developed by researchers and developers under the direction of the U.S. Department of Labor. They, in turn, were assisted by thousands of employers who provided details on the nature of work in the many thousands of job samplings used in the database's development. We used the most recent version of the O*NET database, release 13.0. We appreciate and thank the staff of the U.S. Department of Labor for their efforts and expertise in providing such a rich source of data.

Table of Contents

Summary of Major Sections

Introduction. A short overview to help you better understand and use the book. *Starts on page 1.*

Part I: Renewing a Nation. Explains the major trends that are reshaping the American economy. Describes six major industries that are being renewed and identifies the most important jobs in those industries. *Starts on page 15.*

Part II: The Best Jobs Lists: Jobs in Each of the Six Renewal Industries. Very useful for exploring career options! For each renewal industry, you can see the jobs with the best combination of earnings, job growth, and job openings. You can also see lists that classify the jobs according to education and training required; personality types; and several other features, such as those with the highest percentage of women and of men and jobs with high rates of self-employment and many part-time workers. Although there are a lot of lists, they are easy to understand because they have clear titles and are organized into groupings of related lists. *Starts on page 45.*

Part III: Descriptions of the Best Jobs for Renewing America. Provides descriptions of the 200 jobs that will grow as America's economy is reinvented. Each description contains information on earnings, projected growth, job duties, skills, education and training required, related knowledge and courses, major industries, and many other details. The descriptions are presented in alphabetical order, so you can easily look up a job that you've identified in a list from Part II and that you want to learn more about. *Starts on page 175.*

Appendix A: Definitions of Skills Used in Job Descriptions. Defines the skills used in the Part III job descriptions. *Starts on page 415.*

Appendix B: Definitions of Knowledges/Courses Used in Job Descriptions. Defines the knowledges/courses used in the Part III job descriptions. *Starts on page 417.*

Appendix C: Definitions of Career Clusters Used in Job Descriptions. Lists the career clusters used in the Part III job descriptions. *Starts on page 421.*

Detailed Table of Contents

Part I: Renewing a Nation **15**
Why Renewal Is Necessary 15
The Foundations of Success in the World
   Market 16
Signs of Renewal in America 17
Education 18
   Current State of the Field 18
   Initiatives to Renew Education 19
   Education Jobs Likely to Benefit from
      Renewal Plans 20
Infrastructure 21
   Current State of the Field 22
   Initiatives to Renew the Infrastructure 23
   Infrastructure Jobs Likely to Benefit from
      Renewal Plans 24
Health Care 26
   Current State of the Field 26
   Initiatives to Renew Health Care 27
   Health-Care Jobs Likely to Benefit from
      Renewal Plans 28
Information and Telecommunication
   Technologies 29
   Current State of the Field 29
   Initiatives to Renew the Information and
      Telecommunication Technologies 31
   Information and Telecommunication
      Technologies Jobs Likely to Benefit from
      Renewal Plans 31
Green Technologies 32
   Current State of the Field 33
   Initiatives to Renew Green Technologies 34
   Green Technologies Jobs Likely to Benefit from
      Renewal Plans 35
Advanced Manufacturing 37
   Current State of the Field 37
   Initiatives to Renew Advanced
      Manufacturing 40
   Advanced Manufacturing Jobs Likely to
      Benefit from Renewal Plans 41

Part II: The Best Jobs Lists: Jobs in Each of the Six Renewal Industries 45

Best Jobs Overall in Each Renewal Industry: Jobs with the Highest Pay, Fastest Growth, and Most Openings 46

The 40 Best Advanced Manufacturing Jobs 46

The 50 Best Education Jobs 48

The 50 Best Green Technologies Jobs 49

The 50 Best Health-Care Jobs 51

The 20 Best Information and Telecommunication Technologies Jobs 53

The 50 Best Infrastructure Jobs 53

The 20 Best-Paying Advanced Manufacturing Jobs 55

The 20 Best-Paying Education Jobs 56

The 20 Best-Paying Green Technologies Jobs 57

The 20 Best-Paying Health-Care Jobs 57

The 20 Best-Paying Information and Telecommunication Technologies Jobs 58

The 20 Best-Paying Infrastructure Jobs 59

The 20 Fastest-Growing Advanced Manufacturing Jobs 60

The 20 Fastest-Growing Education Jobs 60

The 20 Fastest-Growing Green Technologies Jobs 61

The 20 Fastest-Growing Health-Care Jobs 62

The 20 Fastest-Growing Information and Telecommunication Technologies Jobs 62

The 20 Fastest-Growing Infrastructure Jobs 63

The 20 Advanced Manufacturing Jobs with the Most Openings 64

The 20 Education Jobs with the Most Openings 65

The 20 Green Technologies Jobs with the Most Openings 65

The 20 Health-Care Jobs with the Most Openings 66

The 20 Information and Telecommunication Technologies Jobs with the Most Openings 67

The 20 Infrastructure Jobs with the Most Openings 67

Best Jobs Lists for Each Renewal Industry by Demographic 68

Advanced Manufacturing Jobs with the Highest Percentage of Workers Age 16–24 69

Best Advanced Manufacturing Jobs Overall Employing 8 Percent or More Workers Age 16–24 70

Education Jobs with the Highest Percentage of Workers Age 16–24 71

Best Education Jobs Overall Employing 8 Percent or More Workers Age 16–24 71

Green Technologies Jobs with the Highest Percentage of Workers Age 16–24 72

Best Green Technologies Jobs Overall Employing 8 Percent or More Workers Age 16–24 73

Health-Care Jobs with the Highest Percentage of Workers Age 16–24 74

Best Health-Care Jobs Overall Employing 8 Percent or More Workers Age 16–24 74

Information and Telecommunication Technologies Jobs with the Highest Percentage of Workers Age 16–24 75

Best Information and Telecommunication Technologies Jobs Overall Employing 8 Percent or More Workers Age 16–24 75

Infrastructure Jobs with the Highest Percentage of Workers Age 16–24 76

Best Infrastructure Jobs Overall Employing 8 Percent or More Workers Age 16–24 76

Advanced Manufacturing Jobs with the Highest Percentage of Workers Age 55 and Over 78

Best Advanced Manufacturing Jobs Overall Employing 15 Percent or More Workers Age 55 and Over 79

Education Jobs with the Highest Percentage of Workers Age 55 and Over 80

Best Education Jobs Overall Employing 15 Percent or More Workers Age 55 and Over 81

Green Technologies Jobs with the Highest Percentage of Workers Age 55 and Over 81

Best Green Technologies Jobs Overall Employing 15 Percent or More Workers Age 55 and Over 82

Health-Care Jobs with the Highest Percentage of Workers Age 55 and Over 83

Best Health-Care Jobs Overall Employing 15 Percent or More Workers Age 55 and Over 85

Information and Telecommunication Technologies Jobs with the Highest Percentage of Workers Age 55 and Over 86

Best Information and Telecommunication Technologies Jobs Overall Employing 15 Percent or More Workers Age 55 and Over 86

Infrastructure Jobs with the Highest Percentage of Workers Age 55 and Over 87

Best Infrastructure Jobs Overall Employing 15 Percent or More Workers Age 55 and Over 88

Advanced Manufacturing Jobs with the Highest Percentage of Part-Time Workers 89

Best Advanced Manufacturing Jobs Overall Employing 15 Percent or More Part-Time Workers 90

Education Jobs with the Highest Percentage of Part-Time Workers 90

Best Education Jobs Overall Employing 15 Percent or More Part-Time Workers 91

Green Technologies Jobs with the Highest Percentage of Part-Time Workers 92

Best Green Technologies Jobs Overall Employing 15 Percent or More Part-Time Workers 93

Health-Care Jobs with the Highest Percentage of Part-Time Workers 93

Best Health-Care Jobs Overall Employing 15 Percent or More Part-Time Workers 94

Information and Telecommunication Technologies Jobs with the Highest Percentage of Part-Time Workers 95

Best Information and Telecommunication Technologies Jobs Overall Employing 15 Percent or More Part-Time Workers 95

Infrastructure Jobs with the Highest Percentage of Part-Time Workers 95

Best Infrastructure Jobs Overall Employing 15 Percent or More Part-Time Workers 96

Advanced Manufacturing Jobs with the Highest Percentage of Self-Employed Workers 97

Best Advanced Manufacturing Jobs Overall with 8 Percent or More Self-Employed Workers 97

Education Jobs with the Highest Percentage of Self-Employed Workers 97

Best Education Jobs Overall with 8 Percent or More Self-Employed Workers 97

Green Technologies Jobs with the Highest Percentage of Self-Employed Workers 98

Best Green Technologies Jobs Overall with 8 Percent or More Self-Employed Workers 98

Health-Care Jobs with the Highest Percentage of Self-Employed Workers 99

Best Health-Care Jobs Overall with 8 Percent or More Self-Employed Workers 99

Information and Telecommunication Technologies Jobs with the Highest Percentage of Self-Employed Workers 100

Best Information and Telecommunication Technologies Jobs Overall with 8 Percent or More Self-Employed Workers 100

Infrastructure Jobs with the Highest Percentage of Self-Employed Workers 100

Best Infrastructure Jobs Overall with 8 Percent or More Self-Employed Workers 101

Advanced Manufacturing Jobs with the Highest Percentage of Men 103

Best Advanced Manufacturing Jobs Overall Employing 70 Percent or More Men 104

Education Jobs with the Highest Percentage of Women 105

Best Education Jobs Overall Employing 70 Percent or More Women 105

Green Technologies Jobs with the Highest Percentage of Men 105

Best Green Technologies Jobs Overall Employing 70 Percent or More Men 107

Health-Care Jobs with the Highest Percentage of Women 108

Best Health-Care Jobs Overall Employing 70 Percent or More Women 108

Health-Care Jobs with the Highest Percentage of Men 109

Best Health-Care Jobs Overall Employing 70 Percent or More Men 110

Information and Telecommunication Technologies Jobs with the Highest Percentage of Men 110

Best Information and Telecommunication Technologies Jobs Overall Employing 70 Percent or More Men 110

Infrastructure Jobs with the Highest Percentage of Men 111

Best Infrastructure Jobs Overall Employing 70 Percent or More Men 113

Advanced Manufacturing Jobs with the Highest Percentage of Urban Workers 114

Best Advanced Manufacturing Jobs Overall Employing 50 Percent or More Urban Workers 115

Advanced Manufacturing Jobs with the Highest Percentage of Rural Workers 116

Best Advanced Manufacturing Jobs Overall Employing 10 Percent or More Rural Workers 117

Education Jobs with the Highest Percentage of Urban Workers 117

Best Education Jobs Overall Employing 50 Percent or More Urban Workers 118

Education Jobs with the Highest Percentage of Rural Workers 118

Best Education Jobs Overall Employing 10 Percent or More Rural Workers 118

Green Technologies Jobs with the Highest Percentage of Urban Workers 119

Best Green Technologies Jobs Overall Employing 50 Percent or More Urban Workers 120

Green Technologies Jobs with the Highest Percentage of Rural Workers 121

Best Green Technologies Jobs Overall Employing 10 Percent or More Rural Workers 122

Health-Care Jobs with the Highest Percentage of Urban Workers 123

Best Health-Care Jobs Overall Employing 50 Percent or More Urban Workers 123

Health-Care Jobs with the Highest Percentage of Rural Workers 124

Best Health-Care Jobs Overall Employing 10 Percent or More Rural Workers 125

Information and Telecommunication Technology Jobs with the Highest Percentage of Urban Workers 126

Best Information and Telecommunication Technologies Jobs Overall Employing 50 Percent or More Urban Workers 127

Information and Telecommunication Technologies Jobs with the Highest Percentage of Rural Workers 128

Best Information and Telecommunication Technologies Jobs Overall Employing 10 Percent or More Rural Workers 128

Infrastructure Jobs with the Highest Percentage of Urban Workers 128

Best Infrastructure Jobs Overall Employing 50 Percent or More Urban Workers 129

Infrastructure Jobs with the Highest Percentage of Rural Workers 130

Best Infrastructure Jobs Overall Employing 10 Percent or More Rural Workers 131

The Best Jobs in Each Renewal Industry Sorted by Education or Training Required 131

The Education Levels 132

Another Warning About the Data 133

Best Advanced Manufacturing Jobs Requiring Short-Term On-the-Job Training 134

Best Advanced Manufacturing Jobs Requiring Moderate-Term On-the-Job Training 134

Best Advanced Manufacturing Jobs Requiring Long-Term On-the-Job Training 134

Best Advanced Manufacturing Jobs Requiring Work Experience in a Related Occupation 135

Best Advanced Manufacturing Jobs Requiring Postsecondary Vocational Training 135

Best Advanced Manufacturing Jobs Requiring an Associate Degree 135

Best Advanced Manufacturing Jobs Requiring a Bachelor's Degree 135

Best Advanced Manufacturing Jobs Requiring Work Experience Plus Degree 136

Best Education Jobs Requiring Work Experience in a Related Occupation 136

Best Education Jobs Requiring Postsecondary Vocational Training 136

Best Education Jobs Requiring a Bachelor's Degree 137

Best Education Jobs Requiring Requiring Work Experience Plus Degree 137

Best Education Jobs Requiring a Master's Degree 137

Best Education Jobs Requiring a Doctoral Degree 137

Best Education Jobs Requiring a First Professional Degree 139

Best Green Technologies Jobs Requiring Short-Term On-the-Job Training 139

Best Green Technologies Jobs Requiring Moderate-Term On-the-Job Training 139

Best Green Technologies Jobs Requiring Long-Term On-the-Job Training 139

Best Green Technologies Jobs Requiring Work Experience in a Related Occupation 140

Best Green Technologies Jobs Requiring Postsecondary Vocational Training 140

Best Green Technologies Jobs Requiring an Associate Degree 141

Best Green Technologies Jobs Requiring a Bachelor's Degree 141

Best Green Technologies Jobs Requiring Work Experience Plus Degree 141

Best Green Technologies Jobs Requiring a Master's Degree 141

Best Health-Care Jobs Requiring Short-Term On-the-Job Training 142

Best Health-Care Jobs Requiring Moderate-Term On-the-Job Training 142

Best Health-Care Jobs Requiring Postsecondary Vocational Training 142

Best Health-Care Jobs Requiring an Associate Degree 143

Best Health-Care Jobs Requiring a Bachelor's Degree 143

Best Health-Care Jobs Requiring Work Experience Plus Degree 143

Best Health-Care Jobs Requiring a Master's Degree 144

Best Health-Care Jobs Requiring a Doctoral Degree 144

Best Health-Care Jobs Requiring a First Professional Degree 144

Best Information and Telecommunication Technologies Jobs Requiring Work Experience in a Related Occupation 145

Best Information and Telecommunication Technologies Jobs Requiring an Associate Degree 145

Best Information and Telecommunication Technologies Jobs Requiring a Bachelor's Degree 145

Best Information and Telecommunication Technologies Jobs Requiring Work Experience Plus Degree 146

Best Information and Telecommunication Technologies Jobs Requiring a Doctoral Degree 146

Best Infrastructure Jobs Requiring Short-Term On-the-Job Training 146

Best Infrastructure Jobs Requiring Moderate-Term On-the-Job Training 146

Best Infrastructure Jobs Requiring Long-Term On-the-Job Training 147

Best Infrastructure Jobs Requiring Work Experience in a Related Occupation 147

Best Infrastructure Jobs Requiring Postsecondary Vocational Training 148

Best Infrastructure Jobs Requiring an Associate Degree 148

Best Infrastructure Jobs Requiring a Bachelor's Degree 148

Best Infrastructure Jobs Requiring Work Experience Plus Degree 149

Best Infrastructure Jobs Requiring a Master's Degree 149

The Best Jobs for Each Renewal Industry Sorted by Personality Types 149

Descriptions of the Six Personality Types 149

Best Advanced Manufacturing Jobs for People with a Realistic Personality Type 150

Best Green Technologies Jobs for People with a Realistic Personality Type 151

Best Health-Care Jobs for People with a Realistic Personality Type 152

Best Information and Telecommunication Technologies Jobs for People with a Realistic Personality Type 152

Best Infrastructure Jobs for People with a Realistic Personality Type 152

Best Advanced Manufacturing Jobs for People with an Investigative Personality Type 153

Best Education Jobs for People with an Investigative Personality Type 154

Best Green Technologies Jobs for People with an Investigative Personality Type 154

Best Health-Care Jobs for People with an Investigative Personality Type 154

Best Information and Telecommunication Technologies Jobs for People with an Investigative Personality Type 155

Best Infrastructure Jobs for People with an Investigative Personality Type 155

Best Advanced Manufacturing Jobs for People with an Artistic Personality Type 156

Best Information and Telecommunication Technologies Jobs for People with an Artistic Personality Type 156

Best Infrastructure Jobs for People with an Artistic Personality Type 156

Best Education Jobs for People with a Social Personality Type 157

Best Health-Care Jobs for People with a Social Personality Type 158

Best Advanced Manufacturing Jobs for People with an Enterprising Personality Type 159

Best Education Jobs for People with an Enterprising Personality Type 159

Best Green Technologies Jobs for People with an Enterprising Personality Type 160

Best Health-Care Jobs for People with an Enterprising Personality Type 160

Best Information and Telecommunication Technologies Jobs for People with an Enterprising Personality Type 160

Best Infrastructure Jobs for People with an Enterprising Personality Type 160

Best Advanced Manufacturing Jobs for People with a Conventional Personality Type 161

Best Green Technologies Jobs for People with a Conventional Personality Type 161

Best Health-Care Jobs for People with a Conventional Personality Type 161

Best Information and Telecommunication Technologies Jobs for People with a Conventional Personality Type 161

Best Infrastructure Jobs for People with a Conventional Personality Type 162

Bonus Lists: Best Jobs Overall in All Renewal Industries 162

The 50 Best Jobs Overall in All Renewal Industries 162

The 50 Best-Paying Jobs in All Renewal Industries 164

The 50 Fastest-Growing Jobs in All Renewal Industries 165

The 50 Jobs with the Most Openings in All Renewal Industries 167

Bonus Lists: Metropolitan Areas with the Highest Concentration of the Best Renewal Jobs 168

Metropolitan Areas with the Highest Concentration of Workers in Advanced Manufacturing 169

Metropolitan Areas with the Highest Concentration of Workers in Education 170

Metropolitan Areas with the Highest Concentration of Workers in Green Technologies 171

Metropolitan Areas with the Highest Concentration of Workers in Health Care 172

Metropolitan Areas with the Highest Concentration of Workers in Information and Telecommunication Technologies 172

Metropolitan Areas with the Highest Concentration of Workers in Infrastructure .. 173

Part III: Descriptions of the Best Jobs for Renewing America **175**

Agricultural Sciences Teachers, Postsecondary .. 177

Aircraft Structure, Surfaces, Rigging, and Systems Assemblers 178

Anesthesiologists 179

Anthropology and Archeology Teachers, Postsecondary 180

Architects, Except Landscape and Naval 181

Architectural and Civil Drafters 181

Architectural Drafters 182

Architecture Teachers, Postsecondary 183

Area, Ethnic, and Cultural Studies Teachers, Postsecondary 184

Art, Drama, and Music Teachers, Postsecondary 185

Atmospheric, Earth, Marine, and Space Sciences Teachers, Postsecondary 186

Biological Science Teachers, Postsecondary 187

Biological Technicians 188

Bus Drivers, Transit and Intercity 189

Business Teachers, Postsecondary 190

Cardiovascular Technologists and Technicians 191

Carpenters 192

Cartographers and Photogrammetrists 192

Cement Masons and Concrete Finishers 193

Chemical Engineers 194

Chemistry Teachers, Postsecondary 195

Chemists 196

Child, Family, and School Social Workers 197

Chiropractors 198

Civil Drafters 199

Civil Engineering Technicians 200

Civil Engineers 201

Clinical Psychologists 202

Clinical, Counseling, and School Psychologists 203

Commercial and Industrial Designers 203

Communications Teachers, Postsecondary 204

Computer and Information Scientists, Research 205

Computer and Information Systems Managers 206

Computer Hardware Engineers 207

Computer Science Teachers, Postsecondary 208

Computer Security Specialists 210

Computer Software Engineers, Applications 211

Computer Software Engineers, Systems Software 212

Computer Specialists, All Other 214

Computer Support Specialists 214

Computer Systems Analysts 215

Computer Systems Engineers/Architects 216

Construction and Building Inspectors 218

Construction Carpenters 219

Construction Laborers 220

Construction Managers 221

Cost Estimators 222

Counseling Psychologists 223

Criminal Justice and Law Enforcement Teachers, Postsecondary 224

Database Administrators 225

Dental Assistants 226

Dental Hygienists 227

Dentists, General 228

Diagnostic Medical Sonographers 229

Dietitians and Nutritionists 230

Drywall and Ceiling Tile Installers 231

Economics Teachers, Postsecondary 232

Education Administrators, Elementary and Secondary School 233

Education Administrators, Postsecondary 234

Education Administrators, Preschool and Child Care Center/Program 235

Education Teachers, Postsecondary 236

Educational, Vocational, and School Counselors 237

Electrical and Electronic Engineering Technicians 238

Electrical and Electronics Drafters 238

Electrical and Electronics Repairers, Commercial and Industrial Equipment 238

Electrical Drafters 240

Electrical Engineering Technicians 241

Electrical Engineers 242

Electrical Power-Line Installers and Repairers 243

Electricians 244

Electronic Drafters 245

Electronics Engineering Technicians 246

Electronics Engineers, Except Computer 247

Elementary School Teachers, Except Special Education 248

Elevator Installers and Repairers 249

Emergency Medical Technicians and Paramedics 250

Engineering Managers 251

Engineering Teachers, Postsecondary 252

English Language and Literature Teachers, Postsecondary 253

Environmental Engineering Technicians 254

Environmental Engineers 255

Environmental Science and Protection Technicians, Including Health 257

Environmental Science Teachers, Postsecondary 258

Environmental Scientists and Specialists, Including Health 259

Family and General Practitioners 260

Fire-Prevention and Protection Engineers 261

First-Line Supervisors/Managers of Construction Trades and Extraction Workers 262

First-Line Supervisors/Managers of Mechanics, Installers, and Repairers 263

First-Line Supervisors/Managers of Production and Operating Workers 264

Foreign Language and Literature Teachers, Postsecondary 265

Forestry and Conservation Science Teachers, Postsecondary 266

Geography Teachers, Postsecondary 267

Geological and Petroleum Technicians 268

Geological Sample Test Technicians 268

Geophysical Data Technicians 269

Geoscientists, Except Hydrologists and Geographers 269

Glaziers 271

Graduate Teaching Assistants 272

Graphic Designers 273

Hazardous Materials Removal Workers 274

Health and Safety Engineers, Except Mining Safety Engineers and Inspectors 275

Health Educators 275

Health Specialties Teachers, Postsecondary 276

Heating, Air Conditioning, and Refrigeration Mechanics and Installers 277

Helpers—Brickmasons, Blockmasons, Stonemasons, and Tile and Marble Setters ... 278

Helpers—Carpenters 279

Helpers—Installation, Maintenance, and Repair Workers 280

Helpers—Pipelayers, Plumbers, Pipefitters, and Steamfitters 281

Highway Maintenance Workers 282

History Teachers, Postsecondary 283

Home Economics Teachers, Postsecondary 284

Hydrologists 285

Industrial Engineering Technicians 286

Industrial Engineers 287

Industrial Machinery Mechanics 288

Industrial Production Managers 289

Industrial Safety and Health Engineers 290

Industrial Truck and Tractor Operators 291

Inspectors, Testers, Sorters, Samplers, and Weighers 292

Instructional Coodinators 293

Insulation Workers, Mechanical 294

Internists, General.............................. 295
Kindergarten Teachers, Except Special
    Education.................................... 296
Laborers and Freight, Stock, and Material
    Movers, Hand................................ 297
Law Teachers, Postsecondary................. 298
Library Science Teachers, Postsecondary.......... 299
Licensed Practical and Licensed Vocational
    Nurses 300
Logisticians 301
Machinists 302
Maintenance and Repair Workers, General.... 304
Maintenance Workers, Machinery................. 305
Mapping Technicians......................... 306
Marriage and Family Therapists 307
Massage Therapists........................... 308
Mathematical Science Teachers,
    Postsecondary............................... 309
Mechanical Drafters........................... 310
Mechanical Engineering Technicians.......... 311
Mechanical Engineers........................ 312
Medical and Clinical Laboratory
    Technicians.................................. 313
Medical and Clinical Laboratory
    Technologists................................ 314
Medical and Health Services Managers 315
Medical and Public Health Social Workers.......316
Medical Assistants 317
Medical Records and Health Information
    Technicians.................................. 318
Medical Scientists, Except Epidemiologists...... 319
Medical Transcriptionists...................... 320
Mental Health and Substance Abuse Social
    Workers 321
Mental Health Counselors 322
Middle School Teachers, Except Special and
    Vocational Education 323
Millwrights 324
Mining and Geological Engineers, Including
    Mining Safety Engineers..................... 325
Mobile Heavy Equipment Mechanics, Except
    Engines...................................... 326
Multi-Media Artists and Animators.............. 327

Network and Computer Systems
    Administrators............................... 329
Network Designers 330
Network Systems and Data Communications
    Analysts 331
Nuclear Engineers 333
Nuclear Medicine Technologists 334
Nursing Aides, Orderlies, and Attendants 335
Nursing Instructors and Teachers,
    Postsecondary............................... 336
Obstetricians and Gynecologists................ 337
Occupational Health and Safety Specialists..... 338
Occupational Therapist Assistants.............. 339
Occupational Therapists........................ 340
Operating Engineers and Other Construction
    Equipment Operators........................ 341
Optometrists.................................. 342
Oral and Maxillofacial Surgeons................ 343
Orthodontists 344
Orthotists and Prosthetists.................... 345
Painters, Construction and Maintenance 346
Painters, Transportation Equipment 347
Pediatricians, General......................... 348
Petroleum Engineers 349
Pharmacists................................... 350
Pharmacy Technicians......................... 351
Philosophy and Religion Teachers,
    Postsecondary............................... 352
Physical Therapist Aides....................... 353
Physical Therapist Assistants................... 354
Physical Therapists............................ 355
Physician Assistants 356
Physicians and Surgeons 357
Physics Teachers, Postsecondary 357
Pipe Fitters and Steamfitters................... 358
Pipelayers..................................... 359
Plumbers...................................... 360
Plumbers, Pipefitters, and Steamfitters.......... 361
Podiatrists.................................... 361
Political Science Teachers, Postsecondary 362
Preschool Teachers, Except Special Education.. 363
Production, Planning, and Expediting
    Clerks....................................... 364

Prosthodontists 365
Psychiatrists 366
Psychology Teachers, Postsecondary 367
Purchasing Agents, Except Wholesale, Retail,
    and Farm Products 368
Purchasing Managers 369
Radiation Therapists 370
Radiologic Technicians 371
Radiologic Technologists 372
Radiologic Technologists and Technicians 373
Recreation and Fitness Studies Teachers,
    Postsecondary 373
Refuse and Recyclable Material Collectors 374
Registered Nurses 375
Rehabilitation Counselors 376
Respiratory Therapists 377
Roofers 379
Rough Carpenters 380
Sales Engineers 381
Sales Representatives, Wholesale and
    Manufacturing, Technical and Scientific
    Products 382
School Psychologists 383
Self-Enrichment Education Teachers 384
Sheet Metal Workers 385
Shipping, Receiving, and Traffic Clerks 386
Social Work Teachers, Postsecondary 387
Sociology Teachers, Postsecondary 388
Software Quality Assurance Engineers and
    Testers 389
Solderers and Brazers 390
Special Education Teachers, Preschool,
    Kindergarten, and Elementary School 391
Speech-Language Pathologists 392
Storage and Distribution Managers 393
Structural Iron and Steel Workers 395
Substance Abuse and Behavioral Disorder
    Counselors 396
Surgeons 397
Surgical Technologists 398
Surveying and Mapping Technicians 399
Surveying Technicians 399

Surveyors 400
Team Assemblers 401
Technical Writers 401
Telecommunications Equipment Installers
    and Repairers, Except Line Installers 402
Telecommunications Line Installers and
    Repairers 404
Transportation Managers 405
Transportation, Storage, and Distribution
    Managers 406
Truck Drivers, Heavy and Tractor-Trailer 406
Truck Drivers, Light or Delivery Services 407
Urban and Regional Planners 408
Vocational Education Teachers,
    Postsecondary 409
Web Administrators 410
Web Developers 411
Welders, Cutters, and Welder Fitters 412
Welders, Cutters, Solderers, and Brazers 413
Appendix A: Definitions of Skills Used in Job
    Descriptions 415
Appendix B: Definitions of Knowledges/
    Courses Used in Job Descriptions 417
Appendix C: Definitions of Career Clusters
    Used in Job Descriptions 421
Index 425

Introduction

Not everybody will want to read this introduction. You may want to skip this background information and go directly to Part I, which discusses why and how America is undergoing renewal, or to Part II, which lists the best renewal jobs.

But if you want to understand how (and why) we put this book together, where the information comes from, and what makes a job "best," this introduction can answer many questions.

How This Book Can Help You in the Renewed Economy

America is now entering a time of renewal. Daunting challenges have forced us to rethink our longstanding ways of doing business and providing services. Now we are transitioning to an economy built on new assumptions and, in doing so, we are discovering great opportunities for becoming a more productive and competitive economic force in the global marketplace. These opportunities translate into job opportunities for you.

This book will help you identify the jobs that are likely to offer the best economic opportunities as America rebuilds. The book focuses on six fast-growing industries and the jobs within those industries with good pay and a need for workers.

When you choose a career and prepare for it, you want some assurances that you will be able to find work in the career. One way to improve your chances is to focus on jobs that are expected to grow and take on many new workers. It also helps to focus on an *industry* with good potential for jobs. You are likely to change jobs several times over the course of your career, but you're less likely to change industries, so it helps to aim for an industry with a bright future.

This book does not cover all jobs and industries with good outlooks. Instead, it concentrates on six industries and the related jobs that are at the center of America's shift toward a forward-looking economy. A lot of innovative and exciting work will be done in these fields. Why not get in on the ground floor?

Where the Information Came From

The information we used in creating the job lists in Part II and the job descriptions in Part III came mostly from databases created by the U.S. Department of Labor:

 ❋ We started with Career Voyages, a Web site that is a collaboration between the Departments of Labor and Education. It is designed to provide information about in-demand occupations, the skills and education needed to attain those jobs, and the industries that will provide employment for those jobs. We largely followed the job-to-industry matches of Career Voyages, although we collapsed some of the 14 specific Career Voyages industries to create six large industries that were key parts of the 2009 economic recovery legislation and budget plans of the Obama administration.

 ❋ We obtained detailed economic data about the jobs from the Bureau of Labor Statistics (BLS). Figures on earnings, job growth, and job openings are reported under a classifying system called Standard Occupational Classification (SOC), which organizes the U.S. workforce into approximately 800 job titles. Some other information reported under SOC titles includes figures on the number of part-time and self-employed workers in each job, on the level of education required, and on sensitivity to recession.

 ❋ To obtain additional information about jobs, we linked the SOC job titles to titles in the O*NET (Occupational Information Network) database, which is now the primary source of detailed information on occupations. The Labor Department updates O*NET regularly, and we used the most recent version available: O*NET release 13. Data from O*NET allowed us to determine the personality types associated with jobs, as well as the important skills, types of knowledge, work tasks, and work conditions. Because O*NET uses a slightly different set of job titles than SOC, we had to match similar titles. In a few cases, we could not obtain data about each of these topics for every occupation. Nevertheless, the information we report here is the most reliable data we could obtain.

 ❋ We used the Classification of Instructional Programs, a system developed by the U.S. Department of Education, to cross-reference the education or training programs related to each job.

Of course, information in a database format can be boring and even confusing, so we did many things to help make the data useful and present it to you in a form that is easy to understand.

How the Best Jobs for Renewing America Were Selected

The Career Voyages Web site (www.careervoyages.gov) was originally based on a program of the George W. Bush administration called the President's High-Growth Job Training Initiative. This program was intended to prepare workers to take advantage of new and increasing job opportunities in high-growth, high-demand, and economically vital sectors of the American economy. As part of this program, the Department of Labor identified 14 high-growth industry sectors and the occupations linked to them.

As explained in the previous section, we collapsed several of these 14 industries to highlight six large industrial groups that we found the Obama administration was encouraging through their policy statements and budget documents. For example, we collapsed Construction and Transportation into one industry called **Infrastructure**. We created a category called **Green Technologies** that draws on several of the Career Voyages industries, especially Energy and Biotechnology. We expanded on Information Technology to create an industry called **Information and Telecommunication Technologies**. Three industries in the book are essentially the same as they are described at the Career Voyages site: **Advanced Manufacturing**, **Education**, and **Health Care**.

It is important to understand that many—even most—of the jobs that are being created in these six major industries are jobs that are found in almost *all* industries—for example, accountants, administrative assistants, janitors, clerks, and security guards. However, to keep the focus of this book on the *new* opportunities that are emerging, we followed the practice of the Career Voyages site and limited this book to the occupations that are *specifically identified with the six renewal industries*. That's why, although Green Technologies companies will employ many accountants, you won't find the occupation Accountants in this book. You will, however, find Glaziers (who are needed to install heat-efficient windows), Geophysical Data Technicians (who are needed to identify promising sites for geothermal energy), and Urban and Regional Planners (who are needed to design public transportation networks). It's true that many Glaziers install heat-inefficient windows, many Geophysical Data Technicians help find coal or other dirty fuels, and many Urban and Regional Planners are more concerned with revitalization of slums than with efficient transportation. Nevertheless, these occupations and the others we include in this book have the potential to help shift our nation's economy toward green technologies, improved health care, a modern infrastructure, and the other trends that are the focus of this book.

Therefore, to choose the 200 renewal jobs for this book, we followed this procedure:

1. We started with a list of 295 O*NET jobs linked to the six major industries covered in the book, largely based on the Career Voyages classifications. We were also influenced by some lists of "green jobs" in publications of industry and research groups, such as the American Solar Energy Society and the Political Economy Research Institute at the University of Massachusetts. Some of the jobs were linked to more than one industry. All 295 jobs had the full range of noneconomic information—work tasks, skills, and work conditions—needed for a reasonably complete description in this book.

2. To obtain economic information about the jobs, we identified 269 unique SOC job titles that are equivalents of the 295 O*NET jobs and that we would use to create our best jobs lists. (As part of this process, we collapsed 6 similar medical jobs into one called Physicians and Surgeons.) For each SOC job, we obtained earnings figures and projections for growth and job openings from BLS databases.

3. Next, we eliminated 4 SOC jobs with annual median earnings of less than $20,270, which is the earnings level that exceeds that of the lowest 25 percent of wage-earners. Although some of these jobs may employ many workers, their low pay makes them unlikely to be of interest to the readers of this book. We also eliminated 2 jobs that cannot be considered best jobs because they are expected to employ fewer than 500 workers per year and to shrink rather than grow in

workforce size; they offer little job opportunity. The list at this point included 263 unique jobs. Infrastructure was the industry with the most job titles, 79; Information and Telecommunication Technologies was the industry with the fewest job titles, 27.

4. For each industry, we ranked the related jobs three times, based on these major criteria: median annual earnings, projected growth through 2016, and number of job openings projected per year through 2016.

5. We then added the three numerical rankings for each job to calculate its overall score within the industry.

6. To emphasize jobs that tend to pay more, are likely to grow more rapidly, and have more job openings, for each industry we selected a subset of job titles with the best total overall scores. As before, the number of jobs remaining for each industry varied: For four industries, we narrowed down the list to the best 50; for Advanced Manufacturing, the best 40; for Information and Telecommunication Technologies, the best 20. The total number of unique jobs was 203. Rounded down just a little, this figure provided the number for the title of this book.

For example, the Infrastructure job with the best combined score for earnings, growth, and number of job openings is Construction Managers, so this job is listed first even though it is not the best-paying Infrastructure job (which is Engineering Managers), the fastest-growing Infrastructure job (which is Environmental Science and Protection Technicians, Including Health), or the Infrastructure job with the most openings (which is Truck Drivers, Heavy and Tractor-Trailer).

Why This Book Has More Than 200 Job Descriptions

We didn't think you would mind that this book actually provides information on more than 200 jobs. We combined several O*NET jobs to create the SOC-based lists in Part II, as mentioned earlier, but in Part III we describe these O*NET jobs separately. This means that although we used 203 unique job titles to construct the lists, Part III actually has a total of 226 job descriptions.

Understand the Limits of the Data in This Book

In this book, we used the most reliable and up-to-date information available on earnings, projected growth, number of openings, and other topics. The earnings data came from the U.S. Department of Labor's Bureau of Labor Statistics. As you look at the figures, keep in mind that they are estimates. They give you a general idea about the number of workers employed, annual earnings, rate of job growth, and annual job openings.

Understand that a problem with such data is that it describes an average. Just as there is no precisely average person, there is no such thing as a statistically average example of a particular job. We say this because data, while helpful, can also be misleading.

Take, for example, the yearly earnings information in this book. This is highly reliable data obtained from a very large U.S. working population sample by the Bureau of Labor Statistics. It tells us the average annual pay received as of May 2007 by people in various job titles (actually, it is the median annual pay, which means that half earned more and half less).

This sounds great, except that half of all people in that occupation earned less than that amount. For example, people who are new to the occupation or with only a few years of work experience often earn much less than the median amount. People who live in rural areas or who work for smaller employers typically earn less than those who do similar work in cities (where the cost of living is higher) or for bigger employers. People in certain areas of the country earn less than those in others. Other factors also influence how much you are likely to earn in a given job in your area. For example, dentists in the New York metropolitan area earn an average of $125,880 per year, whereas dentists in four metropolitan areas in North Carolina earn an average of more than $137,050 per year. Although the cost of living tends to be higher in the New York area, North Carolina has only one dentistry school, and therefore dentists there experience less competition for patients and can command higher fees. So you can see that many factors can cause earnings to vary widely.

Beginning wages also vary greatly, depending not only on location and size of employer, but also on what skills and educational credentials a new hire brings to the job.

Also keep in mind that the figures for job growth and number of openings are projections by labor economists—their best guesses about what we can expect between now and 2016. The same is true for the information about recession sensitivity of jobs. They are not guarantees. A catastrophic economic downturn, war, or technological breakthrough could change the actual outcome.

Finally, don't forget that the job market consists of both job openings and job *seekers*. The figures on job growth and openings don't tell you how many people will be competing with you to be hired. The Department of Labor does not publish figures on the supply of job candidates, so we are unable to provide a number that tells how much competition you can expect. Competition is an important issue that you should research for any tentative career goal. The *Occupational Outlook Handbook* provides informative statements for many occupations, and in the job descriptions in Part III you'll find information extracted from these statements (called "Other Considerations for Job Outlook"). You also should speak to people who educate or train tomorrow's workers; they probably have a good idea of how many graduates find rewarding employment and how quickly. People in the workforce can provide additional insights into this issue. Use your critical thinking skills to evaluate what people tell you. For example, educators or trainers may be trying to recruit you, whereas people in the workforce may be trying to discourage you from competing. Get a variety of opinions to balance out possible biases.

So, in reviewing the information in this book, please understand the limitations of the data. You need to use common sense in career decision making as in most other things in life. We hope that, by using that approach, you find the information helpful and interesting.

The Data Complexities

For those of you who like details, we present some of the complexities inherent in our sources of information and what we did to make sense of them here. You don't need to know this to use the book, so jump to the next section of the Introduction if you are bored with details.

We selected the jobs largely on the basis of economic data, and we include information on earnings, projected growth, and number of job openings for each job throughout this book.

Earnings

The employment security agency of each state gathers information on earnings for various jobs and forwards it to the U.S. Bureau of Labor Statistics. This information is organized in standardized ways by a BLS program called Occupational Employment Statistics (OES). To keep the earnings for the various jobs and regions comparable, the OES screens out certain types of earnings and includes others, so the OES earnings we use in this book represent straight-time gross pay exclusive of premium pay. More specifically, the OES earnings include the job's base rate; cost-of-living allowances; guaranteed pay; hazardous-duty pay; incentive pay, including commissions and production bonuses; on-call pay; and tips. They do not include back pay, jury duty pay, overtime pay, severance pay, shift differentials, nonproduction bonuses, or tuition reimbursements. Also, self-employed workers are not included in the estimates, and they can be a significant segment in certain occupations.

For each job, we report three facts related to earnings:

⚜ The Annual Earnings figure shows the median earnings (half earn more, half earn less).

⚜ The Beginning Wage figure shows the 10th percentile earnings (the figure that exceeds the earnings of the lowest 10 percent of the workers). This is a rough approximation of what a beginning worker may be offered.

⚜ The Earnings Growth Potential statement represents the gap between the 10th percentile and the median. This information answers the question, "If I started at the beginning wage and then got a raise that took me up to the median, how much of a pay boost (in percentage terms) would that be?" If this would be a big boost, the job has great potential for increasing your earnings as you gain experience and skills. If the boost would be small, you probably will need to move on to another occupation to improve your earnings substantially. Because a percentage figure, by itself, might be hard to hard to interpret, we put the figure in parentheses and precede it with an easy-to-understand verbal tag that expresses the Earnings Growth Potential: "very low" when the percentage is less than 25 percent, "low" for 25–35 percent, "medium" for 35–40 percent, "high" for 40–50 percent, and "very high" for any figure higher than 50 percent. For the highest-paying jobs, those for which BLS reports the median earnings as "more than $145,600," we are unable to calculate a figure for Earnings Growth Potential. About one-third of the jobs in this book have high earnings growth potential; another one-third have medium earnings growth potential.

The median earnings for all workers in all occupations were $31,410 in May 2007. The 200 jobs in this book were chosen partly on the basis of good earnings, so their average is a respectable $46,593.

(This is a weighted average, which means that jobs with larger workforces are given greater weight in the computation. It also is based on the assumption that a job with income reported as "more than $145,600" pays exactly $145,600, so the actual average is slightly higher.)

The beginning (that is, 10th percentile) wage for all occupations in May 2007 was $16,060. For the 200 renewal jobs, the weighted average is an impressive $29,279.

The earnings data from the OES survey is reported under the Standard Occupational Classification (SOC) system. As discussed earlier, these are the job titles we use in the lists in Part II, but in Part III we cross-reference these titles to O*NET job titles so that we can provide O*NET-derived information on many useful topics. In some cases, an SOC title cross-references to more than one O*NET job title. For example, the SOC title Electrical and Electronic Engineering Technicians, which we use in Part II, is linked to two jobs described in Part III: Electrical Engineering Technicians and Electronic Engineering Technicians. Because earnings data is available only for the combined job title Electrical and Electronic Engineering Technicians, in Part III you will find the same earnings figure, $52,140, reported for both kinds of technicians. In reality, there probably is a difference between what the two kinds of technicians earn, but this is the best information available.

Projected Growth and Number of Job Openings

This information comes from the Office of Occupational Statistics and Employment Projections, a program within the Bureau of Labor Statistics that develops information about projected trends in the nation's labor market for the next 10 years. As mentioned earlier, the most recent projections available cover the years 2006 to 2016. The projections are based on information about people moving into and out of occupations. The BLS uses data from various sources in projecting the growth and number of openings for each job title; some data comes from the Census Bureau's Current Population Survey and some comes from an OES survey. In making the projections, the BLS economists assume that there will be no major war, depression, or other economic upheaval. They do assume that recessions may occur, in keeping with the business cycles we have experienced for several decades, but because the projections cover 10 years, they are intended to provide an average of both the good times and the bad times.

Like the earnings figures, the figures on projected growth and job openings are reported according to the SOC classification, so again you will find that some of the SOC jobs that we use in Part II are linked to more than one O*NET job in Part III. To continue the example we used earlier, the BLS reports growth (3.6 percent) and openings (12,583) for one SOC occupation called Electrical and Electronic Engineering Technicians, but in Part III of this book we report these figures separately for the O*NET occupations Electrical Engineering Technicians and Electronic Engineering Technicians. In Part III, when you see that both of these occupations have the same 3.6 percent projected growth and the same 12,583 projected job openings, you should realize that the 3.6 percent rate of projected growth represents the *average* of these two occupations—one may actually experience higher growth than the other—and that these two occupations will *share* the 12,583 projected openings.

While salary figures are fairly straightforward, you may not know what to make of job-growth figures. For example, is a projected growth of 15 percent good or bad? Keep in mind that the average (mean) growth projected for all occupations by the Bureau of Labor Statistics is 10.4 percent. One-quarter of the SOC occupations have a growth projection of 3.2 percent or lower. Growth of 11.6 percent is the median, meaning that half of the occupations have more, half less. Only one-quarter of the occupations have growth projected at more than 17.4 percent.

Because the jobs in this book were selected as "best" partly on the basis of job growth, their mean growth is 13.1 percent, which compares favorably to the mean for all jobs. Among these 200 jobs, the job ranked 37th by projected growth has a figure of 23.0 percent, the job ranked 75th (the median) has a projected growth of 22.5 percent, and the job ranked 112th has a projected growth of 13.6 percent.

The average number of annual job openings for the 200 renewal jobs is slightly lower than the average for all occupations. The BLS projects an average of about 35,000 job openings per year for the 750 occupations that it studies, but for the 150 occupations included in this book, the average is about 31,000 openings. The job ranked 37th for job openings has a figure of about 38,000 annual openings, the job ranked 75th (the median) has about 16,000 openings projected, and the job ranked 112th has about 8,000 openings projected.

However, keep in mind that figures for job openings depend on how the BLS defines an occupation. Consider the occupation Clinical, Counseling, and School Psychologists, which employs a workforce of more than 150,000 people and is expected to provide more than 8,000 job openings each year. The BLS regards this as one (SOC) occupation when it reports figures for earnings and job projections, but O*NET divides it into three separate occupations: School Psychologists, Clinical Psychologists, and Counseling Psychologists. If the BLS employment-projection tables were to list these as three separate occupations and divide the 8,000 openings among them, the average number of openings for all occupations would be smaller. So it follows that because the way the BLS defines occupations is somewhat arbitrary, any "average" figure for job openings is also somewhat arbitrary.

Perhaps you're wondering why we present figures on both job growth *and* number of openings. Aren't these two ways of saying the same thing? Actually, you need to know both. Consider the occupation Hydrologists, which is projected to grow at the outstanding rate of 24.3 percent. There should be lots of opportunities in such a fast-growing job, right? Not exactly. This is a tiny occupation, with only about 8,000 people currently employed, so although it is growing rapidly, it will not create many new jobs (about 900 per year). Now consider Team Assemblers. Because many low-tech manufacturing jobs are being offshored, this occupation is almost standing still, with a growth rate of 0.1 percent. Nevertheless, this is a huge occupation that employs more than one million workers, so although its growth rate is insignificant, it is expected to take on more than 264,000 new workers each year as existing workers retire, die, or move on to other jobs. That's why we base our selection of the best jobs on both of these economic indicators and why you should pay attention to both when you scan our lists of best jobs.

Job Security

The recession that began in 2008 has been unusually severe. (As this book goes to press, it is not over yet.) In response, many career decision makers now are particularly concerned about their job security in future recessions. It's true that some occupations are more sensitive to downturns in the economy than others and, if job security is important to you, you may want to focus on job choices that tend to be less sensitive. To help you do this, each job described in Part III is rated for its job security on a scale that ranges from Most Secure to Least Secure.

These ratings are based on an article in the *Occupational Outlook Quarterly* (OOQ), a BLS publication. It rates jobs on a four-point scale, from 0 to 3, for "economic sensitivity," which means how closely the jobs have, in the past, prospered or suffered along with the economy. For an additional check, we consulted the 2008–2009 edition of the *Occupational Outlook Handbook,* another BLS publication, focusing on the outlook statements given for the occupations. When necessary, we adjusted the sensitivity ratings for some jobs. Because many of the job titles are very diverse collections of jobs—for example, Designers, which includes those who work with flowers, interiors, graphics, and industrial products—we did not automatically assume that all the related specific titles deserve to share the same numerical rating for economic sensitivity. To determine separate ratings in these cases, we performed a statistical analysis comparing the historical ups and downs in the workforce size of occupations with the ups and downs in the national economy. For each job in these cases, we also considered the economic outlook projected between 2006 and 2016. In addition, we considered the likelihood that an occupation can be easily offshored. For a more detailed discussion of our methods, see the introduction to *150 Best Recession-Proof Jobs* (JIST).

Other Job Characteristics

Like the figures for earnings, some of the other figures that describe jobs in this book are shared by more than one job title. Usually this is the case for occupations that are so small that the BLS does not release separate statistics for them. For example, the occupation Cardiovascular Technologists and Technicians has a total workforce of only about 45,000 workers, so the BLS does not report a specific figure for the percentage of women workers. In this case, we had to use the figure that the BLS reports for a group of occupations it calls Diagnostic Related Technologists and Technicians. We relied on this same figure for three other jobs: Diagnostic Medical Sonographers, Nuclear Medicine Technologists, and Radiologic Technologists and Technicians. You may notice similar figure-sharing among related jobs in the lists that show percentages of workers in specific age brackets.

How This Book Is Organized

The information in this book about best jobs for renewing America moves from the general to the highly specific.

Part I. Renewing a Nation

Part I explains why this is a time of national renewal and describes the industries that will be most affected by renewal. It describes the factors that will determine whether America is competitive and productive in the twenty-first century and outlines how certain critical industries are receiving encouragement from Washington and from forward-looking people in the private sector.

Part II. The Best Jobs Lists: Jobs in Each of the Six Renewal Industries

For many people, the nearly 200 lists in Part II constitute the book's most interesting feature. Here you can see, for each renewal industry, the titles of jobs with high salaries, fast growth, and plentiful job openings. You can see which jobs are best in terms of each of these factors combined and considered separately. Additional lists highlight renewal jobs with a high percentage of female, male, part-time, self-employed, urban, and rural workers. Look in the Table of Contents for a complete list of lists. Although there are a lot of lists, they are not difficult to understand because they have clear titles and are organized into groupings of related lists.

Depending on your situation, some of the lists in Part II will interest you more than others. For example, if you are young, you may be interested in the best-paying renewal jobs that employ high percentages of people age 16–24. Other lists show jobs within personality types, levels of education, or other ways that you might find helpful in exploring your career options.

Whatever your situation, we suggest you use the lists that make sense for you to help explore career options. Following are the names of each group of lists along with short comments on each group. You will find additional information in a brief introduction provided at the beginning of each group of lists in Part II.

Best Jobs Overall in Each Renewal Industry: Jobs with the Highest Pay, Fastest Growth, and Most Openings

Four sets of lists are in this group, and they are the ones that most people want to see first. The first set of lists presents, for each renewal industry, the top job titles in order of their combined scores for earnings, growth, and number of job openings. Four of these lists cover 50 top jobs each, but two cover fewer because there is a smaller pool of jobs from which to draw. Additional sets of lists in this group are extracted from the best jobs and present, for each renewal industry, the 20 jobs with the highest earnings, the 20 jobs projected to grow most rapidly, and the 20 jobs with the most openings.

Best Jobs Lists for Each Renewal Industry by Demographic

This group of lists presents interesting information for various types of people based on data from the U.S. Census Bureau. The lists are arranged into groups for workers age 16–24, workers 55 and older, part-time workers, self-employed workers, women, men, urban workers, and rural workers. For each group and for each industry, we created two lists:

⚜ The renewal jobs having the highest percentage of people of each type

⚜ The 25 jobs from the previous listing with the highest combined scores for earnings, growth, and number of openings

In some cases there were fewer than 25 jobs that met the cutoff percentage we used to create the list. For example, to create the list of jobs having the highest percentage of workers age 16–24, we set the cutoff at 8 percent. There were only three Information and Telecommunication Technologies jobs with a workforce that met or exceeded this cutoff.

Best Jobs Lists for Each Renewal Industry Sorted by Education or Training Required

We created separate lists for each level of education, training, and experience as defined by the U.S. Department of Labor. For each renewal industry, we put each of the top job titles into one of the lists based on the kind of preparation required for entry. Jobs within these lists are presented in order of their total combined scores for earnings, growth, and number of openings. The lists include renewal jobs in these groupings:

- Short-term on-the-job training
- Moderate-term on-the-job training
- Long-term on-the-job training
- Work experience in a related job
- Postsecondary vocational training
- Associate degree
- Bachelor's degree
- Work experience plus degree
- Master's degree
- Doctoral degree
- First professional degree

Best Jobs for Each Renewal Industry Sorted by Personality Types

These lists organize the 200 best jobs into six personality types described in the introduction to the lists: Realistic, Investigative, Artistic, Social, Enterprising, and Conventional. There's a separate list for each personality type and each industry, so you'd expect 36 lists. However, some lists have no content; for example, our best Advanced Manufacturing jobs include no jobs for people with a Social personality type. The jobs within each list are presented in order of their total scores for earnings, growth, and number of openings.

Bonus Lists: Best Jobs Overall in All Renewal Industries

For this set of lists, we put all 200 jobs into one pool regardless of industry and sorted them to create four lists: best jobs overall, best-paying jobs, fastest-growing jobs, and jobs with the most openings.

Bonus Lists: Metropolitan Areas with the Highest Concentration of the Best Renewal Jobs

For each industry, we identified the metropolitan areas where the best related jobs were most highly concentrated in May 2007. That is the most recent date for which we could obtain information, and in some cases the dominant metro areas may have shifted since.

Part III: Descriptions of the Best Jobs for Renewing America

This part contains descriptions of 227 O*NET job titles related to the 200 best jobs for renewing America, using a format that is informative yet compact and easy to read. The descriptions contain statistics such as earnings and projected percent of growth; lists such as major skills and work tasks; and key descriptors such as personality type and career cluster. Because the jobs in this section are arranged in alphabetical order, you can easily find a job that you've identified from Part II and that you want to learn more about.

In some cases, a job title in Part II cross-references to two or more job titles in Part III. For example, if you look up Physicians and Surgeons in Part III, you'll find a note telling you to look at the descriptions for Anesthesiologists and six other medical specializations. That's why there are 227 descriptions in Part III rather than 200.

As discussed earlier in this introduction, we used the most current information from a variety of government sources to create the descriptions. Although we've tried to make the descriptions easy to understand, the sample that follows—with an explanation of each of its parts—may help you better understand and use the descriptions.

Here are some details on each of the major parts of the job descriptions you will find in Part III:

- **Job Title:** This is the title for the job as defined by the U.S. Department of Labor and used in its O*NET database.
- **Data Elements:** The information comes from various U.S. Department of Labor and Census Bureau databases, as explained elsewhere in this introduction.
- **Renewal Industry:** Of the six renewal industries that we cover in this book, this is the one (or more) that we linked to this job.
- **Industries with Greatest Employment:** These industry titles are taken from the North American Industrial Classification System rather than from the six renewal industry titles we use elsewhere in this book. These industries each employ more than 10 percent of the workforce, ordered with the biggest employers first. Although these industries employ many workers, not all of them are growing fast.
- **Highest-Growth Industries (Projected Growth for This Job):** These industries are expected to show the greatest employment increases for this job between 2006 and 2016. The figure in parentheses shows the projected amount of growth. The fastest-growing industries are listed first, and the list includes all industries offering more than 15 percent growth for the job. For a few booming high-tech jobs, we abbreviated the list. For a few slow-growing jobs, no industries met the 15 percent cutoff.
- **Other Considerations for Job Outlook:** This information, based on the *Occupational Outlook Handbook*, explains some factors that are expected to affect opportunities for job-seekers. Note that these comments apply to the period of time from 2006 to 2016 and have not been written to emphasize the renewal aspects of the occupations.

❋ **Summary Description and Tasks:** The boldfaced sentence provides a summary description of the occupation. It is followed by a listing of tasks generally performed by people who work in this job. This information comes from the O*NET database but, where necessary, has been edited to avoid exceeding 2,200 characters.

❋ **Personality Type:** The O*NET database assigns each job to a primary personality type and to as many as two secondary types. Our job descriptions include the name of the related personality types as well as a brief definition of the primary type.

❋ **Career Cluster and Pathway:** This information cross-references the scheme of career clusters and pathways that was created by the U.S. Department of Education's Office of Vocational and Adult Education around 1999 and is now used by many states to organize career-oriented programs and career information. In identifying a career cluster and pathway for the job, we followed the assignments of the online O*NET database. Your state might assign this job to a different career pathway or even a different cluster. Some jobs are assigned to multiple clusters and pathways. The clusters are defined in Appendix C.

❋ **Skills:** For each job, we included the skills whose level-of-performance scores exceeded the average for all jobs by the greatest amount and whose ratings on the importance scale were higher than very low. We included as many as six such skills for each job, and we ranked them by the extent to which their rating exceeds the average. You'll find a definition for each skill in Appendix A.

❋ **Education/Training Program(s):** This part of the job description provides the name of the educational or training program(s) for the job. It will help you identify sources of formal or informal training for a job that interests you. To get this information, we adapted a crosswalk created by the National Center for O*NET Development to connect information in the Classification of Instructional Programs (CIP) to the O*NET job titles we used in this book. We made various changes to connect the O*NET job titles to the education or training programs related to them and also modified the names of some education and training programs so that they would be more easily understood. In 23 cases, we abbreviated the listing of related programs for the sake of space; such entries end with "others."

❋ **Related Knowledge/Courses:** This entry can help you understand the most important knowledge areas that are required for a job and the types of courses or programs you will likely need to take to prepare for it. We used information in the O*NET database for this entry. For each job, we identified any knowledge area with a rating that was higher than the average rating for that knowledge area for all jobs; then we listed as many as six in descending order. You'll find a definition for each knowledge area in Appendix B.

❋ **Work Environment:** We included any work condition with a rating that exceeds the midpoint of the rating scale. The order does not indicate their frequency on the job. Consider whether you like these conditions and whether any of these conditions would make you uncomfortable. Keep in mind that when hazards are present (such as contaminants), protective equipment and procedures are provided to keep you safe.

Getting all the information we used in the job descriptions was not a simple process, and it is not always perfect. Even so, we used the best and most recent sources of data we could find, and we think that our efforts will be helpful to many people.

Job Title →

Environmental Science Teachers, Postsecondary

Data Elements →

- Education/Training Required: Master's degree
- Annual Earnings: $64,850
- Beginning Wage: $35,120
- Earnings Growth Potential: High (45.8%)
- Growth: 22.9%
- Annual Job Openings: 769
- Job Security: Most Secure
- Self-Employed: 0.4%
- Part-Time: 27.8%

Industry Information →

Renewal Industry: Education.

Industries with Greatest Employment: Educational Services, Public and Private (97.3%).

Highest-Growth Industries (Projected Growth for This Job): Administrative and Support Services (48.3%); Amusement, Gambling, and Recreation Industries (45.2%); Social Assistance (38.6%); Support Activities for Transportation (32.8%); Religious, Grantmaking, Civic, Professional, and Similar Organizations (29.9%); Professional, Scientific, and Technical Services (28.8%); Management of Companies and Enterprises (26.8%); Local Government (23.5%); Educational Services, Public and Private (22.8%); Hospitals, Public and Private (21.4%).

Other Considerations for Job Outlook →

Other Considerations for Job Outlook: Retirements of current postsecondary teachers should create numerous openings for all types of postsecondary teachers, so job opportunities are generally expected to be very good. One of the main reasons why students attend postsecondary institutions is to prepare themselves for careers, so the best job prospects for postsecondary teachers are likely to be in rapidly growing fields that offer many nonacademic career options. Community colleges and other institutions offering career and technical education have been among the most rapidly growing, and these institutions are expected to offer some of the best opportunities for postsecondary teachers.

Summary Description and Tasks →

Teach courses in environmental science. Supervise undergraduate and/or graduate teaching, internship, and research work. Conduct research in a particular field of knowledge and publish findings in professional journals, books, and/or electronic media. Keep abreast of developments in their field by reading current literature, talking with colleagues, and participating in professional conferences. Evaluate and grade students' classwork, laboratory work, assignments, and papers. Write grant proposals to procure external research funding. Supervise students' laboratory work and fieldwork. Prepare course materials such as syllabi, homework assignments, and handouts. Plan, evaluate, and revise curricula, course content, and course materials and methods of instruction. Compile, administer, and grade examinations or assign this work to others. Initiate, facilitate, and moderate classroom discussions. Advise students on academic and vocational curricula and on career issues. Prepare and deliver lectures to undergraduate and/or graduate students on topics such as hazardous waste management, industrial safety, and environmental toxicology. Maintain student attendance records, grades, and other required records. Select and obtain materials and supplies such as textbooks and laboratory equipment. Maintain regularly scheduled office hours in order to advise and assist students. Collaborate with colleagues to address teaching and research issues. Perform administrative duties such as serving as department head. Participate in student recruitment, registration, and placement activities. Provide professional consulting services to government and/or industry. Serve on academic or administrative committees that deal with institutional policies, departmental matters, and academic issues. Compile bibliographies of specialized materials for outside reading assignments. Participate in campus and community events. Act as advisers to student organizations.

← Personality Type

Personality Type: Social-Investigative-Artistic.

← Career Clusters and Pathways

Career Clusters: 01 Agriculture, Food, and Natural Resources; 05 Education and Training. **Career Pathways:** 01.5 Natural Resources Systems; 05.3 Teaching/Training.

← Skills

Skills: Science; Writing; Reading Comprehension; Instructing; Mathematics; Management of Financial Resources.

← Education and Training Programs

Education and Training Programs: Environmental Studies; Environmental Science; Science Teacher Education/General Science Teacher Education. **Related Knowledge/Courses:** Biology; Geography; Chemistry; Education and Training; Physics; History and Archeology.

Work Environment: Indoors; sitting.

↑ Work Environment

↑ Related Knowledge/ Courses

PART I

Renewing a Nation

Anew century may take about 10 years to really get under way. America entered the 21st century holding most of the same assumptions that had guided us for several decades. Then a series of shocks made us realize that we'd have to do things differently to prosper in this new century.

In this part of the book, we'll look at the major changes that America has recently committed to making and how they have created job opportunities in six key industries.

Why Renewal Is Necessary

The two most powerful forces that have changed our nation and our world are **computer technology** and **global trade**. These are not new forces; they have been gathering momentum for several decades. But now they have become so powerful that they are changing everyone's jobs.

Didn't the technology bubble burst 10 years ago? Not at all. *Financial speculation* on technology became a bubble that popped, but use of technology has continued to grow until it now touches every aspect of our lives—and therefore affects jobs of all kinds. Many routine jobs that used to keep thousands of people employed have been reduced or eliminated by technology. Even some jobs that were *created* because of computer technology have been affected. For example, if you have trouble getting on the Internet and call your service provider's help desk, you may connect to an automated system with a recorded voice that will guide you through the steps needed to fix routine problems.

Global trade has exploded partly because of political developments; nations around the world have decided to enter the world market and have lowered tariff barriers. This allows them to sell their products and services to potentially billions of buyers and also gives them access to cheap goods and raw materials from abroad.

Computer technology has reinforced the movement toward world trade, and vice versa. The Internet has made it easier for buyers and sellers to find each other across oceans, and the increased competition created by global trade has forced employers to cut costs (especially payrolls) by using more and more technology. If a job can't be automated but can be done overseas in a country where wages are low, the employer can cut costs by offshoring the job. The example of getting technical help also illustrates that point: If the automated system can't fix your problem, the human technician you eventually get on the phone will probably be talking to you from a foreign country.

One other result of global trade is that when money starts to accumulate anywhere, whether in a government's coffers, a bank's vaults, or a union's pension fund, it can move around the globe instantaneously to wherever the owners of the funds think they can get the highest return on investment. This can cause speculative bubbles to inflate quickly, and we've seen what happens next.

So how can a nation thrive in such a highly competitive and fast-moving economic environment? For a success story, consider Finland.

The Foundations of Success in the World Market

Can you speak Finnish? We didn't think so. Finland has only as many people as Minnesota, and few people in other countries bother to learn Finnish. Yet millions of people around the world speak their own language into cell phones made by Nokia, a Finnish company. Finland used to have many traditional manufacturing industries, but as world trade heated up, they offshored the lower-tech manufacturing jobs, including production of many Nokia phones, which are made in China, Mexico, or other low-wage countries. Instead, Finland concentrated on research and development, creating novel product designs and manufacturing techniques.

In other words, Finland focused its economy on what it does better than most other countries: **creativity** and **innovation**. And to renew America and regain our competitive edge, we're going to need to achieve the same focus. How do we get there?

Creativity and innovation didn't appear in Finland by accident. The Finns laid the foundations: a highly educated population, a world-class infrastructure, and affordable health care. Let's look at how the U.S. compares to Finland in laying these foundations.

The following figures on education apply to 2004 and 2005 and are taken from *Education at a Glance 2007*, a report by the Organization for Economic Cooperation and Development:

* Finns typically graduate from high school at age 19; only 5 percent of students have dropped out by that age. In the U.S., we typically graduate at 18, but 14 percent of students have left school before then. The graduation rate in Finland has doubled over the past 10 years, while ours (which led the world in 1995) has remained unchanged.

* Only a tiny fraction of Finnish college students get the equivalent of an associate degree: 0.2 percent, compared to 9.9 percent of Americans. Instead, 47.3 percent of Finns graduate from bachelor's degree programs; 34.2 percent of Americans do. Two percent of Finns get a Ph.D.; 1.3 percent of Americans do. The figures for Americans, especially at the highest levels of education, are slightly inflated because they include foreign students who graduate here; few foreigners go to Finland to study.

* Of Finns earning a bachelor's degree, 21.3 percent major in engineering, manufacturing, and construction; in the U.S., 6.3 percent do. Among Finns, 5.5 percent major in mathematics and computer science; in the U.S., 4.3 percent do. The U.S. has a slight advantage in the life sciences, physical sciences, and agriculture, with 6.1 percent to the Finns' 5.6 percent.

✳ We actually spend a greater portion of our gross domestic product on education than Finland does—7.4 percent compared to 6.1 percent. (These figures include both public and private expenditures.) At the pre-college level, we spend $9,368 per pupil, compared to $6,660 in Finland. At the college level, the difference is even greater: $22,476 compared to $12,505. As you'll see later in this section of the book, we are not getting better results.

Finland's infrastructure is described by the U.S. Department of Commerce as well-developed, based on an efficient rail and road network. Ports are secure and automated; loading and unloading operations are consistently quick and trouble-free. Their high-tech infrastructure is particularly noteworthy: The telecommunications environment is described as one of the most advanced in Europe. Almost every Finn has access to broadband networks. Fiber-optic cables cover 95 percent of Finnish municipalities, and 99 percent of the population lives in these municipalities.

America's infrastructure suffers by comparison. The American Society of Civil Engineers gives the U.S. an overall grade of D, based on 15 categories. On broadband Internet penetration, the U.S. ranks 15th among nations; Finland ranks sixth.

Finns are not much healthier than Americans; their average life expectancy is not even one year higher than ours. But health-care costs are a much smaller burden on their economy. In 2005, we spent *twice as much* of our gross domestic product on health care: 15.2 percent, compared to Finland's 7.5 percent. On pharmaceuticals, we spent $792 per person, compared to Finland's $380. In the U.S., most health-care insurance is obtained from employers, which means that our high health-care costs are built into the price of every product or service that we sell on the world market.

Finland is not a utopia. The United States has many advantages over Finland, including our large and highly diverse population, our temperate climate, our command of a dominant world language, our natural resources, our outstanding universities, and our influential popular culture. We can compete with any nation on the globe if we lay the same foundations as Finland and thus nurture our own creativity and innovation.

Signs of Renewal in America

The United States has been sorely tried by the recession that set in at the beginning of 2008. But now, as the second decade of the 21st century begins, we have committed ourselves to laying the foundations of renewal.

The arrival of the Obama administration has meant more than just a political changing of the guard; it has brought a new set of priorities that will make America more competitive in the world market. It's only fair to point out that Senator John McCain's presidential campaign gave signs that he would have encouraged some of these same priorities had he been elected, although with different policy tools and without the advantage of being of the same party as the majority in Congress.

You can see signs of renewal in the stimulus plan that was passed by Congress and signed by President Obama in February of 2009. The spending in the bill was intended to do much more than just put people back to work; it was meant to push the economy of the United States in new directions. Another place to find evidence of renewal is in the Obama administration's budget priorities, which encourage many of the same initiatives as the stimulus plan. In President Obama's message that introduced the budget plan in February 2009, he made these remarks (to which we have added emphasis): "...The roots of the problems we face run deeper [than the causes of the current recession]. Government has failed to fully confront the deep, systemic problems that year after year have only become a larger and larger drag on our economy. From the rising costs of **health care** to the state of our **schools**, from the need to revolutionize how we power our economy to our crumbling **infrastructure**, policymakers in Washington have chosen temporary fixes over lasting solutions. The time has come to usher in a new era—a new era of responsibility in which we act not only to save and create new jobs, but also to lay a new foundation of growth upon which we can renew the promise of America."

One factor that is contributing to the momentum of renewal is the winding down of the Iraq war, which plugs an enormous drain on the treasury, removes a flashpoint of partisan ill will, and allows the public and the media to concentrate more on domestic problems and solutions.

In the remainder of this part of the book, we look at the major elements of national renewal currently under way. For each element, we examine the state of the field in the first decade of the century, the initiatives that have been proposed for change, and the kinds of jobs that can be expected to benefit from renewal plans. Note that not all of the jobs mentioned in this part of the book are included in the lists in Part II or the job descriptions in Part III.

We'll start by looking at the three foundations of a healthy economy—Education, Infrastructure, and Health Care—and we'll consider them as job-creating industries in their own right. Then we'll survey three other industries—Information and Telecommunication Technologies, Green Technologies, and Advanced Manufacturing—that are expected to grow during this era of renewal. The lists in Part II of the book are based on these same six fields.

Education

Young people nowadays seem to grow up with an intuitive understanding of how to use the technology that surrounds them. When these youngsters enter the workforce, however, they need to know a lot more than just which buttons to push if they're going to do innovative work in the technology industry or apply high tech to the other industries that use it (essentially *all* industries). They need math and science skills to understand what makes technology work, they need communication skills to be able to collaborate in teams, and they need learning skills to upgrade their other skills on a continuing basis. In short, they need an excellent education, both in their school-age years and in their working years. Adults who have grown up in an era of lower technology need education to bring their skills up to speed, especially if they have to change a job or a career.

Current State of the Field

Every president pledges to improve American education, but in the past several years we have slipped further behind as a nation. You've already seen how we compare unfavorably to Finland in terms of school and college completion. We also lag in educational results, according to most objective measures.

Another report by the Organization for Economic Cooperation and Development, this one on math and science achievement in 2006, found that U.S. teens ranked 17th of 30 countries in science and 23rd in math. The U.S. was not scored on the reading section of the OECD assessment (because of a typo), but in a separate report the same year released by Boston College, the Progress in International Reading Literacy Study, American fourth graders ranked 11th of 40 countries on reading. Compare that to 2001, when Americans ranked in fourth place.

President Obama's budget proposal for 2009 included the following remarks on the state of education in America: "According to the National Assessment of Educational Progress, the Nation's Report Card, in 2007 only one-third of fourth-graders [were] able to demonstrate solid academic performance in reading. Similarly, only 31 percent of eighth-graders demonstrated solid academic performance, a percentage that has remained stagnant since 1992. Achievement levels are similarly disappointing in mathematics."

For the past two decades, school choice has been offered as a remedy to educational underachievement, but charter schools have delivered mixed results. The 2006 National Assessment of Educational Progress found students in public schools scoring higher on reading and math than their charter-school peers. Some studies have produced results more favorable to charter schools, but the NAEP study is thought to have the best methodology. At best, charter schools are useful in certain places and under certain conditions, but they alone will not deliver the reform our educational system needs.

The bipartisan support that the Bush administration enjoyed for its No Child Left Behind legislation in 2001 ebbed as the program became established. Early positive results were reported in 2005, comparing student achievement to that measured in 2001, but these results were actually based on a program that had been in effect only since 2003, and achievement from 2001 to 2003 was as great as that from 2003 to 2005. Although the program was designed to establish accountability by testing students to measure achievement, critics have called the tests too narrow and, because states are free to set their own standards, some states have lowered their passing scores. Most damaging of all, the federal government did not adequately fund the program, and states often were not able to make up the difference, especially once the 2008 recession set in.

American colleges and universities are still the envy of the world, which is why so many foreign students enroll here. However, the skyrocketing costs of college education have contributed to a high dropout rate: about 50 percent total, including 30 percent after the first year. The average recipient of a bachelor's is burdened with $15,000 to $20,000 of debt, and those who drop out before earning a degree must struggle even harder to pay off their loans. Many academically capable young people from low-earning families don't even try to enroll in college. College borrowing also contributed to the bubble of housing-financed debt that undermined the soundness of our banks.

Initiatives to Renew Education

The 2009 stimulus package included $81 billion targeted at education. Of this funding, $53.6 billion was put into the State Fiscal Stabilization Fund to be used at all levels of education from pre-K through (public) college to prevent teacher layoffs, pay for programs such as No Child Left Behind, and modernize school facilities. An additional $10.9 billion was targeted to permit 9,500 schools to be upgraded. Head Start and Early Head Start received $2.1 billion. Programs created for the Individuals with Disabilities Education Act (IDEA) received $12.2 billion. Spending on Title I schools, which serve poor children, was increased by more than 40 percent. The Enhancing Education Through Technology Use program had its funding doubled. (This program was threatened with elimination under the previous administration.) Additional funding made college more affordable by increasing the higher education tax credit by 40 percent, extending that tax credit as a refund to 4 million students who don't pay taxes, increasing the maximum size of Pell Grants, and extending work-study funding to an additional 130,000 students. Funding was also directed at expanding fellowships for graduate students in the sciences.

The budget outline that the White House presented in late February 2009 included additional increases in funding for education. Taken together with the stimulus package, the proposed budget was designed to double the number of children served by Early Head Start. It pushed for reforming the testing in No Child Left Behind so it would measure a broader range of skills and, for the first time, serve English-language learners and students with disabilities. It also encouraged systems to reward strong teacher performance, weed out ineffective teachers, and recruit new teachers. It set aside funds for the expansion of charter schools and the monitoring of existing charter schools so they can be closed if they underperform. The budget plan proposed indexing the size of Pell Grants to inflation and establishing a regular stream of funding so they would become, in effect, an entitlement program like Social Security. It also eliminated the role of private industry in college loans by making the federal loan program the sole lender (with the goal of an estimated saving of $4 billion per year), and it included a new five-year, $2.5 billion Access and Completion Incentive Fund to support innovative state efforts to help low-income students succeed and complete their college education. The stimulus package's higher education tax credit and support of graduate students in science were to be extended.

Young people are not the only beneficiaries of education. Many people in school and training programs are adults who are unemployed, underemployed, or afraid of looming job loss because of changes in the economy. Some states and communities have adopted policies to make it easier for adults to re-educate and retrain. A good example is the CalWORKS program, which administers federal Temporary Assistance for Needy Families (TANF) funding, a result of the welfare-to-work legislation of the Clinton era. Under CalWORKS, time spent in community college classrooms is counted as welfare-to-work activity that preserves the student's eligibility for cash assistance. A research study found that CalWORKS students achieved higher earnings and lower unemployment. The Obama budget proposal of February 2009 included funding for programs such as CalWORKS.

Education Jobs Likely to Benefit from Renewal Plans

The entire economy benefits from a better-educated workforce. But it's worth considering the effects of expanded education funding on the education industry itself, which employed about 13.1 million workers in 2006. Following are the occupations that account for more than 2 percent of the workforce in education.

Job	Workers in 2006	Percentage of Workforce
Postsecondary Teachers	1,626,693	12.4%
Elementary School Teachers, Except Special Education	1,499,293	11.4%
Secondary School Teachers	1,121,498	8.5%
Teacher Assistants	1,085,575	8.3%
Secondary School Teachers, Except Special and Vocational Education	1,027,191	7.8%
Middle School Teachers, Except Special and Vocational Education	650,166	4.9%
Teachers and Instructors, All Other	525,571	4.0%
Janitors and Cleaners, Except Maids and Housekeeping Cleaners	468,838	3.6%
Special Education Teachers	437,624	3.3%
Secretaries, Except Legal, Medical, and Executive	372,548	2.8%
Office Clerks, General	368,529	2.8%
Education Administrators	364,956	2.8%

Although preschool and kindergarten teachers are not listed here (because they make up only 1.7 percent of the workforce), they are expected to grow faster than most other primary and secondary teaching jobs; this high growth was expected even before the Obama administration laid out its stimulus and budget plans. Special education teaching for younger students also has had high growth projections for some time.

Increased funding for education will provide job openings in settings other than the classroom and library, such as the janitorial and secretarial jobs listed here, plus jobs preparing and serving cafeteria food and driving school buses. The expansion of the Enhancing Education Through Technology Use program may increase job opportunities for those who work with computers in educational settings—for example, network managers.

In Part II, you can see lists of the best education-related jobs, including those that pay best and have the best job prospects.

Infrastructure

Our economy is built on an infrastructure of roads, bridges, railways, pipelines, power grids, dams, and telecommunications networks. The initial investment in any wisely constructed component of the infrastructure is rewarded by many years of economic payback: improved transportation, communication, or delivery of a resource as vital as water, electric power, or emergency services. Without the infrastructure, we could not do our jobs, live comfortably in our homes, or be secure from threats to our safety as individuals and as a nation. Most components of the infrastructure are subject to decay and obsolescence, and new technologies sometimes demand the creation of new components—for example, the countless cell-phone towers that have gone up over the past two decades. We are required to invest continuously in the infrastructure if we want a thriving economy.

Current State of the Field

Some components of the infrastructure, such as telephone networks and electric power grids, are privately owned. The owners are able to measure the usage of subscribers and charge them a fee that covers the costs of creating and maintaining the facility and returns a profit to the investors. This is also true for some government-owned infrastructure components, such as toll roads, toll bridges, water works, and sewer systems. These user-supported facilities tend to be well maintained and are upgraded to meet new demands.

For many government-owned facilities, however—especially roads and bridges—it is hard to measure usage or inconvenient to charge a toll, so the government raises the necessary revenue through taxes. Taxation has been unpopular over the past quarter century, and even gasoline taxes, which have a clear relationship to highway and bridge usage, are regarded by many people as burdensome. The federal gasoline tax has not been raised since 1997. You may recall that, when gasoline prices spiked in the summer of 2008, some of the presidential candidates advocated a temporary suspension of this tax. Gasoline taxes have not been eliminated, but neither have they been able to fund all the work that is needed to maintain our highway grid. Over the long run, as we learn to build cars that consume less (or no) gasoline, we will have to develop other sources of revenue to fund this work.

The tattered state of the highway grid became a scandal when a well-traveled bridge in the Minneapolis–St. Paul area collapsed in 2007, killing 13 people, injuring 145, disrupting traffic patterns for more than a year, and causing nearby businesses to lose millions of dollars in sales. The state legislature eventually voted to increase the gasoline tax by 5.5 cents per gallon, but they had to override the veto of the governor.

The 2007 bridge collapse called attention to a nationwide neglect of our bridges. According to the Federal Highway Administration, 12.1 percent of highway bridges were structurally deficient in that same year.

Of course, bridge construction and repair have not been totally forgotten by our legislators. One project that was championed by former Senator Ted Stevens of Alaska was to build a bridge connecting the mainland of Alaska to an island with only 50 residents—the famous "Bridge to Nowhere." Fortunately, opposition to the bridge outside of Alaska succeeded in blocking the project in 2005, but the incident dramatized how decisions about infrastructure spending were being made on the basis of political influence rather than on the basis of economic benefit.

Another infrastructure failure that shocked the nation was the collapse of the New Orleans levees and flood walls when Hurricane Katrina struck in August 2005. Subsequent investigations demonstrated that the U.S. Army Corps of Engineers had used an inadequate design in their construction of the walls and government money had been diverted away from maintenance and repairs. Since Katrina, the Corps has spent more than $1 billion patching up the flood-protection system, but many parts of New Orleans are still considered at risk.

The New Orleans disaster reminded the American people that infrastructure is not just a nice thing to have; it's vital to our survival. Since 2001, we had been mobilized to deal with the threat of another 9/11, but in August 2005 we discovered that our greatest fear—that a whole city might be devastated—did not require a terrorist attack. It required only that we continue to neglect our infrastructure.

In an attempt to address this problem, two senators from opposing parties, Christopher J. Dodd and Chuck Hagel, reached across the aisle in 2007 to propose the creation of a "National Infrastructure Bank." The language of the bill called attention to the need for renewal of the infrastructure:

"According to the Federal Transit Administration, $21.8 billion is needed annually over the next 20 years to maintain and improve the operational capacity of transit systems.

"According to the Department of Housing and Urban Development, there are 1.2 million units of public housing with critical capital needs totaling $18 billion.

"According to the Texas Transportation Institute, the average traveler is delayed 51.5 hours annually due to traffic and infrastructure-related congestion in the nation's 20 largest metropolitan areas. The delays range from 93 hours in Los Angeles to 14 hours in Pittsburgh. Combined, these delays waste 1.78 billion gallons of fuel each year and waste almost $50.3 billion in congestion costs. Furthermore, the average [annual] delay in these metropolitan areas has increased by almost 35.3 hours since 1982.

"According to the Federal Highway Administration, $131.7 billion and $9.4 billion is needed respectively every year over the next 20 years to repair deficient roads and bridges. The average age of bridges is 40 years.

"According to the Environmental Protection Agency, $151 billion and $390 billion is needed respectively every year over the next 20 years to repair obsolete drinking water and wastewater systems. Drinking water and wastewater systems range . . . from 50 to 100 years in age.

"Current federal financing methods do not adequately distribute funding based on an infrastructure project's size, location, cost, usage, or economic benefit to a region or the entire nation."

Initiatives to Renew the Infrastructure

Although the National Infrastructure Bank legislation did not pass in 2007, one of its co-sponsors was Senator Barack Obama. During his presidential campaign, he often mentioned the need to renew our infrastructure and this bill in particular. In a February 2008 speech to anxious workers at a General Motors plant in Janesville, Wisconsin, the candidate Obama predicted that the investment in the National Infrastructure Bank would "multiply into almost half a trillion dollars of additional infrastructure spending and generate nearly two million new jobs—many of them in the construction industry that's been hard hit by this housing crisis."

Therefore it's not at all surprising that, once in office, President Obama made infrastructure renewal a prominent part of his stimulus plan. The package included $27.5 billion for modernizing roads and bridges. To ensure that the money would quickly generate jobs, the bill required states to act within 120 days to commit at least half of their federal funding for highway and bridge maintenance and improvement. And, in fact, states quickly began to use the money for projects, whether repainting bridges or constructing huge new highway interchanges. Most of these projects had already been planned but had been unable to proceed for lack of funding.

The stimulus package also included $8.4 billion to be directed to construction or improvement of commuter and light rail transit facilities. Here, too, there was a backlog of projects that could have spent $16 billion if funded. Another $19 billion of stimulus funding was directed at water pollution prevention, flood control, and environmental restoration, plus $4.5 billion to expand broadband Internet access to rural and underserved areas and $3.1 billion to improve facilities on public lands and parks.

The stimulus spending, large as it was, could not patch up all or even most of the holes in the nation's infrastructure, partly because the goal of the stimulus was rapid job creation. The American Society of Civil Engineers estimates that $2.2 trillion of infrastructure spending is needed over the next five years to repair the infrastructure to a condition that could be called "good." The $101 billion in stimulus funds, added to the $903 billion already allocated, still left a gap of $1.1 trillion in needed spending. However, the budget plan that President Obama unveiled a month later addressed at least a part of that spending gap. The plan proposed creating the National Infrastructure Bank originally proposed by Senators Dodd and Hagel, with funding of $25.5 billion over the next 10 years.

One of the infrastructure initiatives in the budget plan is a $1 billion–a–year grant program for states to use to create a high-speed rail system. This funding is in addition to $8 billion provided in the recovery act for this purpose. (None of this was intended to build a link between Los Angeles and Las Vegas, despite what you may have heard.) Other initiatives are for an overhaul of our antiquated air traffic control system, improved security at our seaports, wastewater and drinking water projects, further expansion of broadband Internet access, and improved security for the Internet.

Some of the projects funded by the stimulus package and proposed for the long-term budget are related to the distribution and conservation of energy. They might logically be discussed in the later section about Green Technologies, but because their effects on job growth will be felt mostly in the construction industry, they deserve to be included here.

One such project is the modernization of our electrical transmission grid; it was addressed in both the stimulus package and the budget plan. The President's economic advisors estimated that breakdowns and inefficiencies in the grid cost the nation $50–100 billion per year. A "smart grid" would be able to integrate electricity generated in distant locations, such as by wind turbines on the Great Plains or on the rooftops of homeowners who install solar panels. It would allow electric power to be priced at different rates depending on the time of day; smart appliances could be designed to draw power at times when rates are lowest. The smart grid would also be less vulnerable to disruption by technical problems or terrorism.

Energy conservation is another such initiative. The stimulus plan included $4.2 billion to make military facilities more energy efficient and $4.0 billion for the same in public housing units. In addition, school districts were allowed to use stimulus money to fund energy-conserving improvements.

Infrastructure Jobs Likely to Benefit from Renewal Plans

It is important to understand that renewal of the infrastructure helps our economy in two ways: It allows us to conduct commerce and live our everyday lives smoothly and efficiently and it provides jobs. Infrastructure jobs are particularly valuable because most of them must be done on site, meaning that they employ Americans and create secondary employment for local suppliers of goods and services—such as the diner where the workers go on their lunch break.

The construction industry, in particular, can be expected to benefit from infrastructure renewal. The industry tends to be sensitive to downturns in the economy, but it was hit particularly hard by the recession that began in 2008, because the collapse of real estate prices and home financing caused a drastic decline in home building. In October of that year, 10.8 percent of workers in the industry (both white- and blue-collar) were unemployed; by January of 2009 the jobless rate had climbed to 18.2 percent.

The construction industry employed about 7.7 million workers in 2006. Following are the occupations that account for more than 2 percent of the workforce.

Job	Workers in 2006	Percentage of Workforce
Carpenters	830,911	10.8%
Construction Laborers	824,489	10.7%
Electricians	476,475	6.2%
First-Line Supervisors/Managers of Construction Trades and Extraction Workers	464,017	6.0%
Helpers—Construction Trades	401,507	5.2%
Plumbers, Pipefitters, and Steamfitters	360,276	4.7%
Operating Engineers and Other Construction Equipment Operators	262,993	3.4%
Painters and Paperhangers	220,554	2.9%
Painters, Construction and Maintenance	216,245	2.8%
Cement Masons and Concrete Finishers	203,711	2.6%
Drywall Installers, Ceiling Tile Installers, and Tapers	181,730	2.4%
Office Clerks, General	179,310	2.3%
Construction Managers	173,235	2.3%
Heating, Air Conditioning, and Refrigeration Mechanics and Installers	172,032	2.2%

The industry provides many opportunities for earning a good living without getting a four-year degree. Many of the skilled trades can be learned through an apprenticeship or a two-year program in a technical school. Opportunities should be particularly good for specializations that require certification or licensure (such as electricians and crane operators) and for those that present uncomfortable work conditions (such as roofers and boilermakers). Competition is expected to be limited, because many young people perceive the work as being low in status. In fact, one consulting firm in this industry predicts that, if the number of new trainees does not expand, the demand for electricians, masons, and pipefitters will exceed the supply by at least 5 percent by 2012.

Of course, every construction project requires design, planning, and supervision, so renewal of the infrastructure should also create jobs for architects, engineers, drafters, surveyors, cost estimators, and managers. Some of these jobs require a bachelor's degree and possibly additional work experience.

Health Care

Health care is one of the basic needs of life, and it is growing in importance as our population gets older and as scientific research discovers new ways to keep people healthy. Any modern economy depends on healthy workers and on providing health care at affordable prices to those who are unwell.

Current State of the Field

Finland is not the only country that spends considerably less than we do on health care while getting results that are equal or superior to ours. We lead the world in per-capita spending on health care: $7,026, which is 16 percent of our gross domestic product. At the present rate of growth, this will reach almost 20 percent by 2017. However, several measures indicate that we are not getting as much health care as we need.

The Commonwealth Fund's *National Scorecard on U.S. Health System Performance, 2008,* gave the U.S. health-care system a grade of 65 out of a possible 100 on 37 measures of performance and noted that performance had not improved since the previous scorecard in 2006. Of greatest concern was the decline in access to health care. "As of 2007, more than 75 million adults—42 percent of all adults ages 19 to 64—were either uninsured during the year or underinsured, up from 35 percent in 2003." This lack of coverage costs us in lives: "The U.S. now ranks last out of 19 countries on a measure of mortality amenable to medical care, falling from 15th as other countries raised the bar on performance. Up to 101,000 fewer people [annually] would die prematurely if the U.S. could achieve leading, benchmark country rates."

One of the great ironies of the Iraq war, often overlooked, is that after all of our sacrifices to establish a democracy there, we helped Iraq write a constitution that included something we still don't have here: guaranteed health insurance for every citizen. The Iraqis expected this provision; every other industrialized nation has it except the United States.

Most Americans who have health-care insurance get it through an employer, but not everyone is employed, and not every worker gets this benefit. Medicare, a federal program, was created in 1965 to provide insurance for people age 65 or older. Although there are concerns about Medicare's funding over the long term, in recent years the real cause for worry was funding for programs that get some or all of their revenue from the states. Medicaid is jointly funded by the states and the federal government, and the State Children's Health Insurance Program (SCHIP), although funded by the federal government, is administered by the states. During the recession that began in 2008, many states began to run out of funds for these programs and had to raise eligibility requirements, cut benefits, raise premiums (such as copayments), or lower reimbursements to health-care providers.

The *National Scorecard on U.S. Health System Performance* also found that people who can access health care often get care that is inefficient. The report notes, "Performance on measures of health system efficiency remains especially low, with the U.S. scoring 53 out of 100 on measures gauging inappropriate, wasteful, or fragmented care; avoidable hospitalizations; variation in quality and costs; administrative costs; and use of information technology."

That last low-scored item, information technology, is particularly glaring considering that America has pioneered so many computer innovations. Our health-care system relies excessively on paper-and-pencil records. In 2004, it was estimated that fewer than 15 percent of hospitals and between 10 and 30 percent of physician practices had implemented electronic health information systems. Most other industries are making much better use of computers and thus are cutting costs.

America's costly health-care system hurts our economy, and not just when workers call in sick. According to a study by economists for the New America Foundation, U.S. manufacturers who provide health-care insurance pay an average of $2.38 per worker per hour for coverage. Health-care insurance premiums continue to rise and are expected to increase by 20 percent in less than four years if nothing is done to reform the system. Employers can pay for these costs by raising the cost of products, but then the products fail to compete with the products of foreign manufacturers, who pay less than half what ours do in health-care costs.

More often, U.S. employers cut workers' wages or trim the workforce, according to the economists Katherine Baicker and Amitabh Chandra. In their 2006 report called "The Labor Market Effects of Rising Health Insurance Premiums," they estimated that "a 20 percent increase in health insurance premiums (smaller than the increase seen in many areas in the last 3 years) would reduce the probability of being employed by 2.4 percentage points—the equivalent of approximately 3.5 million workers. A similar number of workers would move from full-time jobs to part time, reducing the average number of hours worked per week by a little over an hour. Annual (wage) income would be reduced by $1,700 for those who are employed and have [employer-based health insurance]."

Initiatives to Renew Health Care

One of the first pieces of legislation that President Obama signed was reauthorization and expansion of the SCHIP program. At the time, he called the bill "only a first step" and a "down payment on my commitment to cover every single American." The extent of his ambitions became clearer when his February 2009 budget proposal included a ten-year, $630 billion "reserve fund" for expansion of health-care coverage. As this book goes to press, it is still unclear which of several competing models the Obama administration and Congress will follow to achieve the goal of universal coverage.

Some modest expansion of coverage was included in the 2009 stimulus plan. COBRA, which allows laid-off workers to continue the insurance they formerly had at their workplace, was made more affordable through a tax credit. States also received $87.1 billion to close Medicaid budget gaps.

But the recovery act had other provisions related to health care. To encourage hospitals and doctors' offices to convert their medical records to electronic form, the bill offered $17.2 billion in additional Medicare and Medicaid reimbursements to those who comply. Another $2.0 billion was directed to the Office of the National Coordinator for Health Information Technology to oversee this transition, which raises complex privacy issues as well as technical challenges. The President has often noted that the shift to electronic records will save lives as well as money.

The stimulus plan boosted funding for the National Institutes of Health by 36 percent, with the stipulation that the additional $10.4 billion must be allocated by September 2010 on grants and other projects that can extend no more than two years. Coming after six years of nearly flat budgets, the new funding meant that many meritorious but unfunded research projects and laboratory upgrades could proceed.

The stimulus package also included about $1 billion for a "prevention and wellness fund" to fund vaccinations and programs that discourage unhealthy behaviors such as smoking.

One provision that attracted a lot of attention was an expenditure of $1.1 billion for research on the comparative merits of various medical interventions. The idea is that dissemination of this information will discourage expenditures on ineffective procedures. Some alarmist observers have claimed that the purpose is for government to be able to specify what procedures physicians will be allowed to perform, but supporters of the funding say it is designed to make health-care practitioners better informed.

The budget plan that followed the recovery act included a statement that the $630 billion reserve fund being set aside for health-care reform, although huge, will not be enough to accomplish the whole job, but it will get America started on the road toward these eight goals:

- ❋ Protect families' financial health by reducing premium payments and preventing catastrophic health-care debts.
- ❋ Make health coverage affordable by cutting expenditures that do not contribute to health, such as administrative costs and unnecessary tests.
- ❋ Cover everyone.
- ❋ Make coverage portable, so people don't lose it because they lose a job or have a pre-existing condition.
- ❋ Guarantee choice, so people can choose plans or physicians.
- ❋ Invest in prevention and wellness.
- ❋ Improve patient safety and quality care—this includes electronic records and information about comparative effectiveness of interventions.
- ❋ Maintain long-term fiscal sustainability by being self-supporting.

Health-Care Jobs Likely to Benefit from Renewal Plans

Health-care reform is a controversial subject. The Clinton administration suffered a major setback when it wrestled with this issue, and in the 2008 presidential campaign, many different policy ideas were offered. The Obama administration's plans may have some features that you don't like and some that Congress may not pass. However, the purpose of this book is to examine the likely job-market impact of health-care reform—specifically, the impact of expansion of coverage, which seems the most probable outcome.

Like renewal of the infrastructure, expansion of health-care insurance coverage will not only make our economy more competitive but will create many new jobs that have to be done here in America. Keep in mind that health care is already our biggest industry, with about 14 million workers. Seven of the twenty fastest-growing occupations are in this field. It will offer many excellent opportunities for work even if the Obama plans are never implemented in full. Nevertheless, when people are unemployed and lose their health-care insurance, they are less likely to visit a doctor or other practitioner, so plans to expand coverage will give a boost to the already fast-growing health-care industry.

Following are the occupations that account for more than 2 percent of the health-care workforce.

Job	Workers in 2006	Percentage of Workforce
Nursing Aides, Orderlies, and Attendants	821,566	6.0%
Registered Nurses	594,672	4.4%
Home Health Aides	562,614	4.1%
Licensed Practical and Licensed Vocational Nurses	412,341	3.0%
Physicians and Surgeons	355,153	2.6%
Medical Assistants	338,493	2.5%
Receptionists and Information Clerks	318,099	2.3%
Personal and Home Care Aides	302,050	2.2%

This is a very diverse industry, offering several low-paying jobs that require only a little training (such as home care aides), several very high-paying jobs that require many years of advanced education and training (such as orthodontists), and a full range of jobs between these extremes. Expansion of health-insurance coverage will benefit all of these jobs but perhaps will give the biggest boost to nonphysician jobs that offer primary care, such as nurse practitioners, registered nurses, and physician's assistants. Another likely outcome of health-care reform is the increased use of information technology, which will create many high-tech jobs. This is discussed in greater detail in the next section.

Information and Telecommunication Technologies

The field of Information and Telecommunication Technologies is where many of America's most innovative and creative businesses have thrived and where many fast-growing jobs may be found. The transistor, the integrated circuit (computer chip), the Internet, and the cell phone were all invented here.

Unlike the other five large industries covered by this book, the field of Information and Telecommunication Technologies does not need to be pushed toward renewal; it is constantly renewing itself and is a major engine of the renewal of other industries.

Current State of the Field

The field of Information and Telecommunication Technologies is one of the few industries that were not hurt badly by the recession that began in 2008. Between February of 2008 and February of 2009, unemployment in the industry increased by only 1.3 percent, just a little more than one-third of the increase in all industries. Of course, many jobs related to information and telecommunications are in other industries, some of which were affected more severely. But high tech is so important for productivity in today's workplace that even these jobs are more secure than most, especially if they involve tasks that are difficult to offshore, such as working collaboratively or doing on-site installation or troubleshooting.

One of America's competitive advantages in the global economy is the vitality of our high-tech industry, and this advantage is likely to persist despite some of our economic problems. Some observers of economic development, such as Thomas Friedman of *The New York Times,* subscribe to a "flat-world" theory that says modern technology permits people to start up fast-growing companies anywhere in the world. However, as the urban theorist Richard Florida has pointed out, the creative and innovative industries—especially high technology—require a concentration of technical knowledge and creativity that is difficult to construct just anywhere. Creative people like to work together, forming teams for one project and reforming new teams for the next project, so they locate where other creative people already reside. They enjoy cultural amenities, such as a lively arts scene, and they demand an open-minded, tolerant environment. As a result, culturally stagnant communities lose these creative people, and the geographic centers where these innovators are already concentrated and do their work—such as the Silicon Valley in California and the Route 128 Corridor outside Boston—become ever more intense. Another force that concentrates high-tech talent is the availability of investors nearby; venture capitalists prefer to put their money into companies they can drive to in a few minutes. Therefore, the United States is likely to remain home to several of the world's most important centers of high-tech innovation.

On the other hand, a lot of high-tech work is not on the cutting edge. The software applications that people use most, such as word processors or spreadsheets, have added almost no new features for many years. Instead, development work on these applications has focused on making them more stable—less vulnerable to crashes. That effort does not require especially creative workers, so much of the work can be offshored to programmers in India, China, or other countries that combine relatively low wages with a high output of college graduates holding degrees in computer science or engineering. Support jobs have also largely been shipped overseas, with the exception of work that requires hands-on tasks, such as installing a circuit board or connecting a home to a cable network.

The Information and Telecommunication Technologies field consists of several specialized industries:

* The **software publishing** industry is involved in all aspects of producing and distributing computer software, such as designing, providing documentation, assisting in installation, and providing support services to customers.

* The **computer systems design and related services** industry provides custom computer programming services; computer systems design services; computer facilities management services, including facility-support services for computer systems or data processing; and other computer-related services, such as disaster recovery and software installation. People working in this industry support e-commerce, create and manage corporate networks, and deal with computer security threats.

* **Internet service providers, Web search portals, and data processing services** are the backbone of the Internet and provide the infrastructure for it to operate smoothly. By processing and storing data and allowing people to access and sort these data, they facilitate the flow of information that has become vital to the economy.

❋ The **telecommunications** industry delivers voice communications, data, graphics, television, and video at ever-increasing speeds and in an increasing number of ways. Whereas landline telephone communication was once the primary service of the industry, wireless communication services, Internet service, and cable and satellite program distribution make up an increasing share of the industry.

Initiatives to Renew the Information and Telecommunication Technologies

The information and telecommunication industries do not need much direct government encouragement, although it's wise to remember that the Internet started as a government-funded project. High tech is so much a part of efficient industrial practices and our daily lives that almost anything that encourages economic activity in the United States is likely to benefit these industries. But the reverse is also true: Spreading access to these technologies stimulates economic activity of all kinds. That's why the government is funding efforts to extend Internet access.

Some of these funds are intended to help hospitals and physicians' offices computerize their medical records. One health-care chief information officer, blogging on this subject in December 2008, tallied the jobs created when his hospital, Beth Israel Deaconess, computerized their records. He counted 22 jobs created for rollout and support of the system and calculated that the transition to electronic medical records would create tens of thousands of new jobs nationwide. The moderator of Monster.com's discussion forum about the stimulus plan reports, "Health IT leaders are predicting that as many as 200,000 jobs will be created as a result of the stimulus funding."

Government funds are also extending Internet access to many schools that presently do not have it, increasing the user base for educational software and thus spurring innovation in that field.

Information and Telecommunication Technologies Jobs Likely to Benefit from Renewal Plans

Following are the occupations that account for more than 2 percent of the workforce for the field of Information and Telecommunication Technologies.

Job	Workers in 2006	Percentage of Workforce
Customer Service Representatives	137,050	9.7%
Telecommunications Equipment Installers and Repairers, Except Line Installers	126,116	9.0%
Telecommunications Line Installers and Repairers	89,889	6.4%
Sales Representatives, Services, All Other	63,476	4.5%
Retail Salespersons	36,800	2.6%

Note that the job with the largest workforce is also one that is easily offshored and therefore does not have a good outlook. The most promising occupations in Information and Telecommunication Technologies have smaller workforces and do not appear on this list. Also, keep in mind that many high-tech workers are employed in other industries. For example, only about 9,300 systems analysts are employed in this industry, but about five times as many are employed across all industries.

Each segment of the industry is expected to grow overall, but certain specializations should offer better job prospects than others.

The computer systems design and software publishing industries are expected to grow particularly fast and, as the complexity of the technology increases, job opportunities should be favorable for most workers. The best opportunities will be in professional and related occupations, reflecting their growth and the continuing demand for higher-level skills to keep up with changes in technology. In addition, as individuals and organizations continue to conduct business electronically, the importance of maintaining system and network security will increase. Employment opportunities should be excellent for individuals involved in cyberspace security services, such as disaster recovery services, custom security programming, and security software installation services.

At Internet service providers, Web search portals, and data processing services, prospects will be best for computer specialists such as computer software engineers, computer systems analysts, and network and computer system administrators. Applicants for jobs at Internet service providers should face competition, because employment declines will limit the number of openings.

Overall employment in the telecommunications industry will increase as demand swells for an increasing number of its services. In addition, many job opportunities will result from the need to replace a large number of workers who are expected to retire in the coming decade. Job prospects will be best for those with two- or four-year degrees.

Green Technologies

The term "Green Technologies" is not well defined, but it is understood to mean technologies that permit a more sustainable economy. The world's population is nearing 7 billion and is expected to reach about 9 billion by 2050. Most scientists and economists doubt that we will be able to provide for the needs of this huge population using the technologies we now use to maintain our lifestyle. The earth has a finite amount of resources for energy and raw materials. It has a finite amount of breathable air, drinkable water, arable land, edible wild fish, and places to dispose of garbage and sewage. Our environment also has a limited ability to absorb carbon dioxide and other greenhouse gases before climate patterns change drastically.

In a way, we are now realizing that our economic equations have always had a blank space that we need to fill in. When we have computed the costs of various economic activities, we have assumed that clean air had no cost, that another net's load of fish appeared at no cost, and that a river full of clean water had no cost. Now we are recognizing that all components of our economy have costs and that many such costs are rising because of scarcity value. With Green Technologies, we are trying to minimize those costs by reducing the burdens on our natural resources and on other aspects of the environment.

In this way, the Green Technologies industry is like the field of Computer and Telecommunications Technologies: Its innovations will reduce costs of various industries and thus help America to be more competitive.

Current State of the Field

Green technologies affect every industry, because every industry uses energy and water, needs workers to eat well and breathe clean air, and needs to find something to do with waste products. But the energy industry in particular is expected to lead the way to transforming our economy to sustainability, because we are now confronted with many stark reminders of how our current methods of energy production depend on limited resources and inflict damage on the environment. The construction industry also will be greatly affected by the growth of the Green Technologies field, because most solutions to our energy problems will involve building things.

The United States is the world's largest energy consumer, but we do not produce enough energy to meet our needs. The shortfall of oil is especially noteworthy, with domestic consumption of about 21 million barrels per day (and increasing 2 percent per year) but production of only about 6 million barrels per day. Oil accounts for 40 percent of our energy consumption, and for some uses, especially for fueling automobiles, we are heavily committed to technologies that depend on oil and that are not easily convertible to other energy sources.

Our need for massive imports of oil not only drains dollars out of our economy, it requires us to send those dollars to countries that don't share our values and are opposed to our national interests. Our security is also threatened by the possibility of an oil embargo, as happened in 1967 and again in 1973, and by entanglement in Middle Eastern conflicts. Our experience in the summer of 2008 with $4-per-gallon gasoline shows that, even without an embargo, our economy can suffer from price fluctuations on the world oil market.

It is possible for the U.S. to increase domestic oil production to a certain extent, but new domestic oil and gas fields would take many years to come online and at best would serve only a tiny fraction of our energy needs while exacting a high price in environmental degradation of our wildernesses and coastal waters.

Another problem with oil, no matter where it comes from, is that burning it produces carbon dioxide, which contributes to global climate change. Although it is theoretically possible to inject carbon dioxide fumes deep into the earth or encourage deep-water algae blooms that will soak up the gas from the air, these technologies have not yet been demonstrated, and many scientists and engineers doubt that they will ever be feasible. Carbon dioxide release is also a problem (though less so) with natural gas, some of which is imported and which accounts for 23 percent of our energy consumption, and especially with coal, which also provides 23 percent of our energy. We have ample domestic coal reserves, but coal mining is hazardous to workers and often to the environment. Besides carbon dioxide, coal burning releases mercury into the air, and the ash left over contains toxic heavy metals that can pollute the water supply, as happened in the 2008 Tennessee ash spill.

Hydroelectric power produces no carbon dioxide and has comparatively few bad effects on the environment, all of them local rather than global, but it accounts for less than 3 percent of our energy and offers few opportunities for increased production. Nuclear power provides 8 percent of our energy and also does not contribute to global climate change, but no new nuclear plants have come online for many years because of public anxiety about reactor safety and because of political difficulties in creating a permanent nuclear waste storage facility.

Corn-based ethanol has achieved some support as an alternative form of automobile fuel, mostly because it requires only minor changes to automobile and gas-pump technology, can be produced in the U.S., and (perhaps most important) has great political support from the powerful agriculture industry and the states where that industry is clustered. But as a fuel it does not reduce carbon emissions. Growing and processing the corn requires expensive and environmentally destructive inputs of fertilizer, pesticides, and energy, and diversion of a food crop into fuel production probably raises the price of food. So its benefits overall are questionable at best.

Initiatives to Renew Green Technologies

As alternatives to the dirty and limited resources we have traditionally used, various green energy sources are now being encouraged:

* Wind is the leading and fastest-growing source of alternative energy. In 2007, the United States increased its wind-power capacity by 45 percent over the previous year. The next year, the U.S. became the world's largest generator of wind power, although wind turbines still accounted for less than 2 percent of all electric power. A report that year by the U.S. Department of Energy estimated that wind could provide at least 20 percent of our electricity needs by 2030. No technological breakthroughs would be required. Our Great Plains are as rich in wind power as Saudi Arabia is in oil, and offshore winds have potential to help power our coastal states.

* Solar energy is being harnessed in two kinds of facilities: photovoltaic and solar thermal. Photovoltaic arrays convert sunlight directly into electricity. Installations feeding power into the grid grew by more than 48 percent between 2006 and 2007, but the U.S. still ranks fourth among all nations in installed base. Ironically, the top-ranked nation, Germany, gets no more sunlight than southern Alaska but offers its citizens financial incentives to install the arrays on rooftops. Besides having little environmental impact, photovoltaic power can be generated close to where it is consumed and is most abundant when the electricity load is highest: hot summer days. The heat of sunlight is also being exploited for swimming pools, tap water, air that is circulated through buildings, and (when focused by mirrors) steam for electric power. Again, the U.S. ranks fourth in use of solar thermal power, with China in first place. Taken together, photovoltaic and solar thermal facilities still account for less than 1 percent of our electricity generating capacity.

* Biofuels derived from nonfood sources are seen as promising alternatives to corn-based ethanol. The technology for deriving ethanol from such high-cellulose sources as switchgrass and wood chips has not yet matured, but the Obama budget plan includes continuation of the research and development funding that was provided by the stimulus package.

* Fuel cells are another promising technology for producing greener energy, because they generate electricity from fuels without combustion. The stimulus plan directed funding toward research about this technology.

❀ Geothermal energy draws heat from the earth itself. It can be exploited by large-scale power plants located where there are red-hot subsurface rocks; Iceland generates about one-quarter of its electricity this way. In addition, homeowners can take advantage of the constant temperature just a few feet deep by using a geothermal heat pump to extract heat from groundwater or from water circulating in a buried loop of pipe. They can reverse the process to air-condition their houses in summer.

❀ The cheapest and cleanest energy of all is the energy you *don't use*. That's why conservation is an important component of the shift to Green Technologies. The Obama stimulus package and budget plan allocated funding for energy conservation in government buildings and private homes. It also committed funds for research and development of plug-in hybrid automobiles. Expansion of the mass transit infrastructure will also conserve fuel that currently is being consumed by automobiles and jets.

The shift to green energy received a boost when the Obama administration created the Advanced Research Projects Agency—Energy (ARPA-E), modeled on the Defense Department's DARPA, with the goal of bringing together scientists at universities, industry labs, and U.S. national labs to encourage innovative energy-related research.

Not all Green Technologies currently receiving attention are related to energy. Water conservation is an important part of the government's new priorities, to be addressed by the Environmental Protection Agency (through the Clean Water State Revolving Fund), the Department of the Interior (through the Land and Water Conservation Fund) and the Army Corps of Engineers (through the Civil Works program).

Many municipalities have taken steps to encourage recycling of paper, glass, and metal. Instead of adding to the expense of landfills, these materials can be sold as raw materials and thus be turned into revenue streams. Unfortunately, the economics of recycling suffered when recession struck in 2008, causing commodity prices to decline sharply and unsold recyclable materials to pile up. That situation is expected to change, however.

Another green trend is the growing public interest in foods that are locally grown or organic. Some of this interest derives from concerns about health and some from the desire to stimulate local economies while minimizing the environmental impacts of pesticides, chemical fertilizers, and transportation-related energy use. The trend is being seen mostly in consumers' choices, but it is also reflected in President Obama's budget outline, which calls for elimination of large government payments to agribusiness firms. This reversal of a longstanding economic policy will be a hard sell in Congress, as it was when President George W. Bush attempted similar cutbacks and met resistance from farm states.

Green Technologies Jobs Likely to Benefit from Renewal Plans

Green Technologies are not the equivalent of any particular industry or group of industries in our economy, so the Bureau of Labor Statistics does not provide figures on which green jobs currently have the highest employment. However, Management Information Systems, Inc., in conjunction with the American Solar Energy Society, released a 2009 report in which they identified 37 specific jobs in *renewable energy* that they estimated employed a total of about 86,000 workers in 2007. Following are those accounting for more than 2 percent of that total.

Job	Workers in 2006	Percentage of Workforce
Truck Drivers	9,500	11.0%
Bookkeeping and Accounting Clerks	8,228	9.5%
Electricians	6,330	7.3%
Plumbers, Pipefitters, and Steamfitters	4,670	5.4%
Agricultural Equipment Operators	4,260	4.9%
Sales Representatives	4,140	4.8%
Janitors and Cleaners	3,610	4.2%
Business Operations Specialists	3,390	3.9%
Computer Software Engineers	3,260	3.8%
Civil Engineers	3,080	3.6%
Computer Programmers	2,660	3.1%
Inspectors, Testers, and Sorters	2,400	2.8%
Shipping and Receiving Clerks	2,210	2.6%
HVAC Mechanics and Installers	2,130	2.5%
Mechanical Engineers	1,950	2.3%
Chemical Technicians	1,880	2.2%
Machinists	1,820	2.1%

The report that published these figures did not include similar estimates for jobs in the energy efficiency industry—if, indeed, it can be called an industry in its own right. Energy efficiency jobs are better regarded as specializations within other industries, so they are harder to quantify. Nevertheless, the report estimated that work in renewable energy and energy efficiency, taken together, provided more than 9 million jobs in 2007. The report projected that, in the absence of any change in national energy policy, these fields would grow to more than 16 million jobs by 2030; with a high level of commitment, 37 million jobs would be possible.

In the specific field of wind power, the American Wind Energy Association estimated that about 80,000 jobs were related to wind power in January 2009. They expected this figure to grow to 500,000 jobs by 2030.

The White House Office of the Environmental Executive estimated in 1998 that recycling activities employed 2.5 percent of manufacturing workers, which would be a nationwide total of 1 million jobs.

One special advantage of Green Technologies jobs is that they tend to be local. For example, retrofitting buildings for greater energy efficiency or equipping them with rooftop solar panels for electricity or hot water requires on-site work. Wind turbines are so massive that they are difficult and expensive to transport long distances, so they usually are manufactured as close as possible to the sites where they will be deployed. Mass transit jobs, whether in construction, maintenance, or customer service, remain in the community or region being served by the bus or rail network. Many of the raw materials produced by recycling may be shipped to overseas manufacturers, but the pickup and sorting are done locally and are estimated to generate 10 times as many jobs as incineration or landfill dumping.

Advanced Manufacturing

Many of the manufactured products sold in American stores are now made in low-wage countries. In fact, when you're looking for a product other than food or drink, sometimes it's hard to find an item manufactured here. Imports from China alone cost us 2.3 million jobs and $19.4 billion in lost wages between 2001 and 2007, according to an estimate by the Economic Policy Institute. Imported manufactured goods range from cheap dollar-store merchandise to high-tech products such as iPhones, which are manufactured in Taiwan.

Nevertheless, manufacturing continues to be an important domestic industry. U.S. employers are shifting to what is commonly called Advanced Manufacturing. Although there is no precise definition of what makes a manufacturing operation "advanced," it is generally assumed to mean use of the most up-to-date technologies in the manufacturing process, from design through production and distribution. Used intelligently, high tech can bring down costs, improve quality, accelerate the product development schedule, and perform innovative processes, all of which allow a manufacturer to underprice foreign competitors and stay one step ahead of them. The dominant driver of innovation in manufacturing is information technology, often combined with mechanical technology to create robotic equipment or highly precise apparatus, such as computer numerical controlled (CNC) machine tools. Other technologies are emerging, such as nanotechnology, which involves manipulating atoms and molecules. Geospatial technology has already created navigation aids for motorists and promises to deliver many more innovative products. Biotechnology has been used in manufacturing ever since the first batch of beer was brewed but has the potential to produce an endless variety of medicines, foodstuffs, and other commercially valuable products.

Besides the use of technology, another key ingredient that makes a manufacturing operation "advanced" is input from workers, who often are organized into teams. The engineers and managers who create and oversee the manufacturing process recognize that the workers are intimately involved with the operation, observing what works well or poorly on a daily basis. Therefore, managers have learned to welcome workers' suggestions for how to improve the efficiency of the operation (including ways to make it more "green") and the quality of products.

Current State of the Field

Despite the loss of many U.S. manufacturing jobs in recent decades, the production of goods from consumer electronics to industrial equipment still accounts for 14 percent of the U.S. gross domestic product and 11 percent of U.S. employment.

Food manufacturing is a good example of an industry sector that is not experiencing a lot of foreign competition. Most raw food materials can't be shipped overseas without spoilage, so the processing tends to be done near the farms and ranches, or at least within the same country. In addition, American consumers may be suspicious of the quality of processed foods from low-wage countries, especially in the wake of the recent milk contamination scandal in China. Because food is one of the basic necessities of life, this industry sector also seems to be recession-proof. For example, in 2008 the state of Oregon saw an 8.3 percent decrease in manufacturing jobs overall but a 7.9 percent increase in food-manufacturing jobs.

Compared to food manufacturing, automobile manufacturing is more representative of U.S. manufacturing as a whole and can be viewed as a microcosm of what has gone wrong. It is one of the largest sectors of the manufacturing industries and has received a lot of attention as it struggles to survive the recession that began in 2008. Some of the automakers' problems were created by resistance to change on the part of both management and labor. Other problems were caused by the American health-care system, which requires automakers to spend more per car on health care than on steel and thus gives an advantage to foreign car manufacturers.

The mass-production method, which was invented in the United States, broke down the manufacturing process into such small steps that it was possible to "dumb down" jobs to the level where they could be done by low-skilled workers. Some of the jobs in the food manufacturing sector, such as eviscerating chickens, are still at this level because they are difficult to automate. But even in this industry, automation is increasingly being used for tasks such as packaging, inspection, and inventory control. And for many tasks that still require human participation, managers have learned to value the creative contributions of the workers rather than regard them as unthinking robots. In other words, traditional manufacturing is transitioning to Advanced Manufacturing. And as part of that transition, skill requirements are constantly climbing.

The economists Richard Deitz and James Orr, of the Federal Reserve Bank of New York, estimate that low-skilled manufacturing jobs declined by 25 percent between 1983 and 2002, a loss of about 2 million workers, while high-skilled jobs increased by 37 percent, adding about 1.2 million jobs. By 2006, the high-skilled workers accounted for fully one-quarter of the manufacturing workforce. They found this trend toward higher-skilled workers in all sectors of manufacturing and in all regions of the United States.

Unfortunately, the transition to Advanced Manufacturing is threatened by a lack of appropriately trained workers. A 2005 survey by the National Association of Manufacturers reported that 81 percent of respondents were experiencing trouble finding qualified workers; 13 percent reported severe shortages. In 2006, manufacturers surveyed by the Federal Reserve Bank of Philadelphia cited "finding qualified workers" as their worst business problem. This shortage probably diminished somewhat when the recession began in 2008 and demand for manufactured products contracted, but it will remain a problem if manufacturing is to revive as America recovers from recession. Some of this labor shortage can be blamed on the failures of American schools, but some may also be caused by the career choices of talented students who train for other industries. Manufacturing suffers from the perception that it is a career path for low-skilled workers; as we have seen, the trend is actually in the opposite direction.

The lack of trained workers is particularly felt on the factory floor, where a shortage of maintenance technicians is forcing manufacturers to rely on the operators of production equipment to keep the machines running. For example, many high-tech devices have been invented to measure the quality of products continuously as they move through the manufacturing process, rather than requiring that samples be removed at intervals and taken to a lab for testing. However, these sensing devices require highly trained workers who know when and how to clean a sensor or how to rebuild an electrode or recalibrate a device. Technicians who install new equipment sometimes lack the communications skills (perhaps including knowledge of Spanish) needed to train workers in how to use the equipment.

Some industry observers predict that the next wave of high-value manufacturing will be done at the microscopic or even nanotechnology level, requiring still higher levels of skill.

Education reform may help boost the skills of young people graduating from schools, but manufacturers will also need to recruit adults transitioning between jobs. Therefore, it seems likely that Advanced Manufacturing will thrive most in the states that provide the most support for displaced workers to re-educate themselves appropriately.

Here are some of the major specializations within the industry:

* The **aerospace** industry consists of companies producing aircraft, guided missiles, space vehicles, aircraft engines, propulsion units, and related parts. Aircraft overhaul, rebuilding, and conversion also are included.

* **Chemical** manufacturing is divided into seven segments: basic chemicals; synthetic materials, including resin, synthetic rubber, and artificial and synthetic fibers and filaments; agricultural chemicals, including pesticides, fertilizer, and other agricultural chemicals; paint, coatings, and adhesives; cleaning preparations, including soap, cleaning compounds, and toilet preparations; pharmaceuticals and medicines; and other chemical products.

* The **computer and electronic product** manufacturing industry produces computers, computer-related products, including printers, communications equipment, and home electronic equipment, as well as a wide range of goods used for both commercial and military purposes. In addition, many electronics products or components are incorporated into other industries' products, such as cars, toys, and appliances.

* Workers in the **food** manufacturing industry process raw fruits, vegetables, grains, meats, and dairy products into finished goods ready for the grocer or wholesaler to sell to households, restaurants, or institutional food services.

* **Machinery** manufacturing encompasses a vast range of products, ranging from huge industrial turbines costing millions of dollars to the common lawnmower.

* **Motor vehicle and parts** manufacturing produces automobiles, sport-utility vehicles (SUVs), vans and pickup trucks, heavy-duty trucks, buses, truck trailers, and motor homes—plus the parts needed to keep these vehicles running.

* The **printing** industry includes establishments primarily engaged in printing text and images onto paper, metal, glass, and some apparel and other materials.

* **Steel** manufacturing creates the basic materials for automobiles, appliances, bridges, oil pipelines, and buildings

* The **textile, textile product, and apparel** manufacturing industries include establishments that turn fiber into fabric and fabric into clothing and other textile products. The apparel industry has moved mainly to other countries with cheaper labor costs, while the textile industry has been able to automate much of its production to compete effectively with foreign suppliers.

Initiatives to Renew Advanced Manufacturing

As noted earlier, one of the major obstacles confronting Advanced Manufacturing is a lack of trained workers. The efforts to reform America's educational system, if they succeed, will turn out more young graduates and retrained adults who are potential recruits for Advanced Manufacturing jobs. Many community colleges, technical schools, and four-year colleges are developing programs that teach the theory and practices of the new production technologies. For example, have you ever heard of mechatronics? It's a combination of four kinds of engineering—mechanical, electronic, controls, and computer—for designing products and processes, and it is now available as a major in several colleges. Robotics technology is another major aimed at the future workforce for Advanced Manufacturing.

Some government initiatives besides those related to education are aimed specifically at Advanced Manufacturing. The Obama administration's February 2009 budget plan included funding to revive the Manufacturing Extension Partnership (MEP). MEP centers are nonprofit university or state-based organizations that receive a mix of public and private funding and help manufacturers deploy new technologies. Also targeted for funding was the Technology Innovation Program (TIP), which supports high-risk, high-reward research in areas of critical national need.

The growth of the Green Technologies industry, discussed elsewhere in this section of the book, will encourage Advanced Manufacturing by creating demand for new products, many of which will be manufactured here in the U.S. For example, wind turbines are so bulky that it is not practical to build them overseas and ship them here for assembly. As a result, in 2005 the Spanish wind-power company Gamesa bought 24 acres of the shut-down U.S. Steel plant in Fairless Hills, Pennsylvania, and started up three factories to manufacture and assemble components of wind turbines. Although wind turbines are often thought of as low-tech, some of the turbine parts made in the Gamesa plants incorporate the latest technologies, such as use of carbon fiber.

Gamesa's decision to locate factories at the U.S. Steel location resulted partly from government policy. The state of Pennsylvania is committed to getting 18 percent of its electricity from renewable sources by 2020 and wooed Gamesa by offering a combination of grants, loans, and tax breaks. Colorado offered similar incentives to get the Danish company Vestas Wind Systems to locate a plant in that state. It's significant that a Colorado economic development official was quoted by the Associated Press as saying that manufacturers deciding where to locate regard these incentives as "just icing on the cake" compared to the more important fundamentals for Advanced Manufacturing: a trained workforce and a good transportation infrastructure.

Advanced Manufacturing Jobs Likely to Benefit from Renewal Plans

The Bureau of Labor Statistics does not provide separate figures on employment in *Advanced* Manufacturing. Following are the occupations that account for more than 2 percent of the workforce in *all* manufacturing.

Job	Workers in 2006	Percentage of Workforce
Laborers and Material Movers, Hand	158,078	10.7%
Miscellaneous Production Workers	120,199	8.1%
Slaughterers and Meat Packers	117,297	7.9%
Miscellaneous Food Processing Workers	112,500	7.6%
Meat, Poultry, and Fish Cutters and Trimmers	105,620	7.1%
Packaging and Filling Machine Operators and Tenders	103,461	7.0%
Food Batchmakers	74,432	5.0%
Helpers—Production Workers	74,219	5.0%
Industrial Machinery Installation, Repair, and Maintenance Workers	71,567	4.8%
Packers and Packagers, Hand	68,658	4.6%
Laborers and Freight, Stock, and Material Movers, Hand	55,721	3.8%
Driver/Sales Workers and Truck Drivers	51,395	3.5%
Bakers	48,614	3.3%
First-Line Supervisors/Managers of Production and Operating Workers	47,972	3.2%
Maintenance and Repair Workers, General	41,150	2.8%
Industrial Truck and Tractor Operators	39,196	2.6%

Many of the jobs in this list are low-skilled, low-paid, and not associated with *Advanced* Manufacturing. Many are also vulnerable to layoffs during recessions.

So what jobs in advanced manufacturing have good prospects? Let's take another look at what is happening at the former U.S. Steel plant being converted to Advanced Manufacturing facilities, because there's an important lesson hidden in the workforce figures there. Employment at the Gamesa wind turbine factories in Fairless Hills reached 700 workers in early 2009, and another 600 jobs are expected to be created there in a factory opened by Osstem, a South Korean maker of titanium dental implants. The manager of the unsold U.S. Steel property is said to be receiving inquiries from many other potential buyers and believes that the site ultimately could generate 4,000 new jobs. But consider that U.S. Steel once employed 10,000 workers at the site.

The lesson: Advanced Manufacturing typically employs fewer people than low-tech manufacturing. That's why the previous table, which highlights large-workforce occupations, has little relevance for Advanced Manufacturing jobs. Even if you look at the *small*-workforce occupations that are more important for Advanced Manufacturing, you often will find figures for job growth that are small or negative. For example, the occupation Electro-Mechanical Technicians is projected to grow by only 2.6 percent over the coming decade. Even worse, the job is expected to *shrink* in the manufacturing industries taken as a whole, with growth of −8.8 percent. On the other hand, if you look at specific manufacturing industries, especially those that are using advanced techniques, you'll find a somewhat rosier picture. In plastics and rubber products manufacturing, Electro-Mechanical Technicians is projected to grow by 4.0 percent. In medical equipment and supplies manufacturing, 2.3 percent growth is expected.

Of course, single-digit growth figures still are not impressive, compared with the double-digit figures you'll find for some health-care and high-tech occupations. But consider that many of the occupations in the fields of Health Care and Computer and Telecommunication Technologies are growing rapidly because they have emerged only in the last few decades. The manufacturing industry, by contrast, consists largely of occupations such as Electro-Mechanical Technicians that are not newly emerging but rather *are being reinvented.* They consist not of small workforces that are growing rapidly, but rather of large workforces that will experience a lot of turnover as old workers with outmoded skills are laid off, retire, die, or move on to other fields, to be replaced by new workers with advanced skills. Although the net change may be only small growth or even shrinkage, as we have seen at the location of the former U.S. Steel plant, demand for highly skilled workers in some specializations will be good. The fact that manufacturing jobs have sometimes been perceived as having low status may mean less competition for job openings. So don't assume from the modest job-growth figures that Advanced Manufacturing is a bad career choice.

Finally, keep in mind that Advanced Manufacturing depends on some workers in high-status jobs: engineers and industrial designers to develop new products and processes, plus perhaps a dozen technicians for each engineer. In addition, business specialists are needed to connect products and markets—for example, market researchers to anticipate demand for products and logistics specialists to manage the distribution network.

Let's look at prospects in the various manufacturing specializations.

Job opportunities in the aerospace product and parts manufacturing industry are influenced by unique production cycles within the industry, in addition to the general cyclical fluctuations of the economy. Both the civil and military segments of the industry have their own cyclical variations, corresponding to the introduction of major civil aircraft and military aircraft and systems. Because of past reductions in defense expenditures and intense competition in the commercial aircraft sector, there have been and may continue to be mergers in the industry, resulting in layoffs. Even though the number of large firms performing final assembly of aircraft has been reduced, hundreds of smaller manufacturers and subcontractors will remain in this industry.

Employment in chemical manufacturing is projected to decline, and applicants for jobs are expected to face keen competition. Only two segments—pharmaceuticals and cleaning preparations—are projected to grow. Three segments—other chemical products, basic chemical manufacturing, and synthetic materials—are projected to lose jobs. For production jobs, opportunities will be best for those with experience and continuing education. For professional and managerial jobs, applicants with experience and an advanced degree should have the best prospects.

In the computer and electronic product manufacturing industry, prospects are especially good for professional workers, such as engineers. Despite competition from abroad, U.S. companies prefer workers in research and development who have a strong understanding of the domestic marketplace. Although employment in the industry continues to decline, the relatively small number of engineers in the U.S. makes it very difficult for companies to find qualified workers when openings arise. Computer software engineers are also in high demand in this industry because many complicated hardware products will require software.

In food manufacturing, automation and increasing productivity are limiting employment growth in most industry segments, despite the rising demand for manufactured food products by a growing population. Nevertheless, numerous job openings will arise as experienced workers transfer to other industries or retire or leave the labor force for other reasons.

Employment in machinery manufacturing is expected to continue its long-term decline as increases in productivity allow companies to produce more goods with fewer workers. A significant number of job openings will become available because of the need to replace workers who retire or move to jobs outside of the industry, but employers will want to fill these jobs with workers who have good basic educational skills and can be trained for highly skilled jobs. Workers with these skills are expected to experience excellent job prospects.

In motor vehicle and parts manufacturing, continued productivity improvements and more foreign outsourcing of parts will cause overall employment to decline over the next decade. In assembly jobs, opportunities will be best for those with a two-year degree in a technical area. In maintenance jobs, opportunities will be best for those with skills across a range of areas, such as hydraulics, electrical systems, and welding.

Employment in printing is expected to decline rapidly, but the need to replace workers who retire or leave the occupation will create job opportunities, especially for persons with up-to-date printing skills, particularly in electronic prepress work.

In steel manufacturing, job opportunities should be very good for engineers and skilled production and maintenance workers despite a projected decline in employment over the coming decade. Companies report great difficulty in hiring all types of engineers, including mechanical, metallurgical, industrial, electrical, and civil. Also, computer scientists and business majors should be in great demand.

In textile manufacturing, job prospects for skilled production workers, engineers, merchandisers, and designers should be fair as the industry evolves into one that primarily requires people with good communication skills, creativity, and the skills to operate today's sophisticated computer-operated machines. The industry will also create jobs in research and development as biotechnology and nanotechnology lead to the development of new fibers and specialty garments.

The Best Jobs Lists: Jobs in Each of the Six Renewal Industries

This part contains a lot of interesting lists, and it's a good place for you to start using the book. Here are some suggestions for using the lists to explore career options:

* The Table of Contents at the beginning of this book presents a complete listing of the list titles in this section. You can browse the lists or use the Table of Contents to find those that interest you most.

* We gave the lists clear titles, so most require little explanation. We provide comments for each group of lists.

* As you review the lists, one or more of the jobs may appeal to you enough that you want to seek additional information. As this happens, mark that job (or, if someone else will be using this book, write it on a separate sheet of paper) so that you can look up the description of the job in Part III.

* Keep in mind that all jobs in these lists meet our basic criteria for being included in this book. All lists, therefore, are organized by renewal industry and emphasize occupations with high pay, high growth, or large numbers of openings. These economic measures are easily quantified and are often presented in lists of best jobs in the newspapers and other media. While earnings, growth, and openings are important, there are other factors to consider in your career planning. For example, location, having an opportunity to serve others, and enjoying your work are a few of many factors that may define the ideal job for you. These measures are difficult or impossible to quantify and thus are not used in this book, so you will need to consider the importance of these issues yourself. The resources listed in Appendix A may help you research these issues.

* All data used to create these lists comes from the U.S. Department of Labor and the Census Bureau. The earnings figures are based on the average annual pay received by full-time workers. Because the earnings represent the national averages, actual pay rates can vary greatly by location, amount of previous work experience, and other factors.

Best Jobs Overall in Each Renewal Industry: Jobs with the Highest Pay, Fastest Growth, and Most Openings

The four sets of lists that follow are the most important lists in this book. The first set of lists presents, for each renewal industry, the jobs with the highest combined scores for pay, growth, and number of openings. These are very appealing lists because they represent jobs in the renewal industries with the very highest quantifiable measures from our labor market. The 203 jobs in this first set of lists (or, more precisely, the 226 O*NET jobs equivalent to them) are the ones that are described in detail in Part III.

The three additional sets of lists present, for each renewal industry, jobs with the highest scores in each of three measures: annual earnings, projected percentage growth, and largest number of openings.

The Best Jobs in Each Renewal Industry

These are the lists that most people want to see first. For each renewal industry, you can see the jobs that have the highest overall combined ratings for earnings, projected growth, and number of openings. (The "How the Jobs in This Book Were Selected" section in the Introduction explains in detail how we rated jobs to assemble this list.) The number of jobs in each list varies, because some of the six renewal industries are linked to more jobs than others.

Although each list covers one renewal industry, you'll notice a wide variety of jobs on the list. For example, among the top-ranked Advanced Manufacturing jobs you'll find not only engineering jobs, but also several blue-collar and technician jobs that score high because of their plentiful job openings. You'll find a similar mix among the top-ranked Green Technologies and Infrastructure jobs.

A look at one list will clarify how we ordered the jobs—take the Advanced Technologies list as an example. Industrial Engineers is on the top of the list because it was the occupation with the best total score. The second-place job, Logisticians, has lower rewards for all three economic factors. The third-place job, Maintenance and Repair Workers, General, has considerably lower earnings and growth than either of the top two, but it has abundant projected job openings. The other occupations follow in descending order based on their total scores. Many jobs had tied scores and were simply listed one after another, so there are often only very small or even no differences between the scores of jobs that are near each other on the list. All other job lists in this book use these lists as their source.

The 40 Best Advanced Manufacturing Jobs			
Job	Annual Earnings	Percent Growth	Annual Openings
1. Industrial Engineers	$71,430	20.3%	11,272
2. Logisticians	$64,250	17.3%	9,671
3. Maintenance and Repair Workers, General	$32,570	10.1%	165,502

The 40 Best Advanced Manufacturing Jobs

Job	Annual Earnings	Percent Growth	Annual Openings
4. Technical Writers	$60,390	19.5%	7,498
5. Electricians	$44,780	7.4%	79,083
6. Engineering Managers	$111,020	7.3%	7,404
7. Chemists	$63,490	9.1%	9,024
8. Graphic Designers	$41,280	9.8%	26,968
9. Sales Engineers	$80,270	8.5%	7,371
10. Industrial Machinery Mechanics	$42,350	9.0%	23,361
11. Biological Technicians	$37,810	16.0%	15,374
12. Transportation, Storage, and Distribution Managers	$76,310	8.3%	6,994
13. Mechanical Engineers	$72,300	4.2%	12,394
14. Electrical Engineers	$79,240	6.3%	6,806
15. Industrial Engineering Technicians	$47,490	9.9%	6,172
16. Aircraft Structure, Surfaces, Rigging, and Systems Assemblers	$45,420	12.8%	6,550
17. Production, Planning, and Expediting Clerks	$39,690	4.2%	52,735
18. Purchasing Managers	$85,440	3.4%	7,243
19. Purchasing Agents, Except Wholesale, Retail, and Farm Products	$52,460	0.1%	22,349
20. Chemical Engineers	$81,500	7.9%	2,111
21. Electrical and Electronic Engineering Technicians	$52,140	3.6%	12,583
22. Industrial Production Managers	$80,560	−5.9%	14,889
23. Welders, Cutters, Solderers, and Brazers	$32,270	5.1%	61,125
24. Electronics Engineers, Except Computer	$83,340	3.7%	5,699
25. First-Line Supervisors/Managers of Production and Operating Workers	$48,670	−4.8%	46,144
26. Health and Safety Engineers, Except Mining Safety Engineers and Inspectors	$69,580	9.6%	1,105
27. Computer Hardware Engineers	$91,860	4.6%	3,572
28. Mechanical Drafters	$44,740	5.2%	10,902
29. Commercial and Industrial Designers	$56,550	7.2%	4,777
30. Electrical and Electronics Repairers, Commercial and Industrial Equipment	$47,110	6.8%	6,607
31. Shipping, Receiving, and Traffic Clerks	$26,990	3.7%	138,967
32. Mechanical Engineering Technicians	$47,280	6.4%	3,710
33. Electrical and Electronics Drafters	$49,250	4.1%	4,786
34. Laborers and Freight, Stock, and Material Movers, Hand	$21,900	2.1%	630,487
35. Millwrights	$46,090	5.8%	4,758

(continued)

(continued)

The 40 Best Advanced Manufacturing Jobs

Job	Annual Earnings	Percent Growth	Annual Openings
36. Machinists	$35,230	−3.1%	39,505
37. Team Assemblers	$24,630	0.1%	264,135
38. Industrial Truck and Tractor Operators	$28,010	−2.0%	89,547
39. Maintenance Workers, Machinery	$35,590	−1.1%	15,055
40. Painters, Transportation Equipment	$36,000	8.4%	3,268

The 50 Best Education Jobs

Job	Annual Earnings	Percent Growth	Annual Openings
1. Health Specialties Teachers, Postsecondary	$80,700	22.9%	19,617
2. Business Teachers, Postsecondary	$64,900	22.9%	11,643
3. Biological Science Teachers, Postsecondary	$71,780	22.9%	9,039
4. Engineering Teachers, Postsecondary	$79,510	22.9%	5,565
5. Law Teachers, Postsecondary	$87,730	22.9%	2,169
6. Economics Teachers, Postsecondary	$75,300	22.9%	2,208
7. Computer Science Teachers, Postsecondary	$62,020	22.9%	5,820
8. Agricultural Sciences Teachers, Postsecondary	$78,460	22.9%	1,840
9. Art, Drama, and Music Teachers, Postsecondary	$55,190	22.9%	12,707
10. Chemistry Teachers, Postsecondary	$63,870	22.9%	3,405
11. Mathematical Science Teachers, Postsecondary	$58,560	22.9%	7,663
12. Physics Teachers, Postsecondary	$70,090	22.9%	2,155
13. Atmospheric, Earth, Marine, and Space Sciences Teachers, Postsecondary	$73,280	22.9%	1,553
14. Preschool Teachers, Except Special Education	$23,130	26.3%	78,172
15. Psychology Teachers, Postsecondary	$60,610	22.9%	5,261
16. Self-Enrichment Education Teachers	$34,580	23.1%	64,449
17. Education Teachers, Postsecondary	$54,220	22.9%	9,359
18. English Language and Literature Teachers, Postsecondary	$54,000	22.9%	10,475
19. Nursing Instructors and Teachers, Postsecondary	$57,500	22.9%	7,337
20. Political Science Teachers, Postsecondary	$63,100	22.9%	2,435
21. History Teachers, Postsecondary	$59,160	22.9%	3,570
22. Architecture Teachers, Postsecondary	$68,540	22.9%	1,044
23. Vocational Education Teachers, Postsecondary	$45,850	22.9%	19,313
24. Education Administrators, Elementary and Secondary School	$80,580	7.6%	27,143

The 50 Best Education Jobs

Job	Annual Earnings	Percent Growth	Annual Openings
25. Anthropology and Archeology Teachers, Postsecondary	$64,530	22.9%	910
26. Education Administrators, Postsecondary	$75,780	14.2%	17,121
27. Graduate Teaching Assistants	$28,060	22.9%	20,601
28. Environmental Science Teachers, Postsecondary	$64,850	22.9%	769
29. Sociology Teachers, Postsecondary	$58,160	22.9%	2,774
30. Philosophy and Religion Teachers, Postsecondary	$56,380	22.9%	3,120
31. Communications Teachers, Postsecondary	$54,720	22.9%	4,074
32. Foreign Language and Literature Teachers, Postsecondary	$53,610	22.9%	4,317
33. Forestry and Conservation Science Teachers, Postsecondary	$63,790	22.9%	454
34. Area, Ethnic, and Cultural Studies Teachers, Postsecondary	$59,150	22.9%	1,252
35. Geography Teachers, Postsecondary	$61,310	22.9%	697
36. Instructional Coordinators	$55,270	22.5%	21,294
37. Recreation and Fitness Studies Teachers, Postsecondary	$52,170	22.9%	3,010
38. Education Administrators, Preschool and Child Care Center/Program	$38,580	23.5%	8,113
39. Home Economics Teachers, Postsecondary	$58,170	22.9%	820
40. Social Work Teachers, Postsecondary	$56,240	22.9%	1,292
41. Library Science Teachers, Postsecondary	$56,810	22.9%	702
42. Clinical, Counseling, and School Psychologists	$62,210	15.8%	8,309
43. Criminal Justice and Law Enforcement Teachers, Postsecondary	$51,060	22.9%	1,911
44. Speech-Language Pathologists	$60,690	10.6%	11,160
45. Elementary School Teachers, Except Special Education	$47,330	13.6%	181,612
46. Educational, Vocational, and School Counselors	$49,450	12.6%	54,025
47. Middle School Teachers, Except Special and Vocational Education	$47,900	11.2%	75,270
48. Special Education Teachers, Preschool, Kindergarten, and Elementary School	$48,350	19.6%	20,049
49. Child, Family, and School Social Workers	$38,620	19.1%	35,402
50. Kindergarten Teachers, Except Special Education	$45,120	16.3%	27,603

The 50 Best Green Technologies Jobs

Job	Annual Earnings	Percent Growth	Annual Openings
1. Construction Managers	$76,230	15.7%	44,158
2. Industrial Engineers	$71,430	20.3%	11,272

(continued)

(continued)

The 50 Best Green Technologies Jobs

Job	Annual Earnings	Percent Growth	Annual Openings
3. First-Line Supervisors/Managers of Construction Trades and Extraction Workers	$55,950	9.1%	82,923
4. Environmental Scientists and Specialists, Including Health	$58,380	25.1%	6,961
5. Construction and Building Inspectors	$48,330	18.2%	12,606
6. Environmental Engineers	$72,350	25.4%	5,003
7. Plumbers, Pipefitters, and Steamfitters	$44,090	10.6%	68,643
8. Geoscientists, Except Hydrologists and Geographers	$75,800	21.9%	2,471
9. Carpenters	$37,660	10.3%	223,225
10. Electricians	$44,780	7.4%	79,083
11. Environmental Science and Protection Technicians, Including Health	$39,370	28.0%	8,404
12. Engineering Managers	$111,020	7.3%	7,404
13. Roofers	$33,240	14.3%	38,398
14. Hydrologists	$68,140	24.3%	687
15. Urban and Regional Planners	$57,970	14.5%	1,967
16. Mobile Heavy Equipment Mechanics, Except Engines	$41,450	12.3%	11,037
17. Construction Laborers	$27,310	10.9%	257,407
18. Industrial Machinery Mechanics	$42,350	9.0%	23,361
19. Bus Drivers, Transit and Intercity	$33,160	12.5%	27,100
20. Operating Engineers and Other Construction Equipment Operators	$38,130	8.4%	55,468
21. Heating, Air Conditioning, and Refrigeration Mechanics and Installers	$38,360	8.7%	29,719
22. Chemical Engineers	$81,500	7.9%	2,111
23. Electrical Engineers	$79,240	6.3%	6,806
24. Mechanical Engineers	$72,300	4.2%	12,394
25. Surveying and Mapping Technicians	$33,640	19.4%	8,299
26. Industrial Production Managers	$80,560	–5.9%	14,889
27. Helpers—Installation, Maintenance, and Repair Workers	$22,920	11.8%	52,058
28. Helpers—Pipelayers, Plumbers, Pipefitters, and Steamfitters	$25,350	11.9%	29,332
29. Industrial Engineering Technicians	$47,490	9.9%	6,172
30. Mining and Geological Engineers, Including Mining Safety Engineers	$74,330	10.0%	456
31. Sheet Metal Workers	$39,210	6.7%	31,677
32. Electrical and Electronic Engineering Technicians	$52,140	3.6%	12,583
33. Nuclear Engineers	$94,420	7.2%	1,046

The 50 Best Green Technologies Jobs

Job	Annual Earnings	Percent Growth	Annual Openings
34. Architectural and Civil Drafters	$43,310	6.1%	16,238
35. Electrical Power-Line Installers and Repairers	$52,570	7.2%	6,401
36. Glaziers	$35,230	11.9%	6,416
37. Geological and Petroleum Technicians	$50,950	8.6%	1,895
38. Refuse and Recyclable Material Collectors	$29,420	7.4%	37,785
39. Welders, Cutters, Solderers, and Brazers	$32,270	5.1%	61,125
40. Electrical and Electronics Repairers, Commercial and Industrial Equipment	$47,110	6.8%	6,607
41. Petroleum Engineers	$103,960	5.2%	1,016
42. Pipelayers	$31,280	8.7%	8,902
43. Hazardous Materials Removal Workers	$36,330	11.2%	1,933
44. Machinists	$35,230	−3.1%	39,505
45. Insulation Workers, Mechanical	$36,570	8.6%	5,787
46. Structural Iron and Steel Workers	$42,130	6.0%	6,969
47. Industrial Truck and Tractor Operators	$28,010	−2.0%	89,547
48. Mechanical Engineering Technicians	$47,280	6.4%	3,710
49. Electrical and Electronics Drafters	$49,250	4.1%	4,786
50. Inspectors, Testers, Sorters, Samplers, and Weighers	$30,310	−7.0%	75,361

The 50 Best Health-Care Jobs

Job	Annual Earnings	Percent Growth	Annual Openings
1. Registered Nurses	$60,010	23.5%	233,499
2. Physical Therapists	$69,760	27.1%	12,072
3. Dental Hygienists	$64,740	30.1%	10,433
4. Pharmacists	$100,480	21.7%	16,358
5. Physicians and Surgeons	$145,600+	14.2%	38,027
6. Medical and Health Services Managers	$76,990	16.4%	31,877
7. Physician Assistants	$78,450	27.0%	7,147
8. Medical Assistants	$27,430	35.4%	92,977
9. Substance Abuse and Behavioral Disorder Counselors	$35,580	34.3%	20,821
10. Mental Health Counselors	$36,000	30.0%	24,103
11. Mental Health and Substance Abuse Social Workers	$36,640	29.9%	17,289
12. Pharmacy Technicians	$26,720	32.0%	54,453
13. Dental Assistants	$31,550	29.2%	29,482

(continued)

(continued)

The 50 Best Health-Care Jobs

Job	Annual Earnings	Percent Growth	Annual Openings
14. Medical and Public Health Social Workers	$44,670	24.2%	16,429
15. Health Educators	$42,920	26.2%	13,707
16. Medical Scientists, Except Epidemiologists	$64,200	20.2%	10,596
17. Occupational Therapists	$63,790	23.1%	8,338
18. Physical Therapist Assistants	$44,130	32.4%	5,957
19. Surgical Technologists	$37,540	24.5%	15,365
20. Radiation Therapists	$70,010	24.8%	1,461
21. Marriage and Family Therapists	$43,600	29.8%	5,953
22. Rehabilitation Counselors	$29,630	23.0%	32,081
23. Radiologic Technologists and Technicians	$50,260	15.1%	12,836
24. Licensed Practical and Licensed Vocational Nurses	$37,940	14.0%	70,610
25. Clinical, Counseling, and School Psychologists	$62,210	15.8%	8,309
26. Cardiovascular Technologists and Technicians	$44,940	25.5%	3,550
27. Medical Records and Health Information Technicians	$29,290	17.8%	39,048
28. Respiratory Therapists	$50,070	22.6%	5,563
29. Biological Technicians	$37,810	16.0%	15,374
30. Nursing Aides, Orderlies, and Attendants	$23,160	18.2%	321,036
31. Dentists, General	$137,630	9.2%	7,106
32. Occupational Therapist Assistants	$45,050	25.4%	2,634
33. Emergency Medical Technicians and Paramedics	$28,400	19.2%	19,513
34. Speech-Language Pathologists	$60,690	10.6%	11,160
35. Medical and Clinical Laboratory Technologists	$51,720	12.4%	11,457
36. Diagnostic Medical Sonographers	$59,860	19.1%	3,211
37. Chiropractors	$65,890	14.4%	3,179
38. Massage Therapists	$34,870	20.3%	9,193
39. Nuclear Medicine Technologists	$64,670	14.8%	1,290
40. Optometrists	$93,800	11.3%	1,789
41. Medical Transcriptionists	$31,250	13.5%	18,080
42. Medical and Clinical Laboratory Technicians	$34,270	15.0%	10,866
43. Prosthodontists	$145,600+	10.7%	54
44. Orthodontists	$145,600+	9.2%	479
45. Oral and Maxillofacial Surgeons	$145,600+	9.1%	400
46. Podiatrists	$110,510	9.5%	648
47. Physical Therapist Aides	$22,990	24.4%	4,092
48. Occupational Health and Safety Specialists	$60,140	8.1%	3,440
49. Dietitians and Nutritionists	$49,010	8.6%	4,996
50. Orthotists and Prosthetists	$60,520	11.8%	295

The 20 Best Information and Telecommunication Technologies Jobs

Job	Annual Earnings	Percent Growth	Annual Openings
1. Computer Software Engineers, Applications	$83,130	44.6%	58,690
2. Computer Systems Analysts	$73,090	29.0%	63,166
3. Computer Software Engineers, Systems Software	$89,070	28.2%	33,139
4. Computer and Information Systems Managers	$108,070	16.4%	30,887
5. Network Systems and Data Communications Analysts	$68,220	53.4%	35,086
6. Network and Computer Systems Administrators	$64,690	27.0%	37,010
7. Sales Representatives, Wholesale and Manufacturing, Technical and Scientific Products	$68,270	12.4%	43,469
8. Computer Specialists, All Other	$71,510	15.1%	14,374
9. Database Administrators	$67,250	28.6%	8,258
10. Engineering Managers	$111,020	7.3%	7,404
11. Industrial Engineers	$71,430	20.3%	11,272
12. Computer and Information Scientists, Research	$97,970	21.5%	2,901
13. Multi-Media Artists and Animators	$54,550	25.8%	13,182
14. Computer Support Specialists	$42,400	12.9%	97,334
15. Sales Engineers	$80,270	8.5%	7,371
16. Technical Writers	$60,390	19.5%	7,498
17. Mechanical Engineers	$72,300	4.2%	12,394
18. Electrical Engineers	$79,240	6.3%	6,806
19. Computer Hardware Engineers	$91,860	4.6%	3,572
20. Electronics Engineers, Except Computer	$83,340	3.7%	5,699

The 50 Best Infrastructure Jobs

Job	Annual Earnings	Percent Growth	Annual Openings
1. Construction Managers	$76,230	15.7%	44,158
2. Cost Estimators	$54,920	18.5%	38,379
3. Civil Engineers	$71,710	18.0%	15,979
4. Industrial Engineers	$71,430	20.3%	11,272
5. Architects, Except Landscape and Naval	$67,620	17.7%	11,324
6. Surveyors	$51,630	23.7%	14,305
7. First-Line Supervisors/Managers of Construction Trades and Extraction Workers	$55,950	9.1%	82,923
8. Environmental Engineers	$72,350	25.4%	5,003
9. Logisticians	$64,250	17.3%	9,671

(continued)

(continued)

The 50 Best Infrastructure Jobs

Job	Annual Earnings	Percent Growth	Annual Openings
10. Environmental Scientists and Specialists, Including Health	$58,380	25.1%	6,961
11. Technical Writers	$60,390	19.5%	7,498
12. Construction and Building Inspectors	$48,330	18.2%	12,606
13. Plumbers, Pipefitters, and Steamfitters	$44,090	10.6%	68,643
14. Environmental Science and Protection Technicians, Including Health	$39,370	28.0%	8,404
15. Carpenters	$37,660	10.3%	223,225
16. Electricians	$44,780	7.4%	79,083
17. Truck Drivers, Heavy and Tractor-Trailer	$36,220	10.4%	279,032
18. Cartographers and Photogrammetrists	$49,970	20.3%	2,823
19. First-Line Supervisors/Managers of Mechanics, Installers, and Repairers	$55,380	7.3%	24,361
20. Mobile Heavy Equipment Mechanics, Except Engines	$41,450	12.3%	11,037
21. Roofers	$33,240	14.3%	38,398
22. Painters, Construction and Maintenance	$32,080	11.8%	101,140
23. Industrial Machinery Mechanics	$42,350	9.0%	23,361
24. Urban and Regional Planners	$57,970	14.5%	1,967
25. Engineering Managers	$111,020	7.3%	7,404
26. Operating Engineers and Other Construction Equipment Operators	$38,130	8.4%	55,468
27. Construction Laborers	$27,310	10.9%	257,407
28. Cement Masons and Concrete Finishers	$33,840	11.4%	34,625
29. Heating, Air Conditioning, and Refrigeration Mechanics and Installers	$38,360	8.7%	29,719
30. Civil Engineering Technicians	$42,580	10.2%	7,499
31. Environmental Engineering Technicians	$40,690	24.8%	2,162
32. Electrical Engineers	$79,240	6.3%	6,806
33. Elevator Installers and Repairers	$68,000	8.8%	2,850
34. Surveying and Mapping Technicians	$33,640	19.4%	8,299
35. Helpers—Installation, Maintenance, and Repair Workers	$22,920	11.8%	52,058
36. Helpers—Carpenters	$24,340	11.7%	37,731
37. Helpers—Pipelayers, Plumbers, Pipefitters, and Steamfitters	$25,350	11.9%	29,332
38. Architectural and Civil Drafters	$43,310	6.1%	16,238
39. Health and Safety Engineers, Except Mining Safety Engineers and Inspectors	$69,580	9.6%	1,105
40. Sheet Metal Workers	$39,210	6.7%	31,677

The 50 Best Infrastructure Jobs

Job	Annual Earnings	Percent Growth	Annual Openings
41. Telecommunications Equipment Installers and Repairers, Except Line Installers	$54,070	2.5%	13,541
42. Drywall and Ceiling Tile Installers	$36,520	7.3%	30,945
43. Electrical and Electronic Engineering Technicians	$52,140	3.6%	12,583
44. Telecommunications Line Installers and Repairers	$47,220	4.6%	14,719
45. Truck Drivers, Light or Delivery Services	$26,380	8.4%	154,330
46. Highway Maintenance Workers	$32,600	8.9%	24,774
47. Glaziers	$35,230	11.9%	6,416
48. Electrical Power-Line Installers and Repairers	$52,570	7.2%	6,401
49. Helpers—Brickmasons, Blockmasons, Stonemasons, and Tile and Marble Setters	$26,260	11.0%	22,500
50. Mechanical Drafters	$44,740	5.2%	10,902

The 20 Best-Paying Jobs in Each Renewal Industry

In the following six lists you'll find the 20 best-paying jobs for each renewal industry covered by this book. These are popular lists, for obvious reasons.

If you compare these six lists, you may notice that some renewal industries have better income possibilities than others. For example, the best-paying jobs in Health Care command much higher incomes than the best-paying jobs in Education. Keep in mind that these figures are only averages; there are a few educators (for example, college faculty who manage research institutes) who are earning more than obstetricians. Also remember what we said earlier about how earnings can vary by region of the country and amount of experience and because of many other factors. Finally, keep in mind that these earnings figures are the median for *all* workers, not just those in the renewal industry covered by the list.

The 20 Best-Paying Advanced Manufacturing Jobs

Job	Annual Earnings
1. Engineering Managers	$111,020
2. Computer Hardware Engineers	$91,860
3. Purchasing Managers	$85,440
4. Electronics Engineers, Except Computer	$83,340
5. Chemical Engineers	$81,500
6. Industrial Production Managers	$80,560
7. Sales Engineers	$80,270

(continued)

(continued)

The 20 Best-Paying Advanced Manufacturing Jobs

Job	Annual Earnings
8. Electrical Engineers	$79,240
9. Transportation, Storage, and Distribution Managers	$76,310
10. Mechanical Engineers	$72,300
11. Industrial Engineers	$71,430
12. Health and Safety Engineers, Except Mining Safety Engineers and Inspectors	$69,580
13. Logisticians	$64,250
14. Chemists	$63,490
15. Technical Writers	$60,390
16. Commercial and Industrial Designers	$56,550
17. Purchasing Agents, Except Wholesale, Retail, and Farm Products	$52,460
18. Electrical and Electronic Engineering Technicians	$52,140
19. Electrical and Electronics Drafters	$49,250
20. First-Line Supervisors/Managers of Production and Operating Workers	$48,670

The 20 Best-Paying Education Jobs

Job	Annual Earnings
1. Law Teachers, Postsecondary	$87,730
2. Health Specialties Teachers, Postsecondary	$80,700
3. Education Administrators, Elementary and Secondary School	$80,580
4. Engineering Teachers, Postsecondary	$79,510
5. Agricultural Sciences Teachers, Postsecondary	$78,460
6. Education Administrators, Postsecondary	$75,780
7. Economics Teachers, Postsecondary	$75,300
8. Atmospheric, Earth, Marine, and Space Sciences Teachers, Postsecondary	$73,280
9. Biological Science Teachers, Postsecondary	$71,780
10. Physics Teachers, Postsecondary	$70,090
11. Architecture Teachers, Postsecondary	$68,540
12. Business Teachers, Postsecondary	$64,900
13. Environmental Science Teachers, Postsecondary	$64,850
14. Anthropology and Archeology Teachers, Postsecondary	$64,530
15. Chemistry Teachers, Postsecondary	$63,870
16. Forestry and Conservation Science Teachers, Postsecondary	$63,790
17. Political Science Teachers, Postsecondary	$63,100
18. Clinical, Counseling, and School Psychologists	$62,210
19. Computer Science Teachers, Postsecondary	$62,020
20. Geography Teachers, Postsecondary	$61,310

The 20 Best-Paying Green Technologies Jobs

Job	Annual Earnings
1. Engineering Managers	$111,020
2. Petroleum Engineers	$103,960
3. Nuclear Engineers	$94,420
4. Chemical Engineers	$81,500
5. Industrial Production Managers	$80,560
6. Electrical Engineers	$79,240
7. Construction Managers	$76,230
8. Geoscientists, Except Hydrologists and Geographers	$75,800
9. Mining and Geological Engineers, Including Mining Safety Engineers	$74,330
10. Environmental Engineers	$72,350
11. Mechanical Engineers	$72,300
12. Industrial Engineers	$71,430
13. Hydrologists	$68,140
14. Environmental Scientists and Specialists, Including Health	$58,380
15. Urban and Regional Planners	$57,970
16. First-Line Supervisors/Managers of Construction Trades and Extraction Workers	$55,950
17. Electrical Power-Line Installers and Repairers	$52,570
18. Electrical and Electronic Engineering Technicians	$52,140
19. Geological and Petroleum Technicians	$50,950
20. Electrical and Electronics Drafters	$49,250

The 20 Best-Paying Health-Care Jobs

Job	Annual Earnings
1. Oral and Maxillofacial Surgeons	$145,600+
2. Orthodontists	$145,600+
3. Physicians and Surgeons	$145,600+
4. Prosthodontists	$145,600+
5. Dentists, General	$137,630
6. Podiatrists	$110,510
7. Pharmacists	$100,480
8. Optometrists	$93,800
9. Physician Assistants	$78,450
10. Medical and Health Services Managers	$76,990
11. Radiation Therapists	$70,010
12. Physical Therapists	$69,760

(continued)

(continued)

The 20 Best-Paying Health-Care Jobs

Job	Annual Earnings
13. Chiropractors	$65,890
14. Dental Hygienists	$64,740
15. Nuclear Medicine Technologists	$64,670
16. Medical Scientists, Except Epidemiologists	$64,200
17. Occupational Therapists	$63,790
18. Clinical, Counseling, and School Psychologists	$62,210
19. Speech-Language Pathologists	$60,690
20. Orthotists and Prosthetists	$60,520

The 20 Best-Paying Information and Telecommunication Technologies Jobs

Job	Annual Earnings
1. Engineering Managers	$111,020
2. Computer and Information Systems Managers	$108,070
3. Computer and Information Scientists, Research	$97,970
4. Computer Hardware Engineers	$91,860
5. Computer Software Engineers, Systems Software	$89,070
6. Electronics Engineers, Except Computer	$83,340
7. Computer Software Engineers, Applications	$83,130
8. Sales Engineers	$80,270
9. Electrical Engineers	$79,240
10. Computer Systems Analysts	$73,090
11. Mechanical Engineers	$72,300
12. Computer Specialists, All Other	$71,510
13. Industrial Engineers	$71,430
14. Sales Representatives, Wholesale and Manufacturing, Technical and Scientific Products	$68,270
15. Network Systems and Data Communications Analysts	$68,220
16. Database Administrators	$67,250
17. Network and Computer Systems Administrators	$64,690
18. Technical Writers	$60,390
19. Multi-Media Artists and Animators	$54,550
20. Computer Support Specialists	$42,400

The 20 Best-Paying Infrastructure Jobs

Job	Annual Earnings
1. Engineering Managers	$111,020
2. Electrical Engineers	$79,240
3. Construction Managers	$76,230
4. Environmental Engineers	$72,350
5. Civil Engineers	$71,710
6. Industrial Engineers	$71,430
7. Health and Safety Engineers, Except Mining Safety Engineers and Inspectors	$69,580
8. Elevator Installers and Repairers	$68,000
9. Architects, Except Landscape and Naval	$67,620
10. Logisticians	$64,250
11. Technical Writers	$60,390
12. Environmental Scientists and Specialists, Including Health	$58,380
13. Urban and Regional Planners	$57,970
14. First-Line Supervisors/Managers of Construction Trades and Extraction Workers	$55,950
15. First-Line Supervisors/Managers of Mechanics, Installers, and Repairers	$55,380
16. Cost Estimators	$54,920
17. Telecommunications Equipment Installers and Repairers, Except Line Installers	$54,070
18. Electrical Power-Line Installers and Repairers	$52,570
19. Electrical and Electronic Engineering Technicians	$52,140
20. Surveyors	$51,630

The 20 Fastest-Growing Jobs in Each Renewal Industry

From the six lists of best jobs that met our criteria for this book, we extracted these six lists showing the 20 jobs for each renewal industry that are projected to have the highest percentage increases in the numbers of people employed through 2016.

Keep in mind that the figures for growth apply to *all* workers in the occupation, not just those in the particular renewal industry.

You will notice that just as income opportunities vary among the lists of the best-paying jobs, job opportunities vary among the renewal industries. The top jobs in Health Care have better opportunities than do the top jobs in the other groups (with the notable exception of a few jobs in Information and Telecommunication Technologies). This is partly because health-care work typically cannot be done by computers or by overseas workers and partly because an aging population has a growing need for medical care.

The 20 Fastest-Growing Advanced Manufacturing Jobs

Job	Percent Growth
1. Industrial Engineers	20.3%
2. Technical Writers	19.5%
3. Logisticians	17.3%
4. Biological Technicians	16.0%
5. Aircraft Structure, Surfaces, Rigging, and Systems Assemblers	12.8%
6. Maintenance and Repair Workers, General	10.1%
7. Industrial Engineering Technicians	9.9%
8. Graphic Designers	9.8%
9. Health and Safety Engineers, Except Mining Safety Engineers and Inspectors	9.6%
10. Chemists	9.1%
11. Industrial Machinery Mechanics	9.0%
12. Sales Engineers	8.5%
13. Painters, Transportation Equipment	8.4%
14. Transportation, Storage, and Distribution Managers	8.3%
15. Chemical Engineers	7.9%
16. Electricians	7.4%
17. Engineering Managers	7.3%
18. Commercial and Industrial Designers	7.2%
19. Electrical and Electronics Repairers, Commercial and Industrial Equipment	6.8%
20. Mechanical Engineering Technicians	6.4%

The 20 Fastest-Growing Education Jobs

Job	Percent Growth
1. Preschool Teachers, Except Special Education	26.3%
2. Education Administrators, Preschool and Child Care Center/Program	23.5%
3. Self-Enrichment Education Teachers	23.1%
4. Agricultural Sciences Teachers, Postsecondary	22.9%
5. Anthropology and Archeology Teachers, Postsecondary	22.9%
6. Architecture Teachers, Postsecondary	22.9%
7. Area, Ethnic, and Cultural Studies Teachers, Postsecondary	22.9%
8. Art, Drama, and Music Teachers, Postsecondary	22.9%
9. Atmospheric, Earth, Marine, and Space Sciences Teachers, Postsecondary	22.9%
10. Biological Science Teachers, Postsecondary	22.9%

The 20 Fastest-Growing Education Jobs

Job	Percent Growth
11. Business Teachers, Postsecondary	22.9%
12. Chemistry Teachers, Postsecondary	22.9%
13. Communications Teachers, Postsecondary	22.9%
14. Computer Science Teachers, Postsecondary	22.9%
15. Criminal Justice and Law Enforcement Teachers, Postsecondary	22.9%
16. Economics Teachers, Postsecondary	22.9%
17. Education Teachers, Postsecondary	22.9%
18. Engineering Teachers, Postsecondary	22.9%
19. English Language and Literature Teachers, Postsecondary	22.9%
20. Environmental Science Teachers, Postsecondary	22.9%

The 20 Fastest-Growing Green Technologies Jobs

Job	Percent Growth
1. Environmental Science and Protection Technicians, Including Health	28.0%
2. Environmental Engineers	25.4%
3. Environmental Scientists and Specialists, Including Health	25.1%
4. Hydrologists	24.3%
5. Geoscientists, Except Hydrologists and Geographers	21.9%
6. Industrial Engineers	20.3%
7. Surveying and Mapping Technicians	19.4%
8. Construction and Building Inspectors	18.2%
9. Construction Managers	15.7%
10. Urban and Regional Planners	14.5%
11. Roofers	14.3%
12. Bus Drivers, Transit and Intercity	12.5%
13. Mobile Heavy Equipment Mechanics, Except Engines	12.3%
14. Glaziers	11.9%
15. Helpers—Pipelayers, Plumbers, Pipefitters, and Steamfitters	11.9%
16. Helpers—Installation, Maintenance, and Repair Workers	11.8%
17. Hazardous Materials Removal Workers	11.2%
18. Construction Laborers	10.9%
19. Plumbers, Pipefitters, and Steamfitters	10.6%
20. Carpenters	10.3%

The 20 Fastest-Growing Health-Care Jobs

Job	Percent Growth
1. Medical Assistants	35.4%
2. Substance Abuse and Behavioral Disorder Counselors	34.3%
3. Physical Therapist Assistants	32.4%
4. Pharmacy Technicians	32.0%
5. Dental Hygienists	30.1%
6. Mental Health Counselors	30.0%
7. Mental Health and Substance Abuse Social Workers	29.9%
8. Marriage and Family Therapists	29.8%
9. Dental Assistants	29.2%
10. Physical Therapists	27.1%
11. Physician Assistants	27.0%
12. Health Educators	26.2%
13. Cardiovascular Technologists and Technicians	25.5%
14. Occupational Therapist Assistants	25.4%
15. Radiation Therapists	24.8%
16. Surgical Technologists	24.5%
17. Physical Therapist Aides	24.4%
18. Medical and Public Health Social Workers	24.2%
19. Registered Nurses	23.5%
20. Occupational Therapists	23.1%

The 20 Fastest-Growing Information and Telecommunication Technologies Jobs

Job	Percent Growth
1. Network Systems and Data Communications Analysts	53.4%
2. Computer Software Engineers, Applications	44.6%
3. Computer Systems Analysts	29.0%
4. Database Administrators	28.6%
5. Computer Software Engineers, Systems Software	28.2%
6. Network and Computer Systems Administrators	27.0%
7. Multi-Media Artists and Animators	25.8%
8. Computer and Information Scientists, Research	21.5%
9. Industrial Engineers	20.3%
10. Technical Writers	19.5%
11. Computer and Information Systems Managers	16.4%

The 20 Fastest-Growing Information and Telecommunication Technologies Jobs

Job	Percent Growth
12. Computer Specialists, All Other	15.1%
13. Computer Support Specialists	12.9%
14. Sales Representatives, Wholesale and Manufacturing, Technical and Scientific Products	12.4%
15. Sales Engineers	8.5%
16. Engineering Managers	7.3%
17. Electrical Engineers	6.3%
18. Computer Hardware Engineers	4.6%
19. Mechanical Engineers	4.2%
20. Electronics Engineers, Except Computer	3.7%

The 20 Fastest-Growing Infrastructure Jobs

Job	Percent Growth
1. Environmental Science and Protection Technicians, Including Health	28.0%
2. Environmental Engineers	25.4%
3. Environmental Scientists and Specialists, Including Health	25.1%
4. Environmental Engineering Technicians	24.8%
5. Surveyors	23.7%
6. Cartographers and Photogrammetrists	20.3%
7. Industrial Engineers	20.3%
8. Technical Writers	19.5%
9. Surveying and Mapping Technicians	19.4%
10. Cost Estimators	18.5%
11. Construction and Building Inspectors	18.2%
12. Civil Engineers	18.0%
13. Architects, Except Landscape and Naval	17.7%
14. Logisticians	17.3%
15. Construction Managers	15.7%
16. Urban and Regional Planners	14.5%
17. Roofers	14.3%
18. Mobile Heavy Equipment Mechanics, Except Engines	12.3%
19. Glaziers	11.9%
20. Helpers—Pipelayers, Plumbers, Pipefitters, and Steamfitters	11.9%

The 20 Jobs with the Most Openings in Each Renewal Industry

From the six lists of jobs that met our criteria for this book, this list shows the 20 jobs for each renewal industry that are projected to have the largest number of job openings per year through 2016. Like the figures for earnings and growth, the figures for job openings in these lists apply to all workers in the occupations, not just those in the renewal industries.

Jobs with many openings present several advantages that may be attractive to you. Because there are many openings, these jobs can be easier to obtain, particularly for people just entering the job market. These jobs may also offer more opportunities to move from one employer to another with relative ease. Though some of these jobs have average or below-average pay, some also pay quite well and can provide good long-term career opportunities or the ability to move up to more responsible roles.

The renewal industries with the most outstanding figures for job openings are Infrastructure and Advanced Manufacturing. The construction-related jobs in Green Technologies also offer many job openings.

On all the lists, the jobs that are expected to have the greatest number of openings tend to be those that require hands-on or in-person work—for example, truck drivers, teachers, team assemblers, or nurses. These workers are less likely to be replaced by technology or by overseas workers.

The 20 Advanced Manufacturing Jobs with the Most Openings

Job	Annual Openings
1. Laborers and Freight, Stock, and Material Movers, Hand	630,487
2. Team Assemblers	264,135
3. Maintenance and Repair Workers, General	165,502
4. Shipping, Receiving, and Traffic Clerks	138,967
5. Industrial Truck and Tractor Operators	89,547
6. Electricians	79,083
7. Welders, Cutters, Solderers, and Brazers	61,125
8. Production, Planning, and Expediting Clerks	52,735
9. First-Line Supervisors/Managers of Production and Operating Workers	46,144
10. Machinists	39,505
11. Graphic Designers	26,968
12. Industrial Machinery Mechanics	23,361
13. Purchasing Agents, Except Wholesale, Retail, and Farm Products	22,349
14. Biological Technicians	15,374
15. Maintenance Workers, Machinery	15,055
16. Industrial Production Managers	14,889
17. Electrical and Electronic Engineering Technicians	12,583
18. Mechanical Engineers	12,394

The 20 Advanced Manufacturing Jobs with the Most Openings

Job	Annual Openings
19. Industrial Engineers	11,272
20. Mechanical Drafters	10,902

The 20 Education Jobs with the Most Openings

Job	Annual Openings
1. Elementary School Teachers, Except Special Education	181,612
2. Preschool Teachers, Except Special Education	78,172
3. Middle School Teachers, Except Special and Vocational Education	75,270
4. Self-Enrichment Education Teachers	64,449
5. Educational, Vocational, and School Counselors	54,025
6. Child, Family, and School Social Workers	35,402
7. Kindergarten Teachers, Except Special Education	27,603
8. Education Administrators, Elementary and Secondary School	27,143
9. Instructional Coordinators	21,294
10. Graduate Teaching Assistants	20,601
11. Special Education Teachers, Preschool, Kindergarten, and Elementary School	20,049
12. Health Specialties Teachers, Postsecondary	19,617
13. Vocational Education Teachers, Postsecondary	19,313
14. Education Administrators, Postsecondary	17,121
15. Art, Drama, and Music Teachers, Postsecondary	12,707
16. Business Teachers, Postsecondary	11,643
17. Speech-Language Pathologists	11,160
18. English Language and Literature Teachers, Postsecondary	10,475
19. Education Teachers, Postsecondary	9,359
20. Biological Science Teachers, Postsecondary	9,039

The 20 Green Technologies Jobs with the Most Openings

Job	Annual Openings
1. Construction Laborers	257,407
2. Carpenters	223,225
3. Industrial Truck and Tractor Operators	89,547
4. First-Line Supervisors/Managers of Construction Trades and Extraction Workers	82,923
5. Electricians	79,083

(continued)

(continued)

The 20 Green Technologies Jobs with the Most Openings

Job	Annual Openings
6. Inspectors, Testers, Sorters, Samplers, and Weighers	75,361
7. Plumbers, Pipefitters, and Steamfitters	68,643
8. Welders, Cutters, Solderers, and Brazers	61,125
9. Operating Engineers and Other Construction Equipment Operators	55,468
10. Helpers—Installation, Maintenance, and Repair Workers	52,058
11. Construction Managers	44,158
12. Machinists	39,505
13. Roofers	38,398
14. Refuse and Recyclable Material Collectors	37,785
15. Sheet Metal Workers	31,677
16. Heating, Air Conditioning, and Refrigeration Mechanics and Installers	29,719
17. Helpers—Pipelayers, Plumbers, Pipefitters, and Steamfitters	29,332
18. Bus Drivers, Transit and Intercity	27,100
19. Industrial Machinery Mechanics	23,361
20. Architectural and Civil Drafters	16,238

The 20 Health-Care Jobs with the Most Openings

Job	Annual Openings
1. Nursing Aides, Orderlies, and Attendants	321,036
2. Registered Nurses	233,499
3. Medical Assistants	92,977
4. Licensed Practical and Licensed Vocational Nurses	70,610
5. Pharmacy Technicians	54,453
6. Medical Records and Health Information Technicians	39,048
7. Physicians and Surgeons	38,027
8. Rehabilitation Counselors	32,081
9. Medical and Health Services Managers	31,877
10. Dental Assistants	29,482
11. Mental Health Counselors	24,103
12. Substance Abuse and Behavioral Disorder Counselors	20,821
13. Emergency Medical Technicians and Paramedics	19,513
14. Medical Transcriptionists	18,080
15. Mental Health and Substance Abuse Social Workers	17,289
16. Medical and Public Health Social Workers	16,429
17. Pharmacists	16,358

The 20 Health-Care Jobs with the Most Openings

Job	Annual Openings
18. Biological Technicians	15,374
19. Surgical Technologists	15,365
20. Health Educators	13,707

The 20 Information and Telecommunication Technologies Jobs with the Most Openings

Job	Annual Openings
1. Computer Support Specialists	97,334
2. Computer Systems Analysts	63,166
3. Computer Software Engineers, Applications	58,690
4. Sales Representatives, Wholesale and Manufacturing, Technical and Scientific Products	43,469
5. Network and Computer Systems Administrators	37,010
6. Network Systems and Data Communications Analysts	35,086
7. Computer Software Engineers, Systems Software	33,139
8. Computer and Information Systems Managers	30,887
9. Computer Specialists, All Other	14,374
10. Multi-Media Artists and Animators	13,182
11. Mechanical Engineers	12,394
12. Industrial Engineers	11,272
13. Database Administrators	8,258
14. Technical Writers	7,498
15. Engineering Managers	7,404
16. Sales Engineers	7,371
17. Electrical Engineers	6,806
18. Electronics Engineers, Except Computer	5,699
19. Computer Hardware Engineers	3,572
20. Computer and Information Scientists, Research	2,901

The 20 Infrastructure Jobs with the Most Openings

Job	Annual Openings
1. Truck Drivers, Heavy and Tractor-Trailer	279,032
2. Construction Laborers	257,407

(continued)

(continued)

The 20 Infrastructure Jobs with the Most Openings

Job	Annual Openings
3. Carpenters	223,225
4. Truck Drivers, Light or Delivery Services	154,330
5. Painters, Construction and Maintenance	101,140
6. First-Line Supervisors/Managers of Construction Trades and Extraction Workers	82,923
7. Electricians	79,083
8. Plumbers, Pipefitters, and Steamfitters	68,643
9. Operating Engineers and Other Construction Equipment Operators	55,468
10. Helpers—Installation, Maintenance, and Repair Workers	52,058
11. Construction Managers	44,158
12. Roofers	38,398
13. Cost Estimators	38,379
14. Helpers—Carpenters	37,731
15. Cement Masons and Concrete Finishers	34,625
16. Sheet Metal Workers	31,677
17. Drywall and Ceiling Tile Installers	30,945
18. Heating, Air Conditioning, and Refrigeration Mechanics and Installers	29,719
19. Helpers—Pipelayers, Plumbers, Pipefitters, and Steamfitters	29,332
20. Highway Maintenance Workers	24,774

Best Jobs Lists for Each Renewal Industry by Demographic

We decided it would be interesting to include lists in this section that show what sorts of jobs different types of people are most likely to have. For example, what renewal jobs have the highest percentage of men or young workers? We're not saying that men or young people should consider these jobs over others, but it is interesting information to know.

In some cases, the lists can give you ideas for jobs to consider that you might otherwise overlook. For example, perhaps women should consider some jobs that traditionally have high percentages of men in them. Or older workers might consider some jobs typically held by young people. Although these aren't obvious ways of using these lists, the lists may give you some good ideas of jobs to consider. The lists may also help you identify jobs that work well for others in your situation—for example, jobs with plentiful opportunities for part-time work, if that's something you want to do.

All lists in this section were created through a similar process. We began with the best jobs for each renewal industry. Next, we sorted these jobs in order of the primary criterion for each set of lists. For example, we sorted the 50 Education jobs based on the percentage of the workforce age 16–24 from highest to lowest percentage and then selected the jobs with a high percentage (in this case, only 4 jobs met or exceeded the cutoff percentage of 15). From this initial list of jobs with a high percentage of each type of worker, we created a second list ordered to show the best jobs overall, based on their combined scores for earnings, growth rate, and number of openings. When there were a large number of jobs that exceeded the demographic cutoff, we limited this best-of list to 25 jobs.

The same basic process was used to create all the lists in this section. The lists are very interesting, and we hope you find them helpful.

The Best Jobs in Each Renewal Industry with a High Percentage of Workers Age 16–24

In the following lists, we sorted the best jobs for each renewal industry and included only those that employ the highest percentage of workers age 16–24. Workers in this age bracket make up 14.1 percent of the workforce, and jobs in the lists that follow include at least 8 percent of these workers. (As with the economic figures, the figures on age brackets apply to workers in all industries, not just the renewal industries.)

Although young workers are employed in virtually all major occupations, and therefore in settings associated with all six renewal industries, you may notice that the jobs for the Advanced Manufacturing, Green Technologies, and Infrastructure industries are considerably "younger" than those for the other industries, which cannot muster 25 jobs meeting the 8 percent cutoff for young workers. This largely reflects the fact that careers in Education, Health Care, and Information and Telecommunication Technologies often require a lot of prior education, whereas on-the-job training or an educational program requiring a small commitment of time may be sufficient preparation for many jobs in the "younger" renewal industries.

Keep in mind that the young people who hold the jobs listed in this section may not stay in those jobs, or even in jobs related to the same renewal industry, for a whole career. Some people are "late bloomers" who do not recognize at an early age what industry interests them most and how to find a job in that industry. Others may take a job in an uninteresting industry because it offers the opportunity to enter the labor market, earn some money, gain basic job skills, and acquire the experience necessary for moving up to a job that is a better fit.

Advanced Manufacturing Jobs with the Highest Percentage of Workers Age 16–24	
Job	Percent Workers Age 16–24
1. Laborers and Freight, Stock, and Material Movers, Hand	30.3%
2. Painters, Transportation Equipment	16.0%

(continued)

(continued)

Advanced Manufacturing Jobs with the Highest Percentage of Workers Age 16–24

Job	Percent Workers Age 16–24
3. Team Assemblers	14.9%
4. Industrial Truck and Tractor Operators	14.3%
5. Shipping, Receiving, and Traffic Clerks	14.3%
6. Welders, Cutters, Solderers, and Brazers	14.1%
7. Electricians	12.2%
8. Biological Technicians	10.5%
9. Commercial and Industrial Designers	10.3%
10. Graphic Designers	10.3%
11. Electrical and Electronics Drafters	10.0%
12. Mechanical Drafters	10.0%
13. Chemical Engineers	9.8%
14. Maintenance Workers, Machinery	9.7%
15. Electrical and Electronic Engineering Technicians	8.9%
16. Industrial Engineering Technicians	8.9%
17. Mechanical Engineering Technicians	8.9%
18. Electrical and Electronics Repairers, Commercial and Industrial Equipment	8.2%
19. Computer Hardware Engineers	8.0%

Best Advanced Manufacturing Jobs Overall Employing 8 Percent or More Workers Age 16–24

Job	Percent Workers Age 16–24	Annual Earnings	Percent Growth	Annual Openings
1. Electricians	12.2%	$44,780	7.4%	79,083
2. Biological Technicians	10.5%	$37,810	16.0%	15,374
3. Graphic Designers	10.3%	$41,280	9.8%	26,968
4. Industrial Engineering Technicians	8.9%	$47,490	9.9%	6,172
5. Commercial and Industrial Designers	10.3%	$56,550	7.2%	4,777
6. Chemical Engineers	9.8%	$81,500	7.9%	2,111
7. Electrical and Electronics Repairers, Commercial and Industrial Equipment	8.2%	$47,110	6.8%	6,607
8. Electrical and Electronic Engineering Technicians	8.9%	$52,140	3.6%	12,583

Best Advanced Manufacturing Jobs Overall
Employing 8 Percent or More Workers Age 16–24

Job	Percent Workers Age 16–24	Annual Earnings	Percent Growth	Annual Openings
9. Computer Hardware Engineers	8.0%	$91,860	4.6%	3,572
10. Mechanical Drafters	10.0%	$44,740	5.2%	10,902
11. Electrical and Electronics Drafters	10.0%	$49,250	4.1%	4,786
12. Mechanical Engineering Technicians	8.9%	$47,280	6.4%	3,710
13. Welders, Cutters, Solderers, and Brazers	14.1%	$32,270	5.1%	61,125
14. Shipping, Receiving, and Traffic Clerks	14.3%	$26,990	3.7%	138,967
15. Painters, Transportation Equipment	16.0%	$36,000	8.4%	3,268
16. Laborers and Freight, Stock, and Material Movers, Hand	30.3%	$21,900	2.1%	630,487
17. Team Assemblers	14.9%	$24,630	0.1%	264,135
18. Industrial Truck and Tractor Operators	14.3%	$28,010	–2.0%	89,547
19. Maintenance Workers, Machinery	9.7%	$35,590	–1.1%	15,055

Education Jobs with the Highest Percentage of Workers Age 16–24

Job	Percent Workers Age 16–24
1. Self-Enrichment Education Teachers	17.4%
2. Kindergarten Teachers, Except Special Education	13.2%
3. Preschool Teachers, Except Special Education	13.2%

Best Education Jobs Overall Employing
8 Percent or More Workers Age 16–24

Job	Percent Workers Age 16–24	Annual Earnings	Percent Growth	Annual Openings
1. Preschool Teachers, Except Special Education	13.2%	$23,130	26.3%	78,172
2. Self-Enrichment Education Teachers	17.4%	$34,580	23.1%	64,449
3. Educational, Vocational, and School Counselors	8.0%	$49,450	12.6%	54,025
4. Kindergarten Teachers, Except Special Education	13.2%	$45,120	16.3%	27,603

Green Technologies Jobs with the Highest Percentage of Workers Age 16–24

Job	Percent Workers Age 16–24
1. Plumbers, Pipefitters, and Steamfitters	12.8%
2. Carpenters	12.8%
3. Electricians	12.2%
4. Environmental Science and Protection Technicians, Including Health	28.0%
5. Roofers	22.4%
6. Construction Laborers	23.7%
7. Operating Engineers and Other Construction Equipment Operators	8.8%
8. Heating, Air Conditioning, and Refrigeration Mechanics and Installers	10.4%
9. Industrial Engineering Technicians	8.9%
10. Surveying and Mapping Technicians	18.6%
11. Helpers—Installation, Maintenance, and Repair Workers	33.6%
12. Chemical Engineers	9.8%
13. Electrical and Electronic Engineering Technicians	8.9%
14. Glaziers	16.5%
15. Sheet Metal Workers	14.7%
16. Helpers—Pipelayers, Plumbers, Pipefitters, and Steamfitters	41.2%
17. Architectural and Civil Drafters	10.0%
18. Electrical and Electronics Repairers, Commercial and Industrial Equipment	8.2%
19. Pipelayers	12.8%
20. Hazardous Materials Removal Workers	22.6%
21. Mechanical Engineering Technicians	8.9%
22. Refuse and Recyclable Material Collectors	16.7%
23. Welders, Cutters, Solderers, and Brazers	14.1%
24. Electrical and Electronics Drafters	10.0%
25. Structural Iron and Steel Workers	17.1%
26. Insulation Workers, Mechanical	19.0%
27. Industrial Truck and Tractor Operators	14.3%
28. Inspectors, Testers, Sorters, Samplers, and Weighers	9.0%

Best Green Technologies Jobs Overall Employing 8 Percent or More Workers Age 16–24

Job	Percent Workers Age 16–24	Annual Earnings	Percent Growth	Annual Openings
1. Plumbers, Pipefitters, and Steamfitters	12.8%	$44,090	10.6%	68,643
2. Carpenters	12.8%	$37,660	10.3%	223,225
3. Electricians	12.2%	$44,780	7.4%	79,083
4. Environmental Science and Protection Technicians, Including Health	28.0%	$39,370	28.0%	8,404
5. Roofers	22.4%	$33,240	14.3%	38,398
6. Construction Laborers	23.7%	$27,310	10.9%	257,407
7. Operating Engineers and Other Construction Equipment Operators	8.8%	$38,130	8.4%	55,468
8. Heating, Air Conditioning, and Refrigeration Mechanics and Installers	10.4%	$38,360	8.7%	29,719
9. Industrial Engineering Technicians	8.9%	$47,490	9.9%	6,172
10. Surveying and Mapping Technicians	18.6%	$33,640	19.4%	8,299
11. Helpers—Installation, Maintenance, and Repair Workers	33.6%	$22,920	11.8%	52,058
12. Chemical Engineers	9.8%	$81,500	7.9%	2,111
13. Electrical and Electronic Engineering Technicians	8.9%	$52,140	3.6%	12,583
14. Glaziers	16.5%	$35,230	11.9%	6,416
15. Sheet Metal Workers	14.7%	$39,210	6.7%	31,677
16. Helpers—Pipelayers, Plumbers, Pipefitters, and Steamfitters	41.2%	$25,350	11.9%	29,332
17. Architectural and Civil Drafters	10.0%	$43,310	6.1%	16,238
18. Electrical and Electronics Repairers, Commercial and Industrial Equipment	8.2%	$47,110	6.8%	6,607
19. Pipelayers	12.8%	$31,280	8.7%	8,902
20. Hazardous Materials Removal Workers	22.6%	$36,330	11.2%	1,933
21. Mechanical Engineering Technicians	8.9%	$47,280	6.4%	3,710
22. Refuse and Recyclable Material Collectors	16.7%	$29,420	7.4%	37,785
23. Welders, Cutters, Solderers, and Brazers	14.1%	$32,270	5.1%	61,125
24. Electrical and Electronics Drafters	10.0%	$49,250	4.1%	4,786
25. Structural Iron and Steel Workers	17.1%	$42,130	6.0%	6,969

Health-Care Jobs with the Highest Percentage of Workers Age 16–24

Job	Percent Workers Age 16–24
1. Pharmacy Technicians	24.7%
2. Surgical Technologists	24.7%
3. Medical Assistants	19.5%
4. Medical Transcriptionists	19.5%
5. Dental Assistants	18.5%
6. Nursing Aides, Orderlies, and Attendants	17.8%
7. Emergency Medical Technicians and Paramedics	17.3%
8. Physical Therapist Aides	14.8%
9. Physical Therapist Assistants	14.8%
10. Massage Therapists	12.2%
11. Health Educators	10.5%
12. Biological Technicians	10.5%
13. Medical Records and Health Information Technicians	9.1%
14. Marriage and Family Therapists	8.0%
15. Mental Health Counselors	8.0%
16. Rehabilitation Counselors	8.0%
17. Substance Abuse and Behavioral Disorder Counselors	8.0%

Best Health-Care Jobs Overall Employing 8 Percent or More Workers Age 16–24

Job	Percent Workers Age 16–24	Annual Earnings	Percent Growth	Annual Openings
1. Medical Assistants	19.5%	$27,430	35.4%	92,977
2. Substance Abuse and Behavioral Disorder Counselors	8.0%	$35,580	34.3%	20,821
3. Mental Health Counselors	8.0%	$36,000	30.0%	24,103
4. Physical Therapist Assistants	14.8%	$44,130	32.4%	5,957
5. Dental Assistants	18.5%	$31,550	29.2%	29,482
6. Pharmacy Technicians	24.7%	$26,720	32.0%	54,453
7. Health Educators	10.5%	$42,920	26.2%	13,707
8. Marriage and Family Therapists	8.0%	$43,600	29.8%	5,953
9. Surgical Technologists	24.7%	$37,540	24.5%	15,365
10. Rehabilitation Counselors	8.0%	$29,630	23.0%	32,081

Best Health-Care Jobs Overall Employing
8 Percent or More Workers Age 16–24

Job	Percent Workers Age 16–24	Annual Earnings	Percent Growth	Annual Openings
11. Biological Technicians	10.5%	$37,810	16.0%	15,374
12. Medical Records and Health Information Technicians	9.1%	$29,290	17.8%	39,048
13. Nursing Aides, Orderlies, and Attendants	17.8%	$23,160	18.2%	321,036
14. Massage Therapists	12.2%	$34,870	20.3%	9,193
15. Emergency Medical Technicians and Paramedics	17.3%	$28,400	19.2%	19,513
16. Medical Transcriptionists	19.5%	$31,250	13.5%	18,080
17. Physical Therapist Aides	14.8%	$22,990	24.4%	4,092

Information and Telecommunication Technologies
Jobs with the Highest Percentage of Workers Age 16–24

Job	Percent Workers Age 16–24
1. Computer Support Specialists	12.6%
2. Network Systems and Data Communications Analysts	9.1%
3. Computer Hardware Engineers	8.0%

Best Information and Telecommunication Technologies Jobs Overall
Employing 8 Percent or More Workers Age 16–24

Job	Percent Workers Age 16–24	Annual Earnings	Percent Growth	Annual Openings
1. Network Systems and Data Communications Analysts	9.1%	$68,220	53.4%	35,086
2. Computer Support Specialists	12.6%	$42,400	12.9%	97,334
3. Computer Hardware Engineers	8.0%	$91,860	4.6%	3,572

Infrastructure Jobs with the Highest Percentage of Workers Age 16–24

Job	Percent Workers Age 16–24
1. Helpers—Carpenters	41.2%
2. Helpers—Brickmasons, Blockmasons, Stonemasons, and Tile and Marble Setters	41.2%
3. Helpers—Pipelayers, Plumbers, Pipefitters, and Steamfitters	41.2%
4. Helpers—Installation, Maintenance, and Repair Workers	33.6%
5. Environmental Science and Protection Technicians, Including Health	28.0%
6. Construction Laborers	23.7%
7. Roofers	22.4%
8. Surveying and Mapping Technicians	18.6%
9. Glaziers	16.5%
10. Drywall and Ceiling Tile Installers	16.3%
11. Cement Masons and Concrete Finishers	16.3%
12. Sheet Metal Workers	14.7%
13. Carpenters	12.8%
14. Plumbers, Pipefitters, and Steamfitters	12.8%
15. Electricians	12.2%
16. Heating, Air Conditioning, and Refrigeration Mechanics and Installers	10.4%
17. Mechanical Drafters	10.0%
18. Architectural and Civil Drafters	10.0%
19. Cost Estimators	9.0%
20. Highway Maintenance Workers	9.0%
21. Electrical and Electronic Engineering Technicians	8.9%
22. Environmental Engineering Technicians	8.9%
23. Civil Engineering Technicians	8.9%
24. Operating Engineers and Other Construction Equipment Operators	8.8%
25. Telecommunications Equipment Installers and Repairers, Except Line Installers	8.4%

Best Infrastructure Jobs Overall Employing 8 Percent or More Workers Age 16–24

Job	Percent Workers Age 16–24	Annual Earnings	Percent Growth	Annual Openings
1. Cost Estimators	9.0%	$54,920	18.5%	38,379
2. Plumbers, Pipefitters, and Steamfitters	12.8%	$44,090	10.6%	68,643
3. Electricians	12.2%	$44,780	7.4%	79,083

Best Infrastructure Jobs Overall Employing 8 Percent or More Workers Age 16–24

Job	Percent Workers Age 16–24	Annual Earnings	Percent Growth	Annual Openings
4. Carpenters	12.8%	$37,660	10.3%	223,225
5. Roofers	22.4%	$33,240	14.3%	38,398
6. Environmental Science and Protection Technicians, Including Health	28.0%	$39,370	28.0%	8,404
7. Construction Laborers	23.7%	$27,310	10.9%	257,407
8. Environmental Engineering Technicians	8.9%	$40,690	24.8%	2,162
9. Operating Engineers and Other Construction Equipment Operators	8.8%	$38,130	8.4%	55,468
10. Cement Masons and Concrete Finishers	16.3%	$33,840	11.4%	34,625
11. Helpers—Installation, Maintenance, and Repair Workers	33.6%	$22,920	11.8%	52,058
12. Heating, Air Conditioning, and Refrigeration Mechanics and Installers	10.4%	$38,360	8.7%	29,719
13. Helpers—Carpenters	41.2%	$24,340	11.7%	37,731
14. Helpers—Pipelayers, Plumbers, Pipefitters, and Steamfitters	41.2%	$25,350	11.9%	29,332
15. Sheet Metal Workers	14.7%	$39,210	6.7%	31,677
16. Surveying and Mapping Technicians	18.6%	$33,640	19.4%	8,299
17. Telecommunications Equipment Installers and Repairers, Except Line Installers	8.4%	$54,070	2.5%	13,541
18. Architectural and Civil Drafters	10.0%	$43,310	6.1%	16,238
19. Civil Engineering Technicians	8.9%	$42,580	10.2%	7,499
20. Electrical and Electronic Engineering Technicians	8.9%	$52,140	3.6%	12,583
21. Glaziers	16.5%	$35,230	11.9%	6,416
22. Drywall and Ceiling Tile Installers	16.3%	$36,520	7.3%	30,945
23. Mechanical Drafters	10.0%	$44,740	5.2%	10,902
24. Helpers—Brickmasons, Blockmasons, Stonemasons, and Tile and Marble Setters	41.2%	$26,260	11.0%	22,500
25. Highway Maintenance Workers	9.0%	$32,600	8.9%	24,774

The Best Jobs in Each Renewal Industry with a High Percentage of Workers Age 55 and Over

In the following lists, we sorted the best jobs for each renewal industry and included only those jobs that employ the highest percentage of workers age 55 and over. Workers in this age bracket make up roughly 15 percent of the workforce. We included occupations in the lists if the percentage of workers 55 and over was 15 percent or higher. (This is the percentage for workers in all industries, not just the six renewal industries.)

One use for these lists is to help you identify jobs that might be interesting to you as you decide to change careers or approach retirement. Some jobs are on the lists because they are attractive to older workers wanting part-time work to supplement their retirement income—for example, Medical Assistants. Other occupations on the lists, such as several professional-level jobs in health care, require many years of training and experience. People who are established in such careers often have many incentives to continue working at ages when workers in other fields are ready to retire. Some of these jobs also are not as physically demanding as some other jobs, such as construction trades in the Infrastructure industry, and therefore may be easier for older workers to perform.

Advanced Manufacturing Jobs with the Highest Percentage of Workers Age 55 and Over

Job	Percent Workers Age 55 and Over
1. Electrical and Electronics Repairers, Commercial and Industrial Equipment	26.0%
2. Engineering Managers	25.5%
3. Maintenance and Repair Workers, General	25.3%
4. Millwrights	25.2%
5. Chemical Engineers	24.3%
6. Purchasing Managers	24.3%
7. Purchasing Agents, Except Wholesale, Retail, and Farm Products	23.8%
8. Technical Writers	22.4%
9. Maintenance Workers, Machinery	21.7%
10. Industrial Machinery Mechanics	21.6%
11. Machinists	21.4%
12. Electrical Engineers	21.3%
13. Electronics Engineers, Except Computer	21.3%
14. Industrial Engineers	20.8%
15. Health and Safety Engineers, Except Mining Safety Engineers and Inspectors	20.8%
16. Industrial Production Managers	20.6%
17. Sales Engineers	19.7%
18. Electrical and Electronic Engineering Technicians	19.6%
19. Industrial Engineering Technicians	19.6%
20. Mechanical Engineering Technicians	19.6%
21. Production, Planning, and Expediting Clerks	19.2%
22. Transportation, Storage, and Distribution Managers	19.1%
23. Commercial and Industrial Designers	19.0%
24. Graphic Designers	19.0%

Advanced Manufacturing Jobs with the Highest Percentage of Workers Age 55 and Over

Job	Percent Workers Age 55 and Over
25. Logisticians	18.5%
26. Computer Hardware Engineers	17.9%
27. Electrical and Electronics Drafters	16.8%
28. Mechanical Drafters	16.8%
29. Shipping, Receiving, and Traffic Clerks	16.0%
30. Electricians	15.9%
31. Team Assemblers	15.8%

Best Advanced Manufacturing Jobs Overall Employing 15 Percent or More Workers Age 55 and Over

Job	Percent Workers Age 55 and Over	Annual Earnings	Percent Growth	Annual Openings
1. Industrial Engineers	20.8%	$71,430	20.3%	11,272
2. Logisticians	18.5%	$64,250	17.3%	9,671
3. Engineering Managers	25.5%	$111,020	7.3%	7,404
4. Technical Writers	22.4%	$60,390	19.5%	7,498
5. Sales Engineers	19.7%	$80,270	8.5%	7,371
6. Maintenance and Repair Workers, General	25.3%	$32,570	10.1%	165,502
7. Electricians	15.9%	$44,780	7.4%	79,083
8. Graphic Designers	19.0%	$41,280	9.8%	26,968
9. Transportation, Storage, and Distribution Managers	19.1%	$76,310	8.3%	6,994
10. Industrial Machinery Mechanics	21.6%	$42,350	9.0%	23,361
11. Chemical Engineers	24.3%	$81,500	7.9%	2,111
12. Electrical Engineers	21.3%	$79,240	6.3%	6,806
13. Industrial Engineering Technicians	19.6%	$47,490	9.9%	6,172
14. Industrial Production Managers	20.6%	$80,560	–5.9%	14,889
15. Purchasing Managers	24.3%	$85,440	3.4%	7,243
16. Health and Safety Engineers, Except Mining Safety Engineers and Inspectors	20.8%	$69,580	9.6%	1,105
17. Computer Hardware Engineers	17.9%	$91,860	4.6%	3,572

(continued)

(continued)

Best Advanced Manufacturing Jobs Overall
Employing 15 Percent or More Workers Age 55 and Over

Job	Percent Workers Age 55 and Over	Annual Earnings	Percent Growth	Annual Openings
18. Electronics Engineers, Except Computer	21.3%	$83,340	3.7%	5,699
19. Purchasing Agents, Except Wholesale, Retail, and Farm Products	23.8%	$52,460	0.1%	22,349
20. Production, Planning, and Expediting Clerks	19.2%	$39,690	4.2%	52,735
21. Electrical and Electronic Engineering Technicians	19.6%	$52,140	3.6%	12,583
22. Commercial and Industrial Designers	19.0%	$56,550	7.2%	4,777
23. Mechanical Drafters	16.8%	$44,740	5.2%	10,902
24. Shipping, Receiving, and Traffic Clerks	16.0%	$26,990	3.7%	138,967
25. Electrical and Electronics Repairers, Commercial and Industrial Equipment	26.0%	$47,110	6.8%	6,607

Education Jobs with the Highest Percentage of Workers Age 55 and Over

Job	Percent Workers Age 55 and Over
1. Clinical, Counseling, and School Psychologists	35.0%
2. Instructional Coordinators	30.4%
3. Education Administrators, Postsecondary	28.7%
4. Education Administrators, Elementary and Secondary School	28.7%
5. Education Administrators, Preschool and Child Care Center/Program	28.7%
6. Educational, Vocational, and School Counselors	25.3%
7. Self-Enrichment Education Teachers	22.1%
8. Elementary School Teachers, Except Special Education	22.0%
9. Middle School Teachers, Except Special and Vocational Education	22.0%
10. Child, Family, and School Social Workers	19.9%
11. Special Education Teachers, Preschool, Kindergarten, and Elementary School	19.5%
12. Speech-Language Pathologists	17.1%

Best Education Jobs Overall Employing
15 Percent or More Workers Age 55 and Over

Job	Percent Workers Age 55 and Over	Annual Earnings	Percent Growth	Annual Openings
1. Instructional Coordinators	30.4%	$55,270	22.5%	21,294
2. Self-Enrichment Education Teachers	22.1%	$34,580	23.1%	64,449
3. Education Administrators, Postsecondary	28.7%	$75,780	14.2%	17,121
4. Elementary School Teachers, Except Special Education	22.0%	$47,330	13.6%	181,612
5. Education Administrators, Elementary and Secondary School	28.7%	$80,580	7.6%	27,143
6. Educational, Vocational, and School Counselors	25.3%	$49,450	12.6%	54,025
7. Special Education Teachers, Preschool, Kindergarten, and Elementary School	19.5%	$48,350	19.6%	20,049
8. Child, Family, and School Social Workers	19.9%	$38,620	19.1%	35,402
9. Clinical, Counseling, and School Psychologists	35.0%	$62,210	15.8%	8,309
10. Middle School Teachers, Except Special and Vocational Education	22.0%	$47,900	11.2%	75,270
11. Education Administrators, Preschool and Child Care Center/Program	28.7%	$38,580	23.5%	8,113
12. Speech-Language Pathologists	17.1%	$60,690	10.6%	11,160

Green Technologies Jobs with the Highest
Percentage of Workers Age 55 and Over

Job	Percent Workers Age 55 and Over
1. Bus Drivers, Transit and Intercity	38.2%
2. Construction and Building Inspectors	26.8%
3. Electrical and Electronics Repairers, Commercial and Industrial Equipment	26.0%
4. Petroleum Engineers	25.8%
5. Nuclear Engineers	25.5%
6. Engineering Managers	25.5%
7. Chemical Engineers	24.3%
8. Geological and Petroleum Technicians	22.6%
9. Geoscientists, Except Hydrologists and Geographers	22.6%
10. Environmental Scientists and Specialists, Including Health	22.6%

(continued)

(continued)

Green Technologies Jobs with the Highest Percentage of Workers Age 55 and Over

Job	Percent Workers Age 55 and Over
11. Hydrologists	22.6%
12. Industrial Machinery Mechanics	21.6%
13. Machinists	21.4%
14. Electrical Engineers	21.3%
15. Construction Managers	21.1%
16. Urban and Regional Planners	20.9%
17. Industrial Engineers	20.8%
18. Industrial Production Managers	20.6%
19. Hazardous Materials Removal Workers	20.0%
20. Operating Engineers and Other Construction Equipment Operators	19.8%
21. Mechanical Engineering Technicians	19.6%
22. Electrical and Electronic Engineering Technicians	19.6%
23. Industrial Engineering Technicians	19.6%
24. Inspectors, Testers, Sorters, Samplers, and Weighers	18.5%
25. Surveying and Mapping Technicians	17.7%
26. First-Line Supervisors/Managers of Construction Trades and Extraction Workers	17.4%
27. Mobile Heavy Equipment Mechanics, Except Engines	17.4%
28. Electrical and Electronics Drafters	16.8%
29. Architectural and Civil Drafters	16.8%
30. Refuse and Recyclable Material Collectors	16.3%
31. Environmental Engineers	16.2%
32. Electricians	15.9%

Best Green Technologies Jobs Overall Employing 15 Percent or More Workers Age 55 and Over

Job	Percent Workers Age 55 and Over	Annual Earnings	Percent Growth	Annual Openings
1. Construction Managers	21.1%	$76,230	15.7%	44,158
2. First-Line Supervisors/Managers of Construction Trades and Extraction Workers	17.4%	$55,950	9.1%	82,923
3. Industrial Engineers	20.8%	$71,430	20.3%	11,272

Best Green Technologies Jobs Overall Employing 15 Percent or More Workers Age 55 and Over

Job	Percent Workers Age 55 and Over	Annual Earnings	Percent Growth	Annual Openings
4. Environmental Engineers	16.2%	$72,350	25.4%	5,003
5. Environmental Scientists and Specialists, Including Health	22.6%	$58,380	25.1%	6,961
6. Construction and Building Inspectors	26.8%	$48,330	18.2%	12,606
7. Geoscientists, Except Hydrologists and Geographers	22.6%	$75,800	21.9%	2,471
8. Engineering Managers	25.5%	$111,020	7.3%	7,404
9. Electricians	15.9%	$44,780	7.4%	79,083
10. Hydrologists	22.6%	$68,140	24.3%	687
11. Industrial Production Managers	20.6%	$80,560	–5.9%	14,889
12. Operating Engineers and Other Construction Equipment Operators	19.8%	$38,130	8.4%	55,468
13. Bus Drivers, Transit and Intercity	38.2%	$33,160	12.5%	27,100
14. Chemical Engineers	24.3%	$81,500	7.9%	2,111
15. Industrial Machinery Mechanics	21.6%	$42,350	9.0%	23,361
16. Urban and Regional Planners	20.9%	$57,970	14.5%	1,967
17. Electrical Engineers	21.3%	$79,240	6.3%	6,806
18. Mobile Heavy Equipment Mechanics, Except Engines	17.4%	$41,450	12.3%	11,037
19. Surveying and Mapping Technicians	17.7%	$33,640	19.4%	8,299
20. Industrial Engineering Technicians	19.6%	$47,490	9.9%	6,172
21. Nuclear Engineers	25.5%	$94,420	7.2%	1,046
22. Electrical and Electronic Engineering Technicians	19.6%	$52,140	3.6%	12,583
23. Refuse and Recyclable Material Collectors	16.3%	$29,420	7.4%	37,785
24. Architectural and Civil Drafters	16.8%	$43,310	6.1%	16,238
25. Petroleum Engineers	25.8%	$103,960	5.2%	1,016

Health-Care Jobs with the Highest Percentage of Workers Age 55 and Over

Job	Percent Workers Age 55 and Over
1. Clinical, Counseling, and School Psychologists	35.0%
2. Dentists, General	27.4%

(continued)

(continued)

Health-Care Jobs with the Highest Percentage of Workers Age 55 and Over

Job	Percent Workers Age 55 and Over
3. Prosthodontists	27.4%
4. Orthodontists	27.4%
5. Oral and Maxillofacial Surgeons	27.4%
6. Physicians and Surgeons	27.2%
7. Medical Records and Health Information Technicians	26.1%
8. Rehabilitation Counselors	25.3%
9. Substance Abuse and Behavioral Disorder Counselors	25.3%
10. Mental Health Counselors	25.3%
11. Marriage and Family Therapists	25.3%
12. Medical and Health Services Managers	24.7%
13. Optometrists	24.6%
14. Pharmacists	22.5%
15. Licensed Practical and Licensed Vocational Nurses	22.0%
16. Registered Nurses	21.0%
17. Medical and Public Health Social Workers	19.9%
18. Mental Health and Substance Abuse Social Workers	19.9%
19. Medical and Clinical Laboratory Technicians	19.8%
20. Medical and Clinical Laboratory Technologists	19.8%
21. Occupational Therapist Assistants	19.0%
22. Occupational Health and Safety Specialists	18.4%
23. Health Educators	18.3%
24. Chiropractors	17.5%
25. Nursing Aides, Orderlies, and Attendants	17.5%
26. Dietitians and Nutritionists	17.3%
27. Respiratory Therapists	17.1%
28. Speech-Language Pathologists	17.1%

Best Health-Care Jobs Overall Employing 15 Percent or More Workers Age 55 and Over

Job	Percent Workers Age 55 and Over	Annual Earnings	Percent Growth	Annual Openings
1. Registered Nurses	21.0%	$60,010	23.5%	233,499
2. Physicians and Surgeons	27.2%	$145,600+	14.2%	38,027
3. Medical and Health Services Managers	24.7%	$76,990	16.4%	31,877
4. Pharmacists	22.5%	$100,480	21.7%	16,358
5. Mental Health Counselors	25.3%	$36,000	30.0%	24,103
6. Substance Abuse and Behavioral Disorder Counselors	25.3%	$35,580	34.3%	20,821
7. Mental Health and Substance Abuse Social Workers	19.9%	$36,640	29.9%	17,289
8. Medical and Public Health Social Workers	19.9%	$44,670	24.2%	16,429
9. Health Educators	18.3%	$42,920	26.2%	13,707
10. Nursing Aides, Orderlies, and Attendants	17.5%	$23,160	18.2%	321,036
11. Rehabilitation Counselors	25.3%	$29,630	23.0%	32,081
12. Clinical, Counseling, and School Psychologists	35.0%	$62,210	15.8%	8,309
13. Marriage and Family Therapists	25.3%	$43,600	29.8%	5,953
14. Licensed Practical and Licensed Vocational Nurses	22.0%	$37,940	14.0%	70,610
15. Medical Records and Health Information Technicians	26.1%	$29,290	17.8%	39,048
16. Respiratory Therapists	17.1%	$50,070	22.6%	5,563
17. Dentists, General	27.4%	$137,630	9.2%	7,106
18. Occupational Therapist Assistants	19.0%	$45,050	25.4%	2,634
19. Medical and Clinical Laboratory Technologists	19.8%	$51,720	12.4%	11,457
20. Chiropractors	17.5%	$65,890	14.4%	3,179
21. Speech-Language Pathologists	17.1%	$60,690	10.6%	11,160
22. Orthodontists	27.4%	$145,600+	9.2%	479
23. Prosthodontists	27.4%	$145,600+	10.7%	54
24. Optometrists	24.6%	$93,800	11.3%	1,789
25. Oral and Maxillofacial Surgeons	27.4%	$145,600+	9.1%	400

Information and Telecommunication Technologies Jobs with the Highest Percentage of Workers Age 55 and Over

Job	Percent Workers Age 55 and Over
1. Multi-Media Artists and Animators	33.9%
2. Engineering Managers	25.5%
3. Technical Writers	22.4%
4. Electronics Engineers, Except Computer	21.3%
5. Electrical Engineers	21.3%
6. Sales Representatives, Wholesale and Manufacturing, Technical and Scientific Products	21.0%
7. Industrial Engineers	20.8%
8. Database Administrators	20.0%
9. Sales Engineers	19.7%
10. Computer Hardware Engineers	17.9%

Best Information and Telecommunication Technologies Jobs Overall Employing 15 Percent or More Workers Age 55 and Over

Job	Percent Workers Age 55 and Over	Annual Earnings	Percent Growth	Annual Openings
1. Industrial Engineers	20.8%	$71,430	20.3%	11,272
2. Database Administrators	20.0%	$67,250	28.6%	8,258
3. Sales Representatives, Wholesale and Manufacturing, Technical and Scientific Products	21.0%	$68,270	12.4%	43,469
4. Engineering Managers	25.5%	$111,020	7.3%	7,404
5. Multi-Media Artists and Animators	33.9%	$54,550	25.8%	13,182
6. Sales Engineers	19.7%	$80,270	8.5%	7,371
7. Technical Writers	22.4%	$60,390	19.5%	7,498
8. Computer Hardware Engineers	17.9%	$91,860	4.6%	3,572
9. Electrical Engineers	21.3%	$79,240	6.3%	6,806
10. Electronics Engineers, Except Computer	21.3%	$83,340	3.7%	5,699

Infrastructure Jobs with the Highest Percentage of Workers Age 55 and Over

Job	Percent Workers Age 55 and Over
1. Cost Estimators	29.9%
2. Construction and Building Inspectors	26.8%
3. Engineering Managers	25.5%
4. Surveyors	24.2%
5. Cartographers and Photogrammetrists	24.2%
6. Architects, Except Landscape and Naval	23.4%
7. Environmental Scientists and Specialists, Including Health	22.6%
8. Truck Drivers, Light or Delivery Services	22.5%
9. Truck Drivers, Heavy and Tractor-Trailer	22.5%
10. Technical Writers	22.4%
11. First-Line Supervisors/Managers of Mechanics, Installers, and Repairers	22.0%
12. Industrial Machinery Mechanics	21.6%
13. Electrical Engineers	21.3%
14. Construction Managers	21.1%
15. Urban and Regional Planners	20.9%
16. Industrial Engineers	20.8%
17. Health and Safety Engineers, Except Mining Safety Engineers and Inspectors	20.8%
18. Civil Engineers	20.6%
19. Operating Engineers and Other Construction Equipment Operators	19.8%
20. Environmental Engineering Technicians	19.6%
21. Electrical and Electronic Engineering Technicians	19.6%
22. Civil Engineering Technicians	19.6%
23. Telecommunications Equipment Installers and Repairers, Except Line Installers	19.5%
24. Highway Maintenance Workers	18.9%
25. Logisticians	18.5%
26. Surveying and Mapping Technicians	17.7%
27. First-Line Supervisors/Managers of Construction Trades and Extraction Workers	17.4%
28. Mobile Heavy Equipment Mechanics, Except Engines	17.4%
29. Mechanical Drafters	16.8%
30. Architectural and Civil Drafters	16.8%
31. Environmental Engineers	16.2%
32. Electricians	15.9%

Best Infrastructure Jobs Overall Employing
15 Percent or More Workers Age 55 and Over

Job	Percent Workers Age 55 and Over	Annual Earnings	Percent Growth	Annual Openings
1. Construction Managers	21.1%	$76,230	15.7%	44,158
2. Civil Engineers	20.6%	$71,710	18.0%	15,979
3. Industrial Engineers	20.8%	$71,430	20.3%	11,272
4. Cost Estimators	29.9%	$54,920	18.5%	38,379
5. Environmental Engineers	16.2%	$72,350	25.4%	5,003
6. Surveyors	24.2%	$51,630	23.7%	14,305
7. First-Line Supervisors/Managers of Construction Trades and Extraction Workers	17.4%	$55,950	9.1%	82,923
8. Architects, Except Landscape and Naval	23.4%	$67,620	17.7%	11,324
9. Environmental Scientists and Specialists, Including Health	22.6%	$58,380	25.1%	6,961
10. Technical Writers	22.4%	$60,390	19.5%	7,498
11. Logisticians	18.5%	$64,250	17.3%	9,671
12. Construction and Building Inspectors	26.8%	$48,330	18.2%	12,606
13. Truck Drivers, Heavy and Tractor-Trailer	22.5%	$36,220	10.4%	279,032
14. First-Line Supervisors/Managers of Mechanics, Installers, and Repairers	22.0%	$55,380	7.3%	24,361
15. Electricians	15.9%	$44,780	7.4%	79,083
16. Engineering Managers	25.5%	$111,020	7.3%	7,404
17. Cartographers and Photogrammetrists	24.2%	$49,970	20.3%	2,823
18. Industrial Machinery Mechanics	21.6%	$42,350	9.0%	23,361
19. Operating Engineers and Other Construction Equipment Operators	19.8%	$38,130	8.4%	55,468
20. Electrical Engineers	21.3%	$79,240	6.3%	6,806
21. Truck Drivers, Light or Delivery Services	22.5%	$26,380	8.4%	154,330
22. Health and Safety Engineers, Except Mining Safety Engineers and Inspectors	20.8%	$69,580	9.6%	1,105
23. Urban and Regional Planners	20.9%	$57,970	14.5%	1,967
24. Environmental Engineering Technicians	19.6%	$40,690	24.8%	2,162
25. Surveying and Mapping Technicians	17.7%	$33,640	19.4%	8,299

The Best Jobs in Each Renewal Industry with a High Percentage of Part-Time Workers

Starting with the jobs that met our criteria for each renewal industry in this book, we created lists that include those jobs with 15 percent or more part-time workers. (The percentages apply to workers in all industries, not just the renewal industries.)

If you want to work part time, these lists will be helpful in identifying where most others are finding opportunities for this kind of work in the renewal industry that most interests you. Many people prefer to work less than full time. For example, people who are attending school or who have young children may prefer the flexibility of part-time work. People also work part time for money-related reasons, such as supplementing income from a full-time job or working two or more part-time jobs because one desirable full-time job is not available.

If you are interested in Advanced Manufacturing or Green Technologies, you will note that few occupations linked to those industries have a lot of part-timers. For Information and Telecommunication Technologies, only one job is listed. Keep in mind that even in occupations where few people work part-time it may be possible for you to carve out a position for yourself that does not require a 40-hour work week.

Many of these jobs can be learned quickly, offer flexible work schedules, are easy to obtain, and offer other desirable advantages. Although many people think of part-time jobs as requiring few skills and providing low pay, this is not always the case. Some of these jobs pay quite well, require substantial training or experience, or are growing rapidly.

Advanced Manufacturing Jobs with the Highest Percentage of Part-Time Workers	
Job	Percent Part-Time Workers
1. Laborers and Freight, Stock, and Material Movers, Hand	20.8%
2. Commercial and Industrial Designers	16.7%
3. Graphic Designers	16.7%

Best Advanced Manufacturing Jobs Overall Employing 15 Percent or More Part-Time Workers

Job	Percent Part-Time Workers	Annual Earnings	Percent Growth	Annual Openings
1. Graphic Designers	16.7%	$41,280	9.8%	26,968
2. Commercial and Industrial Designers	16.7%	$56,550	7.2%	4,777
3. Laborers and Freight, Stock, and Material Movers, Hand	20.8%	$21,900	2.1%	630,487

Education Jobs with the Highest Percentage of Part-Time Workers

Job	Percent Part-Time Workers
1. Self-Enrichment Education Teachers	41.3%
2. Agricultural Sciences Teachers, Postsecondary	27.8%
3. Anthropology and Archeology Teachers, Postsecondary	27.8%
4. Architecture Teachers, Postsecondary	27.8%
5. Area, Ethnic, and Cultural Studies Teachers, Postsecondary	27.8%
6. Art, Drama, and Music Teachers, Postsecondary	27.8%
7. Atmospheric, Earth, Marine, and Space Sciences Teachers, Postsecondary	27.8%
8. Biological Science Teachers, Postsecondary	27.8%
9. Business Teachers, Postsecondary	27.8%
10. Chemistry Teachers, Postsecondary	27.8%
11. Communications Teachers, Postsecondary	27.8%
12. Computer Science Teachers, Postsecondary	27.8%
13. Criminal Justice and Law Enforcement Teachers, Postsecondary	27.8%
14. Economics Teachers, Postsecondary	27.8%
15. Education Teachers, Postsecondary	27.8%
16. Engineering Teachers, Postsecondary	27.8%
17. English Language and Literature Teachers, Postsecondary	27.8%
18. Environmental Science Teachers, Postsecondary	27.8%
19. Foreign Language and Literature Teachers, Postsecondary	27.8%
20. Forestry and Conservation Science Teachers, Postsecondary	27.8%
21. Geography Teachers, Postsecondary	27.8%
22. Graduate Teaching Assistants	27.8%
23. Health Specialties Teachers, Postsecondary	27.8%
24. History Teachers, Postsecondary	27.8%
25. Home Economics Teachers, Postsecondary	27.8%

Education Jobs with the Highest Percentage of Part-Time Workers

Job	Percent Part-Time Workers
26. Law Teachers, Postsecondary	27.8%
27. Library Science Teachers, Postsecondary	27.8%
28. Mathematical Science Teachers, Postsecondary	27.8%
29. Nursing Instructors and Teachers, Postsecondary	27.8%
30. Philosophy and Religion Teachers, Postsecondary	27.8%
31. Physics Teachers, Postsecondary	27.8%
32. Political Science Teachers, Postsecondary	27.8%
33. Psychology Teachers, Postsecondary	27.8%
34. Recreation and Fitness Studies Teachers, Postsecondary	27.8%
35. Social Work Teachers, Postsecondary	27.8%
36. Sociology Teachers, Postsecondary	27.8%
37. Vocational Education Teachers, Postsecondary	27.8%
38. Kindergarten Teachers, Except Special Education	25.1%
39. Preschool Teachers, Except Special Education	25.1%
40. Speech-Language Pathologists	24.6%
41. Clinical, Counseling, and School Psychologists	24.0%
42. Instructional Coordinators	19.7%
43. Educational, Vocational, and School Counselors	15.4%

Best Education Jobs Overall Employing 15 Percent or More Part-Time Workers

Job	Percent Part-Time Workers	Annual Earnings	Percent Growth	Annual Openings
1. Health Specialties Teachers, Postsecondary	27.8%	$80,700	22.9%	19,617
2. Business Teachers, Postsecondary	27.8%	$64,900	22.9%	11,643
3. Biological Science Teachers, Postsecondary	27.8%	$71,780	22.9%	9,039
4. Engineering Teachers, Postsecondary	27.8%	$79,510	22.9%	5,565
5. Law Teachers, Postsecondary	27.8%	$87,730	22.9%	2,169
6. Economics Teachers, Postsecondary	27.8%	$75,300	22.9%	2,208
7. Computer Science Teachers, Postsecondary	27.8%	$62,020	22.9%	5,820
8. Agricultural Sciences Teachers, Postsecondary	27.8%	$78,460	22.9%	1,840
9. Chemistry Teachers, Postsecondary	27.8%	$63,870	22.9%	3,405
10. Mathematical Science Teachers, Postsecondary	27.8%	$58,560	22.9%	7,663

(continued)

(continued)

Best Education Jobs Overall Employing 15 Percent or More Part-Time Workers

Job	Percent Part-Time Workers	Annual Earnings	Percent Growth	Annual Openings
11. Physics Teachers, Postsecondary	27.8%	$70,090	22.9%	2,155
12. Art, Drama, and Music Teachers, Postsecondary	27.8%	$55,190	22.9%	12,707
13. Atmospheric, Earth, Marine, and Space Sciences Teachers, Postsecondary	27.8%	$73,280	22.9%	1,553
14. Psychology Teachers, Postsecondary	27.8%	$60,610	22.9%	5,261
15. Preschool Teachers, Except Special Education	25.1%	$23,130	26.3%	78,172
16. Self-Enrichment Education Teachers	41.3%	$34,580	23.1%	64,449
17. Nursing Instructors and Teachers, Postsecondary	27.8%	$57,500	22.9%	7,337
18. Political Science Teachers, Postsecondary	27.8%	$63,100	22.9%	2,435
19. History Teachers, Postsecondary	27.8%	$59,160	22.9%	3,570
20. Architecture Teachers, Postsecondary	27.8%	$68,540	22.9%	1,044
21. Education Teachers, Postsecondary	27.8%	$54,220	22.9%	9,359
22. English Language and Literature Teachers, Postsecondary	27.8%	$54,000	22.9%	10,475
23. Vocational Education Teachers, Postsecondary	27.8%	$45,850	22.9%	19,313
24. Graduate Teaching Assistants	27.8%	$28,060	22.9%	20,601
25. Anthropology and Archeology Teachers, Postsecondary	27.8%	$64,530	22.9%	910

Green Technologies Jobs with the Highest Percentage of Part-Time Workers

Job	Percent Part-Time Workers
1. Bus Drivers, Transit and Intercity	34.1%
2. Helpers—Installation, Maintenance, and Repair Workers	22.7%
3. Environmental Science and Protection Technicians, Including Health	19.4%

Best Green Technologies Jobs Overall Employing 15 Percent or More Part-Time Workers

Job	Percent Part-Time Workers	Annual Earnings	Percent Growth	Annual Openings
1. Environmental Science and Protection Technicians, Including Health	19.4%	$39,370	28.0%	8,404
2. Bus Drivers, Transit and Intercity	34.1%	$33,160	12.5%	27,100
3. Helpers—Installation, Maintenance, and Repair Workers	22.7%	$22,920	11.8%	52,058

Health-Care Jobs with the Highest Percentage of Part-Time Workers

Job	Percent Part-Time Workers
1. Dental Hygienists	58.7%
2. Massage Therapists	42.9%
3. Dental Assistants	35.7%
4. Occupational Therapists	29.8%
5. Physical Therapist Aides	27.1%
6. Physical Therapist Assistants	27.1%
7. Dietitians and Nutritionists	27.0%
8. Dentists, General	25.9%
9. Oral and Maxillofacial Surgeons	25.9%
10. Orthodontists	25.9%
11. Prosthodontists	25.9%
12. Speech-Language Pathologists	24.6%
13. Clinical, Counseling, and School Psychologists	24.0%
14. Nursing Aides, Orderlies, and Attendants	24.0%
15. Chiropractors	23.6%
16. Podiatrists	23.6%
17. Medical Assistants	23.2%
18. Medical Transcriptionists	23.2%
19. Physical Therapists	22.7%
20. Registered Nurses	21.8%
21. Optometrists	20.8%
22. Pharmacy Technicians	20.8%
23. Surgical Technologists	20.8%
24. Licensed Practical and Licensed Vocational Nurses	18.3%

(continued)

(continued)

Health-Care Jobs with the Highest Percentage of Part-Time Workers

Job	Percent Part-Time Workers
25. Pharmacists	18.1%
26. Occupational Therapist Assistants	17.8%
27. Cardiovascular Technologists and Technicians	17.3%
28. Diagnostic Medical Sonographers	17.3%
29. Nuclear Medicine Technologists	17.3%
30. Radiologic Technologists and Technicians	17.3%
31. Physician Assistants	15.6%
32. Marriage and Family Therapists	15.4%
33. Mental Health Counselors	15.4%
34. Rehabilitation Counselors	15.4%
35. Substance Abuse and Behavioral Disorder Counselors	15.4%

Best Health-Care Jobs Overall Employing 15 Percent or More Part-Time Workers

Job	Percent Part-Time Workers	Annual Earnings	Percent Growth	Annual Openings
1. Dental Hygienists	58.7%	$64,740	30.1%	10,433
2. Physical Therapists	22.7%	$69,760	27.1%	12,072
3. Registered Nurses	21.8%	$60,010	23.5%	233,499
4. Pharmacists	18.1%	$100,480	21.7%	16,358
5. Medical Assistants	23.2%	$27,430	35.4%	92,977
6. Physician Assistants	15.6%	$78,450	27.0%	7,147
7. Substance Abuse and Behavioral Disorder Counselors	15.4%	$35,580	34.3%	20,821
8. Mental Health Counselors	15.4%	$36,000	30.0%	24,103
9. Pharmacy Technicians	20.8%	$26,720	32.0%	54,453
10. Dental Assistants	35.7%	$31,550	29.2%	29,482
11. Occupational Therapists	29.8%	$63,790	23.1%	8,338
12. Physical Therapist Assistants	27.1%	$44,130	32.4%	5,957
13. Surgical Technologists	20.8%	$37,540	24.5%	15,365
14. Marriage and Family Therapists	15.4%	$43,600	29.8%	5,953
15. Licensed Practical and Licensed Vocational Nurses	18.3%	$37,940	14.0%	70,610

Best Health-Care Jobs Overall Employing 15 Percent or More Part-Time Workers

Job	Percent Part-Time Workers	Annual Earnings	Percent Growth	Annual Openings
16. Radiologic Technologists and Technicians	17.3%	$50,260	15.1%	12,836
17. Rehabilitation Counselors	15.4%	$29,630	23.0%	32,081
18. Clinical, Counseling, and School Psychologists	24.0%	$62,210	15.8%	8,309
19. Nursing Aides, Orderlies, and Attendants	24.0%	$23,160	18.2%	321,036
20. Dentists, General	25.9%	$137,630	9.2%	7,106
21. Cardiovascular Technologists and Technicians	17.3%	$44,940	25.5%	3,550
22. Speech-Language Pathologists	24.6%	$60,690	10.6%	11,160
23. Occupational Therapist Assistants	17.8%	$45,050	25.4%	2,634
24. Chiropractors	23.6%	$65,890	14.4%	3,179
25. Diagnostic Medical Sonographers	17.3%	$59,860	19.1%	3,211

Information and Telecommunication Technologies Jobs with the Highest Percentage of Part-Time Workers

Job	Percent Part-Time Workers
1. Multi-Media Artists and Animators	22.5%

Best Information and Telecommunication Technologies Jobs Overall Employing 15 Percent or More Part-Time Workers

Job	Percent Part-Time Workers	Annual Earnings	Percent Growth	Annual Openings
1. Multi-Media Artists and Animators	22.5%	$54,550	25.8%	13,182

Infrastructure Jobs with the Highest Percentage of Part-Time Workers

Job	Percent Part-Time Workers
1. Helpers—Installation, Maintenance, and Repair Workers	22.7%
2. Environmental Science and Protection Technicians, Including Health	19.4%

	Percent Part-Time Workers	Annual Earnings	Percent Growth	Annual Openings
Best Infrastructure Jobs Overall Employing 15 Percent or More Part-Time Workers				
Job				
1. Environmental Science and Protection Technicians, Including Health	19.4%	$39,370	28.0%	8,404
2. Helpers—Installation, Maintenance, and Repair Workers	22.7%	$22,920	11.8%	52,058

The Best Jobs in Each Renewal Industry with a High Percentage of Self-Employed Workers

About 8 percent of all working people are self-employed or own their own business. This substantial part of our workforce gets little mention in most career books.

The jobs in the lists in this section are selected from the best jobs for each renewal industry, and all have 8 percent or more self-employed workers. (These are the percentages of self-employed workers in all industries, not just the renewal industries.) Many jobs in these lists, such as Graphic Designers, are held by people who operate one- or two-person businesses and who may also do this work part time. Those in other occupations, such as Carpenters, often work on a per-job basis under the supervision of others.

As you will see from these lists, self-employed people hold a wide range of jobs at all levels of pay and skill. Many are in construction (in Green Technologies or Infrastructure), but the health-care professions are also well represented. While the lists do not include data on age and gender, you may be interested to learn that older workers and women make up a rapidly growing part of the self-employed population. For example, some highly experienced older workers set up consulting and other small businesses following a layoff or as an alternative to full retirement. Large numbers of women are forming small businesses or creating self-employment opportunities as an alternative to traditional employment.

Note that the earnings figures in the following lists are based on a survey that *does not include* self-employed workers. The actual earnings of self-employed workers may be higher or lower.

Advanced Manufacturing Jobs with the Highest Percentage of Self-Employed Workers

Job	Percent Self-Employed Workers
1. Commercial and Industrial Designers	29.8%
2. Graphic Designers	25.3%
3. Electricians	10.7%

Best Advanced Manufacturing Jobs Overall with 8 Percent or More Self-Employed Workers

Job	Percent Self-Employed Workers	Annual Earnings	Percent Growth	Annual Openings
1. Electricians	10.7%	$44,780	7.4%	79,083
2. Graphic Designers	25.3%	$41,280	9.8%	26,968
3. Commercial and Industrial Designers	29.8%	$56,550	7.2%	4,777

Education Jobs with the Highest Percentage of Self-Employed Workers

Job	Percent Self-Employed Workers
1. Clinical, Counseling, and School Psychologists	34.2%
2. Self-Enrichment Education Teachers	21.5%
3. Speech-Language Pathologists	8.8%

Best Education Jobs Overall with 8 Percent or More Self-Employed Workers

Job	Percent Self-Employed Workers	Annual Earnings	Percent Growth	Annual Openings
1. Self-Enrichment Education Teachers	21.5%	$34,580	23.1%	64,449
2. Clinical, Counseling, and School Psychologists	34.2%	$62,210	15.8%	8,309
3. Speech-Language Pathologists	8.8%	$60,690	10.6%	11,160

Green Technologies Jobs with the Highest Percentage of Self-Employed Workers

Job	Percent Self-Employed Workers
1. Construction Managers	56.3%
2. Carpenters	31.8%
3. First-Line Supervisors/Managers of Construction Trades and Extraction Workers	24.4%
4. Roofers	20.1%
5. Construction Laborers	16.4%
6. Heating, Air Conditioning, and Refrigeration Mechanics and Installers	12.7%
7. Plumbers, Pipefitters, and Steamfitters	12.3%
8. Pipelayers	11.6%
9. Electricians	10.7%
10. Construction and Building Inspectors	9.4%
11. Petroleum Engineers	9.2%

Best Green Technologies Jobs Overall with 8 Percent or More Self-Employed Workers

Job	Percent Self-Employed Workers	Annual Earnings	Percent Growth	Annual Openings
1. Construction Managers	56.3%	$76,230	15.7%	44,158
2. First-Line Supervisors/Managers of Construction Trades and Extraction Workers	24.4%	$55,950	9.1%	82,923
3. Construction and Building Inspectors	9.4%	$48,330	18.2%	12,606
4. Carpenters	31.8%	$37,660	10.3%	223,225
5. Construction Laborers	16.4%	$27,310	10.9%	257,407
6. Plumbers, Pipefitters, and Steamfitters	12.3%	$44,090	10.6%	68,643
7. Electricians	10.7%	$44,780	7.4%	79,083
8. Roofers	20.1%	$33,240	14.3%	38,398
9. Heating, Air Conditioning, and Refrigeration Mechanics and Installers	12.7%	$38,360	8.7%	29,719
10. Petroleum Engineers	9.2%	$103,960	5.2%	1,016
11. Pipelayers	11.6%	$31,280	8.7%	8,902

Health-Care Jobs with the Highest Percentage of Self-Employed Workers

Job	Percent Self-Employed Workers
1. Massage Therapists	64.0%
2. Chiropractors	51.7%
3. Prosthodontists	51.3%
4. Orthodontists	43.3%
5. Dentists, General	36.6%
6. Clinical, Counseling, and School Psychologists	34.2%
7. Oral and Maxillofacial Surgeons	30.6%
8. Optometrists	25.5%
9. Podiatrists	23.9%
10. Physicians and Surgeons	14.7%
11. Medical Transcriptionists	9.7%
12. Speech-Language Pathologists	8.8%
13. Occupational Therapists	8.6%
14. Physical Therapists	8.4%
15. Medical and Health Services Managers	8.2%

Best Health-Care Jobs Overall with 8 Percent or More Self-Employed Workers

Job	Percent Self-Employed Workers	Annual Earnings	Percent Growth	Annual Openings
1. Physicians and Surgeons	14.7%	$145,600+	14.2%	38,027
2. Medical and Health Services Managers	8.2%	$76,990	16.4%	31,877
3. Physical Therapists	8.4%	$69,760	27.1%	12,072
4. Occupational Therapists	8.6%	$63,790	23.1%	8,338
5. Massage Therapists	64.0%	$34,870	20.3%	9,193
6. Clinical, Counseling, and School Psychologists	34.2%	$62,210	15.8%	8,309
7. Chiropractors	51.7%	$65,890	14.4%	3,179
8. Medical Transcriptionists	9.7%	$31,250	13.5%	18,080
9. Prosthodontists	51.3%	$145,600+	10.7%	54
10. Dentists, General	36.6%	$137,630	9.2%	7,106
11. Optometrists	25.5%	$93,800	11.3%	1,789
12. Orthodontists	43.3%	$145,600+	9.2%	479

(continued)

(continued)

Best Health-Care Jobs Overall with 8 Percent or More Self-Employed Workers

Job	Percent Self-Employed Workers	Annual Earnings	Percent Growth	Annual Openings
13. Speech-Language Pathologists	8.8%	$60,690	10.6%	11,160
14. Oral and Maxillofacial Surgeons	30.6%	$145,600+	9.1%	400
15. Podiatrists	23.9%	$110,510	9.5%	648

Information and Telecommunication Technologies Jobs with the Highest Percentage of Self-Employed Workers

Job	Percent Self-Employed Workers
1. Multi-Media Artists and Animators	69.7%
2. Network Systems and Data Communications Analysts	17.5%

Best Information and Telecommunication Technologies Jobs Overall with 8 Percent or More Self-Employed Workers

Job	Percent Self-Employed Workers	Annual Earnings	Percent Growth	Annual Openings
1. Network Systems and Data Communications Analysts	17.5%	$68,220	53.4%	35,086
2. Multi-Media Artists and Animators	69.7%	$54,550	25.8%	13,182

Infrastructure Jobs with the Highest Percentage of Self-Employed Workers

Job	Percent Self-Employed Workers
1. Construction Managers	56.3%
2. Painters, Construction and Maintenance	42.2%
3. Carpenters	31.8%

Infrastructure Jobs with the Highest Percentage of Self-Employed Workers

Job	Percent Self-Employed Workers
4. First-Line Supervisors/Managers of Construction Trades and Extraction Workers	24.4%
5. Drywall and Ceiling Tile Installers	23.0%
6. Architects, Except Landscape and Naval	20.3%
7. Roofers	20.1%
8. Construction Laborers	16.4%
9. Heating, Air Conditioning, and Refrigeration Mechanics and Installers	12.7%
10. Plumbers, Pipefitters, and Steamfitters	12.3%
11. Electricians	10.7%
12. Construction and Building Inspectors	9.4%
13. Truck Drivers, Light or Delivery Services	9.3%
14. Truck Drivers, Heavy and Tractor-Trailer	8.8%

Best Infrastructure Jobs Overall with 8 Percent or More Self-Employed Workers

Job	Percent Self-Employed Workers	Annual Earnings	Percent Growth	Annual Openings
1. Construction Managers	56.3%	$76,230	15.7%	44,158
2. Architects, Except Landscape and Naval	20.3%	$67,620	17.7%	11,324
3. Construction and Building Inspectors	9.4%	$48,330	18.2%	12.606
4. First-Line Supervisors/Managers of Construction Trades and Extraction Workers	24.4%	$55,950	9.1%	82,923
5. Truck Drivers, Heavy and Tractor-Trailer	8.8%	$36,220	10.4%	279,032
6. Carpenters	31.8%	$37,660	10.3%	223,225
7. Construction Laborers	16.4%	$27,310	10.9%	257,407
8. Plumbers, Pipefitters, and Steamfitters	12.3%	$44,090	10.6%	68,643
9. Painters, Construction and Maintenance	42.2%	$32,080	11.8%	101,140
10. Electricians	10.7%	$44,780	7.4%	79,083
11. Roofers	20.1%	$33,240	14.3%	38,398
12. Heating, Air Conditioning, and Refrigeration Mechanics and Installers	12.7%	$38,360	8.7%	29,719
13. Truck Drivers, Light or Delivery Services	9.3%	$26,380	8.4%	154,330
14. Drywall and Ceiling Tile Installers	23.0%	$36,520	7.3%	30,945

Best Jobs in Each Renewal Industry with a High Percentage of Women or Men

We knew we would create some controversy when we first included the best jobs lists with high percentages of men and women in an earlier *Best Jobs* book. But these lists are not meant to restrict women or men from considering job options—one reason for including these lists is exactly the opposite. We hope the lists will help people see possibilities that they might not otherwise have considered. For example, we suggest that women browse the lists of jobs that employ high percentages of men. Many of these occupations have high rewards, and women who want to do them and are willing to undertake the education or training should consider them.

To create the lists, we sorted the jobs in each renewal industry that met the criteria for this book and we itemized those employing 70 percent or more of women or men. (The figures are based on employment in all industries, not just the renewal industries.) Based on these lists of jobs dominated by one sex or the other, we also present "best overall" lists for each renewal industry in which the jobs are sorted by their combined ranking in terms of annual earnings, percent growth, and annual job openings. In these best-of lists, we show the economic facts for each job so you can compare their potential rewards.

The results were surprising. When we sorted jobs for each renewal industry to find those dominated by one gender or the other, in every industry except one (Health Care), we found *only jobs dominated by a single gender.* For example, we found dozens of Infrastructure jobs with 70 percent or more men, but none with a similarly high percentage of women. For Education jobs, the opposite was true. Even in Health Care, the imbalance is severe, with 28 female-dominated jobs to 5 male-dominated jobs.

Perhaps these great disparities are signs of how badly these industries need to be renewed, especially those with the greatest imbalances. But it seems likely that some gender disparities will remain severe for the foreseeable future. The construction jobs that are so important to Infrastructure (and, to a lesser extent, Green Technologies) are likely to continue to attract men, whereas many jobs in Health Care are likely to remain female-dominated. Of course, that doesn't mean that workers of the opposite sex won't be welcome if they choose these fields. For example, some employers are seeking female recruits to counterbalance a traditional male dominance.

In the following lists, if you compare the occupations employing a high percentage of women with those employing a high percentage of men, you may notice some distinct differences beyond the obvious. For example, you may notice that the jobs with a high percentage of women are growing much faster than those with a high percentage of men. We've done the math and discovered that the difference is an average growth rate of 20.1 percent for the jobs that employ mostly women versus an average rate of 10.0 percent for the jobs that employ mostly men. The number of annual job openings shows a similar pattern, though not as extreme. Occupations with a high percentage of women average 42,000 openings per year, while a slightly smaller number of openings, 39,480, are projected on average for occupations with a high percentage of men.

This discrepancy reflects the trend that men have had more problems than women in adapting to an economy dominated by service and information-based jobs. Many women may simply be better prepared for these jobs, possessing more appropriate skills for the jobs that are now growing rapidly and have more job openings.

On the other hand, you may notice no great difference in earnings between the two groups of jobs. In fact, the jobs with a high percentage of men have only slightly higher wages (an average of $45,906) than do the jobs with a high percentage of women ($43,547). This is a welcome contrast to the comparisons we have found between most job groupings in the *Best Jobs* series, where the male-dominated jobs often have had considerably higher earnings.

Advanced Manufacturing Jobs with the Highest Percentage of Men

Job	Percent Men
1. Electricians	98.1%
2. Millwrights	97.1%
3. Industrial Machinery Mechanics	96.2%
4. Maintenance and Repair Workers, General	96.0%
5. Maintenance Workers, Machinery	95.3%
6. Mechanical Engineers	94.2%
7. Welders, Cutters, Solderers, and Brazers	94.1%
8. Machinists	93.3%
9. Industrial Truck and Tractor Operators	92.8%
10. Engineering Managers	92.7%
11. Electronics Engineers, Except Computer	92.3%
12. Electrical Engineers	92.3%
13. Electrical and Electronics Repairers, Commercial and Industrial Equipment	89.5%
14. Health and Safety Engineers, Except Mining Safety Engineers and Inspectors	88.2%
15. Sales Engineers	86.5%
16. Transportation, Storage, and Distribution Managers	85.4%
17. Computer Hardware Engineers	83.8%
18. Industrial Production Managers	83.6%
19. Painters, Transportation Equipment	83.4%
20. Laborers and Freight, Stock, and Material Movers, Hand	83.1%
21. Chemical Engineers	82.9%
22. Aircraft Structure, Surfaces, Rigging, and Systems Assemblers	82.1%
23. First-Line Supervisors/Managers of Production and Operating Workers	80.6%
24. Mechanical Engineering Technicians	79.4%
25. Industrial Engineering Technicians	79.4%
26. Electrical and Electronic Engineering Technicians	79.4%
27. Electrical and Electronics Drafters	78.2%
28. Mechanical Drafters	78.2%
29. Industrial Engineers	77.4%

Best Advanced Manufacturing Jobs
Overall Employing 70 Percent or More Men

Job	Percent Men	Annual Earnings	Percent Growth	Annual Openings
1. Industrial Engineers	77.4%	$71,430	20.3%	11,272
2. Engineering Managers	92.7%	$111,020	7.3%	7,404
3. Sales Engineers	86.5%	$80,270	8.5%	7,371
4. Maintenance and Repair Workers, General	96.0%	$32,570	10.1%	165,502
5. Transportation, Storage, and Distribution Managers	85.4%	$76,310	8.3%	6,994
6. Electricians	98.1%	$44,780	7.4%	79,083
7. Industrial Machinery Mechanics	96.2%	$42,350	9.0%	23,361
8. Electrical Engineers	92.3%	$79,240	6.3%	6,806
9. Industrial Engineering Technicians	79.4%	$47,490	9.9%	6,172
10. Aircraft Structure, Surfaces, Rigging, and Systems Assemblers	82.1%	$45,420	12.8%	6,550
11. Mechanical Engineers	94.2%	$72,300	4.2%	12,394
12. Chemical Engineers	82.9%	$81,500	7.9%	2,111
13. Industrial Production Managers	83.6%	$80,560	–5.9%	14,889
14. Health and Safety Engineers, Except Mining Safety Engineers and Inspectors	88.2%	$69,580	9.6%	1,105
15. Electrical and Electronic Engineering Technicians	79.4%	$52,140	3.6%	12,583
16. Computer Hardware Engineers	83.8%	$91,860	4.6%	3,572
17. Electronics Engineers, Except Computer	92.3%	$83,340	3.7%	5,699
18. First-Line Supervisors/Managers of Production and Operating Workers	80.6%	$48,670	–4.8%	46,144
19. Electrical and Electronics Repairers, Commercial and Industrial Equipment	89.5%	$47,110	6.8%	6,607
20. Welders, Cutters, Solderers, and Brazers	94.1%	$32,270	5.1%	61,125
21. Mechanical Drafters	78.2%	$44,740	5.2%	10,902
22. Laborers and Freight, Stock, and Material Movers, Hand	83.1%	$21,900	2.1%	630,487
23. Mechanical Engineering Technicians	79.4%	$47,280	6.4%	3,710
24. Electrical and Electronics Drafters	78.2%	$49,250	4.1%	4,786
25. Industrial Truck and Tractor Operators	92.8%	$28,010	–2.0%	89,547

Education Jobs with the Highest Percentage of Women

Job	Percent Women
1. Kindergarten Teachers, Except Special Education	97.7%
2. Preschool Teachers, Except Special Education	97.7%
3. Speech-Language Pathologists	95.3%
4. Instructional Coordinators	91.7%
5. Special Education Teachers, Preschool, Kindergarten, and Elementary School	83.5%
6. Child, Family, and School Social Workers	82.6%
7. Elementary School Teachers, Except Special Education	82.2%
8. Middle School Teachers, Except Special and Vocational Education	82.2%

Best Education Jobs Overall Employing 70 Percent or More Women

Job	Percent Women	Annual Earnings	Percent Growth	Annual Openings
1. Instructional Coordinators	91.7%	$55,270	22.5%	21,294
2. Preschool Teachers, Except Special Education	97.7%	$23,130	26.3%	78,172
3. Elementary School Teachers, Except Special Education	82.2%	$47,330	13.6%	181,612
4. Special Education Teachers, Preschool, Kindergarten, and Elementary School	83.5%	$48,350	19.6%	20,049
5. Middle School Teachers, Except Special and Vocational Education	82.2%	$47,900	11.2%	75,270
6. Child, Family, and School Social Workers	82.6%	$38,620	19.1%	35,402
7. Kindergarten Teachers, Except Special Education	97.7%	$45,120	16.3%	27,603
8. Speech-Language Pathologists	95.3%	$60,690	10.6%	11,160

Green Technologies Jobs with the Highest Percentage of Men

Job	Percent Men
1. Electrical Power-Line Installers and Repairers	99.1%
2. Roofers	98.9%
3. Mobile Heavy Equipment Mechanics, Except Engines	98.6%
4. Operating Engineers and Other Construction Equipment Operators	98.3%
5. Pipelayers	98.2%
6. Plumbers, Pipefitters, and Steamfitters	98.2%
7. Electricians	98.1%
8. Structural Iron and Steel Workers	97.8%

(continued)

(continued)

Green Technologies Jobs with the Highest Percentage of Men

Job	Percent Men
9. Carpenters	97.6%
10. First-Line Supervisors/Managers of Construction Trades and Extraction Workers	97.4%
11. Heating, Air Conditioning, and Refrigeration Mechanics and Installers	97.3%
12. Sheet Metal Workers	96.9%
13. Insulation Workers, Mechanical	96.6%
14. Construction Laborers	96.3%
15. Industrial Machinery Mechanics	96.2%
16. Mechanical Engineers	94.2%
17. Welders, Cutters, Solderers, and Brazers	94.1%
18. Refuse and Recyclable Material Collectors	93.9%
19. Helpers—Pipelayers, Plumbers, Pipefitters, and Steamfitters	93.8%
20. Machinists	93.3%
21. Glaziers	93.2%
22. Industrial Truck and Tractor Operators	92.8%
23. Engineering Managers	92.7%
24. Electrical Engineers	92.3%
25. Construction Managers	92.2%
26. Petroleum Engineers	92.2%
27. Construction and Building Inspectors	91.2%
28. Helpers—Installation, Maintenance, and Repair Workers	90.9%
29. Hazardous Materials Removal Workers	90.8%
30. Mining and Geological Engineers, Including Mining Safety Engineers	90.4%
31. Surveying and Mapping Technicians	90.1%
32. Electrical and Electronics Repairers, Commercial and Industrial Equipment	89.5%
33. Industrial Production Managers	83.6%
34. Chemical Engineers	82.9%
35. Electrical and Electronic Engineering Technicians	79.4%
36. Industrial Engineering Technicians	79.4%
37. Mechanical Engineering Technicians	79.4%
38. Architectural and Civil Drafters	78.2%
39. Electrical and Electronics Drafters	78.2%
40. Environmental Scientists and Specialists, Including Health	78.0%
41. Geoscientists, Except Hydrologists and Geographers	78.0%
42. Hydrologists	78.0%
43. Industrial Engineers	77.4%
44. Environmental Engineers	77.3%
45. Urban and Regional Planners	73.7%

Best Green Technologies Jobs Overall
Employing 70 Percent or More Men

Job	Percent Men	Annual Earnings	Percent Growth	Annual Openings
1. Construction Managers	92.2%	$76,230	15.7%	44,158
2. Industrial Engineers	77.4%	$71,430	20.3%	11,272
3. First-Line Supervisors/Managers of Construction Trades and Extraction Workers	97.4%	$55,950	9.1%	82,923
4. Environmental Scientists and Specialists, Including Health	78.0%	$58,380	25.1%	6,961
5. Construction and Building Inspectors	91.2%	$48,330	18.2%	12,606
6. Environmental Engineers	77.3%	$72,350	25.4%	5,003
7. Plumbers, Pipefitters, and Steamfitters	98.2%	$44,090	10.6%	68,643
8. Geoscientists, Except Hydrologists and Geographers	78.0%	$75,800	21.9%	2,471
9. Carpenters	97.6%	$37,660	10.3%	223,225
10. Electricians	98.1%	$44,780	7.4%	79,083
11. Engineering Managers	92.7%	$111,020	7.3%	7,404
12. Hydrologists	78.0%	$68,140	24.3%	687
13. Construction Laborers	96.3%	$27,310	10.9%	257,407
14. Roofers	98.9%	$33,240	14.3%	38,398
15. Mobile Heavy Equipment Mechanics, Except Engines	98.6%	$41,450	12.3%	11,037
16. Urban and Regional Planners	73.7%	$57,970	14.5%	1,967
17. Industrial Machinery Mechanics	96.2%	$42,350	9.0%	23,361
18. Operating Engineers and Other Construction Equipment Operators	98.3%	$38,130	8.4%	55,468
19. Heating, Air Conditioning, and Refrigeration Mechanics and Installers	97.3%	$38,360	8.7%	29,719
20. Helpers—Installation, Maintenance, and Repair Workers	90.9%	$22,920	11.8%	52,058
21. Industrial Production Managers	83.6%	$80,560	–5.9%	14,889
22. Surveying and Mapping Technicians	90.1%	$33,640	19.4%	8,299
23. Chemical Engineers	82.9%	$81,500	7.9%	2,111
24. Electrical Engineers	92.3%	$79,240	6.3%	6,806
25. Helpers—Pipelayers, Plumbers, Pipefitters, and Steamfitters	93.8%	$25,350	11.9%	29,332

Health-Care Jobs with the Highest Percentage of Women

Job	Percent Women
1. Dental Hygienists	98.6%
2. Dental Assistants	95.4%
3. Speech-Language Pathologists	95.3%
4. Licensed Practical and Licensed Vocational Nurses	94.2%
5. Medical Records and Health Information Technicians	92.0%
6. Registered Nurses	91.3%
7. Dietitians and Nutritionists	91.0%
8. Medical Assistants	91.0%
9. Medical Transcriptionists	91.0%
10. Occupational Therapists	90.3%
11. Nursing Aides, Orderlies, and Attendants	88.9%
12. Occupational Therapist Assistants	85.0%
13. Massage Therapists	84.1%
14. Medical and Public Health Social Workers	82.6%
15. Mental Health and Substance Abuse Social Workers	82.6%
16. Pharmacy Technicians	80.1%
17. Surgical Technologists	80.1%
18. Physical Therapist Aides	78.4%
19. Physical Therapist Assistants	78.4%
20. Medical and Clinical Laboratory Technicians	78.1%
21. Medical and Clinical Laboratory Technologists	78.1%
22. Health Educators	75.1%
23. Radiation Therapists	74.1%
24. Cardiovascular Technologists and Technicians	72.9%
25. Diagnostic Medical Sonographers	72.9%
26. Nuclear Medicine Technologists	72.9%
27. Radiologic Technologists and Technicians	72.9%
28. Physician Assistants	71.7%

Best Health-Care Jobs Overall Employing 70 Percent or More Women

Job	Percent Women	Annual Earnings	Percent Growth	Annual Openings
1. Dental Hygienists	98.6%	$64,740	30.1%	10,433
2. Registered Nurses	91.3%	$60,010	23.5%	233,499
3. Physician Assistants	71.7%	$78,450	27.0%	7,147
4. Medical Assistants	91.0%	$27,430	35.4%	92,977

Best Health-Care Jobs Overall Employing 70 Percent or More Women

Job	Percent Women	Annual Earnings	Percent Growth	Annual Openings
5. Mental Health and Substance Abuse Social Workers	82.6%	$36,640	29.9%	17,289
6. Pharmacy Technicians	80.1%	$26,720	32.0%	54,453
7. Dental Assistants	95.4%	$31,550	29.2%	29,482
8. Health Educators	75.1%	$42,920	26.2%	13,707
9. Medical and Public Health Social Workers	82.6%	$44,670	24.2%	16,429
10. Physical Therapist Assistants	78.4%	$44,130	32.4%	5,957
11. Occupational Therapists	90.3%	$63,790	23.1%	8,338
12. Radiation Therapists	74.1%	$70,010	24.8%	1,461
13. Surgical Technologists	80.1%	$37,540	24.5%	15,365
14. Radiologic Technologists and Technicians	72.9%	$50,260	15.1%	12,836
15. Licensed Practical and Licensed Vocational Nurses	94.2%	$37,940	14.0%	70,610
16. Cardiovascular Technologists and Technicians	72.9%	$44,940	25.5%	3,550
17. Nursing Aides, Orderlies, and Attendants	88.9%	$23,160	18.2%	321,036
18. Occupational Therapist Assistants	85.0%	$45,050	25.4%	2,634
19. Speech-Language Pathologists	95.3%	$60,690	10.6%	11,160
20. Medical and Clinical Laboratory Technologists	78.1%	$51,720	12.4%	11,457
21. Medical Records and Health Information Technicians	92.0%	$29,290	17.8%	39,048
22. Diagnostic Medical Sonographers	72.9%	$59,860	19.1%	3,211
23. Massage Therapists	84.1%	$34,870	20.3%	9,193
24. Nuclear Medicine Technologists	72.9%	$64,670	14.8%	1,290
25. Medical Transcriptionists	91.0%	$31,250	13.5%	18,080

Health-Care Jobs with the Highest Percentage of Men

Job	Percent Men
1. Prosthodontists	77.4%
2. Dentists, General	77.4%
3. Orthodontists	77.4%
4. Oral and Maxillofacial Surgeons	77.4%
5. Chiropractors	76.9%

Best Health-Care Jobs Overall Employing 70 Percent or More Men

Job	Percent Men	Annual Earnings	Percent Growth	Annual Openings
1. Orthodontists	77.4%	$145,600+	9.2%	479
2. Chiropractors	76.9%	$65,890	14.4%	3,179
3. Dentists, General	77.4%	$137,630	9.2%	7,106
4. Prosthodontists	77.4%	$145,600+	10.7%	54
5. Oral and Maxillofacial Surgeons	77.4%	$145,600+	9.1%	400

Information and Telecommunication Technologies Jobs with the Highest Percentage of Men

Job	Percent Men
1. Mechanical Engineers	94.2%
2. Engineering Managers	92.7%
3. Electrical Engineers	92.3%
4. Electronics Engineers, Except Computer	92.3%
5. Sales Engineers	86.5%
6. Computer Hardware Engineers	83.8%
7. Network and Computer Systems Administrators	83.4%
8. Computer Software Engineers, Applications	78.2%
9. Computer Software Engineers, Systems Software	78.2%
10. Industrial Engineers	77.4%
11. Network Systems and Data Communications Analysts	74.5%
12. Computer Specialists, All Other	74.3%
13. Computer and Information Systems Managers	72.8%
14. Sales Representatives, Wholesale and Manufacturing, Technical and Scientific Products	72.8%
15. Computer Support Specialists	71.1%

Best Information and Telecommunication Technologies Jobs Overall Employing 70 Percent or More Men

Job	Percent Men	Annual Earnings	Percent Growth	Annual Openings
1. Computer Software Engineers, Applications	78.2%	$83,130	44.6%	58,690
2. Computer Software Engineers, Systems Software	78.2%	$89,070	28.2%	33,139
3. Computer and Information Systems Managers	72.8%	$108,070	16.4%	30,887

Best Information and Telecommunication Technologies Jobs Overall Employing 70 Percent or More Men

Job	Percent Men	Annual Earnings	Percent Growth	Annual Openings
4. Network Systems and Data Communications Analysts	74.5%	$68,220	53.4%	35,086
5. Network and Computer Systems Administrators	83.4%	$64,690	27.0%	37,010
6. Engineering Managers	92.7%	$111,020	7.3%	7,404
7. Computer Support Specialists	71.1%	$42,400	12.9%	97,334
8. Sales Representatives, Wholesale and Manufacturing, Technical and Scientific Products	72.8%	$68,270	12.4%	43,469
9. Computer Specialists, All Other	74.3%	$71,510	15.1%	14,374
10. Industrial Engineers	77.4%	$71,430	20.3%	11,272
11. Sales Engineers	86.5%	$80,270	8.5%	7,371
12. Computer Hardware Engineers	83.8%	$91,860	4.6%	3,572
13. Mechanical Engineers	94.2%	$72,300	4.2%	12,394
14. Electrical Engineers	92.3%	$79,240	6.3%	6,806
15. Electronics Engineers, Except Computer	92.3%	$83,340	3.7%	5,699

Infrastructure Jobs with the Highest Percentage of Men

Job	Percent Men
1. Cement Masons and Concrete Finishers	99.3%
2. Electrical Power-Line Installers and Repairers	99.1%
3. Roofers	98.9%
4. Mobile Heavy Equipment Mechanics, Except Engines	98.6%
5. Operating Engineers and Other Construction Equipment Operators	98.3%
6. Plumbers, Pipefitters, and Steamfitters	98.2%
7. Electricians	98.1%
8. Carpenters	97.6%
9. First-Line Supervisors/Managers of Construction Trades and Extraction Workers	97.4%
10. Heating, Air Conditioning, and Refrigeration Mechanics and Installers	97.3%
11. Elevator Installers and Repairers	97.3%
12. Drywall and Ceiling Tile Installers	97.1%
13. Sheet Metal Workers	96.9%
14. Construction Laborers	96.3%
15. Highway Maintenance Workers	96.2%
16. Industrial Machinery Mechanics	96.2%
17. Truck Drivers, Heavy and Tractor-Trailer	94.8%

(continued)

(continued)

Infrastructure Jobs with the Highest Percentage of Men

Job	Percent Men
18. Truck Drivers, Light or Delivery Services	94.8%
19. Helpers—Brickmasons, Blockmasons, Stonemasons, and Tile and Marble Setters	93.8%
20. Helpers—Carpenters	93.8%
21. Helpers—Pipelayers, Plumbers, Pipefitters, and Steamfitters	93.8%
22. Glaziers	93.2%
23. Engineering Managers	92.7%
24. Electrical Engineers	92.3%
25. Painters, Construction and Maintenance	92.3%
26. Construction Managers	92.2%
27. First-Line Supervisors/Managers of Mechanics, Installers, and Repairers	91.5%
28. Telecommunications Line Installers and Repairers	91.4%
29. Construction and Building Inspectors	91.2%
30. Helpers—Installation, Maintenance, and Repair Workers	90.9%
31. Surveying and Mapping Technicians	90.1%
32. Health and Safety Engineers, Except Mining Safety Engineers and Inspectors	88.2%
33. Civil Engineers	88.1%
34. Cost Estimators	87.3%
35. Telecommunications Equipment Installers and Repairers, Except Line Installers	84.8%
36. Civil Engineering Technicians	79.4%
37. Electrical and Electronic Engineering Technicians	79.4%
38. Environmental Engineering Technicians	79.4%
39. Architectural and Civil Drafters	78.2%
40. Mechanical Drafters	78.2%
41. Environmental Scientists and Specialists, Including Health	78.0%
42. Architects, Except Landscape and Naval	77.8%
43. Cartographers and Photogrammetrists	77.8%
44. Surveyors	77.8%
45. Industrial Engineers	77.4%
46. Environmental Engineers	77.3%
47. Urban and Regional Planners	73.7%

Best Infrastructure Jobs Overall Employing 70 Percent or More Men

Job	Percent Men	Annual Earnings	Percent Growth	Annual Openings
1. Construction Managers	92.2%	$76,230	15.7%	44,158
2. Cost Estimators	87.3%	$54,920	18.5%	38,379
3. Civil Engineers	88.1%	$71,710	18.0%	15,979
4. Industrial Engineers	77.4%	$71,430	20.3%	11,272
5. Environmental Engineers	77.3%	$72,350	25.4%	5,003
6. First-Line Supervisors/Managers of Construction Trades and Extraction Workers	97.4%	$55,950	9.1%	82,923
7. Surveyors	77.8%	$51,630	23.7%	14,305
8. Environmental Scientists and Specialists, Including Health	78.0%	$58,380	25.1%	6,961
9. Architects, Except Landscape and Naval	77.8%	$67,620	17.7%	11,324
10. Plumbers, Pipefitters, and Steamfitters	98.2%	$44,090	10.6%	68,643
11. Construction and Building Inspectors	91.2%	$48,330	18.2%	12,606
12. Truck Drivers, Heavy and Tractor-Trailer	94.8%	$36,220	10.4%	279,032
13. Carpenters	97.6%	$37,660	10.3%	223,225
14. Painters, Construction and Maintenance	92.3%	$32,080	11.8%	101,140
15. Electricians	98.1%	$44,780	7.4%	79,083
16. Roofers	98.9%	$33,240	14.3%	38,398
17. Construction Laborers	96.3%	$27,310	10.9%	257,407
18. Cartographers and Photogrammetrists	77.8%	$49,970	20.3%	2,823
19. Urban and Regional Planners	73.7%	$57,970	14.5%	1,967
20. First-Line Supervisors/Managers of Mechanics, Installers, and Repairers	91.5%	$55,380	7.3%	24,361
21. Cement Masons and Concrete Finishers	99.3%	$33,840	11.4%	34,625
22. Engineering Managers	92.7%	$111,020	7.3%	7,404
23. Helpers—Installation, Maintenance, and Repair Workers	90.9%	$22,920	11.8%	52,058
24. Operating Engineers and Other Construction Equipment Operators	98.3%	$38,130	8.4%	55,468
25. Mobile Heavy Equipment Mechanics, Except Engines	98.6%	$41,450	12.3%	11,037

Best Jobs in Each Renewal Industry with a High Percentage of Urban or Rural Workers

Some people have a strong preference for an urban setting. They want to live and work where there's more energy and excitement, more access to the arts, more diversity, more really good restaurants, and better public transportation. On the other hand, some prefer the open spaces, closeness to nature, quiet, and inexpensive housing of rural locations. If you are strongly attracted to either setting, you'll be interested in the following lists.

We identified urban jobs as those for which half or more of the workforce is located in the 38 most populous metropolitan areas of the United States. (This means the workforce in all industries, not just the six renewal industries.) These 38 metro areas—the most populous 10 percent of all U.S. metro areas, according to the Census Bureau—consist primarily of built-up communities, unlike smaller metro areas, which consist of a core city surrounded by a lot of countryside. In the following lists of urban jobs, you'll see a figure called the "urban ratio" for each job that represents the percentage of the total U.S. workforce for the job that is located in those 38 huge metro areas.

The Census Bureau also identifies 173 nonmetropolitan areas—areas that have no city of 50,000 people and a total population of less than 100,000. We identified rural jobs as those for which 10 percent or more of the total U.S. workforce is located in these nonmetropolitan areas. In the following lists of rural jobs, you'll see a figure called the "rural ratio" that represents the percentage of the total U.S. workforce for the job that is located in nonmetropolitan areas.

You'll find a few jobs, such as preschool teachers, that appear as both urban *and* rural jobs. These jobs are well represented in all kinds of communities, so if you hold one of these jobs and tire of either the urban or rural lifestyle, you can probably relocate to the opposite setting and still find job opportunities.

The "best-of" lists of both urban and rural jobs are ordered by the usual three economic measures: earnings, growth, and openings.

Advanced Manufacturing Jobs with the Highest Percentage of Urban Workers

Job	Urban Ratio
1. Sales Engineers	72.1%
2. Technical Writers	67.4%
3. Computer Hardware Engineers	65.6%
4. Graphic Designers	64.5%
5. Electronics Engineers, Except Computer	62.7%
6. Chemists	62.5%
7. Electrical Engineers	61.1%
8. Engineering Managers	60.9%
9. Commercial and Industrial Designers	59.9%
10. Biological Technicians	59.4%
11. Purchasing Managers	59.3%
12. Electrical and Electronics Drafters	58.4%
13. Purchasing Agents, Except Wholesale, Retail, and Farm Products	56.9%
14. Shipping, Receiving, and Traffic Clerks	56.5%

Advanced Manufacturing Jobs with the Highest Percentage of Urban Workers

Job	Urban Ratio
15. Transportation, Storage, and Distribution Managers	55.7%
16. Logisticians	55.1%
17. Production, Planning, and Expediting Clerks	54.8%
18. Electrical and Electronic Engineering Technicians	53.6%
19. Health and Safety Engineers, Except Mining Safety Engineers and Inspectors	53.6%
20. Chemical Engineers	52.7%
21. Laborers and Freight, Stock, and Material Movers, Hand	51.3%
22. Electricians	51.2%
23. Mechanical Engineering Technicians	50.6%

Best Advanced Manufacturing Jobs Overall Employing 50 Percent or More Urban Workers

Job	Urban Ratio	Annual Earnings	Percent Growth	Annual Openings
1. Logisticians	55.1%	$64,250	17.3%	9,671
2. Engineering Managers	60.9%	$111,020	7.3%	7,404
3. Technical Writers	67.4%	$60,390	19.5%	7,498
4. Sales Engineers	72.1%	$80,270	8.5%	7,371
5. Chemists	62.5%	$63,490	9.1%	9,024
6. Graphic Designers	64.5%	$41,280	9.8%	26,968
7. Biological Technicians	59.4%	$37,810	16.0%	15,374
8. Electricians	51.2%	$44,780	7.4%	79,083
9. Transportation, Storage, and Distribution Managers	55.7%	$76,310	8.3%	6,994
10. Chemical Engineers	52.7%	$81,500	7.9%	2,111
11. Electrical Engineers	61.1%	$79,240	6.3%	6,806
12. Health and Safety Engineers, Except Mining Safety Engineers and Inspectors	53.6%	$69,580	9.6%	1,105
13. Computer Hardware Engineers	65.6%	$91,860	4.6%	3,572
14. Purchasing Managers	59.3%	$85,440	3.4%	7,243
15. Electronics Engineers, Except Computer	62.7%	$83,340	3.7%	5,699
16. Production, Planning, and Expediting Clerks	54.8%	$39,690	4.2%	52,735
17. Electrical and Electronic Engineering Technicians	53.6%	$52,140	3.6%	12,583

(continued)

(continued)

Best Advanced Manufacturing Jobs Overall
Employing 50 Percent or More Urban Workers

Job	Urban Ratio	Annual Earnings	Percent Growth	Annual Openings
18. Purchasing Agents, Except Wholesale, Retail, and Farm Products	56.9%	$52,460	0.1%	22,349
19. Shipping, Receiving, and Traffic Clerks	56.5%	$26,990	3.7%	138,967
20. Commercial and Industrial Designers	59.9%	$56,550	7.2%	4,777
21. Laborers and Freight, Stock, and Material Movers, Hand	51.3%	$21,900	2.1%	630,487
22. Mechanical Engineering Technicians	50.6%	$47,280	6.4%	3,710
23. Electrical and Electronics Drafters	58.4%	$49,250	4.1%	4,786

Advanced Manufacturing Jobs with the
Highest Percentage of Rural Workers

Job	Rural Ratio
1. Welders, Cutters, Solderers, and Brazers	24.1%
2. Team Assemblers	23.1%
3. Industrial Machinery Mechanics	22.7%
4. First-Line Supervisors/Managers of Production and Operating Workers	20.4%
5. Maintenance Workers, Machinery	20.1%
6. Industrial Truck and Tractor Operators	17.5%
7. Millwrights	17.2%
8. Machinists	16.8%
9. Maintenance and Repair Workers, General	16.7%
10. Industrial Production Managers	15.9%
11. Laborers and Freight, Stock, and Material Movers, Hand	13.2%
12. Electricians	12.6%
13. Industrial Engineers	11.4%
14. Industrial Engineering Technicians	11.2%
15. Shipping, Receiving, and Traffic Clerks	11.0%
16. Production, Planning, and Expediting Clerks	10.4%
17. Mechanical Drafters	10.3%
18. Purchasing Agents, Except Wholesale, Retail, and Farm Products	10.2%
19. Electrical and Electronics Repairers, Commercial and Industrial Equipment	10.1%

Best Advanced Manufacturing Jobs Overall Employing 10 Percent or More Rural Workers

Job	Rural Ratio	Annual Earnings	Percent Growth	Annual Openings
1. Industrial Engineers	11.4%	$71,430	20.3%	11,272
2. Electricians	12.6%	$44,780	7.4%	79,083
3. Maintenance and Repair Workers, General	16.7%	$32,570	10.1%	165,502
4. Industrial Machinery Mechanics	22.7%	$42,350	9.0%	23,361
5. Industrial Engineering Technicians	11.2%	$47,490	9.9%	6,172
6. Purchasing Agents, Except Wholesale, Retail, and Farm Products	10.2%	$52,460	0.1%	22,349
7. Electrical and Electronics Repairers, Commercial and Industrial Equipment	10.1%	$47,110	6.8%	6,607
8. Production, Planning, and Expediting Clerks	10.4%	$39,690	4.2%	52,735
9. First-Line Supervisors/Managers of Production and Operating Workers	20.4%	$48,670	–4.8%	46,144
10. Welders, Cutters, Solderers, and Brazers	24.1%	$32,270	5.1%	61,125
11. Laborers and Freight, Stock, and Material Movers, Hand	13.2%	$21,900	2.1%	630,487
12. Shipping, Receiving, and Traffic Clerks	11.0%	$26,990	3.7%	138,967
13. Mechanical Drafters	10.3%	$44,740	5.2%	10,902
14. Millwrights	17.2%	$46,090	5.8%	4,758
15. Team Assemblers	23.1%	$24,630	0.1%	264,135
16. Industrial Production Managers	15.9%	$80,560	–5.9%	14,889
17. Industrial Truck and Tractor Operators	17.5%	$28,010	–2.0%	89,547
18. Machinists	16.8%	$35,230	–3.1%	39,505
19. Maintenance Workers, Machinery	20.1%	$35,590	–1.1%	15,055

Education Jobs with the Highest Percentage of Urban Workers

Job	Urban Ratio
1. Self-Enrichment Education Teachers	61.5%
2. Education Administrators, Preschool and Child Care Center/Program	57.2%
3. Preschool Teachers, Except Special Education	55.9%
4. Clinical, Counseling, and School Psychologists	54.8%
5. Speech-Language Pathologists	50.8%

Best Education Jobs Overall Employing 50 Percent or More Urban Workers

Job	Urban Ratio	Annual Earnings	Percent Growth	Annual Openings
1. Preschool Teachers, Except Special Education	55.9%	$23,130	26.3%	78,172
2. Clinical, Counseling, and School Psychologists	54.8%	$62,210	15.8%	8,309
3. Self-Enrichment Education Teachers	61.5%	$34,580	23.1%	64,449
4. Education Administrators, Preschool and Child Care Center/Program	57.2%	$38,580	23.5%	8,113
5. Speech-Language Pathologists	50.8%	$60,690	10.6%	11,160

Education Jobs with the Highest Percentage of Rural Workers

Job	Rural Ratio
1. Education Administrators, Elementary and Secondary School	18.7%
2. Kindergarten Teachers, Except Special Education	17.4%
3. Elementary School Teachers, Except Special Education	17.2%
4. Middle School Teachers, Except Special and Vocational Education	16.7%
5. Special Education Teachers, Preschool, Kindergarten, and Elementary School	16.6%
6. Child, Family, and School Social Workers	16.1%
7. Educational, Vocational, and School Counselors	15.4%
8. Speech-Language Pathologists	12.6%
9. Vocational Education Teachers, Postsecondary	11.7%
10. Instructional Coordinators	11.0%
11. Preschool Teachers, Except Special Education	10.9%
12. English Language and Literature Teachers, Postsecondary	10.8%
13. Mathematical Science Teachers, Postsecondary	10.6%
14. Clinical, Counseling, and School Psychologists	10.5%
15. Education Administrators, Postsecondary	10.3%

Best Education Jobs Overall Employing 10 Percent or More Rural Workers

Job	Rural Ratio	Annual Earnings	Percent Growth	Annual Openings
1. Preschool Teachers, Except Special Education	10.9%	$23,130	26.3%	78,172
2. Instructional Coordinators	11.0%	$55,270	22.5%	21,294

Best Education Jobs Overall Employing 10 Percent or More Rural Workers

Job	Rural Ratio	Annual Earnings	Percent Growth	Annual Openings
3. English Language and Literature Teachers, Postsecondary	10.8%	$54,000	22.9%	10,475
4. Mathematical Science Teachers, Postsecondary	10.6%	$58,560	22.9%	7,663
5. Education Administrators, Elementary and Secondary School	18.7%	$80,580	7.6%	27,143
6. Education Administrators, Postsecondary	10.3%	$75,780	14.2%	17,121
7. Elementary School Teachers, Except Special Education	17.2%	$47,330	13.6%	181,612
8. Educational, Vocational, and School Counselors	15.4%	$49,450	12.6%	54,025
9. Special Education Teachers, Preschool, Kindergarten, and Elementary School	16.6%	$48,350	19.6%	20,049
10. Vocational Education Teachers, Postsecondary	11.7%	$45,850	22.9%	19,313
11. Child, Family, and School Social Workers	16.1%	$38,620	19.1%	35,402
12. Clinical, Counseling, and School Psychologists	10.5%	$62,210	15.8%	8,309
13. Middle School Teachers, Except Special and Vocational Education	16.7%	$47,900	11.2%	75,270
14. Kindergarten Teachers, Except Special Education	17.4%	$45,120	16.3%	27,603
15. Speech-Language Pathologists	12.6%	$60,690	10.6%	11,160

Green Technologies Jobs with the Highest Percentage of Urban Workers

Job	Urban Ratio
1. Architectural and Civil Drafters	61.4%
2. Electrical Engineers	61.1%
3. Engineering Managers	60.9%
4. Electrical and Electronics Drafters	58.4%
5. Bus Drivers, Transit and Intercity	58.3%
6. Construction Managers	57.3%
7. Environmental Scientists and Specialists, Including Health	56.0%
8. Construction and Building Inspectors	55.9%
9. Environmental Engineers	55.8%
10. Urban and Regional Planners	55.5%
11. Hazardous Materials Removal Workers	54.7%
12. Glaziers	54.5%

(continued)

(continued)

Green Technologies Jobs with the Highest Percentage of Urban Workers

Job	Urban Ratio
13. Electrical and Electronic Engineering Technicians	53.6%
14. Chemical Engineers	52.7%
15. Construction Laborers	52.4%
16. Roofers	52.2%
17. Electricians	51.2%
18. Carpenters	51.1%
19. Plumbers, Pipefitters, and Steamfitters	50.9%
20. Mechanical Engineering Technicians	50.6%
21. Structural Iron and Steel Workers	50.5%

Best Green Technologies Jobs Overall Employing 50 Percent or More Urban Workers

Job	Urban Ratio	Annual Earnings	Percent Growth	Annual Openings
1. Construction Managers	57.3%	$76,230	15.7%	44,158
2. Environmental Scientists and Specialists, Including Health	56.0%	$58,380	25.1%	6,961
3. Construction and Building Inspectors	55.9%	$48,330	18.2%	12,606
4. Environmental Engineers	55.8%	$72,350	25.4%	5,003
5. Engineering Managers	60.9%	$111,020	7.3%	7,404
6. Plumbers, Pipefitters, and Steamfitters	50.9%	$44,090	10.6%	68,643
7. Electricians	51.2%	$44,780	7.4%	79,083
8. Carpenters	51.1%	$37,660	10.3%	223,225
9. Roofers	52.2%	$33,240	14.3%	38,398
10. Construction Laborers	52.4%	$27,310	10.9%	257,407
11. Urban and Regional Planners	55.5%	$57,970	14.5%	1,967
12. Bus Drivers, Transit and Intercity	58.3%	$33,160	12.5%	27,100
13. Chemical Engineers	52.7%	$81,500	7.9%	2,111
14. Electrical Engineers	61.1%	$79,240	6.3%	6,806
15. Electrical and Electronic Engineering Technicians	53.6%	$52,140	3.6%	12,583
16. Architectural and Civil Drafters	61.4%	$43,310	6.1%	16,238
17. Glaziers	54.5%	$35,230	11.9%	6,416
18. Mechanical Engineering Technicians	50.6%	$47,280	6.4%	3,710

Best Green Technologies Jobs Overall Employing 50 Percent or More Urban Workers

Job	Urban Ratio	Annual Earnings	Percent Growth	Annual Openings
19. Electrical and Electronics Drafters	58.4%	$49,250	4.1%	4,786
20. Structural Iron and Steel Workers	50.5%	$42,130	6.0%	6,969
21. Hazardous Materials Removal Workers	54.7%	$36,330	11.2%	1,933

Green Technologies Jobs with the Highest Percentage of Rural Workers

Job	Rural Ratio
1. Welders, Cutters, Solderers, and Brazers	24.1%
2. Operating Engineers and Other Construction Equipment Operators	23.9%
3. Electrical Power-Line Installers and Repairers	23.1%
4. Industrial Machinery Mechanics	22.7%
5. Refuse and Recyclable Material Collectors	18.2%
6. Inspectors, Testers, Sorters, Samplers, and Weighers	17.9%
7. Industrial Truck and Tractor Operators	17.5%
8. Mobile Heavy Equipment Mechanics, Except Engines	16.8%
9. Machinists	16.8%
10. Industrial Production Managers	15.9%
11. Carpenters	15.3%
12. Helpers—Installation, Maintenance, and Repair Workers	14.7%
13. Surveying and Mapping Technicians	14.6%
14. First-Line Supervisors/Managers of Construction Trades and Extraction Workers	14.1%
15. Construction Laborers	13.8%
16. Mining and Geological Engineers, Including Mining Safety Engineers	13.3%
17. Electricians	12.6%
18. Pipelayers	11.9%
19. Industrial Engineers	11.4%
20. Industrial Engineering Technicians	11.2%
21. Heating, Air Conditioning, and Refrigeration Mechanics and Installers	11.1%
22. Plumbers, Pipefitters, and Steamfitters	10.6%
23. Electrical and Electronics Repairers, Commercial and Industrial Equipment	10.1%
24. Dietitians and Nutritionists	10.0%

Best Green Technologies Jobs Overall
Employing 10 Percent or More Rural Workers

Job	Rural Ratio	Annual Earnings	Percent Growth	Annual Openings
1. First-Line Supervisors/Managers of Construction Trades and Extraction Workers	14.1%	$55,950	9.1%	82,923
2. Industrial Engineers	11.4%	$71,430	20.3%	11,272
3. Plumbers, Pipefitters, and Steamfitters	10.6%	$44,090	10.6%	68,643
4. Carpenters	15.3%	$37,660	10.3%	223,225
5. Construction Laborers	13.8%	$27,310	10.9%	257,407
6. Electricians	12.6%	$44,780	7.4%	79,083
7. Mobile Heavy Equipment Mechanics, Except Engines	16.8%	$41,450	12.3%	11,037
8. Mining and Geological Engineers, Including Mining Safety Engineers	13.3%	$74,330	10.0%	456
9. Industrial Machinery Mechanics	22.7%	$42,350	9.0%	23,361
10. Operating Engineers and Other Construction Equipment Operators	23.9%	$38,130	8.4%	55,468
11. Heating, Air Conditioning, and Refrigeration Mechanics and Installers	11.1%	$38,360	8.7%	29,719
12. Helpers—Installation, Maintenance, and Repair Workers	14.7%	$22,920	11.8%	52,058
13. Industrial Engineering Technicians	11.2%	$47,490	9.9%	6,172
14. Surveying and Mapping Technicians	14.6%	$33,640	19.4%	8,299
15. Industrial Production Managers	15.9%	$80,560	−5.9%	14,889
16. Electrical Power-Line Installers and Repairers	23.1%	$52,570	7.2%	6,401
17. Industrial Truck and Tractor Operators	17.5%	$28,010	−2.0%	89,547
18. Welders, Cutters, Solderers, and Brazers	24.1%	$32,270	5.1%	61,125
19. Electrical and Electronics Repairers, Commercial and Industrial Equipment	10.1%	$47,110	6.8%	6,607
20. Machinists	16.8%	$35,230	−3.1%	39,505
21. Refuse and Recyclable Material Collectors	18.2%	$29,420	7.4%	37,785
22. Inspectors, Testers, Sorters, Samplers, and Weighers	17.9%	$30,310	−7.0%	75,361
23. Pipelayers	11.9%	$31,280	8.7%	8,902

Health-Care Jobs with the Highest Percentage of Urban Workers

Job	Urban Ratio
1. Medical Scientists, Except Epidemiologists	69.3%
2. Biological Technicians	59.4%
3. Massage Therapists	58.6%
4. Dentists, General	58.2%
5. Medical and Clinical Laboratory Technologists	56.4%
6. Clinical, Counseling, and School Psychologists	54.8%
7. Mental Health Counselors	53.9%
8. Dental Assistants	53.5%
9. Occupational Therapists	53.1%
10. Medical and Public Health Social Workers	52.8%
11. Medical Assistants	52.6%
12. Dietitians and Nutritionists	51.6%
13. Physical Therapists	51.6%
14. Medical and Clinical Laboratory Technicians	51.6%
15. Medical and Health Services Managers	51.6%
16. Diagnostic Medical Sonographers	50.8%
17. Speech-Language Pathologists	50.8%
18. Health Educators	50.7%
19. Registered Nurses	50.6%
20. Pharmacists	50.5%
21. Dental Hygienists	50.3%
22. Marriage and Family Therapists	50.3%
23. Nuclear Medicine Technologists	50.1%

Best Health-Care Jobs Overall Employing 50 Percent or More Urban Workers

Job	Urban Ratio	Annual Earnings	Percent Growth	Annual Openings
1. Pharmacists	50.5%	$100,480	21.7%	16,358
2. Physical Therapists	51.6%	$69,760	27.1%	12,072
3. Medical and Health Services Managers	51.6%	$76,990	16.4%	31,877
4. Registered Nurses	50.6%	$60,010	23.5%	233,499
5. Dental Hygienists	50.3%	$64,740	30.1%	10,433
6. Medical Assistants	52.6%	$27,430	35.4%	92,977

(continued)

(continued)

Best Health-Care Jobs Overall Employing 50 Percent or More Urban Workers

Job	Urban Ratio	Annual Earnings	Percent Growth	Annual Openings
7. Mental Health Counselors	53.9%	$36,000	30.0%	24,103
8. Medical and Public Health Social Workers	52.8%	$44,670	24.2%	16,429
9. Dental Assistants	53.5%	$31,550	29.2%	29,482
10. Health Educators	50.7%	$42,920	26.2%	13,707
11. Medical Scientists, Except Epidemiologists	69.3%	$64,200	20.2%	10,596
12. Occupational Therapists	53.1%	$63,790	23.1%	8,338
13. Marriage and Family Therapists	50.3%	$43,600	29.8%	5,953
14. Biological Technicians	59.4%	$37,810	16.0%	15,374
15. Dentists, General	58.2%	$137,630	9.2%	7,106
16. Speech-Language Pathologists	50.8%	$60,690	10.6%	11,160
17. Clinical, Counseling, and School Psychologists	54.8%	$62,210	15.8%	8,309
18. Medical and Clinical Laboratory Technologists	56.4%	$51,720	12.4%	11,457
19. Diagnostic Medical Sonographers	50.8%	$59,860	19.1%	3,211
20. Massage Therapists	58.6%	$34,870	20.3%	9,193
21. Nuclear Medicine Technologists	50.1%	$64,670	14.8%	1,290
22. Medical and Clinical Laboratory Technicians	51.6%	$34,270	15.0%	10,866
23. Dietitians and Nutritionists	51.6%	$49,010	8.6%	4,996

Health-Care Jobs with the Highest Percentage of Rural Workers

Job	Rural Ratio
1. Emergency Medical Technicians and Paramedics	21.9%
2. Licensed Practical and Licensed Vocational Nurses	19.9%
3. Nursing Aides, Orderlies, and Attendants	19.2%
4. Medical Transcriptionists	15.6%
5. Pharmacy Technicians	15.2%
6. Physical Therapist Assistants	15.0%
7. Medical Records and Health Information Technicians	14.4%
8. Pharmacists	13.5%
9. Medical and Health Services Managers	13.4%
10. Radiologic Technologists and Technicians	13.2%
11. Rehabilitation Counselors	13.2%
12. Speech-Language Pathologists	12.6%

Health-Care Jobs with the Highest Percentage of Rural Workers

Job	Rural Ratio
13. Registered Nurses	12.2%
14. Medical and Public Health Social Workers	12.1%
15. Dental Hygienists	12.0%
16. Physical Therapists	12.0%
17. Dental Assistants	12.0%
18. Occupational Health and Safety Specialists	11.9%
19. Substance Abuse and Behavioral Disorder Counselors	11.4%
20. Mental Health and Substance Abuse Social Workers	11.3%
21. Physical Therapist Aides	11.2%
22. Respiratory Therapists	10.7%
23. Clinical, Counseling, and School Psychologists	10.5%
24. Medical and Clinical Laboratory Technologists	10.4%
25. Medical and Clinical Laboratory Technicians	10.2%
26. Medical Assistants	10.2%
27. Dietitians and Nutritionists	10.0%

Best Health-Care Jobs Overall Employing 10 Percent or More Rural Workers

Job	Rural Ratio	Annual Earnings	Percent Growth	Annual Openings
1. Registered Nurses	12.2%	$60,010	23.5%	233,499
2. Medical and Health Services Managers	13.4%	$76,990	16.4%	31,877
3. Medical Assistants	10.2%	$27,430	35.4%	92,977
4. Physical Therapists	12.0%	$69,760	27.1%	12,072
5. Substance Abuse and Behavioral Disorder Counselors	11.4%	$35,580	34.3%	20,821
6. Dental Hygienists	12.0%	$64,740	30.1%	10,433
7. Pharmacists	13.5%	$100,480	21.7%	16,358
8. Pharmacy Technicians	15.2%	$26,720	32.0%	54,453
9. Dental Assistants	12.0%	$31,550	29.2%	29,482
10. Mental Health and Substance Abuse Social Workers	11.3%	$36,640	29.9%	17,289
11. Medical and Public Health Social Workers	12.1%	$44,670	24.2%	16,429
12. Physical Therapist Assistants	15.0%	$44,130	32.4%	5,957

(continued)

(continued)

Best Health-Care Jobs Overall Employing 10 Percent or More Rural Workers

Job	Rural Ratio	Annual Earnings	Percent Growth	Annual Openings
13. Rehabilitation Counselors	13.2%	$29,630	23.0%	32,081
14. Licensed Practical and Licensed Vocational Nurses	19.9%	$37,940	14.0%	70,610
15. Nursing Aides, Orderlies, and Attendants	19.2%	$23,160	18.2%	321,036
16. Medical Records and Health Information Technicians	14.4%	$29,290	17.8%	39,048
17. Clinical, Counseling, and School Psychologists	10.5%	$62,210	15.8%	8,309
18. Radiologic Technologists and Technicians	13.2%	$50,260	15.1%	12,836
19. Respiratory Therapists	10.7%	$50,070	22.6%	5,563
20. Emergency Medical Technicians and Paramedics	21.9%	$28,400	19.2%	19,513
21. Speech-Language Pathologists	12.6%	$60,690	10.6%	11,160
22. Medical and Clinical Laboratory Technologists	10.4%	$51,720	12.4%	11,457
23. Medical Transcriptionists	15.6%	$31,250	13.5%	18,080
24. Medical and Clinical Laboratory Technicians	10.2%	$34,270	15.0%	10,866
25. Occupational Health and Safety Specialists	11.9%	$60,140	8.1%	3,440

Information and Telecommunication Technologies Jobs with the Highest Percentage of Urban Workers

Job	Urban Ratio
1. Computer Software Engineers, Systems Software	76.3%
2. Computer Software Engineers, Applications	75.0%
3. Sales Engineers	72.1%
4. Computer and Information Systems Managers	71.3%
5. Multi-Media Artists and Animators	68.6%
6. Computer Systems Analysts	68.4%
7. Database Administrators	68.3%
8. Computer Specialists, All Other	68.0%
9. Technical Writers	67.4%
10. Computer and Information Scientists, Research	66.9%
11. Network and Computer Systems Administrators	66.5%
12. Network Systems and Data Communications Analysts	66.4%
13. Computer Hardware Engineers	65.6%

Information and Telecommunication Technology Jobs with the Highest Percentage of Urban Workers

Job	Rural Ratio
14. Sales Representatives, Wholesale and Manufacturing, Technical and Scientific Products	64.9%
15. Computer Support Specialists	63.1%
16. Electronics Engineers, Except Computer	62.7%
17. Electrical Engineers	61.1%
18. Engineering Managers	60.9%

Best Information and Telecommunication Technologies Jobs Overall Employing 50 Percent or More Urban Workers

Job	Urban Ratio	Annual Earnings	Percent Growth	Annual Openings
1. Computer Software Engineers, Applications	75.0%	$83,130	44.6%	58,690
2. Computer Systems Analysts	68.4%	$73,090	29.0%	63,166
3. Computer Software Engineers, Systems Software	76.3%	$89,070	28.2%	33,139
4. Computer and Information Systems Managers	71.3%	$108,070	16.4%	30,887
5. Network Systems and Data Communications Analysts	66.4%	$68,220	53.4%	35,086
6. Network and Computer Systems Administrators	66.5%	$64,690	27.0%	37,010
7. Computer and Information Scientists, Research	66.9%	$97,970	21.5%	2,901
8. Database Administrators	68.3%	$67,250	28.6%	8,258
9. Engineering Managers	60.9%	$111,020	7.3%	7,404
10. Sales Representatives, Wholesale and Manufacturing, Technical and Scientific Products	64.9%	$68,270	12.4%	43,469
11. Computer Specialists, All Other	68.0%	$71,510	15.1%	14,374
12. Computer Support Specialists	63.1%	$42,400	12.9%	97,334
13. Multi-Media Artists and Animators	68.6%	$54,550	25.8%	13,182
14. Sales Engineers	72.1%	$80,270	8.5%	7,371
15. Technical Writers	67.4%	$60,390	19.5%	7,498
16. Computer Hardware Engineers	65.6%	$91,860	4.6%	3,572
17. Electrical Engineers	61.1%	$79,240	6.3%	6,806
18. Electronics Engineers, Except Computer	62.7%	$83,340	3.7%	5,699

Information and Telecommunication Technologies Jobs with the Highest Percentage of Rural Workers

Job	Rural Ratio
1. Industrial Engineers	11.4%

Best Information and Telecommunication Technologies Jobs Overall Employing 10 Percent or More Rural Workers

Job	Rural Ratio	Annual Earnings	Percent Growth	Annual Openings
1. Industrial Engineers	11.4%	$71,430	20.3%	11,272

Infrastructure Jobs with the Highest Percentage of Urban Workers

Job	Urban Ratio
1. Architects, Except Landscape and Naval	71.2%
2. Technical Writers	67.4%
3. Telecommunications Equipment Installers and Repairers, Except Line Installers	62.1%
4. Architectural and Civil Drafters	61.4%
5. Electrical Engineers	61.1%
6. Engineering Managers	60.9%
7. Civil Engineers	60.3%
8. Drywall and Ceiling Tile Installers	59.0%
9. Construction Managers	57.3%
10. Environmental Scientists and Specialists, Including Health	56.0%
11. Construction and Building Inspectors	55.9%
12. Environmental Engineers	55.8%
13. Urban and Regional Planners	55.5%
14. Cost Estimators	55.5%
15. Logisticians	55.1%
16. Glaziers	54.5%
17. Health and Safety Engineers, Except Mining Safety Engineers and Inspectors	53.6%
18. Electrical and Electronic Engineering Technicians	53.6%
19. Painters, Construction and Maintenance	53.1%
20. Telecommunications Line Installers and Repairers	52.6%
21. Construction Laborers	52.4%

Infrastructure Jobs with the Highest Percentage of Urban Workers

Job	Urban Ratio
22. Roofers	52.2%
23. Elevator Installers and Repairers	51.6%
24. Electricians	51.2%
25. Carpenters	51.1%
26. Plumbers, Pipefitters, and Steamfitters	50.9%
27. Truck Drivers, Light or Delivery Services	50.4%

Best Infrastructure Jobs Overall Employing 50 Percent or More Urban Workers

Job	Urban Ratio	Annual Earnings	Percent Growth	Annual Openings
1. Construction Managers	57.3%	$76,230	15.7%	44,158
2. Civil Engineers	60.3%	$71,710	18.0%	15,979
3. Cost Estimators	55.5%	$54,920	18.5%	38,379
4. Environmental Engineers	55.8%	$72,350	25.4%	5,003
5. Architects, Except Landscape and Naval	71.2%	$67,620	17.7%	11,324
6. Technical Writers	67.4%	$60,390	19.5%	7,498
7. Environmental Scientists and Specialists, Including Health	56.0%	$58,380	25.1%	6,961
8. Logisticians	55.1%	$64,250	17.3%	9,671
9. Construction and Building Inspectors	55.9%	$48,330	18.2%	12,606
10. Carpenters	51.1%	$37,660	10.3%	223,225
11. Plumbers, Pipefitters, and Steamfitters	50.9%	$44,090	10.6%	68,643
12. Construction Laborers	52.4%	$27,310	10.9%	257,407
13. Engineering Managers	60.9%	$111,020	7.3%	7,404
14. Painters, Construction and Maintenance	53.1%	$32,080	11.8%	101,140
15. Electricians	51.2%	$44,780	7.4%	79,083
16. Roofers	52.2%	$33,240	14.3%	38,398
17. Electrical Engineers	61.1%	$79,240	6.3%	6,806
18. Urban and Regional Planners	55.5%	$57,970	14.5%	1,967
19. Truck Drivers, Light or Delivery Services	50.4%	$26,380	8.4%	154,330
20. Elevator Installers and Repairers	51.6%	$68,000	8.8%	2,850
21. Health and Safety Engineers, Except Mining Safety Engineers and Inspectors	53.6%	$69,580	9.6%	1,105

(continued)

(continued)

Best Infrastructure Jobs Overall Employing 50 Percent or More Urban Workers

Job	Urban Ratio	Annual Earnings	Percent Growth	Annual Openings
22. Drywall and Ceiling Tile Installers	59.0%	$36,520	7.3%	30,945
23. Architectural and Civil Drafters	61.4%	$43,310	6.1%	16,238
24. Telecommunications Equipment Installers and Repairers, Except Line Installers	62.1%	$54,070	2.5%	13,541
25. Telecommunications Line Installers and Repairers	52.6%	$47,220	4.6%	14,719

Infrastructure Jobs with the Highest Percentage of Rural Workers

Job	Rural Ratio
1. Highway Maintenance Workers	40.0%
2. Operating Engineers and Other Construction Equipment Operators	23.9%
3. Electrical Power-Line Installers and Repairers	23.1%
4. Industrial Machinery Mechanics	22.7%
5. Truck Drivers, Heavy and Tractor-Trailer	20.5%
6. Mobile Heavy Equipment Mechanics, Except Engines	16.8%
7. First-Line Supervisors/Managers of Mechanics, Installers, and Repairers	15.5%
8. Carpenters	15.3%
9. Helpers—Installation, Maintenance, and Repair Workers	14.7%
10. Surveying and Mapping Technicians	14.6%
11. First-Line Supervisors/Managers of Construction Trades and Extraction Workers	14.1%
12. Construction Laborers	13.8%
13. Truck Drivers, Light or Delivery Services	13.3%
14. Cement Masons and Concrete Finishers	12.9%
15. Helpers—Carpenters	12.9%
16. Electricians	12.6%
17. Civil Engineering Technicians	12.0%
18. Telecommunications Line Installers and Repairers	11.4%
19. Industrial Engineers	11.4%
20. Heating, Air Conditioning, and Refrigeration Mechanics and Installers	11.1%
21. Surveyors	10.8%
22. Plumbers, Pipefitters, and Steamfitters	10.6%
23. Mechanical Drafters	10.3%

Best Infrastructure Jobs Overall Employing 10 Percent or More Rural Workers

Job	Rural Ratio	Annual Earnings	Percent Growth	Annual Openings
1. First-Line Supervisors/Managers of Construction Trades and Extraction Workers	14.1%	$55,950	9.1%	82,923
2. Industrial Engineers	11.4%	$71,430	20.3%	11,272
3. Surveyors	10.8%	$51,630	23.7%	14,305
4. Plumbers, Pipefitters, and Steamfitters	10.6%	$44,090	10.6%	68,643
5. Truck Drivers, Heavy and Tractor-Trailer	20.5%	$36,220	10.4%	279,032
6. Carpenters	15.3%	$37,660	10.3%	223,225
7. Construction Laborers	13.8%	$27,310	10.9%	257,407
8. Electricians	12.6%	$44,780	7.4%	79,083
9. Cement Masons and Concrete Finishers	12.9%	$33,840	11.4%	34,625
10. Mobile Heavy Equipment Mechanics, Except Engines	16.8%	$41,450	12.3%	11,037
11. First-Line Supervisors/Managers of Mechanics, Installers, and Repairers	15.5%	$55,380	7.3%	24,361
12. Helpers—Installation, Maintenance, and Repair Workers	14.7%	$22,920	11.8%	52,058
13. Helpers—Carpenters	12.9%	$24,340	11.7%	37,731
14. Operating Engineers and Other Construction Equipment Operators	23.9%	$38,130	8.4%	55,468
15. Industrial Machinery Mechanics	22.7%	$42,350	9.0%	23,361
16. Heating, Air Conditioning, and Refrigeration Mechanics and Installers	11.1%	$38,360	8.7%	29,719
17. Surveying and Mapping Technicians	14.6%	$33,640	19.4%	8,299
18. Truck Drivers, Light or Delivery Services	13.3%	$26,380	8.4%	154,330
19. Civil Engineering Technicians	12.0%	$42,580	10.2%	7,499
20. Telecommunications Line Installers and Repairers	11.4%	$47,220	4.6%	14,719
21. Highway Maintenance Workers	40.0%	$32,600	8.9%	24,774
22. Electrical Power-Line Installers and Repairers	23.1%	$52,570	7.2%	6,401
23. Mechanical Drafters	10.3%	$44,740	5.2%	10,902

The Best Jobs in Each Renewal Industry Sorted by Education or Training Required

The lists that follow cover each renewal industry and separate the top jobs that met the criteria for this book into lists based on the education or training typically required for entry. Next to each job title you'll find the job's annual earnings, percent growth, and annual job openings, and these measures are used to order the jobs within each grouping. Thus you can easily find the best overall jobs for a given level of education or training within a given renewal industry.

You can use these lists in a variety of ways. For example, they can help you identify a job that has higher potential than a job you now hold that requires a similar level of education.

You can also use these lists to figure out additional job possibilities that would open up if you were to get additional training, education, or work experience. For example, maybe you are a high school graduate working in a job associated with the Advanced Manufacturing industry. There are several jobs in this field at all levels of education, including five that require long-term on-the-job training. You can identify the job you're interested in and the related training you need (you'll find more details in Part III) so you can move ahead without leaving the Advanced Manufacturing industry.

These lists should also help you when you're planning for future education or training. For example, you might be thinking about a job within the Infrastructure industry, but you aren't sure what kind of work you want to do. The lists show that Glaziers need to get long-term on-the-job training and earn an average of $35,230, whereas Operating Engineers and Other Construction Equipment Operators need only moderate-term on-the-job training but earn an average of $38,130. If you want higher earnings without lengthy training, this information might make a difference in your choice.

The Education Levels

* *Short-term on-the-job training.* It is possible to work in these occupations and achieve an average level of performance within a few days or weeks through on-the-job training.

* *Moderate-term on-the-job training.* Occupations that require this type of training can be performed adequately after a 1- to 12-month period of combined on-the-job and informal training. Typically, untrained workers observe experienced workers performing tasks and are gradually moved into progressively more difficult assignments.

* *Long-term on-the-job training.* This training requires more than 12 months of on-the-job training or combined work experience and formal classroom instruction. This includes occupations that use formal apprenticeships for training workers that may take up to four years. It also includes intensive occupation-specific, employer-sponsored training such as police academies. Furthermore, it includes occupations that require natural talent that must be developed over many years.

* *Work experience in a related occupation.* This type of job requires experience in a related occupation. For example, First-Line Supervisors/Managers of Police and Detectives are selected based on their experience as Police and Sheriff's Patrol Officers.

* *Postsecondary vocational training.* This requirement involves an amount of training that can vary from a few months to about one year. In a few instances, there may be as many as four years of training.

* *Associate degree.* This degree usually requires two years of full-time academic work beyond high school.

- ✸ *Bachelor's degree.* This degree requires approximately four to five years of full-time academic work beyond high school.
- ✸ *Work experience plus degree.* Jobs in this category are often management-related and require some experience in a related nonmanagerial position.
- ✸ *Master's degree.* Completion of a master's degree usually requires one to two years of full-time study beyond the bachelor's degree.
- ✸ *Doctoral degree.* This degree normally requires two or more years of full-time academic work beyond the bachelor's degree.
- ✸ *First professional degree.* This type of degree normally requires a minimum of two years of education beyond the bachelor's degree and frequently requires three years.

Another Warning About the Data

We warned you in the Introduction to use caution in interpreting the data we use, and we want to do it again here. The occupational data we use is the most accurate available anywhere, but it has its limitations. For example, the education or training requirements for entry into a job are those typically required as a minimum—but some people working in those jobs may have considerably more or different credentials. For example, most Registered Nurses now have a four-year bachelor's degree, although the two-year associate degree is the minimum level of training the job requires.

In a similar way, people with jobs that require long-term on-the-job training typically earn more than people with jobs that require short-term on-the-job training. However, some people with short-term on-the-job training do earn more than the average for the highest-paying occupations listed in this book. On the other hand, some people with long-term on-the-job training earn much less than the average shown in this book—this is particularly true early in a person's career.

So as you browse the lists that follow, please use them as a way to be encouraged rather than discouraged. Education and training are very important for success in the labor market of the future, but so are ability, drive, initiative, and, yes, luck.

Having said this, we encourage you to get as much education and training as you can. It used to be that you got your schooling and never went back, but this is not a good attitude to have now. You will probably need to continue learning new things throughout your working life. You can do so by going to school, and this is a good thing for many people to do. But there are also many other ways to learn, such as workshops, certification programs, employer training, professional conferences, Internet training, reading related books and magazines, and many others. Upgrading your computer and other technical skills is particularly important in our rapidly changing workplace, and you avoid doing so at your peril.

An old saying goes, "The harder you work, the luckier you get." It is just as true now as it ever was.

Best Advanced Manufacturing Jobs Requiring Short-Term On-the-Job Training

Job	Annual Earnings	Percent Growth	Annual Openings
1. Shipping, Receiving, and Traffic Clerks	$26,990	3.7%	138,967
2. Laborers and Freight, Stock, and Material Movers, Hand	$21,900	2.1%	630,487
3. Industrial Truck and Tractor Operators	$28,010	–2.0%	89,547

Best Advanced Manufacturing Jobs Requiring Moderate-Term On-the-Job Training

Job	Annual Earnings	Percent Growth	Annual Openings
1. Aircraft Structure, Surfaces, Rigging, and Systems Assemblers	$45,420	12.8%	6,550
2. Maintenance and Repair Workers, General	$32,570	10.1%	165,502
3. Production, Planning, and Expediting Clerks	$39,690	4.2%	52,735
4. Painters, Transportation Equipment	$36,000	8.4%	3,268
5. Team Assemblers	$24,630	0.1%	264,135
6. Maintenance Workers, Machinery	$35,590	–1.1%	15,055

Best Advanced Manufacturing Jobs Requiring Long-Term On-the-Job Training

Job	Annual Earnings	Percent Growth	Annual Openings
1. Electricians	$44,780	7.4%	79,083
2. Industrial Machinery Mechanics	$42,350	9.0%	23,361
3. Purchasing Agents, Except Wholesale, Retail, and Farm Products	$52,460	0.1%	22,349
4. Millwrights	$46,090	5.8%	4,758
5. Machinists	$35,230	–3.1%	39,505

Best Advanced Manufacturing Jobs Requiring Work Experience in a Related Occupation

Job	Annual Earnings	Percent Growth	Annual Openings
1. First-Line Supervisors/Managers of Production and Operating Workers	$48,670	–4.8%	46,144
2. Industrial Production Managers	$80,560	–5.9%	14,889
3. Transportation, Storage, and Distribution Managers	$76,310	8.3%	6,994

Best Advanced Manufacturing Jobs Requiring Postsecondary Vocational Training

Job	Annual Earnings	Percent Growth	Annual Openings
1. Electrical and Electronics Repairers, Commercial and Industrial Equipment	$47,110	6.8%	6,607
2. Mechanical Drafters	$44,740	5.2%	10,902
3. Welders, Cutters, Solderers, and Brazers	$32,270	5.1%	61,125
4. Electrical and Electronics Drafters	$49,250	4.1%	4,786

Best Advanced Manufacturing Jobs Requiring an Associate Degree

Job	Annual Earnings	Percent Growth	Annual Openings
1. Electrical and Electronic Engineering Technicians	$52,140	3.6%	12,583
2. Industrial Engineering Technicians	$47,490	9.9%	6,172
3. Mechanical Engineering Technicians	$47,280	6.4%	3,710

Best Advanced Manufacturing Jobs Requiring a Bachelor's Degree

Job	Annual Earnings	Percent Growth	Annual Openings
1. Biological Technicians	$37,810	16.0%	15,374
2. Industrial Engineers	$71,430	20.3%	11,272
3. Logisticians	$64,250	17.3%	9,671
4. Graphic Designers	$41,280	9.8%	26,968

(continued)

(continued)

Best Advanced Manufacturing Jobs Requiring a Bachelor's Degree

Job	Annual Earnings	Percent Growth	Annual Openings
5. Sales Engineers	$80,270	8.5%	7,371
6. Technical Writers	$60,390	19.5%	7,498
7. Mechanical Engineers	$72,300	4.2%	12,394
8. Chemists	$63,490	9.1%	9,024
9. Chemical Engineers	$81,500	7.9%	2,111
10. Computer Hardware Engineers	$91,860	4.6%	3,572
11. Electrical Engineers	$79,240	6.3%	6,806
12. Electronics Engineers, Except Computer	$83,340	3.7%	5,699
13. Health and Safety Engineers, Except Mining Safety Engineers and Inspectors	$69,580	9.6%	1,105
14. Commercial and Industrial Designers	$56,550	7.2%	4,777

Best Advanced Manufacturing Jobs Requiring Work Experience Plus Degree

Job	Annual Earnings	Percent Growth	Annual Openings
1. Engineering Managers	$111,020	7.3%	7,404
2. Purchasing Managers	$85,440	3.4%	7,243

Best Education Jobs Requiring Work Experience in a Related Occupation

Job	Annual Earnings	Percent Growth	Annual Openings
1. Self-Enrichment Education Teachers	$34,580	23.1%	64,449
2. Vocational Education Teachers, Postsecondary	$45,850	22.9%	19,313

Best Education Jobs Requiring Postsecondary Vocational Training

Job	Annual Earnings	Percent Growth	Annual Openings
1. Preschool Teachers, Except Special Education	$23,130	26.3%	78,172

Best Education Jobs Requiring a Bachelor's Degree

Job	Annual Earnings	Percent Growth	Annual Openings
1. Elementary School Teachers, Except Special Education	$47,330	13.6%	181,612
2. Special Education Teachers, Preschool, Kindergarten, and Elementary School	$48,350	19.6%	20,049
3. Middle School Teachers, Except Special and Vocational Education	$47,900	11.2%	75,270
4. Child, Family, and School Social Workers	$38,620	19.1%	35,402
5. Graduate Teaching Assistants	$28,060	22.9%	20,601
6. Kindergarten Teachers, Except Special Education	$45,120	16.3%	27,603

Best Education Jobs Requiring Work Experience Plus Degree

Job	Annual Earnings	Percent Growth	Annual Openings
1. Education Administrators, Elementary and Secondary School	$80,580	7.6%	27,143
2. Education Administrators, Postsecondary	$75,780	14.2%	17,121
3. Education Administrators, Preschool and Child Care Center/Program	$38,580	23.5%	8,113

Best Education Jobs Requiring a Master's Degree

Job	Annual Earnings	Percent Growth	Annual Openings
1. Instructional Coordinators	$55,270	22.5%	21,294
2. Educational, Vocational, and School Counselors	$49,450	12.6%	54,025
3. Speech-Language Pathologists	$60,690	10.6%	11,160

Best Education Jobs Requiring a Doctoral Degree

Job	Annual Earnings	Percent Growth	Annual Openings
1. Health Specialties Teachers, Postsecondary	$80,700	22.9%	19,617
2. Biological Science Teachers, Postsecondary	$71,780	22.9%	9,039
3. Business Teachers, Postsecondary	$64,900	22.9%	11,643
4. Engineering Teachers, Postsecondary	$79,510	22.9%	5,565

(continued)

(continued)

Best Education Jobs Requiring a Doctoral Degree

Job	Annual Earnings	Percent Growth	Annual Openings
5. Economics Teachers, Postsecondary	$75,300	22.9%	2,208
6. Computer Science Teachers, Postsecondary	$62,020	22.9%	5,820
7. Agricultural Sciences Teachers, Postsecondary	$78,460	22.9%	1,840
8. Chemistry Teachers, Postsecondary	$63,870	22.9%	3,405
9. Mathematical Science Teachers, Postsecondary	$58,560	22.9%	7,663
10. Physics Teachers, Postsecondary	$70,090	22.9%	2,155
11. Art, Drama, and Music Teachers, Postsecondary	$55,190	22.9%	12,707
12. Atmospheric, Earth, Marine, and Space Sciences Teachers, Postsecondary	$73,280	22.9%	1,553
13. Psychology Teachers, Postsecondary	$60,610	22.9%	5,261
14. Nursing Instructors and Teachers, Postsecondary	$57,500	22.9%	7,337
15. History Teachers, Postsecondary	$59,160	22.9%	3,570
16. Political Science Teachers, Postsecondary	$63,100	22.9%	2,435
17. Education Teachers, Postsecondary	$54,220	22.9%	9,359
18. English Language and Literature Teachers, Postsecondary	$54,000	22.9%	10,475
19. Architecture Teachers, Postsecondary	$68,540	22.9%	1,044
20. Anthropology and Archeology Teachers, Postsecondary	$64,530	22.9%	910
21. Environmental Science Teachers, Postsecondary	$64,850	22.9%	769
22. Sociology Teachers, Postsecondary	$58,160	22.9%	2,774
23. Communications Teachers, Postsecondary	$54,720	22.9%	4,074
24. Philosophy and Religion Teachers, Postsecondary	$56,380	22.9%	3,120
25. Foreign Language and Literature Teachers, Postsecondary	$53,610	22.9%	4,317
26. Area, Ethnic, and Cultural Studies Teachers, Postsecondary	$59,150	22.9%	1,252
27. Forestry and Conservation Science Teachers, Postsecondary	$63,790	22.9%	454
28. Geography Teachers, Postsecondary	$61,310	22.9%	697
29. Recreation and Fitness Studies Teachers, Postsecondary	$52,170	22.9%	3,010
30. Home Economics Teachers, Postsecondary	$58,170	22.9%	820
31. Social Work Teachers, Postsecondary	$56,240	22.9%	1,292
32. Clinical, Counseling, and School Psychologists	$62,210	15.8%	8,309
33. Criminal Justice and Law Enforcement Teachers, Postsecondary	$51,060	22.9%	1,911
34. Library Science Teachers, Postsecondary	$56,810	22.9%	702

Best Education Jobs Requiring a First Professional Degree

Job	Annual Earnings	Percent Growth	Annual Openings
1. Law Teachers, Postsecondary	$87,730	22.9%	2,169

Best Green Technologies Jobs Requiring Short-Term On-the-Job Training

Job	Annual Earnings	Percent Growth	Annual Openings
1. Industrial Truck and Tractor Operators	$28,010	–2.0%	89,547
2. Refuse and Recyclable Material Collectors	$29,420	7.4%	37,785
3. Helpers—Installation, Maintenance, and Repair Workers	$22,920	11.8%	52,058
4. Helpers—Pipelayers, Plumbers, Pipefitters, and Steamfitters	$25,350	11.9%	29,332

Best Green Technologies Jobs Requiring Moderate-Term On-the-Job Training

Job	Annual Earnings	Percent Growth	Annual Openings
1. Roofers	$33,240	14.3%	38,398
2. Operating Engineers and Other Construction Equipment Operators	$38,130	8.4%	55,468
3. Surveying and Mapping Technicians	$33,640	19.4%	8,299
4. Bus Drivers, Transit and Intercity	$33,160	12.5%	27,100
5. Construction Laborers	$27,310	10.9%	257,407
6. Hazardous Materials Removal Workers	$36,330	11.2%	1,933
7. Insulation Workers, Mechanical	$36,570	8.6%	5,787
8. Inspectors, Testers, Sorters, Samplers, and Weighers	$30,310	–7.0%	75,361
9. Pipelayers	$31,280	8.7%	8,902

Best Green Technologies Jobs Requiring Long-Term On-the-Job Training

Job	Annual Earnings	Percent Growth	Annual Openings
1. Plumbers, Pipefitters, and Steamfitters	$44,090	10.6%	68,643
2. Electricians	$44,780	7.4%	79,083
3. Carpenters	$37,660	10.3%	223,225

(continued)

(continued)

Best Green Technologies Jobs Requiring Long-Term On-the-Job Training

Job	Annual Earnings	Percent Growth	Annual Openings
4. Mobile Heavy Equipment Mechanics, Except Engines	$41,450	12.3%	11,037
5. Industrial Machinery Mechanics	$42,350	9.0%	23,361
6. Electrical Power-Line Installers and Repairers	$52,570	7.2%	6,401
7. Heating, Air Conditioning, and Refrigeration Mechanics and Installers	$38,360	8.7%	29,719
8. Sheet Metal Workers	$39,210	6.7%	31,677
9. Glaziers	$35,230	11.9%	6,416
10. Structural Iron and Steel Workers	$42,130	6.0%	6,969
11. Machinists	$35,230	–3.1%	39,505

Best Green Technologies Jobs Requiring Work Experience in a Related Occupation

Job	Annual Earnings	Percent Growth	Annual Openings
1. First-Line Supervisors/Managers of Construction Trades and Extraction Workers	$55,950	9.1%	82,923
2. Industrial Production Managers	$80,560	–5.9%	14,889
3. Construction and Building Inspectors	$48,330	18.2%	12,606

Best Green Technologies Jobs Requiring Postsecondary Vocational Training

Job	Annual Earnings	Percent Growth	Annual Openings
1. Electrical and Electronics Repairers, Commercial and Industrial Equipment	$47,110	6.8%	6,607
2. Architectural and Civil Drafters	$43,310	6.1%	16,238
3. Welders, Cutters, Solderers, and Brazers	$32,270	5.1%	61,125
4. Electrical and Electronics Drafters	$49,250	4.1%	4,786

Best Green Technologies Jobs Requiring an Associate Degree

Job	Annual Earnings	Percent Growth	Annual Openings
1. Electrical and Electronic Engineering Technicians	$52,140	3.6%	12,583
2. Environmental Science and Protection Technicians, Including Health	$39,370	28.0%	8,404
3. Industrial Engineering Technicians	$47,490	9.9%	6,172
4. Geological and Petroleum Technicians	$50,950	8.6%	1,895
5. Mechanical Engineering Technicians	$47,280	6.4%	3,710

Best Green Technologies Jobs Requiring a Bachelor's Degree

Job	Annual Earnings	Percent Growth	Annual Openings
1. Construction Managers	$76,230	15.7%	44,158
2. Environmental Engineers	$72,350	25.4%	5,003
3. Chemical Engineers	$81,500	7.9%	2,111
4. Industrial Engineers	$71,430	20.3%	11,272
5. Electrical Engineers	$79,240	6.3%	6,806
6. Nuclear Engineers	$94,420	7.2%	1,046
7. Petroleum Engineers	$103,960	5.2%	1,016
8. Mechanical Engineers	$72,300	4.2%	12,394
9. Mining and Geological Engineers, Including Mining Safety Engineers	$74,330	10.0%	456

Best Green Technologies Jobs Requiring Work Experience Plus Degree

Job	Annual Earnings	Percent Growth	Annual Openings
1. Engineering Managers	$111,020	7.3%	7,404

Best Green Technologies Jobs Requiring a Master's Degree

Job	Annual Earnings	Percent Growth	Annual Openings
1. Environmental Scientists and Specialists, Including Health	$58,380	25.1%	6,961
2. Geoscientists, Except Hydrologists and Geographers	$75,800	21.9%	2,471

(continued)

(continued)

Best Green Technologies Jobs Requiring a Master's Degree

Job	Annual Earnings	Percent Growth	Annual Openings
3. Hydrologists	$68,140	24.3%	687
4. Urban and Regional Planners	$57,970	14.5%	1,967

Best Health-Care Jobs Requiring Short-Term On-the-Job Training

Job	Annual Earnings	Percent Growth	Annual Openings
1. Physical Therapist Aides	$22,990	24.4%	4,092

Best Health-Care Jobs Requiring Moderate-Term On-the-Job Training

Job	Annual Earnings	Percent Growth	Annual Openings
1. Medical Assistants	$27,430	35.4%	92,977
2. Dental Assistants	$31,550	29.2%	29,482
3. Pharmacy Technicians	$26,720	32.0%	54,453

Best Health-Care Jobs Requiring Postsecondary Vocational Training

Job	Annual Earnings	Percent Growth	Annual Openings
1. Licensed Practical and Licensed Vocational Nurses	$37,940	14.0%	70,610
2. Surgical Technologists	$37,540	24.5%	15,365
3. Emergency Medical Technicians and Paramedics	$28,400	19.2%	19,513
4. Massage Therapists	$34,870	20.3%	9,193
5. Nursing Aides, Orderlies, and Attendants	$23,160	18.2%	321,036
6. Medical Transcriptionists	$31,250	13.5%	18,080

Best Health-Care Jobs Requiring an Associate Degree

Job	Annual Earnings	Percent Growth	Annual Openings
1. Dental Hygienists	$64,740	30.1%	10,433
2. Registered Nurses	$60,010	23.5%	233,499
3. Physical Therapist Assistants	$44,130	32.4%	5,957
4. Radiation Therapists	$70,010	24.8%	1,461
5. Radiologic Technologists and Technicians	$50,260	15.1%	12,836
6. Cardiovascular Technologists and Technicians	$44,940	25.5%	3,550
7. Respiratory Therapists	$50,070	22.6%	5,563
8. Diagnostic Medical Sonographers	$59,860	19.1%	3,211
9. Occupational Therapist Assistants	$45,050	25.4%	2,634
10. Medical Records and Health Information Technicians	$29,290	17.8%	39,048
11. Medical and Clinical Laboratory Technicians	$34,270	15.0%	10,866
12. Nuclear Medicine Technologists	$64,670	14.8%	1,290

Best Health-Care Jobs Requiring a Bachelor's Degree

Job	Annual Earnings	Percent Growth	Annual Openings
1. Medical and Public Health Social Workers	$44,670	24.2%	16,429
2. Substance Abuse and Behavioral Disorder Counselors	$35,580	34.3%	20,821
3. Health Educators	$42,920	26.2%	13,707
4. Medical and Clinical Laboratory Technologists	$51,720	12.4%	11,457
5. Biological Technicians	$37,810	16.0%	15,374
6. Dietitians and Nutritionists	$49,010	8.6%	4,996
7. Occupational Health and Safety Specialists	$60,140	8.1%	3,440
8. Orthotists and Prosthetists	$60,520	11.8%	295

Best Health-Care Jobs Requiring Work Experience Plus Degree

Job	Annual Earnings	Percent Growth	Annual Openings
1. Medical and Health Services Managers	$76,990	16.4%	31,877

Best Health-Care Jobs Requiring a Master's Degree

Job	Annual Earnings	Percent Growth	Annual Openings
1. Mental Health Counselors	$36,000	30.0%	24,103
2. Physical Therapists	$69,760	27.1%	12,072
3. Mental Health and Substance Abuse Social Workers	$36,640	29.9%	17,289
4. Physician Assistants	$78,450	27.0%	7,147
5. Occupational Therapists	$63,790	23.1%	8,338
6. Marriage and Family Therapists	$43,600	29.8%	5,953
7. Rehabilitation Counselors	$29,630	23.0%	32,081
8. Speech-Language Pathologists	$60,690	10.6%	11,160

Best Health-Care Jobs Requiring a Doctoral Degree

Job	Annual Earnings	Percent Growth	Annual Openings
1. Medical Scientists, Except Epidemiologists	$64,200	20.2%	10,596
2. Clinical, Counseling, and School Psychologists	$62,210	15.8%	8,309

Best Health-Care Jobs Requiring a First Professional Degree

Job	Annual Earnings	Percent Growth	Annual Openings
1. Physicians and Surgeons	$145,600+	14.2%	38,027
2. Pharmacists	$100,480	21.7%	16,358
3. Chiropractors	$65,890	14.4%	3,179
4. Dentists, General	$137,630	9.2%	7,106
5. Orthodontists	$145,600+	9.2%	479
6. Prosthodontists	$145,600+	10.7%	54
7. Optometrists	$93,800	11.3%	1,789
8. Oral and Maxillofacial Surgeons	$145,600+	9.1%	400
9. Podiatrists	$110,510	9.5%	648

Best Information and Telecommunication Technologies Jobs Requiring Work Experience in a Related Occupation

Job	Annual Earnings	Percent Growth	Annual Openings
1. Sales Representatives, Wholesale and Manufacturing, Technical and Scientific Products	$68,270	12.4%	43,469

Best Information and Telecommunication Technologies Jobs Requiring an Associate Degree

Job	Annual Earnings	Percent Growth	Annual Openings
1. Computer Specialists, All Other	$71,510	15.1%	14,374
2. Computer Support Specialists	$42,400	12.9%	97,334

Best Information and Telecommunication Technologies Jobs Requiring a Bachelor's Degree

Job	Annual Earnings	Percent Growth	Annual Openings
1. Computer Software Engineers, Applications	$83,130	44.6%	58,690
2. Computer Systems Analysts	$73,090	29.0%	63,166
3. Computer Software Engineers, Systems Software	$89,070	28.2%	33,139
4. Network Systems and Data Communications Analysts	$68,220	53.4%	35,086
5. Network and Computer Systems Administrators	$64,690	27.0%	37,010
6. Database Administrators	$67,250	28.6%	8,258
7. Industrial Engineers	$71,430	20.3%	11,272
8. Sales Engineers	$80,270	8.5%	7,371
9. Computer Hardware Engineers	$91,860	4.6%	3,572
10. Multi-Media Artists and Animators	$54,550	25.8%	13,182
11. Mechanical Engineers	$72,300	4.2%	12,394
12. Electrical Engineers	$79,240	6.3%	6,806
13. Electronics Engineers, Except Computer	$83,340	3.7%	5,699
14. Technical Writers	$60,390	19.5%	7,498

Best Information and Telecommunication Technologies Jobs Requiring Work Experience Plus Degree

Job	Annual Earnings	Percent Growth	Annual Openings
1. Computer and Information Systems Managers	$108,070	16.4%	30,887
2. Engineering Managers	$111,020	7.3%	7,404

Best Information and Telecommunication Technologies Jobs Requiring a Doctoral Degree

Job	Annual Earnings	Percent Growth	Annual Openings
1. Computer and Information Scientists, Research	$97,970	21.5%	2,901

Best Infrastructure Jobs Requiring Short-Term On-the-Job Training

Job	Annual Earnings	Percent Growth	Annual Openings
1. Truck Drivers, Light or Delivery Services	$26,380	8.4%	154,330
2. Helpers—Pipelayers, Plumbers, Pipefitters, and Steamfitters	$25,350	11.9%	29,332
3. Helpers—Installation, Maintenance, and Repair Workers	$22,920	11.8%	52,058
4. Helpers—Carpenters	$24,340	11.7%	37,731
5. Helpers—Brickmasons, Blockmasons, Stonemasons, and Tile and Marble Setters	$26,260	11.0%	22,500

Best Infrastructure Jobs Requiring Moderate-Term On-the-Job Training

Job	Annual Earnings	Percent Growth	Annual Openings
1. Truck Drivers, Heavy and Tractor-Trailer	$36,220	10.4%	279,032
2. Operating Engineers and Other Construction Equipment Operators	$38,130	8.4%	55,468
3. Roofers	$33,240	14.3%	38,398
4. Cement Masons and Concrete Finishers	$33,840	11.4%	34,625
5. Painters, Construction and Maintenance	$32,080	11.8%	101,140

Best Infrastructure Jobs Requiring Moderate-Term On-the-Job Training

Job	Annual Earnings	Percent Growth	Annual Openings
6. Surveying and Mapping Technicians	$33,640	19.4%	8,299
7. Construction Laborers	$27,310	10.9%	257,407
8. Drywall and Ceiling Tile Installers	$36,520	7.3%	30,945
9. Highway Maintenance Workers	$32,600	8.9%	24,774

Best Infrastructure Jobs Requiring Long-Term On-the-Job Training

Job	Annual Earnings	Percent Growth	Annual Openings
1. Plumbers, Pipefitters, and Steamfitters	$44,090	10.6%	68,643
2. Electricians	$44,780	7.4%	79,083
3. Carpenters	$37,660	10.3%	223,225
4. Mobile Heavy Equipment Mechanics, Except Engines	$41,450	12.3%	11,037
5. Industrial Machinery Mechanics	$42,350	9.0%	23,361
6. Elevator Installers and Repairers	$68,000	8.8%	2,850
7. Electrical Power-Line Installers and Repairers	$52,570	7.2%	6,401
8. Heating, Air Conditioning, and Refrigeration Mechanics and Installers	$38,360	8.7%	29,719
9. Telecommunications Line Installers and Repairers	$47,220	4.6%	14,719
10. Glaziers	$35,230	11.9%	6,416
11. Sheet Metal Workers	$39,210	6.7%	31,677

Best Infrastructure Jobs Requiring Work Experience in a Related Occupation

Job	Annual Earnings	Percent Growth	Annual Openings
1. First-Line Supervisors/Managers of Construction Trades and Extraction Workers	$55,950	9.1%	82,923
2. Construction and Building Inspectors	$48,330	18.2%	12,606
3. First-Line Supervisors/Managers of Mechanics, Installers, and Repairers	$55,380	7.3%	24,361

Best Infrastructure Jobs Requiring Postsecondary Vocational Training

Job	Annual Earnings	Percent Growth	Annual Openings
1. Architectural and Civil Drafters	$43,310	6.1%	16,238
2. Telecommunications Equipment Installers and Repairers, Except Line Installers	$54,070	2.5%	13,541
3. Mechanical Drafters	$44,740	5.2%	10,902

Best Infrastructure Jobs Requiring an Associate Degree

Job	Annual Earnings	Percent Growth	Annual Openings
1. Electrical and Electronic Engineering Technicians	$52,140	3.6%	12,583
2. Environmental Science and Protection Technicians, Including Health	$39,370	28.0%	8,404
3. Civil Engineering Technicians	$42,580	10.2%	7,499
4. Environmental Engineering Technicians	$40,690	24.8%	2,162

Best Infrastructure Jobs Requiring a Bachelor's Degree

Job	Annual Earnings	Percent Growth	Annual Openings
1. Construction Managers	$76,230	15.7%	44,158
2. Civil Engineers	$71,710	18.0%	15,979
3. Environmental Engineers	$72,350	25.4%	5,003
4. Industrial Engineers	$71,430	20.3%	11,272
5. Surveyors	$51,630	23.7%	14,305
6. Cost Estimators	$54,920	18.5%	38,379
7. Architects, Except Landscape and Naval	$67,620	17.7%	11,324
8. Electrical Engineers	$79,240	6.3%	6,806
9. Technical Writers	$60,390	19.5%	7,498
10. Logisticians	$64,250	17.3%	9,671
11. Cartographers and Photogrammetrists	$49,970	20.3%	2,823
12. Health and Safety Engineers, Except Mining Safety Engineers and Inspectors	$69,580	9.6%	1,105

Best Infrastructure Jobs Requiring Work Experience Plus Degree

Job	Annual Earnings	Percent Growth	Annual Openings
1. Engineering Managers	$111,020	7.3%	7,404

Best Infrastructure Jobs Requiring a Master's Degree

Job	Annual Earnings	Percent Growth	Annual Openings
1. Environmental Scientists and Specialists, Including Health	$58,380	25.1%	6,961
2. Urban and Regional Planners	$57,970	14.5%	1,967

The Best Jobs for Each Renewal Industry Sorted by Personality Types

These lists organize the best jobs in each renewal industry into groups matching six personality types: Realistic, Investigative, Artistic, Social, Enterprising, and Conventional. This system was developed by John L. Holland and is used in the *Self-Directed Search (SDS)* and other career assessment inventories and information systems.

If you have used one of these career inventories or systems, the lists will help you identify jobs that most closely match these personality types. Even if you haven't used one of these systems, the concept of personality types can help you identify jobs that suit the type of person you are.

As we did for the educational and training levels, we have created only one list per renewal industry for each personality type. We've ranked the jobs within each personality type based on the total combined scores for earnings, growth, and annual job openings. As in the other lists in Part II, the economic facts presented here and used for sorting apply to all workers within the occupation, not just those in the renewal industries. Consider reviewing the jobs for more than one personality type so that you don't overlook possible jobs that would interest you. Remember that people often identify with one or two secondary personality types in addition to their primary type.

Descriptions of the Six Personality Types

Following are brief descriptions for each of the six personality types used in the lists, worded in terms of jobs rather than in terms of the workers in the jobs. Select the two or three descriptions that most closely describe your preferences and then use the lists to identify jobs that best fit these personality types.

* **Realistic:** These occupations frequently involve work activities that include practical, hands-on problems and solutions. They often deal with plants; animals; and real-world materials such as

wood, tools, and machinery. Many of the occupations require working outside and don't involve a lot of paperwork or working closely with others.

❋ **Investigative:** These occupations frequently involve working with ideas and require an extensive amount of thinking. These occupations can involve searching for facts and figuring out problems mentally.

❋ **Artistic:** These occupations frequently involve working with forms, designs, and patterns. They often require self-expression, and the work can be done without following a clear set of rules.

❋ **Social:** These occupations frequently involve working with, communicating with, and teaching people. These occupations often involve helping or providing service to others.

❋ **Enterprising:** These occupations frequently involve starting up and carrying out projects. These occupations can involve leading people and making many decisions. They sometimes require risk taking and often deal with business.

❋ **Conventional:** These occupations frequently involve following set procedures and routines. These occupations can include working with data and details more than with ideas. Usually there is a clear line of authority to follow.

Best Advanced Manufacturing Jobs for People with a Realistic Personality Type

Job	Annual Earnings	Percent Growth	Annual Openings
1. Electricians	$44,780	7.4%	79,083
2. Biological Technicians	$37,810	16.0%	15,374
3. Maintenance and Repair Workers, General	$32,570	10.1%	165,502
4. Industrial Machinery Mechanics	$42,350	9.0%	23,361
5. Aircraft Structure, Surfaces, Rigging, and Systems Assemblers	$45,420	12.8%	6,550
6. Electrical and Electronics Repairers, Commercial and Industrial Equipment	$47,110	6.8%	6,607
7. Electrical and Electronic Engineering Technicians	$52,140	3.6%	12,583
8. Electrical and Electronics Drafters	$49,250	4.1%	4,786
9. Mechanical Drafters	$44,740	5.2%	10,902
10. Millwrights	$46,090	5.8%	4,758
11. Welders, Cutters, Solderers, and Brazers	$32,270	5.1%	61,125
12. Laborers and Freight, Stock, and Material Movers, Hand	$21,900	2.1%	630,487
13. Painters, Transportation Equipment	$36,000	8.4%	3,268
14. Team Assemblers	$24,630	0.1%	264,135
15. Industrial Truck and Tractor Operators	$28,010	–2.0%	89,547
16. Machinists	$35,230	–3.1%	39,505
17. Maintenance Workers, Machinery	$35,590	–1.1%	15,055

Best Green Technologies Jobs for People with a Realistic Personality Type

Job	Annual Earnings	Percent Growth	Annual Openings
1. Plumbers, Pipefitters, and Steamfitters	$44,090	10.6%	68,643
2. Construction and Building Inspectors	$48,330	18.2%	12,606
3. Carpenters	$37,660	10.3%	223,225
4. Electricians	$44,780	7.4%	79,083
5. Roofers	$33,240	14.3%	38,398
6. Mobile Heavy Equipment Mechanics, Except Engines	$41,450	12.3%	11,037
7. Construction Laborers	$27,310	10.9%	257,407
8. Industrial Machinery Mechanics	$42,350	9.0%	23,361
9. Operating Engineers and Other Construction Equipment Operators	$38,130	8.4%	55,468
10. Bus Drivers, Transit and Intercity	$33,160	12.5%	27,100
11. Heating, Air Conditioning, and Refrigeration Mechanics and Installers	$38,360	8.7%	29,719
12. Helpers—Installation, Maintenance, and Repair Workers	$22,920	11.8%	52,058
13. Electrical Power-Line Installers and Repairers	$52,570	7.2%	6,401
14. Geological and Petroleum Technicians	$50,950	8.6%	1,895
15. Helpers—Pipelayers, Plumbers, Pipefitters, and Steamfitters	$25,350	11.9%	29,332
16. Sheet Metal Workers	$39,210	6.7%	31,677
17. Electrical and Electronic Engineering Technicians	$52,140	3.6%	12,583
18. Glaziers	$35,230	11.9%	6,416
19. Architectural and Civil Drafters	$43,310	6.1%	16,238
20. Electrical and Electronics Repairers, Commercial and Industrial Equipment	$47,110	6.8%	6,607
21. Hazardous Materials Removal Workers	$36,330	11.2%	1,933
22. Refuse and Recyclable Material Collectors	$29,420	7.4%	37,785
23. Welders, Cutters, Solderers, and Brazers	$32,270	5.1%	61,125
24. Electrical and Electronics Drafters	$49,250	4.1%	4,786
25. Industrial Truck and Tractor Operators	$28,010	–2.0%	89,547
26. Machinists	$35,230	–3.1%	39,505
27. Structural Iron and Steel Workers	$42,130	6.0%	6,969
28. Insulation Workers, Mechanical	$36,570	8.6%	5,787
29. Pipelayers	$31,280	8.7%	8,902

Best Health-Care Jobs for People with a Realistic Personality Type

Job	Annual Earnings	Percent Growth	Annual Openings
1. Biological Technicians	$37,810	16.0%	15,374
2. Surgical Technologists	$37,540	24.5%	15,365
3. Radiologic Technologists and Technicians	$50,260	15.1%	12,836
4. Oral and Maxillofacial Surgeons	$145,600+	9.1%	400

Best Information and Telecommunication Technologies Jobs for People with a Realistic Personality Type

Job	Annual Earnings	Percent Growth	Annual Openings
1. Computer Support Specialists	$42,400	12.9%	97,334

Best Infrastructure Jobs for People with a Realistic Personality Type

Job	Annual Earnings	Percent Growth	Annual Openings
1. Civil Engineers	$71,710	18.0%	15,979
2. Surveyors	$51,630	23.7%	14,305
3. Plumbers, Pipefitters, and Steamfitters	$44,090	10.6%	68,643
4. Construction and Building Inspectors	$48,330	18.2%	12,606
5. Truck Drivers, Heavy and Tractor-Trailer	$36,220	10.4%	279,032
6. Carpenters	$37,660	10.3%	223,225
7. Electricians	$44,780	7.4%	79,083
8. Roofers	$33,240	14.3%	38,398
9. Cartographers and Photogrammetrists	$49,970	20.3%	2,823
10. Painters, Construction and Maintenance	$32,080	11.8%	101,140
11. Construction Laborers	$27,310	10.9%	257,407
12. Cement Masons and Concrete Finishers	$33,840	11.4%	34,625
13. Mobile Heavy Equipment Mechanics, Except Engines	$41,450	12.3%	11,037
14. Environmental Engineering Technicians	$40,690	24.8%	2,162
15. Operating Engineers and Other Construction Equipment Operators	$38,130	8.4%	55,468
16. Helpers—Installation, Maintenance, and Repair Workers	$22,920	11.8%	52,058
17. Industrial Machinery Mechanics	$42,350	9.0%	23,361
18. Elevator Installers and Repairers	$68,000	8.8%	2,850

Best Infrastructure Jobs for People with a Realistic Personality Type

Job	Annual Earnings	Percent Growth	Annual Openings
19. Helpers—Carpenters	$24,340	11.7%	37,731
20. Helpers—Pipelayers, Plumbers, Pipefitters, and Steamfitters	$25,350	11.9%	29,332
21. Heating, Air Conditioning, and Refrigeration Mechanics and Installers	$38,360	8.7%	29,719
22. Truck Drivers, Light or Delivery Services	$26,380	8.4%	154,330
23. Sheet Metal Workers	$39,210	6.7%	31,677
24. Telecommunications Equipment Installers and Repairers, Except Line Installers	$54,070	2.5%	13,541
25. Civil Engineering Technicians	$42,580	10.2%	7,499
26. Glaziers	$35,230	11.9%	6,416
27. Architectural and Civil Drafters	$43,310	6.1%	16,238
28. Drywall and Ceiling Tile Installers	$36,520	7.3%	30,945
29. Electrical Power-Line Installers and Repairers	$52,570	7.2%	6,401
30. Telecommunications Line Installers and Repairers	$47,220	4.6%	14,719
31. Electrical and Electronic Engineering Technicians	$52,140	3.6%	12,583
32. Helpers—Brickmasons, Blockmasons, Stonemasons, and Tile and Marble Setters	$26,260	11.0%	22,500
33. Highway Maintenance Workers	$32,600	8.9%	24,774
34. Mechanical Drafters	$44,740	5.2%	10,902

Best Advanced Manufacturing Jobs for People with an Investigative Personality Type

Job	Annual Earnings	Percent Growth	Annual Openings
1. Industrial Engineers	$71,430	20.3%	11,272
2. Chemists	$63,490	9.1%	9,024
3. Electrical Engineers	$79,240	6.3%	6,806
4. Mechanical Engineers	$72,300	4.2%	12,394
5. Industrial Engineering Technicians	$47,490	9.9%	6,172
6. Computer Hardware Engineers	$91,860	4.6%	3,572
7. Chemical Engineers	$81,500	7.9%	2,111
8. Electronics Engineers, Except Computer	$83,340	3.7%	5,699
9. Occupational Health and Safety Specialists	$60,140	8.1%	3,440
10. Mechanical Engineering Technicians	$47,280	6.4%	3,710

Best Education Jobs for People with an Investigative Personality Type

Job	Annual Earnings	Percent Growth	Annual Openings
1. Clinical, Counseling, and School Psychologists	$62,210	15.8%	8,309

Best Green Technologies Jobs for People with an Investigative Personality Type

Job	Annual Earnings	Percent Growth	Annual Openings
1. Environmental Engineers	$72,350	25.4%	5,003
2. Industrial Engineers	$71,430	20.3%	11,272
3. Environmental Scientists and Specialists, Including Health	$58,380	25.1%	6,961
4. Environmental Science and Protection Technicians, Including Health	$39,370	28.0%	8,404
5. Geoscientists, Except Hydrologists and Geographers	$75,800	21.9%	2,471
6. Electrical Engineers	$79,240	6.3%	6,806
7. Chemical Engineers	$81,500	7.9%	2,111
8. Mechanical Engineers	$72,300	4.2%	12,394
9. Nuclear Engineers	$94,420	7.2%	1,046
10. Hydrologists	$68,140	24.3%	687
11. Industrial Engineering Technicians	$47,490	9.9%	6,172
12. Petroleum Engineers	$103,960	5.2%	1,016
13. Mining and Geological Engineers, Including Mining Safety Engineers	$74,330	10.0%	456
14. Urban and Regional Planners	$57,970	14.5%	1,967
15. Mechanical Engineering Technicians	$47,280	6.4%	3,710

Best Health-Care Jobs for People with an Investigative Personality Type

Job	Annual Earnings	Percent Growth	Annual Openings
1. Pharmacists	$100,480	21.7%	16,358
2. Physicians and Surgeons	$145,600+	14.2%	38,027
3. Physician Assistants	$78,450	27.0%	7,147
4. Medical Scientists, Except Epidemiologists	$64,200	20.2%	10,596
5. Clinical, Counseling, and School Psychologists	$62,210	15.8%	8,309
6. Dentists, General	$137,630	9.2%	7,106

Best Health-Care Jobs for People with an Investigative Personality Type

Job	Annual Earnings	Percent Growth	Annual Openings
7. Medical and Clinical Laboratory Technicians	$34,270	15.0%	10,866
8. Medical and Clinical Laboratory Technologists	$51,720	12.4%	11,457
9. Diagnostic Medical Sonographers	$59,860	19.1%	3,211
10. Prosthodontists	$145,600+	10.7%	54
11. Nuclear Medicine Technologists	$64,670	14.8%	1,290
12. Optometrists	$93,800	11.3%	1,789
13. Orthodontists	$145,600+	9.2%	479
14. Podiatrists	$110,510	9.5%	648
15. Occupational Health and Safety Specialists	$60,140	8.1%	3,440
16. Dietitians and Nutritionists	$49,010	8.6%	4,996

Best Information and Telecommunication Technologies Jobs for People with an Investigative Personality Type

Job	Annual Earnings	Percent Growth	Annual Openings
1. Computer Software Engineers, Applications	$83,130	44.6%	58,690
2. Computer Software Engineers, Systems Software	$89,070	28.2%	33,139
3. Network Systems and Data Communications Analysts	$68,220	53.4%	35,086
4. Computer and Information Scientists, Research	$97,970	21.5%	2,901
5. Network and Computer Systems Administrators	$64,690	27.0%	37,010
6. Computer Hardware Engineers	$91,860	4.6%	3,572
7. Electrical Engineers	$79,240	6.3%	6,806
8. Industrial Engineers	$71,430	20.3%	11,272
9. Mechanical Engineers	$72,300	4.2%	12,394
10. Electronics Engineers, Except Computer	$83,340	3.7%	5,699

Best Infrastructure Jobs for People with an Investigative Personality Type

Job	Annual Earnings	Percent Growth	Annual Openings
1. Industrial Engineers	$71,430	20.3%	11,272
2. Environmental Engineers	$72,350	25.4%	5,003
3. Environmental Science and Protection Technicians, Including Health	$39,370	28.0%	8,404

(continued)

(continued)

Best Infrastructure Jobs for People with an Investigative Personality Type

Job	Annual Earnings	Percent Growth	Annual Openings
4. Environmental Scientists and Specialists, Including Health	$58,380	25.1%	6,961
5. Electrical Engineers	$79,240	6.3%	6,806
6. Health and Safety Engineers, Except Mining Safety Engineers and Inspectors	$69,580	9.6%	1,105
7. Urban and Regional Planners	$57,970	14.5%	1,967

Best Advanced Manufacturing Jobs for People with an Artistic Personality Type

Job	Annual Earnings	Percent Growth	Annual Openings
1. Technical Writers	$60,390	19.5%	7,498
2. Graphic Designers	$41,280	9.8%	26,968
3. Commercial and Industrial Designers	$56,550	7.2%	4,777

Best Information and Telecommunication Technologies Jobs for People with an Artistic Personality Type

Job	Annual Earnings	Percent Growth	Annual Openings
1. Multi-Media Artists and Animators	$54,550	25.8%	13,182
2. Technical Writers	$60,390	19.5%	7,498

Best Infrastructure Jobs for People with an Artistic Personality Type

Job	Annual Earnings	Percent Growth	Annual Openings
1. Architects, Except Landscape and Naval	$67,620	17.7%	11,324
2. Technical Writers	$60,390	19.5%	7,498

Best Education Jobs for People with a Social Personality Type

Job	Annual Earnings	Percent Growth	Annual Openings
1. Health Specialties Teachers, Postsecondary	$80,700	22.9%	19,617
2. Business Teachers, Postsecondary	$64,900	22.9%	11,643
3. Biological Science Teachers, Postsecondary	$71,780	22.9%	9,039
4. Engineering Teachers, Postsecondary	$79,510	22.9%	5,565
5. Law Teachers, Postsecondary	$87,730	22.9%	2,169
6. Computer Science Teachers, Postsecondary	$62,020	22.9%	5,820
7. Economics Teachers, Postsecondary	$75,300	22.9%	2,208
8. Agricultural Sciences Teachers, Postsecondary	$78,460	22.9%	1,840
9. Chemistry Teachers, Postsecondary	$63,870	22.9%	3,405
10. Mathematical Science Teachers, Postsecondary	$58,560	22.9%	7,663
11. Art, Drama, and Music Teachers, Postsecondary	$55,190	22.9%	12,707
12. Physics Teachers, Postsecondary	$70,090	22.9%	2,155
13. Psychology Teachers, Postsecondary	$60,610	22.9%	5,261
14. Atmospheric, Earth, Marine, and Space Sciences Teachers, Postsecondary	$73,280	22.9%	1,553
15. Nursing Instructors and Teachers, Postsecondary	$57,500	22.9%	7,337
16. Preschool Teachers, Except Special Education	$23,130	26.3%	78,172
17. History Teachers, Postsecondary	$59,160	22.9%	3,570
18. Political Science Teachers, Postsecondary	$63,100	22.9%	2,435
19. Self-Enrichment Education Teachers	$34,580	23.1%	64,449
20. Education Teachers, Postsecondary	$54,220	22.9%	9,359
21. English Language and Literature Teachers, Postsecondary	$54,000	22.9%	10,475
22. Architecture Teachers, Postsecondary	$68,540	22.9%	1,044
23. Vocational Education Teachers, Postsecondary	$45,850	22.9%	19,313
24. Anthropology and Archeology Teachers, Postsecondary	$64,530	22.9%	910
25. Environmental Science Teachers, Postsecondary	$64,850	22.9%	769
26. Graduate Teaching Assistants	$28,060	22.9%	20,601
27. Sociology Teachers, Postsecondary	$58,160	22.9%	2,774
28. Philosophy and Religion Teachers, Postsecondary	$56,380	22.9%	3,120
29. Communications Teachers, Postsecondary	$54,720	22.9%	4,074
30. Foreign Language and Literature Teachers, Postsecondary	$53,610	22.9%	4,317
31. Area, Ethnic, and Cultural Studies Teachers, Postsecondary	$59,150	22.9%	1,252
32. Education Administrators, Preschool and Child Care Center/Program	$38,580	23.5%	8,113
33. Forestry and Conservation Science Teachers, Postsecondary	$63,790	22.9%	454
34. Geography Teachers, Postsecondary	$61,310	22.9%	697

(continued)

(continued)

Best Education Jobs for People with a Social Personality Type

Job	Annual Earnings	Percent Growth	Annual Openings
35. Recreation and Fitness Studies Teachers, Postsecondary	$52,170	22.9%	3,010
36. Home Economics Teachers, Postsecondary	$58,170	22.9%	820
37. Social Work Teachers, Postsecondary	$56,240	22.9%	1,292
38. Library Science Teachers, Postsecondary	$56,810	22.9%	702
39. Criminal Justice and Law Enforcement Teachers, Postsecondary	$51,060	22.9%	1,911
40. Instructional Coordinators	$55,270	22.5%	21,294
41. Speech-Language Pathologists	$60,690	10.6%	11,160
42. Elementary School Teachers, Except Special Education	$47,330	13.6%	181,612
43. Educational, Vocational, and School Counselors	$49,450	12.6%	54,025
44. Middle School Teachers, Except Special and Vocational Education	$47,900	11.2%	75,270
45. Special Education Teachers, Preschool, Kindergarten, and Elementary School	$48,350	19.6%	20,049
46. Child, Family, and School Social Workers	$38,620	19.1%	35,402
47. Kindergarten Teachers, Except Special Education	$45,120	16.3%	27,603

Best Health-Care Jobs for People with a Social Personality Type

Job	Annual Earnings	Percent Growth	Annual Openings
1. Dental Hygienists	$64,740	30.1%	10,433
2. Physical Therapists	$69,760	27.1%	12,072
3. Registered Nurses	$60,010	23.5%	233,499
4. Medical Assistants	$27,430	35.4%	92,977
5. Substance Abuse and Behavioral Disorder Counselors	$35,580	34.3%	20,821
6. Mental Health Counselors	$36,000	30.0%	24,103
7. Mental Health and Substance Abuse Social Workers	$36,640	29.9%	17,289
8. Physical Therapist Assistants	$44,130	32.4%	5,957
9. Health Educators	$42,920	26.2%	13,707
10. Medical and Public Health Social Workers	$44,670	24.2%	16,429
11. Occupational Therapists	$63,790	23.1%	8,338
12. Radiation Therapists	$70,010	24.8%	1,461
13. Marriage and Family Therapists	$43,600	29.8%	5,953
14. Cardiovascular Technologists and Technicians	$44,940	25.5%	3,550
15. Licensed Practical and Licensed Vocational Nurses	$37,940	14.0%	70,610

Best Health-Care Jobs for People with a Social Personality Type

Job	Annual Earnings	Percent Growth	Annual Openings
16. Rehabilitation Counselors	$29,630	23.0%	32,081
17. Occupational Therapist Assistants	$45,050	25.4%	2,634
18. Speech-Language Pathologists	$60,690	10.6%	11,160
19. Nursing Aides, Orderlies, and Attendants	$23,160	18.2%	321,036
20. Respiratory Therapists	$50,070	22.6%	5,563
21. Chiropractors	$65,890	14.4%	3,179
22. Emergency Medical Technicians and Paramedics	$28,400	19.2%	19,513
23. Massage Therapists	$34,870	20.3%	9,193
24. Orthotists and Prosthetists	$60,520	11.8%	295
25. Physical Therapist Aides	$22,990	24.4%	4,092

Best Advanced Manufacturing Jobs for People with an Enterprising Personality Type

Job	Annual Earnings	Percent Growth	Annual Openings
1. Engineering Managers	$111,020	7.3%	7,404
2. Logisticians	$64,250	17.3%	9,671
3. Sales Engineers	$80,270	8.5%	7,371
4. Industrial Production Managers	$80,560	–5.9%	14,889
5. Purchasing Managers	$85,440	3.4%	7,243
6. First-Line Supervisors/Managers of Production and Operating Workers	$48,670	–4.8%	46,144
7. Transportation, Storage, and Distribution Managers	$76,310	8.3%	6,994

Best Education Jobs for People with an Enterprising Personality Type

Job	Annual Earnings	Percent Growth	Annual Openings
1. Education Administrators, Elementary and Secondary School	$80,580	7.6%	27,143
2. Education Administrators, Postsecondary	$75,780	14.2%	17,121

Best Green Technologies Jobs for People with an Enterprising Personality Type

Job	Annual Earnings	Percent Growth	Annual Openings
1. Construction Managers	$76,230	15.7%	44,158
2. First-Line Supervisors/Managers of Construction Trades and Extraction Workers	$55,950	9.1%	82,923
3. Engineering Managers	$111,020	7.3%	7,404
4. Industrial Production Managers	$80,560	–5.9%	14,889

Best Health-Care Jobs for People with an Enterprising Personality Type

Job	Annual Earnings	Percent Growth	Annual Openings
1. Medical and Health Services Managers	$76,990	16.4%	31,877

Best Information and Telecommunication Technologies Jobs for People with an Enterprising Personality Type

Job	Annual Earnings	Percent Growth	Annual Openings
1. Computer and Information Systems Managers	$108,070	16.4%	30,887
2. Sales Representatives, Wholesale and Manufacturing, Technical and Scientific Products	$68,270	12.4%	43,469
3. Engineering Managers	$111,020	7.3%	7,404
4. Sales Engineers	$80,270	8.5%	7,371

Best Infrastructure Jobs for People with an Enterprising Personality Type

Job	Annual Earnings	Percent Growth	Annual Openings
1. Construction Managers	$76,230	15.7%	44,158
2. First-Line Supervisors/Managers of Construction Trades and Extraction Workers	$55,950	9.1%	82,923
3. Logisticians	$64,250	17.3%	9,671
4. Engineering Managers	$111,020	7.3%	7,404
5. First-Line Supervisors/Managers of Mechanics, Installers, and Repairers	$55,380	7.3%	24,361

Best Advanced Manufacturing Jobs for People with a Conventional Personality Type

Job	Annual Earnings	Percent Growth	Annual Openings
1. Production, Planning, and Expediting Clerks	$39,690	4.2%	52,735
2. Shipping, Receiving, and Traffic Clerks	$26,990	3.7%	138,967
3. Purchasing Agents, Except Wholesale, Retail, and Farm Products	$52,460	0.1%	22,349

Best Green Technologies Jobs for People with a Conventional Personality Type

Job	Annual Earnings	Percent Growth	Annual Openings
1. Surveying and Mapping Technicians	$33,640	19.4%	8,299
2. Inspectors, Testers, Sorters, Samplers, and Weighers	$30,310	–7.0%	75,361

Best Health-Care Jobs for People with a Conventional Personality Type

Job	Annual Earnings	Percent Growth	Annual Openings
1. Dental Assistants	$31,550	29.2%	29,482
2. Pharmacy Technicians	$26,720	32.0%	54,453
3. Medical Records and Health Information Technicians	$29,290	17.8%	39,048
4. Medical Transcriptionists	$31,250	13.5%	18,080

Best Information and Telecommunication Technologies Jobs for People with a Conventional Personality Type

Job	Annual Earnings	Percent Growth	Annual Openings
1. Computer Systems Analysts	$73,090	29.0%	63,166
2. Computer Specialists, All Other	$71,510	15.1%	14,374
3. Database Administrators	$67,250	28.6%	8,258

Best Infrastructure Jobs for People with a Conventional Personality Type

Job	Annual Earnings	Percent Growth	Annual Openings
1. Cost Estimators	$54,920	18.5%	38,379
2. Surveying and Mapping Technicians	$33,640	19.4%	8,299

Bonus Lists: Best Jobs Overall in All Renewal Industries

In all the preceding lists, the jobs are separated into the six renewal industries. (A few jobs are listed for more than one industry.) We thought you might be curious about how the jobs would compare if all 203 were thrown into the same pot.

In the following lists, you'll find that the high pay, fast growth, and plentiful job openings of the occupations in Information and Telecommunication Technologies and in Health Care cause them to dominate. Nevertheless, you'll find jobs from all six industries among the top 50 in each list.

The jobs listed as best overall are ranked by the three economic measures combined. The remaining lists rank the jobs by one economic measure each.

The 50 Best Jobs Overall in All Renewal Industries

Job	Annual Earnings	Percent Growth	Annual Openings
1. Computer Software Engineers, Applications	$83,130	44.6%	58,690
2. Computer Systems Analysts	$73,090	29.0%	63,166
3. Computer Software Engineers, Systems Software	$89,070	28.2%	33,139
4. Network Systems and Data Communications Analysts	$68,220	53.4%	35,086
5. Registered Nurses	$60,010	23.5%	233,499
6. Network and Computer Systems Administrators	$64,690	27.0%	37,010
7. Health Specialties Teachers, Postsecondary	$80,700	22.9%	19,617
8. Physicians and Surgeons	$145,600+	14.2%	38,027
9. Computer and Information Systems Managers	$108,070	16.4%	30,887
10. Physical Therapists	$69,760	27.1%	12,072
11. Pharmacists	$100,480	21.7%	16,358
12. Construction Managers	$76,230	15.7%	44,158
13. Dental Hygienists	$64,740	30.1%	10,433
14. Physician Assistants	$78,450	27.0%	7,147
15. Medical and Health Services Managers	$76,990	16.4%	31,877

The 50 Best Jobs Overall in All Renewal Industries

Job	Annual Earnings	Percent Growth	Annual Openings
16. Database Administrators	$67,250	28.6%	8,258
17. Biological Science Teachers, Postsecondary	$71,780	22.9%	9,039
18. Business Teachers, Postsecondary	$64,900	22.9%	11,643
19. Sales Representatives, Wholesale and Manufacturing, Technical and Scientific Products	$68,270	12.4%	43,469
20. Engineering Teachers, Postsecondary	$79,510	22.9%	5,565
21. Environmental Engineers	$72,350	25.4%	5,003
22. Medical Assistants	$27,430	35.4%	92,977
23. Multi-Media Artists and Animators	$54,550	25.8%	13,182
24. Civil Engineers	$71,710	18.0%	15,979
25. Occupational Therapists	$63,790	23.1%	8,338
26. Education Administrators, Postsecondary	$75,780	14.2%	17,121
27. Industrial Engineers	$71,430	20.3%	11,272
28. Art, Drama, and Music Teachers, Postsecondary	$55,190	22.9%	12,707
29. Cost Estimators	$54,920	18.5%	38,379
30. Surveyors	$51,630	23.7%	14,305
31. Law Teachers, Postsecondary	$87,730	22.9%	2,169
32. Pharmacy Technicians	$26,720	32.0%	54,453
33. Computer Specialists, All Other	$71,510	15.1%	14,374
34. Self-Enrichment Education Teachers	$34,580	23.1%	64,449
35. Mental Health Counselors	$36,000	30.0%	24,103
36. Instructional Coordinators	$55,270	22.5%	21,294
37. Substance Abuse and Behavioral Disorder Counselors	$35,580	34.3%	20,821
38. Vocational Education Teachers, Postsecondary	$45,850	22.9%	19,313
39. Environmental Scientists and Specialists, Including Health	$58,380	25.1%	6,961
40. Preschool Teachers, Except Special Education	$23,130	26.3%	78,172
41. Mathematical Science Teachers, Postsecondary	$58,560	22.9%	7,663
42. Medical and Public Health Social Workers	$44,670	24.2%	16,429
43. Mental Health and Substance Abuse Social Workers	$36,640	29.9%	17,289
44. Elementary School Teachers, Except Special Education	$47,330	13.6%	181,612
45. Economics Teachers, Postsecondary	$75,300	22.9%	2,208
46. English Language and Literature Teachers, Postsecondary	$54,000	22.9%	10,475
47. Architects, Except Landscape and Naval	$67,620	17.7%	11,324
48. Dental Assistants	$31,550	29.2%	29,482
49. Education Administrators, Elementary and Secondary School	$80,580	7.6%	27,143
50. Education Teachers, Postsecondary	$54,220	22.9%	9,359

The 50 Best-Paying Jobs in All Renewal Industries

Job	Annual Earnings
1. Oral and Maxillofacial Surgeons	$145,600+
2. Orthodontists	$145,600+
3. Physicians and Surgeons	$145,600+
4. Prosthodontists	$145,600+
5. Dentists, General	$137,630
6. Engineering Managers	$111,020
7. Podiatrists	$110,510
8. Computer and Information Systems Managers	$108,070
9. Petroleum Engineers	$103,960
10. Pharmacists	$100,480
11. Computer and Information Scientists, Research	$97,970
12. Nuclear Engineers	$94,420
13. Optometrists	$93,800
14. Computer Hardware Engineers	$91,860
15. Computer Software Engineers, Systems Software	$89,070
16. Law Teachers, Postsecondary	$87,730
17. Purchasing Managers	$85,440
18. Electronics Engineers, Except Computer	$83,340
19. Computer Software Engineers, Applications	$83,130
20. Chemical Engineers	$81,500
21. Health Specialties Teachers, Postsecondary	$80,700
22. Education Administrators, Elementary and Secondary School	$80,580
23. Industrial Production Managers	$80,560
24. Sales Engineers	$80,270
25. Engineering Teachers, Postsecondary	$79,510
26. Electrical Engineers	$79,240
27. Agricultural Sciences Teachers, Postsecondary	$78,460
28. Physician Assistants	$78,450
29. Medical and Health Services Managers	$76,990
30. Transportation, Storage, and Distribution Managers	$76,310
31. Construction Managers	$76,230
32. Geoscientists, Except Hydrologists and Geographers	$75,800
33. Education Administrators, Postsecondary	$75,780
34. Economics Teachers, Postsecondary	$75,300
35. Mining and Geological Engineers, Including Mining Safety Engineers	$74,330
36. Atmospheric, Earth, Marine, and Space Sciences Teachers, Postsecondary	$73,280
37. Computer Systems Analysts	$73,090

The 50 Best-Paying Jobs in All Renewal Industries

Job	Annual Earnings
38. Environmental Engineers	$72,350
39. Mechanical Engineers	$72,300
40. Biological Science Teachers, Postsecondary	$71,780
41. Civil Engineers	$71,710
42. Computer Specialists, All Other	$71,510
43. Industrial Engineers	$71,430
44. Physics Teachers, Postsecondary	$70,090
45. Radiation Therapists	$70,010
46. Physical Therapists	$69,760
47. Health and Safety Engineers, Except Mining Safety Engineers and Inspectors	$69,580
48. Architecture Teachers, Postsecondary	$68,540
49. Sales Representatives, Wholesale and Manufacturing, Technical and Scientific Products	$68,270
50. Network Systems and Data Communications Analysts	$68,220

The 50 Fastest-Growing Jobs in All Renewal Industries

Job	Percent Growth
1. Network Systems and Data Communications Analysts	53.4%
2. Computer Software Engineers, Applications	44.6%
3. Medical Assistants	35.4%
4. Substance Abuse and Behavioral Disorder Counselors	34.3%
5. Physical Therapist Assistants	32.4%
6. Pharmacy Technicians	32.0%
7. Dental Hygienists	30.1%
8. Mental Health Counselors	30.0%
9. Mental Health and Substance Abuse Social Workers	29.9%
10. Marriage and Family Therapists	29.8%
11. Dental Assistants	29.2%
12. Computer Systems Analysts	29.0%
13. Database Administrators	28.6%
14. Computer Software Engineers, Systems Software	28.2%
15. Environmental Science and Protection Technicians, Including Health	28.0%
16. Physical Therapists	27.1%

(continued)

(continued)

The 50 Fastest-Growing Jobs in All Renewal Industries

Job	Percent Growth
17. Network and Computer Systems Administrators	27.0%
18. Physician Assistants	27.0%
19. Preschool Teachers, Except Special Education	26.3%
20. Health Educators	26.2%
21. Multi-Media Artists and Animators	25.8%
22. Cardiovascular Technologists and Technicians	25.5%
23. Environmental Engineers	25.4%
24. Occupational Therapist Assistants	25.4%
25. Environmental Scientists and Specialists, Including Health	25.1%
26. Environmental Engineering Technicians	24.8%
27. Radiation Therapists	24.8%
28. Surgical Technologists	24.5%
29. Physical Therapist Aides	24.4%
30. Hydrologists	24.3%
31. Medical and Public Health Social Workers	24.2%
32. Surveyors	23.7%
33. Education Administrators, Preschool and Child Care Center/Program	23.5%
34. Registered Nurses	23.5%
35. Occupational Therapists	23.1%
36. Self-Enrichment Education Teachers	23.1%
37. Rehabilitation Counselors	23.0%
38. Agricultural Sciences Teachers, Postsecondary	22.9%
39. Anthropology and Archeology Teachers, Postsecondary	22.9%
40. Architecture Teachers, Postsecondary	22.9%
41. Area, Ethnic, and Cultural Studies Teachers, Postsecondary	22.9%
42. Art, Drama, and Music Teachers, Postsecondary	22.9%
43. Atmospheric, Earth, Marine, and Space Sciences Teachers, Postsecondary	22.9%
44. Biological Science Teachers, Postsecondary	22.9%
45. Business Teachers, Postsecondary	22.9%
46. Chemistry Teachers, Postsecondary	22.9%
47. Communications Teachers, Postsecondary	22.9%
48. Computer Science Teachers, Postsecondary	22.9%
49. Criminal Justice and Law Enforcement Teachers, Postsecondary	22.9%
50. Economics Teachers, Postsecondary	22.9%

The 50 Jobs with the Most Openings in All Renewal Industries

Job	Annual Openings
1. Laborers and Freight, Stock, and Material Movers, Hand	630,487
2. Nursing Aides, Orderlies, and Attendants	321,036
3. Truck Drivers, Heavy and Tractor-Trailer	279,032
4. Team Assemblers	264,135
5. Construction Laborers	257,407
6. Registered Nurses	233,499
7. Carpenters	223,225
8. Elementary School Teachers, Except Special Education	181,612
9. Maintenance and Repair Workers, General	165,502
10. Truck Drivers, Light or Delivery Services	154,330
11. Shipping, Receiving, and Traffic Clerks	138,967
12. Painters, Construction and Maintenance	101,140
13. Computer Support Specialists	97,334
14. Medical Assistants	92,977
15. Industrial Truck and Tractor Operators	89,547
16. First-Line Supervisors/Managers of Construction Trades and Extraction Workers	82,923
17. Electricians	79,083
18. Preschool Teachers, Except Special Education	78,172
19. Inspectors, Testers, Sorters, Samplers, and Weighers	75,361
20. Middle School Teachers, Except Special and Vocational Education	75,270
21. Licensed Practical and Licensed Vocational Nurses	70,610
22. Plumbers, Pipefitters, and Steamfitters	68,643
23. Self-Enrichment Education Teachers	64,449
24. Computer Systems Analysts	63,166
25. Welders, Cutters, Solderers, and Brazers	61,125
26. Computer Software Engineers, Applications	58,690
27. Operating Engineers and Other Construction Equipment Operators	55,468
28. Pharmacy Technicians	54,453
29. Educational, Vocational, and School Counselors	54,025
30. Production, Planning, and Expediting Clerks	52,735
31. Helpers—Installation, Maintenance, and Repair Workers	52,058
32. First-Line Supervisors/Managers of Production and Operating Workers	46,144
33. Construction Managers	44,158
34. Sales Representatives, Wholesale and Manufacturing, Technical and Scientific Products	43,469
35. Machinists	39,505

(continued)

(continued)

The 50 Jobs with the Most Openings in All Renewal Industries	
Job	Annual Openings
36. Medical Records and Health Information Technicians	39,048
37. Roofers	38,398
38. Cost Estimators	38,379
39. Physicians and Surgeons	38,027
40. Refuse and Recyclable Material Collectors	37,785
41. Helpers—Carpenters	37,731
42. Network and Computer Systems Administrators	37,010
43. Child, Family, and School Social Workers	35,402
44. Network Systems and Data Communications Analysts	35,086
45. Cement Masons and Concrete Finishers	34,625
46. Computer Software Engineers, Systems Software	33,139
47. Rehabilitation Counselors	32,081
48. Medical and Health Services Managers	31,877
49. Sheet Metal Workers	31,677
50. Drywall and Ceiling Tile Installers	30,945

Bonus Lists: Metropolitan Areas with the Highest Concentration of the Best Renewal Jobs

Jobs in renewal industries are available in all parts of the United States, but you may want to consider relocating to an area that has a high concentration of workers in the particular renewal industry that most appeals to you. To help you plan a possible move, we analyzed the employment in each metropolitan area of the U.S. For each metro area, we computed the ratio between the metro workforce in all jobs and the metro workforce in the 150 best renewal jobs, grouped by industry. Then we sorted the lists to identify the 20 metro areas with the highest ratios for each renewal industry.

Before you start packing your bags, however, you should heed several cautions.

The rankings are based on employment in the renewal jobs held *in all industries*. Therefore, for example, employment of machinists is counted among the Advanced Manufacturing jobs, so any metro area with a lot of machinists gets a boost on that list even if the jobs are mostly in low-tech manufacturing. Many of the workers in jobs linked to Green Technologies are currently employed in the traditional energy industries, so you'll notice that the "Oil Patch" of Texas and Louisiana dominates that listing.

As economic renewal shakes up industries, it may change the geographic regions that they dominate.

This is especially true for the industries that most need renewal. Manufacturing is undergoing drastic change as it becomes truly advanced, so its geographic centers can be expected to shift. As energy output in the U.S. becomes greener, many Green Technologies jobs will cluster in places where sunshine and wind are plentiful. By contrast, the Information and Telecommunication Technologies industry is likely to remain concentrated in California's Silicon Valley and other established hot spots.

Some shifts *have probably occurred already* and are not reflected in the rankings, which are based on figures for paid employment in May 2007. A good example is the Elkhart-Goshen, Indiana, metro area. Based on 2007 employment figures, we ranked it highest among the centers for the jobs linked to Advanced Manufacturing. However, since 2007 there has been a lot of erosion of the local industrial base, which is dominated by the manufacture of recreational vehicles. In February 2008, the unemployment rate there was still only 4.7 percent, but the recession that began about then caused such a steep decline in RV sales that one year later the county's jobless rate was at 15.3 percent, the nation's worst. Other manufacturing areas have also suffered from this recession, but Elkhart-Goshen has probably lost its top ranking. In the listing for Infrastructure, some of the metro areas may have earned their high rankings because of construction work on housing rather than on infrastructure. Now that the home-price bubble has burst, these regions may already deserve lower rankings.

Locating where similar workers are concentrated can be a smarter decision for some jobs and industries than for others. Think about whether you prefer opportunities for collaboration or an absence of competition. As a general rule, jobs in Advanced Manufacturing and Information and Telecommunication Technologies tend to thrive in settings where the industries cluster. Energy-related jobs in Green Technologies tend to do best where workers can collaborate on exploiting local energy resources. In Education and Health Care, on the other hand, it is mostly the lower-skilled technicians and aides who benefit from opportunities for collaboration; professionals may suffer from competition unless they form research teams that bring in funding from outside the community.

If you are serious about relocating, you certainly should consider other aspects of your target location besides just the mix of industries; for example, think about climate, lifestyle, and distance from loved ones.

Metropolitan Areas with the Highest Concentration of Workers in Advanced Manufacturing

Metro Area	Percent of Workers in This Industry
1. Elkhart-Goshen, IN	25.9%
2. Spartanburg, SC	16.7%
3. Dalton, GA	16.2%
4. Columbus, IN	15.1%
5. Sumter, SC	14.9%
6. Rockford, IL	14.8%
7. Morristown, TN	14.4%

(continued)

(continued)

Metropolitan Areas with the Highest Concentration of Workers in Advanced Manufacturing

Metro Area	Percent of Workers in This Industry
8. Evansville, IN-KY	14.3%
9. San German–Cabo Rojo, PR	14.1%
10. Houma–Bayou Cane–Thibodaux, LA	14.0%
11. Hickory-Lenoir-Morganton, NC	13.7%
12. Ponce, PR	13.6%
13. Decatur, AL	13.5%
14. Rocky Mount, NC	13.5%
15. Huntsville, AL	13.4%
16. Wausau, WI	13.3%
17. Holland–Grand Haven, MI	13.2%
18. Greenville, SC	13.1%
19. Gainesville, GA	12.8%
20. Niles–Benton Harbor, MI	12.8%

Metropolitan Areas with the Highest Concentration of Workers in Education

Metro Area	Percent of Workers in This Industry
1. College Station–Bryan, TX	7.2%
2. McAllen-Edinburg-Mission, TX	6.4%
3. El Paso, TX	6.0%
4. Hinesville–Fort Stewart, GA	6.0%
5. Yuba City, CA	6.0%
6. Merced, CA	5.7%
7. Madera, CA	5.5%
8. El Centro, CA	5.5%
9. Brownsville-Harlingen, TX	5.5%
10. Killeen–Temple–Fort Hood, TX	5.5%
11. New Bedford, MA	5.4%
12. Springfield, MA-CT	5.2%
13. Vineland-Millville-Bridgeton, NJ	5.2%
14. Greenville, NC	4.9%
15. Worcester, MA-CT	4.9%

Metropolitan Areas with the Highest Concentration of Workers in Education

Metro Area	Percent of Workers in This Industry
16. Austin–Round Rock, TX	4.9%
17. Utica-Rome, NY	4.9%
18. Bakersfield, CA	4.9%
19. Baltimore-Towson, MD	4.7%
20. Visalia-Porterville, CA	4.7%

Metropolitan Areas with the Highest Concentration of Workers in Green Technologies

Metro Area	Percent of Workers in This Industry
1. Kennewick-Richland-Pasco, WA	12.6%
2. Houma–Bayou Cane–Thibodaux, LA	11.2%
3. Baton Rouge, LA	11.1%
4. Ogden-Clearfield, UT	11.0%
5. Longview, TX	10.8%
6. Beaumont–Port Arthur, TX	10.8%
7. Houston–Sugar Land–Baytown, TX	10.6%
8. Victoria, TX	10.6%
9. Lake Charles, LA	10.5%
10. Farmington, NM	10.5%
11. Kokomo, IN	10.4%
12. Odessa, TX	10.4%
13. Elkhart-Goshen, IN	10.3%
14. Mobile, AL	10.2%
15. Corpus Christi, TX	10.0%
16. Rockford, IL	10.0%
17. Charleston, WV	10.0%
18. Decatur, AL	9.8%
19. Anderson, SC	9.7%
20. Bremerton-Silverdale, WA	9.7%

Metropolitan Areas with the Highest Concentration of Workers in Health Care

Metro Area	Percent of Workers in This Industry
1. Dothan, AL	15.8%
2. Hattiesburg, MS	10.9%
3. Gainesville, FL	10.7%
4. Alexandria, LA	10.7%
5. Huntington-Ashland, WV-KY-OH	10.7%
6. Johnstown, PA	10.5%
7. Johnson City, TN	10.4%
8. Cumberland, MD-WV	10.4%
9. Jackson, TN	10.4%
10. Lima, OH	10.1%
11. Hot Springs, AR	10.1%
12. Punta Gorda, FL	10.1%
13. Worcester, MA-CT	10.1%
14. Tyler, TX	10.0%
15. Duluth, MN-WI	9.9%
16. Monroe, LA	9.9%
17. Toledo, OH	9.8%
18. Utica-Rome, NY	9.6%
19. Florence, SC	9.6%
20. Columbia, MO	9.6%

Metropolitan Areas with the Highest Concentration of Workers in Information and Telecommunication Technologies

Metro Area	Percent of Workers in This Industry
1. San Jose–Sunnyvale–Santa Clara, CA	14.3%
2. Boulder, CO	10.9%
3. Huntsville, AL	9.5%
4. Durham, NC	8.2%
5. Washington-Arlington-Alexandria, DC-VA-MD-WV	8.0%
6. Austin–Round Rock, TX	6.5%
7. Boston-Cambridge-Quincy, MA-NH	6.4%
8. Colorado Springs, CO	6.0%
9. Seattle-Tacoma-Bellevue, WA	5.9%

Metropolitan Areas with the Highest Concentration of Workers in Information and Telecommunication Technologies

Metro Area	Percent of Workers in This Industry
10. San Francisco–Oakland–Fremont, CA	5.6%
11. Cedar Rapids, IA	5.5%
12. Raleigh-Cary, NC	5.4%
13. Denver-Aurora, CO	5.3%
14. Hartford–West Hartford–East Hartford, CT	5.2%
15. Warner Robins, GA	5.2%
16. Minneapolis–St. Paul–Bloomington, MN-WI	5.2%
17. Fort Walton Beach–Crestview–Destin, FL	5.1%
18. Palm Bay–Melbourne–Titusville, FL	5.1%
19. Bridgeport-Stamford-Norwalk, CT	4.9%
20. Olympia, WA	4.6%

Metropolitan Areas with the Highest Concentration of Workers in Infrastructure

Metro Area	Percent of Workers in This Industry
1. Naples–Marco Island, FL	13.8%
2. Fayetteville-Springdale-Rogers, AR-MO	13.7%
3. St. George, UT	13.6%
4. Farmington, NM	13.5%
5. Cape Coral–Fort Myers, FL	13.0%
6. San German–Cabo Rojo, PR	13.0%
7. Charleston, WV	12.5%
8. Fairbanks, AK	12.4%
9. Kennewick-Richland-Pasco, WA	12.4%
10. Lake Charles, LA	12.3%
11. Ogden-Clearfield, UT	12.2%
12. Victoria, TX	12.2%
13. Greeley, CO	12.1%
14. Boise City–Nampa, ID	12.0%
15. Mobile, AL	11.9%

(continued)

(continued)

Metropolitan Areas with the Highest Concentration of Workers in Infrastructure	
Metro Area	Percent of Workers in This Industry
16. Baton Rouge, LA	11.8%
17. Albuquerque, NM	11.8%
18. Odessa, TX	11.8%
19. Prescott, AZ	11.8%
20. Reno-Sparks, NV	11.8%

PART III

Descriptions of the Best Jobs for Renewing America

This part provides descriptions for all the jobs referred to in Part II. The introduction gives more details on how to use and interpret the job descriptions, but here is some additional information:

- Job descriptions are arranged in alphabetical order by job title. This approach allows you to find a description quickly if you know its correct title from one of the lists in Part II.

- Consider the job descriptions in this section as a first step in career exploration. When you find a job that interests you, turn to the appendix for suggestions about resources for further exploration.

- If you are using this section to browse for interesting options, we suggest you begin with the Table of Contents.

Agricultural Sciences Teachers, Postsecondary

* Education/Training Required: Master's degree
* Annual Earnings: $78,460
* Beginning Wage: $43,050
* Earnings Growth Potential: High (45.1%)
* Growth: 22.9%
* Annual Job Openings: 1,840
* Job Security: Most Secure
* Self-Employed: 0.4%
* Part-Time: 27.8%

Renewal Industry: Education.

Industries with Greatest Employment: Educational Services, Public and Private (97.3%).

Highest-Growth Industries (Projected Growth for This Job): Administrative and Support Services (48.3%); Amusement, Gambling, and Recreation Industries (45.2%); Social Assistance (38.6%); Support Activities for Transportation (32.8%); Religious, Grantmaking, Civic, Professional, and Similar Organizations (29.9%); Professional, Scientific, and Technical Services (28.8%); Management of Companies and Enterprises (26.8%); Local Government (23.5%); Educational Services, Public and Private (22.8%); Hospitals, Public and Private (21.4%).

Other Considerations for Job Outlook: Retirements of current postsecondary teachers should create numerous openings for all types of postsecondary teachers, so job opportunities are generally expected to be very good. One of the main reasons why students attend postsecondary institutions is to prepare themselves for careers, so the best job prospects for postsecondary teachers are likely to be in rapidly growing fields, such as agricultural sciences, that offer many nonacademic career options. Community colleges and other institutions offering career and technical education have been among the most rapidly growing, and these institutions are expected to offer some of the best opportunities for postsecondary teachers.

Teach courses in the agricultural sciences, including agronomy, dairy sciences, fisheries management, horticultural sciences, poultry sciences, range management, and agricultural soil conservation. Prepare course materials such as syllabi, homework assignments, and handouts. Evaluate and grade students' classwork, laboratory work, assignments, and papers. Keep abreast of developments in agriculture by reading current literature, talking with colleagues, and participating in professional conferences. Prepare and deliver lectures to undergraduate and/or graduate students on topics such as crop production, plant genetics, and soil chemistry. Initiate, facilitate, and moderate classroom discussions. Conduct research in a particular field of knowledge and publish findings in professional journals, books, and/or electronic media. Supervise laboratory sessions and fieldwork and coordinate laboratory operations. Supervise undergraduate and/or graduate teaching, internship, and research work. Compile, administer, and grade examinations or assign this work to others. Advise students on academic and vocational curricula and on career issues. Plan, evaluate, and revise curricula, course content, and course materials and methods of instruction. Maintain student attendance records, grades, and other required records. Write grant proposals to procure external research funding. Collaborate with colleagues to address teaching and research issues. Maintain regularly scheduled office hours in order to advise and assist students. Participate in student recruitment, registration, and placement activities. Select and obtain materials and supplies such as textbooks and laboratory equipment. Act as advisers to student organizations. Participate in campus and community events. Serve on academic or administrative committees that deal with institutional policies, departmental matters, and academic issues. Provide professional consulting services to government and/or industry. Perform administrative duties such as serving as department head. Compile bibliographies of specialized materials for outside reading assignments.

Personality Type: Social-Investigative-Realistic.

Career Clusters: 01 Agriculture, Food, and Natural Resources; 05 Education and Training. **Career Pathways:** 01.1 Food Products and Processing Systems; 01.2 Plant Systems; 01.3 Animal Systems; 01.4 Power Structure and Technical Systems; 01.7 Agribusiness Systems; 05.3 Teaching/Training.

Skills: Science; Management of Financial Resources; Writing; Reading Comprehension; Instructing; Complex Problem Solving.

Education and Training Programs: Agriculture, General; Agricultural Business and Management, General; Agribusiness/Agricultural Business Operations; Agricultural Economics; Farm/Farm and Ranch Management; Agricultural/Farm Supplies Retailing and Wholesaling; Agricultural Business and Management, Other; Agricultural Mechanization, General; Agricultural Power Machinery Operation; Agricultural Mechanization, Other; others. **Related Knowledge/Courses:** Biology; Food Production; Education and Training; Geography; Chemistry; Communications and Media.

Work Environment: Indoors; sitting.

Aircraft Structure, Surfaces, Rigging, and Systems Assemblers

- ❋ Education/Training Required: Long-term on-the-job training
- ❋ Annual Earnings: $45,420
- ❋ Beginning Wage: $25,050
- ❋ Earnings Growth Potential: High (44.8%)
- ❋ Growth: 12.8%
- ❋ Annual Job Openings: 6,550
- ❋ Job Security: More Secure than Most
- ❋ Self-Employed: 0.0%
- ❋ Part-Time: 1.9%

Renewal Industry: Advanced Manufacturing.

Industries with Greatest Employment: Transportation Equipment Manufacturing (87.5%).

Highest-Growth Industries (Projected Growth for This Job): None met the criteria.

Other Considerations for Job Outlook: Because much of the assembly in the aerospace industry is done in hard-to-reach locations—inside airplane fuselages or gear boxes, for example—which are unsuited to robots, aircraft assemblers will not be easily replaced by automated processes.

Assemble, fit, fasten, and install parts of airplanes, space vehicles, or missiles, such as tails, wings, fuselage, bulkheads, stabilizers, landing gear, rigging and control equipment, or heating and ventilating systems. Form loops or splices in cables, using clamps and fittings, or reweave cable strands. Align and fit structural assemblies manually or signal crane operators to position assemblies for joining. Align, fit, assemble, connect, and install system components, using jigs, fixtures, measuring instruments, hand tools, and power tools. Assemble and fit prefabricated parts to form subassemblies. Assemble, install, and connect parts, fittings, and assemblies on aircraft, using layout tools; hand tools; power tools; and fasteners such as bolts, screws, rivets, and clamps. Attach brackets, hinges, or clips to secure or support components and subassemblies, using bolts, screws, rivets, chemical bonding, or welding. Select and install accessories in swaging machines, using hand tools. Fit and fasten sheet metal coverings to surface areas and other sections of aircraft prior to welding or riveting. Lay out and mark reference points and locations for installation of parts and components, using jigs, templates, and measuring and marking instruments. Inspect and test installed units, parts, systems, and assemblies for fit, alignment, performance, defects, and compliance with standards, using measuring instruments and test equipment. Install mechanical linkages and actuators and verify tension of cables, using tensiometers. Join structural assemblies such as wings, tails, and fuselage. Measure and cut cables and tubing, using master templates, measuring instruments, and cable cutters or saws. Read and interpret blueprints, illustrations, and specifications to determine layouts, sequences of operations, or identities and relationships of parts. Prepare and load live ammunition, missiles, and bombs onto aircraft according to established procedures. Adjust, repair, rework, or replace parts and assemblies to eliminate malfunctions and to ensure proper operation. Cut, trim, file, bend, and smooth parts and verify sizes and fitting tolerances in order to ensure proper fit and clearance of parts. Install and connect control cables to electronically controlled units, using hand tools, ring locks, cotter keys, threaded connectors, turnbuckles, and related devices.

Personality Type: Realistic-Conventional.

Career Cluster: 16 Transportation, Distribution, and Logistics. **Career Pathway:** 16.4 Facility and Mobile Equipment Maintenance.

Skills: Installation; Equipment Maintenance; Repairing; Quality Control Analysis; Equipment Selection; Operation Monitoring.

Education and Training Programs: Airframe Mechanics and Aircraft Maintenance Technology/Technician; Aircraft Powerplant Technology/Technician; Avionics

Maintenance Technology/Technician. **Related Knowledge/Courses:** Mechanical Devices; Design; Chemistry; Public Safety and Security; Production and Processing.

Work Environment: Noisy; contaminants; hazardous conditions; hazardous equipment; standing; using hands on objects, tools, or controls.

Anesthesiologists

- ❋ Education/Training Required: First professional degree
- ❋ Annual Earnings: More than $145,600
- ❋ Beginning Wage: $118,320
- ❋ Earnings Growth Potential: Cannot be calculated
- ❋ Growth: 14.2%
- ❋ Annual Job Openings: 38,027
- ❋ Job Security: Most Secure
- ❋ Self-Employed: 14.7%
- ❋ Part-Time: 8.1%

Our sources did not provide separate job openings data for this occupation. The job openings listed here are shared with Family and General Practitioners; Internists, General; Obstetricians and Gynecologists; Pediatricians, General; Psychiatrists; and Surgeons.

Renewal Industry: Health Care.

Industries with Greatest Employment: Ambulatory Health-Care Services (55.9%); Hospitals, Public and Private (17.8%).

Highest-Growth Industries (Projected Growth for This Job): Social Assistance (58.6%); Administrative and Support Services (26.8%); Professional, Scientific, and Technical Services (22.6%); Nursing and Residential Care Facilities (21.0%); Ambulatory Health-Care Services (19.4%); Religious, Grantmaking, Civic, Professional, and Similar Organizations (16.7%); Management of Companies and Enterprises (15.3%).

Other Considerations for Job Outlook: Opportunities for individuals interested in becoming physicians and surgeons are expected to be very good. Unlike their predecessors, new physicians are much less likely to enter solo practice and more likely to take salaried jobs in group medical practices, clinics, and health networks. Reports of shortages in some specialties, such as general or family practice, internal medicine, and OB/GYN, or in rural or low-income areas should attract new entrants, encouraging schools to expand programs and hospitals to increase available residency slots. However, because physician training is so lengthy, employment change happens gradually. Opportunities should be particularly good in rural and low-income areas, as some physicians find these areas unattractive because of less control over work hours, isolation from medical colleagues, or other reasons.

Administer anesthetics during surgery or other medical procedures. Administer anesthetic or sedation during medical procedures, using local, intravenous, spinal, or caudal methods. Monitor patient before, during, and after anesthesia and counteract adverse reactions or complications. Provide and maintain life support and airway management and help prepare patients for emergency surgery. Record type and amount of anesthesia and patient condition throughout procedure. Examine patient; obtain medical history; and use diagnostic tests to determine risk during surgical, obstetrical, and other medical procedures. Position patient on operating table to maximize patient comfort and surgical accessibility. Decide when patients have recovered or stabilized enough to be sent to another room or ward or to be sent home following outpatient surgery. Coordinate administration of anesthetics with surgeons during operation. Confer with other medical professionals to determine type and method of anesthetic or sedation to render patient insensible to pain. Coordinate and direct work of nurses, medical technicians, and other health-care providers. Order laboratory tests, X-rays, and other diagnostic procedures. Diagnose illnesses, using examinations, tests, and reports. Manage anesthesiological services, coordinating them with other medical activities and formulating plans and procedures. Provide medical care and consultation in many settings, prescribing medication and treatment and referring patients for surgery. Inform students and staff of types and methods of anesthesia administration, signs of complications, and emergency methods to counteract reactions. Schedule and maintain use of surgical suite, including operating, wash-up, and waiting rooms and anesthetic and sterilizing equipment. Instruct individuals and groups on ways to preserve health and prevent disease. Conduct medical research to aid in controlling and curing disease, to investigate new medications, and to develop and test new medical techniques.

Personality Type: Investigative-Realistic-Social.

Career Cluster: 08 Health Science. **Career Pathway:** 08.1 Therapeutic Services.

Skills: Operation Monitoring; Science; Operation and Control; Judgment and Decision Making; Equipment Selection; Monitoring.

Education and Training Programs: Anesthesiology; Critical Care Anesthesiology. **Related Knowledge/Courses:** Medicine and Dentistry; Biology; Chemistry; Psychology; Physics; Therapy and Counseling.

Work Environment: Indoors; contaminants; radiation; disease or infections; standing; using hands on objects, tools, or controls.

Anthropology and Archeology Teachers, Postsecondary

- ✹ Education/Training Required: Master's degree
- ✹ Annual Earnings: $64,530
- ✹ Beginning Wage: $38,840
- ✹ Earnings Growth Potential: Medium (39.8%)
- ✹ Growth: 22.9%
- ✹ Annual Job Openings: 910
- ✹ Job Security: Most Secure
- ✹ Self-Employed: 0.4%
- ✹ Part-Time: 27.8%

Renewal Industry: Education.

Industries with Greatest Employment: Educational Services, Public and Private (97.3%).

Highest-Growth Industries (Projected Growth for This Job): Administrative and Support Services (48.3%); Amusement, Gambling, and Recreation Industries (45.2%); Social Assistance (38.6%); Support Activities for Transportation (32.8%); Religious, Grantmaking, Civic, Professional, and Similar Organizations (29.9%); Professional, Scientific, and Technical Services (28.8%); Management of Companies and Enterprises (26.8%); Local Government (23.5%); Educational Services, Public and Private (22.8%); Hospitals, Public and Private (21.4%).

Other Considerations for Job Outlook: Retirements of current postsecondary teachers should create numerous openings for all types of postsecondary teachers, so job opportunities are generally expected to be very good. However, one of the main reasons why students attend postsecondary institutions is to prepare themselves for careers, so the best job prospects for postsecondary teachers are likely to be in rapidly growing fields that offer many nonacademic career options—unlike anthropology and archeology. Community colleges and other institutions offering career and technical education have been among the most rapidly growing, and these institutions are expected to offer some of the best opportunities for postsecondary teachers.

Teach courses in anthropology or archeology. Conduct research in a particular field of knowledge and publish findings in professional journals, books, and electronic media. Keep abreast of developments in their field by reading current literature, talking with colleagues, and participating in professional conferences. Prepare and deliver lectures to undergraduate and graduate students on topics such as research methods, urban anthropology, and language and culture. Evaluate and grade students' classwork, assignments, and papers. Initiate, facilitate, and moderate classroom discussions. Write grant proposals to procure external research funding. Supervise undergraduate and/or graduate teaching, internship, and research work. Prepare course materials such as syllabi, homework assignments, and handouts. Compile, administer, and grade examinations or assign this work to others. Supervise students' laboratory work or fieldwork. Plan, evaluate, and revise curricula, course content, and course materials and methods of instruction. Advise students on academic and vocational curricula, career issues, and laboratory and field research. Maintain student attendance records, grades, and other required records. Maintain regularly scheduled office hours in order to advise and assist students. Collaborate with colleagues to address teaching and research issues. Compile bibliographies of specialized materials for outside reading assignments. Perform administrative duties such as serving as department head. Select and obtain materials and supplies such as textbooks and laboratory equipment. Serve on academic or administrative committees that deal with institutional policies, departmental matters, and academic issues. Participate in student recruitment, registration, and placement activities. Participate in campus and community events. Provide professional consulting services to government and industry. Act as advisers to student organizations.

Personality Type: Social-Investigative.

Career Clusters: 12 Law, Public Safety, Corrections, and Security; 15 Science, Technology, Engineering, and Mathematics. **Career Pathways:** 12.4 Law Enforcement Services; 15.3 Science and Mathematics.

Skills: Science; Writing; Critical Thinking; Reading Comprehension; Active Learning; Instructing.

Education and Training Programs: Social Science Teacher Education; Anthropology; Physical Anthropology; Archeology. **Related Knowledge/Courses:** Sociology and Anthropology; History and Archeology; Geography; Foreign Language; Philosophy and Theology; English Language.

Work Environment: Indoors; sitting.

Architects, Except Landscape and Naval

- ✸ Education/Training Required: Bachelor's degree
- ✸ Annual Earnings: $67,620
- ✸ Beginning Wage: $40,250
- ✸ Earnings Growth Potential: High (40.5%)
- ✸ Growth: 17.7%
- ✸ Annual Job Openings: 11,324
- ✸ Job Security: Less Secure than Most
- ✸ Self-Employed: 20.3%
- ✸ Part-Time: 6.1%

Renewal Industry: Infrastructure.

Industries with Greatest Employment: Professional, Scientific, and Technical Services (68.7%).

Highest-Growth Industries (Projected Growth for This Job): Administrative and Support Services (25.9%); Professional, Scientific, and Technical Services (22.9%); Real Estate (19.1%); Management of Companies and Enterprises (15.3%).

Other Considerations for Job Outlook: Employment of architects is expected to grow faster than the average for all occupations through 2016. Keen competition is expected for positions at the most prestigious firms, and opportunities will be best for those architects who are able to distinguish themselves with their creativity.

Plan and design structures, such as private residences, office buildings, theaters, factories, and other structural property. Prepare information regarding design, structure specifications, materials, color, equipment, estimated costs, or construction time. Consult with client to determine functional and spatial requirements of structure. Direct activities of workers engaged in preparing drawings and specification documents. Plan layout of project. Prepare contract documents for building contractors. Prepare scale drawings. Integrate engineering element into unified design. Conduct periodic on-site observation of work during construction to monitor compliance with plans. Administer construction contracts. Represent client in obtaining bids and awarding construction contracts. Prepare operating and maintenance manuals, studies, and reports.

Personality Type: Artistic-Investigative.

Career Cluster: 02 Architecture and Construction. **Career Pathway:** 02.1 Design/Pre-Construction.

Skills: Operations Analysis; Management of Financial Resources; Complex Problem Solving; Management of Personnel Resources; Coordination; Negotiation.

Education and Training Programs: Architecture (BArch, BA/BS, MArch, MA/MS, PhD); Environmental Design/Architecture; Architectural History and Criticism, General; Architecture and Related Services, Other. **Related Knowledge/Courses:** Building and Construction; Design; Engineering and Technology; Fine Arts; Law and Government; Physics.

Work Environment: Indoors; sitting.

Architectural and Civil Drafters

See *Architectural Drafters* and *Civil Drafters*, *described separately.*

Architectural Drafters

- ❋ Education/Training Required: Postsecondary vocational training
- ❋ Annual Earnings: $43,310
- ❋ Beginning Wage: $27,680
- ❋ Earnings Growth Potential: Medium (36.1%)
- ❋ Growth: 6.1%
- ❋ Annual Job Openings: 16,238
- ❋ Job Security: Less Secure than Most
- ❋ Self-Employed: 5.0%
- ❋ Part-Time: 5.9%

Our sources did not provide separate job openings data for this occupation. The job openings listed here are shared with Civil Drafters.

Renewal Industries: Green Technologies; Infrastructure.

Industries with Greatest Employment: Professional, Scientific, and Technical Services (76.9%); Construction of Buildings (5.6%).

Highest-Growth Industries (Projected Growth for This Job): Building Material and Garden Equipment and Supplies Dealers (20.9%); Administrative and Support Services (20.4%); Real Estate (16.7%).

Other Considerations for Job Outlook: Demand for particular drafting specialties varies throughout the country because employment usually is contingent on the needs of local industry. Opportunities should be best for individuals with at least two years of postsecondary training in a drafting program that provides strong technical skills and considerable experience with CADD systems.

Prepare detailed drawings of architectural designs and plans for buildings and structures according to specifications provided by architect. Analyze building codes, by-laws, space and site requirements, and other technical documents and reports to determine their effect on architectural designs. Operate computer-aided drafting (CAD) equipment or conventional drafting station to produce designs, working drawings, charts, forms, and records. Coordinate structural, electrical, and mechanical designs and determine a method of presentation to graphically represent building plans. Obtain and assemble data to complete architectural designs, visiting job sites to compile measurements as necessary. Lay out and plan interior room arrangements for commercial buildings, using computer-assisted drafting (CAD) equipment and software. Draw rough and detailed scale plans for foundations, buildings, and structures based on preliminary concepts, sketches, engineering calculations, specification sheets, and other data. Supervise, coordinate, and inspect the work of draftspersons, technicians, and technologists on construction projects. Represent architect on construction site, ensuring builder compliance with design specifications and advising on design corrections under architect's supervision. Check dimensions of materials to be used and assign numbers to lists of materials. Determine procedures and instructions to be followed according to design specifications and quantity of required materials. Analyze technical implications of architect's design concept, calculating weights, volumes, and stress factors. Create freehand drawings and lettering to accompany drawings. Prepare colored drawings of landscape and interior designs for presentation to client. Reproduce drawings on copy machines or trace copies of plans and drawings, using transparent paper or cloth, ink, pencil, and standard drafting instruments. Prepare cost estimates, contracts, bidding documents, and technical reports for specific projects under an architect's supervision. Calculate heat loss and gain of buildings and structures to determine required equipment specifications, following standard procedures. Build landscape, architectural, and display models.

Personality Type: Artistic-Realistic-Investigative.

Career Cluster: 02 Architecture and Construction. **Career Pathway:** 02.1 Design/Pre-Construction.

Skills: Operations Analysis; Coordination; Active Learning; Technology Design; Mathematics; Complex Problem Solving.

Education and Training Programs: Architectural Technology/Technician; Drafting and Design Technology/Technician, General; CAD/CADD Drafting and/or Design Technology/Technician; Architectural Drafting and Architectural CAD/CADD; Civil Drafting and Civil Engineering CAD/CADD. **Related Knowledge/Courses:** Design; Building and Construction; Engineering and Technology; Computers and Electronics; Mathematics; Physics.

Work Environment: Indoors; noisy; sitting; using hands on objects, tools, or controls; repetitive motions.

Architecture Teachers, Postsecondary

- ❀ Education/Training Required: Master's degree
- ❀ Annual Earnings: $68,540
- ❀ Beginning Wage: $41,080
- ❀ Earnings Growth Potential: High (40.1%)
- ❀ Growth: 22.9%
- ❀ Annual Job Openings: 1,044
- ❀ Job Security: Most Secure
- ❀ Self-Employed: 0.4%
- ❀ Part-Time: 27.8%

Renewal Industry: Education.

Industries with Greatest Employment: Educational Services, Public and Private (97.3%).

Highest-Growth Industries (Projected Growth for This Job): Administrative and Support Services (48.3%); Amusement, Gambling, and Recreation Industries (45.2%); Social Assistance (38.6%); Support Activities for Transportation (32.8%); Religious, Grantmaking, Civic, Professional, and Similar Organizations (29.9%); Professional, Scientific, and Technical Services (28.8%); Management of Companies and Enterprises (26.8%); Local Government (23.5%); Educational Services, Public and Private (22.8%); Hospitals, Public and Private (21.4%).

Other Considerations for Job Outlook: Retirements of current postsecondary teachers should create numerous openings for all types of postsecondary teachers, so job opportunities are generally expected to be very good. One of the main reasons why students attend postsecondary institutions is to prepare themselves for careers, so the best job prospects for postsecondary teachers are likely to be in rapidly growing fields that offer many nonacademic career options. Community colleges and other institutions offering career and technical education have been among the most rapidly growing, and these institutions are expected to offer some of the best opportunities for postsecondary teachers.

Teach courses in architecture and architectural design, such as architectural environmental design, interior architecture/design, and landscape architecture. Evaluate and grade students' work, including work performed in design studios. Prepare and deliver lectures to undergraduate and/or graduate students on topics such as architectural design methods, aesthetics and design, and structures and materials. Prepare course materials such as syllabi, homework assignments, and handouts. Initiate, facilitate, and moderate classroom discussions. Plan, evaluate, and revise curricula, course content, and course materials and methods of instruction. Keep abreast of developments in their field by reading current literature, talking with colleagues, and participating in professional conferences. Maintain student attendance records, grades, and other required records. Maintain regularly scheduled office hours to advise and assist students. Compile, administer, and grade examinations or assign this work to others. Conduct research in a particular field of knowledge and publish findings in professional journals, books, and/or electronic media. Supervise undergraduate and/or graduate teaching, internship, and research work. Advise students on academic and vocational curricula and on career issues. Collaborate with colleagues to address teaching and research issues. Compile bibliographies of specialized materials for outside reading assignments. Serve on academic or administrative committees that deal with institutional policies, departmental matters, and academic issues. Participate in student recruitment, registration, and placement activities. Select and obtain materials and supplies such as textbooks and laboratory equipment. Write grant proposals to procure external research funding. Provide professional consulting services to government and/or industry. Perform administrative duties such as serving as department head. Act as advisers to student organizations. Participate in campus and community events.

Personality Type: Social-Artistic.

Career Clusters: 02 Architecture and Construction; 05 Education and Training; 07 Government and Public Administration; 15 Science, Technology, Engineering, and Mathematics. **Career Pathways:** 02.1 Design/Pre-Construction; 05.3 Teaching/Training; 07.4 Planning; 15.1 Engineering and Technology.

Skills: Technology Design; Operations Analysis; Instructing; Writing; Science; Complex Problem Solving.

Education and Training Programs: Architecture (BArch, BA/BS, MArch, MA/MS, PhD); City/Urban, Community and Regional Planning; Environmental Design/Architecture; Interior Architecture; Landscape Architecture (BS, BSLA, BLA, MSLA, MLA, PhD); Teacher Education and

Professional Development, Specific Subject Areas, Other; Architectural Engineering. **Related Knowledge/Courses:** Fine Arts; Design; Building and Construction; History and Archeology; Philosophy and Theology; Geography.

Work Environment: Indoors; sitting.

Area, Ethnic, and Cultural Studies Teachers, Postsecondary

- ❋ Education/Training Required: Master's degree
- ❋ Annual Earnings: $59,150
- ❋ Beginning Wage: $32,940
- ❋ Earnings Growth Potential: High (44.3%)
- ❋ Growth: 22.9%
- ❋ Annual Job Openings: 1,252
- ❋ Job Security: Most Secure
- ❋ Self-Employed: 0.4%
- ❋ Part-Time: 27.8%

Renewal Industry: Education.

Industries with Greatest Employment: Educational Services, Public and Private (97.3%).

Highest-Growth Industries (Projected Growth for This Job): Administrative and Support Services (48.3%); Amusement, Gambling, and Recreation Industries (45.2%); Social Assistance (38.6%); Support Activities for Transportation (32.8%); Religious, Grantmaking, Civic, Professional, and Similar Organizations (29.9%); Professional, Scientific, and Technical Services (28.8%); Management of Companies and Enterprises (26.8%); Local Government (23.5%); Educational Services, Public and Private (22.8%); Hospitals, Public and Private (21.4%).

Other Considerations for Job Outlook: Retirements of current postsecondary teachers should create numerous openings for all types of postsecondary teachers, so job opportunities are generally expected to be very good. However, one of the main reasons why students attend postsecondary institutions is to prepare themselves for careers, so the best job prospects for postsecondary teachers are likely to be in rapidly growing fields that offer many nonacademic career options—unlike area, ethnic, and cultural studies. Community colleges and other institutions offering career and technical education have been among the most rapidly

growing, and these institutions are expected to offer some of the best opportunities for postsecondary teachers.

Teach courses pertaining to the culture and development of an area (e.g., Latin America), an ethnic group, or any other group (e.g., women's studies, urban affairs). Keep abreast of developments in their field by reading current literature, talking with colleagues, and participating in professional conferences. Conduct research in a particular field of knowledge and publish findings in professional journals, books, and/or electronic media. Evaluate and grade students' classwork, assignments, and papers. Prepare course materials such as syllabi, homework assignments, and handouts. Prepare and deliver lectures to undergraduate and/or graduate students on topics such as race and ethnic relations, gender studies, and cross-cultural perspectives. Initiate, facilitate, and moderate classroom discussions. Compile, administer, and grade examinations or assign this work to others. Maintain regularly scheduled office hours in order to advise and assist students. Plan, evaluate, and revise curricula, course content, and course materials and methods of instruction. Maintain student attendance records, grades, and other required records. Advise students on academic and vocational curricula and on career issues. Supervise undergraduate and/or graduate teaching, internship, and research work. Select and obtain materials and supplies such as textbooks. Collaborate with colleagues to address teaching and research issues. Serve on academic or administrative committees that deal with institutional policies, departmental matters, and academic issues. Compile bibliographies of specialized materials for outside reading assignments. Write grant proposals to procure external research funding. Participate in campus and community events. Participate in student recruitment, registration, and placement activities. Act as advisers to student organizations. Incorporate experiential/site visit components into courses. Perform administrative duties such as serving as department head. Provide professional consulting services to government and/or industry.

Personality Type: Social-Investigative-Artistic.

Career Clusters: 10 Human Services; 15 Science, Technology, Engineering, and Mathematics. **Career Pathways:** 10.2 Counseling and Mental Health Services; 15.3 Science and Mathematics.

Skills: Writing; Critical Thinking; Instructing; Persuasion; Active Learning; Learning Strategies.

Education and Training Programs: African Studies; American/United States Studies/Civilization; Asian Studies/Civilization; East Asian Studies; Central/Middle and Eastern European Studies; European Studies/Civilization; Latin American Studies; Near and Middle Eastern Studies; Pacific Area/Pacific Rim Studies; Russian Studies; Scandinavian Studies; South Asian Studies; Southeast Asian Studies; Western European Studies; others. **Related Knowledge/Courses:** History and Archeology; Sociology and Anthropology; Foreign Language; Philosophy and Theology; Geography; Education and Training.

Work Environment: Indoors; sitting.

Art, Drama, and Music Teachers, Postsecondary

- ❈ Education/Training Required: Master's degree
- ❈ Annual Earnings: $55,190
- ❈ Beginning Wage: $30,340
- ❈ Earnings Growth Potential: High (45.0%)
- ❈ Growth: 22.9%
- ❈ Annual Job Openings: 12,707
- ❈ Job Security: Most Secure
- ❈ Self-Employed: 0.4%
- ❈ Part-Time: 27.8%

Renewal Industry: Education.

Industries with Greatest Employment: Educational Services, Public and Private (97.3%).

Highest-Growth Industries (Projected Growth for This Job): Administrative and Support Services (48.3%); Amusement, Gambling, and Recreation Industries (45.2%); Social Assistance (38.6%); Support Activities for Transportation (32.8%); Religious, Grantmaking, Civic, Professional, and Similar Organizations (29.9%); Professional, Scientific, and Technical Services (28.8%); Management of Companies and Enterprises (26.8%); Local Government (23.5%); Educational Services, Public and Private (22.8%); Hospitals, Public and Private (21.4%).

Other Considerations for Job Outlook: Retirements of current postsecondary teachers should create numerous openings for all types of postsecondary teachers, so job opportunities are generally expected to be very good.

However, one of the main reasons why students attend postsecondary institutions is to prepare themselves for careers, so the best job prospects for postsecondary teachers are likely to be in rapidly growing fields that offer many nonacademic career options. Community colleges and other institutions offering career and technical education have been among the most rapidly growing, and these institutions are expected to offer some of the best opportunities for postsecondary teachers.

Teach courses in drama; music; and the arts, including fine and applied art, such as painting and sculpture, or design and crafts. Evaluate and grade students' classwork, performances, projects, assignments, and papers. Explain and demonstrate artistic techniques. Prepare students for performances, exams, or assessments. Prepare and deliver lectures to undergraduate or graduate students on topics such as acting techniques, fundamentals of music, and art history. Organize performance groups and direct their rehearsals. Prepare course materials such as syllabi, homework assignments, and handouts. Initiate, facilitate, and moderate classroom discussions. Keep abreast of developments in their field by reading current literature, talking with colleagues, and participating in professional conferences. Advise students on academic and vocational curricula and on career issues. Maintain student attendance records, grades, and other required records. Conduct research in a particular field of knowledge and publish findings in professional journals, books, or electronic media. Supervise undergraduate and/or graduate teaching, internship, and research work. Plan, evaluate, and revise curricula, course content, and course materials and methods of instruction. Maintain regularly scheduled office hours to advise and assist students. Compile, administer, and grade examinations or assign this work to others. Participate in student recruitment, registration, and placement activities. Select and obtain materials and supplies such as textbooks and performance pieces. Collaborate with colleagues to address teaching and research issues. Serve on academic or administrative committees that deal with institutional policies, departmental matters, and academic issues. Participate in campus and community events. Keep students informed of community events such as plays and concerts. Compile bibliographies of specialized materials for outside reading assignments. Display students' work in schools, galleries, and exhibitions. Perform administrative duties such as serving as department head. Act as advisers to student organizations. Write grant proposals to procure external research funding. Provide professional consulting services to government or industry.

Personality Type: Social-Artistic.

Career Clusters: 03 Arts, Audio/Video Technology, and Communications; 08 Health Science. **Career Pathways:** 03.1 Audio and Video Technology and Film; 03.2 Printing Technology; 03.3 Visual Arts; 03.4 Performing Arts; 08.1 Therapeutic Services.

Skills: Instructing; Social Perceptiveness; Speaking; Active Listening; Persuasion; Learning Strategies.

Education and Training Programs: Visual and Performing Arts, General; Crafts/Craft Design, Folk Art and Artisanry; Dance, General; Design and Visual Communications, General; Industrial Design; Commercial Photography; Fashion/Apparel Design; Interior Design; Graphic Design; Design and Applied Arts, Other; Drama and Dramatics/Theatre Arts, General; Technical Theatre/Theatre Design and Technology; Playwriting and Screenwriting; others. **Related Knowledge/Courses:** Fine Arts; History and Archeology; Philosophy and Theology; Education and Training; Communications and Media; Sociology and Anthropology.

Work Environment: Indoors; noisy; sitting.

Atmospheric, Earth, Marine, and Space Sciences Teachers, Postsecondary

- ✸ Education/Training Required: Master's degree
- ✸ Annual Earnings: $73,280
- ✸ Beginning Wage: $39,840
- ✸ Earnings Growth Potential: High (45.6%)
- ✸ Growth: 22.9%
- ✸ Annual Job Openings: 1,553
- ✸ Job Security: Most Secure
- ✸ Self-Employed: 0.4%
- ✸ Part-Time: 27.8%

Renewal Industry: Education.

Industries with Greatest Employment: Educational Services, Public and Private (97.3%).

Highest-Growth Industries (Projected Growth for This Job): Administrative and Support Services (48.3%); Amusement, Gambling, and Recreation Industries (45.2%); Social Assistance (38.6%); Support Activities for Transportation (32.8%); Religious, Grantmaking, Civic, Professional, and Similar Organizations (29.9%); Professional, Scientific, and Technical Services (28.8%); Management of Companies and Enterprises (26.8%); Local Government (23.5%); Educational Services, Public and Private (22.8%); Hospitals, Public and Private (21.4%).

Other Considerations for Job Outlook: Retirements of current postsecondary teachers should create numerous openings for all types of postsecondary teachers, so job opportunities are generally expected to be very good. One of the main reasons why students attend postsecondary institutions is to prepare themselves for careers, so the best job prospects for postsecondary teachers are likely to be in rapidly growing fields that offer many nonacademic career options. Community colleges and other institutions offering career and technical education have been among the most rapidly growing, and these institutions are expected to offer some of the best opportunities for postsecondary teachers.

Teach courses in the physical sciences, except chemistry and physics. Conduct research in a particular field of knowledge and publish findings in professional journals, books, and/or electronic media. Write grant proposals to procure external research funding. Keep abreast of developments in their field by reading current literature, talking with colleagues, and participating in professional conferences. Supervise undergraduate and/or graduate teaching, internships, and research work. Prepare and deliver lectures to undergraduate and/or graduate students on topics such as structural geology, micrometeorology, and atmospheric thermodynamics. Supervise laboratory work and fieldwork. Evaluate and grade students' classwork, assignments, and papers. Prepare course materials such as syllabi, homework assignments, and handouts. Collaborate with colleagues to address teaching and research issues. Compile, administer, and grade examinations or assign this work to others. Plan, evaluate, and revise curricula, course content, course materials, and methods of instruction. Initiate, facilitate, and moderate classroom discussions. Maintain regularly scheduled office hours to advise and assist students. Advise students on academic and vocational curricula and on career issues. Maintain student attendance records, grades, and other required records. Participate in student recruitment, registration, and placement activities. Perform administrative duties such as serving as department head. Select and obtain materials and supplies such as textbooks and laboratory equipment. Serve on academic or administrative committees that deal with institutional policies, departmental matters, and academic issues. Compile bibliographies of specialized materials for outside reading assignments. Provide professional consulting services to government and/or industry. Act as adviser to student organizations. Participate in campus and community events.

Personality Type: Social-Investigative.

Career Clusters: 05 Education and Training; 15 Science, Technology, Engineering, and Mathematics. **Career Pathways:** 05.3 Teaching/Training; 15.3 Science and Mathematics.

Skills: Science; Programming; Mathematics; Management of Financial Resources; Complex Problem Solving; Writing.

Education and Training Programs: Science Teacher Education/General Science Teacher Education; Physics Teacher Education; Astronomy; Astrophysics; Planetary Astronomy and Science; Atmospheric Sciences and Meteorology, General; Atmospheric Chemistry and Climatology; Atmospheric Physics and Dynamics; Meteorology; Atmospheric Sciences and Meteorology, Other; Geology/Earth Science, General; Geochemistry; Geophysics and Seismology; others. **Related Knowledge/Courses:** Physics; Geography; Chemistry; Biology; Mathematics; Education and Training.

Work Environment: Indoors; sitting.

Biological Science Teachers, Postsecondary

- ❈ Education/Training Required: Master's degree
- ❈ Annual Earnings: $71,780
- ❈ Beginning Wage: $39,100
- ❈ Earnings Growth Potential: High (45.5%)
- ❈ Growth: 22.9%
- ❈ Annual Job Openings: 9,039
- ❈ Job Security: Most Secure
- ❈ Self-Employed: 0.4%
- ❈ Part-Time: 27.8%

Renewal Industry: Education.

Industries with Greatest Employment: Educational Services, Public and Private (97.3%).

Highest-Growth Industries (Projected Growth for This Job): Administrative and Support Services (48.3%); Amusement, Gambling, and Recreation Industries (45.2%); Social Assistance (38.6%); Support Activities for Transportation (32.8%); Religious, Grantmaking, Civic, Professional, and Similar Organizations (29.9%); Professional, Scientific, and Technical Services (28.8%); Management of Companies and Enterprises (26.8%); Local Government (23.5%); Educational Services, Public and Private (22.8%); Hospitals, Public and Private (21.4%).

Other Considerations for Job Outlook: Retirements of current postsecondary teachers should create numerous openings for all types of postsecondary teachers, so job opportunities are generally expected to be very good. One of the main reasons why students attend postsecondary institutions is to prepare themselves for careers, so the best job prospects for postsecondary teachers are likely to be in rapidly growing fields that offer many nonacademic career options. These will include the biological sciences. Community colleges and other institutions offering career and technical education have been among the most rapidly growing, and these institutions are expected to offer some of the best opportunities for postsecondary teachers.

Teach courses in biological sciences. Prepare and deliver lectures to undergraduate and/or graduate students on topics such as molecular biology, marine biology, and botany. Evaluate and grade students' classwork, laboratory work, assignments, and papers. Prepare course materials such as syllabi, homework assignments, and handouts. Compile, administer, and grade examinations or assign this work to others. Supervise students' laboratory work. Keep abreast of developments in their field by reading current literature, talking with colleagues, and participating in professional conferences. Maintain student attendance records, grades, and other required records. Initiate, facilitate, and moderate classroom discussions. Plan, evaluate, and revise curricula, course content, course materials, and methods of instruction. Advise students on academic and vocational curricula and on career issues. Maintain regularly scheduled office hours to advise and assist students. Supervise undergraduate and/or graduate teaching, internships, and research work. Select and obtain materials and supplies such as textbooks and laboratory equipment. Collaborate with colleagues to address teaching and research issues. Conduct research in a particular field of knowledge and publish findings in professional journals, books, and/or electronic media. Serve on academic or administrative committees that deal with institutional policies, departmental matters, and academic issues. Participate in student recruitment, registration, and placement activities. Write grant proposals to procure external research funding. Perform administrative duties such as serving as department head. Act as advisers to student organizations. Compile bibliographies of specialized materials for outside reading assignments. Participate in campus and community events. Provide professional consulting services to government and/or industry.

Personality Type: Social-Investigative.

Career Clusters: 01 Agriculture, Food, and Natural Resources; 15 Science, Technology, Engineering, and Mathematics. **Career Pathways:** 01.5 Natural Resources Systems; 15.3 Science and Mathematics.

Skills: Science; Instructing; Writing; Reading Comprehension; Learning Strategies; Speaking.

Education and Training Programs: Biology/Biological Sciences, General; Biochemistry; Biophysics; Molecular Biology; Radiation Biology/Radiobiology; Botany/Plant Biology; Plant Pathology/Phytopathology; Plant Physiology; Cell/Cellular Biology and Histology; Anatomy; Microbiology, General; Virology; Parasitology; Immunology; Zoology/Animal Biology; Entomology; Animal Physiology; others. **Related Knowledge/Courses:** Biology;

Chemistry; Education and Training; Medicine and Dentistry; Physics; Geography.

Work Environment: Indoors; more often sitting than standing.

Biological Technicians

- ❋ Education/Training Required: Associate degree
- ❋ Annual Earnings: $37,810
- ❋ Beginning Wage: $24,360
- ❋ Earnings Growth Potential: Medium (35.6%)
- ❋ Growth: 16.0%
- ❋ Annual Job Openings: 15,374
- ❋ Job Security: Less Secure than Most
- ❋ Self-Employed: 0.0%
- ❋ Part-Time: 6.2%

Renewal Industries: Advanced Manufacturing; Health Care.

Industries with Greatest Employment: Educational Services, Public and Private (31.0%); Professional, Scientific, and Technical Services (30.1%); Federal Government (15.6%); Chemical Manufacturing (10.0%).

Highest-Growth Industries (Projected Growth for This Job): Museums, Historical Sites, and Similar Institutions (36.6%); Administrative and Support Services (26.6%); Educational Services, Public and Private (22.9%); Ambulatory Health-Care Services (22.7%); Chemical Manufacturing (22.4%); Professional, Scientific, and Technical Services (20.4%); Merchant Wholesalers, Nondurable Goods (15.8%); Religious, Grantmaking, Civic, Professional, and Similar Organizations (15.4%); Management of Companies and Enterprises (15.0%).

Other Considerations for Job Outlook: Job opportunities are expected to be best for graduates of applied science technology programs who are well trained on equipment used in laboratories or production facilities.

Assist biological and medical scientists in laboratories. Set up, operate, and maintain laboratory instruments and equipment; monitor experiments; make observations; and calculate and record results. May analyze organic substances, such as blood, food, and drugs. Keep detailed logs of all work-related activities. Monitor laboratory work to ensure compliance with set standards. Isolate, identify, and prepare specimens for examination. Use computers, computer-interfaced equipment, robotics, or high-technology industrial applications to perform work duties. Conduct research or assist in the conduct of research, including the collection of information and samples such as blood, water, soil, plants, and animals. Set up, adjust, calibrate, clean, maintain, and troubleshoot laboratory and field equipment. Provide technical support and services for scientists and engineers working in fields such as agriculture, environmental science, resource management, biology, and health sciences. Clean, maintain, and prepare supplies and work areas. Participate in the research, development, or manufacturing of medicinal and pharmaceutical preparations. Conduct standardized biological, microbiological, or biochemical tests and laboratory analyses to evaluate the quantity or quality of physical or chemical substances in food or other products. Analyze experimental data and interpret results to write reports and summaries of findings. Measure or weigh compounds and solutions for use in testing or animal feed. Monitor and observe experiments, recording production and test data for evaluation by research personnel. Examine animals and specimens to detect the presence of disease or other problems. Conduct or supervise operational programs such as fish hatcheries, greenhouses, and livestock production programs. Feed livestock or laboratory animals.

Personality Type: Realistic-Investigative-Conventional.

Career Cluster: 13 Manufacturing. **Career Pathway:** 13.3 Maintenance, Installation, and Repair.

Skills: Science; Equipment Maintenance; Quality Control Analysis; Troubleshooting; Mathematics; Active Learning.

Education and Training Program: Biology Technician/Biotechnology Laboratory Technician. **Related Knowledge/Courses:** Chemistry; Biology.

Work Environment: Indoors; standing; using hands on objects, tools, or controls; repetitive motions.

Bus Drivers, Transit and Intercity

- ❋ Education/Training Required: Moderate-term on-the-job training
- ❋ Annual Earnings: $33,160
- ❋ Beginning Wage: $19,660
- ❋ Earnings Growth Potential: High (40.7%)
- ❋ Growth: 12.5%
- ❋ Annual Job Openings: 27,100
- ❋ Job Security: Most Secure
- ❋ Self-Employed: 1.3%
- ❋ Part-Time: 34.1%

Renewal Industry: Green Technologies.

Industries with Greatest Employment: Local Government (55.5%); Transit and Ground Passenger Transportation (31.6%).

Highest-Growth Industries (Projected Growth for This Job): Amusement, Gambling, and Recreation Industries (45.0%); Social Assistance (42.0%); Nursing and Residential Care Facilities (40.9%); Museums, Historical Sites, and Similar Institutions (36.0%); Ambulatory Health-Care Services (35.2%); Scenic and Sightseeing Transportation (34.5%); Religious, Grantmaking, Civic, Professional, and Similar Organizations (18.9%).

Other Considerations for Job Outlook: People seeking jobs as bus drivers likely will have good opportunities. Individuals who have good driving records and who are willing to work a part-time or irregular schedule probably will have the best job prospects. Those seeking higher-paying public transit bus driver positions may encounter competition. Opportunities for intercity driving positions should be good, although employment prospects for motor coach drivers will depend on tourism, which fluctuates with the economy. Full-time bus drivers rarely are laid off during recessions. In local transit and intercity bus systems, if the number of passengers decreases, employers might reduce the hours of part-time bus drivers or consolidate routes since fewer buses would be required. Seasonal layoffs are common.

Drive bus or motor coach, including regular route operations, charters, and private carriage. May assist passengers with baggage. May collect fares or tickets. Inspect vehicles and check gas, oil, and water levels prior to departure. Drive vehicles over specified routes or to specified destinations according to time schedules to transport passengers, complying with traffic regulations. Park vehicles at loading areas so that passengers can board. Assist passengers with baggage and collect tickets or cash fares. Report delays or accidents. Advise passengers to be seated and orderly while on vehicles. Regulate heating, lighting, and ventilating systems for passenger comfort. Load and unload baggage in baggage compartments. Record cash receipts and ticket fares. Make minor repairs to vehicle and change tires.

Personality Type: Realistic-Social.

Career Cluster: 16 Transportation, Distribution, and Logistics. **Career Pathway:** 16.1 Transportation Operations.

Skills: No data available.

Education and Training Program: Truck and Bus Driver/Commercial Vehicle Operation. **Related Knowledge/Courses:** Transportation; Geography; Public Safety and Security; Psychology; Law and Government; Customer and Personal Service.

Work Environment: Outdoors; noisy; contaminants; sitting; using hands on objects, tools, or controls; repetitive motions.

Business Teachers, Postsecondary

- ❀ Education/Training Required: Master's degree
- ❀ Annual Earnings: $64,900
- ❀ Beginning Wage: $32,770
- ❀ Earnings Growth Potential: High (49.5%)
- ❀ Growth: 22.9%
- ❀ Annual Job Openings: 11,643
- ❀ Job Security: Most Secure
- ❀ Self-Employed: 0.4%
- ❀ Part-Time: 27.8%

Renewal Industry: Education.

Industries with Greatest Employment: Educational Services, Public and Private (97.3%).

Highest-Growth Industries (Projected Growth for This Job): Administrative and Support Services (48.3%);

Amusement, Gambling, and Recreation Industries (45.2%); Social Assistance (38.6%); Support Activities for Transportation (32.8%); Religious, Grantmaking, Civic, Professional, and Similar Organizations (29.9%); Professional, Scientific, and Technical Services (28.8%); Management of Companies and Enterprises (26.8%); Local Government (23.5%); Educational Services, Public and Private (22.8%); Hospitals, Public and Private (21.4%).

Other Considerations for Job Outlook: Retirements of current postsecondary teachers should create numerous openings for all types of postsecondary teachers, so job opportunities are generally expected to be very good. One of the main reasons why students attend postsecondary institutions is to prepare themselves for careers, so the best job prospects for postsecondary teachers are likely to be in rapidly growing fields that offer many nonacademic career options. Business is one of the most rapidly growing of these fields. Community colleges and other institutions offering career and technical education have been among the most rapidly growing, and these institutions are expected to offer some of the best opportunities for postsecondary teachers.

Teach courses in business administration and management, such as accounting, finance, human resources, labor relations, marketing, and operations research. Prepare and deliver lectures to undergraduate and/or graduate students on topics such as financial accounting, principles of marketing, and operations management. Evaluate and grade students' classwork, assignments, and papers. Compile, administer, and grade examinations or assign this work to others. Prepare course materials such as syllabi, homework assignments, and handouts. Maintain student attendance records, grades, and other required records. Initiate, facilitate, and moderate classroom discussions. Plan, evaluate, and revise curricula, course content, and course materials and methods of instruction. Keep abreast of developments in their field by reading current literature, talking with colleagues, and participating in professional organizations and conferences. Maintain regularly scheduled office hours to advise and assist students. Advise students on academic and vocational curricula and on career issues. Select and obtain materials and supplies such as textbooks. Collaborate with colleagues to address teaching and research issues. Collaborate with members of the business community to improve programs, to develop new programs, and to provide student access to learning opportunities such as internships. Participate in student recruitment, registration, and placement activities. Serve on academic or administrative committees that deal with institutional policies, departmental matters, and academic issues. Participate in campus and community events. Compile bibliographies of specialized materials for outside reading assignments. Perform administrative duties such as serving as department head. Supervise undergraduate and/or graduate teaching, internship, and research work. Conduct research in a particular field of knowledge and publish findings in professional journals, books, and/or electronic media. Act as advisers to student organizations. Provide professional consulting services to government and/or industry. Write grant proposals to procure external research funding.

Personality Type: Social-Enterprising-Investigative.

Career Clusters: 04 Business, Management, and Administration; 05 Education and Training; 06 Finance; 14 Marketing, Sales, and Service. **Career Pathways:** 04.1 Management; 04.2 Business Financial Management and Accounting; 04.3 Human Resources; 04.5 Marketing; 05.3 Teaching/Training; 06.1 Financial and Investment Planning; 06.4 Insurance Services; 14.1 Management and Entrepreneurship; 14.5 Marketing Information Management and Research.

Skills: Instructing; Learning Strategies; Writing; Monitoring; Speaking; Active Learning.

Education and Training Programs: Business Teacher Education; Business/Commerce, General; Business Administration and Management, General; Purchasing, Procurement/Acquisitions and Contracts Management; Logistics and Materials Management; Operations Management and Supervision; Accounting; Business/Corporate Communications; Entrepreneurship/Entrepreneurial Studies; Franchising and Franchise Operations; Finance, General; others. **Related Knowledge/Courses:** Economics and Accounting; Education and Training; Sociology and Anthropology; Sales and Marketing; Philosophy and Theology; English Language.

Work Environment: Indoors; sitting.

Cardiovascular Technologists and Technicians

* Education/Training Required: Associate degree
* Annual Earnings: $44,940
* Beginning Wage: $24,650
* Earnings Growth Potential: High (45.1%)
* Growth: 25.5%
* Annual Job Openings: 3,550
* Job Security: Most Secure
* Self-Employed: 1.1%
* Part-Time: 17.3%

Renewal Industry: Health Care.

Industries with Greatest Employment: Hospitals, Public and Private (75.2%).

Highest-Growth Industries (Projected Growth for This Job): Administrative and Support Services (39.3%); Management of Companies and Enterprises (25.9%); Local Government (23.3%); Educational Services, Public and Private (23.0%); Hospitals, Public and Private (22.1%).

Other Considerations for Job Outlook: Technologists and technicians trained to perform certain procedures will be in particular demand. Growth will occur as the population ages, because older people have a higher incidence of heart disease and other complications of the heart and vascular system. Employment of vascular technologists and echocardiographers will grow as advances in vascular technology and sonography reduce the need for more costly and invasive procedures. Electrophysiology is also becoming a rapidly growing specialty. However, fewer EKG technicians will be needed as hospitals train nursing aides and others to perform basic EKG procedures. Individuals trained in Holter monitoring and stress testing are expected to have more favorable job prospects than those who can perform only a basic EKG.

Conduct tests on pulmonary or cardiovascular systems of patients for diagnostic purposes. May conduct or assist in electrocardiograms, cardiac catheterizations, pulmonary-functions, lung capacity, and similar tests. Monitor patients' blood pressures and heart rates, using electrocardiogram (EKG) equipment during diagnostic and therapeutic procedures to notify physicians if something appears wrong. Explain testing procedures to patients to obtain cooperation and reduce anxiety. Observe gauges, recorders, and video screens of data analysis systems during imaging of cardiovascular systems. Monitor patients' comfort and safety during tests, alerting physicians to abnormalities or changes in patient responses. Obtain and record patients' identities, medical histories, or test results. Attach electrodes to patients' chests, arms, and legs; connect electrodes to leads from electrocardiogram (EKG) machines; and operate EKG machines to obtain readings. Adjust equipment and controls according to physicians' orders or established protocol. Prepare and position patients for testing. Check, test, and maintain cardiology equipment, making minor repairs when necessary, to ensure proper operation. Supervise and train other cardiology technologists and students. Perform general administrative tasks, such as scheduling appointments or ordering supplies and equipment. Maintain a proper sterile field during surgical procedures. Assist physicians in the diagnosis and treatment of cardiac and peripheral vascular treatments, such as implanting pacemakers or assisting with balloon angioplasties to treat blood vessel blockages. Inject contrast medium into patients' blood vessels. Assess cardiac physiology and calculate valve areas from blood flow velocity measurements. Operate diagnostic imaging equipment to produce contrast-enhanced radiographs of hearts and cardiovascular systems. Observe ultrasound display screens and listen to signals to record vascular information such as blood pressure, limb volume changes, oxygen saturation, and cerebral circulation. Transcribe, type, and distribute reports of diagnostic procedures for interpretation by physician. Conduct electrocardiogram (EKG), phonocardiogram, echocardiogram, stress testing, or other cardiovascular tests to record patients' cardiac activities, using specialized electronic test equipment, recording devices, and laboratory instruments.

Personality Type: Realistic-Investigative-Social.

Career Cluster: 08 Health Science. **Career Pathway:** 08.2 Diagnostics Services.

Skills: No data available.

Education and Training Programs: Cardiovascular Technology/Technologist; Electrocardiograph Technology/Technician; Perfusion Technology/Perfusionist; Cardiopulmonary Technology/Technologist. **Related Knowledge/Courses:** Medicine and Dentistry; Biology; Psychology; Customer and Personal Service; Sociology and Anthropology; Chemistry.

Work Environment: Indoors; radiation; disease or infections; standing; using hands on objects, tools, or controls; repetitive motions.

Carpenters

See *Construction Carpenters* and *Rough Carpenters*, *described separately.*

Cartographers and Photogrammetrists

- ❋ Education/Training Required: Bachelor's degree
- ❋ Annual Earnings: $49,970
- ❋ Beginning Wage: $32,380
- ❋ Earnings Growth Potential: Medium (35.2%)
- ❋ Growth: 20.3%
- ❋ Annual Job Openings: 2,823
- ❋ Job Security: Less Secure than Most
- ❋ Self-Employed: 3.4%
- ❋ Part-Time: 4.6%

Renewal Industry: Infrastructure.

Industries with Greatest Employment: Professional, Scientific, and Technical Services (48.3%); Local Government (22.8%); Federal Government (7.5%).

Highest-Growth Industries (Projected Growth for This Job): Professional, Scientific, and Technical Services (32.9%); Real Estate (26.8%); Administrative and Support Services (20.0%); Management of Companies and Enterprises (15.9%).

Other Considerations for Job Outlook: Cartographers and photogrammetrists should have favorable job prospects. Increasing demand for geographic data, as opposed to traditional surveying services, will mean better opportunities for cartographers and photogrammetrists who are involved in the development and use of geographic and land information systems, but those who produce more basic GIS data may face competition for jobs from offshore firms and contractors.

Collect, analyze, and interpret geographic information provided by geodetic surveys, aerial photographs, and satellite data. Research, study, and prepare maps and other spatial data in digital or graphic form for legal, social, political, educational, and design purposes. May work with Geographic Information Systems (GIS). May design and evaluate algorithms, data structures, and user interfaces for GIS and mapping systems. Identify, scale, and orient geodetic points, elevations, and other planimetric or topographic features, applying standard mathematical formulas. Collect information about specific features of the Earth, using aerial photography and other digital remote sensing techniques. Revise existing maps and charts, making all necessary corrections and adjustments. Compile data required for map preparation, including aerial photographs, survey notes, records, reports, and original maps. Inspect final compositions to ensure completeness and accuracy. Determine map content and layout, as well as production specifications such as scale, size, projection, and colors, and direct production to ensure that specifications are followed. Examine and analyze data from ground surveys, reports, aerial photographs, and satellite images to prepare topographic maps, aerial-photograph mosaics, and related charts. Select aerial photographic and remote sensing techniques and plotting equipment needed to meet required standards of accuracy. Delineate aerial photographic detail such as control points, hydrography, topography, and cultural features, using precision stereoplotting apparatus or drafting instruments. Build and update digital databases. Prepare and alter trace maps, charts, tables, detailed drawings, and three-dimensional optical models of terrain, using stereoscopic plotting and computer graphics equipment. Determine guidelines that specify which source material is acceptable for use. Study legal records to establish boundaries of local, national, and international properties. Travel over photographed areas to observe, identify, record, and verify all relevant features.

Personality Type: Realistic-Investigative-Conventional.

Career Clusters: 02 Architecture and Construction; 15 Science, Technology, Engineering, and Mathematics. **Career Pathways:** 02.1 Design/Pre-Construction; 15.3 Science and Mathematics.

Skills: Science; Technology Design; Mathematics; Active Learning; Troubleshooting; Reading Comprehension.

Education and Training Programs: Surveying Technology/Surveying; Cartography. **Related Knowledge/Courses:** Geography; Design; Engineering and Technology; Computers and Electronics; Production and Processing; Mathematics.

Work Environment: Indoors; sitting; using hands on objects, tools, or controls; repetitive motions.

Cement Masons and Concrete Finishers

- ❊ Education/Training Required: Moderate-term on-the-job training
- ❊ Annual Earnings: $33,840
- ❊ Beginning Wage: $21,980
- ❊ Earnings Growth Potential: Medium (35.0%)
- ❊ Growth: 11.4%
- ❊ Annual Job Openings: 34,625
- ❊ Job Security: Least Secure
- ❊ Self-Employed: 2.0%
- ❊ Part-Time: 6.0%

Renewal Industry: Infrastructure.

Industries with Greatest Employment: Specialty Trade Contractors (69.3%); Construction of Buildings (13.6%); Heavy and Civil Engineering Construction (9.1%).

Highest-Growth Industries (Projected Growth for This Job): Professional, Scientific, and Technical Services (31.7%); Real Estate (26.4%); Administrative and Support Services (23.3%); Management of Companies and Enterprises (15.2%).

Other Considerations for Job Outlook: Opportunities for cement masons and concrete finishers are expected to be good, particularly for those with the most experience and skills. Employers report difficulty in finding workers with the right skills, as many qualified jobseekers often prefer work that is less strenuous and has more comfortable working conditions. There are expected to be a significant number of retirements over the next decade, which will create more job openings. Applicants who take masonry-related courses at technical schools will have better opportunities than those without these courses.

Smooth and finish surfaces of poured concrete, such as floors, walks, sidewalks, roads, or curbs, using a variety of hand and power tools. Align forms for sidewalks, curbs, or gutters; patch voids; and use saws to cut expansion joints. Check the forms that hold the concrete to see that they are properly constructed. Set the forms that hold concrete to the desired pitch and depth and align them. Spread, level, and smooth concrete, using rake, shovel, hand or power trowel, hand or power screed, and float. Mold expansion joints and edges, using edging tools, jointers, and straightedge. Monitor how the wind, heat, or cold affect the curing of the concrete throughout the entire process. Signal truck driver to position truck to facilitate pouring concrete and move chute to direct concrete on forms. Produce rough concrete surface, using broom. Operate power vibrator to compact concrete. Direct the casting of the concrete and supervise laborers who use shovels or special tools to spread it. Mix cement, sand, and water to produce concrete, grout, or slurry, using hoe, trowel, tamper, scraper, or concrete-mixing machine. Cut out damaged areas, drill holes for reinforcing rods, and position reinforcing rods to repair concrete, using power saw and drill. Wet surface to prepare for bonding, fill holes and cracks with grout or slurry, and smooth, using trowel. Wet concrete surface and rub with stone to smooth surface and obtain specified finish. Clean chipped area, using wire brush, and feel and observe surface to determine if it is rough or uneven. Apply hardening and sealing compounds to cure surface of concrete and waterproof or restore surface. Chip, scrape, and grind high spots, ridges, and rough projections to finish concrete, using pneumatic chisels, power grinders, or hand tools. Spread roofing paper on surface of foundation and spread concrete onto roofing paper with trowel to form terrazzo base. Build wooden molds and clamp molds around area to be repaired, using hand tools. Sprinkle colored marble or stone chips, powdered steel, or coloring powder over surface to produce prescribed finish. Cut metal division strips and press them into terrazzo base so that top edges form desired design or pattern. Fabricate concrete beams, columns, and panels. Waterproof or restore concrete surfaces, using appropriate compounds.

Personality Type: Realistic-Enterprising.

Career Cluster: 02 Architecture and Construction. **Career Pathway:** 02.2 Construction.

Skills: No data available.

Education and Training Program: Concrete Finishing/Concrete Finisher. **Related Knowledge/Courses:** Building and Construction; Public Safety and Security; Mechanical Devices; Design; Engineering and Technology.

Work Environment: Outdoors; noisy; hazardous equipment; standing; using hands on objects, tools, or controls; bending or twisting the body.

Chemical Engineers

* Education/Training Required: Bachelor's degree
* Annual Earnings: $81,500
* Beginning Wage: $52,060
* Earnings Growth Potential: Medium (36.1%)
* Growth: 7.9%
* Annual Job Openings: 2,111
* Job Security: More Secure than Most
* Self-Employed: 1.9%
* Part-Time: 3.4%

Renewal Industries: Advanced Manufacturing; Green Technologies.

Industries with Greatest Employment: Professional, Scientific, and Technical Services (30.5%); Chemical Manufacturing (28.9%); Petroleum and Coal Products Manufacturing (5.8%).

Highest-Growth Industries (Projected Growth for This Job): Administrative and Support Services (36.8%); Waste Management and Remediation Services (35.5%); Professional, Scientific, and Technical Services (28.4%); Management of Companies and Enterprises (21.1%); Merchant Wholesalers, Durable Goods (20.0%); Local Government (18.3%); Merchant Wholesalers, Nondurable Goods (18.1%); Educational Services, Public and Private (17.5%).

Other Considerations for Job Outlook: Among manufacturing industries, pharmaceuticals may provide the best opportunities for jobseekers. However, most employment growth for chemical engineers will be in service-providing industries such as professional, scientific, and technical services, particularly for research in energy and the developing fields of biotechnology and nanotechnology. Offshoring of engineering work will likely dampen domestic employment growth to some degree.

Design chemical plant equipment and devise processes for manufacturing chemicals and products, such as gasoline, synthetic rubber, plastics, detergents, cement, paper, and pulp, by applying principles and technology of chemistry, physics, and engineering. Perform tests throughout stages of production to determine degree of control over variables, including temperature, density, specific gravity, and pressure. Develop safety procedures to be employed by workers operating equipment or working in close proximity to ongoing chemical reactions. Determine most effective arrangement of operations such as mixing, crushing, heat transfer, distillation, and drying. Prepare estimate of production costs and production progress reports for management. Direct activities of workers who operate or who are engaged in constructing and improving absorption, evaporation, or electromagnetic equipment. Perform laboratory studies of steps in manufacture of new product and test proposed process in small-scale operation such as a pilot plant. Develop processes to separate components of liquids or gases or generate electrical currents by using controlled chemical processes. Conduct research to develop new and improved chemical manufacturing processes. Design measurement and control systems for chemical plants based on data collected in laboratory experiments and in pilot plant operations. Design and plan layout of equipment.

Personality Type: Investigative-Realistic.

Career Cluster: 15 Science, Technology, Engineering, and Mathematics. **Career Pathway:** 15.1 Engineering and Technology.

Skills: Science; Technology Design; Troubleshooting; Programming; Operations Analysis; Installation.

Education and Training Program: Chemical Engineering. **Related Knowledge/Courses:** Engineering and Technology; Chemistry; Physics; Design; Production and Processing; Mathematics.

Work Environment: Indoors; noisy; hazardous conditions; sitting.

Chemistry Teachers, Postsecondary

- ❀ Education/Training Required: Master's degree
- ❀ Annual Earnings: $63,870
- ❀ Beginning Wage: $37,810
- ❀ Earnings Growth Potential: High (40.8%)
- ❀ Growth: 22.9%
- ❀ Annual Job Openings: 3,405
- ❀ Job Security: Most Secure
- ❀ Self-Employed: 0.4%
- ❀ Part-Time: 27.8%

Renewal Industry: Education.

Industries with Greatest Employment: Educational Services, Public and Private (97.3%).

Highest-Growth Industries (Projected Growth for This Job): Administrative and Support Services (48.3%); Amusement, Gambling, and Recreation Industries (45.2%); Social Assistance (38.6%); Support Activities for Transportation (32.8%); Religious, Grantmaking, Civic, Professional, and Similar Organizations (29.9%); Professional, Scientific, and Technical Services (28.8%); Management of Companies and Enterprises (26.8%); Local Government (23.5%); Educational Services, Public and Private (22.8%); Hospitals, Public and Private (21.4%).

Other Considerations for Job Outlook: Retirements of current postsecondary teachers should create numerous openings for all types of postsecondary teachers, so job opportunities are generally expected to be very good. One of the main reasons why students attend postsecondary institutions is to prepare themselves for careers, so the best job prospects for postsecondary teachers are likely to be in rapidly growing fields that offer many nonacademic career options. Chemistry is a key part of the curriculum for health-care majors. Community colleges and other institutions offering career and technical education have been among the most rapidly growing, and these institutions are expected to offer some of the best opportunities for postsecondary teachers.

Teach courses pertaining to the chemical and physical properties and compositional changes of substances. Work may include instruction in the methods of qualitative and quantitative chemical analysis. Includes both

teachers primarily engaged in teaching and those who do a combination of both teaching and research. Prepare and deliver lectures to undergraduate and/or graduate students on topics such as organic chemistry, analytical chemistry, and chemical separation. Supervise students' laboratory work. Evaluate and grade students' classwork, laboratory performance, assignments, and papers. Compile, administer, and grade examinations or assign this work to others. Maintain student attendance records, grades, and other required records. Prepare course materials such as syllabi, homework assignments, and handouts. Maintain regularly scheduled office hours to advise and assist students. Plan, evaluate, and revise curricula, course content, course materials, and methods of instruction. Supervise undergraduate and/or graduate teaching, internships, and research work. Keep abreast of developments in the field by reading current literature, talking with colleagues, and participating in professional conferences. Initiate, facilitate, and moderate classroom discussions. Select and obtain materials and supplies such as textbooks and laboratory equipment. Conduct research in a particular field of knowledge and publish findings in professional journals, books, and/or electronic media. Advise students on academic and vocational curricula and on career issues. Collaborate with colleagues to address teaching and research issues. Serve on academic or administrative committees that deal with institutional policies, departmental matters, and academic issues. Write grant proposals to procure external research funding. Participate in student recruitment, registration, and placement activities. Prepare and submit required reports related to instruction. Perform administrative duties such as serving as a department head. Act as advisers to student organizations. Compile bibliographies of specialized materials for outside reading assignments. Participate in campus and community events. Provide professional consulting services to government and/or industry.

Personality Type: Social-Investigative-Realistic.

Career Cluster: 15 Science, Technology, Engineering, and Mathematics. **Career Pathway:** 15.3 Science and Mathematics.

Skills: Science; Mathematics; Instructing; Writing; Reading Comprehension; Active Learning.

Education and Training Programs: Chemistry, General; Analytical Chemistry; Inorganic Chemistry; Organic Chemistry; Physical and Theoretical Chemistry; Polymer Chemistry; Chemical Physics; Chemistry, Other; Geochemistry. **Related Knowledge/Courses:** Chemistry; Biology; Physics; Education and Training; Mathematics; English Language.

Work Environment: Indoors; contaminants; hazardous conditions; sitting.

Chemists

- ✹ Education/Training Required: Bachelor's degree
- ✹ Annual Earnings: $63,490
- ✹ Beginning Wage: $36,810
- ✹ Earnings Growth Potential: High (42.0%)
- ✹ Growth: 9.1%
- ✹ Annual Job Openings: 9,024
- ✹ Job Security: Less Secure than Most
- ✹ Self-Employed: 1.2%
- ✹ Part-Time: 3.9%

Renewal Industry: Advanced Manufacturing.

Industries with Greatest Employment: Chemical Manufacturing (34.2%); Professional, Scientific, and Technical Services (29.9%); Federal Government (7.7%).

Highest-Growth Industries (Projected Growth for This Job): Administrative and Support Services (27.5%); Waste Management and Remediation Services (26.5%); Professional, Scientific, and Technical Services (26.1%); Ambulatory Health-Care Services (17.2%); Management of Companies and Enterprises (15.3%).

Other Considerations for Job Outlook: New chemists at all levels may experience competition for jobs, particularly in declining chemical manufacturing industries; graduates with a master's degree, and particularly those with a Ph.D., will enjoy better opportunities at larger pharmaceutical and biotechnology firms.

Conduct qualitative and quantitative chemical analyses or chemical experiments in laboratories for quality or process control or to develop new products or knowledge. Analyze organic and inorganic compounds to determine chemical and physical properties, composition, structure, relationships, and reactions, utilizing chromatography, spectroscopy, and spectrophotometry techniques. Develop, improve, and customize products, equipment, formulas, processes, and analytical methods. Compile and analyze test information to determine process or equipment operating efficiency and to diagnose malfunctions. Confer with scientists and engineers to conduct analyses of research projects, interpret test results, or develop nonstandard tests. Direct, coordinate, and advise personnel in test procedures for analyzing components and physical properties of materials. Induce changes in composition of substances by introducing heat, light, energy, and chemical catalysts for quantitative and qualitative analysis. Write technical papers and reports and prepare standards and specifications for processes, facilities, products, or tests. Study effects of various methods of processing, preserving, and packaging on composition and properties of foods. Prepare test solutions, compounds, and reagents for laboratory personnel to conduct test.

Personality Type: Investigative-Realistic-Conventional.

Career Cluster: 15 Science, Technology, Engineering, and Mathematics. **Career Pathway:** 15.3 Science and Mathematics.

Skills: Science; Quality Control Analysis; Technology Design; Operation Monitoring; Equipment Selection; Management of Material Resources.

Education and Training Programs: Chemistry, General; Analytical Chemistry; Inorganic Chemistry; Organic Chemistry; Physical and Theoretical Chemistry; Polymer Chemistry; Chemical Physics; Chemistry, Other. **Related Knowledge/Courses:** Chemistry; Mathematics; Engineering and Technology; Production and Processing; Computers and Electronics; Law and Government.

Work Environment: Indoors; contaminants; hazardous conditions; standing.

Child, Family, and School Social Workers

* Education/Training Required: Bachelor's degree
* Annual Earnings: $38,620
* Beginning Wage: $25,160
* Earnings Growth Potential: Low (34.9%)
* Growth: 19.1%
* Annual Job Openings: 35,402
* Job Security: Most Secure
* Self-Employed: 2.8%
* Part-Time: 9.4%

Renewal Industry: Education.

Industries with Greatest Employment: Social Assistance (24.4%); State Government (24.1%); Local Government (17.5%); Educational Services, Public and Private (14.0%); Nursing and Residential Care Facilities (5.4%); Religious, Grantmaking, Civic, Professional, and Similar Organizations (5.0%).

Highest-Growth Industries (Projected Growth for This Job): Social Assistance (54.0%); Administrative and Support Services (28.0%); Ambulatory Health-Care Services (22.6%); Nursing and Residential Care Facilities (21.3%); Management of Companies and Enterprises (15.3%); Religious, Grantmaking, Civic, Professional, and Similar Organizations (15.2%).

Other Considerations for Job Outlook: Job prospects are generally expected to be favorable. Social workers, particularly family social workers, will be needed to assist in finding the best care for the aging and to support their families. Furthermore, demand for school social workers will increase and lead to more jobs as efforts are expanded to respond to rising student enrollments as well as the continued emphasis on integrating disabled children into the general school population. There could be competition for school social work jobs in some areas because of the limited number of openings. The availability of federal, state, and local funding will be a major factor in determining the actual job growth in schools. The demand for child and family social workers may also be tied to the availability of government funding.

Provide social services and assistance to improve the social and psychological functioning of children and their families and to maximize the family well-being and the academic functioning of children. May assist single parents, arrange adoptions, and find foster homes for abandoned or abused children. In schools, they address such problems as teenage pregnancy, misbehavior, and truancy. May also advise teachers on how to deal with problem children. Interview clients individually, in families, or in groups, assessing their situations, capabilities, and problems, to determine what services are required to meet their needs. Counsel individuals, groups, families, or communities regarding issues including mental health, poverty, unemployment, substance abuse, physical abuse, rehabilitation, social adjustment, child care, or medical care. Maintain case history records and prepare reports. Counsel students whose behavior, school progress, or mental or physical impairment indicate a need for assistance, diagnosing students' problems and arranging for needed services. Consult with parents, teachers, and other school personnel to determine causes of problems such as truancy and misbehavior and to implement solutions. Counsel parents with child rearing problems, interviewing the child and family to determine whether further action is required. Develop and review service plans in consultation with clients and perform follow-ups assessing the quantity and quality of services provided. Collect supplementary information needed to assist clients, such as employment records, medical records, or school reports. Address legal issues, such as child abuse and discipline, assisting with hearings and providing testimony to inform custody arrangements. Provide, find, or arrange for support services, such as child care, homemaker service, prenatal care, substance abuse treatment, job training, counseling, or parenting classes, to prevent more serious problems from developing. Refer clients to community resources for services such as job placement, debt counseling, legal aid, housing, medical treatment, or financial assistance and provide concrete information, such as where to go and how to apply. Arrange for medical, psychiatric, and other tests that may disclose causes of difficulties and indicate remedial measures. Work in child and adolescent residential institutions. Administer welfare programs. Evaluate personal characteristics and home conditions of foster home or adoption applicants. Serve as liaisons between students, homes, schools, family services, child guidance clinics, courts, protective services, doctors, and other contacts to help children who face problems such as disabilities, abuse, or poverty.

Personality Type: Social-Enterprising.

Career Clusters: 10 Human Services; 12 Law, Public Safety, Corrections, and Security. **Career Pathways:** 10.3 Family and Community Services; 12.1 Correction Services.

Skills: Social Perceptiveness; Service Orientation; Speaking; Monitoring; Writing; Learning Strategies.

Education and Training Programs: Juvenile Corrections; Social Work; Youth Services/Administration. **Related Knowledge/Courses:** Therapy and Counseling; Psychology; Sociology and Anthropology; Philosophy and Theology; Customer and Personal Service; Law and Government.

Work Environment: Indoors; sitting.

Chiropractors

- ✳ Education/Training Required: First professional degree
- ✳ Annual Earnings: $65,890
- ✳ Beginning Wage: $32,530
- ✳ Earnings Growth Potential: Very high (50.6%)
- ✳ Growth: 14.4%
- ✳ Annual Job Openings: 3,179
- ✳ Job Security: Most Secure
- ✳ Self-Employed: 51.7%
- ✳ Part-Time: 23.6%

Renewal Industry: Health Care.

Industries with Greatest Employment: Ambulatory Health-Care Services (46.9%).

Highest-Growth Industries (Projected Growth for This Job): Ambulatory Health-Care Services (23.4%).

Other Considerations for Job Outlook: Job prospects for new chiropractors are expected to be good. In this occupation, replacement needs arise almost entirely from retirements. Chiropractors usually remain in the occupation until they retire; few transfer to other occupations. Establishing a new practice will be easiest in areas with a low concentration of chiropractors. Employment is expected to grow faster than average because of increasing consumer demand for alternative health care. Demand for chiropractic treatment, however, is related to the ability of patients to pay, either directly or through health insurance. Although more insurance plans now cover chiropractic services, the extent of such coverage varies among plans.

Adjust spinal column and other articulations of the body to correct abnormalities of the human body believed to be caused by interference with the nervous system. Examine patients to determine nature and extent of disorders. Manipulate spines or other involved areas. May utilize supplementary measures such as exercise, rest, water, light, heat, and nutritional therapy. Diagnose health problems by reviewing patients' health and medical histories; questioning, observing, and examining patients; and interpreting X-rays. Maintain accurate case histories of patients. Evaluate the functioning of the neuromuscularskeletal system and the spine, using systems of chiropractic diagnosis. Perform a series of manual adjustments to spines, or other articulations of the body, to correct musculoskeletal systems. Obtain and record patients' medical histories. Advise patients about recommended courses of treatment. Consult with and refer patients to appropriate health practitioners when necessary. Analyze X-rays to locate the sources of patients' difficulties and to rule out fractures or diseases as sources of problems. Counsel patients about nutrition, exercise, sleeping habits, stress management, and other matters. Arrange for diagnostic X-rays to be taken. Suggest and apply the use of supports such as straps, tapes, bandages, and braces if necessary.

Personality Type: Social-Investigative-Realistic.

Career Cluster: 08 Health Science. **Career Pathway:** 08.1 Therapeutic Services.

Skills: No data available.

Education and Training Program: Chiropractic (DC). **Related Knowledge/Courses:** Medicine and Dentistry; Therapy and Counseling; Biology; Psychology; Personnel and Human Resources; Sales and Marketing.

Work Environment: Indoors; disease or infections; standing; using hands on objects, tools, or controls; bending or twisting the body; repetitive motions.

Civil Drafters

* Education/Training Required: Postsecondary vocational training
* Annual Earnings: $43,310
* Beginning Wage: $27,680
* Earnings Growth Potential: Medium (36.1%)
* Growth: 6.1%
* Annual Job Openings: 16,238
* Job Security: Less Secure than Most
* Self-Employed: 5.0%
* Part-Time: 5.9%

Our sources did not provide separate job openings data for this occupation. The job openings listed here are shared with Architectural Drafters.

Renewal Industries: Green Technologies; Infrastructure.

Industries with Greatest Employment: Professional, Scientific, and Technical Services (76.9%); Construction of Buildings (5.6%).

Highest-Growth Industries (Projected Growth for This Job): Building Material and Garden Equipment and Supplies Dealers (20.9%); Administrative and Support Services (20.4%); Real Estate (16.7%).

Other Considerations for Job Outlook: Opportunities should be best for individuals with at least two years of postsecondary training in drafting and considerable skill and experience using computer-aided design and drafting systems.

Prepare drawings and topographical and relief maps used in civil engineering projects such as highways, bridges, pipelines, flood control projects, and water and sewerage control systems. Produce drawings by using computer-assisted drafting systems (CAD) or drafting machines or by hand, using compasses, dividers, protractors, triangles, and other drafting devices. Draw maps, diagrams, and profiles, using cross-sections and surveys, to represent elevations, topographical contours, subsurface formations, and structures. Draft plans and detailed drawings for structures, installations, and construction projects such as highways, sewage disposal systems, and dikes, working from sketches or notes. Determine the order of work and method of presentation such as orthographic or isometric drawing. Finish and duplicate drawings and documentation packages according to required mediums and specifications for reproduction, using blueprinting, photography, or other duplication methods. Review rough sketches, drawings, specifications, and other engineering data received from civil engineers to ensure that they conform to design concepts. Calculate excavation tonnage and prepare graphs and fill-hauling diagrams for use in earth-moving operations. Supervise and train other technologists, technicians, and drafters. Correlate, interpret, and modify data obtained from topographical surveys, well logs, and geophysical prospecting reports. Determine quality, cost, strength, and quantity of required materials and enter figures on materials lists. Locate and identify symbols located on topographical surveys to denote geological and geophysical formations or oil field installations. Calculate weights, volumes, and stress factors and their implications for technical aspects of designs. Supervise or conduct field surveys, inspections, or technical investigations to obtain data required to revise construction drawings. Explain drawings to production or construction teams and provide adjustments as necessary. Plot characteristics of boreholes for oil and gas wells from photographic subsurface survey recordings and other data, representing depth, degree, and direction of inclination.

Personality Type: Realistic-Conventional-Investigative.

Career Cluster: 02 Architecture and Construction. **Career Pathway:** 02.1 Design/Pre-Construction.

Skills: No data available.

Education and Training Programs: Architectural Technology/Technician; Drafting and Design Technology/Technician, General; CAD/CADD Drafting and/or Design Technology/Technician; Architectural Drafting and Architectural CAD/CADD; Civil Drafting and Civil Engineering CAD/CADD. **Related Knowledge/Courses:** Design; Engineering and Technology; Building and Construction; Geography; Mathematics; Physics.

Work Environment: Indoors; sitting; using hands on objects, tools, or controls; repetitive motions.

Civil Engineering Technicians

- ❋ Education/Training Required: Associate degree
- ❋ Annual Earnings: $42,580
- ❋ Beginning Wage: $25,390
- ❋ Earnings Growth Potential: High (40.4%)
- ❋ Growth: 10.2%
- ❋ Annual Job Openings: 7,499
- ❋ Job Security: More Secure than Most
- ❋ Self-Employed: 0.9%
- ❋ Part-Time: 5.9%

Renewal Industry: Infrastructure.

Industries with Greatest Employment: Professional, Scientific, and Technical Services (49.0%); State Government (25.5%); Local Government (17.5%).

Highest-Growth Industries (Projected Growth for This Job): Administrative and Support Services (30.4%); Professional, Scientific, and Technical Services (16.2%); Publishing Industries (Except Internet) (15.9%); Management of Companies and Enterprises (15.3%).

Other Considerations for Job Outlook: Because of population growth and the related need to improve the nation's infrastructure, more civil engineering technicians will be needed to expand transportation, water supply, and pollution control systems, as well as large buildings and building complexes. They also will be needed to repair or replace existing roads, bridges, and other public structures. Civil engineering technicians tend to do more on-site work than most engineering technicians and therefore are less threatened by offshoring.

Apply theory and principles of civil engineering in planning, designing, and overseeing construction and maintenance of structures and facilities under the direction of engineering staff or physical scientists. Calculate dimensions, square footage, profile and component specifications, and material quantities, using calculator or computer. Draft detailed dimensional drawings and design layouts for projects and to ensure conformance to specifications. Analyze proposed site factors and design maps, graphs, tracings, and diagrams to illustrate findings. Read and review project blueprints and structural specifications to determine dimensions of structure or system and material requirements. Prepare reports and document project activities and data. Confer with supervisor to determine project details such as plan preparation, acceptance testing, and evaluation of field conditions. Inspect project site and evaluate contractor work to detect design malfunctions and ensure conformance to design specifications and applicable codes. Plan and conduct field surveys to locate new sites and analyze details of project sites. Develop plans and estimate costs for installation of systems, utilization of facilities, or construction of structures. Report maintenance problems occurring at project site to supervisor and negotiate changes to resolve system conflicts. Conduct materials test and analysis, using tools and equipment and applying engineering knowledge. Respond to public suggestions and complaints. Evaluate facility to determine suitability for occupancy and square footage availability.

Personality Type: Realistic-Conventional-Investigative.

Career Clusters: 02 Architecture and Construction; 13 Manufacturing. **Career Pathways:** 02.1 Design/Pre-Construction; 13.3 Maintenance, Installation, and Repair.

Skills: Mathematics; Science; Operations Analysis; Writing; Complex Problem Solving; Reading Comprehension.

Education and Training Programs: Civil Engineering Technology/Technician; Construction Engineering Technology/Technician. **Related Knowledge/Courses:** Building and Construction; Design; Engineering and Technology; Mathematics; Computers and Electronics; Transportation.

Work Environment: More often indoors than outdoors; sitting.

Civil Engineers

- ❋ Education/Training Required: Bachelor's degree
- ❋ Annual Earnings: $71,710
- ❋ Beginning Wage: $46,420
- ❋ Earnings Growth Potential: Medium (35.3%)
- ❋ Growth: 18.0%
- ❋ Annual Job Openings: 15,979
- ❋ Job Security: Less Secure than Most
- ❋ Self-Employed: 4.9%
- ❋ Part-Time: 3.2%

Renewal Industry: Infrastructure.

Industries with Greatest Employment: Professional, Scientific, and Technical Services (51.1%); State Government (11.6%); Local Government (11.5%); Construction of Buildings (6.3%).

Highest-Growth Industries (Projected Growth for This Job): Waste Management and Remediation Services (29.8%); Professional, Scientific, and Technical Services (29.3%); Administrative and Support Services (27.9%); Real Estate (18.5%); Religious, Grantmaking, Civic, Professional, and Similar Organizations (18.4%); Accommodation, Including Hotels and Motels (15.6%); Management of Companies and Enterprises (15.3%).

Other Considerations for Job Outlook: Because construction industries and architectural, engineering, and related services employ many civil engineers, employment opportunities will vary by geographic area and may decrease during economic slowdowns, when construction is often curtailed.

Perform engineering duties in planning, designing, and overseeing construction and maintenance of building structures and facilities such as roads, railroads, airports, bridges, harbors, channels, dams, irrigation projects, pipelines, power plants, water and sewage systems, and waste disposal units. Includes architectural, structural, traffic, ocean, and geo-technical engineers. Manage and direct staff members and construction, operations, or maintenance activities at project site. Provide technical advice regarding design, construction, or program modifications and structural repairs to industrial and managerial personnel. Inspect project sites to monitor progress and ensure conformance to design specifications and safety or sanitation standards. Estimate quantities and cost of materials, equipment, or labor to determine project feasibility. Test soils and materials to determine the adequacy and strength of foundations, concrete, asphalt, or steel. Compute load and grade requirements, water flow rates, and material stress factors to determine design specifications. Plan and design transportation or hydraulic systems and structures, following construction and government standards and using design software and drawing tools. Analyze survey reports, maps, drawings, blueprints, aerial photography, and other topographical or geologic data to plan projects. Prepare or present public reports on topics such as bid proposals, deeds, environmental impact statements, or property and right-of-way descriptions. Direct or participate in surveying to lay out installations and establish reference points, grades, and elevations to guide construction. Conduct studies of traffic patterns or environmental conditions to identify engineering problems and assess the potential impact of projects.

Personality Type: Realistic-Investigative-Conventional.

Career Cluster: 15 Science, Technology, Engineering, and Mathematics. **Career Pathway:** 15.1 Engineering and Technology.

Skills: No data available.

Education and Training Programs: Civil Engineering, General; Transportation and Highway Engineering; Water Resources Engineering; Civil Engineering, Other. **Related Knowledge/Courses:** Engineering and Technology; Design; Building and Construction; Physics; Transportation; Geography.

Work Environment: Indoors; sitting.

Clinical Psychologists

* Education/Training Required: Doctoral degree
* Annual Earnings: $62,210
* Beginning Wage: $37,300
* Earnings Growth Potential: High (40.0%)
* Growth: 15.8%
* Annual Job Openings: 8,309
* Job Security: Most Secure
* Self-Employed: 34.2%
* Part-Time: 24.0%

Our sources did not provide separate job openings data for this occupation. The job openings listed here are shared with Counseling Psychologists and with School Psychologists.

Renewal Industry: Health Care.

Industries with Greatest Employment: Educational Services, Public and Private (30.4%); Ambulatory Health-Care Services (13.2%); Hospitals, Public and Private (6.0%); Social Assistance (5.9%).

Highest-Growth Industries (Projected Growth for This Job): Social Assistance (56.2%); Professional, Scientific, and Technical Services (34.6%); Ambulatory Health-Care Services (26.8%); Nursing and Residential Care Facilities (24.8%); Funds, Trusts, and Other Financial Vehicles (23.3%); Religious, Grantmaking, Civic, Professional, and Similar Organizations (19.4%); Management of Companies and Enterprises (15.2%).

Other Considerations for Job Outlook: Job prospects should be the best for people who have a doctoral degree from a leading university. Master's degree holders will face keen competition for jobs. The rise in health-care costs associated with unhealthy lifestyles, such as smoking, alcoholism, and obesity, has made prevention and treatment more critical. An increase in the number of employee assistance programs, which help workers deal with personal problems, also should lead to employment growth for clinical and counseling specialties. Clinical and counseling psychologists also will be needed to help people deal with depression and other mental disorders, marriage and family problems, job stress, and addiction. The growing number of elderly will increase the demand for psychologists trained in geropsychology to help people deal with the mental and physical changes that occur as individuals grow older. There also will be increased need for psychologists to work with returning veterans.

Diagnose or evaluate mental and emotional disorders of individuals through observation, interview, and psychological tests and formulate and administer programs of treatment. Identify psychological, emotional, or behavioral issues and diagnose disorders, using information obtained from interviews, tests, records, and reference materials. Develop and implement individual treatment plans, specifying type, frequency, intensity, and duration of therapy. Interact with clients to assist them in gaining insight, defining goals, and planning action to achieve effective personal, social, educational, and vocational development and adjustment. Discuss the treatment of problems with clients. Utilize a variety of treatment methods such as psychotherapy, hypnosis, behavior modification, stress reduction therapy, psychodrama, and play therapy. Counsel individuals and groups regarding problems such as stress, substance abuse, and family situations to modify behavior or to improve personal, social, and vocational adjustment. Write reports on clients and maintain required paperwork. Evaluate the effectiveness of counseling or treatments and the accuracy and completeness of diagnoses; then modify plans and diagnoses as necessary. Obtain and study medical, psychological, social, and family histories by interviewing individuals, couples, or families and by reviewing records. Consult reference material such as textbooks, manuals, and journals to identify symptoms, make diagnoses, and develop approaches to treatment. Maintain current knowledge of relevant research. Observe individuals at play, in group interactions, or in other contexts to detect indications of mental deficiency, abnormal behavior, or maladjustment. Select, administer, score, and interpret psychological tests to obtain information on individuals' intelligence, achievements, interests, and personalities. Refer clients to other specialists, institutions, or support services as necessary. Develop, direct, and participate in training programs for staff and students. Provide psychological or administrative services and advice to private firms and community agencies regarding mental health programs or individual cases. Provide occupational, educational, and other information to individuals so that they can make educational and vocational plans.

Personality Type: Investigative-Social-Artistic.

Career Clusters: 08 Health Science; 10 Human Services. **Career Pathways:** 08.1 Therapeutic Services; 08.3 Health Informatics; 10.2 Counseling and Mental Health Services.

Skills: Social Perceptiveness; Service Orientation; Complex Problem Solving; Learning Strategies; Active Listening; Negotiation.

Education and Training Programs: Psychology, General; Clinical Psychology; Counseling Psychology; Developmental and Child Psychology; School Psychology; Clinical Child Psychology; Psychoanalysis and Psychotherapy. **Related Knowledge/Courses:** Therapy and Counseling; Psychology; Sociology and Anthropology; Philosophy and Theology; Customer and Personal Service; Medicine and Dentistry.

Work Environment: Indoors; sitting.

Clinical, Counseling, and School Psychologists

See *Clinical Psychologists*, *Counseling Psychologists*, and *School Psychologists*, described separately.

Commercial and Industrial Designers

- ✽ Education/Training Required: Bachelor's degree
- ✽ Annual Earnings: $56,550
- ✽ Beginning Wage: $31,400
- ✽ Earnings Growth Potential: High (44.5%)
- ✽ Growth: 7.2%
- ✽ Annual Job Openings: 4,777
- ✽ Job Security: Least Secure
- ✽ Self-Employed: 29.8%
- ✽ Part-Time: 16.7%

Renewal Industry: Advanced Manufacturing.

Industries with Greatest Employment: Professional, Scientific, and Technical Services (21.1%); Transportation Equipment Manufacturing (6.1%); Miscellaneous Manufacturing (5.7%); Management of Companies and Enterprises (5.0%).

Highest-Growth Industries (Projected Growth for This Job): Professional, Scientific, and Technical Services (28.4%); Administrative and Support Services (27.4%); Nonstore Retailers (21.1%); Management of Companies and Enterprises (15.3%).

Other Considerations for Job Outlook: Competition for jobs will be keen because many talented individuals are attracted to the design field. The best job opportunities will be in specialized design firms that are used by manufacturers to design products or parts of products. Designers with strong backgrounds in engineering and computer-aided design and extensive business expertise will have the best prospects.

Develop and design manufactured products, such as cars, home appliances, and children's toys. Combine artistic talent with research on product use, marketing, and materials to create the most functional and appealing product design. Prepare sketches of ideas, detailed drawings, illustrations, artwork, or blueprints, using drafting instruments, paints and brushes, or computer-aided design equipment. Direct and coordinate the fabrication of models or samples and the drafting of working drawings and specification sheets from sketches. Modify and refine designs, using working models, to conform with customer specifications, production limitations, or changes in design trends. Coordinate the look and function of product lines.

Confer with engineering, marketing, production, or sales departments, or with customers, to establish and evaluate design concepts for manufactured products. Present designs and reports to customers or design committees for approval and discuss need for modification. Evaluate feasibility of design ideas based on factors such as appearance, safety, function, serviceability, budget, production costs/methods, and market characteristics. Read publications, attend showings, and study competing products and design styles and motifs to obtain perspective and generate design concepts. Research production specifications, costs, production materials, and manufacturing methods and provide cost estimates and itemized production requirements. Design graphic material for use as ornamentation, illustration, or advertising on manufactured materials and packaging or containers. Develop manufacturing procedures and monitor the manufacture of their designs in a factory to improve operations and product quality. Supervise assistants' work throughout the design process. Fabricate models or samples in paper, wood, glass, fabric, plastic, metal, or other materials, using hand or power tools. Investigate product characteristics such as the product's safety and handling qualities; its market appeal; how efficiently it can be produced; and ways of distributing, using, and maintaining it. Develop industrial standards and regulatory guidelines. Participate in new product planning or market research, including studying the potential need for new products. Advise corporations on issues involving corporate image projects or problems.

Personality Type: Artistic-Enterprising-Realistic.

Career Cluster: 03 Arts, Audio/Video Technology, and Communications. **Career Pathways:** 03.1 Audio and Video Technology and Film; 03.3 Visual Arts.

Skills: Technology Design; Operations Analysis; Quality Control Analysis; Troubleshooting; Equipment Selection; Installation.

Education and Training Programs: Design and Visual Communications, General; Commercial and Advertising Art; Industrial Design; Design and Applied Arts, Other. **Related Knowledge/Courses:** Design; Engineering and Technology; Mathematics; Physics; Mechanical Devices; Production and Processing.

Work Environment: Indoors; sitting; using hands on objects, tools, or controls; repetitive motions.

Communications Teachers, Postsecondary

- ❋ Education/Training Required: Master's degree
- ❋ Annual Earnings: $54,720
- ❋ Beginning Wage: $29,700
- ❋ Earnings Growth Potential: High (45.7%)
- ❋ Growth: 22.9%
- ❋ Annual Job Openings: 4,074
- ❋ Job Security: Most Secure
- ❋ Self-Employed: 0.4%
- ❋ Part-Time: 27.8%

Renewal Industry: Education.

Industries with Greatest Employment: Educational Services, Public and Private (97.3%).

Highest-Growth Industries (Projected Growth for This Job): Administrative and Support Services (48.3%); Amusement, Gambling, and Recreation Industries (45.2%); Social Assistance (38.6%); Support Activities for Transportation (32.8%); Religious, Grantmaking, Civic, Professional, and Similar Organizations (29.9%); Professional, Scientific, and Technical Services (28.8%); Management of Companies and Enterprises (26.8%); Local Government (23.5%); Educational Services, Public and Private (22.8%); Hospitals, Public and Private (21.4%).

Other Considerations for Job Outlook: Retirements of current postsecondary teachers should create numerous openings for all types of postsecondary teachers, so job opportunities are generally expected to be very good. One of the main reasons why students attend postsecondary institutions is to prepare themselves for careers, so the best job prospects for postsecondary teachers are likely to be in rapidly growing fields that offer many nonacademic career options. Community colleges and other institutions offering career and technical education have been among the most rapidly growing, and these institutions are expected to offer some of the best opportunities for postsecondary teachers.

Teach courses in communications, such as organizational communications, public relations, radio/television broadcasting, and journalism. Evaluate and grade students' classwork, assignments, and papers. Prepare course materials such as syllabi, homework assignments, and handouts. Initiate, facilitate, and moderate classroom discussions. Prepare and deliver lectures to undergraduate or graduate students on topics such as public speaking, media criticism, and oral traditions. Compile, administer, and grade examinations or assign this work to others. Maintain student attendance records, grades, and other required records. Plan, evaluate, and revise curricula, course content, and course materials and methods of instruction. Maintain regularly scheduled office hours to advise and assist students. Keep abreast of developments in their field by reading current literature, talking with colleagues, and participating in professional conferences. Advise students on academic and vocational curricula and on career issues. Supervise undergraduate or graduate teaching, internship, and research work. Select and obtain materials and supplies such as textbooks. Collaborate with colleagues to address teaching and research issues. Conduct research in a particular field of knowledge and publish findings in professional journals, books, or electronic media. Participate in student recruitment, registration, and placement activities. Serve on academic or administrative committees that deal with institutional policies, departmental matters, and academic issues. Compile bibliographies of specialized materials for outside reading assignments. Act as advisers to student organizations. Participate in campus and community events. Perform administrative duties such as serving as department head. Write grant proposals to procure external research funding. Provide professional consulting services to government or industry.

Personality Type: Social-Artistic.

Career Clusters: 03 Arts, Audio/Video Technology, and Communications; 04 Business, Management, and Administration; 07 Government and Public Administration; 08 Health Science. **Career Pathways:** 03.5 Journalism and Broadcasting; 04.1 Management; 04.5 Marketing; 07.1 Governance; 08.3 Health Informatics.

Skills: Instructing; Writing; Persuasion; Learning Strategies; Monitoring; Speaking.

Education and Training Programs: Communication Studies/Speech Communication and Rhetoric; Mass Communication/Media Studies; Journalism; Broadcast Journalism; Journalism, Other; Radio and Television; Digital Communication and Media/Multimedia; Public Relations/Image Management; Advertising; Political Communication; Health Communication; Communication, Journalism, and Related Programs, Other. **Related Knowledge/Courses:** Communications and Media; Education and Training; Philosophy and Theology; Sociology and Anthropology; English Language; History and Archeology.

Work Environment: Indoors; sitting.

Computer and Information Scientists, Research

- ❋ Education/Training Required: Doctoral degree
- ❋ Annual Earnings: $97,970
- ❋ Beginning Wage: $55,930
- ❋ Earnings Growth Potential: High (42.9%)
- ❋ Growth: 21.5%
- ❋ Annual Job Openings: 2,901
- ❋ Job Security: More Secure than Most
- ❋ Self-Employed: 5.3%
- ❋ Part-Time: 5.6%

Renewal Industry: Information and Telecommunication Technologies.

Industries with Greatest Employment: Professional, Scientific, and Technical Services (48.9%); Publishing Industries (Except Internet) (12.3%); Educational Services, Public and Private (7.7%).

Highest-Growth Industries (Projected Growth for This Job): Publishing Industries (Except Internet) (40.6%); Internet Publishing and Broadcasting (39.8%); Professional, Scientific, and Technical Services (27.2%); Internet Service Providers, Web Search Portals, and Data Processing Services (25.0%); Administrative and Support Services (24.7%); Hospitals, Public and Private (17.6%); Motion Picture, Video, and Sound Recording Industries (17.0%); Management of Companies and Enterprises (15.3%).

Other Considerations for Job Outlook: Computer scientists are projected to be one of the fastest-growing occupations over the next decade. Strong employment growth combined with a limited supply of qualified workers will result in excellent employment prospects for this occupation and a high demand for these workers' skills. Because employers continue to seek computer specialists who can combine strong technical skills with good business skills, individuals with a combination of experience inside and outside the IT arena will have the best job prospects.

Conduct research into fundamental computer and information science as theorists, designers, or inventors. Solve or develop solutions to problems in the field of computer hardware and software. Analyze problems to develop solutions involving computer hardware and software. Assign or schedule tasks in order to meet work priorities and goals. Evaluate project plans and proposals to assess feasibility issues. Apply theoretical expertise and innovation to create or apply new technology, such as adapting principles for applying computers to new uses. Consult with users, management, vendors, and technicians to determine computing needs and system requirements. Meet with managers, vendors, and others to solicit cooperation and resolve problems. Conduct logical analyses of business, scientific, engineering, and other technical problems, formulating mathematical models of problems for solution by computers. Develop and interpret organizational goals, policies, and procedures. Participate in staffing decisions and direct training of subordinates. Develop performance standards and evaluate work in light of established standards. Design computers and the software that runs them. Maintain network hardware and software, direct network security measures, and monitor networks to ensure availability to system users. Participate in multidisciplinary projects in areas such as virtual reality, human-computer interaction, or robotics. Approve, prepare, monitor, and adjust operational budgets. Direct daily operations of departments, coordinating project activities with other departments.

Personality Type: Investigative-Realistic-Conventional.

Career Clusters: 08 Health Science; 11 Information Technology. **Career Pathways:** 08.3 Health Informatics; 11.1 Network Systems; 11.2 Information Support Services; 11.3 Interactive Media; 11.4 Programming and Software Development.

Skills: Programming; Science; Systems Analysis; Operations Analysis; Technology Design; Active Learning.

Education and Training Programs: Computer and Information Sciences, General; Artificial Intelligence and Robotics; Information Science/Studies; Computer Systems Analysis/Analyst; Computer Science; Computer and Information Sciences and Support Services, Other; Medical Informatics. **Related Knowledge/Courses:** Computers and Electronics; Telecommunications; Engineering and Technology; Mathematics; Design; Education and Training.

Work Environment: Indoors; sitting; using hands on objects, tools, or controls; repetitive motions.

Computer and Information Systems Managers

- ❋ Education/Training Required: Work experience plus degree
- ❋ Annual Earnings: $108,070
- ❋ Beginning Wage: $65,760
- ❋ Earnings Growth Potential: Medium (39.2%)
- ❋ Growth: 16.4%
- ❋ Annual Job Openings: 30,887
- ❋ Job Security: Least Secure
- ❋ Self-Employed: 1.4%
- ❋ Part-Time: 2.1%

Renewal Industry: Information and Telecommunication Technologies.

Industries with Greatest Employment: Professional, Scientific, and Technical Services (24.8%); Management of Companies and Enterprises (8.7%); Insurance Carriers and Related Activities (5.4%); Educational Services, Public and Private (5.4%).

Highest-Growth Industries (Projected Growth for This Job): Amusement, Gambling, and Recreation Industries (49.0%); Securities, Commodity Contracts, and Other Financial Investments and Related Activities (45.5%); Social Assistance (43.3%); Internet Publishing and Broadcasting (40.3%); Professional, Scientific, and Technical Services (33.9%); Warehousing and Storage (33.6%); Funds, Trusts, and Other Financial Vehicles (30.2%); Lessors of Nonfinancial Intangible Assets (Except Copyrighted Works) (27.7%); Waste Management and Remediation Services (27.3%); Personal and Laundry Services (27.0%); Administrative and Support Services (26.8%); Ambulatory Health-Care Services (26.5%); Building Material and Garden Equipment and Supplies Dealers (26.3%); Support Activities for Transportation (23.9%); Water Transportation (21.3%); Nursing and Residential Care Facilities (21.3%);

Performing Arts, Spectator Sports, and Related Industries (21.3%); Real Estate (20.8%); Nonstore Retailers (20.7%); Publishing Industries (Except Internet) (20.2%); Religious, Grantmaking, Civic, Professional, and Similar Organizations (18.2%); Rental and Leasing Services (18.1%); Motion Picture, Video, and Sound Recording Industries (17.0%); Accommodation, Including Hotels and Motels (16.9%); Internet Service Providers, Web Search Portals, and Data Processing Services (15.5%); Management of Companies and Enterprises (15.3%); Merchant Wholesalers, Durable Goods (15.2%).

Other Considerations for Job Outlook: Prospects for qualified computer and information systems managers should be excellent. Fast-paced occupational growth and the limited supply of technical workers will lead to a wealth of opportunities for qualified individuals. While technical workers remain relatively scarce in the United States, the demand for them continues to rise. Workers with specialized technical knowledge and strong communications skills will have the best prospects. People with management skills and an understanding of business practices and principles will have excellent opportunities, as companies are increasingly looking to technology to drive their revenue.

Plan, direct, or coordinate activities in such fields as electronic data processing, information systems, systems analysis, and computer programming. Review project plans to plan and coordinate project activity. Manage backup, security, and user help systems. Develop and interpret organizational goals, policies, and procedures. Develop computer information resources, providing for data security and control, strategic computing, and disaster recovery. Consult with users, management, vendors, and technicians to assess computing needs and system requirements. Stay abreast of advances in technology. Meet with department heads, managers, supervisors, vendors, and others to solicit cooperation and resolve problems. Provide users with technical support for computer problems. Recruit, hire, train, and supervise staff or participate in staffing decisions. Evaluate data-processing proposals to assess project feasibility and requirements. Review and approve all systems charts and programs prior to their implementation. Control operational budget and expenditures. Direct daily operations of department, analyzing workflow, establishing priorities, developing standards, and setting deadlines. Assign and review the work of systems analysts, programmers, and other computer-related

workers. Evaluate the organization's technology use and needs and recommend improvements such as hardware and software upgrades. Prepare and review operational reports or project progress reports. Purchase necessary equipment.

Personality Type: Enterprising-Conventional-Investigative.

Career Clusters: 04 Business, Management, and Administration; 11 Information Technology. **Career Pathways:** 04.1 Management; 04.4 Business Analysis; 11.1 Network Systems; 11.2 Information Support Services.

Skills: Programming; Systems Analysis; Management of Financial Resources; Systems Evaluation; Management of Material Resources; Management of Personnel Resources.

Education and Training Programs: Computer and Information Sciences, General; Information Science/Studies; Computer Science; System Administration/Administrator; Operations Management and Supervision; Management Information Systems, General; Information Resources Management/CIO Training; Knowledge Management. **Related Knowledge/Courses:** Telecommunications; Computers and Electronics; Economics and Accounting; Personnel and Human Resources; Production and Processing; Administration and Management.

Work Environment: Indoors; sitting; using hands on objects, tools, or controls.

Computer Hardware Engineers

- ❋ Education/Training Required: Bachelor's degree
- ❋ Annual Earnings: $91,860
- ❋ Beginning Wage: $55,880
- ❋ Earnings Growth Potential: Medium (39.2%)
- ❋ Growth: 4.6%
- ❋ Annual Job Openings: 3,572
- ❋ Job Security: Less Secure than Most
- ❋ Self-Employed: 3.6%
- ❋ Part-Time: 2.7%

Renewal Industries: Advanced Manufacturing; Information and Telecommunication Technologies.

Industries with Greatest Employment: Computer and Electronic Product Manufacturing (41.0%); Professional,

Scientific, and Technical Services (29.7%); Federal Government (5.6%); Merchant Wholesalers, Durable Goods (5.3%).

Highest-Growth Industries (Projected Growth for This Job): Professional, Scientific, and Technical Services (29.5%); Publishing Industries (Except Internet) (26.9%); Administrative and Support Services (26.8%); Internet Service Providers, Web Search Portals, and Data Processing Services (22.4%); Merchant Wholesalers, Durable Goods (16.7%); Management of Companies and Enterprises (15.3%).

Other Considerations for Job Outlook: As computer and chip manufacturers contract out more of their engineering needs to both domestic and foreign design firms, much of the growth in employment of hardware engineers is expected in the computer systems design and related services industry.

Research, design, develop, and test computer or computer-related equipment for commercial, industrial, military, or scientific use. May supervise the manufacturing and installation of computer or computer-related equipment and components. Update knowledge and skills to keep up with rapid advancements in computer technology. Provide technical support to designers, marketing and sales departments, suppliers, engineers, and other team members throughout the product development and implementation process. Test and verify hardware and support peripherals to ensure that they meet specifications and requirements, analyzing and recording test data. Monitor functioning of equipment and make necessary modifications to ensure system operates in conformance with specifications. Analyze information to determine, recommend, and plan layout, including type of computers and peripheral equipment modifications. Build, test, and modify product prototypes, using working models or theoretical models constructed using computer simulation. Analyze user needs and recommend appropriate hardware. Direct technicians, engineering designers, or other technical support personnel as needed. Confer with engineering staff and consult specifications to evaluate interface between hardware and software and operational and performance requirements of overall system. Select hardware and material, assuring compliance with specifications and product requirements. Store, retrieve, and manipulate data for analysis of system capabilities and requirements. Write detailed functional specifications that document the hardware development process and support hardware introduction. Specify power supply requirements and configuration, drawing on system performance expectations and design specifications. Provide training and support to system designers and users. Assemble and modify existing pieces of equipment to meet special needs. Evaluate factors such as reporting formats required, cost constraints, and need for security restrictions to determine hardware configuration. Design and develop computer hardware and support peripherals, including central processing units (CPUs), support logic, microprocessors, custom integrated circuits, and printers and disk drives. Recommend purchase of equipment to control dust, temperature, and humidity in area of system installation.

Personality Type: Investigative-Realistic-Conventional.

Career Clusters: 11 Information Technology; 15 Science, Technology, Engineering, and Mathematics. **Career Pathways:** 11.4 Programming and Software Development; 15.1 Engineering and Technology.

Skills: Programming; Operations Analysis; Systems Analysis; Systems Evaluation; Troubleshooting; Technology Design.

Education and Training Programs: Computer Engineering, General; Computer Hardware Engineering. **Related Knowledge/Courses:** Computers and Electronics; Engineering and Technology; Telecommunications; Design; Physics; Communications and Media.

Work Environment: Indoors; sitting.

Computer Science Teachers, Postsecondary

- ❋ Education/Training Required: Master's degree
- ❋ Annual Earnings: $62,020
- ❋ Beginning Wage: $33,720
- ❋ Earnings Growth Potential: High (45.6%)
- ❋ Growth: 22.9%
- ❋ Annual Job Openings: 5,820
- ❋ Job Security: Most Secure
- ❋ Self-Employed: 0.4%
- ❋ Part-Time: 27.8%

Renewal Industry: Education.

Industries with Greatest Employment: Educational Services, Public and Private (97.3%).

Highest-Growth Industries (Projected Growth for This Job): Administrative and Support Services (48.3%); Amusement, Gambling, and Recreation Industries (45.2%); Social Assistance (38.6%); Support Activities for Transportation (32.8%); Religious, Grantmaking, Civic, Professional, and Similar Organizations (29.9%); Professional, Scientific, and Technical Services (28.8%); Management of Companies and Enterprises (26.8%); Local Government (23.5%); Educational Services, Public and Private (22.8%); Hospitals, Public and Private (21.4%).

Other Considerations for Job Outlook: Retirements of current postsecondary teachers should create numerous openings for all types of postsecondary teachers, so job opportunities are generally expected to be very good. However, one of the main reasons why students attend postsecondary institutions is to prepare themselves for careers, so the best job prospects for postsecondary teachers are likely to be in rapidly growing fields that offer many non-academic career options. Computer science courses are commonly required as part of many business, science, and technology majors. Community colleges and other institutions offering career and technical education have been among the most rapidly growing, and these institutions are expected to offer some of the best opportunities for postsecondary teachers.

Teach courses in computer science. May specialize in a field of computer science, such as the design and function of computers or operations and research analysis. Evaluate and grade students' classwork, laboratory work, assignments, and papers. Maintain student attendance records, grades, and other required records. Prepare and deliver lectures to undergraduate and/or graduate students on topics such as programming, data structures, and software design. Prepare course materials such as syllabi, homework assignments, and handouts. Compile, administer, and grade examinations or assign this work to others. Keep abreast of developments in their field by reading current literature, talking with colleagues, and participating in professional conferences. Initiate, facilitate, and moderate classroom discussions. Plan, evaluate, and revise curricula, course content, and course materials and methods of instruction. Supervise students' laboratory work.

Maintain regularly scheduled office hours to advise and assist students. Select and obtain materials and supplies such as textbooks and laboratory equipment. Advise students on academic and vocational curricula and on career issues. Participate in student recruitment, registration, and placement activities. Collaborate with colleagues to address teaching and research issues. Serve on academic or administrative committees that deal with institutional policies, departmental matters, and academic issues. Act as advisers to student organizations. Supervise undergraduate and/or graduate teaching, internship, and research work. Perform administrative duties such as serving as department head. Conduct research in a particular field of knowledge and publish findings in professional journals, books, and/or electronic media. Direct research of other teachers or of graduate students working for advanced academic degrees. Provide professional consulting services to government and/or industry. Participate in campus and community events. Compile bibliographies of specialized materials for outside reading assignments. Write grant proposals to procure external research funding.

Personality Type: Social-Investigative-Conventional.

Career Cluster: 11 Information Technology. **Career Pathways:** 11.1 Network Systems; 11.2 Information Support Services; 11.4 Programming and Software Development.

Skills: Programming; Instructing; Operations Analysis; Technology Design; Science; Mathematics.

Education and Training Programs: Computer and Information Sciences, General; Computer Programming/Programmer, General; Information Science/Studies; Computer Systems Analysis/Analyst; Computer Science. **Related Knowledge/Courses:** Computers and Electronics; Education and Training; Telecommunications; Mathematics; Engineering and Technology; English Language.

Work Environment: Indoors; sitting.

Computer Security Specialists

- ❋ Education/Training Required: Bachelor's degree
- ❋ Annual Earnings: $64,690
- ❋ Beginning Wage: $39,970
- ❋ Earnings Growth Potential: Medium (38.2%)
- ❋ Growth: 27.0%
- ❋ Annual Job Openings: 37,010
- ❋ Job Security: More Secure than Most
- ❋ Self-Employed: 0.4%
- ❋ Part-Time: 3.1%

Our sources did not provide separate job openings data for this occupation. The job openings listed here are shared with Network and Computer Systems Administrators.

Renewal Industry: Information and Telecommunication Technologies.

Industries with Greatest Employment: Professional, Scientific, and Technical Services (25.0%); Educational Services, Public and Private (10.0%); Management of Companies and Enterprises (6.0%).

Highest-Growth Industries (Projected Growth for This Job): Amusement, Gambling, and Recreation Industries (66.1%); Social Assistance (58.3%); Securities, Commodity Contracts, and Other Financial Investments and Related Activities (58.2%); Internet Publishing and Broadcasting (54.3%); Museums, Historical Sites, and Similar Institutions (49.6%); Professional, Scientific, and Technical Services (47.2%); Warehousing and Storage (46.9%); Personal and Laundry Services (40.4%); Lessors of Nonfinancial Intangible Assets (Except Copyrighted Works) (40.1%); Building Material and Garden Equipment and Supplies Dealers (39.8%); Waste Management and Remediation Services (39.7%); Administrative and Support Services (39.0%); Ambulatory Health-Care Services (38.7%); Performing Arts, Spectator Sports, and Related Industries (38.0%); Nursing and Residential Care Facilities (37.4%); Support Activities for Transportation (34.5%); Water Transportation (33.7%); Real Estate (32.9%); Nonstore Retailers (31.7%); Religious, Grantmaking, Civic, Professional, and Similar Organizations (30.4%); Publishing Industries (Except Internet) (28.8%); Accommodation, Including Hotels and Motels (27.8%); Motion Picture, Video, and Sound Recording Industries (27.7%); Rental and Leasing Services (27.5%); General Merchandise Stores (26.9%); Broadcasting (Except Internet) (26.8%); Management of Companies and Enterprises (26.8%); Merchant Wholesalers, Durable Goods (26.1%); Transit and Ground Passenger Transportation (25.4%); Motor Vehicle and Parts Dealers (24.9%); Wholesale Electronic Markets and Agents and Brokers (24.8%); Truck Transportation (24.3%); Construction of Buildings (23.6%); Local Government (23.6%); Food Services and Drinking Places (21.9%); Air Transportation (21.6%); Chemical Manufacturing (21.6%); Hospitals, Public and Private (21.3%); Internet Service Providers, Web Search Portals, and Data Processing Services (21.2%); Educational Services, Public and Private (21.0%); Couriers and Messengers (19.1%); Credit Intermediation and Related Activities (19.0%); Food and Beverage Stores (18.8%); Specialty Trade Contractors (18.2%); Insurance Carriers and Related Activities (18.0%); Health and Personal Care Stores (17.8%); Furniture and Home Furnishings Stores (16.5%); Mining (Except Oil and Gas) (15.7%); Merchant Wholesalers, Nondurable Goods (15.5%).

Other Considerations for Job Outlook: Strong employment growth combined with a limited supply of qualified workers will result in excellent employment prospects for this occupation and a high demand for their skills. Demand for computer security specialists will grow as businesses and government continue to invest heavily in "cyber security," protecting vital computer networks and electronic infrastructures from attack. Job prospects should be best for college graduates who possess the latest technological skills, particularly graduates who have supplemented their formal education with relevant work experience. Employers will continue to seek computer specialists who possess strong fundamental computer skills combined with good interpersonal and communication skills. Due to the demand for computer support specialists and systems administrators over the next decade, those who have strong computer skills but do not have a college degree should continue to qualify for some entry-level positions.

Plan, coordinate, and implement security measures for information systems to regulate access to computer data files and prevent unauthorized modification, destruction, or disclosure of information. Train users and promote security awareness to ensure system security and to improve server and network efficiency. Develop plans to safeguard computer files against accidental or unauthorized modification, destruction, or disclosure and to meet emergency data processing needs. Confer with users to discuss issues such as computer data access needs, security violations, and programming changes. Monitor current reports of computer viruses to determine when to update virus protection systems. Modify computer security files to incorporate new software, correct errors, or change individual access status. Coordinate implementation of computer system plan with establishment personnel and outside vendors. Monitor use of data files and regulate access to safeguard information in computer files. Perform risk assessments and execute tests of data-processing system to ensure functioning of data-processing activities and security measures. Encrypt data transmissions and erect firewalls to conceal confidential information as it is being transmitted and to keep out tainted digital transfers. Document computer security and emergency measures policies, procedures, and tests. Review violations of computer security procedures and discuss procedures with violators to ensure violations are not repeated. Maintain permanent fleet cryptologic and carry-on direct support systems required in special land, sea surface, and subsurface operations.

Personality Type: Conventional-Investigative-Realistic.

Career Cluster: 11 Information Technology. **Career Pathway:** 11.4 Programming and Software Development.

Skills: Systems Evaluation; Systems Analysis; Operations Analysis; Programming; Installation; Management of Material Resources.

Education and Training Programs: Computer and Information Sciences, General; Information Science/Studies; Computer Systems Analysis/Analyst; Computer Systems Networking and Telecommunications; System Administration/Administrator; System, Networking, and LAN/WAN Management/Manager; Computer and Information Systems Security; Computer and Information Sciences and Support Services, Other. **Related Knowledge/Courses:** Computers and Electronics; Telecommunications; Engineering and Technology; Design; Education and Training; Therapy and Counseling.

Work Environment: Indoors; sitting.

Computer Software Engineers, Applications

- ❋ Education/Training Required: Bachelor's degree
- ❋ Annual Earnings: $83,130
- ❋ Beginning Wage: $52,090
- ❋ Earnings Growth Potential: Medium (37.3%)
- ❋ Growth: 44.6%
- ❋ Annual Job Openings: 58,690
- ❋ Job Security: More Secure than Most
- ❋ Self-Employed: 2.0%
- ❋ Part-Time: 2.6%

Renewal Industry: Information and Telecommunication Technologies.

Industries with Greatest Employment: Professional, Scientific, and Technical Services (40.0%); Publishing Industries (Except Internet) (8.2%); Computer and Electronic Product Manufacturing (7.6%).

Highest-Growth Industries (Projected Growth for This Job): Social Assistance (68.7%); Internet Publishing and Broadcasting (68.4%); Museums, Historical Sites, and Similar Institutions (63.3%); Professional, Scientific, and Technical Services (63.3%); Warehousing and Storage (60.3%); Personal and Laundry Services (54.7%); Administrative and Support Services (53.7%); Lessors of Nonfinancial Intangible Assets (Except Copyrighted Works) (53.1%); Waste Management and Remediation Services (52.8%); Funds, Trusts, and Other Financial Vehicles (51.4%); Publishing Industries (Except Internet) (50.8%); Nonstore Retailers (50.0%); Ambulatory Health-Care Services (48.9%); Support Activities for Transportation (46.8%); Real Estate (44.8%); Rental and Leasing Services (44.6%); Religious, Grantmaking, Civic, Professional, and Similar Organizations (41.9%); Motion Picture, Video, and Sound Recording Industries (40.9%); Merchant Wholesalers, Durable Goods (39.2%); Management of Companies and Enterprises (38.3%); Wholesale Electronic Markets and Agents and Brokers (36.2%); Broadcasting (Except Internet) (35.9%); Truck Transportation (35.8%); Internet Service Providers, Web Search Portals, and Data Processing Services (35.6%); Credit Intermediation and Related Activities (35.3%); Educational Services, Public and Private (35.1%); Local Government (34.8%); Hospitals, Public and Private

(34.6%); Chemical Manufacturing (34.5%); Construction of Buildings (34.5%); Merchant Wholesalers, Nondurable Goods (33.1%); Health and Personal Care Stores (29.8%); Couriers and Messengers (29.1%); Specialty Trade Contractors (27.7%); Heavy and Civil Engineering Construction (26.1%); Motor Vehicle and Parts Dealers (25.5%); Telecommunications (21.3%); Transportation Equipment Manufacturing (20.6%); Plastics and Rubber Products Manufacturing (20.6%); Food Manufacturing (20.0%); State Government (17.8%); Other Information Services (17.4%); Miscellaneous Manufacturing (16.9%).

Other Considerations for Job Outlook: Very good opportunities are expected for college graduates with at least a bachelor's degree in computer engineering or computer science and with practical work experience.

Develop, create, and modify general computer applications software or specialized utility programs. Analyze user needs and develop software solutions. Design software or customize software for client use with the aim of optimizing operational efficiency. May analyze and design databases within an application area, working individually or coordinating database development as part of a team. Confer with systems analysts, engineers, programmers, and others to design system and to obtain information on project limitations and capabilities, performance requirements, and interfaces. Modify existing software to correct errors, allow it to adapt to new hardware, or improve its performance. Analyze user needs and software requirements to determine feasibility of design within time and cost constraints. Consult with customers about software system design and maintenance. Coordinate software system installation and monitor equipment functioning to ensure specifications are met. Design, develop, and modify software systems, using scientific analysis and mathematical models to predict and measure outcome and consequences of design. Develop and direct software system testing and validation procedures, programming, and documentation. Analyze information to determine, recommend, and plan computer specifications and layouts and peripheral equipment modifications. Supervise the work of programmers, technologists, and technicians and other engineering and scientific personnel. Obtain and evaluate information on factors such as reporting formats required, costs, and security needs to determine hardware configuration. Determine system performance standards. Train users to use new or modified equipment. Store, retrieve, and manipulate data

for analysis of system capabilities and requirements. Specify power supply requirements and configuration. Recommend purchase of equipment to control dust, temperature, and humidity in area of system installation.

Personality Type: Investigative-Realistic-Conventional.

Career Clusters: 08 Health Science; 11 Information Technology; 13 Manufacturing; 15 Science, Technology, Engineering, and Mathematics. **Career Pathways:** 08.3 Health Informatics; 11.1 Network Systems; 11.2 Information Support Services; 11.3 Interactive Media; 11.4 Programming and Software Development; 13.3 Maintenance, Installation, and Repair; 15.3 Science and Mathematics.

Skills: Programming; Troubleshooting; Technology Design; Systems Analysis; Quality Control Analysis; Operations Analysis.

Education and Training Programs: Artificial Intelligence and Robotics; Information Technology; Computer Science; Computer Engineering, General; Computer Software Engineering; Computer Engineering Technologies/Technicians, Other; Bioinformatics; Medical Informatics; Medical Illustration and Informatics, Other. **Related Knowledge/Courses:** Computers and Electronics; Telecommunications; Engineering and Technology; Design; Mathematics; Physics.

Work Environment: Indoors; sitting; using hands on objects, tools, or controls; repetitive motions.

Computer Software Engineers, Systems Software

- ❋ Education/Training Required: Bachelor's degree
- ❋ Annual Earnings: $89,070
- ❋ Beginning Wage: $55,870
- ❋ Earnings Growth Potential: Medium (37.3%)
- ❋ Growth: 28.2%
- ❋ Annual Job Openings: 33,139
- ❋ Job Security: More Secure than Most
- ❋ Self-Employed: 2.1%
- ❋ Part-Time: 2.6%

Renewal Industry: Information and Telecommunication Technologies.

Industries with Greatest Employment: Professional, Scientific, and Technical Services (38.5%); Computer and Electronic Product Manufacturing (13.1%); Internet Service Providers, Web Search Portals, and Data Processing Services (6.8%); Publishing Industries (Except Internet) (6.6%).

Highest-Growth Industries (Projected Growth for This Job): Securities, Commodity Contracts, and Other Financial Investments and Related Activities (61.7%); Internet Publishing and Broadcasting (54.3%); Professional, Scientific, and Technical Services (47.5%); Warehousing and Storage (46.7%); Funds, Trusts, and Other Financial Vehicles (42.1%); Ambulatory Health-Care Services (41.5%); Publishing Industries (Except Internet) (39.3%); Support Activities for Transportation (33.6%); Nonstore Retailers (33.0%); Religious, Grantmaking, Civic, Professional, and Similar Organizations (32.6%); Broadcasting (Except Internet) (29.0%); Merchant Wholesalers, Durable Goods (27.4%); Management of Companies and Enterprises (26.8%); Internet Service Providers, Web Search Portals, and Data Processing Services (26.8%); Chemical Manufacturing (26.1%); Motion Picture, Video, and Sound Recording Industries (25.6%); Wholesale Electronic Markets and Agents and Brokers (24.8%); Local Government (23.5%); Educational Services, Public and Private (22.4%); Merchant Wholesalers, Nondurable Goods (21.8%); Hospitals, Public and Private (21.8%); Credit Intermediation and Related Activities (17.8%); Specialty Trade Contractors (17.3%); Insurance Carriers and Related Activities (15.4%).

Other Considerations for Job Outlook: Computer software engineers must continually strive to acquire new skills in conjunction with the rapid changes that are occurring in computer technology.

Research, design, develop, and test operating systems-level software, compilers, and network distribution software for medical, industrial, military, communications, aerospace, business, scientific, and general computing applications. Set operational specifications and formulate and analyze software requirements. Apply principles and techniques of computer science, engineering, and mathematical analysis. Modify existing software to correct errors, to adapt it to new hardware, or to upgrade interfaces and improve performance. Design and develop software systems, using scientific analysis and mathematical models to predict and measure outcome and consequences of design. Consult with engineering staff to evaluate interface between hardware and software, develop specifications and performance requirements, and resolve customer problems. Analyze information to determine, recommend, and plan installation of a new system or modification of an existing system. Develop and direct software system testing and validation procedures. Direct software programming and development of documentation. Consult with customers or other departments on project status, proposals, and technical issues such as software system design and maintenance. Advise customer about, or perform, maintenance of software system. Coordinate installation of software system. Monitor functioning of equipment to ensure system operates in conformance with specifications. Store, retrieve, and manipulate data for analysis of system capabilities and requirements. Confer with data processing and project managers to obtain information on limitations and capabilities for data-processing projects. Prepare reports and correspondence concerning project specifications, activities, and status. Evaluate factors such as reporting formats required, cost constraints, and need for security restrictions to determine hardware configuration. Supervise and assign work to programmers, designers, technologists and technicians, and other engineering and scientific personnel. Train users to use new or modified equipment. Utilize microcontrollers to develop control signals; implement control algorithms; and measure process variables such as temperatures, pressures, and positions. Recommend purchase of equipment to control dust, temperature, and humidity in area of system installation. Specify power supply requirements and configuration.

Personality Type: Investigative-Conventional-Realistic.

Career Clusters: 02 Architecture and Construction; 11 Information Technology. **Career Pathways:** 02.1 Design/Pre-Construction; 11.1 Network Systems; 11.2 Information Support Services; 11.3 Interactive Media; 11.4 Programming and Software Development.

Skills: Programming; Technology Design; Systems Analysis; Troubleshooting; Operations Analysis; Complex Problem Solving.

Education and Training Programs: Artificial Intelligence and Robotics; Information Technology; Information Science/Studies; Computer Science; System, Networking, and LAN/WAN Management/Manager; Computer Engineering, General; Computer Engineering Technologies/

Technicians, Other. **Related Knowledge/Courses:** Computers and Electronics; Design; Engineering and Technology; Telecommunications; Mathematics; Communications and Media.

Work Environment: Indoors; sitting; using hands on objects, tools, or controls; repetitive motions.

Computer Specialists, All Other

See *Computer Systems Engineers/Architects*, *Network Designers*, *Software Quality Assurance Engineers and Testers*, *Web Administrators*, and *Web Developers*, *described separately*.

Computer Support Specialists

- ❋ Education/Training Required: Associate degree
- ❋ Annual Earnings: $42,400
- ❋ Beginning Wage: $25,950
- ❋ Earnings Growth Potential: Medium (38.8%)
- ❋ Growth: 12.9%
- ❋ Annual Job Openings: 97,334
- ❋ Job Security: More Secure than Most
- ❋ Self-Employed: 1.3%
- ❋ Part-Time: 6.9%

Renewal Industry: Information and Telecommunication Technologies.

Industries with Greatest Employment: Professional, Scientific, and Technical Services (22.5%); Educational Services, Public and Private (13.1%); Administrative and Support Services (6.2%).

Highest-Growth Industries (Projected Growth for This Job): Amusement, Gambling, and Recreation Industries (45.5%); Securities, Commodity Contracts, and Other Financial Investments and Related Activities (42.8%); Social Assistance (41.1%); Internet Publishing and Broadcasting (40.4%); Museums, Historical Sites, and Similar Institutions (36.2%); Funds, Trusts, and Other Financial Vehicles (34.1%); Warehousing and Storage (33.6%); Waste Management and Remediation Services (28.4%); Lessors of Nonfinancial Intangible Assets (Except Copyrighted Works) (27.6%); General Merchandise Stores (27.2%); Ambulatory Health-Care Services (25.9%); Professional, Scientific, and Technical Services (25.4%); Support Activities for Transportation (23.8%); Administrative and Support Services (22.7%); Nursing and Residential Care Facilities (22.5%); Personal and Laundry Services (22.0%); Nonstore Retailers (21.2%); Real Estate (21.2%); Water Transportation (19.5%); Performing Arts, Spectator Sports, and Related Industries (18.7%); Religious, Grantmaking, Civic, Professional, and Similar Organizations (18.0%); Rental and Leasing Services (17.5%); Broadcasting (Except Internet) (17.1%); Accommodation, Including Hotels and Motels (16.9%); Motion Picture, Video, and Sound Recording Industries (16.3%); Management of Companies and Enterprises (15.3%).

Other Considerations for Job Outlook: Job prospects should be best for college graduates who are up to date with the latest skills and technologies; certifications and practical experience are essential for persons without degrees.

Provide technical assistance to computer system users. Answer questions or resolve computer problems for clients in person, via telephone, or from remote locations. May provide assistance concerning the use of computer hardware and software, including printing, installation, word processing, e-mail, and operating systems. Oversee the daily performance of computer systems. Answer user inquiries regarding computer software or hardware operation to resolve problems. Enter commands and observe system functioning to verify correct operations and detect errors. Set up equipment for employee use, performing or ensuring proper installation of cables, operating systems, or appropriate software. Install and perform minor repairs to hardware, software, or peripheral equipment, following design or installation specifications. Maintain records of daily data communication transactions, problems and remedial actions taken, or installation activities. Read technical manuals, confer with users, or conduct computer diagnostics to investigate and resolve problems or to provide technical assistance and support. Refer major hardware or software problems or defective products to vendors or technicians for service. Develop training materials and procedures or train users in the proper use of hardware or software. Confer with staff, users, and management to establish requirements for new systems or modifications. Prepare evaluations of software or hardware and recommend improvements or upgrades. Read trade magazines and technical manuals or attend conferences and seminars to maintain knowledge of hardware and software. Hire, supervise, and direct workers engaged in special project work, problem solving, monitoring, and installing data communication equipment and software. Inspect equipment and read order sheets to prepare for delivery to users. Modify and customize commercial programs for internal needs. Conduct office automation feasibility studies, including workflow analysis, space design, or cost comparison analysis.

Personality Type: Realistic-Investigative-Conventional.

Career Clusters: 01 Agriculture, Food, and Natural Resources; 08 Health Science; 11 Information Technology; 13 Manufacturing; 15 Science, Technology, Engineering, and Mathematics. **Career Pathways:** 01.1 Food Products and Processing Systems; 08.3 Health Informatics; 11.2 Information Support Services; 13.3 Maintenance, Installation, and Repair; 15.3 Science and Mathematics.

Skills: Programming; Installation; Systems Analysis; Operation Monitoring; Repairing; Systems Evaluation.

Education and Training Programs: Agricultural Business Technology; Data Processing and Data Processing Technology/Technician; Computer Hardware Technology/Technician; Computer Software Technology/Technician; Accounting and Computer Science; Medical Office Computer Specialist/Assistant. **Related Knowledge/Courses:** Computers and Electronics; Telecommunications; Engineering and Technology; Clerical Practices; Customer and Personal Service; Communications and Media.

Work Environment: Indoors; sitting; using hands on objects, tools, or controls.

Computer Systems Analysts

- ❋ Education/Training Required: Bachelor's degree
- ❋ Annual Earnings: $73,090
- ❋ Beginning Wage: $43,930
- ❋ Earnings Growth Potential: Medium (39.9%)
- ❋ Growth: 29.0%
- ❋ Annual Job Openings: 63,166
- ❋ Job Security: More Secure than Most
- ❋ Self-Employed: 5.8%
- ❋ Part-Time: 5.6%

Renewal Industry: Information and Telecommunication Technologies.

Industries with Greatest Employment: Professional, Scientific, and Technical Services (29.3%); Management of Companies and Enterprises (7.3%); Insurance Carriers and Related Activities (6.6%).

Highest-Growth Industries (Projected Growth for This Job): Amusement, Gambling, and Recreation Industries (63.0%); Social Assistance (60.3%); Securities, Commodity Contracts, and Other Financial Investments and Related Activities (58.4%); Internet Publishing and Broadcasting (54.3%); Museums, Historical Sites, and Similar Institutions (51.0%); Professional, Scientific, and Technical Services (49.6%); Warehousing and Storage (46.9%); Personal and Laundry Services (44.0%); Waste Management and Remediation Services (42.6%); Funds, Trusts, and Other Financial Vehicles (40.3%); Lessors of Nonfinancial Intangible Assets (Except Copyrighted Works) (40.1%); Administrative and Support Services (38.6%); Ambulatory Health-Care Services (38.0%); Nonstore Retailers (36.5%); Internet Service Providers, Web Search Portals, and Data Processing Services (36.3%); Support Activities for Transportation (35.4%); Publishing Industries (Except Internet) (34.7%); Nursing and Residential Care Facilities (32.7%); Real Estate (31.2%); Performing Arts, Spectator Sports, and Related Industries (31.1%); Religious, Grantmaking, Civic, Professional, and Similar Organizations (30.3%); Motion Picture, Video, and Sound Recording Industries (29.9%); Rental and Leasing Services (29.0%); Accommodation, Including Hotels and Motels (28.8%); Broadcasting (Except Internet) (28.7%); Merchant Wholesalers, Durable Goods (27.5%); Management of Companies and Enterprises (26.8%); Wholesale Electronic Markets and Agents and Brokers (24.8%); Truck Transportation (24.5%); Food Services and Drinking Places (24.4%); Educational Services, Public and Private (23.9%); Local Government (23.6%); Construction of Buildings (23.4%); Hospitals, Public and Private (22.5%); Air Transportation (21.6%); Chemical Manufacturing (21.5%); Health and Personal Care Stores (20.0%); Credit Intermediation and Related Activities (19.5%); Food and Beverage Stores (19.4%); Couriers and Messengers (18.5%); Specialty Trade Contractors (17.0%); Mining (Except Oil and Gas) (16.0%); Insurance Carriers and Related Activities (15.5%); Merchant Wholesalers, Nondurable Goods (15.4%).

Other Considerations for Job Outlook: Job prospects should be very good. Job growth will not be as rapid as during the preceding decade, however, as the information technology sector matures and as routine work is increasingly outsourced offshore to foreign countries with lower prevailing wages. Individuals with an advanced degree in computer science or computer engineering or with an MBA with a concentration in information systems should have the best prospects. College graduates with a bachelor's degree in computer science, computer engineering, information science, or management information systems also should enjoy very good prospects, particularly if they have supplemented their formal education with practical experience.

Analyze science, engineering, business, and all other data-processing problems for application to electronic data processing systems. Analyze user requirements, procedures, and problems to automate or improve existing systems and review computer system capabilities, workflow, and scheduling limitations. May analyze or recommend commercially available software. May supervise computer programmers. Provide staff and users with assistance solving computer-related problems, such as malfunctions and program problems. Test, maintain, and monitor computer programs and systems, including coordinating the installation of computer programs and systems. Use object-oriented programming languages as well as client and server applications development processes and multimedia and Internet technology. Confer with clients regarding the nature of the information processing or computation needs a computer program is to address. Coordinate and link the computer systems within an organization to increase compatibility and so information can be shared. Consult with management to ensure agreement on system principles. Expand or modify system to serve new purposes or improve workflow. Interview or survey workers, observe job performance, or perform the job to determine what information is processed and how it is processed. Determine computer software or hardware needed to set up or alter system. Train staff and users to work with computer systems and programs. Analyze information processing or computation needs and plan and design computer systems, using techniques such as structured analysis, data modeling, and information engineering. Assess the usefulness of pre-developed application packages and adapt them to a user environment. Define the goals of the system and devise flow charts and diagrams describing logical operational steps of programs. Develop, document, and revise system design procedures, test procedures, and quality standards. Review and analyze computer printouts and performance indicators to locate code problems; correct errors by correcting codes. Recommend new equipment or software packages. Read manuals, periodicals, and technical reports to learn how to develop programs that meet staff and user requirements. Supervise computer programmers or other systems analysts or serve as project leaders for particular systems projects. Utilize the computer in the analysis and solution of business problems such as development of integrated production and inventory control and cost analysis systems.

Personality Type: Investigative-Conventional-Realistic.

Career Cluster: 11 Information Technology. **Career Pathways:** 11.2 Information Support Services; 11.3 Interactive Media; 11.4 Programming and Software Development.

Skills: Installation; Quality Control Analysis; Technology Design; Programming; Systems Analysis; Troubleshooting.

Education and Training Programs: Computer and Information Sciences, General; Information Technology; Computer Systems Analysis/Analyst; Web/Multimedia Management and Webmaster. **Related Knowledge/Courses:** Computers and Electronics; Telecommunications; Design; Customer and Personal Service; Law and Government; Communications and Media.

Work Environment: Indoors; sitting.

Computer Systems Engineers/ Architects

- ❀ Education/Training Required: No data available.
- ❀ Annual Earnings: $71,510
- ❀ Beginning Wage: $37,600
- ❀ Earnings Growth Potential: High (47.4%)
- ❀ Growth: 15.1%
- ❀ Annual Job Openings: 14,374
- ❀ Job Security: More Secure than Most
- ❀ Self-Employed: 6.6%
- ❀ Part-Time: 5.6%

Our sources did not provide separate job openings data for this occupation. The job openings listed here are shared with Network Designers, Software Quality Assurance Engineers and Testers, Web Administrators, and Web Developers.

Renewal Industry: Information and Telecommunication Technologies.

Industries with Greatest Employment: Professional, Scientific, and Technical Services (22.9%); Educational Services, Public and Private (10.0%); Management of Companies and Enterprises (8.0%); State Government (5.5%).

Highest-Growth Industries (Projected Growth for This Job): Amusement, Gambling, and Recreation Industries (53.3%); Securities, Commodity Contracts, and Other Financial Investments and Related Activities (46.9%); Social Assistance (44.2%); Internet Publishing and Broadcasting (40.3%); Warehousing and Storage (33.3%); Professional, Scientific, and Technical Services (31.4%); Real Estate (25.8%); General Merchandise Stores (25.0%); Nursing and Residential Care Facilities (24.8%); Ambulatory Health-Care Services (24.7%); Building Material and Garden Equipment and Supplies Dealers (24.2%); Publishing Industries (Except Internet) (21.7%); Nonstore Retailers (21.4%); Religious, Grantmaking, Civic, Professional, and Similar Organizations (19.6%); Chemical Manufacturing (19.0%); Merchant Wholesalers, Durable Goods (15.9%); Management of Companies and Enterprises (15.3%).

Other Considerations for Job Outlook: Individuals with an advanced degree in computer science or computer engineering or with an MBA with a concentration in information systems should enjoy favorable employment prospects. College graduates with a bachelor's degree in computer science, computer engineering, information science, or MIS also should enjoy favorable prospects, particularly if they have supplemented their formal education with practical experience. Because employers continue to seek computer specialists who can combine strong technical skills with good business skills, individuals with a combination of experience inside and outside the IT arena will have the best job prospects.

Design and develop solutions to complex applications problems, system administration issues, or network concerns. Perform systems management and integration functions. Communicate with staff or clients to understand specific system requirements. Provide advice on project costs, design concepts, or design changes. Document design specifications, installation instructions, and other system-related information. Verify stability, interoperability, portability, security, or scalability of system architecture. Collaborate with engineers or software developers to select appropriate design solutions or ensure the compatibility of system components. Provide technical guidance or support for the development or troubleshooting of systems. Evaluate current or emerging technologies to consider factors such as cost, portability, compatibility, or usability. Identify system data, hardware, or software components required to meet user needs. Provide guidelines for implementing secure systems to customers or installation teams. Monitor system operation to detect potential problems. Direct the analysis, development, and operation of complete computer systems. Investigate system component suitability for specified purposes and make recommendations regarding component use. Perform ongoing hardware and software maintenance operations, including installing or upgrading hardware or software. Develop or approve project plans, schedules, or budgets. Configure servers to meet functional specifications. Design and conduct hardware or software tests. Define and analyze objectives, scope, issues, or organizational impact of information systems. Develop system engineering, software engineering, system integration, or distributed system architectures. Establish functional or system standards to ensure operational requirements, quality requirements, and design constraints are addressed. Evaluate existing systems to determine effectiveness and suggest changes to meet organizational requirements. Research, test, or verify proper functioning of software patches and fixes. Communicate project information through presentations, technical reports, or white papers. Complete models and simulations, using manual or automated tools, to analyze or predict system performance under different operating conditions.

Personality Type: Investigative-Realistic-Conventional.

Career Cluster: 11 Information Technology. **Career Pathway:** 11.2 Programming and Software Development.

Skills: Programming; Systems Evaluation; Technology Design; Systems Analysis; Troubleshooting; Operations Analysis.

Education and Training Programs: Computer Engineering, General; Computer Software Engineering. **Related**

Knowledge/Courses: Computers and Electronics; Engineering and Technology; Telecommunications; Design; Mathematics; Sales and Marketing.

Work Environment: Indoors; sitting; repetitive motions.

Construction and Building Inspectors

- ❋ Education/Training Required: Work experience in a related occupation
- ❋ Annual Earnings: $48,330
- ❋ Beginning Wage: $30,450
- ❋ Earnings Growth Potential: Medium (37.0%)
- ❋ Growth: 18.2%
- ❋ Annual Job Openings: 12,606
- ❋ Job Security: More Secure than Most
- ❋ Self-Employed: 9.4%
- ❋ Part-Time: 4.6%

Renewal Industries: Green Technologies; Infrastructure.

Industries with Greatest Employment: Local Government (41.4%); Professional, Scientific, and Technical Services (28.8%); State Government (8.0%).

Highest-Growth Industries (Projected Growth for This Job): Professional, Scientific, and Technical Services (40.5%); Social Assistance (36.4%); Waste Management and Remediation Services (31.9%); Administrative and Support Services (24.1%); Real Estate (22.6%); Religious, Grantmaking, Civic, Professional, and Similar Organizations (15.7%); Management of Companies and Enterprises (15.3%).

Other Considerations for Job Outlook: Opportunities should be best for experienced construction supervisors and craftworkers who have some college education, engineering or architectural training, or certification as construction inspectors or plan examiners.

Inspect structures using engineering skills to determine structural soundness and compliance with specifications, building codes, and other regulations. Inspections may be general in nature or may be limited to a specific area, such as electrical systems or plumbing. Issue violation notices and stop-work orders, conferring with owners, violators, and authorities to explain regulations and recommend rectifications. Inspect bridges, dams, highways, buildings, wiring, plumbing, electrical circuits, sewers, heating systems, and foundations during and after construction for structural quality, general safety, and conformance to specifications and codes. Approve and sign plans that meet required specifications. Review and interpret plans, blueprints, site layouts, specifications, and construction methods to ensure compliance to legal requirements and safety regulations. Monitor installation of plumbing, wiring, equipment, and appliances to ensure that installation is performed properly and is in compliance with applicable regulations. Inspect and monitor construction sites to ensure adherence to safety standards, building codes, and specifications. Measure dimensions and verify level, alignment, and elevation of structures and fixtures to ensure compliance to building plans and codes. Maintain daily logs and supplement inspection records with photographs. Use survey instruments, metering devices, tape measures, and test equipment such as concrete strength measurers to perform inspections. Train, direct, and supervise other construction inspectors. Issue permits for construction, relocation, demolition, and occupancy. Examine lifting and conveying devices such as elevators, escalators, moving sidewalks, lifts and hoists, inclined railways, ski lifts, and amusement rides to ensure safety and proper functioning. Compute estimates of work completed or of needed renovations or upgrades and approve payment for contractors. Evaluate premises for cleanliness, including proper garbage disposal and lack of vermin infestation.

Personality Type: Realistic-Conventional-Investigative.

Career Cluster: 02 Architecture and Construction. **Career Pathway:** 02.2 Construction.

Skills: No data available.

Education and Training Program: Building/Home/Construction Inspection/Inspector. **Related Knowledge/Courses:** Building and Construction; Engineering and Technology; Design; Physics; Public Safety and Security; Mechanical Devices.

Work Environment: More often outdoors than indoors; very hot or cold; very bright or dim lighting; contaminants; cramped work space, awkward positions.

Construction Carpenters

- ❋ Education/Training Required: Long-term on-the-job training
- ❋ Annual Earnings: $37,660
- ❋ Beginning Wage: $23,370
- ❋ Earnings Growth Potential: Medium (37.9%)
- ❋ Growth: 10.3%
- ❋ Annual Job Openings: 223,225
- ❋ Job Security: Least Secure
- ❋ Self-Employed: 31.8%
- ❋ Part-Time: 6.1%

Our sources did not provide separate job openings data for this occupation. The job openings listed here are shared with Rough Carpenters.

Renewal Industries: Green Technologies; Infrastructure.

Industries with Greatest Employment: Construction of Buildings (31.8%); Specialty Trade Contractors (23.1%).

Highest-Growth Industries (Projected Growth for This Job): Securities, Commodity Contracts, and Other Financial Investments and Related Activities (41.0%); Museums, Historical Sites, and Similar Institutions (36.3%); Professional, Scientific, and Technical Services (35.7%); Nursing and Residential Care Facilities (33.3%); Warehousing and Storage (33.3%); Amusement, Gambling, and Recreation Industries (32.7%); Waste Management and Remediation Services (31.4%); Social Assistance (28.7%); Building Material and Garden Equipment and Supplies Dealers (27.7%); Administrative and Support Services (27.5%); Rental and Leasing Services (20.8%); Accommodation, Including Hotels and Motels (17.6%); Support Activities for Transportation (17.3%); Real Estate (17.3%); Religious, Grantmaking, Civic, Professional, and Similar Organizations (17.0%); Food Services and Drinking Places (15.6%); Management of Companies and Enterprises (15.3%).

Other Considerations for Job Outlook: About one-third of all carpenters—the largest construction trade—are self-employed.

Construct, erect, install, and repair structures and fixtures of wood, plywood, and wallboard, using carpenter's hand tools and power tools. Measure and mark cutting lines on materials, using ruler, pencil, chalk, and marking gauge. Follow established safety rules and regulations and maintain a safe and clean environment. Verify trueness of structure, using plumb bob and level. Shape or cut materials to specified measurements, using hand tools, machines, or power saw. Study specifications in blueprints, sketches, or building plans to prepare project layout and determine dimensions and materials required. Assemble and fasten materials to make framework or props, using hand tools and wood screws, nails, dowel pins, or glue. Build or repair cabinets, doors, frameworks, floors, and other wooden fixtures used in buildings, using woodworking machines, carpenter's hand tools, and power tools. Erect scaffolding and ladders for assembling structures above ground level. Remove damaged or defective parts or sections of structures and repair or replace, using hand tools. Install structures and fixtures, such as windows, frames, floorings, and trim, or hardware, using carpenter's hand and power tools. Select and order lumber and other required materials. Maintain records, document actions, and present written progress reports. Finish surfaces of woodwork or wallboard in houses and buildings, using paint, hand tools, and paneling. Prepare cost estimates for clients or employers. Arrange for subcontractors to deal with special areas such as heating and electrical wiring work. Inspect ceiling or floor tile, wall coverings, siding, glass, or woodwork to detect broken or damaged structures. Work with or remove hazardous material. Construct forms and chutes for pouring concrete. Cover subfloors with building paper to keep out moisture and lay hardwood, parquet, and wood-strip-block floors by nailing floors to subfloor or cementing them to mastic or asphalt base. Fill cracks and other defects in plaster or plasterboard and sand patch, using patching plaster, trowel, and sanding tool. Perform minor plumbing, welding, or concrete mixing work. Apply shock-absorbing, sound-deadening, and decorative paneling to ceilings and walls.

Personality Type: Realistic-Conventional-Investigative.

Career Cluster: 02 Architecture and Construction. **Career Pathway:** 02.2 Construction.

Skills: Management of Personnel Resources; Management of Material Resources; Management of Financial Resources; Repairing; Equipment Maintenance; Quality Control Analysis.

Education and Training Program: Carpentry/Carpenter. **Related Knowledge/Courses:** Building and Construction;

Mechanical Devices; Design; Engineering and Technology; Production and Processing; Public Safety and Security.

Work Environment: Outdoors; noisy; hazardous equipment; standing; walking and running; using hands on objects, tools, or controls.

Construction Laborers

- ❋ Education/Training Required: Moderate-term on-the-job training
- ❋ Annual Earnings: $27,310
- ❋ Beginning Wage: $17,410
- ❋ Earnings Growth Potential: Medium (36.3%)
- ❋ Growth: 10.9%
- ❋ Annual Job Openings: 257,407
- ❋ Job Security: Least Secure
- ❋ Self-Employed: 16.4%
- ❋ Part-Time: 8.7%

Renewal Industries: Green Technologies; Infrastructure.

Industries with Greatest Employment: Specialty Trade Contractors (30.1%); Construction of Buildings (20.5%); Heavy and Civil Engineering Construction (16.3%); Administrative and Support Services (8.4%).

Highest-Growth Industries (Projected Growth for This Job): Social Assistance (40.0%); Warehousing and Storage (33.8%); Professional, Scientific, and Technical Services (33.4%); Waste Management and Remediation Services (31.0%); Amusement, Gambling, and Recreation Industries (28.8%); Building Material and Garden Equipment and Supplies Dealers (27.7%); Administrative and Support Services (25.8%); Rental and Leasing Services (19.8%); Real Estate (17.8%); Management of Companies and Enterprises (15.3%); Religious, Grantmaking, Civic, Professional, and Similar Organizations (15.2%); Accommodation, Including Hotels and Motels (15.2%).

Other Considerations for Job Outlook: In many geographic areas there will be competition, especially for jobs requiring limited skills, due to a plentiful supply of workers who are willing to work as day laborers. In other areas, however, opportunities will be better. Overall opportunities will be best for those with experience and specialized skills and for those who can relocate to areas with new construction projects. Opportunities will also be better for laborers specializing in road construction.

Perform tasks involving physical labor at building, highway, and heavy construction projects; tunnel and shaft excavations; and demolition sites. May operate hand and power tools of all types: air hammers, earth tampers, cement mixers, small mechanical hoists, surveying and measuring equipment, and various other types of equipment and instruments. May clean and prepare sites; dig trenches; set braces to support the sides of excavations; erect scaffolding; clean up rubble and debris; and remove asbestos, lead, and other hazardous waste materials. May assist other craft workers. Clean and prepare construction sites to eliminate possible hazards. Read and interpret plans, instructions, and specifications to determine work activities. Control traffic passing near, in, and around work zones. Signal equipment operators to facilitate alignment, movement, and adjustment of machinery, equipment, and materials. Dig ditches or trenches, backfill excavations, and compact and level earth to grade specifications, using picks, shovels, pneumatic tampers, and rakes. Measure, mark, and record openings and distances to lay out areas where construction work will be performed. Position, join, align, and seal structural components, such as concrete wall sections and pipes. Load, unload, and identify building materials, machinery, and tools and distribute them to the appropriate locations according to project plans and specifications. Erect and disassemble scaffolding, shoring, braces, traffic barricades, ramps, and other temporary structures. Build and position forms for pouring concrete and dismantle forms after use, using saws, hammers, nails, or bolts. Lubricate, clean, and repair machinery, equipment, and tools. Operate jackhammers and drills to break up concrete or pavement. Smooth and finish freshly poured cement or concrete, using floats, trowels, screeds, or powered cement finishing tools. Operate, read, and maintain air monitoring and other sampling devices in confined or hazardous environments. Install sewer, water, and storm drain pipes, using pipe-laying machinery and laser guidance equipment. Transport and set explosives for tunnel, shaft, and road construction. Provide assistance to craft workers, such as carpenters, plasterers, and masons. Tend pumps, compressors, and generators to provide power for tools, machinery, and equipment or to heat and move materials such as asphalt. Mop, brush, or spread paints, cleaning solutions, or other compounds over surfaces to clean them or to provide protection. Place, consolidate, and protect case-in-place concrete or masonry structures. Identify, pack, and transport hazardous and/

or radioactive materials. Use computers and other input devices to control robotic pipe cutters and cleaners.

Personality Type: Realistic-Conventional.

Career Cluster: 02 Architecture and Construction. **Career Pathway:** 02.2 Construction.

Skills: No data available.

Education and Training Program: Construction Trades, Other. **Related Knowledge/Courses:** Building and Construction; Design; Mechanical Devices; Transportation; Engineering and Technology; Public Safety and Security.

Work Environment: Outdoors; noisy; very hot or cold; contaminants; standing; using hands on objects, tools, or controls.

Construction Managers

* Education/Training Required: Bachelor's degree
* Annual Earnings: $76,230
* Beginning Wage: $44,630
* Earnings Growth Potential: High (41.5%)
* Growth: 15.7%
* Annual Job Openings: 44,158
* Job Security: Least Secure
* Self-Employed: 56.3%
* Part-Time: 4.9%

Renewal Industries: Green Technologies; Infrastructure.

Industries with Greatest Employment: Construction of Buildings (18.0%); Specialty Trade Contractors (12.8%).

Highest-Growth Industries (Projected Growth for This Job): Professional, Scientific, and Technical Services (33.9%); Waste Management and Remediation Services (31.1%); Building Material and Garden Equipment and Supplies Dealers (27.7%); Administrative and Support Services (26.7%); Construction of Buildings (23.9%); Ambulatory Health-Care Services (22.8%); Real Estate (19.2%); Religious, Grantmaking, Civic, Professional, and Similar Organizations (18.4%); Social Assistance (17.9%); Accommodation, Including Hotels and Motels (17.8%); Management of Companies and Enterprises (15.3%).

Other Considerations for Job Outlook: Although certification is not required, there is a growing movement toward certification of construction managers.

Plan, direct, coordinate, or budget, usually through subordinate supervisory personnel, activities concerned with the construction and maintenance of structures, facilities, and systems. Participate in the conceptual development of a construction project and oversee its organization, scheduling, and implementation. Schedule the project in logical steps and budget time required to meet deadlines. Confer with supervisory personnel, owners, contractors, and design professionals to discuss and resolve matters such as work procedures, complaints, and construction problems. Prepare contracts and negotiate revisions, changes, and additions to contractual agreements with architects, consultants, clients, suppliers, and subcontractors. Prepare and submit budget estimates and progress and cost tracking reports. Interpret and explain plans and contract terms to administrative staff, workers, and clients, representing the owner or developer. Plan, organize, and direct activities concerned with the construction and maintenance of structures, facilities, and systems. Take actions to deal with the results of delays, bad weather, or emergencies at construction sites. Inspect and review projects to monitor compliance with building and safety codes and other regulations. Study job specifications to determine appropriate construction methods. Select, contract, and oversee workers who complete specific pieces of the project, such as painting or plumbing. Obtain all necessary permits and licenses. Direct and supervise workers. Develop and implement quality control programs. Investigate damage, accidents, or delays at construction sites to ensure that proper procedures are being carried out. Determine labor requirements and dispatch workers to construction sites. Evaluate construction methods and determine cost-effectiveness of plans, using computers. Requisition supplies and materials to complete construction projects. Direct acquisition of land for construction projects.

Personality Type: Enterprising-Realistic-Conventional.

Career Clusters: 02 Architecture and Construction; 04 Business, Management, and Administration. **Career Pathways:** 02.2 Construction; 04.1 Management.

Skills: Management of Financial Resources; Management of Material Resources; Management of Personnel Resources; Systems Analysis; Systems Evaluation; Negotiation.

Education and Training Programs: Construction Engineering Technology/Technician; Business/Commerce, General; Business Administration and Management, General; Operations Management and Supervision; Construction Management. **Related Knowledge/Courses:** Building and Construction; Design; Engineering and Technology; Mechanical Devices; Administration and Management; Personnel and Human Resources.

Work Environment: More often outdoors than indoors; noisy; contaminants; hazardous equipment; sitting.

Cost Estimators

- ❋ Education/Training Required: Work experience in a related occupation
- ❋ Annual Earnings: $54,920
- ❋ Beginning Wage: $32,470
- ❋ Earnings Growth Potential: High (40.9%)
- ❋ Growth: 18.5%
- ❋ Annual Job Openings: 38,379
- ❋ Job Security: Less Secure than Most
- ❋ Self-Employed: 1.1%
- ❋ Part-Time: 5.8%

Renewal Industry: Infrastructure.

Industries with Greatest Employment: Specialty Trade Contractors (37.8%); Construction of Buildings (18.3%); Heavy and Civil Engineering Construction (5.5%); Repair and Maintenance (5.1%).

Highest-Growth Industries (Projected Growth for This Job): Social Assistance (51.5%); Warehousing and Storage (44.5%); Internet Service Providers, Web Search Portals, and Data Processing Services (43.8%); Professional, Scientific, and Technical Services (42.6%); Waste Management and Remediation Services (41.6%); Building Material and Garden Equipment and Supplies Dealers (36.9%); Administrative and Support Services (32.4%); Support Activities for Transportation (31.8%); Real Estate (29.6%); Rental and Leasing Services (27.6%); Repair and Maintenance (24.8%); Management of Companies and Enterprises (24.5%); Furniture and Home Furnishings Stores (23.9%); Credit Intermediation and Related Activities (23.7%); Wholesale Electronic Markets and Agents and Brokers (22.6%); Merchant Wholesalers, Durable Goods (22.6%); Motor Vehicle and Parts Dealers (22.4%); Truck Transportation (21.8%); Local Government (21.5%); Construction of Buildings (21.3%); Educational Services, Public and Private (20.8%); Hospitals, Public and Private (19.8%); Specialty Trade Contractors (19.3%); Merchant Wholesalers, Nondurable Goods (17.7%); Mining (Except Oil and Gas) (16.2%); Insurance Carriers and Related Activities (15.8%); Heavy and Civil Engineering Construction (15.3%).

Other Considerations for Job Outlook: Voluntary certification can be valuable to cost estimators; some individual employers may require professional certification for employment.

Prepare cost estimates for product manufacturing, construction projects, or services to aid management in bidding on or determining prices of products or services. May specialize according to particular service performed or type of product manufactured. Consult with clients, vendors, personnel in other departments, or construction foremen to discuss and formulate estimates and resolve issues. Analyze blueprints and other documentation to prepare time, cost, materials, and labor estimates. Prepare estimates for use in selecting vendors or subcontractors. Confer with engineers, architects, owners, contractors, and subcontractors on changes and adjustments to cost estimates. Prepare estimates used by management for purposes such as planning, organizing, and scheduling work. Prepare cost and expenditure statements and other necessary documentation at regular intervals for the duration of the project. Assess cost-effectiveness of products, projects, or services, tracking actual costs relative to bids as projects develop. Set up cost-monitoring and cost-reporting systems and procedures. Conduct special studies to develop and establish standard hour and related cost data or to effect cost reductions. Review material and labor requirements to decide whether it is more cost-effective to produce or purchase components. Prepare and maintain a directory of suppliers, contractors, and subcontractors. Establish and maintain tendering processes and conduct negotiations. Visit sites and record information about access, drainage and topography, and availability of services such as water and electricity.

Personality Type: Conventional-Enterprising.

Career Clusters: 02 Architecture and Construction; 04 Business, Management, and Administration; 15 Science, Technology, Engineering, and Mathematics. **Career**

Pathways: 02.2 Construction; 04.1 Management; 15.1 Engineering and Technology.

Skills: No data available.

Education and Training Programs: Materials Engineering; Mechanical Engineering; Construction Engineering; Manufacturing Engineering; Construction Engineering Technology/Technician; Business/Commerce, General; Business Administration and Management, General. **Related Knowledge/Courses:** Engineering and Technology; Mathematics; Economics and Accounting; Building and Construction; Design; Computers and Electronics.

Work Environment: Indoors; sitting.

Counseling Psychologists

- ❀ Education/Training Required: Doctoral degree
- ❀ Annual Earnings: $62,210
- ❀ Beginning Wage: $37,300
- ❀ Earnings Growth Potential: High (40.0%)
- ❀ Growth: 15.8%
- ❀ Annual Job Openings: 8,309
- ❀ Job Security: Most Secure
- ❀ Self-Employed: 34.2%
- ❀ Part-Time: 24.0%

Our sources did not provide separate job openings data for this occupation. The job openings listed here are shared with Clinical Psychologists and with School Psychologists.

Renewal Industry: Health Care.

Industries with Greatest Employment: Educational Services, Public and Private (30.4%); Ambulatory Health-Care Services (13.2%); Hospitals, Public and Private (6.0%); Social Assistance (5.9%).

Highest-Growth Industries (Projected Growth for This Job): Social Assistance (56.2%); Professional, Scientific, and Technical Services (34.6%); Ambulatory Health-Care Services (26.8%); Nursing and Residential Care Facilities (24.8%); Funds, Trusts, and Other Financial Vehicles (23.3%); Religious, Grantmaking, Civic, Professional, and Similar Organizations (19.4%); Management of Companies and Enterprises (15.2%).

Other Considerations for Job Outlook: Job prospects should be the best for people who have a doctoral degree from a leading university. Master's degree holders will face keen competition for jobs. The rise in health-care costs associated with unhealthy lifestyles, such as smoking, alcoholism, and obesity, has made prevention and treatment more critical. An increase in the number of employee assistance programs, which help workers deal with personal problems, also should lead to employment growth for clinical and counseling specialties. Clinical and counseling psychologists also will be needed to help people deal with depression and other mental disorders, marriage and family problems, job stress, and addiction. The growing number of elderly will increase the demand for psychologists trained in geropsychology to help people deal with the mental and physical changes that occur as individuals grow older. There also will be increased need for psychologists to work with returning veterans.

Assess and evaluate individuals' problems through the use of case history, interview, and observation and provide individual or group counseling services to assist individuals in achieving more effective personal, social, educational, and vocational development and adjustment. Collect information about individuals or clients, using interviews, case histories, observational techniques, and other assessment methods. Counsel individuals, groups, or families to help them understand problems, define goals, and develop realistic action plans. Develop therapeutic and treatment plans based on clients' interests, abilities, and needs. Consult with other professionals to discuss therapies, treatments, counseling resources, or techniques and to share occupational information. Analyze data such as interview notes, test results, and reference manuals in order to identify symptoms and to diagnose the nature of clients' problems. Advise clients on how they could be helped by counseling. Evaluate the results of counseling methods to determine the reliability and validity of treatments. Provide consulting services to schools, social service agencies, and businesses. Refer clients to specialists or to other institutions for non-counseling treatment of problems. Select, administer, and interpret psychological tests to assess intelligence, aptitudes, abilities, or interests. Conduct research to develop or improve diagnostic or therapeutic counseling techniques.

Personality Type: Social-Investigative-Artistic.

Career Clusters: 08 Health Science; 10 Human Services.
Career Pathways: 08.1 Therapeutic Services; 10.2 Counseling and Mental Health Services.

Skills: Social Perceptiveness; Active Listening; Persuasion; Service Orientation; Coordination; Monitoring.

Education and Training Programs: Psychology, General; Clinical Psychology; Counseling Psychology; Developmental and Child Psychology; School Psychology; Clinical Child Psychology; Psychoanalysis and Psychotherapy.
Related Knowledge/Courses: Therapy and Counseling; Philosophy and Theology; Sociology and Anthropology; Psychology; English Language; Customer and Personal Service.

Work Environment: Indoors; sitting.

Criminal Justice and Law Enforcement Teachers, Postsecondary

- ❋ Education/Training Required: Master's degree
- ❋ Annual Earnings: $51,060
- ❋ Beginning Wage: $30,420
- ❋ Earnings Growth Potential: High (40.4%)
- ❋ Growth: 22.9%
- ❋ Annual Job Openings: 1,911
- ❋ Job Security: Most Secure
- ❋ Self-Employed: 0.4%
- ❋ Part-Time: 27.8%

Renewal Industry: Education.

Industries with Greatest Employment: Educational Services, Public and Private (97.3%).

Highest-Growth Industries (Projected Growth for This Job): Administrative and Support Services (48.3%); Amusement, Gambling, and Recreation Industries (45.2%); Social Assistance (38.6%); Support Activities for Transportation (32.8%); Religious, Grantmaking, Civic, Professional, and Similar Organizations (29.9%); Professional, Scientific, and Technical Services (28.8%); Management of Companies and Enterprises (26.8%); Local Government (23.5%); Educational Services, Public and Private (22.8%); Hospitals, Public and Private (21.4%).

Other Considerations for Job Outlook: Retirements of current postsecondary teachers should create numerous openings for all types of postsecondary teachers. However, one of the main reasons why students attend postsecondary institutions is to prepare themselves for careers, so the best job prospects for postsecondary teachers are likely to be in rapidly growing fields that offer many nonacademic career options, such as criminal justice and law enforcement. Community colleges and other institutions offering career and technical education have been among the most rapidly growing, and these institutions are expected to offer some of the best opportunities for postsecondary teachers.

Teach courses in criminal justice, corrections, and law enforcement administration. Initiate, facilitate, and moderate classroom discussions. Keep abreast of developments in their field by reading current literature, talking with colleagues, and participating in professional conferences. Evaluate and grade students' classwork, assignments, and papers. Compile, administer, and grade examinations or assign this work to others. Prepare and deliver lectures to undergraduate or graduate students on topics such as criminal law, defensive policing, and investigation techniques. Prepare course materials such as syllabi, homework assignments, and handouts. Conduct research in a particular field of knowledge and publish findings in professional journals, books, and/or electronic media. Plan, evaluate, and revise curricula, course content, and course materials and methods of instruction. Supervise undergraduate and/or graduate teaching, internship, and research work. Maintain student attendance records, grades, and other required records. Select and obtain materials and supplies such as textbooks. Advise students on academic and vocational curricula and on career issues. Maintain regularly scheduled office hours to advise and assist students. Collaborate with colleagues to address teaching and research issues. Write grant proposals to procure external research funding. Serve on academic or administrative committees that deal with institutional policies, departmental matters, and academic issues. Compile bibliographies of specialized materials for outside reading assignments. Participate in student recruitment, registration, and placement activities. Provide professional consulting services to government and/or industry. Perform administrative duties such as serving as department head. Participate in campus and community events. Act as advisers to student organizations.

Personality Type: Social-Investigative.

Career Clusters: 05 Education and Training; 12 Law, Public Safety, Corrections, and Security. **Career Pathways:** 05.3 Teaching/Training; 12.1 Correction Services; 12.3 Security and Protective Services; 12.4 Law Enforcement Services.

Skills: Writing; Critical Thinking; Instructing; Active Learning; Reading Comprehension; Persuasion.

Education and Training Programs: Teacher Education and Professional Development, Specific Subject Areas, Other; Corrections; Criminal Justice/Law Enforcement Administration; Criminal Justice/Safety Studies; Forensic Science and Technology; Criminal Justice/Police Science; Security and Loss Prevention Services; Juvenile Corrections; Criminalistics and Criminal Science; Corrections Administration; Corrections and Criminal Justice, Other. **Related Knowledge/Courses:** Sociology and Anthropology; Philosophy and Theology; History and Archeology; Law and Government; English Language; Education and Training.

Work Environment: Indoors; sitting.

Database Administrators

- ❋ Education/Training Required: Bachelor's degree
- ❋ Annual Earnings: $67,250
- ❋ Beginning Wage: $38,890
- ❋ Earnings Growth Potential: High (42.2%)
- ❋ Growth: 28.6%
- ❋ Annual Job Openings: 8,258
- ❋ Job Security: More Secure than Most
- ❋ Self-Employed: 1.3%
- ❋ Part-Time: 5.3%

Renewal Industry: Information and Telecommunication Technologies.

Industries with Greatest Employment: Professional, Scientific, and Technical Services (23.2%); Educational Services, Public and Private (8.5%); Management of Companies and Enterprises (6.9%); Administrative and Support Services (5.7%); Insurance Carriers and Related Activities (5.1%).

Highest-Growth Industries (Projected Growth for This Job): Amusement, Gambling, and Recreation Industries (85.1%); Social Assistance (59.7%); Securities, Commodity Contracts, and Other Financial Investments and Related Activities (58.1%); Internet Publishing and Broadcasting (54.0%); Museums, Historical Sites, and Similar Institutions (49.3%); Professional, Scientific, and Technical Services (48.3%); Warehousing and Storage (46.9%); Waste Management and Remediation Services (43.1%); Administrative and Support Services (42.0%); Lessors of Nonfinancial Intangible Assets (Except Copyrighted Works) (40.2%); Funds, Trusts, and Other Financial Vehicles (39.8%); Ambulatory Health-Care Services (37.2%); Support Activities for Transportation (36.4%); Nonstore Retailers (34.8%); Nursing and Residential Care Facilities (34.5%); Real Estate (33.2%); Religious, Grantmaking, Civic, Professional, and Similar Organizations (29.1%); Motion Picture, Video, and Sound Recording Industries (29.0%); Rental and Leasing Services (28.9%); Performing Arts, Spectator Sports, and Related Industries (28.2%); Internet Service Providers, Web Search Portals, and Data Processing Services (27.1%); Management of Companies and Enterprises (26.5%); Publishing Industries (Except Internet) (26.4%); Truck Transportation (24.1%); Construction of Buildings (23.7%); Local Government (23.3%); Hospitals, Public and Private (22.7%); Broadcasting (Except Internet) (21.9%); Air Transportation (21.1%); Educational Services, Public and Private (20.7%); Motor Vehicle and Parts Dealers (20.7%); Credit Intermediation and Related Activities (20.2%); Merchant Wholesalers, Nondurable Goods (20.1%); Chemical Manufacturing (20.0%); Furniture and Home Furnishings Stores (18.9%); Couriers and Messengers (18.5%); Specialty Trade Contractors (18.3%); Insurance Carriers and Related Activities (17.3%).

Other Considerations for Job Outlook: Database administrators are projected to be one of the fastest-growing occupations over the next decade. Strong employment growth combined with a limited supply of qualified workers will result in excellent employment prospects for this occupation and a high demand for these workers' skills. Expansion of electronic commerce—doing business on the Internet—and the continuing need to build and maintain databases that store critical information on customers, inventory, and projects are fueling demand for database administrators familiar with the latest technology. Individuals with an advanced degree in computer science or computer engineering or with an MBA with a concentration in information systems should enjoy favorable employment prospects. College graduates with a bachelor's degree in

D

computer science, computer engineering, information science, or MIS also should enjoy favorable prospects, particularly if they have supplemented their formal education with practical experience.

Coordinate changes to computer databases. Test and implement the databases, applying knowledge of database management systems. May plan, coordinate, and implement security measures to safeguard computer databases. Test programs or databases, correct errors, and make necessary modifications. Modify existing databases and database management systems or direct programmers and analysts to make changes. Plan, coordinate, and implement security measures to safeguard information in computer files against accidental or unauthorized damage, modification, or disclosure. Work as part of project teams to coordinate database development and determine project scope and limitations. Write and code logical and physical database descriptions and specify identifiers of database to management system or direct others in coding descriptions. Train users and answer questions. Specify users and user access levels for each segment of databases. Approve, schedule, plan, and supervise the installation and testing of new products and improvements to computer systems such as the installation of new databases. Review project requests describing database user needs to estimate time and cost required to accomplish project. Develop standards and guidelines to guide the use and acquisition of software and to protect vulnerable information. Review procedures in database management system manuals for making changes to database. Develop methods for integrating different products so they work properly together such as customizing commercial databases to fit specific needs. Develop data models describing data elements and how they are used, following procedures and using pen, template, or computer software. Select and enter codes to monitor database performances and to create production databases. Establish and calculate optimum values for database parameters, using manuals and calculators. Revise company definition of data as defined in data dictionary. Review workflow charts developed by programmer analysts to understand tasks computer will perform, such as updating records. Identify and evaluate industry trends in database systems to serve as a source of information and advice for upper management.

Personality Type: Conventional-Investigative.

Career Clusters: 04 Business, Management, and Administration; 11 Information Technology. **Career Pathways:** 04.4 Business Analysis; 11.2 Information Support Services; 11.4 Programming and Software Development.

Skills: No data available.

Education and Training Programs: Computer and Information Sciences, General; Computer Systems Analysis/Analyst; Data Modeling/Warehousing and Database Administration; Computer and Information Systems Security; Management Information Systems, General. **Related Knowledge/Courses:** Computers and Electronics; Telecommunications; Clerical Practices; Communications and Media; Engineering and Technology; Mathematics.

Work Environment: Indoors; noisy; sitting; using hands on objects, tools, or controls; repetitive motions.

Dental Assistants

- ❋ Education/Training Required: Moderate-term on-the-job training
- ❋ Annual Earnings: $31,550
- ❋ Beginning Wage: $21,550
- ❋ Earnings Growth Potential: Low (31.7%)
- ❋ Growth: 29.2%
- ❋ Annual Job Openings: 29,482
- ❋ Job Security: Most Secure
- ❋ Self-Employed: 0.0%
- ❋ Part-Time: 35.7%

Renewal Industry: Health Care.

Industries with Greatest Employment: Ambulatory Health-Care Services (94.8%).

Highest-Growth Industries (Projected Growth for This Job): Ambulatory Health-Care Services (30.4%); Administrative and Support Services (26.9%).

Other Considerations for Job Outlook: Job prospects for dental assistants should be excellent. In addition to job openings due to employment growth, numerous job openings will arise out of the need to replace assistants who transfer to other occupations, retire, or leave for other reasons. Many opportunities for entry-level positions offer on-the-job training, but some dentists prefer to hire experienced assistants or those who have completed a dental-assisting program.

Assist dentist, set up patient and equipment, and keep records. Prepare patient, sterilize and disinfect instruments, set up instrument trays, prepare materials, and assist dentist during dental procedures. Expose dental diagnostic X-rays. Record treatment information in patient records. Take and record medical and dental histories and vital signs of patients. Provide postoperative instructions prescribed by dentist. Assist dentist in management of medical and dental emergencies. Pour, trim, and polish study casts. Instruct patients in oral hygiene and plaque control programs. Make preliminary impressions for study casts and occlusal registrations for mounting study casts. Clean and polish removable appliances. Clean teeth, using dental instruments. Apply protective coating of fluoride to teeth. Fabricate temporary restorations and custom impressions from preliminary impressions. Schedule appointments, prepare bills, and receive payment for dental services; complete insurance forms; and maintain records, manually or using computer.

Personality Type: Conventional-Realistic-Social.

Career Cluster: 08 Health Science. **Career Pathway:** 08.1 Therapeutic Services.

Skills: Equipment Maintenance; Operation and Control; Social Perceptiveness; Management of Material Resources; Operation Monitoring; Equipment Selection.

Education and Training Program: Dental Assisting/Assistant. **Related Knowledge/Courses:** Medicine and Dentistry; Chemistry; Clerical Practices; Customer and Personal Service; Psychology.

Work Environment: Indoors; contaminants; disease or infections; using hands on objects, tools, or controls; bending or twisting the body; repetitive motions.

Dental Hygienists

- ❋ Education/Training Required: Associate degree
- ❋ Annual Earnings: $64,740
- ❋ Beginning Wage: $42,480
- ❋ Earnings Growth Potential: Low (34.4%)
- ❋ Growth: 30.1%
- ❋ Annual Job Openings: 10,433
- ❋ Job Security: Most Secure
- ❋ Self-Employed: 0.1%
- ❋ Part-Time: 58.7%

Renewal Industry: Health Care.

Industries with Greatest Employment: Ambulatory Health-Care Services (97.2%).

Highest-Growth Industries (Projected Growth for This Job): Social Assistance (49.2%); Ambulatory Health-Care Services (30.5%); Administrative and Support Services (26.7%).

Other Considerations for Job Outlook: Job prospects are expected to remain excellent. Older dentists, who have been less likely to employ dental hygienists, are leaving the occupation and will be replaced by recent graduates, who are more likely to employ one or more hygienists. In addition, as dentists' workloads increase, they are expected to hire more hygienists to perform preventive dental care, such as cleaning, so that they may devote their own time to more complex procedures.

Clean teeth and examine oral areas, head, and neck for signs of oral disease. May educate patients on oral hygiene, take and develop X-rays, or apply fluoride or sealants. Clean calcareous deposits, accretions, and stains from teeth and beneath margins of gums, using dental instruments. Feel and visually examine gums for sores and signs of disease. Chart conditions of decay and disease for diagnosis and treatment by dentist. Feel lymph nodes under patient's chin to detect swelling or tenderness that could indicate presence of oral cancer. Apply fluorides and other cavity-preventing agents to arrest dental decay. Examine gums, using probes, to locate periodontal recessed gums and signs of gum disease. Expose and develop X-ray film. Provide clinical services and health education to improve and maintain oral health of schoolchildren. Remove excess cement from coronal surfaces of teeth. Make impressions for study casts. Place, carve, and finish amalgam restorations. Administer local anesthetic agents. Conduct dental health clinics for community groups to augment services of dentist. Remove sutures and dressings. Place and remove rubber dams, matrices, and temporary restorations.

Personality Type: Social-Realistic-Conventional.

Career Cluster: 08 Health Science. **Career Pathway:** 08.1 Therapeutic Services.

Skills: Science; Active Learning; Reading Comprehension; Time Management; Equipment Selection; Persuasion.

Education and Training Program: Dental Hygiene/ Hygienist. **Related Knowledge/Courses:** Biology; Medicine and Dentistry; Chemistry; Psychology; Therapy and Counseling; Sales and Marketing.

Work Environment: Indoors; radiation; disease or infections; sitting; using hands on objects, tools, or controls; repetitive motions.

Dentists, General

- ❋ Education/Training Required: First professional degree
- ❋ Annual Earnings: $137,630
- ❋ Beginning Wage: $71,520
- ❋ Earnings Growth Potential: High (48.0%)
- ❋ Growth: 9.2%
- ❋ Annual Job Openings: 7,106
- ❋ Job Security: Less Secure than Most
- ❋ Self-Employed: 36.6%
- ❋ Part-Time: 25.9%

Renewal Industry: Health Care.

Industries with Greatest Employment: Ambulatory Health-Care Services (60.4%).

Highest-Growth Industries (Projected Growth for This Job): Social Assistance (52.9%); Administrative and Support Services (27.4%).

Other Considerations for Job Outlook: Job prospects should be good. Average employment growth will generate some job openings, but most openings will result from the need to replace the large number of dentists expected to retire.

Diagnose and treat diseases, injuries, and malformations of teeth and gums and related oral structures. May treat diseases of nerve, pulp, and other dental tissues affecting vitality of teeth. Use masks, gloves, and safety glasses to protect themselves and their patients from infectious diseases. Administer anesthetics to limit the amount of pain experienced by patients during procedures. Examine teeth, gums, and related tissues, using dental instruments, X-rays, and other diagnostic equipment, to evaluate dental health, diagnose diseases or abnormalities, and plan appropriate treatments. Formulate plan of treatment for patient's teeth and mouth tissue. Use air turbine and hand instruments, dental appliances, and surgical implements. Advise and instruct patients regarding preventive dental care, the causes and treatment of dental problems, and oral health-care services. Design, make, and fit prosthodontic appliances such as space maintainers, bridges, and dentures or write fabrication instructions or prescriptions for denturists and dental technicians. Diagnose and treat diseases, injuries, and malformations of teeth, gums, and related oral structures and provide preventive and corrective services. Fill pulp chamber and canal with endodontic materials. Write prescriptions for antibiotics and other medications. Analyze and evaluate dental needs to determine changes and trends in patterns of dental disease. Treat exposure of pulp by pulp capping, removal of pulp from pulp chamber, or root canal, using dental instruments. Eliminate irritating margins of fillings and correct occlusions, using dental instruments. Perform oral and periodontal surgery on the jaw or mouth. Remove diseased tissue, using surgical instruments. Apply fluoride and sealants to teeth. Manage business, employing and supervising staff and handling paperwork and insurance claims. Bleach, clean, or polish teeth to restore natural color. Plan, organize, and maintain dental health programs. Produce and evaluate dental health educational materials.

Personality Type: Investigative-Realistic-Social.

Career Cluster: 08 Health Science. **Career Pathway:** 08.1 Therapeutic Services.

Skills: Science; Management of Financial Resources; Management of Material Resources; Equipment Selection; Complex Problem Solving; Reading Comprehension.

Education and Training Programs: Dentistry (DDS, DMD); Dental Clinical Sciences, General (MS, PhD); Advanced General Dentistry (Cert, MS, PhD); Oral

Biology and Oral Pathology (MS, PhD); Dental Public Health and Education (Cert, MS/MPH, PhD/DPH); Dental Materials (MS, PhD); Pediatric Dentistry/Pedodontics (Cert, MS, PhD); Dental Public Health Specialty; Pedodontics Specialty. **Related Knowledge/Courses:** Medicine and Dentistry; Biology; Psychology; Chemistry; Personnel and Human Resources; Economics and Accounting.

Work Environment: Indoors; contaminants; radiation; disease or infections; sitting; using hands on objects, tools, or controls.

Diagnostic Medical Sonographers

- ❋ Education/Training Required: Associate degree
- ❋ Annual Earnings: $59,860
- ❋ Beginning Wage: $42,250
- ❋ Earnings Growth Potential: Low (29.4%)
- ❋ Growth: 19.1%
- ❋ Annual Job Openings: 3,211
- ❋ Job Security: Most Secure
- ❋ Self-Employed: 1.1%
- ❋ Part-Time: 17.3%

Renewal Industry: Health Care.

Industries with Greatest Employment: Hospitals, Public and Private (58.9%); Ambulatory Health-Care Services (36.9%).

Highest-Growth Industries (Projected Growth for This Job): Ambulatory Health-Care Services (32.4%); Administrative and Support Services (28.8%).

Other Considerations for Job Outlook: Job opportunities should be favorable. In addition to job openings from growth, some openings will arise from the need to replace sonographers who retire or leave the occupation permanently for some other reason. Sonographic technology is expected to evolve rapidly and to spawn many new sonography procedures, such as 3D and 4D sonography for use in obstetric and ophthalmologic diagnosis. However, high costs and approval by the federal government may limit the rate at which some promising new technologies are adopted.

Produce ultrasonic recordings of internal organs for use by physicians. Provide sonograms and oral or written summaries of technical findings to physicians for use in medical diagnosis. Decide which images to include, looking for differences between healthy and pathological areas. Operate ultrasound equipment to produce and record images of the motion, shape, and composition of blood, organs, tissues, and bodily masses such as fluid accumulations. Select appropriate equipment settings and adjust patient positions to obtain the best sites and angles. Observe screens during scans to ensure that images produced are satisfactory for diagnostic purposes, making adjustments to equipment as required. Prepare patients for exams by explaining procedures, transferring them to ultrasound tables, scrubbing skin and applying gel, and positioning them properly. Observe and care for patients throughout examinations to ensure their safety and comfort. Obtain and record accurate patient histories, including prior test results and information from physical examinations. Determine whether scope of exams should be extended, based on findings. Maintain records that include patient information; sonographs and interpretations; files of correspondence; publications and regulations; or quality assurance records such as pathology, biopsy, or post-operative reports. Record and store suitable images, using camera unit connected to the ultrasound equipment. Coordinate work with physicians and other health-care team members, including providing assistance during invasive procedures. Perform clerical duties such as scheduling exams and special procedures, keeping records, and archiving computerized images. Perform legal and ethical duties, including preparing safety and accident reports, obtaining written consent from patients to perform invasive procedures, and reporting symptoms of abuse and neglect. Clean, check, and maintain sonographic equipment, submitting maintenance requests or performing minor repairs as necessary. Supervise and train students and other medical sonographers. Maintain stock and supplies, preparing supplies for special examinations and ordering supplies when necessary. Process and code film from procedures and complete appropriate documentation.

Personality Type: Investigative-Social-Realistic.

Career Cluster: 08 Health Science. **Career Pathways:** 08.1 Therapeutic Services; 08.2 Diagnostics Services.

Skills: No data available.

Education and Training Programs: Diagnostic Medical Sonography/Sonographer and Ultrasound Technician;

Allied Health Diagnostic, Intervention, and Treatment Professions, Other. **Related Knowledge/Courses:** Medicine and Dentistry; Physics; Biology; Psychology; Customer and Personal Service; Clerical Practices.

Work Environment: Indoors; disease or infections; standing; using hands on objects, tools, or controls; bending or twisting the body; repetitive motions.

Dietitians and Nutritionists

- ✲ Education/Training Required: Bachelor's degree
- ✲ Annual Earnings: $49,010
- ✲ Beginning Wage: $31,830
- ✲ Earnings Growth Potential: Medium (35.1%)
- ✲ Growth: 8.6%
- ✲ Annual Job Openings: 4,996
- ✲ Job Security: Most Secure
- ✲ Self-Employed: 7.9%
- ✲ Part-Time: 27.0%

Renewal Industry: Health Care.

Industries with Greatest Employment: Hospitals, Public and Private (33.9%); Ambulatory Health-Care Services (15.9%); Nursing and Residential Care Facilities (10.7%); Local Government (7.2%).

Highest-Growth Industries (Projected Growth for This Job): Social Assistance (51.4%); Professional, Scientific, and Technical Services (35.7%); Amusement, Gambling, and Recreation Industries (33.3%); Administrative and Support Services (30.6%); Ambulatory Health-Care Services (28.9%); Religious, Grantmaking, Civic, Professional, and Similar Organizations (15.7%); Management of Companies and Enterprises (15.3%).

Other Considerations for Job Outlook: Overall, job opportunities will be good for dietitians and nutritionists, particularly for licensed and registered dietitians. Job opportunities should be particularly good in outpatient care facilities, offices of physicians, and food service management. Dietitians and nutritionists without a bachelor's degree will face keen competition for jobs. Dietitians with specialized training, an advanced degree, or certifications beyond the particular state's minimum requirement will experience the best job opportunities. Those specializing in renal and diabetic nutrition or gerontological nutrition will benefit from the growing number of diabetics and the aging of the population.

Plan and conduct food service or nutritional programs to assist in the promotion of health and control of disease. May supervise activities of a department providing quantity food services, counsel individuals, or conduct nutritional research. Assess nutritional needs, diet restrictions, and current health plans to develop and implement dietary-care plans and provide nutritional counseling. Consult with physicians and health-care personnel to determine nutritional needs and diet restrictions of patient or client. Advise patients and their families on nutritional principles, dietary plans and diet modifications, and food selection and preparation. Counsel individuals and groups on basic rules of good nutrition, healthy eating habits, and nutrition monitoring to improve their quality of life. Monitor food service operations to ensure conformance to nutritional, safety, sanitation, and quality standards. Coordinate recipe development and standardization and develop new menus for independent food service operations. Develop policies for food service or nutritional programs to assist in health promotion and disease control. Inspect meals served for conformance to prescribed diets and standards of palatability and appearance. Develop curriculum and prepare manuals, visual aids, course outlines, and other materials used in teaching. Prepare and administer budgets for food, equipment, and supplies. Purchase food in accordance with health and safety codes. Select, train, and supervise workers who plan, prepare, and serve meals. Manage quantity food service departments or clinical and community nutrition services. Coordinate diet counseling services. Advise food service managers and organizations on sanitation, safety procedures, menu development, budgeting, and planning to assist with the establishment, operation, and evaluation of food service facilities and nutrition programs. Organize, develop, analyze, test, and prepare special meals such as low-fat, low-cholesterol, and chemical-free meals. Plan, conduct, and evaluate dietary, nutritional, and epidemiological research. Plan and conduct training programs in dietetics, nutrition, and institutional management and administration for medical students, health-care personnel, and the general public. Make recommendations regarding public policy, such as nutrition labeling, food fortification, and nutrition standards for school programs.

Personality Type: Investigative-Social.

Career Clusters: 05 Education and Training; 08 Health Science; 15 Science, Technology, Engineering, and Mathematics. **Career Pathways:** 05.3 Teaching/Training; 08.1 Therapeutic Services; 08.4 Support Services; 15.3 Science and Mathematics.

Skills: Science; Writing; Social Perceptiveness; Instructing; Reading Comprehension; Speaking.

Education and Training Programs: Foods, Nutrition, and Wellness Studies, General; Human Nutrition; Foodservice Systems Administration/Management; Foods, Nutrition, and Related Services, Other; Nutrition Sciences; Dietetics/Dietitian (RD); Clinical Nutrition/Nutritionist; Dietetics and Clinical Nutrition Services, Other. **Related Knowledge/Courses:** Food Production; Therapy and Counseling; Sociology and Anthropology; Medicine and Dentistry; Philosophy and Theology; Psychology.

Work Environment: Indoors; more often sitting than standing.

Drywall and Ceiling Tile Installers

- ❋ Education/Training Required: Moderate-term on-the-job training
- ❋ Annual Earnings: $36,520
- ❋ Beginning Wage: $23,480
- ❋ Earnings Growth Potential: Medium (35.7%)
- ❋ Growth: 7.3%
- ❋ Annual Job Openings: 30,945
- ❋ Job Security: Least Secure
- ❋ Self-Employed: 23.0%
- ❋ Part-Time: 6.1%

Renewal Industry: Infrastructure.

Industries with Greatest Employment: Specialty Trade Contractors (68.8%); Construction of Buildings (7.1%).

Highest-Growth Industries (Projected Growth for This Job): Administrative and Support Services (26.6%); Real Estate (20.0%).

Other Considerations for Job Outlook: Job opportunities for drywall installers and ceiling tile installers are expected to be good. Many potential workers are not attracted to this occupation because they prefer work that is less strenuous and has more comfortable working conditions. Experienced workers will have especially favorable opportunities.

Apply plasterboard or other wallboard to ceilings or interior walls of buildings. Apply or mount acoustical tiles or blocks, strips, or sheets of shock-absorbing materials to ceilings and walls of buildings to reduce or reflect sound. Materials may be of decorative quality. Includes lathers who fasten wooden, metal, or rockboard lath to walls, ceilings, or partitions of buildings to provide support base for plaster, fireproofing, or acoustical material. Inspect furrings, mechanical mountings, and masonry surface for plumbness and level, using spirit or water levels. Install metal lath where plaster applications will be exposed to weather or water or for curved or irregular surfaces. Install blanket insulation between studs and tack plastic moisture barriers over insulation. Coordinate work with drywall finishers who cover the seams between drywall panels. Trim rough edges from wallboard to maintain even joints, using knives. Seal joints between ceiling tiles and walls. Scribe and cut edges of tile to fit walls where wall molding is not specified. Read blueprints and other specifications to determine methods of installation, work procedures, and material and tool requirements. Nail channels or wood furring strips to surfaces to provide mounting for tile. Mount tile by using adhesives or by nailing, screwing, stapling, or wire-tying lath directly to structural frameworks. Measure and mark surfaces to lay out work according to blueprints and drawings, using tape measures, straightedges or squares, and marking devices. Hang drywall panels on metal frameworks of walls and ceilings in offices, schools, and other large buildings, using lifts or hoists to adjust panel heights when necessary. Install horizontal and vertical metal or wooden studs to frames so that wallboard can be attached to interior walls. Fasten metal or rockboard lath to the structural framework of walls, ceilings, and partitions of buildings, using nails, screws, staples, or wire-ties. Apply or mount acoustical tile or blocks, strips, or sheets of shock-absorbing materials to ceilings and walls of buildings to reduce reflection of sound or to decorate rooms. Apply cement to backs of tiles and press tiles into place, aligning them with layout marks or joints of previously laid tile. Hang dry lines (stretched string) to wall moldings in order to guide positioning of main runners. Assemble and install metal framing and decorative trim for windows, doorways, and vents. Fit and fasten wallboard or drywall into position on wood or metal frameworks, using glue, nails, or screws.

Personality Type: Realistic-Conventional.

Career Cluster: 02 Architecture and Construction. **Career Pathway:** 02.2 Construction.

Skills: Installation; Management of Personnel Resources; Management of Material Resources; Management of Financial Resources; Mathematics; Repairing.

Education and Training Program: Drywall Installation/Drywaller. **Related Knowledge/Courses:** Building and Construction; Design; Mechanical Devices; Mathematics; Production and Processing; Public Safety and Security.

Work Environment: High places; standing; walking and running; using hands on objects, tools, or controls; bending or twisting the body; repetitive motions.

Economics Teachers, Postsecondary

- ❋ Education/Training Required: Master's degree
- ❋ Annual Earnings: $75,300
- ❋ Beginning Wage: $41,650
- ❋ Earnings Growth Potential: High (44.7%)
- ❋ Growth: 22.9%
- ❋ Annual Job Openings: 2,208
- ❋ Job Security: Most Secure
- ❋ Self-Employed: 0.4%
- ❋ Part-Time: 27.8%

Renewal Industry: Education.

Industries with Greatest Employment: Educational Services, Public and Private (97.3%).

Highest-Growth Industries (Projected Growth for This Job): Administrative and Support Services (48.3%); Amusement, Gambling, and Recreation Industries (45.2%); Social Assistance (38.6%); Support Activities for Transportation (32.8%); Religious, Grantmaking, Civic, Professional, and Similar Organizations (29.9%); Professional, Scientific, and Technical Services (28.8%); Management of Companies and Enterprises (26.8%); Local Government (23.5%); Educational Services, Public and Private (22.8%); Hospitals, Public and Private (21.4%).

Other Considerations for Job Outlook: Retirements of current postsecondary teachers should create numerous openings for all types of postsecondary teachers, so job

opportunities are generally expected to be very good. However, one of the main reasons why students attend postsecondary institutions is to prepare themselves for careers, so the best job prospects for postsecondary teachers are likely to be in rapidly growing fields that offer many non-academic career options. Economics courses are commonly required as part of business majors. Community colleges and other institutions offering career and technical education have been among the most rapidly growing, and these institutions are expected to offer some of the best opportunities for postsecondary teachers.

Teach courses in economics. Prepare and deliver lectures to undergraduate and/or graduate students on topics such as econometrics, price theory, and macroeconomics. Prepare course materials such as syllabi, homework assignments, and handouts. Evaluate and grade students' classwork, assignments, and papers. Compile, administer, and grade examinations or assign this work to others. Keep abreast of developments in their field by reading current literature, talking with colleagues, and participating in professional conferences. Maintain student attendance records, grades, and other required records. Initiate, facilitate, and moderate classroom discussions. Maintain regularly scheduled office hours in order to advise and assist students. Select and obtain materials and supplies such as textbooks. Plan, evaluate, and revise curricula, course content, and course materials and methods of instruction. Conduct research in a particular field of knowledge and publish findings in professional journals, books, and/or electronic media. Supervise undergraduate and/or graduate teaching, internship, and research work. Advise students on academic and vocational curricula and on career issues. Serve on academic or administrative committees that deal with institutional policies, departmental matters, and academic issues. Collaborate with colleagues to address teaching and research issues. Compile bibliographies of specialized materials for outside reading assignments. Participate in student recruitment, registration, and placement activities. Perform administrative duties such as serving as department head. Write grant proposals to procure external research funding. Participate in campus and community events. Provide professional consulting services to government and/or industry. Act as advisers to student organizations.

Personality Type: Social-Investigative.

Career Clusters: 04 Business, Management, and Administration; 15 Science, Technology, Engineering, and Mathematics.

Career Pathways: 04.1 Management; 15.3 Science and Mathematics.

Skills: Mathematics; Writing; Instructing; Speaking; Reading Comprehension; Critical Thinking.

Education and Training Programs: Social Science Teacher Education; Economics, General; Applied Economics; Econometrics and Quantitative Economics; Development Economics and International Development; International Economics; Economics, Other; Business/Managerial Economics. **Related Knowledge/Courses:** Economics and Accounting; History and Archeology; Mathematics; Philosophy and Theology; Education and Training; English Language.

Work Environment: Indoors; sitting.

Education Administrators, Elementary and Secondary School

- ❋ Education/Training Required: Work experience plus degree
- ❋ Annual Earnings: $80,580
- ❋ Beginning Wage: $52,940
- ❋ Earnings Growth Potential: Low (34.3%)
- ❋ Growth: 7.6%
- ❋ Annual Job Openings: 27,143
- ❋ Job Security: Most Secure
- ❋ Self-Employed: 3.3%
- ❋ Part-Time: 8.3%

Renewal Industry: Education.

Industries with Greatest Employment: Educational Services, Public and Private (94.4%).

Highest-Growth Industries (Projected Growth for This Job): Professional, Scientific, and Technical Services (51.8%); Social Assistance (33.6%); Administrative and Support Services (29.0%); Nursing and Residential Care Facilities (22.2%); Religious, Grantmaking, Civic, Professional, and Similar Organizations (19.9%).

Other Considerations for Job Outlook: Job opportunities should be very good because a large proportion of education administrators are expected to retire over the next 10 years. Job growth will mainly depend on growth in enrollments of school-age children, but growth at the elementary and secondary level is expected to slow. Principals and assistant principals should have very favorable job prospects because the job has seen a sharp increase in responsibilities in recent years that has made the job more stressful and has discouraged some teachers from taking positions in administration. Enrollments are expected to increase the fastest in the West and South, where the population is growing faster, and to decline or remain stable in the Northeast and the Midwest. School administrators also are in greater demand in rural and urban areas, where pay is generally lower than in the suburbs.

Plan, direct, or coordinate the academic, clerical, or auxiliary activities of public or private elementary or secondary-level schools. Review and approve new programs or recommend modifications to existing programs, submitting program proposals for school board approval as necessary. Prepare, maintain, or oversee the preparation and maintenance of attendance, activity, planning, or personnel reports and records. Confer with parents and staff to discuss educational activities, policies, and student behavioral or learning problems. Prepare and submit budget requests and recommendations or grant proposals to solicit program funding. Direct and coordinate school maintenance services and the use of school facilities. Counsel and provide guidance to students regarding personal, academic, vocational, or behavioral issues. Organize and direct committees of specialists, volunteers, and staff to provide technical and advisory assistance for programs. Teach classes or courses to students. Advocate for new schools to be built or for existing facilities to be repaired or remodeled. Plan and develop instructional methods and content for educational, vocational, or student activity programs. Develop partnerships with businesses, communities, and other organizations to help meet identified educational needs and to provide school-to-work programs. Direct and coordinate activities of teachers, administrators, and support staff at schools, public agencies, and institutions. Evaluate curricula, teaching methods, and programs to determine their effectiveness, efficiency, and utilization and to ensure that school activities comply with federal, state, and local regulations. Set educational standards and goals and help establish policies and procedures to carry them out. Recruit, hire, train, and evaluate primary and supplemental staff. Enforce discipline and attendance rules. Observe teaching methods and examine learning materials to evaluate and standardize curricula and teaching techniques and to determine areas where improvement is needed. Establish, coordinate, and oversee particular programs across school districts, such as programs to evaluate student academic achievement. Review and interpret government codes and develop programs to ensure adherence to codes and facility safety, security, and maintenance.

Personality Type: Enterprising-Social-Conventional.

Career Cluster: 05 Education and Training. **Career Pathway:** 05.1 Administration and Administrative Support.

Skills: Management of Personnel Resources; Management of Financial Resources; Negotiation; Learning Strategies; Monitoring; Management of Material Resources.

Education and Training Programs: Educational Leadership and Administration, General; Educational, Instructional, and Curriculum Supervision; Elementary and Middle School Administration/Principalship; Secondary School Administration/Principalship; Educational Administration and Supervision, Other. **Related Knowledge/Courses:** Therapy and Counseling; Education and Training; Personnel and Human Resources; Psychology; Sociology and Anthropology; History and Archeology.

Work Environment: Indoors; standing.

Education Administrators, Postsecondary

- ✳ Education/Training Required: Work experience plus degree
- ✳ Annual Earnings: $75,780
- ✳ Beginning Wage: $41,910
- ✳ Earnings Growth Potential: High (44.7%)
- ✳ Growth: 14.2%
- ✳ Annual Job Openings: 17,121
- ✳ Job Security: Most Secure
- ✳ Self-Employed: 3.3%
- ✳ Part-Time: 8.3%

Renewal Industry: Education.

Industries with Greatest Employment: Educational Services, Public and Private (95.3%).

Highest-Growth Industries (Projected Growth for This Job): Professional, Scientific, and Technical Services (23.5%); Religious, Grantmaking, Civic, Professional, and Similar Organizations (22.5%); Management of Companies and Enterprises (18.2%).

Other Considerations for Job Outlook: Job opportunities should be excellent because a large proportion of education administrators are expected to retire over the next 10 years. Job growth will mainly depend on growth in enrollments of school-age children, and growth will be especially fast at the postsecondary level, including private and for-profit institutions that serve adults. Enrollments are expected to increase the fastest in the West and South, where the population is growing faster, and to decline or remain stable in the Northeast and the Midwest.

Plan, direct, or coordinate research, instructional, student administration and services, and other educational activities at postsecondary institutions, including universities, colleges, and junior and community colleges. Recruit, hire, train, and terminate departmental personnel. Plan, administer, and control budgets; maintain financial records; and produce financial reports. Represent institutions at community and campus events, in meetings with other institution personnel, and during accreditation processes. Participate in faculty and college committee activities. Provide assistance to faculty and staff in duties such as teaching classes, conducting orientation programs, issuing transcripts, and scheduling events. Establish operational policies and procedures and make any necessary modifications, based on analysis of operations, demographics, and other research information. Confer with other academic staff to explain and formulate admission requirements and course credit policies. Appoint individuals to faculty positions and evaluate their performance. Direct activities of administrative departments such as admissions, registration, and career services. Develop curricula and recommend curricula revisions and additions. Determine course schedules and coordinate teaching assignments and room assignments to ensure optimum use of buildings and equipment. Consult with government regulatory and licensing agencies to ensure the institution's conformance with applicable standards. Direct, coordinate, and evaluate the activities of personnel engaged in administering academic institutions, departments, and/or alumni organizations. Teach courses within their department. Participate in student recruitment, selection, and admission, making admissions recommendations when required to do so. Review student misconduct reports requiring disciplinary action and counsel students regarding such reports. Supervise coaches. Assess and collect tuition and fees. Direct scholarship, fellowship, and loan programs, performing activities such as selecting recipients and distributing aid. Coordinate the production and dissemination of university publications such as course catalogs and class schedules. Review registration statistics and consult with faculty officials to develop registration policies. Audit the financial status of student organizations and facility accounts.

Personality Type: Enterprising-Conventional-Social.

Career Cluster: 05 Education and Training. **Career Pathway:** 05.1 Administration and Administrative Support.

Skills: Management of Financial Resources; Management of Personnel Resources; Systems Evaluation; Persuasion; Monitoring; Judgment and Decision Making.

Education and Training Programs: Educational Leadership and Administration, General; Educational, Instructional, and Curriculum Supervision; Higher Education/Higher Education Administration; Community College Education; Educational Administration and Supervision, Other. **Related Knowledge/Courses:** Personnel and Human Resources; Education and Training; Sociology and Anthropology; Administration and Management; Philosophy and Theology; English Language.

Work Environment: Indoors; sitting.

Education Administrators, Preschool and Child Care Center/Program

- ❋ Education/Training Required: Work experience plus degree
- ❋ Annual Earnings: $38,580
- ❋ Beginning Wage: $25,340
- ❋ Earnings Growth Potential: Low (34.3%)
- ❋ Growth: 23.5%
- ❋ Annual Job Openings: 8,113
- ❋ Job Security: Most Secure
- ❋ Self-Employed: 3.4%
- ❋ Part-Time: 8.3%

Renewal Industry: Education.

Industries with Greatest Employment: Social Assistance (63.1%); Religious, Grantmaking, Civic, Professional, and Similar Organizations (15.6%); Educational Services, Public and Private (14.3%).

Highest-Growth Industries (Projected Growth for This Job): Professional, Scientific, and Technical Services (39.3%); Social Assistance (30.3%); Ambulatory Health-Care Services (27.1%); Nursing and Residential Care Facilities (19.6%); Religious, Grantmaking, Civic, Professional, and Similar Organizations (17.6%); Management of Companies and Enterprises (15.2%).

Other Considerations for Job Outlook: Job opportunities should be excellent because a large proportion of education administrators are expected to retire over the next 10 years. Job growth will mainly depend on growth in enrollments of school-age children, and growth will be especially fast at preschool and child-care centers. Enrollments are expected to increase the fastest in the West and South, where the population is growing faster, and to decline or remain stable in the Northeast and the Midwest. School administrators also are in greater demand in rural and urban areas, where pay is generally lower than in the suburbs.

Plan, direct, or coordinate the academic and nonacademic activities of preschool and child care centers or programs. Confer with parents and staff to discuss educational activities and policies and students' behavioral or learning problems. Prepare and maintain attendance, activity, planning, accounting, or personnel reports and records for officials and agencies or direct preparation and maintenance activities. Set educational standards and goals and help establish policies, procedures, and programs to carry them out. Monitor students' progress and provide students and teachers with assistance in resolving any problems. Determine allocations of funds for staff, supplies, materials, and equipment and authorize purchases. Recruit, hire, train, and evaluate primary and supplemental staff and recommend personnel actions for programs and services. Direct and coordinate activities of teachers or administrators at daycare centers, schools, public agencies, or institutions. Plan, direct, and monitor instructional methods and content of educational, vocational, or student activity programs. Review and interpret government codes and develop procedures to meet codes and to ensure facility safety, security, and maintenance. Determine the scope of educational program offerings and prepare drafts of program schedules and descriptions to estimate staffing and facility requirements. Review and evaluate new and current programs to determine their efficiency; effectiveness;

and compliance with state, local, and federal regulations, and recommend any necessary modifications. Teach classes or courses or provide direct care to children. Prepare and submit budget requests or grant proposals to solicit program funding. Write articles, manuals, and other publications and assist in the distribution of promotional literature about programs and facilities. Collect and analyze survey data, regulatory information, and demographic and employment trends to forecast enrollment patterns and the need for curriculum changes. Inform businesses, community groups, and governmental agencies about educational needs, available programs, and program policies. Organize and direct committees of specialists, volunteers, and staff to provide technical and advisory assistance for programs.

Personality Type: Social-Enterprising-Conventional.

Career Cluster: 05 Education and Training. **Career Pathway:** 05.1 Administration and Administrative Support.

Skills: Management of Financial Resources; Management of Personnel Resources; Management of Material Resources; Learning Strategies; Monitoring; Social Perceptiveness.

Education and Training Programs: Educational Leadership and Administration, General; Educational, Instructional, and Curriculum Supervision; Elementary and Middle School Administration/Principalship; Educational Administration and Supervision, Other. **Related Knowledge/Courses:** Personnel and Human Resources; Education and Training; Clerical Practices; Philosophy and Theology; Therapy and Counseling; Sociology and Anthropology.

Work Environment: Indoors; standing.

Education Teachers, Postsecondary

- ✸ Education/Training Required: Master's degree
- ✸ Annual Earnings: $54,220
- ✸ Beginning Wage: $29,060
- ✸ Earnings Growth Potential: High (46.4%)
- ✸ Growth: 22.9%
- ✸ Annual Job Openings: 9,359
- ✸ Job Security: Most Secure
- ✸ Self-Employed: 0.4%
- ✸ Part-Time: 27.8%

Renewal Industry: Education.

Industries with Greatest Employment: Educational Services, Public and Private (97.3%).

Highest-Growth Industries (Projected Growth for This Job): Administrative and Support Services (48.3%); Amusement, Gambling, and Recreation Industries (45.2%); Social Assistance (38.6%); Support Activities for Transportation (32.8%); Religious, Grantmaking, Civic, Professional, and Similar Organizations (29.9%); Professional, Scientific, and Technical Services (28.8%); Management of Companies and Enterprises (26.8%); Local Government (23.5%); Educational Services, Public and Private (22.8%); Hospitals, Public and Private (21.4%).

Other Considerations for Job Outlook: Retirements of current postsecondary teachers should create numerous openings for all types of postsecondary teachers, so job opportunities are generally expected to be very good. However, one of the main reasons why students attend postsecondary institutions is to prepare themselves for careers, and the education industry is growing rapidly, so many prospective teachers and teacher aides will come to colleges. Community colleges and other institutions offering career and technical education have been among the most rapidly growing, and these institutions are expected to offer some of the best opportunities for postsecondary teachers.

Teach courses pertaining to education, such as counseling, curriculum, guidance, instruction, teacher education, and teaching English as a second language. Prepare course materials such as syllabi, homework assignments, and handouts. Prepare and deliver lectures to undergraduate and/or graduate students on topics such as children's literature, learning and development, and reading instruction. Initiate, facilitate, and moderate classroom discussions. Evaluate and grade students' classwork, assignments, and papers. Plan, evaluate, and revise curricula, course content, and course materials and methods of instruction. Supervise students' fieldwork, internship, and research work. Keep abreast of developments in their field by reading current literature, talking with colleagues, and participating in professional conferences. Advise students on academic and vocational curricula and on career issues. Maintain regularly scheduled office hours to advise and assist students. Maintain student attendance records, grades, and other required records. Collaborate with colleagues to address teaching and research issues. Compile, administer, and grade examinations or assign this work to others. Conduct research in a particular field of knowledge and publish findings in professional journals, books, or electronic media. Select and obtain materials and supplies such as textbooks. Participate in student recruitment, registration, and placement activities. Advise and instruct teachers employed in school systems by providing activities such as in-service seminars. Serve on academic or administrative committees that deal with institutional policies, departmental matters, and academic issues. Compile bibliographies of specialized materials for outside reading assignments. Write grant proposals to procure external research funding. Participate in campus and community events. Perform administrative duties such as serving as department head. Act as advisers to student organizations. Provide professional consulting services to government and/or industry.

Personality Type: Social-Artistic-Investigative.

Career Cluster: 05 Education and Training. **Career Pathway:** 05.3 Teaching/Training.

Skills: Learning Strategies; Instructing; Writing; Social Perceptiveness; Speaking; Persuasion.

Education and Training Programs: Education, General; Indian/Native American Education; Social and Philosophical Foundations of Education; Agricultural Teacher Education; Art Teacher Education; Business Teacher Education; Driver and Safety Teacher Education; English/Language Arts Teacher Education; Foreign Language Teacher Education; Health Teacher Education; Family and Consumer Sciences/Home Economics Teacher Education; others. **Related Knowledge/Courses:** Therapy and Counseling; Education and Training; Sociology and Anthropology; Philosophy and Theology; Psychology; English Language.

Work Environment: Indoors; sitting.

Educational, Vocational, and School Counselors

- ❋ Education/Training Required: Master's degree
- ❋ Annual Earnings: $49,450
- ❋ Beginning Wage: $28,430
- ❋ Earnings Growth Potential: High (42.5%)
- ❋ Growth: 12.6%
- ❋ Annual Job Openings: 54,025
- ❋ Job Security: Most Secure
- ❋ Self-Employed: 6.1%
- ❋ Part-Time: 15.4%

Renewal Industry: Education.

Industries with Greatest Employment: Educational Services, Public and Private (73.3%); Social Assistance (9.8%).

Highest-Growth Industries (Projected Growth for This Job): Professional, Scientific, and Technical Services (46.3%); Social Assistance (32.9%); Ambulatory Health-Care Services (26.2%); Nursing and Residential Care Facilities (22.3%); Religious, Grantmaking, Civic, Professional, and Similar Organizations (16.9%); Management of Companies and Enterprises (15.3%).

Other Considerations for Job Outlook: Demand for vocational or career counselors should grow as multiple job and career changes become common and as workers become increasingly aware of counseling services. In addition, state and local governments will employ growing numbers of counselors to assist beneficiaries of welfare programs who exhaust their eligibility and must find jobs. Demand for school counselors may increase due in large part to increases in student enrollments at postsecondary schools and colleges and as more states require elementary schools to employ counselors. Expansion of the responsibilities of school counselors should also lead to increases in their employment. Federal grants and subsidies may help to offset tight budgets and allow the reduction in student-to-counselor ratios to continue. For school counselors, job prospects should be good because many people are leaving the occupation to retire; however, opportunities may be more favorable in rural and urban areas, rather than the suburbs.

E

Counsel individuals and provide group educational and vocational guidance services. Counsel students regarding educational issues such as course and program selection, class scheduling, school adjustment, truancy, study habits, and career planning. Counsel individuals to help them understand and overcome personal, social, or behavioral problems affecting their educational or vocational situations. Maintain accurate and complete student records as required by laws, district policies, and administrative regulations. Confer with parents or guardians, teachers, other counselors, and administrators to resolve students' behavioral, academic, and other problems. Provide crisis intervention to students when difficult situations occur at schools. Identify cases involving domestic abuse or other family problems affecting students' development. Meet with parents and guardians to discuss their children's progress and to determine their priorities for their children and their resource needs. Prepare students for later educational experiences by encouraging them to explore learning opportunities and to persevere with challenging tasks. Encourage students and/or parents to seek additional assistance from mental health professionals when necessary. Observe and evaluate students' performance, behavior, social development, and physical health. Enforce all administration policies and rules governing students. Meet with other professionals to discuss individual students' needs and progress. Provide students with information on such topics as college degree programs and admission requirements, financial aid opportunities, trade and technical schools, and apprenticeship programs. Evaluate individuals' abilities, interests, and personality characteristics, using tests, records, interviews, and professional sources. Collaborate with teachers and administrators in the development, evaluation, and revision of school programs. Establish and enforce behavioral rules and procedures to maintain order among students. Teach classes and present self-help or information sessions on subjects related to education and career planning. Attend professional meetings, educational conferences, and teacher training workshops to maintain and improve professional competence.

Personality Type: Social.

Career Cluster: 05 Education and Training. **Career Pathway:** 05.2 Professional Support Services.

Skills: Social Perceptiveness; Service Orientation; Negotiation; Active Listening; Persuasion; Learning Strategies.

Education and Training Programs: Counselor Education/School Counseling and Guidance Services; College Student Counseling and Personnel Services. **Related Knowledge/Courses:** Therapy and Counseling; Psychology; Sociology and Anthropology; Education and Training; Philosophy and Theology; Clerical Practices.

Work Environment: Indoors; sitting.

Electrical and Electronic Engineering Technicians

See *Electrical Engineering Technicians* and *Electronics Engineering Technicians*, described separately.

Electrical and Electronics Drafters

See *Electrical Drafters* and *Electronic Drafters*, described separately.

Electrical and Electronics Repairers, Commercial and Industrial Equipment

- ❋ Education/Training Required: Postsecondary vocational training
- ❋ Annual Earnings: $47,110
- ❋ Beginning Wage: $28,830
- ❋ Earnings Growth Potential: Medium (38.8%)
- ❋ Growth: 6.8%
- ❋ Annual Job Openings: 6,607
- ❋ Job Security: Most Secure
- ❋ Self-Employed: 0.0%
- ❋ Part-Time: 0.6%

Renewal Industries: Advanced Manufacturing; Green Technologies.

Industries with Greatest Employment: Federal Government (14.8%); Merchant Wholesalers, Durable Goods (10.3%); Computer and Electronic Product Manufacturing (9.9%); Specialty Trade Contractors (9.0%); Repair and Maintenance (8.4%); Chemical Manufacturing (7.5%).

Highest-Growth Industries (Projected Growth for This Job): Amusement, Gambling, and Recreation Industries (41.3%); Professional, Scientific, and Technical Services (34.6%); Telecommunications (30.6%); Support Activities for Transportation (27.1%); Rental and Leasing Services (24.0%); Management of Companies and Enterprises (23.0%); Merchant Wholesalers, Durable Goods (21.6%); Wholesale Electronic Markets and Agents and Brokers (20.9%); Local Government (19.7%); Construction of Buildings (19.5%); Broadcasting (Except Internet) (18.7%); Hospitals, Public and Private (17.6%); Educational Services, Public and Private (16.2%).

Other Considerations for Job Outlook: Job opportunities should be best for applicants with an associate degree in electronics, certification, and related experience. In addition to employment growth, the need to replace workers who transfer to other occupations or leave the labor force will result in some openings. Commercial and industrial equipment will become more sophisticated and will be used more frequently as businesses strive to lower costs by increasing and improving automation. Companies will install electronic controls, robots, sensors, and other equipment to automate processes such as assembly and testing. In addition, as prices decline, this equipment will be used more frequently throughout a number of industries, including services, utilities, and construction, as well as manufacturing. Improved reliability of equipment should not constrain employment growth, however: Companies increasingly will rely on repairers because malfunctions that idle commercial and industrial equipment will continue to be costly.

Repair, test, adjust, or install electronic equipment, such as industrial controls, transmitters, and antennas. Perform scheduled preventive maintenance tasks, such as checking, cleaning, and repairing equipment, to detect and prevent problems. Examine work orders and converse with equipment operators to detect equipment problems and to ascertain whether mechanical or human errors contributed to the problems. Operate equipment to demonstrate proper use and to analyze malfunctions. Set up and test industrial equipment to ensure that it functions properly. Test faulty equipment to diagnose malfunctions, using test equipment and software and applying knowledge of the functional operation of electronic units and systems. Repair and adjust equipment, machines, and defective components, replacing worn parts such as gaskets and seals in watertight electrical equipment. Calibrate testing instruments and installed or repaired equipment to prescribed specifications. Advise management regarding customer satisfaction, product performance, and suggestions for product improvements. Study blueprints, schematics, manuals, and other specifications to determine installation procedures. Inspect components of industrial equipment for accurate assembly and installation and for defects such as loose connections and frayed wires. Maintain equipment logs that record performance problems, repairs, calibrations, and tests. Coordinate efforts with other workers involved in installing and maintaining equipment or components. Maintain inventory of spare parts. Consult with customers, supervisors, and engineers to plan layout of equipment and to resolve problems in system operation and maintenance. Install repaired equipment in various settings, such as industrial or military establishments. Send defective units to the manufacturer or to a specialized repair shop for repair. Determine feasibility of using standardized equipment and develop specifications for equipment required to perform additional functions. Enter information into computer to copy program or to draw, modify, or store schematics, applying knowledge of software package used. Sign overhaul documents for equipment replaced or repaired. Develop or modify industrial electronic devices, circuits, and equipment according to available specifications.

Personality Type: Realistic-Investigative-Conventional.

Career Cluster: 13 Manufacturing. **Career Pathway:** 13.3 Maintenance, Installation, and Repair.

Skills: Installation; Repairing; Operation Monitoring; Troubleshooting; Equipment Maintenance; Operation and Control.

Education and Training Programs: Computer Installation and Repair Technology/Technician; Industrial Electronics Technology/Technician. **Related Knowledge/Courses:** Mechanical Devices; Computers and Electronics; Telecommunications; Engineering and Technology.

Work Environment: Indoors; noisy; cramped work space, awkward positions; hazardous conditions; standing; using hands on objects, tools, or controls.

Electrical Drafters

- ❋ Education/Training Required: Postsecondary vocational training
- ❋ Annual Earnings: $49,250
- ❋ Beginning Wage: $30,490
- ❋ Earnings Growth Potential: Medium (38.1%)
- ❋ Growth: 4.1%
- ❋ Annual Job Openings: 4,786
- ❋ Job Security: Less Secure than Most
- ❋ Self-Employed: 5.7%
- ❋ Part-Time: 5.9%

Our sources did not provide separate job openings data for this occupation. The job openings listed here are shared with Electronic Drafters.

Renewal Industries: Advanced Manufacturing; Green Technologies.

Industries with Greatest Employment: Professional, Scientific, and Technical Services (28.0%); Specialty Trade Contractors (17.7%); Computer and Electronic Product Manufacturing (17.0%); Electrical Equipment, Appliance, and Component Manufacturing (7.5%); Utilities (7.0%).

Highest-Growth Industries (Projected Growth for This Job): Administrative and Support Services (31.4%); Professional, Scientific, and Technical Services (17.5%); Merchant Wholesalers, Durable Goods (15.8%); Management of Companies and Enterprises (15.4%).

Other Considerations for Job Outlook: Demand for particular drafting specialties varies throughout the country because employment usually is contingent on the needs of local industry. Opportunities should be best for individuals with at least two years of postsecondary training in a drafting program that provides strong technical skills and considerable experience with CADD systems.

Develop specifications and instructions for installation of voltage transformers, overhead or underground cables, and related electrical equipment used to conduct electrical energy from transmission lines or high-voltage distribution lines to consumers. Use computer-aided drafting equipment and/or conventional drafting stations; technical handbooks; tables; calculators; and traditional drafting tools such as boards, pencils, protractors, and T-squares. Draft working drawings, wiring diagrams, wiring connection specifications, or cross-sections of underground cables as required for instructions to installation crew. Confer with engineering staff and other personnel to resolve problems. Draw master sketches to scale, showing relation of proposed installations to existing facilities and exact specifications and dimensions. Measure factors that affect installation and arrangement of equipment, such as distances to be spanned by wire and cable. Assemble documentation packages and produce drawing sets, which are then checked by an engineer or an architect. Review completed construction drawings and cost estimates for accuracy and conformity to standards and regulations. Prepare and interpret specifications, calculating weights, volumes, and stress factors. Explain drawings to production or construction teams and provide adjustments as necessary. Supervise and train other technologists, technicians, and drafters. Study work order requests to determine type of service, such as lighting or power, demanded by installation. Visit proposed installation sites and draw rough sketches of location. Determine the order of work and the method of presentation, such as orthographic or isometric drawing. Reproduce working drawings on copy machines or trace drawings in ink. Write technical reports and draw charts that display statistics and data.

Personality Type: Realistic-Investigative-Conventional.

Career Cluster: 02 Architecture and Construction. **Career Pathway:** 02.1 Design/Pre-Construction.

Skills: Mathematics; Installation; Active Learning; Critical Thinking; Quality Control Analysis; Technology Design.

Education and Training Program: Electrical/Electronics Drafting and Electrical/Electronics CAD/CADD. **Related Knowledge/Courses:** Design; Engineering and Technology; Building and Construction; Computers and Electronics; Telecommunications; Clerical Practices.

Work Environment: Indoors; sitting.

Electrical Engineering Technicians

❊ Education/Training Required: Associate degree
❊ Annual Earnings: $52,140
❊ Beginning Wage: $31,310
❊ Earnings Growth Potential: High (40.0%)
❊ Growth: 3.6%
❊ Annual Job Openings: 12,583
❊ Job Security: More Secure than Most
❊ Self-Employed: 0.9%
❊ Part-Time: 5.9%

Our sources did not provide separate job openings data for this occupation. The job openings listed here are shared with Electronics Engineering Technicians.

Renewal Industries: Advanced Manufacturing; Green Technologies; Infrastructure.

Industries with Greatest Employment: Computer and Electronic Product Manufacturing (24.8%); Professional, Scientific, and Technical Services (15.3%); Federal Government (9.5%); Telecommunications (7.9%); Merchant Wholesalers, Durable Goods (6.4%).

Highest-Growth Industries (Projected Growth for This Job): Warehousing and Storage (33.8%); Professional, Scientific, and Technical Services (25.2%); Support Activities for Transportation (19.9%); Motion Picture, Video, and Sound Recording Industries (17.5%); Internet Service Providers, Web Search Portals, and Data Processing Services (17.3%); Publishing Industries (Except Internet) (16.2%); Management of Companies and Enterprises (15.3%).

Other Considerations for Job Outlook: Although rising demand for electronic goods—including communications equipment, defense-related equipment, medical electronics, and consumer products—should continue to drive demand, foreign competition in design and manufacturing will limit employment growth.

Apply electrical theory and related knowledge to test and modify developmental or operational electrical machinery and electrical control equipment and circuitry in industrial or commercial plants and laboratories. Usually work under direction of engineering staff. Assemble electrical and electronic systems and prototypes according to engineering data and knowledge of electrical principles, using hand tools and measuring instruments. Provide technical assistance and resolution when electrical or engineering problems are encountered before, during, and after construction. Install and maintain electrical control systems and solid state equipment. Modify electrical prototypes, parts, assemblies, and systems to correct functional deviations. Set up and operate test equipment to evaluate performance of developmental parts, assemblies, or systems under simulated operating conditions and record results. Collaborate with electrical engineers and other personnel to identify, define, and solve developmental problems. Build, calibrate, maintain, troubleshoot, and repair electrical instruments or testing equipment. Analyze and interpret test information to resolve design-related problems. Write commissioning procedures for electrical installations. Prepare project cost and work-time estimates. Evaluate engineering proposals, shop drawings, and design comments for sound electrical engineering practice and conformance with established safety and design criteria and recommend approval or disapproval. Draw or modify diagrams and write engineering specifications to clarify design details and functional criteria of experimental electronics units. Conduct inspections for quality control and assurance programs, reporting findings and recommendations. Prepare contracts and initiate, review, and coordinate modifications to contract specifications and plans throughout the construction process. Plan, schedule, and monitor work of support personnel to assist supervisor. Review existing electrical engineering criteria to identify necessary revisions, deletions, or amendments to outdated material. Perform supervisory duties such as recommending work assignments, approving leaves, and completing performance evaluations. Plan method and sequence of operations for developing and testing experimental electronic and electrical equipment. Visit construction sites to observe conditions impacting design and to identify solutions to technical design problems involving electrical systems equipment that arise during construction.

Personality Type: Realistic-Investigative-Conventional.

Career Cluster: 13 Manufacturing. **Career Pathways:** 13.2 Manufacturing Production Process Development; 13.3 Maintenance, Installation, and Repair.

Skills: Repairing; Installation; Troubleshooting; Science; Operations Analysis; Technology Design.

E

Education and Training Programs: Electrical, Electronic, and Communications Engineering Technology/Technician; Telecommunications Technology/Technician; Electrical and Electronic Engineering Technologies/Technicians, Other; Computer Engineering Technology/Technician; Computer Technology/Computer Systems Technology. **Related Knowledge/Courses:** Engineering and Technology; Design; Computers and Electronics; Physics; Mechanical Devices; Telecommunications.

Work Environment: Indoors; noisy; sitting; using hands on objects, tools, or controls.

Electrical Engineers

- ❈ Education/Training Required: Bachelor's degree
- ❈ Annual Earnings: $79,240
- ❈ Beginning Wage: $51,220
- ❈ Earnings Growth Potential: Medium (35.4%)
- ❈ Growth: 6.3%
- ❈ Annual Job Openings: 6,806
- ❈ Job Security: More Secure than Most
- ❈ Self-Employed: 2.1%
- ❈ Part-Time: 2.0%

Renewal Industries: Advanced Manufacturing; Green Technologies; Information and Telecommunication Technologies; Infrastructure.

Industries with Greatest Employment: Professional, Scientific, and Technical Services (29.3%); Computer and Electronic Product Manufacturing (22.3%); Utilities (8.4%); Machinery Manufacturing (6.5%).

Highest-Growth Industries (Projected Growth for This Job): Waste Management and Remediation Services (30.1%); Administrative and Support Services (28.2%); Professional, Scientific, and Technical Services (26.4%); Publishing Industries (Except Internet) (26.3%); Support Activities for Transportation (19.7%); Internet Service Providers, Web Search Portals, and Data Processing Services (19.3%); Motion Picture, Video, and Sound Recording Industries (18.5%); Merchant Wholesalers, Durable Goods (15.8%); Management of Companies and Enterprises (15.3%).

Other Considerations for Job Outlook: Electrical engineers working in firms providing engineering expertise and design services to manufacturers should have the best job prospects.

Design, develop, test, or supervise the manufacturing and installation of electrical equipment, components, or systems for commercial, industrial, military, or scientific use. Confer with engineers, customers, and others to discuss existing or potential engineering projects and products. Design, implement, maintain, and improve electrical instruments, equipment, facilities, components, products, and systems for commercial, industrial, and domestic purposes. Operate computer-assisted engineering and design software and equipment to perform engineering tasks. Direct and coordinate manufacturing, construction, installation, maintenance, support, documentation, and testing activities to ensure compliance with specifications, codes, and customer requirements. Perform detailed calculations to compute and establish manufacturing, construction, and installation standards and specifications. Inspect completed installations and observe operations to ensure conformance to design and equipment specifications and compliance with operational and safety standards. Plan and implement research methodology and procedures to apply principles of electrical theory to engineering projects. Prepare specifications for purchase of materials and equipment. Supervise and train project team members as necessary. Investigate and test vendors' and competitors' products. Oversee project production efforts to assure projects are completed satisfactorily, on time, and within budget. Prepare and study technical drawings, specifications of electrical systems, and topographical maps to ensure that installation and operations conform to standards and customer requirements. Investigate customer or public complaints, determine nature and extent of problem, and recommend remedial measures. Plan layout of electric-power-generating plants and distribution lines and stations. Assist in developing capital project programs for new equipment and major repairs. Develop budgets, estimating labor, material, and construction costs. Compile data and write reports regarding existing and potential engineering studies and projects. Collect data relating to commercial and residential development, population, and power system interconnection to determine operating efficiency of electrical systems. Conduct field surveys and study maps, graphs, diagrams, and other data to identify and correct power system problems.

Personality Type: Investigative-Realistic.

Career Cluster: 15 Science, Technology, Engineering, and Mathematics. **Career Pathway:** 15.1 Engineering and Technology.

Skills: Technology Design; Science; Systems Analysis; Troubleshooting; Systems Evaluation; Equipment Selection.

Education and Training Program: Electrical, Electronic, and Communications Engineering. **Related Knowledge/ Courses:** Engineering and Technology; Design; Physics; Telecommunications; Computers and Electronics; Mathematics.

Work Environment: Indoors; sitting.

Electrical Power-Line Installers and Repairers

- ❋ Education/Training Required: Long-term on-the-job training
- ❋ Annual Earnings: $52,570
- ❋ Beginning Wage: $29,780
- ❋ Earnings Growth Potential: High (43.4%)
- ❋ Growth: 7.2%
- ❋ Annual Job Openings: 6,401
- ❋ Job Security: More Secure than Most
- ❋ Self-Employed: 0.6%
- ❋ Part-Time: 1.3%

Renewal Industries: Green Technologies; Infrastructure.

Industries with Greatest Employment: Utilities (51.1%); Heavy and Civil Engineering Construction (21.5%); Local Government (11.4%); Telecommunications (5.0%).

Highest-Growth Industries (Projected Growth for This Job): Administrative and Support Services (43.2%); Educational Services, Public and Private (22.2%); Local Government (18.6%); Heavy and Civil Engineering Construction (15.7%).

Other Considerations for Job Outlook: Most new jobs for electrical power-line installers and repairers are expected to arise among contracting firms in the construction industry.

Install or repair cables or wires used in electrical power or distribution systems. May erect poles and light- or heavy-duty transmission towers. Adhere to safety practices and procedures, such as checking equipment regularly and erecting barriers around work areas. Open switches or attach grounding devices to remove electrical hazards from disturbed or fallen lines or to facilitate repairs. Climb poles or use truck-mounted buckets to access equipment. Place insulating or fireproofing materials over conductors and joints. Install, maintain, and repair electrical distribution and transmission systems, including conduits; cables; wires; and related equipment such as transformers, circuit breakers, and switches. Identify defective sectionalizing devices, circuit breakers, fuses, voltage regulators, transformers, switches, relays, or wiring, using wiring diagrams and electrical-testing instruments. Drive vehicles equipped with tools and materials to job sites. Coordinate work assignment preparation and completion with other workers. String wire conductors and cables between poles, towers, trenches, pylons, and buildings, setting lines in place and using winches to adjust tension. Inspect and test power lines and auxiliary equipment to locate and identify problems, using reading and testing instruments. Test conductors according to electrical diagrams and specifications to identify corresponding conductors and to prevent incorrect connections. Replace damaged poles with new poles and straighten the poles. Install watt-hour meters and connect service drops between power lines and consumers' facilities. Attach crossarms, insulators, and auxiliary equipment to poles prior to installing them. Travel in trucks, helicopters, and airplanes to inspect lines for freedom from obstruction and adequacy of insulation. Dig holes, using augers, and set poles, using cranes and power equipment. Trim trees that could be hazardous to the functioning of cables or wires. Splice or solder cables together or to overhead transmission lines, customer service lines, or street light lines, using hand tools, epoxies, or specialized equipment. Cut and peel lead sheathing and insulation from defective or newly installed cables and conduits prior to splicing.

Personality Type: Realistic-Investigative-Conventional.

Career Cluster: 02 Architecture and Construction. **Career Pathway:** 02.2 Construction.

Skills: Repairing; Installation; Equipment Maintenance; Operation Monitoring; Troubleshooting; Operation and Control.

Education and Training Programs: Electrical and Power Transmission Installation/Installer, General; Lineworker; Electrical and Power Transmission Installers, Other. **Related Knowledge/Courses:** Building and Construction; Mechanical Devices; Customer and Personal Service; Engineering and Technology; Transportation; Design.

Work Environment: Outdoors; very hot or cold; high places; hazardous conditions; hazardous equipment; using hands on objects, tools, or controls.

Electricians

- ❋ Education/Training Required: Long-term on-the-job training
- ❋ Annual Earnings: $44,780
- ❋ Beginning Wage: $27,330
- ❋ Earnings Growth Potential: Medium (39.0%)
- ❋ Growth: 7.4%
- ❋ Annual Job Openings: 79,083
- ❋ Job Security: Least Secure
- ❋ Self-Employed: 10.7%
- ❋ Part-Time: 2.3%

Renewal Industries: Advanced Manufacturing; Green Technologies; Infrastructure.

Industries with Greatest Employment: Specialty Trade Contractors (64.6%).

Highest-Growth Industries (Projected Growth for This Job): Nursing and Residential Care Facilities (46.8%); Museums, Historical Sites, and Similar Institutions (41.2%); Amusement, Gambling, and Recreation Industries (40.4%); Warehousing and Storage (38.4%); Waste Management and Remediation Services (34.3%); Professional, Scientific, and Technical Services (33.9%); Building Material and Garden Equipment and Supplies Dealers (32.5%); Telecommunications (29.5%); Ambulatory Health-Care Services (26.9%); Real Estate (25.6%); Rental and Leasing Services (24.2%); Support Activities for Transportation (23.5%); Religious, Grantmaking, Civic, Professional, and Similar Organizations (22.6%); Accommodation, Including Hotels and Motels (21.8%); Management of Companies and Enterprises (19.5%); Food Services and Drinking Places (18.8%); Broadcasting (Except Internet) (18.8%); Furniture and Home Furnishings Stores (18.6%); Performing Arts, Spectator Sports, and Related Industries (18.1%);

Wholesale Electronic Markets and Agents and Brokers (17.6%); Water Transportation (17.5%); Merchant Wholesalers, Durable Goods (17.3%); Local Government (16.5%); Construction of Buildings (16.4%).

Other Considerations for Job Outlook: Most electricians acquire their skills by completing an apprenticeship program lasting four to five years.

Install, maintain, and repair electrical wiring, equipment, and fixtures. Ensure that work is in accordance with relevant codes. May install or service street lights, intercom systems, or electrical control systems. Maintain current electrician's license or identification card to meet governmental regulations. Connect wires to circuit breakers, transformers, or other components. Repair or replace wiring, equipment, and fixtures, using hand tools and power tools. Assemble, install, test, and maintain electrical or electronic wiring, equipment, appliances, apparatus, and fixtures, using hand tools and power tools. Test electrical systems and continuity of circuits in electrical wiring, equipment, and fixtures, using testing devices such as ohmmeters, voltmeters, and oscilloscopes, to ensure compatibility and safety of system. Use a variety of tools and equipment such as power construction equipment, measuring devices, power tools, and testing equipment, including oscilloscopes, ammeters, and test lamps. Plan layout and installation of electrical wiring, equipment, and fixtures based on job specifications and local codes. Inspect electrical systems, equipment, and components to identify hazards, defects, and the need for adjustment or repair and to ensure compliance with codes. Direct and train workers to install, maintain, or repair electrical wiring, equipment, and fixtures. Diagnose malfunctioning systems, apparatus, and components, using test equipment and hand tools, to locate the cause of a breakdown and correct the problem. Prepare sketches or follow blueprints to determine the location of wiring and equipment and to ensure conformance to building and safety codes. Install ground leads and connect power cables to equipment such as motors. Work from ladders, scaffolds, and roofs to install, maintain, or repair electrical wiring, equipment, and fixtures. Perform business management duties such as maintaining records and files, preparing reports, and ordering supplies and equipment. Fasten small metal or plastic boxes to walls to house electrical switches or outlets. Place conduit, pipes, or tubing inside designated partitions, walls, or other concealed areas and pull insulated wires or cables through the conduit to complete circuits between boxes. Advise management on whether continued operation of equipment could be hazardous.

Personality Type: Realistic-Investigative-Conventional.

Career Cluster: 02 Architecture and Construction. **Career Pathway:** 02.2 Construction.

Skills: No data available.

Education and Training Program: Electrician. **Related Knowledge/Courses:** Building and Construction; Mechanical Devices; Design; Physics; Telecommunications; Engineering and Technology.

Work Environment: Noisy; cramped work space, awkward positions; hazardous conditions; hazardous equipment; standing; using hands on objects, tools, or controls.

Electronic Drafters

- ❋ Education/Training Required: Postsecondary vocational training
- ❋ Annual Earnings: $49,250
- ❋ Beginning Wage: $30,490
- ❋ Earnings Growth Potential: Medium (38.1%)
- ❋ Growth: 4.1%
- ❋ Annual Job Openings: 4,786
- ❋ Job Security: Less Secure than Most
- ❋ Self-Employed: 5.7%
- ❋ Part-Time: 5.9%

Our sources did not provide separate job openings data for this occupation. The job openings listed here are shared with Electrical Drafters.

Renewal Industries: Advanced Manufacturing; Green Technologies.

Industries with Greatest Employment: Professional, Scientific, and Technical Services (28.0%); Specialty Trade Contractors (17.7%); Computer and Electronic Product Manufacturing (17.0%); Electrical Equipment, Appliance, and Component Manufacturing (7.5%); Utilities (7.0%).

Highest-Growth Industries (Projected Growth for This Job): Administrative and Support Services (31.4%); Professional, Scientific, and Technical Services (17.5%);

Merchant Wholesalers, Durable Goods (15.8%); Management of Companies and Enterprises (15.4%).

Other Considerations for Job Outlook: Demand for particular drafting specialties varies throughout the country because employment usually is contingent on the needs of local industry. Opportunities should be best for individuals with at least two years of postsecondary training in a drafting program that provides strong technical skills and considerable experience with CADD systems.

Draw wiring diagrams, circuit board assembly diagrams, schematics, and layout drawings used for manufacture, installation, and repair of electronic equipment. Draft detail and assembly drawings of design components, circuitry, and printed circuit boards, using computer-assisted equipment or standard drafting techniques and devices. Consult with engineers to discuss and interpret design concepts and determine requirements of detailed working drawings. Locate files relating to specified design project in database library, load program into computer, and record completed job data. Examine electronic schematics and supporting documents to develop, compute, and verify specifications for drafting data, such as configuration of parts, dimensions, and tolerances. Supervise and coordinate work activities of workers engaged in drafting, designing layouts, assembling, and testing printed circuit boards. Compare logic element configuration on display screen with engineering schematics and calculate figures to convert, redesign, and modify element. Review work orders and procedural manuals and confer with vendors and design staff to resolve problems and modify design. Review blueprints to determine customer requirements and consult with assembler regarding schematics, wiring procedures, and conductor paths. Train students to use drafting machines and to prepare schematic diagrams, block diagrams, control drawings, logic diagrams, integrated circuit drawings, and interconnection diagrams. Generate computer tapes of final layout design to produce layered photo masks and photo plotting design onto film. Select drill size to drill test head, according to test design and specifications, and submit guide layout to designated department. Key and program specified commands and engineering specifications into computer system to change functions and test final layout. Copy drawings of printed circuit board fabrication, using print machine or blueprinting procedure. Plot electrical test points on layout sheets and draw schematics for wiring test fixture heads to frames.

Personality Type: Conventional-Realistic-Investigative.

Career Cluster: 02 Architecture and Construction. **Career Pathway:** 02.1 Design/Pre-Construction.

Skills: Technology Design; Operations Analysis; Installation; Equipment Selection; Mathematics; Coordination.

Education and Training Program: Electrical/Electronics Drafting and Electrical/Electronics CAD/CADD. **Related Knowledge/Courses:** Design; Engineering and Technology; Mechanical Devices; Physics; Telecommunications; Mathematics.

Work Environment: Indoors; noisy; sitting; using hands on objects, tools, or controls; repetitive motions.

Electronics Engineering Technicians

- ❋ Education/Training Required: Associate degree
- ❋ Annual Earnings: $52,140
- ❋ Beginning Wage: $31,310
- ❋ Earnings Growth Potential: High (40.0%)
- ❋ Growth: 3.6%
- ❋ Annual Job Openings: 12,583
- ❋ Job Security: More Secure than Most
- ❋ Self-Employed: 0.9%
- ❋ Part-Time: 5.9%

Our sources did not provide separate job openings data for this occupation. The job openings listed here are shared with Electrical Engineering Technicians.

Renewal Industries: Advanced Manufacturing; Green Technologies; Infrastructure.

Industries with Greatest Employment: Computer and Electronic Product Manufacturing (24.8%); Professional, Scientific, and Technical Services (15.3%); Federal Government (9.5%); Telecommunications (7.9%); Merchant Wholesalers, Durable Goods (6.4%).

Highest-Growth Industries (Projected Growth for This Job): Warehousing and Storage (33.8%); Professional, Scientific, and Technical Services (25.2%); Support Activities for Transportation (19.9%); Motion Picture, Video, and Sound Recording Industries (17.5%); Internet Service Providers, Web Search Portals, and Data Processing Services

(17.3%); Publishing Industries (Except Internet) (16.2%); Management of Companies and Enterprises (15.3%).

Other Considerations for Job Outlook: Although rising demand for electronic goods—including communications equipment, defense-related equipment, medical electronics, and consumer products—should continue to drive demand, foreign competition in design and manufacturing will limit employment growth.

Lay out, build, test, troubleshoot, repair, and modify developmental and production electronic components, parts, equipment, and systems, such as computer equipment, missile control instrumentation, electron tubes, test equipment, and machine tool numerical controls, applying principles and theories of electronics, electrical circuitry, engineering mathematics, electronic and electrical testing, and physics. Usually work under direction of engineering staff. Read blueprints, wiring diagrams, schematic drawings, and engineering instructions for assembling electronics units, applying knowledge of electronic theory and components. Test electronics units, using standard test equipment, and analyze results to evaluate performance and determine need for adjustment. Perform preventative maintenance and calibration of equipment and systems. Assemble, test, and maintain circuitry or electronic components according to engineering instructions, technical manuals, and knowledge of electronics, using hand and power tools. Adjust and replace defective or improperly functioning circuitry and electronics components, using hand tools and soldering iron. Write reports and record data on testing techniques, laboratory equipment, and specifications to assist engineers. Identify and resolve equipment malfunctions, working with manufacturers and field representatives as necessary to procure replacement parts. Provide user applications and engineering support and recommendations for new and existing equipment with regard to installation, upgrades, and enhancement. Maintain system logs and manuals to document testing and operation of equipment. Provide customer support and education, working with users to identify needs, determine sources of problems, and provide information on product use. Maintain working knowledge of state-of-the-art tools or software by reading or by attending conferences, workshops, or other training. Build prototypes from rough sketches or plans. Design basic circuitry and draft sketches for clarification of details and design documentation under engineers' direction, using drafting instruments and computer-aided design (CAD) equipment. Procure parts and maintain inventory and related documentation. Research equipment and component needs, sources, competitive prices, delivery times, and ongoing operational costs. Write computer or microprocessor software programs. Fabricate parts such as coils, terminal boards, and chassis, using bench lathes, drills, or other machine tools. Develop and upgrade preventative maintenance procedures for components, equipment, parts, and systems.

Personality Type: Realistic-Investigative.

Career Cluster: 13 Manufacturing. **Career Pathway:** 13.3 Maintenance, Installation, and Repair.

Skills: No data available.

Education and Training Programs: Electrical, Electronic, and Communications Engineering Technology/Technician; Telecommunications Technology/Technician; Electrical and Electronic Engineering Technologies/Technicians, Other; Computer Engineering Technology/Technician. **Related Knowledge/Courses:** Telecommunications; Engineering and Technology; Design; Mechanical Devices; Computers and Electronics; Physics.

Work Environment: Indoors; noisy; sitting; using hands on objects, tools, or controls.

Electronics Engineers, Except Computer

- ❀ Education/Training Required: Bachelor's degree
- ❀ Annual Earnings: $83,340
- ❀ Beginning Wage: $53,710
- ❀ Earnings Growth Potential: Medium (35.6%)
- ❀ Growth: 3.7%
- ❀ Annual Job Openings: 5,699
- ❀ Job Security: More Secure than Most
- ❀ Self-Employed: 2.2%
- ❀ Part-Time: 2.0%

Renewal Industries: Advanced Manufacturing; Information and Telecommunication Technologies.

Industries with Greatest Employment: Computer and Electronic Product Manufacturing (26.2%); Professional,

Scientific, and Technical Services (18.8%); Telecommunications (15.2%); Federal Government (13.4%); Merchant Wholesalers, Durable Goods (5.7%).

Highest-Growth Industries (Projected Growth for This Job): Securities, Commodity Contracts, and Other Financial Investments and Related Activities (41.3%); Administrative and Support Services (28.4%); Professional, Scientific, and Technical Services (27.3%); Publishing Industries (Except Internet) (25.8%); Merchant Wholesalers, Durable Goods (15.4%); Management of Companies and Enterprises (15.3%).

Other Considerations for Job Outlook: Although rising demand for electronic goods should continue to increase demand for electronics engineers, foreign competition in electronic products development and the use of engineering services performed in other countries will limit employment growth. Growth is expected to be fastest in service-providing industries—particularly in firms that provide engineering and design services.

Research, design, develop, and test electronic components and systems for commercial, industrial, military, or scientific use, utilizing knowledge of electronic theory and materials properties. Design electronic circuits and components for use in fields such as telecommunications, aerospace guidance and propulsion control, acoustics, or instruments and controls. Design electronic components, software, products, or systems for commercial, industrial, medical, military, or scientific applications. Provide technical support and instruction to staff or customers regarding equipment standards, assisting with specific, difficult in-service engineering. Operate computer-assisted engineering and design software and equipment to perform engineering tasks. Analyze system requirements, capacity, cost, and customer needs to determine feasibility of project and develop system plan. Confer with engineers, customers, vendors, or others to discuss existing and potential engineering projects or products. Review and evaluate work of others inside and outside the organization to ensure effectiveness, technical adequacy, and compatibility in the resolution of complex engineering problems. Determine material and equipment needs and order supplies. Inspect electronic equipment, instruments, products, and systems to ensure conformance to specifications, safety standards, and applicable codes and regulations. Evaluate operational systems, prototypes, and proposals and recommend repair or design modifications based on factors such as environment, service, cost, and system capabilities. Prepare documentation containing information such as confidential descriptions and specifications of proprietary hardware and software, product development and introduction schedules, product costs, and information about product performance weaknesses. Direct and coordinate activities concerned with manufacture, construction, installation, maintenance, operation, and modification of electronic equipment, products, and systems. Develop and perform operational, maintenance, and testing procedures for electronic products, components, equipment, and systems. Plan and develop applications and modifications for electronic properties used in components, products, and systems to improve technical performance. Plan and implement research, methodology, and procedures to apply principles of electronic theory to engineering projects. Prepare engineering sketches and specifications for construction, relocation, and installation of equipment, facilities, products, and systems.

Personality Type: Investigative-Realistic.

Career Cluster: 15 Science, Technology, Engineering, and Mathematics. **Career Pathway:** 15.1 Engineering and Technology.

Skills: Troubleshooting; Installation; Science; Operations Analysis; Technology Design; Equipment Selection.

Education and Training Program: Electrical, Electronic, and Communications Engineering. **Related Knowledge/Courses:** Engineering and Technology; Design; Physics; Computers and Electronics; Telecommunications; Production and Processing.

Work Environment: Indoors; noisy; sitting.

Elementary School Teachers, Except Special Education

- ❋ Education/Training Required: Bachelor's degree
- ❋ Annual Earnings: $47,330
- ❋ Beginning Wage: $31,480
- ❋ Earnings Growth Potential: Low (33.5%)
- ❋ Growth: 13.6%
- ❋ Annual Job Openings: 181,612
- ❋ Job Security: More Secure than Most
- ❋ Self-Employed: 0.0%
- ❋ Part-Time: 9.5%

Renewal Industry: Education.

Industries with Greatest Employment: Educational Services, Public and Private (97.3%).

Highest-Growth Industries (Projected Growth for This Job): Social Assistance (30.6%); Administrative and Support Services (26.6%); Nursing and Residential Care Facilities (21.7%); Religious, Grantmaking, Civic, Professional, and Similar Organizations (20.0%).

Other Considerations for Job Outlook: Job prospects should be better in inner cities and rural areas than in suburban districts.

Teach pupils in public or private schools at the elementary level basic academic, social, and other formative skills. Establish and enforce rules for behavior and procedures for maintaining order among the students for whom they are responsible. Observe and evaluate students' performance, behavior, social development, and physical health. Prepare materials and classrooms for class activities. Adapt teaching methods and instructional materials to meet students' varying needs and interests. Plan and conduct activities for a balanced program of instruction, demonstration, and work time that provides students with opportunities to observe, question, and investigate. Instruct students individually and in groups, using various teaching methods such as lectures, discussions, and demonstrations. Establish clear objectives for all lessons, units, and projects and communicate those objectives to students. Assign and grade classwork and homework. Read books to entire classes or small groups. Prepare, administer, and grade tests and assignments in order to evaluate students' progress. Confer with parents or guardians, teachers, counselors, and administrators to resolve students' behavioral and academic problems. Meet with parents and guardians to discuss their children's progress and to determine their priorities for their children and their resource needs. Prepare students for later grades by encouraging them to explore learning opportunities and to persevere with challenging tasks. Maintain accurate and complete student records as required by laws, district policies, and administrative regulations. Guide and counsel students with adjustment or academic problems or special academic interests. Prepare and implement remedial programs for students requiring extra help. Prepare objectives and outlines for courses of study, following curriculum guidelines or requirements of states and schools. Provide a variety of materials and resources for children to explore, manipulate, and use, both in learning activities and in imaginative play. Enforce administration policies and rules governing students. Confer with other staff members to plan and schedule lessons promoting learning, following approved curricula.

Personality Type: Social-Artistic-Conventional.

Career Cluster: 05 Education and Training. **Career Pathway:** 05.3 Teaching/Training.

Skills: Instructing; Learning Strategies; Monitoring; Social Perceptiveness; Speaking; Persuasion.

Education and Training Programs: Elementary Education and Teaching; Teacher Education, Multiple Levels; Montessori Teacher Education. **Related Knowledge/ Courses:** Geography; History and Archeology; Sociology and Anthropology; Therapy and Counseling; Philosophy and Theology; Education and Training.

Work Environment: Indoors; noisy; disease or infections; standing.

Elevator Installers and Repairers

- ❋ Education/Training Required: Long-term on-the-job training
- ❋ Annual Earnings: $68,000
- ❋ Beginning Wage: $39,120
- ❋ Earnings Growth Potential: High (42.5%)
- ❋ Growth: 8.8%
- ❋ Annual Job Openings: 2,850
- ❋ Job Security: Least Secure
- ❋ Self-Employed: 0.0%
- ❋ Part-Time: 0.4%

Renewal Industry: Infrastructure.

Industries with Greatest Employment: Specialty Trade Contractors (92.2%).

Highest-Growth Industries (Projected Growth for This Job): None met the criteria.

Other Considerations for Job Outlook: Workers should have excellent opportunities when seeking to enter this occupation. Elevator installer and repairer jobs have relatively high earnings and good benefits. However, the dangerous and physically challenging nature of this occupation and the significant training it requires reduces the number of applicants and creates better opportunities for those who apply. Job prospects should be best for those with postsecondary education in electronics or experience in the military.

Assemble, install, repair, or maintain electric or hydraulic freight or passenger elevators, escalators, or dumbwaiters. Assemble, install, repair, and maintain elevators, escalators, moving sidewalks, and dumbwaiters, using hand and power tools and testing devices such as test lamps, ammeters, and voltmeters. Test newly installed equipment to ensure that it meets specifications such as stopping at floors for set amounts of time. Check that safety regulations and building codes are met and complete service reports verifying conformance to standards. Locate malfunctions in brakes, motors, switches, and signal and control systems, using test equipment. Connect electrical wiring to control panels and electric motors. Read and interpret blueprints to determine the layout of system components, frameworks, and foundations, and to select installation equipment. Adjust safety controls, counterweights,

E

door mechanisms, and components such as valves, ratchets, seals, and brake linings. Inspect wiring connections, control panel hookups, door installations, and alignments and clearances of cars and hoistways to ensure that equipment will operate properly. Disassemble defective units, and repair or replace parts such as locks, gears, cables, and electric wiring. Maintain log books that detail all repairs and checks performed. Participate in additional training to keep skills up-to-date. Attach guide shoes and rollers to minimize the lateral motion of cars as they travel through shafts. Connect car frames to counterweights, using steel cables. Bolt or weld steel rails to the walls of shafts to guide elevators, working from scaffolding or platforms. Assemble elevator cars, installing each car's platform, walls, and doors. Install outer doors and door frames at elevator entrances on each floor of a structure. Install electrical wires and controls by attaching conduit along shaft walls from floor to floor, then pulling plastic-covered wires through the conduit. Cut prefabricated sections of framework, rails, and other components to specified dimensions. Operate elevators to determine power demands, and test power consumption to detect overload factors. Assemble electrically powered stairs, steel frameworks, and tracks, and install associated motors and electrical wiring.

Personality Type: Realistic-Investigative-Conventional.

Career Cluster: 13 Manufacturing. **Career Pathway:** 13.3 Maintenance, Installation, and Repair.

Skills: Installation; Repairing; Equipment Maintenance; Troubleshooting; Quality Control Analysis; Technology Design.

Education and Training Program: Industrial Mechanics and Maintenance Technology. **Related Knowledge/Courses:** Building and Construction; Mechanical Devices; Physics; Design; Engineering and Technology; Public Safety and Security.

Work Environment: Very bright or dim lighting; contaminants; high places; hazardous conditions; hazardous equipment; using hands on objects, tools, or controls.

Emergency Medical Technicians and Paramedics

* Education/Training Required: Postsecondary vocational training
* Annual Earnings: $28,400
* Beginning Wage: $18,150
* Earnings Growth Potential: Medium (36.1%)
* Growth: 19.2%
* Annual Job Openings: 19,513
* Job Security: Most Secure
* Self-Employed: 0.2%
* Part-Time: 10.5%

Renewal Industry: Health Care.

Industries with Greatest Employment: Ambulatory Health-Care Services (44.6%); Local Government (30.9%); Hospitals, Public and Private (20.2%).

Highest-Growth Industries (Projected Growth for This Job): Amusement, Gambling, and Recreation Industries (42.4%); Professional, Scientific, and Technical Services (39.7%); Administrative and Support Services (34.3%); Ambulatory Health-Care Services (27.5%); Waste Management and Remediation Services (25.3%); Performing Arts, Spectator Sports, and Related Industries (24.3%); Transit and Ground Passenger Transportation (19.3%); Accommodation, Including Hotels and Motels (17.5%); Management of Companies and Enterprises (15.6%).

Other Considerations for Job Outlook: Job prospects should be favorable. Many job openings will arise from growth and from the need to replace workers who leave the occupation because of the limited potential for advancement, as well as the modest pay and benefits in private-sector jobs. Job opportunities should be best in private ambulance services. Competition will be greater for jobs in local government, including fire, police, and independent third-service rescue squad departments, which tend to have better salaries and benefits. EMTs and paramedics who have advanced education and certifications, such as Paramedic level certification, should enjoy the most favorable job prospects as clients and patients demand higher levels of care before arriving at the hospital.

Assess injuries, administer emergency medical care, and extricate trapped individuals. Transport injured or sick persons to medical facilities. Administer first-aid treatment and life-support care to sick or injured persons in prehospital setting. Perform emergency diagnostic and treatment procedures, such as stomach suction, airway management, or heart monitoring, during ambulance ride. Observe, record, and report to physician the patient's condition or injury, the treatment provided, and reactions to drugs and treatment. Immobilize patient for placement on stretcher and ambulance transport, using backboard or other spinal immobilization device. Maintain vehicles and medical and communication equipment and replenish first-aid equipment and supplies. Assess nature and extent of illness or injury to establish and prioritize medical procedures. Communicate with dispatchers and treatment center personnel to provide information about situation, to arrange reception of victims, and to receive instructions for further treatment. Comfort and reassure patients. Decontaminate ambulance interior following treatment of patient with infectious disease and report case to proper authorities. Operate equipment such as electrocardiograms (EKGs), external defibrillators, and bag-valve mask resuscitators in advanced life-support environments. Drive mobile intensive care unit to specified location, following instructions from emergency medical dispatcher. Coordinate with treatment center personnel to obtain patients' vital statistics and medical history, to determine the circumstances of the emergency, and to administer emergency treatment. Coordinate work with other emergency medical team members and police and fire department personnel. Attend training classes to maintain certification licensure, keep abreast of new developments in the field, or maintain existing knowledge. Administer drugs orally or by injection and perform intravenous procedures under a physician's direction.

Personality Type: Social-Investigative-Realistic.

Career Cluster: 08 Health Science. **Career Pathway:** 08.2 Diagnostics Services.

Skills: No data available.

Education and Training Programs: Emergency Care Attendant (EMT Ambulance); Emergency Medical Technology/Technician (EMT Paramedic). **Related Knowledge/Courses:** Medicine and Dentistry; Customer and Personal Service; Therapy and Counseling; Psychology; Transportation; Education and Training.

Work Environment: More often outdoors than indoors; noisy; very hot or cold; very bright or dim lighting; disease or infections.

Engineering Managers

- ❋ Education/Training Required: Work experience plus degree
- ❋ Annual Earnings: $111,020
- ❋ Beginning Wage: $70,640
- ❋ Earnings Growth Potential: Medium (36.4%)
- ❋ Growth: 7.3%
- ❋ Annual Job Openings: 7,404
- ❋ Job Security: Less Secure than Most
- ❋ Self-Employed: 0.0%
- ❋ Part-Time: 2.0%

Renewal Industries: Advanced Manufacturing; Green Technologies; Information and Telecommunication Technologies; Infrastructure.

Industries with Greatest Employment: Professional, Scientific, and Technical Services (29.9%); Computer and Electronic Product Manufacturing (15.8%); Transportation Equipment Manufacturing (9.4%); Machinery Manufacturing (5.4%).

Highest-Growth Industries (Projected Growth for This Job): Warehousing and Storage (33.7%); Waste Management and Remediation Services (29.7%); Professional, Scientific, and Technical Services (28.3%); Administrative and Support Services (28.2%); Lessors of Nonfinancial Intangible Assets (Except Copyrighted Works) (28.1%); Publishing Industries (Except Internet) (25.1%); Real Estate (24.7%); Water Transportation (20.8%); Support Activities for Transportation (20.2%); Religious, Grantmaking, Civic, Professional, and Similar Organizations (19.1%); Motion Picture, Video, and Sound Recording Industries (16.4%); Accommodation, Including Hotels and Motels (15.7%); Management of Companies and Enterprises (15.3%).

Other Considerations for Job Outlook: Opportunities will be best for workers with strong communication and business management skills.

Plan, direct, or coordinate activities or research and development in such fields as architecture and engineering. Coordinate and direct projects, making detailed plans to accomplish goals and directing the integration of technical activities. Consult or negotiate with clients to prepare project specifications. Present and explain proposals, reports, and findings to clients. Direct, review, and approve product design and changes. Recruit employees; assign, direct, and evaluate their work; and oversee the development and maintenance of staff competence. Perform administrative functions such as reviewing and writing reports, approving expenditures, enforcing rules, and making decisions about the purchase of materials or services. Prepare budgets, bids, and contracts and direct the negotiation of research contracts. Analyze technology, resource needs, and market demand to plan and assess the feasibility of projects. Confer with management, production, and marketing staff to discuss project specifications and procedures. Review and recommend or approve contracts and cost estimates. Develop and implement policies, standards, and procedures for the engineering and technical work performed in the department, service, laboratory, or firm. Plan and direct the installation, testing, operation, maintenance, and repair of facilities and equipment. Administer highway planning, construction, and maintenance. Confer with and report to officials and the public to provide information and solicit support for projects. Set scientific and technical goals within broad outlines provided by top management. Direct the engineering of water control, treatment, and distribution projects. Plan, direct, and coordinate survey work with other staff activities, certifying survey work, and writing land legal descriptions.

Personality Type: Enterprising-Realistic-Investigative.

Career Clusters: 02 Architecture and Construction; 07 Government and Public Administration; 11 Information Technology; 15 Science, Technology, Engineering, and Mathematics. **Career Pathways:** 02.1 Design/Pre-Construction; 07.4 Planning; 11.4 Programming and Software Development; 15.1 Engineering and Technology; 15.3 Science and Mathematics.

Skills: Management of Financial Resources; Management of Personnel Resources; Systems Analysis; Management of Material Resources; Systems Evaluation; Negotiation.

Education and Training Programs: Architecture (BArch, BA/BS, MArch, MA/MS, PhD); City/Urban, Community and Regional Planning; Environmental Design/Architecture; Interior Architecture; Landscape Architecture (BS, BSLA, BLA, MSLA, MLA, PhD); Engineering, General;

Aerospace, Aeronautical and Astronautical Engineering; Agricultural/Biological Engineering and Bioengineering; Architectural Engineering; Biomedical/Medical Engineering; others. **Related Knowledge/Courses:** Engineering and Technology; Design; Physics; Building and Construction; Computers and Electronics; Mathematics.

Work Environment: Indoors; noisy; sitting.

Engineering Teachers, Postsecondary

- ❋ Education/Training Required: Master's degree
- ❋ Annual Earnings: $79,510
- ❋ Beginning Wage: $43,090
- ❋ Earnings Growth Potential: High (45.8%)
- ❋ Growth: 22.9%
- ❋ Annual Job Openings: 5,565
- ❋ Job Security: Most Secure
- ❋ Self-Employed: 0.4%
- ❋ Part-Time: 27.8%

Renewal Industry: Education.

Industries with Greatest Employment: Educational Services, Public and Private (97.3%).

Highest-Growth Industries (Projected Growth for This Job): Administrative and Support Services (48.3%); Amusement, Gambling, and Recreation Industries (45.2%); Social Assistance (38.6%); Support Activities for Transportation (32.8%); Religious, Grantmaking, Civic, Professional, and Similar Organizations (29.9%); Professional, Scientific, and Technical Services (28.8%); Management of Companies and Enterprises (26.8%); Local Government (23.5%); Educational Services, Public and Private (22.8%); Hospitals, Public and Private (21.4%).

Other Considerations for Job Outlook: Retirements of current postsecondary teachers should create numerous openings for all types of postsecondary teachers, so job opportunities are generally expected to be very good. However, one of the main reasons why students attend postsecondary institutions is to prepare themselves for careers, so the best job prospects for postsecondary teachers are likely to be in rapidly growing fields that offer many nonacademic career options. Community colleges and other institutions offering career and technical education have been among the most rapidly growing, and these institutions are expected to offer some of the best opportunities for post-secondary teachers.

Teach courses pertaining to the application of physical laws and principles of engineering for the development of machines, materials, instruments, processes, and services. Includes teachers of subjects such as chemical, civil, electrical, industrial, mechanical, mineral, and petroleum engineering. Includes both teachers primarily engaged in teaching and those who do a combination of both teaching and research. Prepare and deliver lectures to undergraduate and/or graduate students on topics such as mechanics, hydraulics, and robotics. Keep abreast of developments in their field by reading current literature, talking with colleagues, and participating in professional conferences. Supervise undergraduate and/or graduate teaching, internship, and research work. Evaluate and grade students' classwork, laboratory work, assignments, and papers. Conduct research in a particular field of knowledge and publish findings in professional journals, books, and/or electronic media. Prepare course materials such as syllabi, homework assignments, and handouts. Compile, administer, and grade examinations or assign this work to others. Write grant proposals to procure external research funding. Supervise students' laboratory work. Initiate, facilitate, and moderate class discussions. Maintain regularly scheduled office hours to advise and assist students. Plan, evaluate, and revise curricula, course content, and course materials and methods of instruction. Advise students on academic and vocational curricula and on career issues. Maintain student attendance records, grades, and other required records. Collaborate with colleagues to address teaching and research issues. Select and obtain materials and supplies such as textbooks and laboratory equipment. Participate in student recruitment, registration, and placement activities. Serve on academic or administrative committees that deal with institutional policies, departmental matters, and academic issues. Perform administrative duties such as serving as department head. Provide professional consulting services to government and/or industry. Compile bibliographies of specialized materials for outside reading assignments. Act as advisers to student organizations. Participate in campus and community events.

Personality Type: Investigative-Realistic-Social.

Career Clusters: 02 Architecture and Construction; 04 Business, Management, and Administration; 05 Education and Training; 11 Information Technology; 15 Science, Technology, Engineering, and Mathematics. **Career Pathways:** 02.1 Design/Pre-Construction; 04.4 Business Analysis; 05.3 Teaching/Training; 11.4 Programming and Software Development; 15.1 Engineering and Technology; 15.3 Science and Mathematics.

Skills: Science; Programming; Mathematics; Technology Design; Complex Problem Solving; Management of Financial Resources.

Education and Training Programs: Teacher Education and Professional Development, Specific Subject Areas, Other; Engineering, General; Aerospace, Aeronautical and Astronautical Engineering; Agricultural/Biological Engineering and Bioengineering; Architectural Engineering; Biomedical/Medical Engineering; Ceramic Sciences and Engineering; Chemical Engineering; Civil Engineering, General; Geotechnical Engineering; Structural Engineering; others. **Related Knowledge/Courses:** Engineering and Technology; Physics; Design; Mathematics; Education and Training; Telecommunications.

Work Environment: Indoors; sitting.

English Language and Literature Teachers, Postsecondary

* Education/Training Required: Master's degree
* Annual Earnings: $54,000
* Beginning Wage: $30,680
* Earnings Growth Potential: High (43.2%)
* Growth: 22.9%
* Annual Job Openings: 10,475
* Job Security: Most Secure
* Self-Employed: 0.4%
* Part-Time: 27.8%

Renewal Industry: Education.

Industries with Greatest Employment: Educational Services, Public and Private (97.3%).

Highest-Growth Industries (Projected Growth for This Job): Administrative and Support Services (48.3%);

Amusement, Gambling, and Recreation Industries (45.2%); Social Assistance (38.6%); Support Activities for Transportation (32.8%); Religious, Grantmaking, Civic, Professional, and Similar Organizations (29.9%); Professional, Scientific, and Technical Services (28.8%); Management of Companies and Enterprises (26.8%); Local Government (23.5%); Educational Services, Public and Private (22.8%); Hospitals, Public and Private (21.4%).

Other Considerations for Job Outlook: Retirements of current postsecondary teachers should create numerous openings for all types of postsecondary teachers, so job opportunities are generally expected to be very good. One of the main reasons why students attend postsecondary institutions is to prepare themselves for careers, so the best job prospects for postsecondary teachers are likely to be in rapidly growing fields that offer many nonacademic career options. English composition is a key part of the curriculum for most majors. Community colleges and other institutions offering career and technical education have been among the most rapidly growing, and these institutions are expected to offer some of the best opportunities for postsecondary teachers.

Teach courses in English language and literature, including linguistics and comparative literature. Initiate, facilitate, and moderate classroom discussions. Evaluate and grade students' classwork, assignments, and papers. Prepare course materials such as syllabi, homework assignments, and handouts. Prepare and deliver lectures to undergraduate and graduate students on topics such as poetry, novel structure, and translation and adaptation. Maintain student attendance records, grades, and other required records. Plan, evaluate, and revise curricula, course content, and course materials and methods of instruction. Compile, administer, and grade examinations or assign this work to others. Maintain regularly scheduled office hours in order to advise and assist students. Keep abreast of developments in their field by reading current literature, talking with colleagues, and participating in professional conferences. Select and obtain materials and supplies such as textbooks. Advise students on academic and vocational curricula and on career issues. Conduct research in a particular field of knowledge and publish findings in professional journals, books, or electronic media. Collaborate with colleagues to address teaching and research issues. Serve on academic or administrative committees that deal with institutional policies, departmental matters, and academic issues. Participate in campus and community events. Participate in student recruitment, registration, and placement activities. Compile bibliographies of specialized materials for outside reading assignments. Supervise undergraduate and/or graduate teaching, internship, and research work. Provide assistance to students in college writing centers. Perform administrative duties such as serving as department head. Recruit, train, and supervise student writing instructors. Act as advisers to student organizations. Write grant proposals to procure external research funding. Provide professional consulting services to government or industry.

Personality Type: Social-Artistic-Investigative.

Career Clusters: 03 Arts, Audio/Video Technology, and Communications; 05 Education and Training. **Career Pathways:** 03.5 Journalism and Broadcasting; 05.3 Teaching/Training.

Skills: Instructing; Writing; Learning Strategies; Social Perceptiveness; Reading Comprehension; Persuasion.

Education and Training Programs: Comparative Literature; English Language and Literature, General; English Composition; Creative Writing; American Literature (United States); American Literature (Canadian); English Literature (British and Commonwealth); Technical and Business Writing; English Language and Literature/Letters, Other. **Related Knowledge/Courses:** Philosophy and Theology; English Language; History and Archeology; Education and Training; Fine Arts; Sociology and Anthropology.

Work Environment: Indoors; sitting.

Environmental Engineering Technicians

* Education/Training Required: Associate degree
* Annual Earnings: $40,690
* Beginning Wage: $25,360
* Earnings Growth Potential: Medium (37.7%)
* Growth: 24.8%
* Annual Job Openings: 2,162
* Job Security: More Secure than Most
* Self-Employed: 0.8%
* Part-Time: 5.9%

Renewal Industry: Infrastructure.

Industries with Greatest Employment: Professional, Scientific, and Technical Services (56.8%); Local Government (11.7%); Waste Management and Remediation Services (8.3%); State Government (5.3%).

Highest-Growth Industries (Projected Growth for This Job): Waste Management and Remediation Services (38.7%); Professional, Scientific, and Technical Services (34.7%); Administrative and Support Services (26.5%); Management of Companies and Enterprises (15.6%).

Other Considerations for Job Outlook: More environmental engineering technicians will be needed to comply with environmental regulations and to develop methods of cleaning up existing hazards. A shift in emphasis toward preventing problems rather than controlling those that already exist, as well as increasing public health concerns resulting from population growth, also will spur demand. Opportunities will be best for individuals with an associate degree or extensive job training in engineering technology. As technology becomes more sophisticated, employers will continue to look for technicians who are skilled in new technology and require little additional training.

Apply theory and principles of environmental engineering to modify, test, and operate equipment and devices used in the prevention, control, and remediation of environmental pollution, including waste treatment and site remediation. May assist in the development of environmental pollution remediation devices under direction of engineer. Receive, set up, test, and decontaminate equipment. Maintain project logbook records and computer program files. Perform environmental quality work in field and office settings. Conduct pollution surveys, collecting and analyzing samples such as air and groundwater. Review technical documents to ensure completeness and conformance to requirements. Perform laboratory work such as logging numerical and visual observations, preparing and packaging samples, recording test results, and performing photo documentation. Review work plans to schedule activities. Obtain product information, identify vendors and suppliers, and order materials and equipment to maintain inventory. Arrange for the disposal of lead, asbestos, and other hazardous materials. Inspect facilities to monitor compliance with regulations governing substances such as asbestos, lead, and wastewater. Provide technical engineering support in the planning of projects such as wastewater treatment plants to ensure compliance with environmental regulations and policies. Improve chemical processes to reduce toxic emissions. Oversee support staff. Assist in the cleanup of hazardous material spills. Produce environmental assessment reports, tabulating data and preparing charts, graphs, and sketches. Maintain process parameters and evaluate process anomalies. Work with customers to assess the environmental impact of proposed construction and to develop pollution prevention programs. Perform statistical analysis and correction of air or water pollution data submitted by industry and other agencies. Develop work plans, including writing specifications and establishing material, manpower, and facilities needs.

Personality Type: Realistic-Investigative-Conventional.

Career Clusters: 01 Agriculture, Food, and Natural Resources; 13 Manufacturing. **Career Pathways:** 01.6 Environmental Service Systems; 13.4 Quality Assurance.

Skills: Science; Repairing; Troubleshooting; Equipment Maintenance; Operation Monitoring; Mathematics.

Education and Training Programs: Environmental Engineering Technology/Environmental Technology; Hazardous Materials Information Systems Technology/ Technician. **Related Knowledge/Courses:** Engineering and Technology; Building and Construction; Physics; Design; Biology; Chemistry.

Work Environment: More often indoors than outdoors; contaminants; hazardous conditions; hazardous equipment; standing.

Environmental Engineers

- ❋ Education/Training Required: Bachelor's degree
- ❋ Annual Earnings: $72,350
- ❋ Beginning Wage: $44,090
- ❋ Earnings Growth Potential: Medium (39.1%)
- ❋ Growth: 25.4%
- ❋ Annual Job Openings: 5,003
- ❋ Job Security: Most Secure
- ❋ Self-Employed: 2.7%
- ❋ Part-Time: 3.0%

E

Renewal Industries: Green Technologies; Infrastructure.

Industries with Greatest Employment: Professional, Scientific, and Technical Services (50.3%); State Government (12.5%); Local Government (8.9%); Federal Government (7.8%).

Highest-Growth Industries (Projected Growth for This Job): Professional, Scientific, and Technical Services (46.6%); Waste Management and Remediation Services (40.5%); Administrative and Support Services (33.7%); Religious, Grantmaking, Civic, Professional, and Similar Organizations (19.5%); Management of Companies and Enterprises (15.3%); Merchant Wholesalers, Nondurable Goods (15.1%).

Other Considerations for Job Outlook: More environmental engineers will be needed to comply with environmental regulations and to develop methods of cleaning up existing hazards. A shift in emphasis toward preventing problems rather than controlling those that already exist, as well as increasing public health concerns resulting from population growth, also are expected to spur demand for environmental engineers. Because of this employment growth, job opportunities should be good even as more students earn degrees. Even though employment of environmental engineers should be less affected by economic conditions than most other types of engineers, a significant economic downturn could reduce the emphasis on environmental protection, reducing job opportunities.

Design, plan, or perform engineering duties in the prevention, control, and remediation of environmental health hazards, using various engineering disciplines. Work may include waste treatment, site remediation, or pollution control technology. Collaborate with environmental scientists, planners, hazardous waste technicians, engineers, and other specialists and experts in law and business to address environmental problems. Inspect industrial and municipal facilities and programs to evaluate operational effectiveness and ensure compliance with environmental regulations. Prepare, review, and update environmental investigation and recommendation reports. Design and supervise the development of systems processes or equipment for control, management, or remediation of water, air, or soil quality. Provide environmental engineering assistance in network analysis, regulatory analysis, and planning or reviewing database development. Obtain, update, and maintain plans, permits, and standard operating procedures. Provide technical-level support for environmental remediation and litigation projects, including remediation system design and determination of regulatory applicability. Monitor progress of environmental improvement programs. Inform company employees and other interested parties of environmental issues. Advise corporations and government agencies of procedures to follow in cleaning up contaminated sites to protect people and the environment. Develop proposed project objectives and targets and report to management on progress in attaining them. Request bids from suppliers or consultants. Advise industries and government agencies about environmental policies and standards. Assess the existing or potential environmental impact of land use projects on air, water, and land. Assist in budget implementation, forecasts, and administration. Serve on teams conducting multimedia inspections at complex facilities, providing assistance with planning, quality assurance, safety inspection protocols, and sampling. Coordinate and manage environmental protection programs and projects, assigning and evaluating work. Maintain, write, and revise quality assurance documentation and procedures. Provide administrative support for projects by collecting data, providing project documentation, training staff, and performing other general administrative duties.

Personality Type: Investigative-Realistic-Conventional.

Career Cluster: 15 Science, Technology, Engineering, and Mathematics. **Career Pathway:** 15.1 Engineering and Technology.

Skills: Management of Financial Resources; Systems Analysis; Mathematics; Systems Evaluation; Management of Personnel Resources; Writing.

Education and Training Program: Environmental/Environmental Health Engineering. **Related Knowledge/Courses:** Engineering and Technology; Physics; Design; Chemistry; Building and Construction; Biology.

Work Environment: More often indoors than outdoors; noisy; contaminants; sitting; using hands on objects, tools, or controls.

Environmental Science and Protection Technicians, Including Health

❋ Education/Training Required: Associate degree

❋ Annual Earnings: $39,370

❋ Beginning Wage: $25,090

❋ Earnings Growth Potential: Medium (36.3%)

❋ Growth: 28.0%

❋ Annual Job Openings: 8,404

❋ Job Security: Less Secure than Most

❋ Self-Employed: 1.5%

❋ Part-Time: 19.4%

Renewal Industries: Green Technologies; Infrastructure.

Industries with Greatest Employment: Professional, Scientific, and Technical Services (42.8%); Local Government (21.2%); State Government (13.1%); Educational Services, Public and Private (5.1%).

Highest-Growth Industries (Projected Growth for This Job): Professional, Scientific, and Technical Services (53.1%); Waste Management and Remediation Services (28.9%); Administrative and Support Services (27.7%).

Other Considerations for Job Outlook: These workers will be needed to help regulate waste products; to collect air, water, and soil samples for measuring levels of pollutants; to monitor compliance with environmental regulations; and to clean up contaminated sites. Over 80 percent of this growth is expected to be in professional, scientific, and technical services as environmental monitoring, management, and regulatory compliance increase.

Perform laboratory and field tests to monitor the environment and investigate sources of pollution, including those that affect health. Under direction of environmental scientists or specialists, may collect samples of gases, soil, water, and other materials for testing and take corrective actions as assigned. Collect samples of gases, soils, water, industrial wastewater, and asbestos products to conduct tests on pollutant levels and identify sources of pollution. Record test data and prepare reports, summaries, and charts that interpret test results. Develop and implement programs for monitoring of environmental pollution and radiation. Discuss test results and analyses with customers. Set up equipment or stations to monitor and collect pollutants from sites such as smokestacks, manufacturing plants, or mechanical equipment. Maintain files, such as hazardous waste databases, chemical usage data, personnel exposure information, and diagrams showing equipment locations. Develop testing procedures or direct activities of workers in laboratory. Prepare samples or photomicrographs for testing and analysis. Calibrate microscopes and test instruments. Examine and analyze material for presence and concentration of contaminants such as asbestos, using variety of microscopes. Calculate amount of pollutant in samples or compute air pollution or gas flow in industrial processes, using chemical and mathematical formulas. Make recommendations to control or eliminate unsafe conditions at workplaces or public facilities. Weigh, analyze, and measure collected sample particles such as lead, coal dust, or rock to determine concentration of pollutants. Provide information and technical and program assistance to government representatives, employers, and the general public on the issues of public health, environmental protection, or workplace safety. Conduct standardized tests to ensure materials and supplies used throughout power supply systems meet processing and safety specifications. Perform statistical analysis of environmental data. Respond to and investigate hazardous conditions or spills or outbreaks of disease or food poisoning, collecting samples for analysis. Determine amounts and kinds of chemicals to use in destroying harmful organisms and removing impurities from purification systems. Inspect sanitary conditions at public facilities. Inspect workplaces to ensure the absence of health and safety hazards such as high noise levels, radiation, or lighting that is too bright or dim.

Personality Type: Investigative-Realistic-Conventional.

Career Clusters: 01 Agriculture, Food, and Natural Resources; 13 Manufacturing. **Career Pathways:** 01.5 Natural Resources Systems; 13.2 Manufacturing Production Process Development.

Skills: No data available.

Education and Training Programs: Environmental Studies; Environmental Science; Physical Science Technologies/Technicians, Other; Science Technologies/Technicians, Other. **Related Knowledge/Courses:** Biology; Chemistry; Geography; Physics; Computers and Electronics; Building and Construction.

Work Environment: More often outdoors than indoors; very hot or cold; contaminants; hazardous equipment; standing.

Environmental Science Teachers, Postsecondary

- ❋ Education/Training Required: Master's degree
- ❋ Annual Earnings: $64,850
- ❋ Beginning Wage: $35,120
- ❋ Earnings Growth Potential: High (45.8%)
- ❋ Growth: 22.9%
- ❋ Annual Job Openings: 769
- ❋ Job Security: Most Secure
- ❋ Self-Employed: 0.4%
- ❋ Part-Time: 27.8%

Renewal Industry: Education.

Industries with Greatest Employment: Educational Services, Public and Private (97.3%).

Highest-Growth Industries (Projected Growth for This Job): Administrative and Support Services (48.3%); Amusement, Gambling, and Recreation Industries (45.2%); Social Assistance (38.6%); Support Activities for Transportation (32.8%); Religious, Grantmaking, Civic, Professional, and Similar Organizations (29.9%); Professional, Scientific, and Technical Services (28.8%); Management of Companies and Enterprises (26.8%); Local Government (23.5%); Educational Services, Public and Private (22.8%); Hospitals, Public and Private (21.4%).

Other Considerations for Job Outlook: Retirements of current postsecondary teachers should create numerous openings for all types of postsecondary teachers, so job opportunities are generally expected to be very good. One of the main reasons why students attend postsecondary institutions is to prepare themselves for careers, so the best job prospects for postsecondary teachers are likely to be in rapidly growing fields that offer many nonacademic career options. Community colleges and other institutions offering career and technical education have been among the most rapidly growing, and these institutions are expected to offer some of the best opportunities for postsecondary teachers.

Teach courses in environmental science. Supervise undergraduate and/or graduate teaching, internship, and research work. Conduct research in a particular field of knowledge and publish findings in professional journals, books, and/or electronic media. Keep abreast of developments in their field by reading current literature, talking with colleagues, and participating in professional conferences. Evaluate and grade students' classwork, laboratory work, assignments, and papers. Write grant proposals to procure external research funding. Supervise students' laboratory work and fieldwork. Prepare course materials such as syllabi, homework assignments, and handouts. Plan, evaluate, and revise curricula, course content, and course materials and methods of instruction. Compile, administer, and grade examinations or assign this work to others. Initiate, facilitate, and moderate classroom discussions. Advise students on academic and vocational curricula and on career issues. Prepare and deliver lectures to undergraduate and/or graduate students on topics such as hazardous waste management, industrial safety, and environmental toxicology. Maintain student attendance records, grades, and other required records. Select and obtain materials and supplies such as textbooks and laboratory equipment. Maintain regularly scheduled office hours in order to advise and assist students. Collaborate with colleagues to address teaching and research issues. Perform administrative duties such as serving as department head. Participate in student recruitment, registration, and placement activities. Provide professional consulting services to government and/or industry. Serve on academic or administrative committees that deal with institutional policies, departmental matters, and academic issues. Compile bibliographies of specialized materials for outside reading assignments. Participate in campus and community events. Act as advisers to student organizations.

Personality Type: Social-Investigative-Artistic.

Career Clusters: 01 Agriculture, Food, and Natural Resources; 05 Education and Training. **Career Pathways:** 01.5 Natural Resources Systems; 05.3 Teaching/Training.

Skills: Science; Writing; Reading Comprehension; Instructing; Mathematics; Management of Financial Resources.

Education and Training Programs: Environmental Studies; Environmental Science; Science Teacher Education/General Science Teacher Education. **Related Knowledge/Courses:** Biology; Geography; Chemistry; Education and Training; Physics; History and Archeology.

Work Environment: Indoors; sitting.

Environmental Scientists and Specialists, Including Health

- ❀ Education/Training Required: Master's degree
- ❀ Annual Earnings: $58,380
- ❀ Beginning Wage: $35,630
- ❀ Earnings Growth Potential: Medium (39.0%)
- ❀ Growth: 25.1%
- ❀ Annual Job Openings: 6,961
- ❀ Job Security: More Secure than Most
- ❀ Self-Employed: 2.2%
- ❀ Part-Time: 5.3%

Renewal Industries: Green Technologies; Infrastructure.

Industries with Greatest Employment: Professional, Scientific, and Technical Services (42.4%); State Government (23.7%); Local Government (11.6%); Federal Government (7.5%); Educational Services, Public and Private (5.5%).

Highest-Growth Industries (Projected Growth for This Job): Professional, Scientific, and Technical Services (54.3%); Administrative and Support Services (32.1%); Waste Management and Remediation Services (29.3%); Management of Companies and Enterprises (15.3%); Religious, Grantmaking, Civic, Professional, and Similar Organizations (15.2%).

Other Considerations for Job Outlook: Job prospects for environmental scientists will be good. Funding for federal and state geological surveys depend largely on the political climate and the current budget. Thus, job security for environmental scientists may vary. During periods of economic recession, layoffs of environmental scientists may occur in consulting firms; layoffs are much less likely in government.

Conduct research or perform investigation for the purpose of identifying, abating, or eliminating sources of pollutants or hazards that affect either the environment or the health of the population. Using knowledge of various scientific disciplines, may collect, synthesize, study, report, and take action based on data derived from measurements or observations of air, food, soil, water, and other sources. Collect, synthesize, analyze, manage, and report environmental data such as pollution emission measurements, atmospheric monitoring measurements, meteorological and mineralogical information, and soil or water samples. Analyze data to determine validity, quality, and scientific significance and to interpret correlations between human activities and environmental effects. Communicate scientific and technical information to the public, organizations, or internal audiences through oral briefings, written documents, workshops, conferences, training sessions, or public hearings. Provide scientific and technical guidance, support, coordination, and oversight to governmental agencies, environmental programs, industry, or the public. Process and review environmental permits, licenses, and related materials. Review and implement environmental technical standards, guidelines, policies, and formal regulations that meet all appropriate requirements. Prepare charts or graphs from data samples, providing summary information on the environmental relevance of the data. Determine data collection methods to be employed in research projects and surveys. Investigate and report on accidents affecting the environment. Research sources of pollution to determine their effects on the environment and to develop theories or methods of pollution abatement or control. Provide advice on proper standards and regulations or the development of policies, strategies, and codes of practice for environmental management. Monitor effects of pollution and land degradation and recommend means of prevention or control. Supervise or train students, environmental technologists, technicians, or other related staff. Evaluate violations or problems discovered during inspections to determine appropriate regulatory actions or to provide advice on the development and prosecution of regulatory cases. Conduct environmental audits and inspections and investigate violations. Plan and develop research models, using knowledge of mathematical and statistical concepts. Conduct applied research on environmental topics such as waste control and treatment and pollution abatement methods.

Personality Type: Investigative-Realistic-Conventional.

Career Cluster: 01 Agriculture, Food, and Natural Resources. **Career Pathway:** 01.5 Natural Resources Systems.

Skills: No data available.

Education and Training Programs: Environmental Studies; Environmental Science. **Related Knowledge/Courses:** Biology; Geography; Chemistry; Physics; Law and Government; Engineering and Technology.

Work Environment: More often indoors than outdoors; noisy; sitting.

Family and General Practitioners

- ❋ Education/Training Required: First professional degree
- ❋ Annual Earnings: More than $145,600
- ❋ Beginning Wage: $67,400
- ❋ Earnings Growth Potential: Cannot be calculated
- ❋ Growth: 14.2%
- ❋ Annual Job Openings: 38,027
- ❋ Job Security: Most Secure
- ❋ Self-Employed: 14.7%
- ❋ Part-Time: 8.1%

Our sources did not provide separate job openings data for this occupation. The job openings listed here are shared with Anesthesiologists; Internists, General; Obstetricians and Gynecologists; Pediatricians, General; Psychiatrists; and Surgeons.

Renewal Industry: Health Care.

Industries with Greatest Employment: Ambulatory Health-Care Services (55.9%); Hospitals, Public and Private (17.8%).

Highest-Growth Industries (Projected Growth for This Job): Social Assistance (58.6%); Administrative and Support Services (26.8%); Professional, Scientific, and Technical Services (22.6%); Nursing and Residential Care Facilities (21.0%); Ambulatory Health-Care Services (19.4%); Religious, Grantmaking, Civic, Professional, and Similar Organizations (16.7%); Management of Companies and Enterprises (15.3%).

Other Considerations for Job Outlook: Opportunities for individuals interested in becoming physicians and surgeons are expected to be very good. Unlike their predecessors, new physicians are much less likely to enter solo practice and more likely to take salaried jobs in group medical practices, clinics, and health networks. Reports of shortages in some specialties, such as general or family practice, internal medicine, and OB/GYN, or in rural or low-income areas should attract new entrants, encouraging schools to expand programs and hospitals to increase available residency slots. However, because physician training is so lengthy, employment change happens gradually. Opportunities should be particularly good in rural and low-income areas, as some physicians find these areas unattractive because of less control over work hours, isolation from medical colleagues, or other reasons.

Diagnose, treat, and help prevent diseases and injuries that commonly occur in the general population. Prescribe or administer treatment, therapy, medication, vaccination, and other specialized medical care to treat or prevent illness, disease, or injury. Order, perform, and interpret tests and analyze records, reports, and examination information to diagnose patients' condition. Monitor the patients' conditions and progress and re-evaluate treatments as necessary. Explain procedures and discuss test results or prescribed treatments with patients. Collect, record, and maintain patient information, such as medical history, reports, and examination results. Advise patients and community members concerning diet, activity, hygiene, and disease prevention. Refer patients to medical specialists or other practitioners when necessary. Direct and coordinate activities of nurses, students, assistants, specialists, therapists, and other medical staff. Coordinate work with nurses, social workers, rehabilitation therapists, pharmacists, psychologists, and other health-care providers. Deliver babies. Operate on patients to remove, repair, or improve functioning of diseased or injured body parts and systems. Plan, implement, or administer health programs or standards in hospital, business, or community for information, prevention, or treatment of injury or illness. Prepare reports for government or management of birth, death, and disease statistics; workforce evaluations; or medical status of individuals. Conduct research to study anatomy and develop or test medications, treatments, or procedures to prevent or control disease or injury.

Personality Type: Investigative-Social.

Career Clusters: 08 Health Science; 15 Science, Technology, Engineering, and Mathematics. **Career Pathways:** 08.1 Therapeutic Services; 15.3 Science and Mathematics.

Skills: Science; Social Perceptiveness; Reading Comprehension; Complex Problem Solving; Persuasion; Service Orientation.

Education and Training Programs: Medicine (MD); Osteopathic Medicine/Osteopathy (DO); Family Medicine.

Related Knowledge/Courses: Medicine and Dentistry; Biology; Therapy and Counseling; Psychology; Sociology and Anthropology; Chemistry.

Work Environment: Indoors; disease or infections; standing; using hands on objects, tools, or controls.

Fire-Prevention and Protection Engineers

- ❋ Education/Training Required: Bachelor's degree
- ❋ Annual Earnings: $69,580
- ❋ Beginning Wage: $42,200
- ❋ Earnings Growth Potential: Medium (39.4%)
- ❋ Growth: 9.6%
- ❋ Annual Job Openings: 1,105
- ❋ Job Security: More Secure than Most
- ❋ Self-Employed: 1.1%
- ❋ Part-Time: 2.0%

Our sources did not provide separate job openings data for this occupation. The job openings listed here are shared with Industrial Safety and Health Engineers and with another occupation not included in this book.

Renewal Industry: Infrastructure.

Industries with Greatest Employment: Professional, Scientific, and Technical Services (15.3%); Chemical Manufacturing (11.5%); Construction of Buildings (9.2%); Heavy and Civil Engineering Construction (7.2%); State Government (5.2%).

Highest-Growth Industries (Projected Growth for This Job): Professional, Scientific, and Technical Services (40.5%); Waste Management and Remediation Services (28.3%); Support Activities for Transportation (20.1%); Merchant Wholesalers, Durable Goods (15.3%); Management of Companies and Enterprises (15.3%).

Other Considerations for Job Outlook: Fire-prevention and protection engineers tend to do more on-site work than most engineers and therefore are less threatened by offshoring. Engineers who have not kept current in their field may find themselves at a disadvantage when seeking promotions or during layoffs.

Research causes of fires, determine fire protection methods, and design or recommend materials or equipment such as structural components or fire-detection equipment to assist organizations in safeguarding life and property against fire, explosion, and related hazards. Design fire detection equipment, alarm systems, and fire extinguishing devices and systems. Inspect buildings or building designs to determine fire protection system requirements and potential problems in areas such as water supplies, exit locations, and construction materials. Advise architects, builders, and other construction personnel on fire prevention equipment and techniques and on fire code and standard interpretation and compliance. Prepare and write reports detailing specific fire prevention and protection issues, such as work performed and proposed review schedules. Determine causes of fires and ways in which they could have been prevented. Direct the purchase, modification, installation, maintenance, and operation of fire protection systems. Consult with authorities to discuss safety regulations and to recommend changes as necessary. Develop plans for the prevention of destruction by fire, wind, and water. Study the relationships between ignition sources and materials to determine how fires start. Attend workshops, seminars, or conferences to present or obtain information regarding fire prevention and protection. Develop training materials and conduct training sessions on fire protection. Evaluate fire department performance and the laws and regulations affecting fire prevention or fire safety. Conduct research on fire retardants and the fire safety of materials and devices.

Personality Type: Investigative-Realistic-Enterprising.

Career Cluster: 15 Science, Technology, Engineering, and Mathematics. **Career Pathway:** 15.1 Engineering and Technology.

Skills: Science; Management of Financial Resources; Operations Analysis; Mathematics; Systems Analysis; Negotiation.

Education and Training Program: Environmental/Environmental Health Engineering. **Related Knowledge/Courses:** Design; Engineering and Technology; Building and Construction; Physics; Chemistry; Public Safety and Security.

Work Environment: Indoors; sitting.

First-Line Supervisors/Managers of Construction Trades and Extraction Workers

* ✷ Education/Training Required: Work experience in a related occupation
* ✷ Annual Earnings: $55,950
* ✷ Beginning Wage: $34,870
* ✷ Earnings Growth Potential: Medium (37.7%)
* ✷ Growth: 9.1%
* ✷ Annual Job Openings: 82,923
* ✷ Job Security: Least Secure
* ✷ Self-Employed: 24.4%
* ✷ Part-Time: 3.0%

Renewal Industries: Green Technologies; Infrastructure.

Industries with Greatest Employment: Specialty Trade Contractors (29.9%); Construction of Buildings (21.7%); Heavy and Civil Engineering Construction (8.5%).

Highest-Growth Industries (Projected Growth for This Job): Securities, Commodity Contracts, and Other Financial Investments and Related Activities (41.3%); Amusement, Gambling, and Recreation Industries (35.8%); Warehousing and Storage (33.9%); Professional, Scientific, and Technical Services (32.5%); Waste Management and Remediation Services (31.1%); Building Material and Garden Equipment and Supplies Dealers (27.7%); Performing Arts, Spectator Sports, and Related Industries (26.5%); Social Assistance (25.4%); Administrative and Support Services (25.2%); Real Estate (20.4%); Rental and Leasing Services (20.2%); Religious, Grantmaking, Civic, Professional, and Similar Organizations (17.0%); Accommodation, Including Hotels and Motels (16.9%); Management of Companies and Enterprises (15.3%).

Other Considerations for Job Outlook: Outlook depends on the outlook for the construction trade being supervised. See the job descriptions for those trades.

Directly supervise and coordinate activities of construction or extraction workers. Examine and inspect work progress, equipment, and construction sites to verify safety and to ensure that specifications are met. Read specifications such as blueprints to determine construction requirements and to plan procedures. Estimate material and worker requirements to complete jobs. Supervise, coordinate, and schedule the activities of construction or extractive workers. Confer with managerial and technical personnel, other departments, and contractors in order to resolve problems and to coordinate activities. Coordinate work activities with other construction project activities. Locate, measure, and mark site locations and placement of structures and equipment, using measuring and marking equipment. Order or requisition materials and supplies. Record information such as personnel, production, and operational data on specified forms and reports. Assign work to employees, based on material and worker requirements of specific jobs. Provide assistance to workers engaged in construction or extraction activities, using hand tools and equipment. Train workers in construction methods, operation of equipment, safety procedures, and company policies. Analyze worker and production problems and recommend solutions such as improving production methods or implementing motivational plans. Arrange for repairs of equipment and machinery. Suggest or initiate personnel actions such as promotions, transfers, and hires.

Personality Type: Enterprising-Realistic-Conventional.

Career Cluster: 02 Architecture and Construction. **Career Pathway:** 02.2 Construction.

Skills: Management of Material Resources; Installation; Equipment Maintenance; Repairing; Coordination; Equipment Selection.

Education and Training Programs: Blasting/Blaster; Building/Construction Finishing, Management, and Inspection, Other; Building/Construction Site Management/Manager; Building/Construction Trades, Other; Building/Home/Construction Inspection/Inspector; Building/Property Maintenance and Management; Carpentry/Carpenter; Concrete Finishing/Concrete Finisher; Drywall Installation/Drywaller; others. **Related Knowledge/Courses:** Building and Construction; Mechanical Devices; Design; Engineering and Technology; Production and Processing; Administration and Management.

Work Environment: Outdoors; noisy; very hot or cold; contaminants; hazardous equipment; standing.

First-Line Supervisors/Managers of Mechanics, Installers, and Repairers

- ✺ Education/Training Required: Work experience in a related occupation
- ✺ Annual Earnings: $55,380
- ✺ Beginning Wage: $33,620
- ✺ Earnings Growth Potential: Medium (39.3%)
- ✺ Growth: 7.3%
- ✺ Annual Job Openings: 24,361
- ✺ Job Security: Less Secure than Most
- ✺ Self-Employed: 1.5%
- ✺ Part-Time: 0.9%

Renewal Industry: Infrastructure.

Industries with Greatest Employment: Repair and Maintenance (11.6%); Motor Vehicle and Parts Dealers (10.7%); Specialty Trade Contractors (6.4%); Merchant Wholesalers, Durable Goods (5.5%); Local Government (5.3%).

Highest-Growth Industries (Projected Growth for This Job): Social Assistance (37.7%); Museums, Historical Sites, and Similar Institutions (36.4%); Amusement, Gambling, and Recreation Industries (34.5%); Professional, Scientific, and Technical Services (33.9%); Warehousing and Storage (33.6%); Administrative and Support Services (29.4%); Ambulatory Health-Care Services (29.3%); Scenic and Sightseeing Transportation (27.6%); Waste Management and Remediation Services (27.0%); Performing Arts, Spectator Sports, and Related Industries (25.3%); Nursing and Residential Care Facilities (24.1%); Water Transportation (20.0%); Religious, Grantmaking, Civic, Professional, and Similar Organizations (19.4%); Broadcasting (Except Internet) (19.3%); Support Activities for Transportation (18.7%); Real Estate (17.2%); Rental and Leasing Services (16.2%); Repair and Maintenance (16.0%); Accommodation, Including Hotels and Motels (15.9%); Management of Companies and Enterprises (15.3%).

Other Considerations for Job Outlook: Outlook depends on the industry. Prospects are probably better in repairs than in manufacturing.

Supervise and coordinate the activities of mechanics, installers, and repairers. Determine schedules, sequences, and assignments for work activities, based on work priority, quantity of equipment, and skill of personnel. Monitor employees' work levels and review work performance. Monitor tool and part inventories and the condition and maintenance of shops to ensure adequate working conditions. Recommend or initiate personnel actions such as hires, promotions, transfers, discharges, and disciplinary measures. Investigate accidents and injuries and prepare reports of findings. Compile operational and personnel records such as time and production records, inventory data, repair and maintenance statistics, and test results. Develop, implement, and evaluate maintenance policies and procedures. Counsel employees about work-related issues and assist employees in correcting job-skill deficiencies. Examine objects, systems, or facilities and analyze information to determine needed installations, services, or repairs. Conduct or arrange for worker training in safety, repair, and maintenance techniques; operational procedures; or equipment use. Inspect and monitor work areas; examine tools and equipment; and provide employee safety training to prevent, detect, and correct unsafe conditions or violations of procedures and safety rules. Inspect, test, and measure completed work, using devices such as hand tools and gauges to verify conformance to standards and repair requirements. Requisition materials and supplies such as tools, equipment, and replacement parts. Participate in budget preparation and administration, coordinating purchasing and documentation and monitoring departmental expenditures. Perform skilled repair and maintenance operations, using equipment such as hand and power tools, hydraulic presses and shears, and welding equipment. Meet with vendors and suppliers to discuss products used in repair work. Compute estimates and actual costs of factors such as materials, labor, and outside contractors. Review, evaluate, accept, and coordinate completion of work bid from contractors. Confer with personnel such as management, engineering, quality control, customer, and union workers' representatives to coordinate work activities, resolve employee grievances, and identify and review resource needs.

Personality Type: Enterprising-Conventional-Realistic.

Career Cluster: 04 Business, Management, and Administration. **Career Pathway:** 04.1 Management.

Skills: Repairing; Operation Monitoring; Management of Personnel Resources; Equipment Maintenance; Management of Financial Resources; Systems Analysis.

Education and Training Program: Operations Management and Supervision. **Related Knowledge/Courses:**

Mechanical Devices; Personnel and Human Resources; Production and Processing; Engineering and Technology; Building and Construction; Economics and Accounting.

Work Environment: More often indoors than outdoors; noisy; contaminants; hazardous conditions; standing.

First-Line Supervisors/Managers of Production and Operating Workers

- ❋ Education/Training Required: Work experience in a related occupation
- ❋ Annual Earnings: $48,670
- ❋ Beginning Wage: $29,830
- ❋ Earnings Growth Potential: Medium (38.7%)
- ❋ Growth: –4.8%
- ❋ Annual Job Openings: 46,144
- ❋ Job Security: Least Secure
- ❋ Self-Employed: 2.4%
- ❋ Part-Time: 1.9%

Renewal Industry: Advanced Manufacturing.

Industries with Greatest Employment: Fabricated Metal Product Manufacturing (10.0%); Transportation Equipment Manufacturing (7.7%); Food Manufacturing (6.9%); Machinery Manufacturing (6.3%).

Highest-Growth Industries (Projected Growth for This Job): Internet Service Providers, Web Search Portals, and Data Processing Services (34.3%); Warehousing and Storage (33.6%); Administrative and Support Services (30.9%); Amusement, Gambling, and Recreation Industries (30.3%); Performing Arts, Spectator Sports, and Related Industries (27.7%); Waste Management and Remediation Services (26.8%); Building Material and Garden Equipment and Supplies Dealers (26.7%); General Merchandise Stores (24.9%); Professional, Scientific, and Technical Services (24.5%); Ambulatory Health-Care Services (23.7%); Social Assistance (23.2%); Nursing and Residential Care Facilities (21.4%); Religious, Grantmaking, Civic, Professional, and Similar Organizations (19.2%); Real Estate (18.3%); Accommodation, Including Hotels and Motels (16.2%); Support Activities for Transportation (16.1%); Management of Companies and Enterprises (15.3%).

Other Considerations for Job Outlook: Outlook information is limited. Prospects are probably better in advanced manufacturing than in low-tech manufacturing.

Supervise and coordinate the activities of production and operating workers, such as inspectors, precision workers, machine setters and operators, assemblers, fabricators, and plant and system operators. Enforce safety and sanitation regulations. Direct and coordinate the activities of employees engaged in the production or processing of goods, such as inspectors, machine setters, and fabricators. Read and analyze charts, work orders, production schedules, and other records and reports to determine production requirements and to evaluate current production estimates and outputs. Confer with other supervisors to coordinate operations and activities within or between departments. Plan and establish work schedules, assignments, and production sequences to meet production goals. Inspect materials, products, or equipment to detect defects or malfunctions. Demonstrate equipment operations and work and safety procedures to new employees or assign employees to experienced workers for training. Observe work and monitor gauges, dials, and other indicators to ensure that operators conform to production or processing standards. Interpret specifications, blueprints, job orders, and company policies and procedures for workers. Confer with management or subordinates to resolve worker problems, complaints, or grievances. Maintain operations data such as time, production, and cost records and prepare management reports of production results. Recommend or implement measures to motivate employees and to improve production methods, equipment performance, product quality, or efficiency. Determine standards, budgets, production goals, and rates based on company policies, equipment and labor availability, and workloads. Requisition materials, supplies, equipment parts, or repair services. Recommend personnel actions such as hirings and promotions. Set up and adjust machines and equipment. Calculate labor and equipment requirements and production specifications, using standard formulas. Plan and develop new products and production processes.

Personality Type: Enterprising-Realistic-Conventional.

Career Cluster: 04 Business, Management, and Administration. **Career Pathway:** 04.1 Management.

Skills: Management of Personnel Resources; Operation Monitoring; Operation and Control; Quality Control Analysis; Operations Analysis; Systems Analysis.

Education and Training Program: Operations Management and Supervision. **Related Knowledge/Courses:**

Production and Processing; Mechanical Devices; Personnel and Human Resources; Engineering and Technology; Administration and Management; Psychology.

Work Environment: Indoors; noisy; contaminants; hazardous equipment; standing; walking and running.

Foreign Language and Literature Teachers, Postsecondary

- ❋ Education/Training Required: Master's degree
- ❋ Annual Earnings: $53,610
- ❋ Beginning Wage: $30,590
- ❋ Earnings Growth Potential: High (42.9%)
- ❋ Growth: 22.9%
- ❋ Annual Job Openings: 4,317
- ❋ Job Security: Most Secure
- ❋ Self-Employed: 0.4%
- ❋ Part-Time: 27.8%

Renewal Industry: Education.

Industries with Greatest Employment: Educational Services, Public and Private (97.3%).

Highest-Growth Industries (Projected Growth for This Job): Administrative and Support Services (48.3%); Amusement, Gambling, and Recreation Industries (45.2%); Social Assistance (38.6%); Support Activities for Transportation (32.8%); Religious, Grantmaking, Civic, Professional, and Similar Organizations (29.9%); Professional, Scientific, and Technical Services (28.8%); Management of Companies and Enterprises (26.8%); Local Government (23.5%); Educational Services, Public and Private (22.8%); Hospitals, Public and Private (21.4%).

Other Considerations for Job Outlook: Retirements of current postsecondary teachers should create numerous openings for all types of postsecondary teachers, so job opportunities are generally expected to be very good. However, one of the main reasons why students attend postsecondary institutions is to prepare themselves for careers, so the best job prospects for postsecondary teachers are likely to be in rapidly growing fields that offer many non-academic career options—unlike foreign language and literature. On the other hand, foreign language courses are required for many majors. Community colleges and other institutions offering career and technical education have been among the most rapidly growing, and these institutions are expected to offer some of the best opportunities for postsecondary teachers.

Teach courses in foreign (i.e., other than English) languages and literature. Evaluate and grade students' classwork, assignments, and papers. Prepare course materials such as syllabi, homework assignments, and handouts. Initiate, facilitate, and moderate classroom discussions. Maintain student attendance records, grades, and other required records. Compile, administer, and grade examinations or assign this work to others. Plan, evaluate, and revise curricula, course content, and course materials and methods of instruction. Prepare and deliver lectures to undergraduate and graduate students on topics such as how to speak and write a foreign language and the cultural aspects of areas where a particular language is used. Maintain regularly scheduled office hours to advise and assist students. Select and obtain materials and supplies such as textbooks. Keep abreast of developments in their field by reading current literature, talking with colleagues, and participating in professional organizations and activities. Advise students on academic and vocational curricula and on career issues. Conduct research in a particular field of knowledge and publish findings in scholarly journals, books, and/or electronic media. Collaborate with colleagues to address teaching and research issues. Serve on academic or administrative committees that deal with institutional policies, departmental matters, and academic issues. Participate in student recruitment, registration, and placement activities. Compile bibliographies of specialized materials for outside reading assignments. Participate in campus and community events. Act as advisers to student organizations. Perform administrative duties such as serving as department head. Supervise undergraduate and graduate teaching, internship, and research work. Write grant proposals to procure external research funding. Provide professional consulting services to government or industry.

Personality Type: Social-Artistic-Investigative.

Career Cluster: 05 Education and Training. **Career Pathway:** 05.3 Teaching/Training.

Skills: Learning Strategies; Instructing; Writing; Reading Comprehension; Speaking; Persuasion.

Education and Training Programs: Latin Teacher Education; Foreign Languages and Literatures, General;

Linguistics; Language Interpretation and Translation; African Languages, Literatures, and Linguistics; East Asian Languages, Literatures, and Linguistics, General; Chinese Language and Literature; Japanese Language and Literature; Korean Language and Literature; Tibetan Language and Literature; others. **Related Knowledge/Courses:** Foreign Language; Philosophy and Theology; History and Archeology; Sociology and Anthropology; Geography; English Language.

Work Environment: Indoors; sitting.

Forestry and Conservation Science Teachers, Postsecondary

- ❈ Education/Training Required: Master's degree
- ❈ Annual Earnings: $63,790
- ❈ Beginning Wage: $36,270
- ❈ Earnings Growth Potential: High (43.1%)
- ❈ Growth: 22.9%
- ❈ Annual Job Openings: 454
- ❈ Job Security: Most Secure
- ❈ Self-Employed: 0.4%
- ❈ Part-Time: 27.8%

Renewal Industry: Education.

Industries with Greatest Employment: Educational Services, Public and Private (97.3%).

Highest-Growth Industries (Projected Growth for This Job): Administrative and Support Services (48.3%); Amusement, Gambling, and Recreation Industries (45.2%); Social Assistance (38.6%); Support Activities for Transportation (32.8%); Religious, Grantmaking, Civic, Professional, and Similar Organizations (29.9%); Professional, Scientific, and Technical Services (28.8%); Management of Companies and Enterprises (26.8%); Local Government (23.5%); Educational Services, Public and Private (22.8%); Hospitals, Public and Private (21.4%).

Other Considerations for Job Outlook: Retirements of current postsecondary teachers should create numerous openings for all types of postsecondary teachers, so job opportunities are generally expected to be very good. One of the main reasons why students attend postsecondary institutions is to prepare themselves for careers, so the best job prospects for postsecondary teachers are likely to be in rapidly growing fields that offer many nonacademic career options. Community colleges and other institutions offering career and technical education have been among the most rapidly growing, and these institutions are expected to offer some of the best opportunities for postsecondary teachers.

Teach courses in environmental and conservation science. Conduct research in a particular field of knowledge and publish findings in books, professional journals, and/or electronic media. Keep abreast of developments in their field by reading current literature, talking with colleagues, and participating in professional conferences. Prepare and deliver lectures to undergraduate and/or graduate students on topics such as forest resource policy, forest pathology, and mapping. Evaluate and grade students' classwork, assignments, and papers. Write grant proposals to procure external research funding. Supervise undergraduate and/or graduate teaching, internship, and research work. Plan, evaluate, and revise curricula, course content, and course materials and methods of instruction. Prepare course materials such as syllabi, homework assignments, and handouts. Compile, administer, and grade examinations or assign this work to others. Advise students on academic and vocational curricula and on career issues. Initiate, facilitate, and moderate classroom discussions. Supervise students' laboratory work and fieldwork. Maintain student attendance records, grades, and other required records. Collaborate with colleagues to address teaching and research issues. Maintain regularly scheduled office hours in order to advise and assist students. Select and obtain materials and supplies such as textbooks and laboratory equipment. Participate in student recruitment, registration, and placement activities. Serve on academic or administrative committees that deal with institutional policies, departmental matters, and academic issues. Provide professional consulting services to government and/or industry. Perform administrative duties such as serving as department head. Compile bibliographies of specialized materials for outside reading assignments. Act as advisers to student organizations. Participate in campus and community events.

Personality Type: Social-Investigative-Realistic.

Career Cluster: 05 Education and Training. **Career Pathway:** 05.3 Teaching/Training.

Skills: Science; Management of Financial Resources; Writing; Instructing; Mathematics; Management of Personnel Resources.

Education and Training Program: Science Teacher Education/General Science Teacher Education. **Related Knowledge/Courses:** Biology; Geography; Education and Training; Mathematics; Chemistry; History and Archeology.

Work Environment: Indoors; sitting.

Geography Teachers, Postsecondary

- ✵ Education/Training Required: Master's degree
- ✵ Annual Earnings: $61,310
- ✵ Beginning Wage: $36,070
- ✵ Earnings Growth Potential: High (41.2%)
- ✵ Growth: 22.9%
- ✵ Annual Job Openings: 697
- ✵ Job Security: Most Secure
- ✵ Self-Employed: 0.4%
- ✵ Part-Time: 27.8%

Renewal Industry: Education.

Industries with Greatest Employment: Educational Services, Public and Private (97.3%).

Highest-Growth Industries (Projected Growth for This Job): Administrative and Support Services (48.3%); Amusement, Gambling, and Recreation Industries (45.2%); Social Assistance (38.6%); Support Activities for Transportation (32.8%); Religious, Grantmaking, Civic, Professional, and Similar Organizations (29.9%); Professional, Scientific, and Technical Services (28.8%); Management of Companies and Enterprises (26.8%); Local Government (23.5%); Educational Services, Public and Private (22.8%); Hospitals, Public and Private (21.4%).

Other Considerations for Job Outlook: Retirements of current postsecondary teachers should create numerous openings for all types of postsecondary teachers. However, one of the main reasons why students attend postsecondary institutions is to prepare themselves for careers, so the best job prospects for postsecondary teachers are likely to be in rapidly growing fields that offer many nonacademic career options. Community colleges and other institutions offering career and technical education have been among the most rapidly growing, and these institutions are expected to offer some of the best opportunities for postsecondary teachers.

Teach courses in geography. Prepare and deliver lectures to undergraduate and/or graduate students on topics such as urbanization, environmental systems, and cultural geography. Evaluate and grade students' classwork, assignments, and papers. Compile, administer, and grade examinations or assign this work to others. Initiate, facilitate, and moderate classroom discussions. Maintain student attendance records, grades, and other required records. Prepare course materials such as syllabi, homework assignments, and handouts. Keep abreast of developments in their field by reading current literature, talking with colleagues, and participating in professional conferences. Supervise undergraduate and/or graduate teaching, internship, and research work. Plan, evaluate, and revise curricula, course content, and course materials and methods of instruction. Maintain regularly scheduled office hours to advise and assist students. Supervise students' laboratory work and fieldwork. Conduct research in a particular field of knowledge and publish findings in professional journals, books, and electronic media. Collaborate with colleagues to address teaching and research issues. Select and obtain materials and supplies such as textbooks. Advise students on academic and vocational curricula and on career issues. Serve on academic or administrative committees that deal with institutional policies, departmental matters, and academic issues. Participate in student recruitment, registration, and placement activities. Participate in campus and community events. Compile bibliographies of specialized materials for outside reading assignments. Perform administrative duties such as serving as department head. Write grant proposals to procure external research funding. Maintain geographic information systems laboratories, performing duties such as updating software. Perform spatial analysis and modeling, using geographic information system techniques. Act as advisers to student organizations. Provide professional consulting services to government and industry.

Personality Type: Social-Investigative.

Career Clusters: 05 Education and Training; 15 Science, Technology, Engineering, and Mathematics. **Career Pathways:** 05.3 Teaching/Training; 15.3 Science and Mathematics.

Skills: Science; Writing; Instructing; Learning Strategies; Reading Comprehension; Speaking.

Education and Training Programs: Geography Teacher Education; Geography. **Related Knowledge/Courses:** Geography; Sociology and Anthropology; History and Archeology; Philosophy and Theology; Education and Training; Communications and Media.

Work Environment: Indoors; sitting.

Geological and Petroleum Technicians

See *Geological Sample Test Technicians* and *Geophysical Data Technicians*, described separately.

Geological Sample Test Technicians

* Education/Training Required: Associate degree
* Annual Earnings: $50,950
* Beginning Wage: $25,160
* Earnings Growth Potential: Very high (50.6%)
* Growth: 8.6%
* Annual Job Openings: 1,895
* Job Security: Less Secure than Most
* Self-Employed: 0.0%
* Part-Time: 1.0%

Our sources did not provide separate job openings data for this occupation. The job openings listed here are shared with Geophysical Data Technicians.

Renewal Industry: Green Technologies.

Industries with Greatest Employment: Oil and Gas Extraction (36.5%); Professional, Scientific, and Technical Services (24.5%); Support Activities for Mining (19.6%).

Highest-Growth Industries (Projected Growth for This Job): Professional, Scientific, and Technical Services (33.2%); Administrative and Support Services (26.4%); Management of Companies and Enterprises (15.4%).

Other Considerations for Job Outlook: Trained job applicants should experience little competition for positions because of the relatively small number of new entrants.

Test and analyze geological samples, crude oil, or petroleum products to detect presence of petroleum, gas, or mineral deposits indicating potential for exploration and production or to determine physical and chemical properties to ensure that products meet quality standards. Test and analyze samples in order to determine their content and characteristics, using laboratory apparatus and testing equipment. Collect and prepare solid and fluid samples for analysis. Assemble, operate, and maintain field and laboratory testing, measuring, and mechanical equipment, working as part of a crew when required. Compile and record testing and operational data for review and further analysis. Adjust and repair testing, electrical, and mechanical equipment and devices. Supervise well exploration and drilling activities and well completions. Inspect engines for wear and defective parts, using equipment and measuring devices. Prepare notes, sketches, geological maps, and cross sections. Participate in geological, geophysical, geochemical, hydrographic, or oceanographic surveys; prospecting field trips; exploratory drilling; well logging; or underground mine survey programs. Plot information from aerial photographs, well logs, section descriptions, and other databases. Assess the environmental impacts of development projects on subsurface materials. Collaborate with hydrogeologists to evaluate groundwater and well circulation. Prepare, transcribe, and/or analyze seismic, gravimetric, well log, or other geophysical and survey data. Participate in the evaluation of possible mining locations.

Personality Type: Realistic-Investigative-Conventional.

Career Cluster: 01 Agriculture, Food, and Natural Resources. **Career Pathway:** 01.5 Natural Resources Systems.

Skills: Science; Equipment Maintenance; Operation Monitoring; Quality Control Analysis; Mathematics; Operations Analysis.

Education and Training Program: Petroleum Technology/Technician. **Related Knowledge/Courses:** Chemistry; Geography; Physics; Mechanical Devices; Mathematics; Computers and Electronics.

Work Environment: Indoors; noisy; contaminants; more often standing than sitting; using hands on objects, tools, or controls.

Geophysical Data Technicians

* ❋ Education/Training Required: Associate degree
* ❋ Annual Earnings: $50,950
* ❋ Beginning Wage: $25,160
* ❋ Earnings Growth Potential: Very high (50.6%)
* ❋ Growth: 8.6%
* ❋ Annual Job Openings: 1,895
* ❋ Job Security: Less Secure than Most
* ❋ Self-Employed: 0.0%
* ❋ Part-Time: 1.0%

Our sources did not provide separate job openings data for this occupation. The job openings listed here are shared with Geological Sample Test Technicians.

Renewal Industry: Green Technologies.

Industries with Greatest Employment: Oil and Gas Extraction (36.5%); Professional, Scientific, and Technical Services (24.5%); Support Activities for Mining (19.6%).

Highest-Growth Industries (Projected Growth for This Job): Professional, Scientific, and Technical Services (33.2%); Administrative and Support Services (26.4%); Management of Companies and Enterprises (15.4%).

Other Considerations for Job Outlook: Trained job applicants should experience little competition for positions because of the relatively small number of new entrants.

Measure, record, and evaluate geological data by using sonic, electronic, electrical, seismic, or gravity-measuring instruments to prospect for oil or gas. May collect and evaluate core samples and cuttings. Prepare notes, sketches, geological maps, and cross-sections. Read and study reports in order to compile information and data for geological and geophysical prospecting. Interview individuals and research public databases in order to obtain information. Assemble, maintain, and distribute information for library or record systems. Operate and adjust equipment and apparatus used to obtain geological data. Plan and direct activities of workers who operate equipment to collect data. Set up or direct setup of instruments used to collect geological data. Record readings in order to compile data used in prospecting for oil or gas. Supervise oil, water, and gas well drilling activities. Collect samples and cuttings, using equipment and hand tools. Develop and print photographic recordings of information, using equipment. Measure geological characteristics used in prospecting for oil or gas, using measuring instruments. Evaluate and interpret core samples and cuttings and other geological data used in prospecting for oil or gas. Diagnose and repair malfunctioning instruments and equipment, using manufacturers' manuals and hand tools. Prepare and attach packing instructions to shipping containers. Develop and design packing materials and handling procedures for shipping of objects.

Personality Type: Conventional-Realistic-Investigative.

Career Cluster: 01 Agriculture, Food, and Natural Resources. **Career Pathway:** 01.5 Natural Resources Systems.

Skills: Science; Technology Design; Mathematics; Operations Analysis; Operation Monitoring; Persuasion.

Education and Training Program: Petroleum Technology/Technician. **Related Knowledge/Courses:** Geography; Engineering and Technology; Physics; Computers and Electronics; Mathematics; Chemistry.

Work Environment: Indoors; sitting.

Geoscientists, Except Hydrologists and Geographers

* ❋ Education/Training Required: Master's degree
* ❋ Annual Earnings: $75,800
* ❋ Beginning Wage: $41,020
* ❋ Earnings Growth Potential: High (45.9%)
* ❋ Growth: 21.9%
* ❋ Annual Job Openings: 2,471
* ❋ Job Security: Most Secure
* ❋ Self-Employed: 2.2%
* ❋ Part-Time: 5.3%

Renewal Industry: Green Technologies.

Industries with Greatest Employment: Professional, Scientific, and Technical Services (43.7%); Oil and Gas Extraction (17.9%); State Government (9.4%); Federal Government (8.4%); Support Activities for Mining (6.5%).

Highest-Growth Industries (Projected Growth for This Job): Professional, Scientific, and Technical Services (45.2%); Securities, Commodity Contracts, and Other Financial Investments and Related Activities (40.7%); Waste Management and Remediation Services (32.1%); Administrative and Support Services (26.8%); Management of Companies and Enterprises (15.4%).

Other Considerations for Job Outlook: Graduates with a master's degree can expect excellent job opportunities; very few geoscientist jobs are available to bachelor's degree holders. Ph.D.s should face competition for basic research and college teaching jobs. Historically, employment of petroleum geologists, geophysicists, and some other geoscientists has been cyclical and affected considerably by the price of oil and gas. When prices are low, oil and gas producers curtail exploration activities and lay off geologists. When prices were higher, companies had the funds and incentive to renew exploration efforts and to hire geoscientists in larger numbers. In recent years, however, a growing worldwide demand for oil and gas and for new exploration and recovery techniques has created some stability in the petroleum industry. Geoscientists who speak a foreign language and who are willing to work abroad should enjoy the best opportunities.

Study the composition, structure, and other physical aspects of the Earth. May use knowledge of geology, physics, and mathematics in exploration for oil, gas, minerals, or underground water or in waste disposal, land reclamation, or other environmental problems. May study the Earth's internal composition, atmospheres, and oceans and its magnetic, electrical, and gravitational forces. Includes mineralogists, crystallographers, paleontologists, stratigraphers, geodesists, and seismologists. Analyze and interpret geological, geochemical, and geophysical information from sources such as survey data, well logs, bore holes, and aerial photos. Locate and estimate probable natural gas, oil, and mineral ore deposits and underground water resources, using aerial photographs, charts, or research and survey results. Plan and conduct geological, geochemical, and geophysical field studies and surveys, sample collection, or drilling and testing programs used to collect data for research or application. Analyze and interpret geological data, using computer software. Search for and review research articles or environmental, historical, and technical reports. Assess ground and surface water movement to provide advice regarding issues such as waste management, route and site selection, and the restoration of contaminated sites. Prepare geological maps, cross-sectional diagrams, charts, and reports concerning mineral extraction, land use, and resource management, using results of field work and laboratory research. Investigate the composition, structure, and history of the Earth's crust through the collection, examination, measurement, and classification of soils, minerals, rocks, or fossil remains. Conduct geological and geophysical studies to provide information for use in regional development, site selection, and development of public works projects. Measure characteristics of the Earth, such as gravity and magnetic fields, using equipment such as seismographs, gravimeters, torsion balances, and magnetometers. Inspect construction projects to analyze engineering problems, applying geological knowledge and using test equipment and drilling machinery. Design geological mine maps, monitor mine structural integrity, or advise and monitor mining crews. Identify risks for natural disasters such as mudslides, earthquakes, and volcanic eruptions, providing advice on mitigation of potential damage. Advise construction firms and government agencies on dam and road construction, foundation design, or land use and resource management. Test industrial diamonds and abrasives, soil, or rocks to determine their geological characteristics, using optical, X-ray, heat, acid, and precision instruments.

Personality Type: Investigative-Realistic.

Career Cluster: 15 Science, Technology, Engineering, and Mathematics. **Career Pathway:** 15.3 Science and Mathematics.

Skills: No data available.

Education and Training Programs: Geology/Earth Science, General; Geochemistry; Geophysics and Seismology; Paleontology; Geochemistry and Petrology; Oceanography, Chemical and Physical; Geological and Earth Sciences/Geosciences, Other. **Related Knowledge/Courses:** Geography; Engineering and Technology; Physics; Chemistry; Mathematics; Design.

Work Environment: Indoors; sitting.

Glaziers

- ❀ Education/Training Required: Long-term on-the-job training
- ❀ Annual Earnings: $35,230
- ❀ Beginning Wage: $21,670
- ❀ Earnings Growth Potential: Medium (38.5%)
- ❀ Growth: 11.9%
- ❀ Annual Job Openings: 6,416
- ❀ Job Security: Least Secure
- ❀ Self-Employed: 5.3%
- ❀ Part-Time: 2.7%

Renewal Industries: Green Technologies; Infrastructure.

Industries with Greatest Employment: Specialty Trade Contractors (66.1%); Building Material and Garden Equipment and Supplies Dealers (16.1%).

Highest-Growth Industries (Projected Growth for This Job): Building Material and Garden Equipment and Supplies Dealers (25.5%); Administrative and Support Services (25.2%).

Other Considerations for Job Outlook: Job opportunities for glaziers are expected to be good. Since employers prefer workers who can do a variety of tasks, glaziers with a range of skills will have the best opportunities.

Install glass in windows, skylights, storefronts, and display cases or on surfaces such as building fronts, interior walls, ceilings, and tabletops. Read and interpret blueprints and specifications to determine size, shape, color, type, and thickness of glass; location of framing; installation procedures; and staging and scaffolding materials required. Determine plumb of walls or ceilings, using plumb-lines and levels. Fabricate and install metal sashes and moldings for glass installation, using aluminum or steel framing. Measure mirrors and dimensions of areas to be covered to determine work procedures. Fasten glass panes into wood sashes or frames with clips, points, or moldings, adding weather seals or putty around pane edges to seal joints. Secure mirrors in position, using mastic cement, putty, bolts, or screws. Cut, fit, install, repair, and replace glass and glass substitutes such as plastic and aluminum in building interiors or exteriors and in furniture or other products. Cut and remove broken glass prior to installing replacement glass. Set glass doors into frames and bolt metal hinges, handles, locks, and other hardware to attach doors to frames and walls. Score glass with cutters' wheels, breaking off excess glass by hand or with notched tools. Cut, assemble, fit, and attach metal-framed glass enclosures for showers, bathtubs, display cases, skylights, solariums, and other structures. Drive trucks to installation sites and unload mirrors, glass equipment, and tools. Install pre-assembled metal or wood frameworks for windows or doors to be fitted with glass panels, using hand tools. Cut and attach mounting strips, metal or wood moldings, rubber gaskets, or metal clips to surfaces in preparation for mirror installation. Assemble, erect, and dismantle scaffolds, rigging, and hoisting equipment. Load and arrange glass and mirrors onto delivery trucks, using suction cups or cranes to lift glass. Measure and mark outlines or patterns on glass to indicate cutting lines. Grind and polish glass, smoothing edges when necessary. Prepare glass for cutting by resting it on rack edges or against cutting tables and by brushing a thin layer of oil along cutting lines or by dipping cutting tools in oil. Pack spaces between moldings and glass with glazing compounds, and trim excess material with glazing knives.

Personality Type: Realistic-Conventional.

Career Cluster: 02 Architecture and Construction. **Career Pathway:** 02.2 Construction.

Skills: No data available.

Education and Training Program: Glazier. **Related Knowledge/Courses:** Building and Construction; Mechanical Devices; Design; Engineering and Technology; Mathematics; Public Safety and Security.

Work Environment: Outdoors; noisy; very hot or cold; contaminants; standing; using hands on objects, tools, or controls.

Graduate Teaching Assistants

- ❋ Education/Training Required: Master's degree
- ❋ Annual Earnings: $28,060
- ❋ Beginning Wage: $15,660
- ❋ Earnings Growth Potential: High (44.2%)
- ❋ Growth: 22.9%
- ❋ Annual Job Openings: 20,601
- ❋ Job Security: Most Secure
- ❋ Self-Employed: 0.4%
- ❋ Part-Time: 27.8%

Renewal Industry: Education.

Industries with Greatest Employment: Educational Services, Public and Private (97.3%).

Highest-Growth Industries (Projected Growth for This Job): Administrative and Support Services (48.3%); Amusement, Gambling, and Recreation Industries (45.2%); Social Assistance (38.6%); Support Activities for Transportation (32.8%); Religious, Grantmaking, Civic, Professional, and Similar Organizations (29.9%); Professional, Scientific, and Technical Services (28.8%); Management of Companies and Enterprises (26.8%); Local Government (23.5%); Educational Services, Public and Private (22.8%); Hospitals, Public and Private (21.4%).

Other Considerations for Job Outlook: Retirements of current postsecondary teachers should create numerous openings for all types of postsecondary teachers, so job opportunities are generally expected to be very good. However, one of the main reasons why students attend postsecondary institutions is to prepare themselves for careers, so the best job prospects for postsecondary teachers are likely to be in rapidly growing fields that offer many nonacademic career options. Community colleges and other institutions offering career and technical education have been among the most rapidly growing, and these institutions are expected to offer some of the best opportunities for postsecondary teachers.

Assist department chairperson, faculty members, or other professional staff members in colleges or universities by performing teaching or teaching-related duties such as teaching lower-level courses, developing teaching materials, preparing and giving examinations, and grading examinations or papers. Graduate assistants must be enrolled in graduate school programs. Graduate assistants who primarily perform non-teaching duties such as laboratory research should be reported in the occupational category related to the work performed. Lead discussion sections, tutorials, and laboratory sections. Evaluate and grade examinations, assignments, and papers and record grades. Return assignments to students in accordance with established deadlines. Schedule and maintain regular office hours to meet with students. Inform students of the procedures for completing and submitting class work such as lab reports. Prepare and proctor examinations. Notify instructors of errors or problems with assignments. Meet with supervisors to discuss students' grades and to complete required grade-related paperwork. Copy and distribute classroom materials. Demonstrate use of laboratory equipment and enforce laboratory rules. Teach undergraduate-level courses. Complete laboratory projects prior to assigning them to students so that any needed modifications can be made. Develop teaching materials such as syllabi, visual aids, answer keys, supplementary notes, and course Web sites. Provide assistance to faculty members or staff with laboratory or field research. Arrange for supervisors to conduct teaching observations; meet with supervisors to receive feedback about teaching performance. Attend lectures given by the instructors whom they are assisting. Order or obtain materials needed for classes. Provide instructors with assistance in the use of audiovisual equipment. Assist faculty members or staff with student conferences.

Personality Type: Social-Conventional.

Career Cluster: 05 Education and Training. **Career Pathway:** 05.3 Teaching/Training.

Skills: Learning Strategies; Instructing; Social Perceptiveness; Reading Comprehension; Writing; Speaking.

Education and Training Program: Education, General. **Related Knowledge/Courses:** Sociology and Anthropology; Education and Training; English Language; Philosophy and Theology; Communications and Media; Psychology.

Work Environment: Indoors; sitting.

Graphic Designers

- ❋ Education/Training Required: Bachelor's degree
- ❋ Annual Earnings: $41,280
- ❋ Beginning Wage: $25,090
- ❋ Earnings Growth Potential: Medium (39.2%)
- ❋ Growth: 9.8%
- ❋ Annual Job Openings: 26,968
- ❋ Job Security: More Secure than Most
- ❋ Self-Employed: 25.3%
- ❋ Part-Time: 16.7%

Renewal Industry: Advanced Manufacturing.

Industries with Greatest Employment: Professional, Scientific, and Technical Services (28.2%); Publishing Industries (Except Internet) (10.7%); Printing and Related Support Activities (6.9%).

Highest-Growth Industries (Projected Growth for This Job): Securities, Commodity Contracts, and Other Financial Investments and Related Activities (44.8%); Amusement, Gambling, and Recreation Industries (40.9%); Internet Publishing and Broadcasting (40.3%); Museums, Historical Sites, and Similar Institutions (36.2%); Social Assistance (35.4%); Funds, Trusts, and Other Financial Vehicles (33.3%); Warehousing and Storage (33.0%); Administrative and Support Services (30.6%); Personal and Laundry Services (29.6%); Lessors of Nonfinancial Intangible Assets (Except Copyrighted Works) (28.1%); Ambulatory Health-Care Services (28.0%); Professional, Scientific, and Technical Services (27.1%); Building Material and Garden Equipment and Supplies Dealers (23.0%); Real Estate (22.5%); Nonstore Retailers (22.1%); Religious, Grantmaking, Civic, Professional, and Similar Organizations (19.4%); Nursing and Residential Care Facilities (18.3%); Rental and Leasing Services (17.2%); Accommodation, Including Hotels and Motels (17.1%); Repair and Maintenance (16.5%); Motion Picture, Video, and Sound Recording Industries (16.4%); Management of Companies and Enterprises (15.3%); General Merchandise Stores (15.2%).

Other Considerations for Job Outlook: Job seekers are expected to face keen competition; individuals with a bachelor's degree and knowledge of computer design software, particularly those with Web site design and animation experience, will have the best opportunities.

Design or create graphics to meet specific commercial or promotional needs such as packaging, displays, or logos. May use a variety of media to achieve artistic or decorative effects. Create designs, concepts, and sample layouts based on knowledge of layout principles and esthetic design concepts. Determine size and arrangement of illustrative material and copy; and select style and size of type. Confer with clients to discuss and determine layout designs. Develop graphics and layouts for product illustrations, company logos, and Internet Web sites. Review final layouts and suggest improvements as needed. Prepare illustrations or rough sketches of material, discussing them with clients or supervisors and making necessary changes. Use computer software to generate new images. Key information into computer equipment to create layouts for client or supervisor. Maintain archive of images, photos, or previous work products. Prepare notes and instructions for workers who assemble and prepare final layouts for printing. Draw and print charts, graphs, illustrations, and other artwork, using computer. Study illustrations and photographs to plan presentations of materials, products, or services. Research new software or design concepts. Mark up, paste, and assemble final layouts to prepare layouts for printer. Produce still and animated graphics for on-air and taped portions of television news broadcasts, using electronic video equipment. Photograph layouts, using cameras, to make layout prints for supervisors or clients. Develop negatives and prints to produce layout photographs, using negative and print developing equipment and tools.

Personality Type: Artistic-Realistic-Enterprising.

Career Clusters: 01 Agriculture, Food, and Natural Resources; 03 Arts, Audio/Video Technology, and Communications; 11 Information Technology. **Career Pathways:** 01.7 Agribusiness Systems; 03.1 Audio and Video Technology and Film; 03.3 Visual Arts; 11.1 Network Systems.

Skills: No data available.

Education and Training Programs: Agricultural Communication/Journalism; Web Page, Digital/Multimedia, and Information Resources Design; Computer Graphics; Design and Visual Communications, General; Commercial and Advertising Art; Industrial Design; Graphic Design. **Related Knowledge/Courses:** Fine Arts; Design;

Communications and Media; Sales and Marketing; Sociology and Anthropology; Computers and Electronics.

Work Environment: Indoors; sitting; using hands on objects, tools, or controls; repetitive motions.

Hazardous Materials Removal Workers

- ❋ Education/Training Required: Moderate-term on-the-job training
- ❋ Annual Earnings: $36,330
- ❋ Beginning Wage: $23,200
- ❋ Earnings Growth Potential: Medium (36.1%)
- ❋ Growth: 11.2%
- ❋ Annual Job Openings: 1,933
- ❋ Job Security: Most Secure
- ❋ Self-Employed: 1.6%
- ❋ Part-Time: 5.7%

Renewal Industry: Green Technologies.

Industries with Greatest Employment: Waste Management and Remediation Services (79.5%).

Highest-Growth Industries (Projected Growth for This Job): Professional, Scientific, and Technical Services (37.4%).

Other Considerations for Job Outlook: In addition to some job openings from employment growth, many openings are expected for hazardous materials removal workers because of the need to replace workers who leave the occupation, leading to good opportunities. The often dangerous aspects of the job lead to high turnover because many workers do not stay in the occupation long. Opportunities for decontamination technicians, radiation safety technicians, and decontamination workers should be particularly good. Lead and asbestos workers will have some opportunities at specialty remediation companies as restoration of federal buildings and historic structures continues, although at a slower pace. The best employment opportunities for mold remediation workers will be in the Southeast, and parts of the Northeast and Northwest, where mold tends to thrive. These workers are not greatly affected by economic fluctuations because the facilities in which they work must operate, regardless of the state of the economy.

Identify, remove, pack, transport, or dispose of hazardous materials, including asbestos, lead-based paint, waste oil, fuel, transmission fluid, radioactive materials, contaminated soil, and so on. Specialized training and certification in hazardous materials handling or a confined entry permit are generally required. May operate earth-moving equipment or trucks. Follow prescribed safety procedures and comply with federal laws regulating waste disposal methods. Record numbers of containers stored at disposal sites and specify amounts and types of equipment and waste disposed. Drive trucks or other heavy equipment to convey contaminated waste to designated sea or ground locations. Operate machines and equipment to remove, package, store, or transport loads of waste materials. Load and unload materials into containers and onto trucks, using hoists or forklifts. Clean contaminated equipment or areas for reuse, using detergents and solvents, sandblasters, filter pumps, and steam cleaners. Construct scaffolding or build containment areas prior to beginning abatement or decontamination work. Remove asbestos and/or lead from surfaces, using hand and power tools such as scrapers, vacuums, and high-pressure sprayers. Unload baskets of irradiated elements onto packaging machines that automatically insert fuel elements into canisters and secure lids. Apply chemical compounds to lead-based paint, allow compounds to dry, and then scrape the hazardous material into containers for removal or storage. Identify asbestos, lead, or other hazardous materials that need to be removed, using monitoring devices. Pull tram cars along underwater tracks and position cars to receive irradiated fuel elements; then pull loaded cars to mechanisms that automatically unload elements onto underwater tables. Package, store, and move irradiated fuel elements in the underwater storage basin of a nuclear reactor plant, using machines and equipment. Organize and track the locations of hazardous items in landfills. Operate cranes to move and load baskets, casks, and canisters. Manipulate handgrips of mechanical arms to place irradiated fuel elements into baskets. Mix and pour concrete into forms to encase waste material for disposal.

Personality Type: Realistic-Conventional.

Career Clusters: 01 Agriculture, Food, and Natural Resources; 13 Manufacturing. **Career Pathways:** 01.6 Environmental Service Systems; 13.1 Production; 13.3 Maintenance, Installation, and Repair.

Skills: Equipment Maintenance; Operation Monitoring; Repairing; Operation and Control; Science; Troubleshooting.

Education and Training Programs: Hazardous Materials Management and Waste Technology/Technician; Construction Trades, Other; Mechanic and Repair Technologies/Technicians, Other. **Related Knowledge/Courses:** Chemistry; Mechanical Devices; Building and Construction; Transportation; Physics; Public Safety and Security.

Work Environment: Outdoors; very hot or cold; contaminants; hazardous conditions; using hands on objects, tools, or controls; repetitive motions.

Health and Safety Engineers, Except Mining Safety Engineers and Inspectors

See *Fire-Prevention and Protection Engineers* and *Industrial Safety and Health Engineers*, *described separately.*

Health Educators

- ❋ Education/Training Required: Master's degree
- ❋ Annual Earnings: $42,920
- ❋ Beginning Wage: $25,340
- ❋ Earnings Growth Potential: High (41.0%)
- ❋ Growth: 26.2%
- ❋ Annual Job Openings: 13,707
- ❋ Job Security: Most Secure
- ❋ Self-Employed: 0.1%
- ❋ Part-Time: 12.0%

Renewal Industry: Health Care.

Industries with Greatest Employment: Hospitals, Public and Private (18.8%); Social Assistance (17.0%); Ambulatory Health-Care Services (14.1%); Local Government (11.9%); Religious, Grantmaking, Civic, Professional, and Similar Organizations (9.7%); State Government (8.1%); Educational Services, Public and Private (8.1%).

Highest-Growth Industries (Projected Growth for This Job): Social Assistance (74.7%); Ambulatory Health-Care Services (34.5%); Religious, Grantmaking, Civic, Professional, and Similar Organizations (29.7%); Administrative and Support Services (29.0%); Professional, Scientific, and Technical Services (27.5%); Nursing and Residential Care Facilities (23.3%); Management of Companies and Enterprises (15.2%).

Other Considerations for Job Outlook: The rising cost of health care has increased the need for health educators. Demand for health educators will increase in most industries, but their employment may decrease in secondary schools. Many schools, facing budget cuts, ask teachers trained in other fields, like science or physical education, to teach the subject of health education. Job prospects for health educators with bachelor's degrees will be favorable, but better for those who have acquired experience through internships or volunteer jobs. A graduate degree is preferred by many employers.

Promote, maintain, and improve individual and community health by assisting individuals and communities to adopt healthy behaviors. Collect and analyze data to identify community needs prior to planning, implementing, monitoring, and evaluating programs designed to encourage healthy lifestyles, policies, and environments. May also serve as a resource to assist individuals, other professionals, or the community and may administer fiscal resources for health education programs. Document activities, recording information such as the numbers of applications completed, presentations conducted, and persons assisted. Develop and present health education and promotion programs such as training workshops, conferences, and school or community presentations. Develop and maintain cooperative working relationships with agencies and organizations interested in public health care. Prepare and distribute health education materials, including reports; bulletins; and visual aids such as films, videotapes, photographs, and posters. Develop operational plans and policies necessary to achieve health education objectives and services. Collaborate with health specialists and civic groups to determine community health needs and the availability of services and to develop goals for meeting needs. Maintain databases, mailing lists, telephone networks, and other information to facilitate the functioning of health education programs. Supervise professional and technical staff in implementing health programs, objectives, and goals. Design and conduct evaluations and diagnostic studies to assess the quality and performance of health education programs. Provide program information to the public by preparing and presenting press releases, conducting media campaigns, and/or maintaining program-related Web sites. Develop, prepare, and coordinate grant applications and grant-related activities to obtain funding for health education programs and related work. Provide guidance to agencies and organizations in the assessment of health education needs and in the development and delivery of health education programs. Develop and maintain health education libraries to provide resources for staff and community agencies. Develop, conduct, or coordinate health needs assessments and other public health surveys.

Personality Type: Social-Enterprising.

Career Clusters: 08 Health Science; 10 Human Services. **Career Pathways:** 08.3 Health Informatics; 10.2 Counseling and Mental Health Services.

Skills: Service Orientation; Social Perceptiveness; Monitoring; Learning Strategies; Instructing; Speaking.

Education and Training Programs: Health Communication; Community Health Services/Liaison/Counseling; Public Health Education and Promotion; Maternal and Child Health; International Public Health/International Health; Bioethics/Medical Ethics. **Related Knowledge/Courses:** Sociology and Anthropology; Customer and Personal Service; Education and Training; Personnel and Human Resources; Psychology; Therapy and Counseling.

Work Environment: Indoors; disease or infections; sitting; using hands on objects, tools, or controls.

Health Specialties Teachers, Postsecondary

- ❋ Education/Training Required: Master's degree
- ❋ Annual Earnings: $80,700
- ❋ Beginning Wage: $37,890
- ❋ Earnings Growth Potential: Very high (53.0%)
- ❋ Growth: 22.9%
- ❋ Annual Job Openings: 19,617
- ❋ Job Security: Most Secure
- ❋ Self-Employed: 0.4%
- ❋ Part-Time: 27.8%

Renewal Industry: Education.

Industries with Greatest Employment: Educational Services, Public and Private (97.3%).

Highest-Growth Industries (Projected Growth for This Job): Administrative and Support Services (48.3%); Amusement, Gambling, and Recreation Industries (45.2%); Social Assistance (38.6%); Support Activities for Transportation (32.8%); Religious, Grantmaking, Civic, Professional, and Similar Organizations (29.9%); Professional, Scientific, and Technical Services (28.8%); Management of Companies and Enterprises (26.8%); Local Government (23.5%); Educational Services, Public and Private (22.8%); Hospitals, Public and Private (21.4%).

Other Considerations for Job Outlook: Retirements of current postsecondary teachers should create numerous openings for all types of postsecondary teachers, so job opportunities are generally expected to be very good. However, one of the main reasons why students attend postsecondary institutions is to prepare themselves for careers, so the best job prospects for postsecondary teachers are likely to be in rapidly growing fields that offer many nonacademic career options, such as the health sciences. Community colleges and other institutions offering career and technical education have been among the most rapidly growing, and these institutions are expected to offer some of the best opportunities for postsecondary teachers.

Teach courses in health specialties, such as veterinary medicine, dentistry, pharmacy, therapy, laboratory technology, and public health. Initiate, facilitate, and moderate classroom discussions. Keep abreast of developments in their field by reading current literature, talking with colleagues, and participating in professional conferences. Compile, administer, and grade examinations or assign this work to others. Evaluate and grade students' classwork, assignments, and papers. Prepare course materials such as syllabi, homework assignments, and handouts. Prepare and deliver lectures to undergraduate or graduate students on topics such as public health, stress management, and worksite health promotion. Plan, evaluate, and revise curricula, course content, and course materials and methods of instruction. Supervise undergraduate or graduate teaching, internship, and research work. Conduct research in a particular field of knowledge and publish findings in professional journals, books, or electronic media. Collaborate with colleagues to address teaching and research issues. Supervise laboratory sessions. Maintain student attendance records, grades, and other required records. Maintain regularly scheduled office hours in order to advise and assist students. Advise students on academic and vocational curricula and on career issues. Participate in student recruitment, registration, and placement activities. Write grant proposals to procure external research funding. Serve on academic or administrative committees that deal with institutional policies, departmental matters, and academic issues. Select and obtain materials and supplies such as textbooks and laboratory equipment. Act as advisers to student organizations. Perform administrative duties such as serving as department head. Compile bibliographies of specialized materials for outside reading assignments. Provide professional consulting services to government and industry. Participate in campus and community events.

Personality Type: Social-Investigative.

Career Clusters: 05 Education and Training; 08 Health Science; 15 Science, Technology, Engineering, and Mathematics. **Career Pathways:** 05.3 Teaching/Training; 08.1 Therapeutic Services; 08.2 Diagnostics Services; 08.3 Health Informatics; 08.5 Biotechnology Research and Development; 15.3 Science and Mathematics.

Skills: Science; Instructing; Writing; Reading Comprehension; Learning Strategies; Complex Problem Solving.

Education and Training Programs: Health Occupations Teacher Education; Biostatistics; Epidemiology; Chiropractic (DC); Communication Disorders, General; Audiology/Audiologist and Hearing Sciences; Speech-Language Pathology/Pathologist; Audiology/Audiologist and Speech-Language Pathology/Pathologist; Dentistry (DDS, DMD); Dental Clinical Sciences, General (MS, PhD); Dental Assisting/Assistant; Dental Hygiene/Hygienist; others. **Related Knowledge/Courses:** Biology; Medicine and Dentistry; Education and Training; Therapy and Counseling; Sociology and Anthropology; Psychology.

Work Environment: Indoors; sitting.

Heating, Air Conditioning, and Refrigeration Mechanics and Installers

- ❋ Education/Training Required: Long-term on-the-job training
- ❋ Annual Earnings: $38,360
- ❋ Beginning Wage: $24,240
- ❋ Earnings Growth Potential: Medium (36.8%)
- ❋ Growth: 8.7%
- ❋ Annual Job Openings: 29,719
- ❋ Job Security: Less Secure than Most
- ❋ Self-Employed: 12.7%
- ❋ Part-Time: 3.6%

Our sources did not provide separate job openings data for this occupation. The job openings listed here are shared with another occupation not included in this book.

Renewal Industries: Green Technologies; Infrastructure.

Industries with Greatest Employment: Specialty Trade Contractors (58.4%).

Highest-Growth Industries (Projected Growth for This Job): Amusement, Gambling, and Recreation Industries (35.9%); Museums, Historical Sites, and Similar Institutions (35.8%); Professional, Scientific, and Technical Services (33.8%); Warehousing and Storage (33.6%); Nursing and Residential Care Facilities (30.5%); Administrative and Support Services (30.5%); Performing Arts, Spectator Sports, and Related Industries (29.1%); Social Assistance (23.2%); Building Material and Garden Equipment and Supplies Dealers (22.1%); Real Estate (17.9%); Accommodation, Including Hotels and Motels (16.8%); Support Activities for Transportation (16.0%); Rental and Leasing Services (15.6%); Management of Companies and Enterprises (15.3%); Food Services and Drinking Places (15.2%); Furniture and Home Furnishings Stores (15.1%).

Other Considerations for Job Outlook: Job prospects for heating, air-conditioning, and refrigeration mechanics and installers are expected to be excellent, particularly for those who have completed training from an accredited technical school or a formal apprenticeship. Job opportunities should be best in the fastest-growing areas of the country. A growing number of retirements of highly skilled technicians are expected to generate many job openings. Many contractors have reported problems finding enough workers to meet the demand for service and installation of HVACR systems.

Install, service, and repair heating and air conditioning systems in residences and commercial establishments. Obtain and maintain required certifications. Comply with all applicable standards, policies, and procedures, including safety procedures and the maintenance of a clean work area. Repair or replace defective equipment, components, or wiring. Test electrical circuits and components for continuity, using electrical test equipment. Reassemble and test equipment following repairs. Inspect and test system to verify system compliance with plans and specifications and to detect and locate malfunctions. Discuss heating-cooling system malfunctions with users to isolate problems or to verify that malfunctions have been corrected. Test pipe or tubing joints and connections for leaks, using pressure gauge or soap-and-water solution. Record and report all faults, deficiencies, and other unusual occurrences, as well as the time and materials expended on work orders. Adjust system controls to setting recommended by manufacturer to balance system, using hand tools. Recommend, develop, and perform preventive and general maintenance procedures such as cleaning, power-washing, and vacuuming equipment; oiling parts; and changing filters. Lay out and connect electrical wiring between controls and equipment according to wiring diagram, using electrician's hand tools. Install auxiliary components to heating-cooling equipment, such as expansion and discharge valves, air ducts, pipes, blowers, dampers, flues, and stokers, following blueprints. Assist with other work in coordination with repair and maintenance teams. Install, connect, and adjust thermostats, humidistats, and timers, using hand tools. Generate work orders that address deficiencies in need of correction. Join pipes or tubing to equipment and to fuel, water, or refrigerant source to form complete circuit. Assemble, position, and mount heating or cooling equipment, following blueprints. Study blueprints, design specifications, and manufacturers' recommendations to ascertain the configuration of heating or cooling equipment components and to ensure the proper installation of components. Cut and drill holes in floors, walls, and roof to install equipment, using power saws and drills.

Personality Type: Realistic-Conventional-Investigative.

Career Cluster: 02 Architecture and Construction. **Career Pathways:** 02.2 Construction; 02.3 Maintenance/Operations.

Skills: Repairing; Installation; Equipment Maintenance; Troubleshooting; Systems Evaluation; Science.

Education and Training Programs: Heating, Air Conditioning, and Refrigeration Technology/Technician (ACH/ACR/ACHR/HRAC/HVAC); Solar Energy Technology/Technician; Heating, Air Conditioning, Ventilation, and Refrigeration Maintenance Technology/Technician. **Related Knowledge/Courses:** Mechanical Devices; Building and Construction; Design; Physics; Engineering and Technology; Sales and Marketing.

Work Environment: Outdoors; contaminants; hazardous conditions; minor burns, cuts, bites, or stings; standing; using hands on objects, tools, or controls.

Helpers—Brickmasons, Blockmasons, Stonemasons, and Tile and Marble Setters

- ✱ Education/Training Required: Short-term on-the-job training
- ✱ Annual Earnings: $26,260
- ✱ Beginning Wage: $18,340
- ✱ Earnings Growth Potential: Low (30.2%)
- ✱ Growth: 11.0%
- ✱ Annual Job Openings: 22,500
- ✱ Job Security: Least Secure
- ✱ Self-Employed: 3.0%
- ✱ Part-Time: 10.4%

Renewal Industry: Infrastructure.

Industries with Greatest Employment: Specialty Trade Contractors (87.6%); Construction of Buildings (6.1%).

Highest-Growth Industries (Projected Growth for This Job): Building Material and Garden Equipment and

Supplies Dealers (27.7%); Administrative and Support Services (26.0%); Furniture and Home Furnishings Stores (16.1%).

Other Considerations for Job Outlook: Opportunities are expected to be good, particularly for those with the most experience and skills. Employers report difficulty in finding workers with the right skills, as many qualified jobseekers often prefer work that is less strenuous and has more comfortable working conditions.

Help brickmasons, blockmasons, stonemasons, or tile and marble setters by performing duties of lesser skill. Duties include using, supplying, or holding materials or tools and cleaning work area and equipment. Transport materials, tools, and machines to installation sites, manually or using conveyance equipment. Move or position materials such as marble slabs, using cranes, hoists, or dollies. Modify material moving, mixing, grouting, grinding, polishing, or cleaning procedures according to installation or material requirements. Correct surface imperfections or fill chipped, cracked, or broken bricks or tiles, using fillers, adhesives, and grouting materials. Arrange and store materials, machines, tools, and equipment. Apply caulk, sealants, or other agents to installed surfaces. Select or locate and supply materials to masons for installation, following drawings or numbered sequences. Remove excess grout and residue from tile or brick joints, using sponges or trowels. Remove damaged tile, brick, or mortar and clean and prepare surfaces, using pliers, hammers, chisels, drills, wire brushes, and metal wire anchors. Provide assistance in the preparation, installation, repair, and/or rebuilding of tile, brick, or stone surfaces. Mix mortar, plaster, and grout, manually or using machines, according to standard formulas. Erect scaffolding or other installation structures. Cut materials to specified sizes for installation, using power saws or tile cutters. Clean installation surfaces, equipment, tools, work sites, and storage areas, using water, chemical solutions, oxygen lances, or polishing machines. Apply grout between joints of bricks or tiles, using grouting trowels.

Personality Type: Realistic.

Career Cluster: 02 Architecture and Construction. **Career Pathway:** 02.2 Construction.

Skills: No data available.

Education and Training Program: Mason/Masonry. **Related Knowledge/Courses:** Building and Construction; Chemistry; Transportation; Production and Processing; Mechanical Devices; Design.

Work Environment: Outdoors; noisy; very hot or cold; high places; using hands on objects, tools, or controls; repetitive motions.

Helpers—Carpenters

- ❋ Education/Training Required: Short-term on-the-job training
- ❋ Annual Earnings: $24,340
- ❋ Beginning Wage: $16,790
- ❋ Earnings Growth Potential: Low (31.0%)
- ❋ Growth: 11.7%
- ❋ Annual Job Openings: 37,731
- ❋ Job Security: Less Secure than Most
- ❋ Self-Employed: 3.2%
- ❋ Part-Time: 10.4%

Renewal Industry: Infrastructure.

Industries with Greatest Employment: Construction of Buildings (54.1%); Specialty Trade Contractors (31.6%).

Highest-Growth Industries (Projected Growth for This Job): Waste Management and Remediation Services (32.2%); Building Material and Garden Equipment and Supplies Dealers (27.7%); Administrative and Support Services (26.3%); Professional, Scientific, and Technical Services (22.9%); Real Estate (17.4%).

Other Considerations for Job Outlook: Like carpenters, helpers with all-around skills will have better opportunities for steady work than those who can perform only a few relatively simple, routine tasks.

Help carpenters by performing duties of lesser skill. Duties include using, supplying, or holding materials or tools and cleaning work area and equipment. Position and hold timbers, lumber, and paneling in place for fastening or cutting. Erect scaffolding, shoring, and braces. Select tools, equipment, and materials from storage and transport items to worksite. Fasten timbers or lumber with glue, screws, pegs, or nails and install hardware. Clean work areas, machines, and equipment to maintain a clean and safe jobsite. Align, straighten, plumb, and square forms for installation. Hold plumb bobs, sighting rods, and other equipment to aid in establishing reference points and lines. Cut timbers, lumber, or paneling to specified dimensions and drill holes in timbers or lumber. Smooth and sand surfaces to remove ridges, tool marks, glue, or caulking. Perform tie spacing layout; then measure, mark, drill, and cut. Secure stakes to grids for constructions of footings, nail scabs to footing forms, and vibrate and float concrete. Construct forms; then assist in raising them to the required elevation. Install handrails under the direction of a carpenter. Glue and clamp edges or joints of assembled parts. Cut and install insulating or sound-absorbing material. Cut tile or linoleum to fit and spread adhesives on flooring to install tile or linoleum. Cover surfaces with laminated-plastic covering material.

Personality Type: Realistic-Conventional.

Career Cluster: 02 Architecture and Construction. **Career Pathway:** 02.2 Construction.

Skills: No data available.

Education and Training Program: Carpentry/Carpenter. **Related Knowledge/Courses:** Building and Construction; Design; Engineering and Technology.

Work Environment: Noisy; very hot or cold; hazardous equipment; standing; walking and running; using hands on objects, tools, or controls.

Helpers—Installation, Maintenance, and Repair Workers

- ❋ Education/Training Required: Short-term on-the-job training
- ❋ Annual Earnings: $22,920
- ❋ Beginning Wage: $15,530
- ❋ Earnings Growth Potential: Low (32.2%)
- ❋ Growth: 11.8%
- ❋ Annual Job Openings: 52,058
- ❋ Job Security: Least Secure
- ❋ Self-Employed: 0.1%
- ❋ Part-Time: 22.7%

Renewal Industries: Green Technologies; Infrastructure.

Industries with Greatest Employment: Repair and Maintenance (15.4%); Specialty Trade Contractors (14.9%);

Motor Vehicle and Parts Dealers (12.3%); Local Government (7.8%); Merchant Wholesalers, Durable Goods (5.7%).

Highest-Growth Industries (Projected Growth for This Job): Professional, Scientific, and Technical Services (37.0%); Warehousing and Storage (33.5%); Amusement, Gambling, and Recreation Industries (31.5%); Administrative and Support Services (29.4%); Scenic and Sightseeing Transportation (27.2%); Waste Management and Remediation Services (27.0%); Ambulatory Health-Care Services (26.4%); Nursing and Residential Care Facilities (24.6%); Social Assistance (24.5%); Performing Arts, Spectator Sports, and Related Industries (23.7%); General Merchandise Stores (22.1%); Religious, Grantmaking, Civic, Professional, and Similar Organizations (19.7%); Real Estate (19.3%); Building Material and Garden Equipment and Supplies Dealers (19.2%); Support Activities for Transportation (18.3%); Telecommunications (18.1%); Broadcasting (Except Internet) (17.0%); Rental and Leasing Services (15.9%); Accommodation, Including Hotels and Motels (15.8%); Management of Companies and Enterprises (15.3%); Repair and Maintenance (15.3%).

Other Considerations for Job Outlook: Job opportunities should be excellent, especially for helpers with experience in maintenance or related fields. General maintenance and repair is a large occupation, generating many job openings for helpers due to growth and the need to replace those who leave the occupation or get promoted to more skilled positions.

Help installation, maintenance, and repair workers in maintenance, parts replacement, and repair of vehicles, industrial machinery, and electrical and electronic equipment. Perform duties such as furnishing tools, materials, and supplies to other workers; cleaning work area, machines, and tools; and holding materials or tools for other workers. Tend and observe equipment and machinery to verify efficient and safe operation. Examine and test machinery, equipment, components, and parts for defects and to ensure proper functioning. Adjust, connect, or disconnect wiring, piping, tubing, and other parts, using hand tools or power tools. Install or replace machinery, equipment, and new or replacement parts and instruments, using hand tools or power tools. Clean or lubricate vehicles, machinery, equipment, instruments, tools, work areas, and other objects, using hand tools, power tools, and cleaning equipment. Apply protective materials to equipment, components, and parts to prevent defects and corrosion. Transfer tools, parts, equipment, and supplies to and from workstations and other areas. Disassemble broken or defective equipment in order to facilitate repair; reassemble equipment when repairs are complete. Assemble and maintain physical structures, using hand tools or power tools. Provide assistance to more skilled workers involved in the adjustment, maintenance, part replacement, and repair of tools, equipment, and machines. Position vehicles, machinery, equipment, physical structures, and other objects for assembly or installation, using hand tools, power tools, and moving equipment. Hold or supply tools, parts, equipment, and supplies for other workers. Prepare work stations so mechanics and repairers can conduct work.

Personality Type: Realistic-Conventional-Investigative.

Career Cluster: 13 Manufacturing. **Career Pathway:** 13.3 Maintenance, Installation, and Repair.

Skills: Installation; Operation Monitoring; Repairing; Equipment Maintenance; Troubleshooting; Operations Analysis.

Education and Training Program: Industrial Mechanics and Maintenance Technology. **Related Knowledge/Courses:** Mechanical Devices; Engineering and Technology; Building and Construction; Chemistry; Design; Public Safety and Security.

Work Environment: Noisy; hazardous conditions; hazardous equipment; standing; using hands on objects, tools, or controls; bending or twisting the body.

Helpers—Pipelayers, Plumbers, Pipefitters, and Steamfitters

- ❋ Education/Training Required: Short-term on-the-job training
- ❋ Annual Earnings: $25,350
- ❋ Beginning Wage: $17,700
- ❋ Earnings Growth Potential: Low (30.2%)
- ❋ Growth: 11.9%
- ❋ Annual Job Openings: 29,332
- ❋ Job Security: Less Secure than Most
- ❋ Self-Employed: 2.9%
- ❋ Part-Time: 10.4%

Renewal Industries: Green Technologies; Infrastructure.

Industries with Greatest Employment: Specialty Trade Contractors (79.7%); Heavy and Civil Engineering Construction (8.6%).

Highest-Growth Industries (Projected Growth for This Job): Waste Management and Remediation Services (32.1%); Professional, Scientific, and Technical Services (27.9%); Building Material and Garden Equipment and Supplies Dealers (27.6%); Administrative and Support Services (26.0%).

Other Considerations for Job Outlook: Workers with welding experience should have especially good opportunities.

Help plumbers, pipefitters, steamfitters, or pipelayers by performing duties of lesser skill. Duties include using, supplying, or holding materials or tools and cleaning work area and equipment. Assist plumbers by performing rough-ins, repairing and replacing fixtures, and locating and repairing leaking or broken pipes. Cut or drill holes in walls or floors to accommodate the passage of pipes. Measure, cut, thread, and assemble new pipe, placing the assembled pipe in hangers or other supports. Mount brackets and hangers on walls and ceilings to hold pipes and set sleeves or inserts to provide support for pipes. Requisition tools and equipment, select type and size of pipe, and collect and transport materials and equipment to worksite. Fit or assist in fitting valves, couplings, or assemblies to tanks, pumps, or systems, using hand tools. Assist pipe fitters in the layout, assembly, and installation of piping for air, ammonia, gas, and water systems. Excavate and grade ditches and lay and join pipe for water and sewer service. Cut pipe and lift up to fitters. Disassemble and remove damaged or worn pipe. Clean shop, work area, and machines, using solvent and rags. Install gas burners to convert furnaces from wood, coal, or oil. Immerse pipe in chemical solution to remove dirt, oil, and scale. Clean and renew steam traps. Fill pipes with sand or resin to prevent distortion and hold pipes during bending and installation.

Personality Type: Realistic.

Career Cluster: 02 Architecture and Construction. **Career Pathway:** 02.2 Construction.

Skills: Installation; Repairing; Equipment Maintenance; Troubleshooting; Mathematics; Quality Control Analysis.

Education and Training Program: Plumbing Technology/Plumber. **Related Knowledge/Courses:** Building and Construction; Mechanical Devices; Design; Public Safety and Security; Engineering and Technology; Law and Government.

Work Environment: Outdoors; noisy; contaminants; hazardous equipment; standing; using hands on objects, tools, or controls.

Highway Maintenance Workers

- ✲ Education/Training Required: Moderate-term on-the-job training
- ✲ Annual Earnings: $32,600
- ✲ Beginning Wage: $20,960
- ✲ Earnings Growth Potential: Medium (35.7%)
- ✲ Growth: 8.9%
- ✲ Annual Job Openings: 24,774
- ✲ Job Security: More Secure than Most
- ✲ Self-Employed: 0.9%
- ✲ Part-Time: 1.9%

Renewal Industry: Infrastructure.

Industries with Greatest Employment: Local Government (71.3%); State Government (24.0%).

Highest-Growth Industries (Projected Growth for This Job): Administrative and Support Services (23.0%).

Other Considerations for Job Outlook: The amount of money budgeted for highway repair varies each year. Government agencies budget more money for highway repairs when the economy is strong and they collect more taxes. Regardless of the state of the economy, job openings will occur each year as workers leave this occupation.

Maintain highways, municipal and rural roads, airport runways, and rights-of-way. Duties include patching broken or eroded pavement and repairing guardrails, highway markers, and snow fences. May also mow or clear brush from along road or plow snow from roadway. Flag motorists to warn them of obstacles or repair work ahead. Set out signs and cones around work areas to divert traffic. Drive trucks or tractors with adjustable attachments to sweep debris from paved surfaces, mow grass and weeds, and remove snow and ice. Dump, spread, and tamp asphalt, using pneumatic tampers, to repair joints and patch broken pavement. Drive trucks to transport crews and equipment to worksites. Inspect, clean, and repair drainage systems, bridges, tunnels, and other structures. Haul and spread sand, gravel, and clay to fill washouts and repair road shoulders. Erect, install, or repair guardrails, road shoulders, berms, highway markers, warning signals, and highway lighting, using hand tools and power tools. Remove litter and debris from roadways, including debris from rock slides and mudslides. Clean and clear debris from culverts, catch basins, drop inlets, ditches, and other drain structures. Perform roadside landscaping work, such as clearing weeds and brush and planting and trimming trees. Paint traffic control lines and place pavement traffic messages by hand or using machines. Inspect markers to verify accurate installation. Apply poisons along roadsides and in animal burrows to eliminate unwanted roadside vegetation and rodents. Measure and mark locations for installation of markers, using tape, string, or chalk. Apply oil to road surfaces, using sprayers. Blend compounds to form adhesive mixtures used for marker installation. Place and remove snow fences used to prevent the accumulation of drifting snow on highways.

Personality Type: Realistic-Conventional.

Career Cluster: 02 Architecture and Construction. **Career Pathway:** 02.2 Construction.

Skills: Equipment Maintenance; Repairing; Installation; Operation and Control; Management of Material Resources; Equipment Selection.

Education and Training Program: Construction/Heavy Equipment/Earthmoving Equipment Operation. **Related Knowledge/Courses:** Building and Construction; Transportation; Mechanical Devices; Public Safety and Security; Customer and Personal Service; Geography.

Work Environment: Outdoors; noisy; very hot or cold; contaminants; hazardous equipment; using hands on objects, tools, or controls.

History Teachers, Postsecondary

- ❁ Education/Training Required: Master's degree
- ❁ Annual Earnings: $59,160
- ❁ Beginning Wage: $33,540
- ❁ Earnings Growth Potential: High (43.3%)
- ❁ Growth: 22.9%
- ❁ Annual Job Openings: 3,570
- ❁ Job Security: Most Secure
- ❁ Self-Employed: 0.4%
- ❁ Part-Time: 27.8%

Renewal Industry: Education.

Industries with Greatest Employment: Educational Services, Public and Private (97.3%).

Highest-Growth Industries (Projected Growth for This Job): Administrative and Support Services (48.3%); Amusement, Gambling, and Recreation Industries (45.2%); Social Assistance (38.6%); Support Activities for Transportation (32.8%); Religious, Grantmaking, Civic, Professional, and Similar Organizations (29.9%); Professional, Scientific, and Technical Services (28.8%); Management of Companies and Enterprises (26.8%); Local Government (23.5%); Educational Services, Public and Private (22.8%); Hospitals, Public and Private (21.4%).

Other Considerations for Job Outlook: Retirements of current postsecondary teachers should create numerous openings for all types of postsecondary teachers, so job opportunities are generally expected to be very good. However, one of the main reasons why students attend postsecondary institutions is to prepare themselves for careers, so the best job prospects for postsecondary teachers are likely to be in rapidly growing fields that offer many nonacademic career options—unlike history. On the other hand, history courses are required for many majors. Community colleges and other institutions offering career and technical education have been among the most rapidly growing, and these institutions are expected to offer some of the best opportunities for postsecondary teachers.

Teach courses in human history and historiography. Prepare and deliver lectures to undergraduate and/or graduate students on topics such as ancient history, postwar civilizations, and the history of third-world countries. Evaluate and grade students' classwork, assignments, and papers. Prepare course materials such as syllabi, homework assignments, and handouts. Compile, administer, and grade examinations or assign this work to others. Initiate, facilitate, and moderate classroom discussions. Keep abreast of developments in their field by reading current literature, talking with colleagues, and participating in professional conferences. Plan, evaluate, and revise curricula, course content, and course materials and methods of instruction. Maintain student attendance records, grades, and other required records. Maintain regularly scheduled office hours to advise and assist students. Conduct research in a particular field of knowledge and publish findings in professional journals, books, or electronic media. Select and obtain materials and supplies such as textbooks. Advise students on academic and vocational curricula and on career issues. Collaborate with colleagues to address teaching and research issues. Serve on academic or administrative committees that deal with institutional policies, departmental matters, and academic issues. Participate in campus and community events. Act as advisers to student organizations. Participate in student recruitment, registration, and placement activities. Compile bibliographies of specialized materials for outside reading assignments. Supervise undergraduate and graduate teaching, internship, and research work. Perform administrative duties such as serving as department head. Write grant proposals to procure external research funding. Provide professional consulting services to government, educational institutions, and industry.

Personality Type: Social-Investigative-Artistic.

Career Cluster: 15 Science, Technology, Engineering, and Mathematics. **Career Pathway:** 15.3 Science and Mathematics.

Skills: Writing; Instructing; Learning Strategies; Reading Comprehension; Speaking; Persuasion.

Education and Training Programs: History, General; American History (United States); European History; History and Philosophy of Science and Technology; Public/Applied History and Archival Administration; Asian History; Canadian History; History, Other. **Related Knowledge/Courses:** History and Archeology; Philosophy and Theology; Geography; Sociology and Anthropology; Education and Training; English Language.

Work Environment: Indoors; sitting.

Home Economics Teachers, Postsecondary

- ❋ Education/Training Required: Master's degree
- ❋ Annual Earnings: $58,170
- ❋ Beginning Wage: $29,510
- ❋ Earnings Growth Potential: High (49.3%)
- ❋ Growth: 22.9%
- ❋ Annual Job Openings: 820
- ❋ Job Security: Most Secure
- ❋ Self-Employed: 0.4%
- ❋ Part-Time: 27.8%

Renewal Industry: Education.

Industries with Greatest Employment: Educational Services, Public and Private (97.3%).

Highest-Growth Industries (Projected Growth for This Job): Administrative and Support Services (48.3%); Amusement, Gambling, and Recreation Industries (45.2%); Social Assistance (38.6%); Support Activities for Transportation (32.8%); Religious, Grantmaking, Civic, Professional, and Similar Organizations (29.9%); Professional, Scientific, and Technical Services (28.8%); Management of Companies and Enterprises (26.8%); Local Government (23.5%); Educational Services, Public and Private (22.8%); Hospitals, Public and Private (21.4%).

Other Considerations for Job Outlook: Retirements of current postsecondary teachers should create numerous openings for all types of postsecondary teachers, so job opportunities are generally expected to be very good. One of the main reasons why students attend postsecondary institutions is to prepare themselves for careers, so the best job prospects for postsecondary teachers are likely to be in rapidly growing fields that offer many nonacademic career options. Many home economics majors, such as textiles and culinary arts, are very career-oriented. Community colleges and other institutions offering career and technical education have been among the most rapidly growing, and these institutions are expected to offer some of the best opportunities for postsecondary teachers.

Teach courses in child care, family relations, finance, nutrition, and related subjects as pertaining to home management. Evaluate and grade students' classwork, laboratory work, projects, assignments, and papers. Initiate, facilitate, and moderate classroom discussions. Prepare and deliver lectures to undergraduate or graduate students on topics such as food science, nutrition, and child care. Prepare course materials such as syllabi, homework assignments, and handouts. Keep abreast of developments in their field by reading current literature, talking with colleagues, and participating in professional conferences. Maintain student attendance records, grades, and other required records. Plan, evaluate, and revise curricula, course content, and course materials and methods of instruction. Compile, administer, and grade examinations or assign this work to others. Advise students on academic and vocational curricula and on career issues. Maintain regularly scheduled office hours to advise and assist students. Supervise undergraduate or graduate teaching, internship, and research work. Select and obtain materials and supplies such as textbooks. Conduct research in a particular field of knowledge and publish findings in professional journals, books, and/or electronic media. Collaborate with colleagues to address teaching and research issues. Act as advisers to student organizations. Participate in student recruitment, registration, and placement activities. Serve on academic or administrative committees that deal with institutional policies, departmental matters, and academic issues. Participate in campus and community events. Compile bibliographies of specialized materials for outside reading assignments. Perform administrative duties such as serving as department head. Write grant proposals to procure external research funding. Provide professional consulting services to government and industry.

Personality Type: Social-Investigative-Artistic.

Career Clusters: 08 Health Science; 10 Human Services. **Career Pathways:** 08.4 Support Services; 10.1 Early Childhood Development and Services; 10.3 Family and Community Services; 10.5 Consumer Services Career.

Skills: Writing; Instructing; Learning Strategies; Service Orientation; Active Learning; Operations Analysis.

Education and Training Programs: Family and Consumer Sciences/Human Sciences, General; Business Family and Consumer Sciences/Human Sciences; Foodservice Systems Administration/Management; Human Development and Family Studies, General; Child Care and Support Services Management. **Related Knowledge/Courses:** Sociology and Anthropology; Philosophy and Theology;

Education and Training; Therapy and Counseling; Psychology; English Language.

Work Environment: Indoors; sitting.

Hydrologists

- ❀ Education/Training Required: Master's degree
- ❀ Annual Earnings: $68,140
- ❀ Beginning Wage: $42,450
- ❀ Earnings Growth Potential: Medium (37.7%)
- ❀ Growth: 24.3%
- ❀ Annual Job Openings: 687
- ❀ Job Security: More Secure than Most
- ❀ Self-Employed: 2.4%
- ❀ Part-Time: 5.3%

Renewal Industry: Green Technologies.

Industries with Greatest Employment: Professional, Scientific, and Technical Services (46.7%); Federal Government (28.0%); State Government (15.4%); Local Government (5.4%).

Highest-Growth Industries (Projected Growth for This Job): Professional, Scientific, and Technical Services (53.9%).

Other Considerations for Job Outlook: Job prospects for hydrologists should be favorable, particularly for those with field experience. Demand for hydrologists who understand both the scientific and engineering aspects of waste remediation should be strong. Few colleges and universities offer programs in hydrology, so the number of qualified workers may be limited. Funding for federal and state geological surveys depend largely on the political climate and the current budget. Thus, job security for hydrologists may vary. During periods of economic recession, layoffs of hydrologists may occur in consulting firms; layoffs are much less likely in government.

Research the distribution, circulation, and physical properties of underground and surface waters; study the form and intensity of precipitation, its rate of infiltration into the soil, its movement through the earth, and its return to the ocean and atmosphere. Study and document quantities, distribution, disposition, and development of underground and surface waters. Draft final reports describing research results, including illustrations, appendices, maps, and other attachments. Coordinate and supervise the work of professional and technical staff, including research assistants, technologists, and technicians. Prepare hydrogeologic evaluations of known or suspected hazardous waste sites and land treatment and feedlot facilities. Design and conduct scientific hydrogeological investigations to ensure that accurate and appropriate information is available for use in water resource management decisions. Study public water supply issues, including flood and drought risks, water quality, wastewater, and impacts on wetland habitats. Collect and analyze water samples as part of field investigations and/or to validate data from automatic monitors. Apply research findings to help minimize the environmental impacts of pollution, water-borne diseases, erosion, and sedimentation. Measure and graph phenomena such as lake levels, stream flows, and changes in water volumes. Investigate complaints or conflicts related to the alteration of public waters, gathering information, recommending alternatives, informing participants of progress, and preparing draft orders. Develop or modify methods of conducting hydrologic studies. Answer questions and provide technical assistance and information to contractors and/or the public regarding issues such as well drilling, code requirements, hydrology, and geology. Install, maintain, and calibrate instruments such as those that monitor water levels, rainfall, and sediments. Evaluate data and provide recommendations regarding the feasibility of municipal projects such as hydroelectric power plants, irrigation systems, flood warning systems, and waste treatment facilities. Conduct short-term and long-term climate assessments and study storm occurrences. Study and analyze the physical aspects of the Earth in terms of the hydrological components, including atmosphere, hydrosphere, and interior structure. Conduct research and communicate information to promote the conservation and preservation of water resources.

Personality Type: Investigative-Realistic.

Career Cluster: 15 Science, Technology, Engineering, and Mathematics. **Career Pathway:** 15.3 Science and Mathematics.

Skills: Science; Programming; Management of Financial Resources; Mathematics; Management of Personnel Resources; Complex Problem Solving.

Education and Training Programs: Geology/Earth Science, General; Hydrology and Water Resources Science;

Oceanography, Chemical and Physical. **Related Knowledge/Courses:** Geography; Physics; Engineering and Technology; Biology; Chemistry; Mathematics.

Work Environment: More often indoors than outdoors; sitting.

Industrial Engineering Technicians

* Education/Training Required: Associate degree
* Annual Earnings: $47,490
* Beginning Wage: $31,130
* Earnings Growth Potential: Low (34.4%)
* Growth: 9.9%
* Annual Job Openings: 6,172
* Job Security: More Secure than Most
* Self-Employed: 0.8%
* Part-Time: 5.9%

Renewal Industries: Advanced Manufacturing; Green Technologies.

Industries with Greatest Employment: Computer and Electronic Product Manufacturing (20.1%); Transportation Equipment Manufacturing (18.0%); Professional, Scientific, and Technical Services (8.8%); Machinery Manufacturing (8.6%); Chemical Manufacturing (5.0%).

Highest-Growth Industries (Projected Growth for This Job): Internet Service Providers, Web Search Portals, and Data Processing Services (45.5%); Professional, Scientific, and Technical Services (41.2%); Support Activities for Transportation (32.4%); Insurance Carriers and Related Activities (30.3%); Ambulatory Health-Care Services (29.1%); Management of Companies and Enterprises (26.8%); Merchant Wholesalers, Durable Goods (25.4%); Truck Transportation (24.2%); Educational Services, Public and Private (23.3%); Local Government (23.2%); Chemical Manufacturing (21.3%); Mining (Except Oil and Gas) (18.1%); Heavy and Civil Engineering Construction (17.6%).

Other Considerations for Job Outlook: As firms continue to seek new means of reducing costs and increasing productivity, demand for industrial engineering technicians to analyze and improve production processes should increase. This should lead to some job growth even in manufacturing industries with slowly growing or declining employment.

Apply engineering theory and principles to problems of industrial layout or manufacturing production, usually under the direction of engineering staff. May study and record time, motion, method, and speed involved in performance of production, maintenance, clerical, and other worker operations for such purposes as establishing standard production rates or improving efficiency. Recommend revision to methods of operation, material handling, equipment layout, or other changes to increase production or improve standards. Study time, motion, methods, and speed involved in maintenance, production, and other operations to establish standard production rate and improve efficiency. Interpret engineering drawings, schematic diagrams, or formulas and confer with management or engineering staff to determine quality and reliability standards. Recommend modifications to existing quality or production standards to achieve optimum quality within limits of equipment capability. Aid in planning work assignments in accordance with worker performance, machine capacity, production schedules, and anticipated delays. Observe workers using equipment to verify that equipment is being operated and maintained according to quality assurance standards. Observe workers operating equipment or performing tasks to determine time involved and fatigue rate, using timing devices. Prepare charts, graphs, and diagrams to illustrate workflow, routing, floor layouts, material handling, and machine utilization. Evaluate data and write reports to validate or indicate deviations from existing standards. Read worker logs, product processing sheets, and specification sheets to verify that records adhere to quality assurance specifications. Prepare graphs or charts of data or enter data into computer for analysis. Record test data, applying statistical quality control procedures. Select products for tests at specified stages in production process and test products for performance characteristics and adherence to specifications. Compile and evaluate statistical data to determine and maintain quality and reliability of products.

Personality Type: Investigative-Realistic-Conventional.

Career Clusters: 13 Manufacturing; 15 Science, Technology, Engineering, and Mathematics. **Career Pathways:** 13.3 Maintenance, Installation, and Repair; 15.1 Engineering and Technology.

Skills: Operations Analysis; Technology Design; Repairing; Troubleshooting; Systems Evaluation; Systems Analysis.

Education and Training Programs: Industrial Technology/Technician; Manufacturing Technology/Technician; Industrial Production Technologies/Technicians, Other; Engineering/Industrial Management. **Related Knowledge/Courses:** Production and Processing; Engineering and Technology; Design; Clerical Practices; Mathematics; Mechanical Devices.

Work Environment: Indoors; noisy; contaminants; hazardous equipment; standing; walking and running.

Industrial Engineers

- ❋ Education/Training Required: Bachelor's degree
- ❋ Annual Earnings: $71,430
- ❋ Beginning Wage: $46,340
- ❋ Earnings Growth Potential: Medium (35.1%)
- ❋ Growth: 20.3%
- ❋ Annual Job Openings: 11,272
- ❋ Job Security: More Secure than Most
- ❋ Self-Employed: 0.9%
- ❋ Part-Time: 2.0%

Renewal Industries: Advanced Manufacturing; Green Technologies; Information and Telecommunication Technologies; Infrastructure.

Industries with Greatest Employment: Transportation Equipment Manufacturing (17.7%); Computer and Electronic Product Manufacturing (15.2%); Professional, Scientific, and Technical Services (12.6%); Machinery Manufacturing (7.6%); Fabricated Metal Product Manufacturing (6.7%).

Highest-Growth Industries (Projected Growth for This Job): Social Assistance (84.8%); Warehousing and Storage (62.2%); Professional, Scientific, and Technical Services (57.9%); Administrative and Support Services (56.6%); Waste Management and Remediation Services (56.5%); Ambulatory Health-Care Services (51.6%); Support Activities for Transportation (47.2%); Publishing Industries (Except Internet) (46.5%); Management of Companies and Enterprises (40.0%); Wholesale Electronic Markets

and Agents and Brokers (37.8%); Merchant Wholesalers, Durable Goods (37.7%); Educational Services, Public and Private (37.6%); Truck Transportation (37.2%); Local Government (36.4%); Construction of Buildings (36.1%); Hospitals, Public and Private (35.4%); Air Transportation (34.0%); Specialty Trade Contractors (33.2%); Merchant Wholesalers, Nondurable Goods (33.0%); Heavy and Civil Engineering Construction (30.3%); Mining (Except Oil and Gas) (29.1%); Repair and Maintenance (27.5%); Insurance Carriers and Related Activities (26.6%); Plastics and Rubber Products Manufacturing (21.2%); Oil and Gas Extraction (19.4%); Miscellaneous Manufacturing (19.3%); State Government (19.3%); Nonmetallic Mineral Product Manufacturing (18.8%); Food Manufacturing (18.1%); Wood Product Manufacturing (18.1%); Chemical Manufacturing (17.1%); Federal Government (16.1%).

Other Considerations for Job Outlook: Because their work is similar to that done in management occupations, many industrial engineers leave the occupation to become managers. Many openings will be created by the need to replace industrial engineers who transfer to other occupations or leave the labor force.

Design, develop, test, and evaluate integrated systems for managing industrial production processes, including human work factors, quality control, inventory control, logistics and material flow, cost analysis, and production coordination. Analyze statistical data and product specifications to determine standards and establish quality and reliability objectives of finished product. Develop manufacturing methods, labor utilization standards, and cost analysis systems to promote efficient staff and facility utilization. Recommend methods for improving utilization of personnel, material, and utilities. Plan and establish sequence of operations to fabricate and assemble parts or products and to promote efficient utilization. Apply statistical methods and perform mathematical calculations to determine manufacturing processes, staff requirements, and production standards. Coordinate quality control objectives and activities to resolve production problems, maximize product reliability, and minimize cost. Confer with vendors, staff, and management personnel regarding purchases, procedures, product specifications, manufacturing capabilities, and project status. Draft and design layout of equipment, materials, and workspace to illustrate maximum efficiency, using drafting tools and computer. Review production schedules, engineering specifications, orders, and related information to obtain knowledge of manufacturing methods, procedures, and activities. Communicate with management and user personnel to develop production and design standards. Estimate production cost and effect of product design changes for management review, action, and control. Formulate sampling procedures and designs and develop forms and instructions for recording, evaluating, and reporting quality and reliability data. Record or oversee recording of information to ensure currency of engineering drawings and documentation of production problems. Study operations sequence, material flow, functional statements, organization charts, and project information to determine worker functions and responsibilities. Direct workers engaged in product measurement, inspection, and testing activities to ensure quality control and reliability. Implement methods and procedures for disposition of discrepant material and defective or damaged parts and assess cost and responsibility.

Personality Type: Investigative-Conventional-Enterprising.

Career Cluster: 15 Science, Technology, Engineering, and Mathematics. **Career Pathway:** 15.1 Engineering and Technology.

Skills: Equipment Selection; Technology Design; Troubleshooting; Installation; Systems Analysis; Mathematics.

Education and Training Program: Industrial Engineering. **Related Knowledge/Courses:** Engineering and Technology; Design; Production and Processing; Mechanical Devices; Physics; Mathematics.

Work Environment: Indoors; noisy; contaminants; hazardous equipment; more often sitting than standing.

Industrial Machinery Mechanics

- ❋ Education/Training Required: Long-term on-the-job training
- ❋ Annual Earnings: $42,350
- ❋ Beginning Wage: $27,650
- ❋ Earnings Growth Potential: Low (34.7%)
- ❋ Growth: 9.0%
- ❋ Annual Job Openings: 23,361
- ❋ Job Security: More Secure than Most
- ❋ Self-Employed: 2.5%
- ❋ Part-Time: 1.7%

Renewal Industries: Advanced Manufacturing; Green Technologies; Infrastructure.

Industries with Greatest Employment: Food Manufacturing (9.3%); Merchant Wholesalers, Durable Goods (8.2%); Repair and Maintenance (8.1%); Transportation Equipment Manufacturing (6.5%); Chemical Manufacturing (6.2%); Fabricated Metal Product Manufacturing (5.3%).

Highest-Growth Industries (Projected Growth for This Job): Warehousing and Storage (53.6%); Administrative and Support Services (51.6%); Amusement, Gambling, and Recreation Industries (48.2%); Waste Management and Remediation Services (45.5%); Real Estate (40.5%); Professional, Scientific, and Technical Services (38.2%); Rental and Leasing Services (37.9%); Support Activities for Transportation (35.0%); Accommodation, Including Hotels and Motels (32.8%); Management of Companies and Enterprises (32.6%); Wholesale Electronic Markets and Agents and Brokers (30.5%); Truck Transportation (29.6%); Local Government (29.2%); Construction of Buildings (29.0%); Nonstore Retailers (28.3%); Educational Services, Public and Private (26.1%); Specialty Trade Contractors (25.7%); Hospitals, Public and Private (23.9%); Support Activities for Agriculture and Forestry (23.2%); Heavy and Civil Engineering Construction (22.9%); Repair and Maintenance (21.9%); Merchant Wholesalers, Durable Goods (21.6%); Food and Beverage Stores (20.2%); Mining (Except Oil and Gas) (19.9%); Personal and Laundry Services (18.9%); Merchant Wholesalers, Nondurable Goods (18.5%); Plastics and Rubber Products Manufacturing (15.8%).

Other Considerations for Job Outlook: Job candidates usually need some education after high school plus experience working on specific machines. Applicants with broad skills in machine repair and maintenance should have favorable job prospects.

Repair, install, adjust, or maintain industrial production and processing machinery or refinery and pipeline distribution systems. Disassemble machinery and equipment to remove parts and make repairs. Repair and replace broken or malfunctioning components of machinery and equipment. Repair and maintain the operating condition of industrial production and processing machinery and equipment. Examine parts for defects such as breakage and excessive wear. Reassemble equipment after completion of inspections, testing, or repairs. Observe and test the operation of machinery and equipment to diagnose malfunctions, using voltmeters and other testing devices. Operate newly repaired machinery and equipment to verify the adequacy of repairs. Clean, lubricate, and adjust parts, equipment, and machinery. Analyze test results, machine error messages, and information obtained from operators to diagnose equipment problems. Record repairs and maintenance performed. Study blueprints and manufacturers' manuals to determine correct installation and operation of machinery. Record parts and materials used, ordering or requisitioning new parts and materials as necessary. Cut and weld metal to repair broken metal parts, fabricate new parts, and assemble new equipment. Demonstrate equipment functions and features to machine operators. Enter codes and instructions to program computer-controlled machinery.

Personality Type: Realistic-Investigative-Conventional.

Career Cluster: 13 Manufacturing. **Career Pathway:** 13.3 Maintenance, Installation, and Repair.

Skills: Installation; Repairing; Equipment Maintenance; Operation Monitoring; Troubleshooting; Technology Design.

Education and Training Programs: Industrial Mechanics and Maintenance Technology; Heavy/Industrial Equipment Maintenance Technologies, Other. **Related Knowledge/Courses:** Mechanical Devices; Engineering and Technology; Building and Construction; Design; Chemistry; Physics.

Work Environment: Noisy; contaminants; hazardous conditions; hazardous equipment; standing; using hands on objects, tools, or controls.

Industrial Production Managers

- ✸ Education/Training Required: Work experience in a related occupation
- ✸ Annual Earnings: $80,560
- ✸ Beginning Wage: $48,670
- ✸ Earnings Growth Potential: Medium (39.6%)
- ✸ Growth: −5.9%
- ✸ Annual Job Openings: 14,889
- ✸ Job Security: More Secure than Most
- ✸ Self-Employed: 2.0%
- ✸ Part-Time: 1.6%

Renewal Industries: Advanced Manufacturing; Green Technologies.

Industries with Greatest Employment: Fabricated Metal Product Manufacturing (10.8%); Transportation Equipment Manufacturing (9.5%); Computer and Electronic Product Manufacturing (7.8%); Chemical Manufacturing (7.3%); Machinery Manufacturing (7.1%); Food Manufacturing (6.4%); Plastics and Rubber Products Manufacturing (5.1%).

Highest-Growth Industries (Projected Growth for This Job): Warehousing and Storage (33.7%); Administrative and Support Services (29.6%); Waste Management and Remediation Services (26.6%); Social Assistance (24.9%); Professional, Scientific, and Technical Services (24.6%); Building Material and Garden Equipment and Supplies Dealers (23.9%); Nonstore Retailers (20.2%); Support Activities for Transportation (16.4%); Management of Companies and Enterprises (15.3%).

Other Considerations for Job Outlook: Employers are likely to seek candidates who have excellent communication skills and related work experience and who are personable, flexible, and eager to enhance their knowledge and skills through ongoing training.

Plan, direct, or coordinate the work activities and resources necessary for manufacturing products in accordance with specifications for cost, quality, and quantity. Direct and coordinate production, processing, distribution, and marketing activities of industrial organization. Review processing schedules and production orders to make decisions concerning inventory requirements, staffing requirements, work procedures, and duty assignments, considering budgetary limitations and time constraints. Review operations and confer with technical or administrative staff to resolve production or processing problems. Develop and implement production tracking and quality control systems, analyzing reports on production, quality control, maintenance, and other aspects of operations to detect problems. Hire, train, evaluate, and discharge staff, and resolve personnel grievances. Set and monitor product standards, examining samples of raw products or directing testing during processing, to ensure finished products are of prescribed quality. Prepare and maintain production reports and personnel records. Coordinate and recommend procedures for maintenance or modification of facilities and equipment, including the replacement of machines.

Initiate and coordinate inventory and cost control programs. Institute employee suggestion or involvement programs. Maintain current knowledge of the quality control field, relying on current literature pertaining to materials use, technological advances, and statistical studies. Review plans and confer with research and support staff to develop new products and processes. Develop budgets and approve expenditures for supplies, materials, and human resources, ensuring that materials, labor, and equipment are used efficiently to meet production targets. Negotiate prices of materials with suppliers.

Personality Type: Enterprising-Conventional.

Career Cluster: 04 Business, Management, and Administration. **Career Pathway:** 04.1 Management.

Skills: No data available.

Education and Training Programs: Business/Commerce, General; Business Administration and Management, General; Operations Management and Supervision. **Related Knowledge/Courses:** Production and Processing; Mechanical Devices; Administration and Management; Design; Personnel and Human Resources; Engineering and Technology.

Work Environment: Indoors; noisy; contaminants; hazardous equipment; minor burns, cuts, bites, or stings; standing.

Industrial Safety and Health Engineers

- ❀ Education/Training Required: Bachelor's degree
- ❀ Annual Earnings: $69,580
- ❀ Beginning Wage: $42,200
- ❀ Earnings Growth Potential: Medium (39.4%)
- ❀ Growth: 9.6%
- ❀ Annual Job Openings: 1,105
- ❀ Job Security: More Secure than Most
- ❀ Self-Employed: 1.1%
- ❀ Part-Time: 2.0%

Our sources did not provide separate job openings data for this occupation. The job openings listed here are shared with Fire-Prevention and Protection Engineers and with another occupation not included in this book.

Renewal Industry: Infrastructure.

Industries with Greatest Employment: Professional, Scientific, and Technical Services (15.3%); Chemical Manufacturing (11.5%); Construction of Buildings (9.2%); Heavy and Civil Engineering Construction (7.2%); State Government (5.2%).

Highest-Growth Industries (Projected Growth for This Job): Professional, Scientific, and Technical Services (40.5%); Waste Management and Remediation Services (28.3%); Support Activities for Transportation (20.1%); Merchant Wholesalers, Durable Goods (15.3%); Management of Companies and Enterprises (15.3%).

Other Considerations for Job Outlook: Because health and safety engineers make production processes and products as safe as possible, their services should be in demand as concern increases for health and safety within work environments. As new technologies for production or processing are developed, health and safety engineers will be needed to ensure that they are safe. They tend to do more on-site work than most engineers and therefore are less threatened by offshoring.

Plan, implement, and coordinate safety programs requiring application of engineering principles and technology to prevent or correct unsafe environmental working conditions. Investigate industrial accidents, injuries, or occupational diseases to determine causes and preventive measures. Report or review findings from accident investigations, facilities inspections, or environmental testing. Maintain and apply knowledge of current policies, regulations, and industrial processes. Inspect facilities, machinery, and safety equipment to identify and correct potential hazards and to ensure safety regulation compliance. Conduct or coordinate worker training in areas such as safety laws and regulations, hazardous condition monitoring, and use of safety equipment. Review employee safety programs to determine their adequacy. Interview employers and employees to obtain information about work environments and workplace incidents. Review plans and specifications for construction of new machinery or equipment to determine whether all safety requirements have been met. Compile, analyze, and interpret statistical data related to occupational illnesses and accidents. Interpret safety regulations for others interested in industrial safety, such as safety engineers, labor representatives, and safety inspectors. Recommend process and product safety features that will reduce employees' exposure to chemical, physical, and biological work hazards. Conduct or direct testing of air quality, noise, temperature, or radiation levels to verify compliance with health and safety regulations. Provide technical advice and guidance to organizations on how to handle health-related problems and make needed changes. Confer with medical professionals to assess health risks and to develop ways to manage health issues and concerns. Install safety devices on machinery or direct device installation. Maintain liaisons with outside organizations such as fire departments, mutual aid societies, and rescue teams so that emergency responses can be facilitated. Evaluate adequacy of actions taken to correct health inspection violations. Write and revise safety regulations and codes. Check floors of plants to ensure that they are strong enough to support heavy machinery. Plan and conduct industrial hygiene research.

Personality Type: Investigative-Conventional-Realistic.

Career Cluster: 15 Science, Technology, Engineering, and Mathematics. **Career Pathway:** 15.1 Engineering and Technology.

Skills: Management of Financial Resources; Science; Systems Analysis; Persuasion; Operations Analysis; Systems Evaluation.

Education and Training Program: Environmental/Environmental Health Engineering. **Related Knowledge/Courses:** Building and Construction; Physics; Chemistry; Biology; Engineering and Technology; Education and Training.

Work Environment: More often indoors than outdoors; noisy; sitting.

Industrial Truck and Tractor Operators

- ❋ Education/Training Required: Short-term on-the-job training
- ❋ Annual Earnings: $28,010
- ❋ Beginning Wage: $19,510
- ❋ Earnings Growth Potential: Low (30.3%)
- ❋ Growth: –2.0%
- ❋ Annual Job Openings: 89,547
- ❋ Job Security: Least Secure
- ❋ Self-Employed: 0.3%
- ❋ Part-Time: 2.7%

Renewal Industries: Advanced Manufacturing; Green Technologies.

Industries with Greatest Employment: Warehousing and Storage (12.4%); Building Material and Garden Equipment and Supplies Dealers (8.3%); Merchant Wholesalers, Nondurable Goods (8.2%); Merchant Wholesalers, Durable Goods (7.7%); Administrative and Support Services (7.0%); Food Manufacturing (6.2%).

Highest-Growth Industries (Projected Growth for This Job): Professional, Scientific, and Technical Services (33.9%); Warehousing and Storage (20.2%); General Merchandise Stores (18.1%); Telecommunications (15.4%).

Other Considerations for Job Outlook: Workers must receive specialized training in safety awareness and procedures and be evaluated at least once every three years.

Operate industrial trucks or tractors equipped to move materials around a warehouse, storage yard, factory, construction site, or similar location. Inspect product load for accuracy and safely move it around the warehouse or facility to ensure timely and complete delivery. Move controls to drive gasoline- or electric-powered trucks, cars, or tractors and transport materials between loading, processing, and storage areas. Move levers and controls that operate lifting devices such as forklifts, lift beams and swivel-hooks, hoists, and elevating platforms to load, unload, transport, and stack material. Position lifting devices under, over, or around loaded pallets, skids, and boxes and secure material or products for transport to designated areas. Manually or mechanically load and unload materials from pallets, skids, platforms, cars, lifting devices, or other transport vehicles. Perform routine maintenance on vehicles and auxiliary equipment, such as cleaning, lubricating, recharging batteries, fueling, or replacing liquefied-gas tank. Weigh materials or products and record weight and other production data on tags or labels. Operate or tend automatic stacking, loading, packaging, or cutting machines. Turn valves and open chutes to dump, spray, or release materials from dump cars or storage bins into hoppers. Signal workers to discharge, dump, or level materials. Hook tow trucks to trailer hitches and fasten attachments such as graders, plows, rollers, and winch cables to tractors, using hitchpins.

Personality Type: Realistic-Conventional.

Career Cluster: 01 Agriculture, Food, and Natural Resources. **Career Pathway:** 01.5 Natural Resources Systems.

Skills: No data available.

Education and Training Program: Ground Transportation, Other. **Related Knowledge/Course:** Production and Processing.

Work Environment: Very hot or cold; contaminants; sitting; using hands on objects, tools, or controls; bending or twisting the body; repetitive motions.

Inspectors, Testers, Sorters, Samplers, and Weighers

* Education/Training Required: Moderate-term on-the-job training
* Annual Earnings: $30,310
* Beginning Wage: $18,630
* Earnings Growth Potential: Medium (38.5%)
* Growth: –7.0%
* Annual Job Openings: 75,361
* Job Security: Most Secure
* Self-Employed: 1.5%
* Part-Time: 4.9%

Renewal Industry: Green Technologies.

Industries with Greatest Employment: Transportation Equipment Manufacturing (10.8%); Administrative and Support Services (9.3%); Fabricated Metal Product Manufacturing (7.8%); Computer and Electronic Product Manufacturing (7.3%); Plastics and Rubber Products Manufacturing (5.9%); Food Manufacturing (5.3%); Machinery Manufacturing (5.1%).

Highest-Growth Industries (Projected Growth for This Job): Professional, Scientific, and Technical Services (27.1%); Warehousing and Storage (26.0%); Internet Service Providers, Web Search Portals, and Data Processing Services (23.7%); Ambulatory Health-Care Services (23.3%); Telecommunications (22.2%); Administrative and Support Services (21.7%); Waste Management and Remediation Services (19.6%); Repair and Maintenance (19.3%); Social Assistance (16.0%).

Other Considerations for Job Outlook: Although numerous job openings will arise due to the need to replace workers who move out of this large occupation, many of these jobs will be open only to experienced workers with advanced skills. Because the majority of inspectors, testers, sorters, samplers, and weighers work in the manufacturing sector, their outlook is greatly affected by what happens to manufacturing companies. As this sector becomes more automated and productive and as some production moves offshore, the number of inspectors, testers, sorters, samplers, and weighers is expected to decline. However, the continuing emphasis on producing quality goods and the need for accuracy in the growing medical and biotechnology fields will positively affect this occupation and moderate the decline.

Inspect, test, sort, sample, or weigh nonagricultural raw materials or processed, machined, fabricated, or assembled parts or products for defects, wear, and deviations from specifications. May use precision measuring instruments and complex test equipment. Discard or reject products, materials, and equipment not meeting specifications. Analyze and interpret blueprints, data, manuals, and other materials to determine specifications, inspection and testing procedures, adjustment and certification methods, formulas, and measuring instruments required. Inspect, test, or measure materials, products, installations, and work for conformance to specifications. Notify supervisors and other personnel of production problems and assist in identifying and correcting these problems. Discuss inspection results with those responsible for products and recommend necessary corrective actions. Record inspection or test data, such as weights, temperatures, grades, or moisture content, and quantities inspected or graded. Mark items with details such as grade and acceptance or rejection status. Observe and monitor production operations and equipment to ensure conformance to specifications and make or order necessary process or assembly adjustments. Measure dimensions of products to verify conformance to specifications, using measuring instruments such as rulers, calipers, gauges, or micrometers. Analyze test data and make computations as necessary to determine test results. Collect or select samples for testing or for use as models. Check arriving materials to ensure that they match purchase orders and submit discrepancy reports when problems are found. Compare colors, shapes, textures, or grades of products or materials with color charts, templates, or samples to verify conformance to standards. Write test and inspection reports describing results, recommendations, and needed repairs. Read dials and meters to verify that equipment is functioning at specified levels. Remove defects, such as chips and burrs, and lap corroded or pitted surfaces. Clean, maintain, repair, and calibrate measuring instruments and test equipment such as dial indicators, fixed gauges, and height gauges. Adjust, clean, or repair products or processing equipment to correct defects found during inspections. Stack and arrange tested products for further processing, shipping, or packaging and transport products to other work stations as necessary.

Personality Type: Conventional-Realistic.

Career Cluster: 13 Manufacturing. **Career Pathway:** 13.4 Quality Assurance.

Skills: No data available.

Education and Training Program: Quality Control Technology/Technician. **Related Knowledge/Course:** Production and Processing.

Work Environment: Noisy; standing; using hands on objects, tools, or controls; repetitive motions.

Instructional Coodinators

* Education/Training Required: Master's degree
* Annual Earnings: $55,270
* Beginning Wage: $30,580
* Earnings Growth Potential: High (44.7%)
* Growth: 22.5%
* Annual Job Openings: 21,294
* Job Security: Most Secure
* Self-Employed: 3.1%
* Part-Time: 19.7%

Renewal Industry: Education.

Industries with Greatest Employment: Educational Services, Public and Private (69.4%); Social Assistance (5.9%); State Government (5.2%).

Highest-Growth Industries (Projected Growth for This Job): Internet Publishing and Broadcasting (40.9%); Museums, Historical Sites, and Similar Institutions (36.2%); Local Government (34.8%); Social Assistance (33.2%); Amusement, Gambling, and Recreation Industries

(32.6%); Professional, Scientific, and Technical Services (31.9%); Administrative and Support Services (28.1%); Ambulatory Health-Care Services (26.9%); Nursing and Residential Care Facilities (23.1%); Educational Services, Public and Private (22.8%); Performing Arts, Spectator Sports, and Related Industries (18.2%); State Government (17.7%); Religious, Grantmaking, Civic, Professional, and Similar Organizations (17.5%); Management of Companies and Enterprises (15.3%).

Other Considerations for Job Outlook: Job opportunities generally should be favorable. Opportunities should be best for those who specialize in subjects targeted for improvement by the No Child Left Behind Act—namely, reading, math, and science. There also will be a need for more instructional coordinators to show teachers how to use technology in the classroom.

Develop instructional material, coordinate educational content, and incorporate current technology in specialized fields that provide guidelines to educators and instructors for developing curricula and conducting courses. Conduct or participate in workshops, committees, and conferences designed to promote the intellectual, social, and physical welfare of students. Plan and conduct teacher training programs and conferences dealing with new classroom procedures, instructional materials and equipment, and teaching aids. Advise teaching and administrative staff in curriculum development, use of materials and equipment, and implementation of state and federal programs and procedures. Recommend, order, or authorize purchase of instructional materials, supplies, equipment, and visual aids designed to meet student educational needs and district standards. Interpret and enforce provisions of state education codes and rules and regulations of state education boards. Confer with members of educational committees and advisory groups to obtain knowledge of subject areas and to relate curriculum materials to specific subjects, individual student needs, and occupational areas. Organize production and design of curriculum materials. Research, evaluate, and prepare recommendations on curricula, instructional methods, and materials for school systems. Observe work of teaching staff to evaluate performance and to recommend changes that could strengthen teaching skills. Develop instructional materials to be used by educators and instructors. Prepare grant proposals, budgets, and program policies and goals or assist in their preparation. Develop tests, questionnaires, and procedures that measure the effectiveness of curricula and use these tools to determine whether program objectives are being met. Update the content of educational programs to ensure that students are being trained with equipment and processes that are technologically current. Address public audiences to explain program objectives and to elicit support. Advise and teach students. Prepare or approve manuals, guidelines, and reports on state educational policies and practices for distribution to school districts. Develop classroom-based and distance-learning training courses, using needs assessments and skill level analyses. Inspect instructional equipment to determine if repairs are needed and authorize necessary repairs.

Personality Type: Social-Investigative-Enterprising.

Career Cluster: 05 Education and Training. **Career Pathways:** 05.1 Administration and Administrative Support; 05.3 Teaching/Training.

Skills: Management of Financial Resources; Learning Strategies; Monitoring; Social Perceptiveness; Coordination; Time Management.

Education and Training Programs: Curriculum and Instruction; Educational/Instructional Media Design; International and Comparative Education. **Related Knowledge/Courses:** Education and Training; Sociology and Anthropology; English Language; Personnel and Human Resources; Communications and Media; Psychology.

Work Environment: Indoors; sitting.

Insulation Workers, Mechanical

* Education/Training Required: Moderate-term on-the-job training
* Annual Earnings: $36,570
* Beginning Wage: $22,840
* Earnings Growth Potential: Medium (37.5%)
* Growth: 8.6%
* Annual Job Openings: 5,787
* Job Security: Least Secure
* Self-Employed: 0.7%
* Part-Time: 3.1%

Renewal Industry: Green Technologies.

Industries with Greatest Employment: Specialty Trade Contractors (81.1%); Heavy and Civil Engineering Construction (8.4%).

Highest-Growth Industries (Projected Growth for This Job): Administrative and Support Services (32.2%); Waste Management and Remediation Services (32.1%).

Other Considerations for Job Outlook: Job opportunities for insulation workers are expected to be excellent. In addition to opportunities created by job growth, there will be a need to replace many workers. The irritating nature of many insulation materials, combined with the often difficult working conditions, causes many insulation workers to leave the occupation each year. Job openings will also arise from the need to replace workers who retire or leave the labor force for other reasons.

Apply insulating materials to pipes or ductwork or other mechanical systems to help control and maintain temperature. Cover, seal, or finish insulated surfaces or access holes with plastic covers, canvas strips, sealants, tape, cement, or asphalt mastic. Measure and cut insulation for covering surfaces, using tape measures, handsaws, knives, and scissors. Prepare surfaces for insulation application by brushing or spreading on adhesives, cement, or asphalt, or by attaching metal pins to surfaces. Select appropriate insulation such as fiberglass, Styrofoam, or cork, based on the heat-retaining or -excluding characteristics of the material. Read blueprints and specifications to determine job requirements. Install sheet metal around insulated pipes with screws to protect the insulation from weather conditions or physical damage. Determine the amounts and types of insulation needed, and methods of installation, based on factors such as location, surface shape, and equipment use. Apply, remove, and repair insulation on industrial equipment, pipes, ductwork, or other mechanical systems, such as heat exchangers, tanks, and vessels, to help control noise and maintain temperatures. Remove or seal off old asbestos insulation, following safety procedures. Move controls, buttons, or levers to start blowers and to regulate flow of materials through nozzles. Fill blower hoppers with insulating materials. Distribute insulating materials evenly into small spaces within floors, ceilings, or walls, using blowers and hose attachments or cement mortar. Fit insulation around obstructions, and shape insulating materials and protective coverings as required.

Personality Type: Realistic-Conventional-Investigative.

Career Cluster: 02 Architecture and Construction. **Career Pathway:** 02.2 Construction.

Skills: Installation; Repairing; Mathematics; Coordination; Management of Personnel Resources; Equipment Selection.

Education and Training Program: Construction Trades, Other. **Related Knowledge/Courses:** Building and Construction; Design; Mechanical Devices; Transportation; Education and Training; Public Safety and Security.

Work Environment: Noisy; contaminants; cramped work space, awkward positions; high places; standing; using hands on objects, tools, or controls.

Internists, General

- ❋ Education/Training Required: First professional degree
- ❋ Annual Earnings: More than $145,600
- ❋ Beginning Wage: $89,130
- ❋ Earnings Growth Potential: Cannot be calculated
- ❋ Growth: 14.2%
- ❋ Annual Job Openings: 38,027
- ❋ Job Security: Most Secure
- ❋ Self-Employed: 14.7%
- ❋ Part-Time: 8.1%

Our sources did not provide separate job openings data for this occupation. The job openings listed here are shared with Anesthesiologists; Family and General Practitioners; Obstetricians and Gynecologists; Pediatricians, General; Psychiatrists; and Surgeons.

Renewal Industry: Health Care.

Industries with Greatest Employment: Ambulatory Health-Care Services (55.9%); Hospitals, Public and Private (17.8%).

Highest-Growth Industries (Projected Growth for This Job): Social Assistance (58.6%); Administrative and Support Services (26.8%); Professional, Scientific, and Technical Services (22.6%); Nursing and Residential Care Facilities (21.0%); Ambulatory Health-Care Services

(19.4%); Religious, Grantmaking, Civic, Professional, and Similar Organizations (16.7%); Management of Companies and Enterprises (15.3%).

Other Considerations for Job Outlook: Opportunities for individuals interested in becoming physicians and surgeons are expected to be very good. Unlike their predecessors, new physicians are much less likely to enter solo practice and more likely to take salaried jobs in group medical practices, clinics, and health networks. Reports of shortages in some specialties, such as general or family practice, internal medicine, and OB/GYN, or in rural or low-income areas should attract new entrants, encouraging schools to expand programs and hospitals to increase available residency slots. However, because physician training is so lengthy, employment change happens gradually. Opportunities should be particularly good in rural and low-income areas, as some physicians find these areas unattractive because of less control over work hours, isolation from medical colleagues, or other reasons.

Diagnose and provide non-surgical treatment of diseases and injuries of internal organ systems. Provide care mainly for adults who have a wide range of problems associated with the internal organs. Treat internal disorders, such as hypertension; heart disease; diabetes; and problems of the lung, brain, kidney, and gastrointestinal tract. Analyze records, reports, test results, or examination information to diagnose medical condition of patient. Prescribe or administer medication, therapy, and other specialized medical care to treat or prevent illness, disease, or injury. Provide and manage long-term, comprehensive medical care, including diagnosis and non-surgical treatment of diseases, for adult patients in an office or hospital. Manage and treat common health problems, such as infections, influenza and pneumonia, as well as serious, chronic, and complex illnesses, in adolescents, adults, and the elderly. Monitor patients' conditions and progress and re-evaluate treatments as necessary. Collect, record, and maintain patient information, such as medical history, reports, and examination results. Make diagnoses when different illnesses occur together or in situations where the diagnosis may be obscure. Explain procedures and discuss test results or prescribed treatments with patients. Advise patients and community members concerning diet, activity, hygiene, and disease prevention. Refer patient to medical specialist or other practitioner when necessary. Immunize patients to protect them from preventable diseases. Advise surgeon of a patient's risk status and recommend appropriate intervention to minimize risk. Direct and coordinate activities of nurses, students, assistants, specialists, therapists, and other medical staff. Provide consulting services to other doctors caring for patients with special or difficult problems. Operate on patients to remove, repair, or improve functioning of diseased or injured body parts and systems. Plan, implement, or administer health programs in hospitals, businesses, or communities for prevention and treatment of injuries or illnesses. Conduct research to develop or test medications, treatments, or procedures to prevent or control disease or injury. Prepare government or organizational reports on birth, death, and disease statistics; workforce evaluations; or the medical status of individuals.

Personality Type: Investigative-Social-Realistic.

Career Cluster: 08 Health Science. **Career Pathway:** 08.1 Therapeutic Services.

Skills: Science; Judgment and Decision Making; Complex Problem Solving; Reading Comprehension; Social Perceptiveness; Service Orientation.

Education and Training Programs: Cardiology; Critical Care Medicine; Endocrinology and Metabolism; Gastroenterology; Geriatric Medicine; Hematology; Infectious Disease; Internal Medicine; Nephrology; Neurology; Nuclear Medicine; Oncology; Pulmonary Disease; Rheumatology. **Related Knowledge/Courses:** Medicine and Dentistry; Biology; Therapy and Counseling; Psychology; Chemistry; Education and Training.

Work Environment: Indoors; disease or infections; standing.

Kindergarten Teachers, Except Special Education

- ❋ Education/Training Required: Bachelor's degree
- ❋ Annual Earnings: $45,120
- ❋ Beginning Wage: $29,300
- ❋ Earnings Growth Potential: Medium (35.1%)
- ❋ Growth: 16.3%
- ❋ Annual Job Openings: 27,603
- ❋ Job Security: Most Secure
- ❋ Self-Employed: 1.1%
- ❋ Part-Time: 25.1%

Renewal Industry: Education.

Industries with Greatest Employment: Educational Services, Public and Private (92.9%).

Highest-Growth Industries (Projected Growth for This Job): Social Assistance (25.8%); Religious, Grantmaking, Civic, Professional, and Similar Organizations (18.8%); Educational Services, Public and Private (15.9%).

Other Considerations for Job Outlook: Job prospects are expected to be favorable, with particularly good prospects for teachers in less desirable urban or rural school districts and for those with licensure in more than one subject. Fast-growing states in the South and West—led by Nevada, Arizona, Texas, and Georgia—will experience the largest enrollment increases. Enrollments in the Midwest are expected to hold relatively steady, while those in the Northeast are expected to decline. The number of teachers employed is dependent on state and local expenditures for education and on the enactment of legislation to increase the quality and scope of public education. At the federal level, there has been a large increase in funding for education, particularly for the hiring of qualified teachers in lower-income areas. Also, some states are instituting programs to improve early childhood education, such as offering full day kindergarten and universal preschool.

Teach elemental natural and social science, personal hygiene, music, art, and literature to children from 4 to 6 years of age. Promote physical, mental, and social development. May be required to hold state certification. Teach basic skills such as color, shape, number, and letter recognition; personal hygiene; and social skills. Establish and enforce rules for behavior and policies and procedures to maintain order among students. Observe and evaluate children's performance, behavior, social development, and physical health. Instruct students individually and in groups, adapting teaching methods to meet students' varying needs and interests. Read books to entire classes or to small groups. Demonstrate activities to children. Provide a variety of materials and resources for children to explore, manipulate, and use, both in learning activities and in imaginative play. Plan and conduct activities for a balanced program of instruction, demonstration, and work time that provides students with opportunities to observe, question, and investigate. Confer with parents or guardians, other teachers, counselors, and administrators to resolve students' behavioral and academic problems.

Prepare children for later grades by encouraging them to explore learning opportunities and to persevere with challenging tasks. Establish clear objectives for all lessons, units, and projects and communicate those objectives to children. Prepare and implement remedial programs for students requiring extra help. Meet with parents and guardians to discuss their children's progress and to determine their priorities for their children and their resource needs. Prepare objectives and outlines for courses of study, following curriculum guidelines or requirements of states and schools. Organize and lead activities designed to promote physical, mental, and social development such as games, arts and crafts, music, and storytelling. Guide and counsel students with adjustment or academic problems or special academic interests. Identify children showing signs of emotional, developmental, or health-related problems and discuss them with supervisors, parents or guardians, and child development specialists. Instruct and monitor students in the use and care of equipment and materials to prevent injuries and damage. Assimilate arriving children to the school environment by greeting them, helping them remove outerwear, and selecting activities of interest to them.

Personality Type: Social-Artistic.

Career Cluster: 05 Education and Training. **Career Pathway:** 05.3 Teaching/Training.

Skills: Learning Strategies; Instructing; Monitoring; Social Perceptiveness; Writing; Time Management.

Education and Training Programs: Montessori Teacher Education; Waldorf/Steiner Teacher Education; Kindergarten/Preschool Education and Teaching; Early Childhood Education and Teaching. **Related Knowledge/Courses:** History and Archeology; Geography; Sociology and Anthropology; Philosophy and Theology; Psychology; Education and Training.

Work Environment: Indoors; disease or infections; standing.

Laborers and Freight, Stock, and Material Movers, Hand

- ✿ Education/Training Required: Short-term on-the-job training
- ✿ Annual Earnings: $21,900
- ✿ Beginning Wage: $15,420
- ✿ Earnings Growth Potential: Low (29.6%)
- ✿ Growth: 2.1%
- ✿ Annual Job Openings: 630,487
- ✿ Job Security: Least Secure
- ✿ Self-Employed: 1.1%
- ✿ Part-Time: 20.8%

Renewal Industry: Advanced Manufacturing.

Industries with Greatest Employment: Administrative and Support Services (20.8%); Merchant Wholesalers, Durable Goods (8.2%); Merchant Wholesalers, Nondurable Goods (7.6%); Warehousing and Storage (5.9%); Couriers and Messengers (5.4%); General Merchandise Stores (5.0%).

Highest-Growth Industries (Projected Growth for This Job): Professional, Scientific, and Technical Services (29.4%); Ambulatory Health-Care Services (23.0%); Museums, Historical Sites, and Similar Institutions (22.6%); Internet Service Providers, Web Search Portals, and Data Processing Services (21.6%); Warehousing and Storage (20.2%); Amusement, Gambling, and Recreation Industries (19.4%); Nursing and Residential Care Facilities (16.1%).

Other Considerations for Job Outlook: Despite the little or no employment growth expected, job openings should be plentiful due to the fact that these occupations are very large and there will be a relatively high number of openings created by the need replace workers who transfer to other occupations or who retire or leave the labor force for other reasons—characteristic of occupations requiring little prior or formal training.

Manually move freight, stock, or other materials or perform other unskilled general labor. Includes all unskilled manual laborers not elsewhere classified. Attach identifying tags to containers or mark them with identifying information. Read work orders or receive oral instructions to determine work assignments and material and equipment needs. Record numbers of units handled and moved, using daily production sheets or work tickets. Move freight, stock, and other materials to and from storage and production areas, loading docks, delivery vehicles, ships, and containers by hand or using trucks, tractors, and other equipment. Sort cargo before loading and unloading. Assemble product containers and crates, using hand tools and precut lumber. Load and unload ship cargo, using winches and other hoisting devices. Connect hoses and operate equipment to move liquid materials into and out of storage tanks on vessels. Pack containers and re-pack damaged containers. Carry needed tools and supplies from storage or trucks and return them after use. Install protective devices, such as bracing, padding, or strapping, to prevent shifting or damage to items being transported. Maintain equipment storage areas to ensure that inventory is protected. Attach slings, hooks, and other devices to lift cargo and guide loads. Carry out general yard duties such as performing shunting on railway lines. Adjust controls to guide, position, and move equipment such as cranes, booms, and cameras. Guide loads being lifted to prevent swinging. Adjust or replace equipment parts such as rollers, belts, plugs, and caps, using hand tools. Stack cargo in locations such as transit sheds or in holds of ships as directed, using pallets or cargo boards. Connect electrical equipment to power sources so that it can be tested before use. Set up the equipment needed to produce special lighting and sound effects during performances. Bundle and band material such as fodder and tobacco leaves, using banding machines. Rig and dismantle props and equipment such as frames, scaffolding, platforms, or backdrops, using hand tools. Check out, rent, or requisition all equipment needed for productions or for set construction. Direct spouts and position receptacles such as bins, carts, and containers so they can be loaded.

Personality Type: Realistic.

Career Cluster: 16 Transportation, Distribution, and Logistics. **Career Pathway:** 16.1 Transportation Operations.

Skills: No data available.

Education and Training Program: No related CIP programs; this job is learned through informal short-term on-the-job training. **Related Knowledge/Courses:** Transportation; Public Safety and Security; Production and Processing.

Work Environment: Outdoors; noisy; very hot or cold; contaminants; standing; using hands on objects, tools, or controls.

Law Teachers, Postsecondary

* Education/Training Required: First professional degree
* Annual Earnings: $87,730
* Beginning Wage: $39,670
* Earnings Growth Potential: Very high (54.8%)
* Growth: 22.9%
* Annual Job Openings: 2,169
* Job Security: Most Secure
* Self-Employed: 0.4%
* Part-Time: 27.8%

Renewal Industry: Education.

Industries with Greatest Employment: Educational Services, Public and Private (97.3%).

Highest-Growth Industries (Projected Growth for This Job): Administrative and Support Services (48.3%); Amusement, Gambling, and Recreation Industries (45.2%); Social Assistance (38.6%); Support Activities for Transportation (32.8%); Religious, Grantmaking, Civic, Professional, and Similar Organizations (29.9%); Professional, Scientific, and Technical Services (28.8%); Management of Companies and Enterprises (26.8%); Local Government (23.5%); Educational Services, Public and Private (22.8%); Hospitals, Public and Private (21.4%).

Other Considerations for Job Outlook: Retirements of current postsecondary teachers should create numerous openings for all types of postsecondary teachers, so job opportunities are generally expected to be very good. One of the main reasons why students attend postsecondary institutions is to prepare themselves for careers, so the best job prospects for postsecondary teachers are likely to be in rapidly growing fields that offer many nonacademic career options. Enrollments in law schools seem likely to remain high.

Teach courses in law. Evaluate and grade students' classwork, assignments, papers, and oral presentations. Compile, administer, and grade examinations or assign this work to others. Prepare and deliver lectures to undergraduate or graduate students on topics such as civil procedure, contracts, and torts. Initiate, facilitate, and moderate classroom discussions. Prepare course materials such as syllabi, homework assignments, and handouts. Keep abreast of developments in their field by reading current literature, talking with colleagues, and participating in professional conferences. Plan, evaluate, and revise curricula, course content, and course materials and methods of instruction. Maintain regularly scheduled office hours to advise and assist students. Conduct research in a particular field of knowledge and publish findings in professional journals, books, or electronic media. Advise students on academic and vocational curricula and on career issues. Supervise undergraduate and/or graduate teaching, internship, and research work. Select and obtain materials and supplies such as textbooks. Maintain student attendance records, grades, and other required records. Serve on academic or administrative committees that deal with institutional policies, departmental matters, and academic issues. Perform administrative duties such as serving as department head. Collaborate with colleagues to address teaching and research issues. Participate in student recruitment, registration, and placement activities. Compile bibliographies of specialized materials for outside reading assignments. Participate in campus and community events. Act as advisers to student organizations. Assign cases for students to hear and try. Provide professional consulting services to government or industry. Write grant proposals to procure external research funding.

Personality Type: Social-Investigative-Enterprising.

Career Cluster: 12 Law, Public Safety, Corrections, and Security. **Career Pathway:** 12.5 Legal Services.

Skills: Instructing; Critical Thinking; Writing; Reading Comprehension; Persuasion; Speaking.

Education and Training Programs: Legal Studies, General; Law (LL.B., J.D.). **Related Knowledge/Courses:** Law and Government; English Language; History and Archeology; Education and Training; Philosophy and Theology; Communications and Media.

Work Environment: Indoors; sitting.

Library Science Teachers, Postsecondary

* Education/Training Required: Master's degree
* Annual Earnings: $56,810
* Beginning Wage: $34,850
* Earnings Growth Potential: Medium (38.7%)
* Growth: 22.9%
* Annual Job Openings: 702
* Job Security: Most Secure
* Self-Employed: 0.4%
* Part-Time: 27.8%

Renewal Industry: Education.

Industries with Greatest Employment: Educational Services, Public and Private (97.3%).

Highest-Growth Industries (Projected Growth for This Job): Administrative and Support Services (48.3%); Amusement, Gambling, and Recreation Industries (45.2%); Social Assistance (38.6%); Support Activities for Transportation (32.8%); Religious, Grantmaking, Civic, Professional, and Similar Organizations (29.9%); Professional, Scientific, and Technical Services (28.8%); Management of Companies and Enterprises (26.8%); Local Government (23.5%); Educational Services, Public and Private (22.8%); Hospitals, Public and Private (21.4%).

Other Considerations for Job Outlook: Retirements of current postsecondary teachers should create numerous openings for all types of postsecondary teachers. However, one of the main reasons why students attend postsecondary institutions is to prepare themselves for careers, so the best job prospects for postsecondary teachers are likely to be in rapidly growing fields that offer many nonacademic career options. Community colleges and other institutions offering career and technical education have been among the most rapidly growing, and these institutions are expected to offer some of the best opportunities for postsecondary teachers.

Teach courses in library science. Prepare course materials such as syllabi, homework assignments, and handouts. Prepare and deliver lectures to undergraduate or graduate students on topics such as collection development, archival methods, and indexing and abstracting. Evaluate and grade students' classwork, assignments, and papers. Keep abreast of developments in their field by reading current literature, talking with colleagues, and participating in professional conferences. Initiate, facilitate, and moderate classroom discussions. Plan, evaluate, and revise curricula, course content, and course materials and methods of instruction. Conduct research in a particular field of knowledge and publish findings in professional journals, books, and/or electronic media. Maintain student attendance records, grades, and other required records. Collaborate with colleagues to address teaching and research issues. Advise students on academic and vocational curricula and on career issues. Compile, administer, and grade examinations or assign this work to others. Supervise undergraduate or graduate teaching, internship, and research work. Maintain regularly scheduled office hours in order to advise and assist students. Write grant proposals to procure external research funding. Select and obtain materials and supplies such as textbooks. Serve on academic or administrative committees that deal with institutional policies, departmental matters, and academic issues. Compile bibliographies of specialized materials for outside reading assignments. Participate in student recruitment, registration, and placement activities. Perform administrative duties such as serving as department head. Participate in campus and community events. Act as advisers to student organizations. Provide professional consulting services to government and/or industry.

Personality Type: Social-Investigative-Conventional.

Career Cluster: 05 Education and Training. **Career Pathways:** 05.2 Professional Support Services; 05.3 Teaching/Training.

Skills: Writing; Learning Strategies; Instructing; Reading Comprehension; Active Learning; Monitoring.

Education and Training Programs: Teacher Education and Professional Development, Specific Subject Areas, Other; Library Science/Librarianship. **Related Knowledge/Courses:** Education and Training; Sociology and Anthropology; English Language; Communications and Media; History and Archeology; Philosophy and Theology.

Work Environment: Indoors; sitting.

Licensed Practical and Licensed Vocational Nurses

- ❋ Education/Training Required: Postsecondary vocational training
- ❋ Annual Earnings: $37,940
- ❋ Beginning Wage: $27,370
- ❋ Earnings Growth Potential: Low (27.9%)
- ❋ Growth: 14.0%
- ❋ Annual Job Openings: 70,610
- ❋ Job Security: Most Secure
- ❋ Self-Employed: 1.5%
- ❋ Part-Time: 18.3%

Renewal Industry: Health Care.

Industries with Greatest Employment: Nursing and Residential Care Facilities (32.1%); Hospitals, Public and Private (25.8%); Ambulatory Health-Care Services (22.9%); Administrative and Support Services (7.5%).

Highest-Growth Industries (Projected Growth for This Job): Social Assistance (50.0%); Professional, Scientific, and Technical Services (44.2%); Amusement, Gambling, and Recreation Industries (31.9%); Administrative and Support Services (26.9%); Nursing and Residential Care Facilities (23.4%); Ambulatory Health-Care Services (23.4%); Religious, Grantmaking, Civic, Professional, and Similar Organizations (19.7%); Management of Companies and Enterprises (15.3%).

Other Considerations for Job Outlook: Replacement needs will be a major source of job openings, as many workers leave the occupation permanently. Very good job opportunities are expected. Rapid employment growth is projected in most health care industries, with the best job opportunities occurring in nursing care facilities and in home health care services. However, applicants for jobs in hospitals may face competition as the number of hospital jobs for LPNs declines.

Care for ill, injured, convalescent, or disabled persons in hospitals, nursing homes, clinics, private homes, group homes, and similar institutions. May work under the supervision of a registered nurse. Licensing required. Administer prescribed medications or start intravenous fluids, recording times and amounts on patients' charts. Observe patients, charting and reporting changes in patients' conditions, such as adverse reactions to medication or treatment, and taking any necessary actions. Provide basic patient care and treatments such as taking temperatures or blood pressures, dressing wounds, treating bedsores, giving enemas or douches, rubbing with alcohol, massaging, or performing catheterizations. Sterilize equipment and supplies, using germicides, sterilizer, or autoclave. Answer patients' calls and determine how to assist them. Work as part of a health-care team to assess patient needs, plan and modify care, and implement interventions. Measure and record patients' vital signs, such as height, weight, temperature, blood pressure, pulse, and respiration. Collect samples such as blood, urine, and sputum from patients and perform routine laboratory tests on samples. Prepare patients for examinations, tests, or treatments and explain procedures. Assemble and use equipment such as catheters, tracheotomy tubes, and oxygen suppliers. Evaluate nursing intervention outcomes, conferring with other health-care team members as necessary. Record food and fluid intake and output. Help patients with bathing, dressing, maintaining personal hygiene, moving in bed, or standing and walking. Apply compresses, ice bags, and hot water bottles. Inventory and requisition supplies and instruments. Clean rooms and make beds. Supervise nurses' aides and assistants. Make appointments, keep records, and perform other clerical duties in doctors' offices and clinics. In private home settings, provide medical treatment and personal care, such as cooking for patients, keeping their rooms orderly, seeing that patients are comfortable and in good spirits, and instructing family members in simple nursing tasks. Set up equipment and prepare medical treatment rooms. Prepare food trays and examine them for conformance to prescribed diet. Wash and dress bodies of deceased persons. Assist in delivery, care, and feeding of infants.

Personality Type: Social-Realistic.

Career Cluster: 08 Health Science. **Career Pathway:** 08.1 Therapeutic Services.

Skills: No data available.

Education and Training Program: Licensed Practical/Vocational Nurse Training (LPN, LVN, Cert, Dipl, AAS). **Related Knowledge/Courses:** Psychology; Medicine and Dentistry; Therapy and Counseling; Biology; Philosophy and Theology; Customer and Personal Service.

Work Environment: Indoors; contaminants; disease or infections; standing; walking and running; using hands on objects, tools, or controls.

Logisticians

- ❋ Education/Training Required: Bachelor's degree
- ❋ Annual Earnings: $64,250
- ❋ Beginning Wage: $38,280
- ❋ Earnings Growth Potential: High (40.4%)
- ❋ Growth: 17.3%
- ❋ Annual Job Openings: 9,671
- ❋ Job Security: More Secure than Most
- ❋ Self-Employed: 1.5%
- ❋ Part-Time: 3.6%

Renewal Industries: Advanced Manufacturing; Infrastructure.

Industries with Greatest Employment: Federal Government (28.1%); Professional, Scientific, and Technical Services (13.4%); Transportation Equipment Manufacturing (8.1%); Computer and Electronic Product Manufacturing (7.7%); Management of Companies and Enterprises (6.3%).

Highest-Growth Industries (Projected Growth for This Job): Securities, Commodity Contracts, and Other Financial Investments and Related Activities (60.4%); Professional, Scientific, and Technical Services (56.8%); Warehousing and Storage (46.9%); Ambulatory Health-Care Services (43.1%); Social Assistance (38.7%); Support Activities for Transportation (38.1%); Nonstore Retailers (33.8%); Water Transportation (32.8%); Motion Picture, Video, and Sound Recording Industries (30.3%); Religious, Grantmaking, Civic, Professional, and Similar Organizations (29.9%); Publishing Industries (Except Internet) (27.6%); Management of Companies and Enterprises (26.8%); Rental and Leasing Services (26.3%); Merchant Wholesalers, Durable Goods (26.1%); Credit Intermediation and Related Activities (25.2%); Wholesale Electronic Markets and Agents and Brokers (24.8%); Truck Transportation (24.2%); Local Government (23.6%); Construction of Buildings (23.3%); Air Transportation (21.5%); Hospitals, Public and Private (21.4%); Broadcasting (Except Internet) (20.8%); Educational Services, Public and Private

(20.0%); Specialty Trade Contractors (19.2%); Couriers and Messengers (18.8%); Merchant Wholesalers, Nondurable Goods (18.8%); Support Activities for Agriculture and Forestry (17.9%); Insurance Carriers and Related Activities (16.8%); Furniture and Home Furnishings Stores (16.4%).

Other Considerations for Job Outlook: Employment is projected to grow as fast as the national average due to the increasingly widespread use of logisticians to increase workplace efficiencies.

Analyze and coordinate the logistical functions of a firm or organization. Responsible for the entire life cycle of a product, including acquisition, distribution, internal allocation, delivery, and final disposal of resources. Maintain and develop positive business relationships with a customer's key personnel involved in or directly relevant to a logistics activity. Develop an understanding of customers' needs and take actions to ensure that such needs are met. Direct availability and allocation of materials, supplies, and finished products. Collaborate with other departments as necessary to meet customer requirements, to take advantage of sales opportunities, or, in the case of shortages, to minimize negative impacts on a business. Protect and control proprietary materials. Review logistics performance with customers against targets, benchmarks, and service agreements. Develop and implement technical project management tools such as plans, schedules, and responsibility and compliance matrices. Direct team activities, establishing task priorities, scheduling and tracking work assignments, providing guidance, and ensuring the availability of resources. Report project plans, progress, and results. Direct and support the compilation and analysis of technical source data necessary for product development. Explain proposed solutions to customers, management, or other interested parties through written proposals and oral presentations. Provide project management services, including the provision and analysis of technical data. Develop proposals that include documentation for estimates. Plan, organize, and execute logistics support activities such as maintenance planning, repair analysis, and test equipment recommendations. Participate in the assessment and review of design alternatives and design change proposal impacts. Support the development of training materials and technical manuals. Stay informed of logistics technology advances and apply appropriate technology in order to improve logistics processes. Redesign the movement of goods in order to maximize value and minimize

costs. Manage subcontractor activities, reviewing proposals, developing performance specifications, and serving as liaisons between subcontractors and organizations. Manage the logistical aspects of product life cycles, including coordination or provisioning of samples and the minimization of obsolescence.

Personality Type: Enterprising-Conventional.

Career Clusters: 04 Business, Management, and Administration; 16 Transportation, Distribution, and Logistics. **Career Pathways:** 04.1 Management; 16.2 Logistics Planning and Management Services.

Skills: Management of Financial Resources; Management of Material Resources; Systems Analysis; Operations Analysis; Management of Personnel Resources; Service Orientation.

Education and Training Programs: Logistics and Materials Management; Operations Management and Supervision; Transportation/Transportation Management. **Related Knowledge/Courses:** Telecommunications; Geography; Computers and Electronics; Administration and Management; Economics and Accounting; Public Safety and Security.

Work Environment: Indoors; sitting.

Machinists

- ❋ Education/Training Required: Long-term on-the-job training
- ❋ Annual Earnings: $35,230
- ❋ Beginning Wage: $21,670
- ❋ Earnings Growth Potential: Medium (38.5%)
- ❋ Growth: –3.1%
- ❋ Annual Job Openings: 39,505
- ❋ Job Security: More Secure than Most
- ❋ Self-Employed: 1.7%
- ❋ Part-Time: 1.7%

Renewal Industries: Advanced Manufacturing; Green Technologies.

Industries with Greatest Employment: Fabricated Metal Product Manufacturing (29.1%); Machinery Manufacturing (18.8%); Transportation Equipment Manufacturing

(13.1%); Administrative and Support Services (6.3%); Merchant Wholesalers, Durable Goods (5.2%).

Highest-Growth Industries (Projected Growth for This Job): Administrative and Support Services (33.2%); Building Material and Garden Equipment and Supplies Dealers (32.8%); Waste Management and Remediation Services (32.4%); Rental and Leasing Services (26.5%); Professional, Scientific, and Technical Services (25.4%); Support Activities for Transportation (23.2%); Management of Companies and Enterprises (21.0%); Wholesale Electronic Markets and Agents and Brokers (19.2%); Air Transportation (18.0%); Local Government (17.9%); Construction of Buildings (17.5%); Educational Services, Public and Private (16.8%); Specialty Trade Contractors (16.1%); Merchant Wholesalers, Nondurable Goods (16.0%); Merchant Wholesalers, Durable Goods (15.4%).

Other Considerations for Job Outlook: Although employment is projected to decline, job opportunities are expected to be good. The number of workers learning to be machinists is expected to be less than the number of job openings arising each year from the need to replace experienced machinists who retire or transfer to other occupations.

Set up and operate a variety of machine tools to produce precision parts and instruments. Includes precision instrument makers who fabricate, modify, or repair mechanical instruments. May also fabricate and modify parts to make or repair machine tools or maintain industrial machines, applying knowledge of mechanics, shop mathematics, metal properties, layout, and machining procedures. Calculate dimensions and tolerances, using knowledge of mathematics and instruments such as micrometers and vernier calipers. Align and secure holding fixtures, cutting tools, attachments, accessories, and materials onto machines. Select the appropriate tools, machines, and materials to be used in preparation of machinery work. Monitor the feed and speed of machines during the machining process. Machine parts to specifications, using machine tools such as lathes, milling machines, shapers, or grinders. Set up, adjust, and operate all of the basic machine tools and many specialized or advanced variation tools to perform precision machining operations. Measure, examine, and test completed units to detect defects and ensure conformance to specifications, using precision instruments such as micrometers. Set controls to regulate machining or enter commands to retrieve, input, or edit computerized machine control media. Position and fasten work pieces. Maintain industrial machines, applying knowledge of mechanics, shop mathematics, metal properties, layout, and machining procedures. Observe and listen to operating machines or equipment to diagnose machine malfunctions and to determine need for adjustments or repairs. Check work pieces to ensure that they are properly lubricated and cooled. Lay out, measure, and mark metal stock to display placement of cuts. Study sample parts, blueprints, drawings, and engineering information to determine methods and sequences of operations needed to fabricate products and determine product dimensions and tolerances. Confer with engineering, supervisory, and manufacturing personnel to exchange technical information. Program computers and electronic instruments such as numerically controlled machine tools. Operate equipment to verify operational efficiency. Clean and lubricate machines, tools, and equipment to remove grease, rust, stains, and foreign matter. Design fixtures, tooling, and experimental parts to meet special engineering needs. Evaluate experimental procedures and recommend changes or modifications for improved efficiency and adaptability to setup and production.

Personality Type: Realistic-Conventional-Investigative.

Career Cluster: 13 Manufacturing. **Career Pathway:** 13.1 Production.

Skills: No data available.

Education and Training Programs: Machine Tool Technology/Machinist; Machine Shop Technology/Assistant. **Related Knowledge/Courses:** Mechanical Devices; Design; Engineering and Technology; Production and Processing; Mathematics.

Work Environment: Noisy; contaminants; hazardous equipment; minor burns, cuts, bites, or stings; standing; using hands on objects, tools, or controls.

Maintenance and Repair Workers, General

- ❈ Education/Training Required: Moderate-term on-the-job training
- ❈ Annual Earnings: $32,570
- ❈ Beginning Wage: $19,590
- ❈ Earnings Growth Potential: Medium (39.9%)
- ❈ Growth: 10.1%
- ❈ Annual Job Openings: 165,502
- ❈ Job Security: Most Secure
- ❈ Self-Employed: 1.5%
- ❈ Part-Time: 5.2%

Renewal Industry: Advanced Manufacturing.

Industries with Greatest Employment: Real Estate (15.9%); Educational Services, Public and Private (7.5%); Local Government (7.3%); Accommodation, Including Hotels and Motels (5.0%).

Highest-Growth Industries (Projected Growth for This Job): Securities, Commodity Contracts, and Other Financial Investments and Related Activities (43.8%); Funds, Trusts, and Other Financial Vehicles (37.0%); Museums, Historical Sites, and Similar Institutions (36.2%); Social Assistance (35.9%); Professional, Scientific, and Technical Services (35.8%); Warehousing and Storage (33.6%); Amusement, Gambling, and Recreation Industries (32.5%); Scenic and Sightseeing Transportation (30.6%); Lessors of Nonfinancial Intangible Assets (Except Copyrighted Works) (27.8%); Administrative and Support Services (27.6%); Waste Management and Remediation Services (27.4%); Performing Arts, Spectator Sports, and Related Industries (27.1%); Ambulatory Health-Care Services (26.5%); Nursing and Residential Care Facilities (26.0%); Water Transportation (21.6%); Religious, Grant-making, Civic, Professional, and Similar Organizations (19.3%); Support Activities for Transportation (18.8%); Building Material and Garden Equipment and Supplies Dealers (18.5%); Real Estate (17.1%); Rental and Leasing Services (16.1%); Accommodation, Including Hotels and Motels (15.7%); Management of Companies and Enterprises (15.3%).

Other Considerations for Job Outlook: Job opportunities should be excellent, especially for those with experience in maintenance or related fields. General maintenance and repair is a large occupation, generating many job openings due to growth and the need to replace those who leave the occupation. Many job openings are expected to result from the retirement of experienced maintenance workers over the next decade. Employment is related to the number of buildings—for example, office and apartment buildings, stores, schools, hospitals, hotels, and factories—and the amount of equipment needing maintenance and repair. One factor limiting job growth is that computers allow buildings to be monitored more efficiently, partially reducing the need for workers.

Perform work involving the skills of two or more maintenance or craft occupations to keep machines, mechanical equipment, or the structure of an establishment in repair. Duties may involve pipe fitting; boiler making; insulating; welding; machining; carpentry; repairing electrical or mechanical equipment; installing, aligning, and balancing new equipment; and repairing buildings, floors, or stairs. Repair or replace defective equipment parts, using hand tools and power tools, and reassemble equipment. Perform routine preventive maintenance to ensure that machines continue to run smoothly, building systems operate efficiently, and the physical condition of buildings does not deteriorate. Inspect drives, motors, and belts; check fluid levels; replace filters; and perform other maintenance actions, following checklists. Use tools ranging from common hand and power tools, such as hammers, hoists, saws, drills, and wrenches, to precision measuring instruments and electrical and electronic testing devices. Assemble, install, or repair wiring, electrical and electronic components, pipe systems and plumbing, machinery, and equipment. Diagnose mechanical problems and determine how to correct them, checking blueprints, repair manuals, and parts catalogs as necessary. Inspect, operate, and test machinery and equipment to diagnose machine malfunctions. Record maintenance and repair work performed and the costs of the work. Clean and lubricate shafts, bearings, gears, and other parts of machinery. Dismantle devices to gain access to and remove defective parts, using hoists, cranes, hand tools, and power tools. Plan and lay out repair work, using diagrams, drawings, blueprints, maintenance manuals, and schematic diagrams. Adjust functional parts of devices and control instruments, using hand tools, levels, plumb bobs, and straightedges. Order parts, supplies, and equipment from catalogs and suppliers or obtain them from storerooms.

Paint and repair roofs, windows, doors, floors, woodwork, plaster, drywall, and other parts of building structures. Operate cutting torches or welding equipment to cut or join metal parts. Align and balance new equipment after installation. Inspect used parts to determine changes in dimensional requirements, using rules, calipers, micrometers, and other measuring instruments. Set up and operate machine tools to repair or fabricate machine parts, jigs and fixtures, and tools. Maintain and repair specialized equipment and machinery found in cafeterias, laundries, hospitals, stores, offices, and factories.

Personality Type: Realistic-Conventional-Investigative.

Career Cluster: 02 Architecture and Construction. **Career Pathway:** 02.2 Construction.

Skills: Equipment Maintenance; Installation; Repairing; Troubleshooting; Operation Monitoring; Operation and Control.

Education and Training Program: Building/Construction Site Management/Manager. **Related Knowledge/Courses:** Building and Construction; Mechanical Devices; Design; Physics; Engineering and Technology; Public Safety and Security.

Work Environment: Indoors; noisy; minor burns, cuts, bites, or stings; standing; walking and running; using hands on objects, tools, or controls.

Maintenance Workers, Machinery

- ❋ Education/Training Required: Short-term on-the-job training
- ❋ Annual Earnings: $35,590
- ❋ Beginning Wage: $21,890
- ❋ Earnings Growth Potential: Medium (38.5%)
- ❋ Growth: −1.1%
- ❋ Annual Job Openings: 15,055
- ❋ Job Security: More Secure than Most
- ❋ Self-Employed: 0.0%
- ❋ Part-Time: 4.0%

Renewal Industry: Advanced Manufacturing.

Industries with Greatest Employment: Merchant Wholesalers, Durable Goods (7.3%); Food Manufacturing (6.9%); Local Government (6.4%); Transportation Equipment Manufacturing (6.0%); Chemical Manufacturing (5.8%).

Highest-Growth Industries (Projected Growth for This Job): Warehousing and Storage (33.6%); Amusement, Gambling, and Recreation Industries (31.3%); Waste Management and Remediation Services (28.0%); Administrative and Support Services (24.6%); Professional, Scientific, and Technical Services (21.0%); Rental and Leasing Services (20.7%); Motor Vehicle and Parts Dealers (20.0%); Support Activities for Transportation (19.9%); Accommodation, Including Hotels and Motels (16.1%); Food Services and Drinking Places (15.6%); Management of Companies and Enterprises (15.4%).

Other Considerations for Job Outlook: Applicants with broad skills in machine repair and maintenance should have favorable job prospects. Many mechanics are expected to retire in coming years, and employers have reported difficulty in recruiting young workers with the necessary skills to be industrial machinery mechanics. In addition to openings from growth, most job openings will stem from the need to replace workers who transfer to other occupations or who retire or leave the labor force for other reasons.

Lubricate machinery, change parts, or perform other routine machinery maintenance. Reassemble machines after the completion of repair or maintenance work. Start machines and observe mechanical operation to determine efficiency and to detect problems. Inspect or test damaged machine parts and mark defective areas or advise supervisors of repair needs. Lubricate or apply adhesives or other materials to machines, machine parts, or other equipment, according to specified procedures. Install, replace, or change machine parts and attachments, according to production specifications. Dismantle machines and remove parts for repair, using hand tools, chain falls, jacks, cranes, or hoists. Record production, repair, and machine maintenance information. Read work orders and specifications to determine machines and equipment requiring repair or maintenance. Set up and operate machines and adjust controls to regulate operations. Collaborate with other workers to repair or move machines, machine parts, or equipment. Inventory and requisition machine parts, equipment, and other supplies so that stock can be maintained and replenished. Transport machine parts, tools, equipment, and other material between work areas and storage, using cranes, hoists, or dollies. Clean machines and machine parts, using cleaning solvents, cloths, air guns, hoses, vacuums, or other equipment. Collect and discard worn machine parts and other refuse to maintain machinery and work areas. Replace or repair metal, wood, leather, glass, or other lining in machines or in equipment compartments or containers. Remove hardened material from machines or machine parts, using abrasives, power and hand tools, jackhammers, sledgehammers, or other equipment. Measure, mix, prepare, and test chemical solutions used to clean or repair machinery and equipment. Replace, empty, or replenish machine and equipment containers, such as gas tanks or boxes.

Personality Type: Realistic-Conventional-Investigative.

Career Cluster: 13 Manufacturing. **Career Pathway:** 13.3 Maintenance, Installation, and Repair.

Skills: Installation; Repairing; Equipment Maintenance; Troubleshooting; Operation Monitoring; Operation and Control.

Education and Training Programs: Industrial Mechanics and Maintenance Technology; Heavy/Industrial Equipment Maintenance Technologies, Other. **Related Knowledge/Courses:** Mechanical Devices; Building and Construction; Engineering and Technology; Physics; Chemistry; Design.

Work Environment: Noisy; very hot or cold; contaminants; hazardous equipment; standing; using hands on objects, tools, or controls.

Mapping Technicians

- ❀ Education/Training Required: Moderate-term on-the-job training
- ❀ Annual Earnings: $33,640
- ❀ Beginning Wage: $20,670
- ❀ Earnings Growth Potential: Medium (38.6%)
- ❀ Growth: 19.4%
- ❀ Annual Job Openings: 8,299
- ❀ Job Security: Less Secure than Most
- ❀ Self-Employed: 4.2%
- ❀ Part-Time: 4.5%

Our sources did not provide separate job openings data for this occupation. The job openings listed here are shared with Surveying Technicians.

Renewal Industries: Green Technologies; Infrastructure.

Industries with Greatest Employment: Professional, Scientific, and Technical Services (71.8%); Local Government (10.3%).

Highest-Growth Industries (Projected Growth for This Job): Real Estate (25.4%); Professional, Scientific, and Technical Services (24.7%); Management of Companies and Enterprises (15.3%).

Other Considerations for Job Outlook: Opportunities should be stronger for professional surveyors than for mapping technicians. Advancements in technology, such as total stations and GPS, have made surveying parties smaller than they once were. In addition, mapping technicians who produce more basic GIS data may face competition for jobs from offshore firms and contractors.

Calculate mapmaking information from field notes and draw and verify accuracy of topographical maps. Check all layers of maps to ensure accuracy, identifying and marking errors and making corrections. Determine scales, line sizes, and colors to be used for hard copies of computerized maps, using plotters. Monitor mapping work and the updating of maps to ensure accuracy, the inclusion of new and/or changed information, and compliance with rules and regulations. Identify and compile database information to create maps in response to requests. Produce and update overlay maps to show information boundaries, water locations, and topographic features on various base maps and at different scales. Trace contours and topographic details to generate maps that denote specific land and property locations and geographic attributes. Lay out and match aerial photographs in sequences in which they were taken and identify any areas missing from photographs. Compare topographical features and contour lines with images from aerial photographs, old maps, and other reference materials to verify the accuracy of their identification. Compute and measure scaled distances between reference points to establish relative positions of adjoining prints and enable the creation of photographic mosaics. Research resources such as survey maps and legal descriptions to verify property lines and to obtain information needed for mapping. Form three-dimensional images of aerial photographs taken from different locations, using mathematical techniques and plotting instruments. Enter GPS data, legal deeds, field notes, and land survey reports into GIS workstations so that information can be transformed into graphic land descriptions such as maps and drawings. Analyze aerial photographs to detect and interpret significant military, industrial, resource, or topographical data. Redraw and correct maps, such as revising parcel maps to reflect tax code area changes, using information from official records and surveys. Train staff members in duties such as tax mapping, the use of computerized mapping equipment, and the interpretation of source documents.

Personality Type: Conventional-Realistic.

Career Clusters: 07 Government and Public Administration; 13 Manufacturing. **Career Pathways:** 07.1 Governance; 13.3 Maintenance, Installation, and Repair.

Skills: Technology Design; Operations Analysis; Programming; Quality Control Analysis; Science; Troubleshooting.

Education and Training Programs: Surveying Technology/Surveying; Cartography. **Related Knowledge/Courses:** Geography; Design; Computers and Electronics; Engineering and Technology; Mathematics; Clerical Practices.

Work Environment: Indoors; sitting; using hands on objects, tools, or controls; repetitive motions.

Marriage and Family Therapists

- ❋ Education/Training Required: Master's degree
- ❋ Annual Earnings: $43,600
- ❋ Beginning Wage: $26,080
- ❋ Earnings Growth Potential: High (40.2%)
- ❋ Growth: 29.8%
- ❋ Annual Job Openings: 5,953
- ❋ Job Security: Most Secure
- ❋ Self-Employed: 6.2%
- ❋ Part-Time: 15.4%

Renewal Industry: Health Care.

Industries with Greatest Employment: Social Assistance (35.6%); Ambulatory Health-Care Services (19.4%); State Government (18.1%); Local Government (7.1%); Religious, Grantmaking, Civic, Professional, and Similar Organizations (6.6%).

Highest-Growth Industries (Projected Growth for This Job): Social Assistance (63.4%); Nursing and Residential Care Facilities (23.6%); Ambulatory Health-Care Services (20.4%); Religious, Grantmaking, Civic, Professional, and Similar Organizations (19.8%); Management of Companies and Enterprises (15.6%).

Other Considerations for Job Outlook: Marriage and family therapists will experience fast growth in part because of an increased recognition of the field. It is more common for people to seek help for their marital and family problems than it was in the past. Job prospects should be good due to growth and the need to replace people leaving the field.

Diagnose and treat mental and emotional disorders, whether cognitive, affective, or behavioral, within the context of marriage and family systems. Apply psychotherapeutic and family systems theories and techniques in the delivery of professional services to individuals, couples, and families for the purpose of treating such diagnosed nervous and mental disorders. Ask questions that will help clients identify their feelings and behaviors. Counsel clients on concerns such as unsatisfactory relationships, divorce and separation, child rearing, home management, and financial difficulties. Encourage individuals and family members to develop and use skills and strategies for confronting their problems in a constructive manner. Maintain case files that include activities, progress notes, evaluations, and recommendations. Collect information about clients, using techniques such as testing, interviewing, discussion, and observation. Develop and implement individualized treatment plans addressing family relationship problems. Determine whether clients should be counseled or referred to other specialists in such fields as medicine, psychiatry, and legal aid. Confer with clients in order to develop plans for post-treatment activities. Confer with other counselors to analyze individual cases and to coordinate counseling services. Follow up on results of counseling programs and clients' adjustments to determine effectiveness of programs. Provide instructions to clients on how to obtain help with legal, financial, and other personal issues. Contact doctors, schools, social workers, juvenile counselors, law enforcement personnel, and others to gather information in order to make recommendations to courts for the resolution of child custody or visitation disputes. Provide public education and consultation to other professionals or groups regarding counseling services, issues, and methods. Supervise other counselors, social service staff, and assistants. Provide family counseling and treatment services to inmates participating in substance abuse programs. Write evaluations of parents and children for use by courts deciding divorce and custody cases, testifying in court if necessary.

Personality Type: Social-Artistic-Investigative.

Career Cluster: 10 Human Services. **Career Pathways:** 10.2 Counseling and Mental Health Services; 10.3 Family and Community Services.

Skills: Social Perceptiveness; Negotiation; Active Listening; Persuasion; Service Orientation; Monitoring.

Education and Training Programs: Social Work; Marriage and Family Therapy/Counseling; Clinical Pastoral Counseling/Patient Counseling. **Related Knowledge/Courses:** Therapy and Counseling; Psychology; Philosophy and Theology; Sociology and Anthropology; Medicine and Dentistry; Customer and Personal Service.

Work Environment: Indoors; sitting.

Massage Therapists

- ❋ Education/Training Required: Postsecondary vocational training
- ❋ Annual Earnings: $34,870
- ❋ Beginning Wage: $16,000
- ❋ Earnings Growth Potential: Very high (54.1%)
- ❋ Growth: 20.3%
- ❋ Annual Job Openings: 9,193
- ❋ Job Security: Most Secure
- ❋ Self-Employed: 64.0%
- ❋ Part-Time: 42.9%

Renewal Industry: Health Care.

Industries with Greatest Employment: Personal and Laundry Services (14.4%); Ambulatory Health-Care Services (9.9%).

Highest-Growth Industries (Projected Growth for This Job): Amusement, Gambling, and Recreation Industries (33.0%); Ambulatory Health-Care Services (26.3%); Administrative and Support Services (26.1%); Nursing and Residential Care Facilities (18.5%); Accommodation, Including Hotels and Motels (16.1%).

Other Considerations for Job Outlook: In states that regulate massage therapy, therapists who complete formal training programs and pass the national certification exam are likely to have very good opportunities. However, new massage therapists should expect to work only part-time in spas, hotels, hospitals, physical therapy centers, and other businesses until they can build a client base of their own. Because referrals are a very important source of work for massage therapists, networking will increase the number of job opportunities. Joining a state or local chapter of a professional association can also help build strong contacts and further increase the likelihood of steady work. Female massage therapists will continue to enjoy slightly better job prospects, as some clients—both male and female—are uncomfortable with male physical contact.

Massage customers for hygienic or remedial purposes. Confer with clients about their medical histories and any problems with stress or pain to determine whether massage would be helpful. Apply finger and hand pressure to specific points of the body. Massage and knead the muscles and soft tissues of the human body to provide courses of treatment for medical conditions and injuries or wellness maintenance. Maintain treatment records. Provide clients with guidance and information about techniques for postural improvement and stretching, strengthening, relaxation, and rehabilitative exercises. Assess clients' soft tissue condition, joint quality and function, muscle strength, and range of motion. Develop and propose client treatment plans that specify which types of massage are to be used. Refer clients to other types of therapists when necessary. Use complementary aids, such as infrared lamps, wet compresses, ice, and whirlpool baths, to promote clients' recovery, relaxation, and well-being. Treat clients in own offices or travel to clients' offices and homes. Consult with other health-care professionals such as physiotherapists, chiropractors, physicians, and psychologists to develop treatment plans for clients. Prepare and blend oils and apply the blends to clients' skin.

Personality Type: Social-Realistic.

Career Cluster: 08 Health Science. **Career Pathway:** 08.1 Therapeutic Services.

Skills: No data available.

Education and Training Programs: Massage Therapy/Therapeutic Massage; Asian Bodywork Therapy; Somatic Bodywork; Somatic Bodywork and Related Therapeutic

Services, Other. **Related Knowledge/Courses:** Therapy and Counseling; Psychology; Sales and Marketing; Medicine and Dentistry; Chemistry; English Language.

Work Environment: Indoors; standing; using hands on objects, tools, or controls; repetitive motions.

Mathematical Science Teachers, Postsecondary

- ❋ Education/Training Required: Master's degree
- ❋ Annual Earnings: $58,560
- ❋ Beginning Wage: $32,690
- ❋ Earnings Growth Potential: High (44.2%)
- ❋ Growth: 22.9%
- ❋ Annual Job Openings: 7,663
- ❋ Job Security: Most Secure
- ❋ Self-Employed: 0.4%
- ❋ Part-Time: 27.8%

Renewal Industry: Education.

Industries with Greatest Employment: Educational Services, Public and Private (97.3%).

Highest-Growth Industries (Projected Growth for This Job): Administrative and Support Services (48.3%); Amusement, Gambling, and Recreation Industries (45.2%); Social Assistance (38.6%); Support Activities for Transportation (32.8%); Religious, Grantmaking, Civic, Professional, and Similar Organizations (29.9%); Professional, Scientific, and Technical Services (28.8%); Management of Companies and Enterprises (26.8%); Local Government (23.5%); Educational Services, Public and Private (22.8%); Hospitals, Public and Private (21.4%).

Other Considerations for Job Outlook: Retirements of current postsecondary teachers should create numerous openings for all types of postsecondary teachers, so job opportunities are generally expected to be very good. However, one of the main reasons why students attend postsecondary institutions is to prepare themselves for careers, so the best job prospects for postsecondary teachers are likely to be in rapidly growing fields that offer many nonacademic career options. Community colleges and other institutions offering career and technical education have been among the most rapidly growing, and these institutions are

expected to offer some of the best opportunities for postsecondary teachers.

Teach courses pertaining to mathematical concepts, statistics, and actuarial science and to the application of original and standardized mathematical techniques in solving specific problems and situations. Evaluate and grade students' classwork, assignments, and papers. Compile, administer, and grade examinations or assign this work to others. Prepare and deliver lectures to undergraduate and/or graduate students on topics such as linear algebra, differential equations, and discrete mathematics. Prepare course materials such as syllabi, homework assignments, and handouts. Maintain student attendance records, grades, and other required records. Maintain regularly scheduled office hours to advise and assist students. Plan, evaluate, and revise curricula, course content, and course materials and methods of instruction. Initiate, facilitate, and moderate classroom discussions. Select and obtain materials and supplies such as textbooks. Keep abreast of developments in their field by reading current literature, talking with colleagues, and participating in professional conferences. Advise students on academic and vocational curricula and on career issues. Collaborate with colleagues to address teaching and research issues. Serve on academic or administrative committees that deal with institutional policies, departmental matters, and academic issues. Participate in student recruitment, registration, and placement activities. Perform administrative duties such as serving as department head. Conduct research in a particular field of knowledge and publish findings in books, professional journals, and/or electronic media. Supervise undergraduate and/or graduate teaching, internship, and research work. Act as advisers to student organizations. Participate in campus and community events. Write grant proposals to procure external research funding. Compile bibliographies of specialized materials for outside reading assignments. Provide professional consulting services to government and/or industry.

Personality Type: Social-Investigative-Artistic.

Career Clusters: 04 Business, Management, and Administration; 10 Human Services; 15 Science, Technology, Engineering, and Mathematics. **Career Pathways:** 04.2 Business Financial Management and Accounting; 10.2 Counseling and Mental Health Services; 15.3 Science and Mathematics.

Skills: Mathematics; Instructing; Science; Learning Strategies; Critical Thinking; Complex Problem Solving.

Education and Training Programs: Mathematics, General; Algebra and Number Theory; Analysis and Functional Analysis; Geometry/Geometric Analysis; Topology and Foundations; Mathematics, Other; Applied Mathematics; Statistics, General; Mathematical Statistics and Probability; Mathematics and Statistics, Other; Logic; Business Statistics. **Related Knowledge/Courses:** Mathematics; Education and Training; Physics; Computers and Electronics; English Language; Communications and Media.

Work Environment: Indoors; more often standing than sitting.

Mechanical Drafters

- ❋ Education/Training Required: Postsecondary vocational training
- ❋ Annual Earnings: $44,740
- ❋ Beginning Wage: $28,540
- ❋ Earnings Growth Potential: Medium (36.2%)
- ❋ Growth: 5.2%
- ❋ Annual Job Openings: 10,902
- ❋ Job Security: More Secure than Most
- ❋ Self-Employed: 5.5%
- ❋ Part-Time: 5.9%

Renewal Industries: Advanced Manufacturing; Infrastructure.

Industries with Greatest Employment: Professional, Scientific, and Technical Services (28.4%); Machinery Manufacturing (18.2%); Transportation Equipment Manufacturing (12.8%); Fabricated Metal Product Manufacturing (12.5%).

Highest-Growth Industries (Projected Growth for This Job): Building Material and Garden Equipment and Supplies Dealers (29.0%); Real Estate (26.5%); Support Activities for Transportation (23.1%); Professional, Scientific, and Technical Services (18.6%); Administrative and Support Services (18.1%); Management of Companies and Enterprises (16.6%); Rental and Leasing Services (16.3%).

Other Considerations for Job Outlook: Demand for particular drafting specialties varies throughout the country because employment usually is contingent on the needs of local industry. Opportunities should be best for individuals with at least 2 years of postsecondary training in a drafting program that provides strong technical skills and considerable experience with CADD systems.

Prepare detailed working diagrams of machinery and mechanical devices, including dimensions, fastening methods, and other engineering information. Develop detailed design drawings and specifications for mechanical equipment, dies, tools, and controls, using computer-assisted drafting (CAD) equipment. Coordinate with and consult other workers to design, lay out, or detail components and systems and to resolve design or other problems. Review and analyze specifications, sketches, drawings, ideas, and related data to assess factors affecting component designs and the procedures and instructions to be followed. Position instructions and comments onto drawings. Compute mathematical formulas to develop and design detailed specifications for components or machinery, using computer-assisted equipment. Modify and revise designs to correct operating deficiencies or to reduce production problems. Design scale or full-size blueprints of specialty items such as furniture and automobile body or chassis components. Check dimensions of materials to be used and assign numbers to the materials. Lay out and draw schematic, orthographic, or angle views to depict functional relationships of components, assemblies, systems, and machines. Confer with customer representatives to review schematics and answer questions pertaining to installation of systems. Draw freehand sketches of designs, trace finished drawings onto designated paper for the reproduction of blueprints, and reproduce working drawings on copy machines. Supervise and train other drafters, technologists, and technicians. Lay out, draw, and reproduce illustrations for reference manuals and technical publications to describe operation and maintenance of mechanical systems. Shade or color drawings to clarify and emphasize details and dimensions or eliminate background, using ink, crayon, airbrush, and overlays.

Personality Type: Realistic-Conventional-Investigative.

Career Cluster: 02 Architecture and Construction. **Career Pathway:** 02.1 Design/Pre-Construction.

Skills: Technology Design; Installation; Equipment Selection; Operations Analysis; Quality Control Analysis; Mathematics.

Education and Training Program: Mechanical Drafting and Mechanical Drafting CAD/CADD. **Related Knowledge/Courses:** Design; Engineering and Technology; Building and Construction; Physics; Mathematics; English Language.

Work Environment: Indoors; noisy; sitting; using hands on objects, tools, or controls; repetitive motions.

Mechanical Engineering Technicians

- ❈ Education/Training Required: Associate degree
- ❈ Annual Earnings: $47,280
- ❈ Beginning Wage: $30,960
- ❈ Earnings Growth Potential: Low (34.5%)
- ❈ Growth: 6.4%
- ❈ Annual Job Openings: 3,710
- ❈ Job Security: More Secure than Most
- ❈ Self-Employed: 0.8%
- ❈ Part-Time: 5.9%

Renewal Industries: Advanced Manufacturing; Green Technologies.

Industries with Greatest Employment: Professional, Scientific, and Technical Services (38.1%); Machinery Manufacturing (16.8%); Computer and Electronic Product Manufacturing (12.5%); Transportation Equipment Manufacturing (7.7%).

Highest-Growth Industries (Projected Growth for This Job): Administrative and Support Services (27.4%); Professional, Scientific, and Technical Services (23.0%); Management of Companies and Enterprises (15.2%).

Other Considerations for Job Outlook: Growth is expected to be limited by foreign competition in both design services and manufacturing.

Apply theory and principles of mechanical engineering to modify, develop, and test machinery and equipment under direction of engineering staff or physical scientists. Prepare parts sketches and write work orders and purchase requests to be furnished by outside contractors. Draft detail drawing or sketch for drafting room completion or to request parts fabrication by machine, sheet, or wood shops. Review project instructions and blueprints to ascertain test specifications, procedures, and objectives and test nature of technical problems such as redesign. Review project instructions and specifications to identify, modify, and plan requirements fabrication, assembly, and testing. Devise, fabricate, and assemble new or modified mechanical components for products such as industrial machinery or equipment and measuring instruments. Discuss changes in design, method of manufacture and assembly, and drafting techniques and procedures with staff and coordinate corrections. Set up and conduct tests of complete units and components under operational conditions to investigate proposals for improving equipment performance. Inspect lines and figures for clarity and return erroneous drawings to designer for correction. Analyze test results in relation to design or rated specifications and test objectives and modify or adjust equipment to meet specifications. Evaluate tool drawing designs by measuring drawing dimensions and comparing with original specifications for form and function, using engineering skills. Confer with technicians and submit reports of test results to engineering department and recommend design or material changes. Calculate required capacities for equipment of proposed system to obtain specified performance and submit data to engineering personnel for approval. Record test procedures and results, numerical and graphical data, and recommendations for changes in product or test methods. Read dials and meters to determine amperage, voltage, and electrical output and input at specific operating temperature to analyze parts performance. Estimate cost factors, including labor and material, for purchased and fabricated parts and costs for assembly, testing, or installing. Set up prototype and test apparatus and operate test-controlling equipment to observe and record prototype test results.

Personality Type: Realistic-Investigative.

Career Clusters: 01 Agriculture, Food, and Natural Resources; 13 Manufacturing. **Career Pathways:** 01.5 Natural Resources Systems; 13.3 Maintenance, Installation, and Repair.

Skills: Installation; Troubleshooting; Technology Design; Operations Analysis; Equipment Selection; Science.

Education and Training Programs: Mechanical Engineering/Mechanical Technology/Technician; Mechanical Engineering Related Technologies/Technicians, Other. **Related Knowledge/Courses:** Engineering and

Technology; Design; Mechanical Devices; Physics; Chemistry; Production and Processing.

Work Environment: Indoors; noisy; contaminants; hazardous equipment; sitting.

Mechanical Engineers

- ❋ Education/Training Required: Bachelor's degree
- ❋ Annual Earnings: $72,300
- ❋ Beginning Wage: $46,560
- ❋ Earnings Growth Potential: Medium (35.6%)
- ❋ Growth: 4.2%
- ❋ Annual Job Openings: 12,394
- ❋ Job Security: More Secure than Most
- ❋ Self-Employed: 2.2%
- ❋ Part-Time: 1.9%

Renewal Industries: Advanced Manufacturing; Green Technologies; Information and Telecommunication Technologies.

Industries with Greatest Employment: Professional, Scientific, and Technical Services (28.0%); Transportation Equipment Manufacturing (14.4%); Machinery Manufacturing (13.2%); Computer and Electronic Product Manufacturing (9.2%); Fabricated Metal Product Manufacturing (5.8%).

Highest-Growth Industries (Projected Growth for This Job): Waste Management and Remediation Services (29.1%); Building Material and Garden Equipment and Supplies Dealers (28.1%); Administrative and Support Services (27.6%); Professional, Scientific, and Technical Services (25.6%); Nonstore Retailers (25.0%); Performing Arts, Spectator Sports, and Related Industries (25.0%); Publishing Industries (Except Internet) (23.0%); Religious, Grantmaking, Civic, Professional, and Similar Organizations (21.2%); Rental and Leasing Services (20.8%); Support Activities for Transportation (18.3%); Management of Companies and Enterprises (15.3%).

Other Considerations for Job Outlook: Some new job opportunities will be created due to emerging technologies in biotechnology, materials science, and nanotechnology. Additional opportunities outside of mechanical engineering will exist because the skills acquired through earning a

degree in mechanical engineering often can be applied in other engineering specialties.

Perform engineering duties in planning and designing tools, engines, machines, and other mechanically functioning equipment. Oversee installation, operation, maintenance, and repair of such equipment as centralized heat, gas, water, and steam systems. Read and interpret blueprints, technical drawings, schematics, and computer-generated reports. Confer with engineers and other personnel to implement operating procedures, resolve system malfunctions, and provide technical information. Research and analyze customer design proposals, specifications, manuals, and other data to evaluate the feasibility, cost, and maintenance requirements of designs or applications. Specify system components or direct modification of products to ensure conformance with engineering design and performance specifications. Research, design, evaluate, install, operate, and maintain mechanical products, equipment, systems, and processes to meet requirements, applying knowledge of engineering principles. Investigate equipment failures and difficulties to diagnose faulty operation and to make recommendations to maintenance crew. Assist drafters in developing the structural design of products, using drafting tools or computer-assisted design (CAD) or drafting equipment and software. Provide feedback to design engineers on customer problems and needs. Oversee installation, operation, maintenance, and repair to ensure that machines and equipment are installed and functioning according to specifications. Conduct research that tests and analyzes the feasibility, design, operation, and performance of equipment, components, and systems. Recommend design modifications to eliminate machine or system malfunctions. Develop and test models of alternate designs and processing methods to assess feasibility, operating condition effects, possible new applications, and necessity of modification. Develop, coordinate, and monitor all aspects of production, including selection of manufacturing methods, fabrication, and operation of product designs. Estimate costs and submit bids for engineering, construction, or extraction projects and prepare contract documents. Perform personnel functions such as supervision of production workers, technicians, technologists, and other engineers or design of evaluation programs. Solicit new business and provide technical customer service. Establish and coordinate the maintenance and safety procedures, service schedule, and supply of materials required to maintain machines and equipment in the prescribed condition.

Personality Type: Investigative-Realistic-Conventional.

Career Cluster: 15 Science, Technology, Engineering, and Mathematics. **Career Pathway:** 15.1 Engineering and Technology.

Skills: Science; Operations Analysis; Installation; Complex Problem Solving; Mathematics; Systems Analysis.

Education and Training Program: Mechanical Engineering. **Related Knowledge/Courses:** Design; Engineering and Technology; Mechanical Devices; Production and Processing; Physics; Administration and Management.

Work Environment: Indoors; sitting.

Medical and Clinical Laboratory Technicians

- ❋ Education/Training Required: Associate degree
- ❋ Annual Earnings: $34,270
- ❋ Beginning Wage: $22,670
- ❋ Earnings Growth Potential: Low (33.8%)
- ❋ Growth: 15.0%
- ❋ Annual Job Openings: 10,866
- ❋ Job Security: Most Secure
- ❋ Self-Employed: 0.7%
- ❋ Part-Time: 14.3%

Renewal Industry: Health Care.

Industries with Greatest Employment: Hospitals, Public and Private (43.3%); Ambulatory Health-Care Services (37.1%); Educational Services, Public and Private (9.6%).

Highest-Growth Industries (Projected Growth for This Job): Social Assistance (54.3%); Administrative and Support Services (26.9%); Chemical Manufacturing (25.1%); Nursing and Residential Care Facilities (23.4%); Merchant Wholesalers, Nondurable Goods (18.4%); Ambulatory Health-Care Services (17.8%); Merchant Wholesalers, Durable Goods (17.0%); Religious, Grantmaking, Civic, Professional, and Similar Organizations (16.7%); Professional, Scientific, and Technical Services (15.2%).

Other Considerations for Job Outlook: Job opportunities are expected to be excellent because the number of job openings is expected to continue to exceed the number of job seekers. Although significant, job growth will not be the only source of opportunities. As in most occupations, many additional openings will result from the need to replace workers who transfer to other occupations, retire, or stop working for some other reason. The volume of laboratory tests continues to increase with both population growth and the development of new types of tests. Technological advances will continue to have opposing effects on employment. On the one hand, new, increasingly powerful diagnostic tests will encourage additional testing and spur employment. On the other, research and development efforts targeted at simplifying routine testing procedures may enhance the ability of nonlaboratory personnel—physicians and patients in particular—to perform tests now conducted in laboratories.

Perform routine medical laboratory tests for the diagnosis, treatment, and prevention of disease. May work under the supervision of a medical technologist. Conduct chemical analyses of bodily fluids, such as blood and urine, using microscope or automatic analyzer to detect abnormalities or diseases, and enter findings into computer. Set up, adjust, maintain, and clean medical laboratory equipment. Analyze the results of tests and experiments to ensure conformity to specifications, using special mechanical and electrical devices. Analyze and record test data to issue reports that use charts, graphs and narratives. Conduct blood tests for transfusion purposes and perform blood counts. Perform medical research to further control and cure disease. Obtain specimens, cultivating, isolating, and identifying microorganisms for analysis. Examine cells stained with dye to locate abnormalities. Collect blood or tissue samples from patients, observing principles of asepsis to obtain blood sample. Consult with a pathologist to determine a final diagnosis when abnormal cells are found. Inoculate fertilized eggs, broths, or other bacteriological media with organisms. Cut, stain, and mount tissue samples for examination by pathologists. Supervise and instruct other technicians and laboratory assistants. Prepare standard volumetric solutions and reagents to be combined with samples, following standardized formulas or experimental procedures. Prepare vaccines and serums by standard laboratory methods, testing for virus inactivity and sterility. Test raw materials, processes, and finished products to determine quality and quantity of materials or characteristics of a substance.

Personality Type: Realistic-Investigative-Conventional.

Career Cluster: 08 Health Science. **Career Pathways:** 08.1 Therapeutic Services; 08.2 Diagnostics Services.

Skills: Science; Equipment Maintenance; Troubleshooting; Quality Control Analysis; Operation Monitoring; Operation and Control.

Education and Training Programs: Clinical/Medical Laboratory Assistant; Blood Bank Technology Specialist; Hematology Technology/Technician; Clinical/Medical Laboratory Technician; Histologic Technician. **Related Knowledge/Courses:** Medicine and Dentistry; Therapy and Counseling; Biology; Clerical Practices.

Work Environment: Indoors; disease or infections; standing; walking and running; using hands on objects, tools, or controls.

Medical and Clinical Laboratory Technologists

- ❋ Education/Training Required: Bachelor's degree
- ❋ Annual Earnings: $51,720
- ❋ Beginning Wage: $35,460
- ❋ Earnings Growth Potential: Low (31.4%)
- ❋ Growth: 12.4%
- ❋ Annual Job Openings: 11,457
- ❋ Job Security: Most Secure
- ❋ Self-Employed: 0.7%
- ❋ Part-Time: 14.3%

Renewal Industry: Health Care.

Industries with Greatest Employment: Hospitals, Public and Private (60.6%); Ambulatory Health-Care Services (25.3%); Educational Services, Public and Private (5.2%).

Highest-Growth Industries (Projected Growth for This Job): Social Assistance (46.7%); Ambulatory Health-Care Services (36.8%); Professional, Scientific, and Technical Services (27.1%); Administrative and Support Services (26.5%); Chemical Manufacturing (26.1%); Nursing and Residential Care Facilities (15.7%); Management of Companies and Enterprises (15.3%).

Other Considerations for Job Outlook: Job opportunities are expected to be excellent because the number of job openings is expected to continue to exceed the number of job seekers. Although significant, job growth will not be the only source of opportunities. As in most occupations, many additional openings will result from the need to replace workers who transfer to other occupations, retire, or stop working for some other reason. The volume of laboratory tests continues to increase with both population growth and the development of new types of tests. Technological advances will continue to have opposing effects on employment. On the one hand, new, increasingly powerful diagnostic tests will encourage additional testing and spur employment. On the other, research and development efforts targeted at simplifying routine testing procedures may enhance the ability of nonlaboratory personnel—physicians and patients in particular—to perform tests now conducted in laboratories.

Perform complex medical laboratory tests for diagnosis, treatment, and prevention of disease. May train or supervise staff. Conduct chemical analysis of bodily fluids, including blood, urine, and spinal fluid, to determine presence of normal and abnormal components. Analyze laboratory findings to check the accuracy of the results. Enter data from analysis of medical tests and clinical results into computer for storage. Operate, calibrate, and maintain equipment used in quantitative and qualitative analysis, such as spectrophotometers, calorimeters, flame photometers, and computer-controlled analyzers. Establish and monitor quality assurance programs and activities to ensure the accuracy of laboratory results. Set up, clean, and maintain laboratory equipment. Provide technical information about test results to physicians, family members, and researchers. Supervise, train, and direct lab assistants, medical and clinical laboratory technicians and technologists, and other medical laboratory workers engaged in laboratory testing. Collect and study blood samples to determine the number of cells, their morphology, or their blood group, blood type, and compatibility for transfusion purposes, using microscopic techniques. Analyze samples of biological material for chemical content or reaction. Cultivate, isolate, and assist in identifying microbial organisms and perform various tests on these microorganisms. Obtain, cut, stain, and mount biological material on slides for microscopic study and diagnosis, following standard laboratory procedures. Select and prepare specimen and media for cell culture, using aseptic technique and knowledge of medium components and cell requirements. Develop, standardize, evaluate, and modify procedures, techniques, and tests used in the analysis of specimens and in medical laboratory experiments. Harvest cell cultures at optimum time based on knowledge of cell cycle differences and culture conditions. Conduct medical research under direction of microbiologist or biochemist.

Personality Type: Investigative-Realistic-Conventional.

Career Cluster: 08 Health Science. **Career Pathway:** 08.2 Diagnostics Services.

Skills: No data available.

Education and Training Programs: Cytotechnology/ Cytotechnologist; Clinical Laboratory Science/Medical Technology/Technologist; Histologic Technology/His-totechnologist; Cytogenetics/Genetics/Clinical Genetics Technology/Technologist; Renal/Dialysis Technologist/ Technician; Clinical/Medical Laboratory Science and Allied Professions, Other. **Related Knowledge/Courses:** Biology; Chemistry; Medicine and Dentistry; Mechanical Devices; Clerical Practices; Mathematics.

Work Environment: Indoors; noisy; contaminants; disease or infections; standing; using hands on objects, tools, or controls.

Medical and Health Services Managers

- ✳ Education/Training Required: Work experience plus degree
- ✳ Annual Earnings: $76,990
- ✳ Beginning Wage: $46,860
- ✳ Earnings Growth Potential: Medium (39.1%)
- ✳ Growth: 16.4%
- ✳ Annual Job Openings: 31,877
- ✳ Job Security: Most Secure
- ✳ Self-Employed: 8.2%
- ✳ Part-Time: 5.5%

Renewal Industry: Health Care.

Industries with Greatest Employment: Hospitals, Public and Private (37.3%); Ambulatory Health-Care Services (21.7%); Nursing and Residential Care Facilities (11.7%).

Highest-Growth Industries (Projected Growth for This Job): Social Assistance (51.7%); Professional, Scientific, and Technical Services (35.2%); Ambulatory Health-Care Services (31.0%); Administrative and Support Services (28.5%); Funds, Trusts, and Other Financial Vehicles (23.2%); Nonstore Retailers (22.8%); Nursing and Residential Care Facilities (22.1%); Merchant Wholesalers, Nondurable Goods (18.8%); Religious, Grantmaking, Civic, Professional, and Similar Organizations (18.1%); Management of Companies and Enterprises (15.3%).

Other Considerations for Job Outlook: Job opportunities for medical and health services managers should be good, especially for applicants with work experience in the health care field and strong business management skills. Hospitals will continue to employ the most medical and health services managers, but the number of new jobs created is expected to increase at a slower rate in hospitals than in many other industries because of the growing use of clinics and other outpatient care sites. Despite relatively slow employment growth, a large number of new jobs will be created because of the industry's large size. Employment will grow fastest in practitioners' offices and in home health care agencies. Medical and health services managers also will be employed by HMOs. Competition for jobs at the highest management levels will be keen because of the high pay and prestige.

Plan, direct, or coordinate medicine and health services in hospitals, clinics, managed care organizations, public health agencies, or similar organizations. Conduct and administer fiscal operations, including accounting, planning budgets, authorizing expenditures, establishing rates for services, and coordinating financial reporting. Direct, supervise, and evaluate work activities of medical, nursing, technical, clerical, service, maintenance, and other personnel. Maintain communication between governing boards, medical staff, and department heads by attending board meetings and coordinating interdepartmental functioning. Review and analyze facility activities and data to aid planning and cash and risk management and to improve service utilization. Plan, implement, and administer programs and services in a health-care or medical facility, including personnel administration, training, and coordination of medical, nursing, and physical plant staff. Direct or conduct recruitment, hiring, and training of personnel. Establish work schedules and assignments for staff according to workload, space, and equipment availability. Maintain awareness of advances in medicine, computerized diagnostic and treatment equipment, data processing technology, government regulations, health insurance changes, and financing options. Monitor the use of diagnostic services, inpatient beds, facilities, and staff to ensure effective use of resources and assess the need for additional staff, equipment, and services. Develop and maintain computerized record management systems to store and process data such as personnel activities and information and to produce reports. Establish and evaluative objectives and evaluative operational criteria for units they manage. Prepare activity reports to inform management of the status and implementation plans of programs, services, and quality initiatives. Inspect facilities and recommend building or equipment modifications to ensure emergency readiness and compliance to access, safety, and sanitation regulations. Develop and implement organizational policies and procedures for the facility or medical unit. Manage change in integrated health-care delivery systems such as work restructuring, technological innovations, and shifts in the focus of care.

Personality Type: Enterprising-Conventional-Social.

Career Cluster: 08 Health Science. **Career Pathways:** 08.1 Therapeutic Services; 08.2 Diagnostics Services; 08.3 Health Informatics.

Skills: Management of Financial Resources; Management of Personnel Resources; Systems Analysis; Systems Evaluation; Management of Material Resources; Negotiation.

Education and Training Programs: Health/Health Care Administration/Management; Hospital and Health Care Facilities Administration/Management; Health Unit Manager/Ward Supervisor; Health Information/Medical Records Administration/Administrator; Medical Staff Services Technology/Technician; Health and Medical Administrative Services, Other; Nursing Administration (MSN, MS, PhD); Public Health, General (MPH, DPH); Community Health and Preventive Medicine; others. **Related Knowledge/Courses:** Economics and Accounting; Personnel and Human Resources; Administration and Management; Sales and Marketing; Medicine and Dentistry; Law and Government.

Work Environment: Indoors; disease or infections; sitting.

Medical and Public Health Social Workers

❋ Education/Training Required: Bachelor's degree
❋ Annual Earnings: $44,670
❋ Beginning Wage: $28,160
❋ Earnings Growth Potential: Medium (37.0%)
❋ Growth: 24.2%
❋ Annual Job Openings: 16,429
❋ Job Security: More Secure than Most
❋ Self-Employed: 2.6%
❋ Part-Time: 9.4%

Renewal Industry: Health Care.

Industries with Greatest Employment: Hospitals, Public and Private (30.9%); Ambulatory Health-Care Services (19.0%); Nursing and Residential Care Facilities (13.8%); Social Assistance (13.4%); Local Government (8.5%).

Highest-Growth Industries (Projected Growth for This Job): Ambulatory Health-Care Services (57.1%); Social Assistance (56.4%); Administrative and Support Services (26.9%); Nursing and Residential Care Facilities (25.2%); Personal and Laundry Services (16.7%); Religious, Grantmaking, Civic, Professional, and Similar Organizations (16.0%); Professional, Scientific, and Technical Services (15.8%); Management of Companies and Enterprises (15.3%).

Other Considerations for Job Outlook: Job prospects are generally expected to be favorable. Opportunities should be good in rural areas, which often find it difficult to attract and retain qualified staff. Hospitals continue to limit the length of patient stays, so the demand for social workers in hospitals will grow more slowly than in other areas. But hospitals are releasing patients earlier than in the past, so social worker employment in home health care services is growing. However, the expanding senior population is an even larger factor. Employment opportunities for social workers with backgrounds in gerontology should be good in the growing numbers of assisted-living and senior-living communities. The expanding senior population also will spur demand for social workers in nursing homes, long-term care facilities, and hospices. However, in these settings other types of workers are often being given tasks that were previously done by social workers.

Provide persons, families, or vulnerable populations with the psychosocial support needed to cope with chronic, acute, or terminal illnesses such as Alzheimer's, cancer, or AIDS. Services include advising family caregivers, providing patient education and counseling, and making necessary referrals for other social services. Advocate for clients or patients to resolve crises. Collaborate with other professionals to evaluate patients' medical or physical condition and to assess client needs. Refer patients, clients, or families to community resources to assist in recovery from mental or physical illnesses and to provide access to services such as financial assistance, legal aid, housing, job placement, or education. Counsel clients and patients in individual and group sessions to help them overcome dependencies, recover from illnesses, and adjust to life. Use consultation data and social work experience to plan and coordinate client or patient care and rehabilitation, following through to ensure service efficacy. Plan discharge from care facility to home or other care facility. Organize support groups or counsel family members to assist them in understanding, dealing with, and supporting clients or patients. Modify treatment plans to comply with changes in clients' statuses. Monitor, evaluate, and record client progress according to measurable goals described in treatment and care plans. Identify environmental impediments to client or patient progress through interviews and review of patient records. Supervise and direct other workers providing services to clients or patients. Develop or advise on social policy and assist in community development. Investigate child abuse or neglect cases and take authorized protective action when necessary. Oversee Medicaid- and Medicare-related paperwork and recordkeeping in hospitals. Plan and conduct programs to combat social problems, prevent substance abuse, or improve community health and counseling services. Conduct social research to advance knowledge in the social work field.

Personality Type: Social-Investigative.

Career Cluster: 10 Human Services. **Career Pathway:** 10.2 Counseling and Mental Health Services.

Skills: No data available.

Education and Training Program: Clinical/Medical Social Work. **Related Knowledge/Courses:** Therapy and Counseling; Sociology and Anthropology; Psychology; Philosophy and Theology; Customer and Personal Service; Medicine and Dentistry.

Work Environment: Indoors; noisy; disease or infections; sitting.

Medical Assistants

- ❋ Education/Training Required: Moderate-term on-the-job training
- ❋ Annual Earnings: $27,430
- ❋ Beginning Wage: $19,850
- ❋ Earnings Growth Potential: Low (27.6%)
- ❋ Growth: 35.4%
- ❋ Annual Job Openings: 92,977
- ❋ Job Security: Most Secure
- ❋ Self-Employed: 0.0%
- ❋ Part-Time: 23.2%

Renewal Industry: Health Care.

Industries with Greatest Employment: Ambulatory Health-Care Services (79.8%); Hospitals, Public and Private (12.3%).

Highest-Growth Industries (Projected Growth for This Job): Social Assistance (69.7%); Professional, Scientific, and Technical Services (40.5%); Administrative and Support Services (39.6%); Chemical Manufacturing (38.9%); Ambulatory Health-Care Services (38.3%); Nursing and Residential Care Facilities (37.3%); Management of Companies and Enterprises (26.8%); Local Government (23.6%); Real Estate (22.6%); Educational Services, Public and Private (22.4%); Hospitals, Public and Private (21.9%); Insurance Carriers and Related Activities (19.9%).

Other Considerations for Job Outlook: Job seekers who want to work as a medical assistant should find excellent job prospects. Medical assistants are projected to account for a very large number of new jobs, and many other opportunities will come from the need to replace workers leaving the occupation. Those with formal training or experience—particularly those with certification—should have the best job opportunities.

Perform administrative and certain clinical duties under the direction of physicians. Administrative duties may include scheduling appointments, maintaining medical records, billing, and coding for insurance purposes. Clinical duties may include taking and recording vital signs and medical histories, preparing

patients for examination, drawing blood, and administering medications as directed by physician. Record patients' medical history, vital statistics, and information such as test results in medical records. Prepare treatment rooms for patient examinations, keeping the rooms neat and clean. Interview patients to obtain medical information and measure their vital signs, weights, and heights. Authorize drug refills and provide prescription information to pharmacies. Clean and sterilize instruments and dispose of contaminated supplies. Prepare and administer medications as directed by a physician. Show patients to examination rooms and prepare them for the physician. Explain treatment procedures, medications, diets, and physicians' instructions to patients. Help physicians examine and treat patients, handing them instruments and materials or performing such tasks as giving injections or removing sutures. Collect blood, tissue, or other laboratory specimens, log the specimens, and prepare them for testing. Perform routine laboratory tests and sample analyses. Contact medical facilities or departments to schedule patients for tests or admission. Operate X-ray, electrocardiogram (EKG), and other equipment to administer routine diagnostic tests. Change dressings on wounds. Set up medical laboratory equipment. Perform general office duties such as answering telephones, taking dictation, or completing insurance forms. Greet and log in patients arriving at office or clinic. Schedule appointments for patients. Inventory and order medical, lab, or office supplies and equipment. Keep financial records and perform other bookkeeping duties, such as handling credit and collections and mailing monthly statements to patients.

Personality Type: Social-Conventional-Realistic.

Career Cluster: 08 Health Science. **Career Pathways:** 08.2 Diagnostics Services; 08.3 Health Informatics.

Skills: No data available.

Education and Training Programs: Medical Office Management/Administration; Medical Office Assistant/Specialist; Medical Reception/Receptionist; Medical Insurance Coding Specialist/Coder; Medical Administrative/Executive Assistant and Medical Secretary; Medical/Clinical Assistant; Anesthesiologist Assistant; Chiropractic Assistant/Technician; Allied Health and Medical Assisting Services, Other; Optomeric Technician/Assistant; others. **Related Knowledge/Courses:** Medicine and Dentistry; Clerical Practices; Psychology; Therapy and

Counseling; Customer and Personal Service; Public Safety and Security.

Work Environment: Indoors; disease or infections; standing; walking and running; using hands on objects, tools, or controls; repetitive motions.

Medical Records and Health Information Technicians

* Education/Training Required: Associate degree
* Annual Earnings: $29,290
* Beginning Wage: $19,690
* Earnings Growth Potential: Low (32.8%)
* Growth: 17.8%
* Annual Job Openings: 39,048
* Job Security: Most Secure
* Self-Employed: 0.2%
* Part-Time: 12.5%

Renewal Industry: Health Care.

Industries with Greatest Employment: Hospitals, Public and Private (39.0%); Ambulatory Health-Care Services (35.5%); Nursing and Residential Care Facilities (9.5%).

Highest-Growth Industries (Projected Growth for This Job): Social Assistance (57.6%); Internet Service Providers, Web Search Portals, and Data Processing Services (32.7%); Professional, Scientific, and Technical Services (31.2%); Ambulatory Health-Care Services (28.5%); Chemical Manufacturing (25.6%); Religious, Grantmaking, Civic, Professional, and Similar Organizations (18.9%); Merchant Wholesalers, Nondurable Goods (18.9%); Management of Companies and Enterprises (15.3%); Nursing and Residential Care Facilities (15.2%).

Other Considerations for Job Outlook: Job prospects should be very good. In addition to job growth, openings will result from the need to replace technicians who retire or leave the occupation permanently. Technicians with a strong background in medical coding will be in particularly high demand. Changing government regulations and the growth of managed care have increased the amount of paperwork involved in filing insurance claims. Additionally, health-care facilities are having some difficulty attracting qualified workers, primarily because employers prefer trained and experienced technicians prepared to work in an increasingly electronic environment with the integration of electronic health records. Job opportunities may be especially good for coders employed through temporary help agencies or by professional services firms.

Compile, process, and maintain medical records of hospital and clinic patients in a manner consistent with medical, administrative, ethical, legal, and regulatory requirements of the health-care system. Process, maintain, compile, and report patient information for health requirements and standards. Protect the security of medical records to ensure that confidentiality is maintained. Review records for completeness, accuracy, and compliance with regulations. Retrieve patient medical records for physicians, technicians, or other medical personnel. Release information to persons and agencies according to regulations. Plan, develop, maintain, and operate a variety of health record indexes and storage and retrieval systems to collect, classify, store, and analyze information. Enter data such as demographic characteristics, history and extent of disease, diagnostic procedures, and treatment into computer. Process and prepare business and government forms. Compile and maintain patients' medical records to document condition and treatment and to provide data for research or cost control and care improvement efforts. Process patient admission and discharge documents. Assign the patient to diagnosis-related groups (DRGs), using appropriate computer software. Transcribe medical reports. Identify, compile, abstract, and code patient data, using standard classification systems. Resolve or clarify codes and diagnoses with conflicting, missing, or unclear information by consulting with doctors or others or by participating in the coding team's regular meetings. Compile medical care and census data for statistical reports on diseases treated, surgeries performed, or use of hospital beds. Post medical insurance billings. Train medical records staff. Prepare statistical reports, narrative reports, and graphic presentations of information such as tumor registry data for use by hospital staff, researchers, or other users. Manage the department and supervise clerical workers, directing and controlling activities of personnel in the medical records department. Develop in-service educational materials. Consult classification manuals to locate information about disease processes.

Personality Type: Conventional-Enterprising.

Career Cluster: 08 Health Science. **Career Pathway:** 08.3 Health Informatics.

Skills: No data available.

Education and Training Programs: Health Information/Medical Records Technology/Technician; Medical Insurance Coding Specialist/Coder. **Related Knowledge/ Courses:** Clerical Practices; Law and Government; Customer and Personal Service.

Work Environment: Indoors; disease or infections; sitting; using hands on objects, tools, or controls; repetitive motions.

Medical Scientists, Except Epidemiologists

- ❋ Education/Training Required: Doctoral degree
- ❋ Annual Earnings: $64,200
- ❋ Beginning Wage: $36,730
- ❋ Earnings Growth Potential: High (42.8%)
- ❋ Growth: 20.2%
- ❋ Annual Job Openings: 10,596
- ❋ Job Security: More Secure than Most
- ❋ Self-Employed: 2.0%
- ❋ Part-Time: 5.9%

Renewal Industry: Health Care.

Industries with Greatest Employment: Educational Services, Public and Private (33.6%); Professional, Scientific, and Technical Services (30.8%); Chemical Manufacturing (11.6%); Hospitals, Public and Private (9.2%).

Highest-Growth Industries (Projected Growth for This Job): Administrative and Support Services (26.8%); Chemical Manufacturing (25.9%); Educational Services, Public and Private (23.0%); Ambulatory Health-Care Services (23.0%); Professional, Scientific, and Technical Services (20.2%); Merchant Wholesalers, Nondurable Goods (18.9%); Merchant Wholesalers, Durable Goods (17.1%); Religious, Grantmaking, Civic, Professional, and Similar Organizations (16.9%); Management of Companies and Enterprises (15.3%).

Other Considerations for Job Outlook: Doctoral degree holders can expect to face considerable competition for basic research positions and for research grants. If the number of advanced degrees awarded continues to grow, applicants are likely to face even more competition. However, those with both doctoral and medical degrees are likely to experience very good opportunities.

Conduct research dealing with the understanding of human diseases and the improvement of human health. Engage in clinical investigation or other research, production, technical writing, or related activities. Conduct research to develop methodologies, instrumentation, and procedures for medical application, analyzing data and presenting findings. Plan and direct studies to investigate human or animal disease, preventive methods, and treatments for disease. Follow strict safety procedures when handling toxic materials to avoid contamination. Evaluate effects of drugs, gases, pesticides, parasites, and microorganisms at various levels. Teach principles of medicine and medical and laboratory procedures to physicians, residents, students, and technicians. Prepare and analyze organ, tissue, and cell samples to identify toxicity, bacteria, or microorganisms or to study cell structure. Standardize drug dosages, methods of immunization, and procedures for manufacture of drugs and medicinal compounds. Investigate cause, progress, life cycle, or mode of transmission of diseases or parasites. Confer with health department, industry personnel, physicians, and others to develop health safety standards and public health improvement programs. Study animal and human health and physiological processes. Consult with and advise physicians, educators, researchers, and others regarding medical applications of physics, biology, and chemistry. Use equipment such as atomic absorption spectrometers, electron microscopes, flow cytometers, and chromatography systems.

Personality Type: Investigative-Realistic-Artistic.

Career Clusters: 08 Health Science; 15 Science, Technology, Engineering, and Mathematics. **Career Pathways:** 08.1 Therapeutic Services; 15.3 Science and Mathematics.

Skills: Science; Management of Financial Resources; Judgment and Decision Making; Reading Comprehension; Writing; Time Management.

Education and Training Programs: Biomedical Sciences, General; Biochemistry; Biophysics; Molecular Biology; Cell/Cellular Biology and Histology; Anatomy; Medical Microbiology and Bacteriology; Immunology; Human/Medical Genetics; Physiology, General; Molecular Physiology; Cell Physiology; Endocrinology; Reproductive Biology; Neurobiology and Neurophysiology; Cardiovascular Science; others. **Related Knowledge/Courses:** Biology; Medicine and Dentistry; Chemistry; Communications and Media; Personnel and Human Resources; Sociology and Anthropology.

Work Environment: Indoors; sitting; using hands on objects, tools, or controls.

Medical Transcriptionists

- ❇ Education/Training Required: Postsecondary vocational training
- ❇ Annual Earnings: $31,250
- ❇ Beginning Wage: $22,160
- ❇ Earnings Growth Potential: Low (29.1%)
- ❇ Growth: 13.5%
- ❇ Annual Job Openings: 18,080
- ❇ Job Security: More Secure than Most
- ❇ Self-Employed: 9.7%
- ❇ Part-Time: 23.2%

Renewal Industry: Health Care.

Industries with Greatest Employment: Hospitals, Public and Private (41.1%); Ambulatory Health-Care Services (36.3%); Administrative and Support Services (8.8%).

Highest-Growth Industries (Projected Growth for This Job): Professional, Scientific, and Technical Services (50.6%); Administrative and Support Services (46.4%); Ambulatory Health-Care Services (19.5%); Management of Companies and Enterprises (15.2%).

Other Considerations for Job Outlook: Job opportunities will be good, especially for those who are certified. Hospitals will continue to employ a large percentage of medical transcriptionists, but job growth there will not be as fast as in other industries. An increasing demand for standardized records should result in rapid employment growth in physicians' offices, especially in large group practices.

Use transcribing machines with headset and foot pedal to listen to recordings by physicians and other health-care professionals dictating a variety of medical reports, such as emergency room visits, diagnostic imaging studies, operations, chart reviews, and final summaries. Transcribe dictated reports and translate medical

jargon and abbreviations into their expanded forms. Edit as necessary and return reports in either printed or electronic form to the dictator for review and signature or correction. Transcribe dictation for a variety of medical reports such as patient histories, physical examinations, emergency room visits, operations, chart reviews, consultation, or discharge summaries. Review and edit transcribed reports or dictated material for spelling, grammar, clarity, consistency, and proper medical terminology. Distinguish between homonyms and recognize inconsistencies and mistakes in medical terms, referring to dictionaries; drug references; and other sources on anatomy, physiology, and medicine. Return dictated reports in printed or electronic form for physicians' review, signature, and corrections and for inclusion in patients' medical records. Translate medical jargon and abbreviations into their expanded forms to ensure the accuracy of patient and health-care facility records. Take dictation, using either shorthand or a stenotype machine or using headsets and transcribing machines; then convert dictated materials or rough notes to written form. Identify mistakes in reports and check with doctors to obtain the correct information. Perform data entry and data retrieval services, providing data for inclusion in medical records and for transmission to physicians. Produce medical reports, correspondence, records, patient-care information, statistics, medical research, and administrative material. Answer inquiries concerning the progress of medical cases within the limits of confidentiality laws. Set up and maintain medical files and databases, including records such as X-ray, lab, and procedure reports; medical histories; diagnostic workups; admission and discharge summaries; and clinical resumes. Perform a variety of clerical and office tasks, such as handling incoming and outgoing mail, completing and submitting insurance claims, typing, filing, and operating office machines. Decide which information should be included or excluded in reports. Receive patients, schedule appointments, and maintain patient records. Receive and screen telephone calls and visitors.

Personality Type: Conventional-Realistic.

Career Cluster: 08 Health Science. **Career Pathway:** 08.3 Health Informatics.

Skills: No data available.

Education and Training Program: Medical Transcription/Transcriptionist. **Related Knowledge/Courses:**

Clerical Practices; English Language; Medicine and Dentistry; Computers and Electronics.

Work Environment: Indoors; sitting; using hands on objects, tools, or controls; repetitive motions.

Mental Health and Substance Abuse Social Workers

- ✱ Education/Training Required: Master's degree
- ✱ Annual Earnings: $36,640
- ✱ Beginning Wage: $23,820
- ✱ Earnings Growth Potential: Medium (35.0%)
- ✱ Growth: 29.9%
- ✱ Annual Job Openings: 17,289
- ✱ Job Security: Most Secure
- ✱ Self-Employed: 2.8%
- ✱ Part-Time: 9.4%

Renewal Industry: Health Care.

Industries with Greatest Employment: Ambulatory Health-Care Services (21.5%); Social Assistance (21.4%); Nursing and Residential Care Facilities (17.8%); Hospitals, Public and Private (15.7%); Local Government (10.7%).

Highest-Growth Industries (Projected Growth for This Job): Professional, Scientific, and Technical Services (68.4%); Social Assistance (55.5%); Nursing and Residential Care Facilities (51.2%); Ambulatory Health-Care Services (33.0%); Administrative and Support Services (29.6%); Religious, Grantmaking, Civic, Professional, and Similar Organizations (16.0%); Management of Companies and Enterprises (15.3%).

Other Considerations for Job Outlook: Job prospects are expected to be favorable, particularly for social workers who specialize in substance abuse. Substance abusers are increasingly being placed into treatment programs instead of being sentenced to prison. Also, growing numbers of the substance abusers sentenced to prison or probation are, increasingly being required by correctional systems to have substance abuse treatment added as a condition to their sentence or probation. As this trend grows, demand will strengthen for treatment programs and social workers to assist abusers on the road to recovery.

Assess and treat individuals with mental, emotional, or substance abuse problems, including abuse of alcohol, tobacco, and/or other drugs. Activities may include individual and group therapy, crisis intervention, case management, client advocacy, prevention, and education. Counsel clients in individual and group sessions to assist them in dealing with substance abuse, mental and physical illness, poverty, unemployment, or physical abuse. Interview clients, review records, and confer with other professionals to evaluate mental or physical condition of client or patient. Collaborate with counselors, physicians, and nurses to plan and coordinate treatment, drawing on social work experience and patient needs. Monitor, evaluate, and record client progress with respect to treatment goals. Refer patient, client, or family to community resources for housing or treatment to assist in recovery from mental or physical illness, following through to ensure service efficacy. Counsel and aid family members to assist them in understanding, dealing with, and supporting the client or patient. Modify treatment plans according to changes in client status. Plan and conduct programs to prevent substance abuse, to combat social problems, or to improve health and counseling services in community. Supervise and direct other workers who provide services to clients or patients. Develop or advise on social policy and assist in community development. Conduct social research to advance knowledge in the social work field.

Personality Type: Social-Investigative-Artistic.

Career Cluster: 10 Human Services. **Career Pathway:** 10.2 Counseling and Mental Health Services.

Skills: Social Perceptiveness; Service Orientation; Negotiation; Judgment and Decision Making; Active Listening; Persuasion.

Education and Training Program: Clinical/Medical Social Work. **Related Knowledge/Courses:** Psychology; Therapy and Counseling; Sociology and Anthropology; Customer and Personal Service.

Work Environment: Indoors; noisy; sitting.

Mental Health Counselors

* Education/Training Required: Master's degree
* Annual Earnings: $36,000
* Beginning Wage: $22,900
* Earnings Growth Potential: Medium (36.4%)
* Growth: 30.0%
* Annual Job Openings: 24,103
* Job Security: Most Secure
* Self-Employed: 6.1%
* Part-Time: 15.4%

Renewal Industry: Health Care.

Industries with Greatest Employment: Ambulatory Health-Care Services (28.5%); Nursing and Residential Care Facilities (20.2%); Social Assistance (18.9%); Hospitals, Public and Private (11.3%); Local Government (9.2%).

Highest-Growth Industries (Projected Growth for This Job): Social Assistance (57.9%); Nursing and Residential Care Facilities (39.2%); Ambulatory Health-Care Services (33.1%); Administrative and Support Services (30.3%); Management of Companies and Enterprises (15.4%); Religious, Grantmaking, Civic, Professional, and Similar Organizations (15.0%).

Other Considerations for Job Outlook: Job prospects should be good due to growth and the need to replace people leaving the field. Employment of mental health counselors is expected to grow much faster than the average for all occupations. Mental health counselors will be needed to staff statewide networks that are being established to improve services for children and adolescents with serious emotional disturbances and for their families. Under managed care systems, insurance companies are increasingly providing for reimbursement of counselors as a less costly alternative to psychiatrists and psychologists.

Counsel with emphasis on prevention. Work with individuals and groups to promote optimum mental health. May help individuals deal with addictions and substance abuse; family, parenting, and marital problems; suicide; stress management; problems with self-esteem; and issues associated with aging and mental and emotional health. Maintain confidentiality of records relating to clients' treatment. Guide clients in the development of skills and strategies for dealing with their problems. Encourage clients to express their feelings and discuss what is happening in their lives and help them to develop insight into themselves and their relationships. Prepare and maintain all required treatment records and reports. Counsel clients and patients, individually and in group sessions, to assist in overcoming dependencies, adjusting to life, and making changes. Collect information about clients through interviews, observation, and tests. Act as client advocates to coordinate required services or to resolve emergency problems in crisis situations. Develop and implement treatment plans based on clinical experience and knowledge. Collaborate with other staff members to perform clinical assessments and develop treatment plans. Evaluate clients' physical or mental condition based on review of client information. Meet with families, probation officers, police, and other interested parties to exchange necessary information during the treatment process. Refer patients, clients, or family members to community resources or to specialists as necessary. Evaluate the effectiveness of counseling programs and clients' progress in resolving identified problems and moving towards defined objectives. Counsel family members to assist them in understanding, dealing with, and supporting clients or patients. Plan, organize, and lead structured programs of counseling, work, study, recreation, and social activities for clients. Modify treatment activities and approaches as needed to comply with changes in clients' status. Learn about new developments in their field by reading professional literature, attending courses and seminars, and establishing and maintaining contact with other social service agencies. Discuss with individual patients their plans for life after leaving therapy. Gather information about community mental health needs and resources that could be used in conjunction with therapy. Monitor clients' use of medications. Supervise other counselors, social service staff, and assistants.

Personality Type: Social-Investigative-Artistic.

Career Clusters: 08 Health Science; 10 Human Services. **Career Pathways:** 08.3 Health Informatics; 10.2 Counseling and Mental Health Services.

Skills: Social Perceptiveness; Service Orientation; Negotiation; Active Listening; Persuasion; Learning Strategies.

Education and Training Programs: Substance Abuse/Addiction Counseling; Clinical/Medical Social Work;

Mental Health Counseling/Counselor; Mental and Social Health Services and Allied Professions, Other. **Related Knowledge/Courses:** Therapy and Counseling; Psychology; Sociology and Anthropology; Philosophy and Theology; Medicine and Dentistry; Law and Government.

Work Environment: Indoors; noisy; sitting.

Middle School Teachers, Except Special and Vocational Education

- ✸ Education/Training Required: Bachelor's degree
- ✸ Annual Earnings: $47,900
- ✸ Beginning Wage: $32,630
- ✸ Earnings Growth Potential: Low (31.9%)
- ✸ Growth: 11.2%
- ✸ Annual Job Openings: 75,270
- ✸ Job Security: Most Secure
- ✸ Self-Employed: 0.0%
- ✸ Part-Time: 9.5%

Renewal Industry: Education.

Industries with Greatest Employment: Educational Services, Public and Private (98.8%).

Highest-Growth Industries (Projected Growth for This Job): Social Assistance (27.7%); Administrative and Support Services (26.6%); Nursing and Residential Care Facilities (22.4%); Religious, Grantmaking, Civic, Professional, and Similar Organizations (20.0%).

Other Considerations for Job Outlook: Job prospects are expected to be favorable, with particularly good prospects for teachers in high-demand fields like math, science, and bilingual education, or in less desirable urban or rural school districts. Fast-growing states in the South and West—led by Nevada, Arizona, Texas, and Georgia—will experience the largest enrollment increases. Enrollments in the Midwest are expected to hold relatively steady, while those in the Northeast are expected to decline. The number of teachers employed is dependent on state and local expenditures for education and on the enactment of legislation to increase the quality and scope of public education. At the federal level, there has been a large increase in funding for education, particularly for the hiring of qualified teachers in lower-income areas.

Teach students in public or private schools in one or more subjects at the middle, intermediate, or junior high level, which falls between elementary and senior high school as defined by applicable state laws and regulations. Establish and enforce rules for behavior and procedures for maintaining order among the students for whom they are responsible. Adapt teaching methods and instructional materials to meet students' varying needs and interests. Instruct through lectures, discussions, and demonstrations in one or more subjects such as English, mathematics, or social studies. Prepare, administer, and grade tests and assignments to evaluate students' progress. Establish clear objectives for all lessons, units, and projects and communicate these objectives to students. Plan and conduct activities for a balanced program of instruction, demonstration, and work time that provides students with opportunities to observe, question, and investigate. Maintain accurate, complete, and correct student records as required by laws, district policies, and administrative regulations. Observe and evaluate students' performance, behavior, social development, and physical health. Assign lessons and correct homework. Prepare materials and classrooms for class activities. Enforce all administration policies and rules governing students. Confer with parents or guardians, other teachers, counselors, and administrators to resolve students' behavioral and academic problems. Prepare students for later grades by encouraging them to explore learning opportunities and to persevere with challenging tasks. Prepare objectives and outlines for courses of study, following curriculum guidelines or requirements of states and schools. Guide and counsel students with adjustment or academic problems or special academic interests. Meet with parents and guardians to discuss their children's progress and to determine their priorities for their children and their resource needs. Meet with other professionals to discuss individual students' needs and progress. Prepare and implement remedial programs for students requiring extra help. Prepare for assigned classes and show written evidence of preparation upon request of immediate supervisors. Instruct and monitor students in the use and care of equipment and materials to prevent injury and damage.

Personality Type: Social-Artistic.

Career Cluster: 05 Education and Training. **Career Pathway:** 05.3 Teaching/Training.

Skills: Learning Strategies; Instructing; Monitoring; Social Perceptiveness; Time Management; Persuasion.

Education and Training Programs: Junior High/Intermediate/Middle School Education and Teaching; Montessori Teacher Education; Waldorf/Steiner Teacher Education; Art Teacher Education; English/Language Arts Teacher Education; Foreign Language Teacher Education; Health Teacher Education; Family and Consumer Sciences/Home Economics Teacher Education; Technology Teacher Education/Industrial Arts Teacher Education; Mathematics Teacher Education; others. **Related Knowledge/Courses:** Sociology and Anthropology; History and Archeology; Philosophy and Theology; Education and Training; Geography; Therapy and Counseling.

Work Environment: Indoors; noisy; standing.

Millwrights

- ❋ Education/Training Required: Long-term on-the-job training
- ❋ Annual Earnings: $46,090
- ❋ Beginning Wage: $28,940
- ❋ Earnings Growth Potential: Medium (37.2%)
- ❋ Growth: 5.8%
- ❋ Annual Job Openings: 4,758
- ❋ Job Security: Least Secure
- ❋ Self-Employed: 3.2%
- ❋ Part-Time: 1.5%

Renewal Industry: Advanced Manufacturing.

Industries with Greatest Employment: Specialty Trade Contractors (28.1%); Transportation Equipment Manufacturing (17.0%); Primary Metal Manufacturing (8.9%); Construction of Buildings (8.8%); Wood Product Manufacturing (7.4%); Paper Manufacturing (6.3%).

Highest-Growth Industries (Projected Growth for This Job): Warehousing and Storage (44.6%); Amusement, Gambling, and Recreation Industries (43.3%); Waste Management and Remediation Services (42.9%); Building Material and Garden Equipment and Supplies Dealers (38.2%); Administrative and Support Services (37.8%); Professional, Scientific, and Technical Services (31.9%); Management of Companies and Enterprises (24.9%); Wholesale Electronic Markets and Agents and Brokers (22.9%); Local Government (21.7%); Construction of Buildings (21.5%); Merchant Wholesalers, Durable Goods

(19.8%); Specialty Trade Contractors (18.4%); Heavy and Civil Engineering Construction (15.8%).

Other Considerations for Job Outlook: The large number of expected retirements and the difficulty of recruiting new workers will create excellent job opportunities for well-qualified applicants. Job prospects should be especially good for those who have experience in machining, welding, or doing mechanical work. Employment prospects for millwrights are better than for some other manufacturing workers because they work across a wide range of industries, including power generation, paper mills, mining, and motor vehicle parts manufacturing. When a downturn occurs in one industry, millwrights can more easily switch to another industry. There will always be a need to maintain and repair existing machinery, dismantle old machinery, and install new equipment.

Install, dismantle, or move machinery and heavy equipment according to layout plans, blueprints, or other drawings. Replace defective parts of machine or adjust clearances and alignment of moving parts. Align machines and equipment, using hoists, jacks, hand tools, squares, rules, micrometers, and plumb bobs. Connect power unit to machines or steam piping to equipment and test unit to evaluate its mechanical operation. Repair and lubricate machines and equipment. Assemble and install equipment, using hand tools and power tools. Position steel beams to support bedplates of machines and equipment, using blueprints and schematic drawings to determine work procedures. Signal crane operator to lower basic assembly units to bedplate and align unit to centerline. Insert shims, adjust tension on nuts and bolts, or position parts, using hand tools and measuring instruments to set specified clearances between moving and stationary parts. Move machinery and equipment, using hoists, dollies, rollers, and trucks. Attach moving parts and subassemblies to basic assembly unit, using hand tools and power tools. Assemble machines and bolt, weld, rivet, or otherwise fasten them to foundation or other structures, using hand tools and power tools. Lay out mounting holes, using measuring instruments, and drill holes with power drill. Bolt parts, such as side and deck plates, jaw plates, and journals, to basic assembly unit. Dismantle machines, using hammers, wrenches, crowbars, and other hand tools. Level bedplate and establish centerline, using straightedge, levels, and transit. Shrink-fit bushings, sleeves, rings, liners, gears, and wheels to specified items, using portable gas heating equipment. Dismantle

machinery and equipment for shipment to installation site, usually performing installation and maintenance work as part of team. Construct foundation for machines, using hand tools and building materials such as wood, cement, and steel. Install robot and modify its program, using teach pendant. Operate engine lathe to grind, file, and turn machine parts to dimensional specifications.

Personality Type: Realistic-Conventional-Investigative.

Career Cluster: 13 Manufacturing. **Career Pathway:** 13.3 Maintenance, Installation, and Repair.

Skills: Installation; Repairing; Troubleshooting; Equipment Maintenance; Equipment Selection; Mathematics.

Education and Training Programs: Industrial Mechanics and Maintenance Technology; Heavy/Industrial Equipment Maintenance Technologies, Other. **Related Knowledge/Courses:** Mechanical Devices; Building and Construction; Physics; Engineering and Technology; Design; Public Safety and Security.

Work Environment: Noisy; very hot or cold; very bright or dim lighting; contaminants; hazardous equipment; using hands on objects, tools, or controls.

Mining and Geological Engineers, Including Mining Safety Engineers

- ✳ Education/Training Required: Bachelor's degree
- ✳ Annual Earnings: $74,330
- ✳ Beginning Wage: $44,690
- ✳ Earnings Growth Potential: Medium (39.9%)
- ✳ Growth: 10.0%
- ✳ Annual Job Openings: 456
- ✳ Job Security: Less Secure than Most
- ✳ Self-Employed: 0.0%
- ✳ Part-Time: 5.3%

Renewal Industry: Green Technologies.

Industries with Greatest Employment: Mining (Except Oil and Gas) (28.5%); Professional, Scientific, and Technical Services (27.6%); Oil and Gas Extraction (24.3%).

Highest-Growth Industries (Projected Growth for This Job): Professional, Scientific, and Technical Services

(24.8%); Management of Companies and Enterprises (15.3%).

Other Considerations for Job Outlook: Many mining engineers currently employed are approaching retirement age. Furthermore, relatively few schools offer mining engineering programs, resulting in good job opportunities for graduates. The best opportunities may require frequent travel or even living overseas for extended periods of time as mining operations around the world recruit graduates of U.S. mining engineering programs.

Determine the location and plan the extraction of coal, metallic ores, nonmetallic minerals, and building materials such as stone and gravel. Work involves conducting preliminary surveys of deposits or undeveloped mines and planning their development; examining deposits or mines to determine whether they can be worked at a profit; making geological and topographical surveys; evolving methods of mining best suited to character, type, and size of deposits; and supervising mining operations. Inspect mining areas for unsafe structures, equipment, and working conditions. Select locations and plan underground or surface mining operations, specifying processes, labor usage, and equipment that will result in safe, economical, and environmentally sound extraction of minerals and ores. Examine maps, deposits, drilling locations, or mines to determine the location, size, accessibility, contents, value, and potential profitability of mineral, oil, and gas deposits. Supervise and coordinate the work of technicians, technologists, survey personnel, engineers, scientists, and other mine personnel. Prepare schedules, reports, and estimates of the costs involved in developing and operating mines. Monitor mine production rates to assess operational effectiveness. Design, implement, and monitor the development of mines, facilities, systems, or equipment. Select or develop mineral location, extraction, and production methods based on factors such as safety, cost, and deposit characteristics. Prepare technical reports for use by mining, engineering, and management personnel. Implement and coordinate mine safety programs, including the design and maintenance of protective and rescue equipment and safety devices. Test air to detect toxic gases and recommend measures to remove them, such as installation of ventilation shafts. Design, develop, and implement computer applications for use in mining operations such as mine design, modeling, or mapping or for monitoring mine conditions. Select or devise materials-handling methods and equipment to transport ore, waste materials, and mineral products efficiently and economically. Devise solutions to problems of land reclamation and water and air pollution, such as methods of storing excavated soil and returning exhausted mine sites to natural states. Lay out, direct, and supervise mine construction operations, such as the construction of shafts and tunnels. Evaluate data to develop new mining products, equipment, or processes. Conduct or direct mining experiments to test or prove research findings. Design mining and mineral treatment equipment and machinery in collaboration with other engineering specialists.

Personality Type: Investigative-Realistic-Enterprising.

Career Cluster: 15 Science, Technology, Engineering, and Mathematics. **Career Pathway:** 15.1 Engineering and Technology.

Skills: Operations Analysis; Science; Programming; Management of Financial Resources; Mathematics; Management of Material Resources.

Education and Training Program: Mining and Mineral Engineering. **Related Knowledge/Courses:** Engineering and Technology; Design; Chemistry; Physics; Production and Processing; Geography.

Work Environment: More often indoors than outdoors; very hot or cold; contaminants; hazardous equipment; sitting.

Mobile Heavy Equipment Mechanics, Except Engines

* Education/Training Required: Postsecondary vocational training
* Annual Earnings: $41,450
* Beginning Wage: $27,200
* Earnings Growth Potential: Low (34.4%)
* Growth: 12.3%
* Annual Job Openings: 11,037
* Job Security: Least Secure
* Self-Employed: 5.0%
* Part-Time: 2.3%

Renewal Industries: Green Technologies; Infrastructure.

Industries with Greatest Employment: Merchant Wholesalers, Durable Goods (26.0%); Heavy and Civil Engineering Construction (9.6%); Specialty Trade Contractors (9.0%); Federal Government (7.3%); Rental and Leasing Services (6.9%); Local Government (6.3%); Mining (Except Oil and Gas) (5.7%).

Highest-Growth Industries (Projected Growth for This Job): Warehousing and Storage (33.4%); Motor Vehicle and Parts Dealers (32.6%); Professional, Scientific, and Technical Services (32.0%); Administrative and Support Services (29.1%); Amusement, Gambling, and Recreation Industries (28.1%); Merchant Wholesalers, Durable Goods (27.3%); Waste Management and Remediation Services (27.0%); Rental and Leasing Services (20.3%); Accommodation, Including Hotels and Motels (16.0%); Support Activities for Transportation (15.7%); Management of Companies and Enterprises (15.4%).

Other Considerations for Job Outlook: Opportunities for heavy vehicle and mobile equipment service technicians and mechanics should be excellent for those who have completed formal training programs in diesel or heavy equipment mechanics. People without formal training are expected to encounter growing difficulty entering these jobs.

Diagnose, adjust, repair, or overhaul mobile mechanical, hydraulic, and pneumatic equipment, such as cranes, bulldozers, graders, and conveyors, used in construction, logging, and surface mining. Test mechanical products and equipment after repair or assembly to ensure proper performance and compliance with manufacturers' specifications. Repair and replace damaged or worn parts. Diagnose faults or malfunctions to determine required repairs, using engine diagnostic equipment such as computerized test equipment and calibration devices. Operate and inspect machines or heavy equipment to diagnose defects. Dismantle and reassemble heavy equipment, using hoists and hand tools. Clean, lubricate, and perform other routine maintenance work on equipment and vehicles. Examine parts for damage or excessive wear, using micrometers and gauges. Read and understand operating manuals, blueprints, and technical drawings. Schedule maintenance for industrial machines and equipment and keep equipment service records. Overhaul and test machines or equipment to ensure operating efficiency. Assemble gear systems and align frames and gears. Fit bearings to adjust, repair, or overhaul mobile mechanical, hydraulic, and pneumatic equipment. Weld or solder broken parts and structural members, using electric or gas welders and soldering tools. Clean parts by spraying them with grease solvent or immersing them in tanks of solvent. Adjust, maintain, and repair or replace subassemblies, such as transmissions and crawler heads, using hand tools, jacks, and cranes. Adjust and maintain industrial machinery, using control and regulating devices. Fabricate needed parts or items from sheet metal. Direct workers who are assembling or disassembling equipment or cleaning parts.

Personality Type: Realistic-Conventional.

Career Clusters: 01 Agriculture, Food, and Natural Resources; 13 Manufacturing. **Career Pathways:** 01.4 Power Structure and Technical Systems; 13.3 Maintenance, Installation, and Repair.

Skills: Installation; Repairing; Equipment Maintenance; Operation Monitoring; Troubleshooting; Operation and Control.

Education and Training Programs: Agricultural Mechanics and Equipment/Machine Technology; Heavy Equipment Maintenance Technology/Technician. **Related Knowledge/Courses:** Mechanical Devices; Engineering and Technology; Physics.

Work Environment: Noisy; contaminants; hazardous equipment; minor burns, cuts, bites, or stings; standing; using hands on objects, tools, or controls.

Multi-Media Artists and Animators

- ❋ Education/Training Required: Bachelor's degree
- ❋ Annual Earnings: $54,550
- ❋ Beginning Wage: $30,620
- ❋ Earnings Growth Potential: High (43.9%)
- ❋ Growth: 25.8%
- ❋ Annual Job Openings: 13,182
- ❋ Job Security: Less Secure than Most
- ❋ Self-Employed: 69.7%
- ❋ Part-Time: 22.5%

Renewal Industry: Information and Telecommunication Technologies.

Industries with Greatest Employment: Professional, Scientific, and Technical Services (10.9%); Motion Picture, Video, and Sound Recording Industries (7.5%).

Highest-Growth Industries (Projected Growth for This Job): Internet Publishing and Broadcasting (58.8%); Motion Picture, Video, and Sound Recording Industries (47.3%); Professional, Scientific, and Technical Services (46.8%); Administrative and Support Services (45.3%); Telecommunications (45.3%); Nonstore Retailers (38.5%); Publishing Industries (Except Internet) (33.8%); Management of Companies and Enterprises (30.4%); Merchant Wholesalers, Durable Goods (30.1%); Educational Services, Public and Private (29.1%); Local Government (27.2%); Broadcasting (Except Internet) (24.0%); Merchant Wholesalers, Nondurable Goods (23.9%).

Other Considerations for Job Outlook: Demand for multimedia artists and animators will increase as consumers continue to demand more realistic video games, movie and television special effects, and 3D animated movies. Additional job openings will arise from an increasing demand for Web site development and for computer graphics adaptation from the growing number of mobile technologies. Animators are also increasingly finding work in alternative areas such as scientific research or design services. Multi-media artists and animators should have better job opportunities than other artists, but still will experience competition. Job opportunities for animators of lower-technology cartoons could be hampered as these jobs continue to be outsourced overseas.

Create special effects, animation, or other visual images, using film, video, computers, or other electronic tools and media, for use in products or creations such as computer games, movies, music videos, and commercials. Design complex graphics and animation, using independent judgment, creativity, and computer equipment. Create two-dimensional and three-dimensional images depicting objects in motion or illustrating a process, using computer animation or modeling programs. Make objects or characters appear lifelike by manipulating light, color, texture, shadow, and transparency or manipulating static images to give the illusion of motion. Apply story development, directing, cinematography, and editing to animation to create storyboards that show the flow of the animation and map out key scenes and characters. Assemble, typeset, scan, and produce digital camera-ready art or film negatives and printer's proofs. Script, plan, and create animated narrative sequences under tight deadlines, using computer software and hand-drawing techniques. Create basic designs, drawings, and illustrations for product labels, cartons, direct mail, or television. Create pen-and-paper images to be scanned, edited, colored, textured, or animated by computer. Develop briefings, brochures, multimedia presentations, Web pages, promotional products, technical illustrations, and computer artwork for use in products, technical manuals, literature, newsletters, and slide shows. Use models to simulate the behavior of animated objects in the finished sequence. Create and install special effects as required by the script, mixing chemicals and fabricating needed parts from wood, metal, plaster, and clay. Participate in design and production of multimedia campaigns, handling budgeting and scheduling and assisting with such responsibilities as production coordination, background design, and progress tracking. Convert real objects to animated objects through modeling, using techniques such as optical scanning. Implement and maintain configuration control systems.

Personality Type: Artistic-Investigative.

Career Clusters: 03 Arts, Audio/Video Technology, and Communications; 11 Information Technology. **Career Pathways:** 03.1 Audio and Video Technology and Film; 03.2 Printing Technology; 03.3 Visual Arts; 11.1 Network Systems.

Skills: Operations Analysis; Technology Design; Time Management; Judgment and Decision Making; Science; Reading Comprehension.

Education and Training Programs: Animation, Interactive Technology, Video Graphics and Special Effects; Web Page, Digital/Multimedia and Information Resources Design; Graphic Design; Drawing; Intermedia/Multimedia; Painting; Printmaking. **Related Knowledge/Courses:** Fine Arts; Design; Computers and Electronics; Communications and Media; English Language.

Work Environment: Indoors; sitting; using hands on objects, tools, or controls; repetitive motions.

Network and Computer Systems Administrators

- ❋ Education/Training Required: Bachelor's degree
- ❋ Annual Earnings: $64,690
- ❋ Beginning Wage: $39,970
- ❋ Earnings Growth Potential: Medium (38.2%)
- ❋ Growth: 27.0%
- ❋ Annual Job Openings: 37,010
- ❋ Job Security: More Secure than Most
- ❋ Self-Employed: 0.4%
- ❋ Part-Time: 3.1%

Our sources did not provide separate job openings data for this occupation. The job openings listed here are shared with Computer Security Specialists.

Renewal Industry: Information and Telecommunication Technologies.

Industries with Greatest Employment: Professional, Scientific, and Technical Services (25.0%); Educational Services, Public and Private (10.0%); Management of Companies and Enterprises (6.0%).

Highest-Growth Industries (Projected Growth for This Job): Amusement, Gambling, and Recreation Industries (66.1%); Social Assistance (58.3%); Securities, Commodity Contracts, and Other Financial Investments and Related Activities (58.2%); Internet Publishing and Broadcasting (54.3%); Museums, Historical Sites, and Similar Institutions (49.6%); Professional, Scientific, and Technical Services (47.2%); Warehousing and Storage (46.9%); Personal and Laundry Services (40.4%); Lessors of Nonfinancial Intangible Assets (Except Copyrighted Works) (40.1%); Building Material and Garden Equipment and Supplies Dealers (39.8%); Waste Management and Remediation Services (39.7%); Administrative and Support Services (39.0%); Ambulatory Health-Care Services (38.7%); Performing Arts, Spectator Sports, and Related Industries (38.0%); Nursing and Residential Care Facilities (37.4%); Support Activities for Transportation (34.5%); Water Transportation (33.7%); Real Estate (32.9%); Nonstore Retailers (31.7%); Religious, Grantmaking, Civic, Professional, and Similar Organizations (30.4%); Publishing Industries (Except Internet) (28.8%); Accommodation, Including Hotels and Motels (27.8%); Motion Picture, Video, and Sound Recording Industries (27.7%); Rental and Leasing Services (27.5%); General Merchandise Stores (26.9%); Broadcasting (Except Internet) (26.8%); Management of Companies and Enterprises (26.8%); Merchant Wholesalers, Durable Goods (26.1%); Transit and Ground Passenger Transportation (25.4%); Motor Vehicle and Parts Dealers (24.9%); Wholesale Electronic Markets and Agents and Brokers (24.8%); Truck Transportation (24.3%); Construction of Buildings (23.6%); Local Government (23.6%); Food Services and Drinking Places (21.9%); Air Transportation (21.6%); Chemical Manufacturing (21.6%); Hospitals, Public and Private (21.3%); Internet Service Providers, Web Search Portals, and Data Processing Services (21.2%); Educational Services, Public and Private (21.0%); Couriers and Messengers (19.1%); Credit Intermediation and Related Activities (19.0%); Food and Beverage Stores (18.8%); Specialty Trade Contractors (18.2%); Insurance Carriers and Related Activities (18.0%); Health and Personal Care Stores (17.8%); Furniture and Home Furnishings Stores (16.5%); Mining (Except Oil and Gas) (15.7%); Merchant Wholesalers, Nondurable Goods (15.5%).

Other Considerations for Job Outlook: Although employment may be tempered somewhat by offshore outsourcing, strong employment growth combined with a limited supply of qualified workers will result in very good employment prospects for this occupation. Individuals with an advanced degree in computer science or computer engineering or with an MBA with a concentration in information systems should enjoy favorable employment prospects. College graduates with a bachelor's degree in computer science, computer engineering, information science, or MIS also should enjoy favorable prospects, particularly if they have supplemented their formal education with practical experience.

Install, configure, and support organizations' local area networks (LANs), wide area networks (WANs), and Internet systems or segments of network systems. Maintain network hardware and software. Monitor networks to ensure network availability to all system users and perform necessary maintenance to support network availability. May supervise other network support and client server specialists and plan, coordinate, and implement network security measures. Maintain and administer computer networks and related computing environments, including computer hardware, systems software, applications software, and all configurations. Perform data backups and disaster recovery operations. Diagnose, troubleshoot, and resolve hardware, software, or other network and system problems and replace defective components when necessary. Plan, coordinate, and implement network security measures to protect data, software, and hardware. Configure, monitor, and maintain e-mail applications or virus protection software. Operate master consoles to monitor the performance of computer systems and networks and to coordinate computer network access and use. Load computer tapes and disks and install software and printer paper or forms. Design, configure, and test computer hardware, networking software, and operating system software. Monitor network performance to determine whether adjustments need to be made and to determine where changes will need to be made in the future. Confer with network users about how to solve existing system problems. Research new technologies by attending seminars, reading trade articles, or taking classes and implement or recommend the implementation of new technologies. Analyze equipment performance records to determine the need for repair or replacement. Implement and provide technical support for voice services and equipment such as private branch exchanges, voice mail systems, and telecom systems. Maintain inventories of parts for emergency repairs. Recommend changes to improve systems and network configurations and determine hardware or software requirements related to such changes. Gather data pertaining to customer needs and use the information to identify, predict, interpret, and evaluate system and network requirements. Train people in computer system use. Coordinate with vendors and with company personnel to facilitate purchases. Perform routine network startup and shutdown procedures and maintain control records. Maintain logs related to network functions, as well as maintenance and repair records.

Personality Type: Investigative-Realistic-Conventional.

Career Cluster: 11 Information Technology. **Career Pathways:** 11.1 Network Systems; 11.2 Information Support Services; 11.4 Programming and Software Development.

Skills: No data available.

Education and Training Programs: Computer and Information Sciences and Support Services, Other; Computer and Information Sciences, General; Computer and

Information Systems Security; Computer Systems Analysis/Analyst; Computer Systems Networking and Telecommunications; Information Science/Studies; System Administration/Administrator; System, Networking, and LAN/WAN Management/Manager. **Related Knowledge/Courses:** Telecommunications; Computers and Electronics; Clerical Practices; Administration and Management; Engineering and Technology.

Work Environment: Indoors; noisy; sitting; using hands on objects, tools, or controls; repetitive motions.

Network Designers

- ✳ Education/Training Required: No data available.
- ✳ Annual Earnings: $71,510
- ✳ Beginning Wage: $37,600
- ✳ Earnings Growth Potential: High (47.4%)
- ✳ Growth: 15.1%
- ✳ Annual Job Openings: 14,374
- ✳ Job Security: More Secure than Most
- ✳ Self-Employed: 6.6%
- ✳ Part-Time: 5.6%

Our sources did not provide separate job openings data for this occupation. The job openings listed here are shared with Computer Systems Engineers/Architects, Software Quality Assurance Engineers and Testers, Web Administrators, and Web Developers.

Renewal Industry: Information and Telecommunication Technologies.

Industries with Greatest Employment: Professional, Scientific, and Technical Services (22.9%); Educational Services, Public and Private (10.0%); Management of Companies and Enterprises (8.0%); State Government (5.5%).

Highest-Growth Industries (Projected Growth for This Job): Amusement, Gambling, and Recreation Industries (53.3%); Securities, Commodity Contracts, and Other Financial Investments and Related Activities (46.9%); Social Assistance (44.2%); Internet Publishing and Broadcasting (40.3%); Warehousing and Storage (33.3%); Professional, Scientific, and Technical Services (31.4%); Real Estate (25.8%); General Merchandise Stores (25.0%);

Nursing and Residential Care Facilities (24.8%); Ambulatory Health-Care Services (24.7%); Building Material and Garden Equipment and Supplies Dealers (24.2%); Publishing Industries (Except Internet) (21.7%); Nonstore Retailers (21.4%); Religious, Grantmaking, Civic, Professional, and Similar Organizations (19.6%); Chemical Manufacturing (19.0%); Merchant Wholesalers, Durable Goods (15.9%); Management of Companies and Enterprises (15.3%).

Other Considerations for Job Outlook: Given the rate at which the computer systems design and related services industry is expected to grow, and the increasing complexity of technology, job opportunities should be favorable for most workers. The best opportunities will be in professional and related occupations, reflecting their growth and the continuing demand for higher level skills to keep up with changes in technology. In addition, as individuals and organizations continue to conduct business electronically, the importance of maintaining system and network security will increase.

Determine user requirements and design specifications for computer networks. Plan and implement network upgrades. Develop network-related documentation. Design, build, or operate equipment configuration prototypes, including network hardware, software, servers, or server operation systems. Coordinate network operations, maintenance, repairs, or upgrades. Adjust network sizes to meet volume or capacity demands. Communicate with vendors to gather information about products, to alert them to future needs, to resolve problems, or to address system maintenance issues. Coordinate installation of new equipment. Coordinate network or design activities with designers of associated networks. Design, organize, and deliver product awareness, skills transfer, and product education sessions for staff and suppliers. Determine specific network hardware or software requirements, such as platforms, interfaces, bandwidths, or routine schemas. Develop disaster recovery plans. Communicate with customers, sales staff, or marketing staff to determine customer needs. Explain design specifications to integration or test engineers. Develop plans or budgets for network equipment replacement. Prepare design presentations and proposals for staff or customers. Supervise engineers and other staff in the design or implementation of network solutions. Use network computer-aided design (CAD) software packages to optimize network designs. Develop or maintain

project reporting systems. Participate in network technology upgrade or expansion projects, including installation of hardware and software and integration testing. Research and test new or modified hardware or software products to determine performance and interoperability. Develop and implement solutions for network problems. Prepare or monitor project schedules, budgets, or cost control systems. Monitor and analyze network performance and data input/output reports to detect problems, identify inefficient use of computer resources, or perform capacity planning. Evaluate network designs to determine whether customer requirements are met efficiently and effectively. Estimate time and materials needed to complete projects. Develop or recommend network security measures, such as firewalls, network security audits, or automated security probes.

Personality Type: Conventional-Investigative-Realistic.

Career Cluster: 11 Information Technology. **Career Pathway:** 11.2 Programming and Software Development.

Skills: No data available.

Education and Training Programs: Computer and Information Sciences, General; Computer Science; Computer Systems Networking and Telecommunications; Computer Engineering, General; Computer Software Engineering.

Work Environment: No data available.

Network Systems and Data Communications Analysts

- ✸ Education/Training Required: Bachelor's degree
- ✸ Annual Earnings: $68,220
- ✸ Beginning Wage: $40,100
- ✸ Earnings Growth Potential: High (41.2%)
- ✸ Growth: 53.4%
- ✸ Annual Job Openings: 35,086
- ✸ Job Security: More Secure than Most
- ✸ Self-Employed: 17.5%
- ✸ Part-Time: 8.6%

Renewal Industry: Information and Telecommunication Technologies.

Industries with Greatest Employment: Professional, Scientific, and Technical Services (21.1%);

Telecommunications (8.1%); Management of Companies and Enterprises (6.1%).

Highest-Growth Industries (Projected Growth for This Job): Securities, Commodity Contracts, and Other Financial Investments and Related Activities (94.4%); Social Assistance (90.4%); Internet Publishing and Broadcasting (89.4%); Amusement, Gambling, and Recreation Industries (84.3%); Museums, Historical Sites, and Similar Institutions (83.8%); Professional, Scientific, and Technical Services (83.8%); Warehousing and Storage (80.4%); Waste Management and Remediation Services (76.9%); Personal and Laundry Services (72.9%); Lessors of Nonfinancial Intangible Assets (Except Copyrighted Works) (72.4%); Administrative and Support Services (71.7%); Funds, Trusts, and Other Financial Vehicles (70.9%); Ambulatory Health-Care Services (70.0%); Nursing and Residential Care Facilities (69.3%); Performing Arts, Spectator Sports, and Related Industries (69.2%); Nonstore Retailers (66.7%); Building Material and Garden Equipment and Supplies Dealers (66.7%); Real Estate (64.7%); Support Activities for Transportation (62.4%); Religious, Grantmaking, Civic, Professional, and Similar Organizations (60.3%); Rental and Leasing Services (59.0%); Accommodation, Including Hotels and Motels (57.8%); Merchant Wholesalers, Durable Goods (56.2%); Management of Companies and Enterprises (55.6%); Wholesale Electronic Markets and Agents and Brokers (53.2%); Publishing Industries (Except Internet) (52.5%); Construction of Buildings (51.7%); Local Government (51.7%); Food Services and Drinking Places (51.6%); Motor Vehicle and Parts Dealers (50.7%); Educational Services, Public and Private (50.5%); Broadcasting (Except Internet) (50.2%); Hospitals, Public and Private (49.5%); Air Transportation (49.2%); Motion Picture, Video, and Sound Recording Industries (47.8%); Merchant Wholesalers, Nondurable Goods (47.0%); Credit Intermediation and Related Activities (46.4%); Furniture and Home Furnishings Stores (45.6%); Health and Personal Care Stores (44.3%); Specialty Trade Contractors (42.9%); Chemical Manufacturing (42.6%); Insurance Carriers and Related Activities (42.6%); Heavy and Civil Engineering Construction (40.6%); Internet Service Providers, Web Search Portals, and Data Processing Services (39.7%); Sporting Goods, Hobby, Book, and Music Stores (36.3%); Plastics and Rubber Products Manufacturing (36.2%); Food Manufacturing (35.4%); Clothing and Clothing Accessories Stores (33.3%); Oil and Gas Extraction (32.7%); State Government (32.5%); Transportation Equipment Manufacturing (32.3%); Nonmetallic Mineral Product Manufacturing (30.2%); Miscellaneous Manufacturing (29.2%); Wood Product Manufacturing (29.2%); Federal Government (28.4%); Furniture and Related Product Manufacturing (26.8%); Telecommunications (26.1%); Repair and Maintenance (25.6%); Utilities (23.5%); Machinery Manufacturing (20.1%); Monetary Authorities–Central Bank (18.7%); Fabricated Metal Product Manufacturing (18.7%); Computer and Electronic Product Manufacturing (16.7%); Rail Transportation (16.1%).

Other Considerations for Job Outlook: Strong employment growth combined with a limited supply of qualified workers will result in excellent employment prospects for this occupation and a high demand for their skills. There is growing demand for network systems and data communication analysts to help firms maximize their efficiency with available technology. Individuals with an advanced degree in computer science or computer engineering or with an MBA with a concentration in information systems should enjoy favorable employment prospects. College graduates with a bachelor's degree in computer science, computer engineering, information science, or MIS also should enjoy favorable prospects, particularly if they have supplemented their formal education with practical experience.

Analyze, design, test, and evaluate network systems, such as local area networks (LAN); wide area networks (WAN); and Internet, intranet, and other data communications systems. Perform network modeling, analysis, and planning. Research and recommend network and data communications hardware and software. Includes telecommunications specialists who deal with the interfacing of computer and communications equipment. May supervise computer programmers. Maintain needed files by adding and deleting files on the network server and backing up files to guarantee their safety in the event of problems with the network. Monitor system performance and provide security measures, troubleshooting, and maintenance as needed. Assist users to diagnose and solve data communication problems. Set up user accounts, regulating and monitoring file access to ensure confidentiality and proper use. Design and implement systems, network configurations, and network architecture, including hardware and software technology, site locations, and integration of technologies. Maintain the peripherals, such as printers, that are connected to the network. Identify areas of operation that need upgraded equipment such as modems, fiber-optic cables, and telephone wires. Train users in use of equipment. Develop and write procedures for installation, use, and troubleshooting of communications hardware and software. Adapt and modify existing software to meet specific needs. Work with other engineers, systems analysts, programmers, technicians, scientists, and top-level managers in the design, testing, and evaluation of systems. Test and evaluate hardware and software to determine efficiency, reliability, and compatibility with existing system and make purchase recommendations. Read technical manuals and brochures to determine which equipment meets establishment requirements. Consult customers, visit workplaces, or conduct surveys to determine present and future user needs. Visit vendors, attend conferences or training, and study technical journals to keep up with changes in technology.

Personality Type: Investigative-Conventional.

Career Cluster: 11 Information Technology. **Career Pathways:** 11.1 Network Systems; 11.2 Information Support Services; 11.4 Programming and Software Development.

Skills: Installation; Technology Design; Troubleshooting; Systems Analysis; Programming; Systems Evaluation.

Education and Training Programs: Computer and Information Sciences, General; Information Technology; Computer Systems Analysis/Analyst; Computer Systems Networking and Telecommunications; System, Networking, and LAN/WAN Management/Manager; Computer and Information Systems Security. **Related Knowledge/Courses:** Telecommunications; Computers and Electronics; Customer and Personal Service; Engineering and Technology; Education and Training; Design.

Work Environment: Indoors; sitting.

Nuclear Engineers

- ❈ Education/Training Required: Bachelor's degree
- ❈ Annual Earnings: $94,420
- ❈ Beginning Wage: $66,460
- ❈ Earnings Growth Potential: Low (29.6%)
- ❈ Growth: 7.2%
- ❈ Annual Job Openings: 1,046
- ❈ Job Security: More Secure than Most
- ❈ Self-Employed: 0.0%
- ❈ Part-Time: 2.9%

Renewal Industry: Green Technologies.

Industries with Greatest Employment: Professional, Scientific, and Technical Services (42.7%); Utilities (28.9%); Federal Government (14.0%).

Highest-Growth Industries (Projected Growth for This Job): None met the criteria.

Other Considerations for Job Outlook: Most job growth will be in research and development and engineering services. Although no commercial nuclear power plants have been built in the United States for many years, nuclear engineers will be needed to operate existing plants and design new ones, including researching future nuclear power sources. They also will be needed to work in defense-related areas, to develop nuclear medical technology, and to improve and enforce waste management and safety standards. Nuclear engineers are expected to have good employment opportunities because the small number of nuclear engineering graduates is likely to be in rough balance with the number of job openings.

Conduct research on nuclear engineering problems or apply principles and theory of nuclear science to problems concerned with release, control, and utilization of nuclear energy and nuclear waste disposal. Examine accidents to obtain data that can be used to design preventive measures. Monitor nuclear facility operations to identify any design, construction, or operation practices that violate safety regulations and laws or that could jeopardize the safety of operations. Keep abreast of developments and changes in the nuclear field by reading technical journals and by independent study and research. Perform experiments that will provide information about acceptable methods of nuclear material usage, nuclear fuel reclamation, and waste disposal. Design and oversee construction and operation of nuclear reactors and power plants and nuclear fuels reprocessing and reclamation systems. Design and develop nuclear equipment such as reactor cores, radiation shielding, and associated instrumentation and control mechanisms. Initiate corrective actions or order plant shutdowns in emergency situations. Recommend preventive measures to be taken in the handling of nuclear technology, based on data obtained from operations monitoring or from evaluation of test results. Write operational instructions to be used in nuclear plant operation and nuclear fuel and waste handling and disposal. Conduct tests of nuclear fuel behavior and cycles and performance of nuclear machinery and equipment to optimize performance of existing plants. Direct operating and maintenance activities of operational nuclear power plants to ensure efficiency and conformity to safety standards. Synthesize analyses of test results and use the results to prepare technical reports of findings and recommendations. Prepare construction project proposals that include cost estimates and discuss proposals with interested parties such as vendors, contractors, and nuclear facility review boards. Analyze available data and consult with other scientists to determine parameters of experimentation and suitability of analytical models. Design and direct nuclear research projects to discover facts, to test or modify theoretical models, or to develop new theoretical models or new uses for current models.

Personality Type: Investigative-Realistic-Conventional.

Career Cluster: 15 Science, Technology, Engineering, and Mathematics. **Career Pathway:** 15.1 Engineering and Technology.

Skills: Operation Monitoring; Technology Design; Systems Evaluation; Systems Analysis; Operations Analysis; Quality Control Analysis.

Education and Training Program: Nuclear Engineering. **Related Knowledge/Courses:** Engineering and Technology; Physics; Design; Chemistry; Mechanical Devices; Building and Construction.

Work Environment: Indoors; noisy; radiation; sitting.

Nuclear Medicine Technologists

- ❀ Education/Training Required: Associate degree
- ❀ Annual Earnings: $64,670
- ❀ Beginning Wage: $47,370
- ❀ Earnings Growth Potential: Low (26.8%)
- ❀ Growth: 14.8%
- ❀ Annual Job Openings: 1,290
- ❀ Job Security: Most Secure
- ❀ Self-Employed: 1.0%
- ❀ Part-Time: 17.3%

Renewal Industry: Health Care.

Industries with Greatest Employment: Hospitals, Public and Private (66.8%); Ambulatory Health-Care Services (29.5%).

Highest-Growth Industries (Projected Growth for This Job): Ambulatory Health-Care Services (23.8%).

Other Considerations for Job Outlook: In spite of fast growth in nuclear medicine, the number of openings into the occupation each year will be relatively low because of the small size of the occupation. Technologists who have additional training in other diagnostic methods, such as radiologic technology or diagnostic medical sonography, will have the best prospects.

Prepare, administer, and measure radioactive isotopes in therapeutic, diagnostic, and tracer studies, using a variety of radioisotope equipment. Prepare stock solutions of radioactive materials and calculate doses to be administered by radiologists. Subject patients to radiation. Execute blood volume, red cell survival, and fat absorption studies, following standard laboratory techniques. Detect and map radiopharmaceuticals in patients' bodies, using a camera to produce photographic or computer images. Administer radiopharmaceuticals or radiation intravenously to detect or treat diseases, using radioisotope equipment, under direction of a physician. Produce computer-generated or film images for interpretation by physicians. Calculate, measure, and record radiation dosages or radiopharmaceuticals received, used, and disposed, using computers and following physicians' prescriptions. Perform quality control checks on laboratory equipment and cameras. Maintain and calibrate radioisotope and laboratory equipment. Dispose of radioactive materials and store radiopharmaceuticals, following radiation safety procedures. Process cardiac function studies, using computers. Prepare stock radiopharmaceuticals, adhering to safety standards that minimize radiation exposure to workers and patients. Record and process results of procedures. Explain test procedures and safety precautions to patients and provide them with assistance during test procedures. Gather information on patients' illnesses and medical histories to guide choices of diagnostic procedures for therapies. Measure glandular activity, blood volume, red cell survival, and radioactivity of patient, using scanners, Geiger counters, scintillation counters, and other laboratory equipment. Train and supervise student or subordinate nuclear medicine technologists. Position radiation fields, radiation beams, and patients to allow for most effective treatment of patients' diseases, using computers. Add radioactive substances to biological specimens such as blood, urine, and feces to determine therapeutic drug or hormone levels. Develop treatment procedures for nuclear medicine treatment programs.

Personality Type: Investigative-Realistic-Social.

Career Cluster: 08 Health Science. **Career Pathways:** 08.1 Therapeutic Services; 08.2 Diagnostics Services.

Skills: No data available.

Education and Training Programs: Nuclear Medical Technology/Technologist; Radiation Protection/Health Physics Technician. **Related Knowledge/Courses:** Medicine and Dentistry; Biology; Chemistry; Physics; Customer and Personal Service; Therapy and Counseling.

Work Environment: Indoors; contaminants; radiation; disease or infections; standing; using hands on objects, tools, or controls.

Nursing Aides, Orderlies, and Attendants

- ❋ Education/Training Required: Postsecondary vocational training
- ❋ Annual Earnings: $23,160
- ❋ Beginning Wage: $16,850
- ❋ Earnings Growth Potential: Low (27.2%)
- ❋ Growth: 18.2%
- ❋ Annual Job Openings: 321,036
- ❋ Job Security: Most Secure
- ❋ Self-Employed: 2.4%
- ❋ Part-Time: 24.0%

Renewal Industry: Health Care.

Industries with Greatest Employment: Nursing and Residential Care Facilities (52.0%); Hospitals, Public and Private (28.9%).

Highest-Growth Industries (Projected Growth for This Job): Social Assistance (55.0%); Ambulatory Health-Care Services (42.3%); Administrative and Support Services (26.7%); Professional, Scientific, and Technical Services (24.4%); Hospitals, Public and Private (21.8%); Religious, Grantmaking, Civic, Professional, and Similar Organizations (19.9%); Management of Companies and Enterprises (15.3%).

Other Considerations for Job Outlook: Excellent job opportunities for nursing, psychiatric, and home health aides will arise from a combination of rapid employment growth and the need to replace the many workers who leave the occupation each year. The occupation has high turnover because of the modest entry requirements, low pay, high physical and emotional demands, and limited opportunities for advancement within the occupation. For these same reasons, the number of people looking to enter the occupation will be limited. Many aides leave the occupation to attend training programs for other health care occupations. Therefore, people who are interested in, and suited for, this work should have excellent job opportunities.

Provide basic patient care under direction of nursing staffs. Perform duties such as feeding, bathing, dressing, grooming, or moving patients or changing linens. Answer patients' call signals. Turn and reposition bedridden patients, alone or with assistance, to prevent bedsores.

Observe patients' conditions, measuring and recording food and liquid intake and output and vital signs, reporting changes to professionals. Feed patients who are unable to feed themselves. Provide patients with help walking, exercising, and moving in and out of bed. Provide patient care by supplying and emptying bed pans, applying dressings, and supervising exercise routines. Bathe, groom, shave, dress, or drape patients to prepare them for surgery, treatment, or examination. Transport patients to treatment units, using a wheelchair or stretcher. Clean rooms and change linens. Collect specimens such as urine, feces, or sputum. Prepare, serve, and collect food trays. Deliver messages, documents, and specimens. Answer phones and direct visitors. Restrain patients if necessary. Set up equipment such as oxygen tents, portable X-ray machines, and overhead irrigation bottles. Explain medical instructions to patients and family members. Work as part of a medical team that examines and treats clinic outpatients. Maintain inventories by storing, preparing, sterilizing, and issuing supplies such as dressing packs and treatment trays. Administer medications and treatments such as catheterizations, suppositories, irrigations, enemas, massages, and douches as directed by a physician or nurse. Perform clerical duties such as processing documents and scheduling appointments.

Personality Type: Social-Realistic-Conventional.

Career Cluster: 08 Health Science. **Career Pathway:** 08.1 Therapeutic Services.

Skills: No data available.

Education and Training Programs: Nurse/Nursing Assistant/Aide and Patient Care Assistant; Health Aide. **Related Knowledge/Courses:** Medicine and Dentistry; Psychology; Therapy and Counseling; Customer and Personal Service.

Work Environment: Disease or infections; standing; walking and running; using hands on objects, tools, or controls; bending or twisting the body; repetitive motions.

Nursing Instructors and Teachers, Postsecondary

* Education/Training Required: Master's degree
* Annual Earnings: $57,500
* Beginning Wage: $36,020
* Earnings Growth Potential: Medium (37.4%)
* Growth: 22.9%
* Annual Job Openings: 7,337
* Job Security: Most Secure
* Self-Employed: 0.4%
* Part-Time: 27.8%

Renewal Industry: Education.

Industries with Greatest Employment: Educational Services, Public and Private (97.3%).

Highest-Growth Industries (Projected Growth for This Job): Administrative and Support Services (48.3%); Amusement, Gambling, and Recreation Industries (45.2%); Social Assistance (38.6%); Support Activities for Transportation (32.8%); Religious, Grantmaking, Civic, Professional, and Similar Organizations (29.9%); Professional, Scientific, and Technical Services (28.8%); Management of Companies and Enterprises (26.8%); Local Government (23.5%); Educational Services, Public and Private (22.8%); Hospitals, Public and Private (21.4%).

Other Considerations for Job Outlook: Retirements of current postsecondary teachers should create numerous openings for all types of postsecondary teachers. However, one of the main reasons why students attend postsecondary institutions is to prepare themselves for careers, so the best job prospects for postsecondary teachers are likely to be in rapidly growing fields that offer many nonacademic career options, such as nursing. The demand for nurses continues to grow, and many who are qualified to teach are finding work outside of education, so job opportunities should be excellent. Community colleges and other institutions offering career and technical education have been among the most rapidly growing, and these institutions are expected to offer some of the best opportunities for postsecondary teachers.

Demonstrate and teach patient care in classroom and clinical units to nursing students. Includes both

teachers primarily engaged in teaching and those who do a combination of both teaching and research. Initiate, facilitate, and moderate classroom discussions. Prepare and deliver lectures to undergraduate or graduate students on topics such as pharmacology, mental health nursing, and community health-care practices. Keep abreast of developments in their field by reading current literature, talking with colleagues, and participating in professional conferences. Prepare course materials such as syllabi, homework assignments, and handouts. Supervise students' laboratory and clinical work. Evaluate and grade students' classwork, laboratory and clinic work, assignments, and papers. Collaborate with colleagues to address teaching and research issues. Plan, evaluate, and revise curricula, course content, and course materials and methods of instruction. Assess clinical education needs and patient and client teaching needs, utilizing a variety of methods. Compile, administer, and grade examinations or assign this work to others. Advise students on academic and vocational curricula and on career issues. Maintain student attendance records, grades, and other required records. Maintain regularly scheduled office hours to advise and assist students. Supervise undergraduate or graduate teaching, internship, and research work. Conduct research in a particular field of knowledge and publish findings in professional journals, books, and/or electronic media. Participate in student recruitment, registration, and placement activities. Serve on academic or administrative committees that deal with institutional policies, departmental matters, and academic issues. Coordinate training programs with area universities, clinics, hospitals, health agencies, and/or vocational schools. Compile bibliographies of specialized materials for outside reading assignments. Select and obtain materials and supplies such as textbooks and laboratory equipment. Participate in campus and community events. Write grant proposals to procure external research funding. Act as advisers to student organizations. Demonstrate patient care in clinical units of hospitals. Perform administrative duties such as serving as department head.

Personality Type: Social-Investigative.

Career Cluster: 08 Health Science. **Career Pathway:** 08.1 Therapeutic Services.

Skills: Science; Instructing; Writing; Social Perceptiveness; Reading Comprehension; Learning Strategies.

Education and Training Programs: Pre-Nursing Studies; Nursing—Registered Nurse Training (RN, ASN, BSN, MSN); Adult Health Nurse/Nursing; Nurse Anesthetist; Family Practice Nurse/Nurse Practitioner; Maternal/Child Health and Neonatal Nurse/Nursing; Nurse Midwife/Nursing Midwifery; Nursing Science (MS, PhD); Pediatric Nurse/Nursing; Psychiatric/Mental Health Nurse/Nursing; Public Health/Community Nurse/Nursing; others. **Related Knowledge/Courses:** Therapy and Counseling; Biology; Sociology and Anthropology; Medicine and Dentistry; Philosophy and Theology; Psychology.

Work Environment: Indoors; disease or infections; sitting.

Obstetricians and Gynecologists

- ✸ Education/Training Required: First professional degree
- ✸ Annual Earnings: More than $145,600
- ✸ Beginning Wage: $100,770
- ✸ Earnings Growth Potential: Cannot be calculated
- ✸ Growth: 14.2%
- ✸ Annual Job Openings: 38,027
- ✸ Job Security: Most Secure
- ✸ Self-Employed: 14.7%
- ✸ Part-Time: 8.1%

Our sources did not provide separate job openings data for this occupation. The job openings listed here are shared with Anesthesiologists; Family and General Practitioners; Internists, General; Pediatricians, General; Psychiatrists; and Surgeons.

Renewal Industry: Health Care.

Industries with Greatest Employment: Ambulatory Health-Care Services (55.9%); Hospitals, Public and Private (17.8%).

Highest-Growth Industries (Projected Growth for This Job): Social Assistance (58.6%); Administrative and Support Services (26.8%); Professional, Scientific, and Technical Services (22.6%); Nursing and Residential Care Facilities (21.0%); Ambulatory Health-Care Services (19.4%); Religious, Grantmaking, Civic, Professional, and

Similar Organizations (16.7%); Management of Companies and Enterprises (15.3%).

Other Considerations for Job Outlook: Opportunities for individuals interested in becoming physicians and surgeons are expected to be very good. Unlike their predecessors, new physicians are much less likely to enter solo practice and more likely to take salaried jobs in group medical practices, clinics, and health networks. Reports of shortages in some specialties, such as general or family practice, internal medicine, and OB/GYN, or in rural or low-income areas should attract new entrants, encouraging schools to expand programs and hospitals to increase available residency slots. However, because physician training is so lengthy, employment change happens gradually. Opportunities should be particularly good in rural and low-income areas, as some physicians find these areas unattractive because of less control over work hours, isolation from medical colleagues, or other reasons.

Diagnose, treat, and help prevent diseases of women, especially those affecting the reproductive system and the process of childbirth. Care for and treat women during prenatal, natal, and post-natal periods. Explain procedures and discuss test results or prescribed treatments with patients. Treat diseases of female organs. Monitor patients' condition and progress and re-evaluate treatments as necessary. Perform cesarean sections or other surgical procedures as needed to preserve patients' health and deliver babies safely. Prescribe or administer therapy, medication, and other specialized medical care to treat or prevent illness, disease, or injury. Analyze records, reports, test results, or examination information to diagnose medical condition of patient. Collect, record, and maintain patient information, such as medical histories, reports, and examination results. Advise patients and community members concerning diet, activity, hygiene, and disease prevention. Refer patient to medical specialist or other practitioner when necessary. Consult with, or provide consulting services to, other physicians. Direct and coordinate activities of nurses, students, assistants, specialists, therapists, and other medical staff. Plan, implement, or administer health programs in hospitals, businesses, or communities for prevention and treatment of injuries or illnesses. Prepare government and organizational reports on birth, death, and disease statistics; workforce evaluations; or the medical status of individuals. Conduct research to develop or test medications, treatments, or procedures to prevent or control disease or injury.

Personality Type: Investigative-Social-Realistic.

Career Cluster: 08 Health Science. **Career Pathway:** 08.1 Therapeutic Services.

Skills: Science; Judgment and Decision Making; Reading Comprehension; Complex Problem Solving; Active Learning; Social Perceptiveness.

Education and Training Programs: Neonatal-Perinatal Medicine; Obstetrics and Gynecology. **Related Knowledge/Courses:** Medicine and Dentistry; Therapy and Counseling; Biology; Psychology; Sociology and Anthropology; Chemistry.

Work Environment: Indoors; disease or infections; standing; using hands on objects, tools, or controls.

Occupational Health and Safety Specialists

- ❀ Education/Training Required: Bachelor's degree
- ❀ Annual Earnings: $60,140
- ❀ Beginning Wage: $35,990
- ❀ Earnings Growth Potential: High (40.2%)
- ❀ Growth: 8.1%
- ❀ Annual Job Openings: 3,440
- ❀ Job Security: More Secure than Most
- ❀ Self-Employed: 2.4%
- ❀ Part-Time: 8.0%

Renewal Industries: Advanced Manufacturing; Health Care.

Industries with Greatest Employment: Federal Government (15.4%); Local Government (14.6%); State Government (13.3%); Professional, Scientific, and Technical Services (8.3%); Hospitals, Public and Private (6.2%).

Highest-Growth Industries (Projected Growth for This Job): Professional, Scientific, and Technical Services (51.4%); Amusement, Gambling, and Recreation Industries (47.3%); Warehousing and Storage (33.6%); Ambulatory Health-Care Services (29.8%); Administrative and Support Services (28.3%); Waste Management and Remediation Services (27.8%); Social Assistance (27.0%); Real Estate (24.6%); Support Activities for Transportation (23.5%); Nursing and Residential Care Facilities (23.4%);

Religious, Grantmaking, Civic, Professional, and Similar Organizations (18.9%); Management of Companies and Enterprises (15.3%).

Other Considerations for Job Outlook: An aging population paired with a decline in the number of postsecondary students studying the sciences, especially health physics, will create opportunities for those with technical skill. Federal, state, and local governments, which employ about 2 out of 5 of all specialists and technicians, provide considerable job security; workers in the private sector may be affected by changes in the economy.

Review, evaluate, and analyze work environments and design programs and procedures to control, eliminate, and prevent diseases or injuries caused by chemical, physical, and biological agents or ergonomic factors. May conduct inspections and enforce adherence to laws and regulations governing health and safety of individuals. May be employed in public or private sector. Order suspension of activities that pose threats to workers' health and safety. Recommend measures to help protect workers from potentially hazardous work methods, processes, or materials. Investigate accidents to identify causes and to determine how such accidents might be prevented in the future. Investigate the adequacy of ventilation, exhaust equipment, lighting, and other conditions that could affect employee health, comfort, or performance. Develop and maintain hygiene programs such as noise surveys, continuous atmosphere monitoring, ventilation surveys, and asbestos management plans. Inspect and evaluate workplace environments, equipment, and practices in order to ensure compliance with safety standards and government regulations. Collaborate with engineers and physicians to institute control and remedial measures for hazardous and potentially hazardous conditions or equipment. Conduct safety training and education programs and demonstrate the use of safety equipment. Provide new-employee health and safety orientations and develop materials for these presentations. Collect samples of dust, gases, vapors, and other potentially toxic materials for analysis. Investigate health-related complaints and inspect facilities to ensure that they comply with public health legislation and regulations. Coordinate "right-to-know" programs regarding hazardous chemicals and other substances. Maintain and update emergency response plans and procedures. Develop and maintain medical monitoring programs for employees. Inspect specified areas to ensure the presence of fire prevention equipment, safety equipment, and first-aid supplies. Conduct audits at hazardous waste sites or industrial sites and participate in hazardous waste site investigations. Collect samples of hazardous materials or arrange for sample collection. Maintain inventories of hazardous materials and hazardous wastes, using waste tracking systems, to ensure that materials are handled properly. Prepare hazardous, radioactive, and mixed waste samples for transportation and storage by treating, compacting, packaging, and labeling them.

Personality Type: Investigative-Conventional.

Career Clusters: 01 Agriculture, Food, and Natural Resources; 08 Health Science; 13 Manufacturing; 16 Transportation, Distribution, and Logistics. **Career Pathways:** 01.6 Environmental Service Systems; 08.3 Health Informatics; 13.4 Quality Assurance; 16.1 Transportation Operations.

Skills: Science; Management of Financial Resources; Technology Design; Persuasion; Systems Analysis; Management of Material Resources.

Education and Training Programs: Occupational Safety and Health Technology/Technician; Industrial Safety Technology/Technician; Quality Control and Safety Technologies/Technicians, Other; Environmental Health; Occupational Health and Industrial Hygiene. **Related Knowledge/Courses:** Chemistry; Biology; Physics; Engineering and Technology; Public Safety and Security; Psychology.

Work Environment: More often indoors than outdoors; noisy; contaminants; sitting.

Occupational Therapist Assistants

* Education/Training Required: Associate degree
* Annual Earnings: $45,050
* Beginning Wage: $27,870
* Earnings Growth Potential: Medium (38.1%)
* Growth: 25.4%
* Annual Job Openings: 2,634
* Job Security: Most Secure
* Self-Employed: 3.5%
* Part-Time: 17.8%

Renewal Industry: Health Care.

Industries with Greatest Employment: Hospitals, Public and Private (29.6%); Ambulatory Health-Care Services (29.3%); Nursing and Residential Care Facilities (20.6%); Educational Services, Public and Private (6.8%).

Highest-Growth Industries (Projected Growth for This Job): Ambulatory Health-Care Services (45.3%); Social Assistance (36.6%); Administrative and Support Services (26.6%); Hospitals, Public and Private (20.2%); Management of Companies and Enterprises (15.1%).

Other Considerations for Job Outlook: Opportunities for individuals interested in becoming occupational therapist assistants are expected to be very good. In addition to employment growth, job openings will result from the need to replace occupational therapist assistants and aides who leave the occupation permanently over the 2006–2016 period. Occupational therapist assistants and aides with prior experience working in an occupational therapy office or other health care setting will have the best job opportunities. However, individuals with only a high school diploma may face keen competition for occupational therapist aide jobs.

Assist occupational therapists in providing occupational therapy treatments and procedures. May, in accordance with state laws, assist in development of treatment plans, carry out routine functions, direct activity programs, and document the progress of treatments. Generally requires formal training. Observe and record patients' progress, attitudes, and behavior and maintain this information in client records. Maintain and promote a positive attitude toward clients and their treatment programs. Monitor patients' performance in therapy activities, providing encouragement. Select therapy activities to fit patients' needs and capabilities. Instruct, or assist in instructing, patients and families in home programs, basic living skills, and the care and use of adaptive equipment. Evaluate the daily living skills and capacities of physically, developmentally, or emotionally disabled clients. Aid patients in dressing and grooming themselves. Implement, or assist occupational therapists with implementing, treatment plans designed to help clients function independently. Report to supervisors, verbally or in writing, on patients' progress, attitudes, and behavior. Alter treatment programs to obtain better results if treatment is not having the intended effect. Work under the direction of occupational therapists to plan, implement, and administer educational, vocational, and recreational programs that restore and enhance performance in individuals with functional impairments. Design, fabricate, and repair assistive devices and make adaptive changes to equipment and environments. Assemble, clean, and maintain equipment and materials for patient use. Teach patients how to deal constructively with their emotions. Perform clerical duties such as scheduling appointments, collecting data, and documenting health insurance billings. Transport patients to and from the occupational therapy work area. Demonstrate therapy techniques such as manual and creative arts or games. Order any needed educational or treatment supplies. Assist educational specialists or clinical psychologists in administering situational or diagnostic tests to measure client's abilities or progress.

Personality Type: Social-Realistic.

Career Cluster: 08 Health Science. **Career Pathway:** 08.1 Therapeutic Services.

Skills: Social Perceptiveness; Operations Analysis; Equipment Selection; Service Orientation; Writing; Persuasion.

Education and Training Program: Occupational Therapist Assistant. **Related Knowledge/Courses:** Therapy and Counseling; Psychology; Sociology and Anthropology; Philosophy and Theology; Medicine and Dentistry; Biology.

Work Environment: Indoors; disease or infections; standing; walking and running; using hands on objects, tools, or controls; bending or twisting the body.

Occupational Therapists

- ❀ Education/Training Required: Master's degree
- ❀ Annual Earnings: $63,790
- ❀ Beginning Wage: $42,330
- ❀ Earnings Growth Potential: Low (33.6%)
- ❀ Growth: 23.1%
- ❀ Annual Job Openings: 8,338
- ❀ Job Security: Most Secure
- ❀ Self-Employed: 8.6%
- ❀ Part-Time: 29.8%

Renewal Industry: Health Care.

Industries with Greatest Employment: Hospitals, Public and Private (29.2%); Ambulatory Health-Care Services (27.8%); Educational Services, Public and Private (12.7%); Nursing and Residential Care Facilities (9.9%); Social Assistance (5.2%).

Highest-Growth Industries (Projected Growth for This Job): Professional, Scientific, and Technical Services (64.0%); Social Assistance (38.0%); Ambulatory Health-Care Services (37.2%); Administrative and Support Services (26.6%); Nursing and Residential Care Facilities (23.9%); Hospitals, Public and Private (21.5%); Management of Companies and Enterprises (15.3%).

Other Considerations for Job Outlook: Job opportunities should be good for licensed occupational therapists in all settings, particularly in acute hospital, rehabilitation, and orthopedic settings because the elderly receive most of their treatment in these settings. Occupational therapists with specialized knowledge in a treatment area also will have increased job prospects. Driver rehabilitation and fall-prevention training for the elderly are emerging practice areas for occupational therapy.

Assess, plan, organize, and participate in rehabilitative programs that help restore vocational, homemaking, and daily living skills, as well as general independence, to disabled persons. Plan, organize, and conduct occupational therapy programs in hospital, institutional, or community settings to help rehabilitate those impaired because of illness, injury, or psychological or developmental problems. Test and evaluate patients' physical and mental abilities and analyze medical data to determine realistic rehabilitation goals for patients. Select activities that will help individuals learn work and life-management skills within limits of their mental and physical capabilities. Evaluate patients' progress and prepare reports that detail progress. Complete and maintain necessary records. Train caregivers to provide for the needs of patients during and after therapies. Recommend changes in patients' work or living environments consistent with their needs and capabilities. Develop and participate in health promotion programs, group activities, or discussions to promote client health, facilitate social adjustment, alleviate stress, and prevent physical or mental disability. Consult with rehabilitation team to select activity programs and coordinate occupational therapy with other therapeutic activities. Plan and implement programs and social activities to help patients learn work and school skills and adjust to handicaps. Design and create, or requisition, special supplies and equipment such as splints, braces, and computer-aided adaptive equipment. Conduct research in occupational therapy. Provide training and supervision in therapy techniques and objectives for students and nurses and other medical staff. Help clients improve decision making, abstract reasoning, memory, sequencing, coordination, and perceptual skills, using computer programs. Advise on health risks in the workplace and on health-related transition to retirement. Lay out materials such as puzzles, scissors, and eating utensils for use in therapy and clean and repair these tools after therapy sessions. Provide patients with assistance in locating and holding jobs.

Personality Type: Social-Investigative.

Career Cluster: 08 Health Science. **Career Pathway:** 08.3 Health Informatics.

Skills: No data available.

Education and Training Program: Occupational Therapy/Therapist. **Related Knowledge/Courses:** Therapy and Counseling; Psychology; Sociology and Anthropology; Medicine and Dentistry; Biology; Education and Training.

Work Environment: Indoors; disease or infections; standing; using hands on objects, tools, or controls; bending or twisting the body.

Operating Engineers and Other Construction Equipment Operators

- ❋ Education/Training Required: Moderate-term on-the-job training
- ❋ Annual Earnings: $38,130
- ❋ Beginning Wage: $24,840
- ❋ Earnings Growth Potential: Low (34.9%)
- ❋ Growth: 8.4%
- ❋ Annual Job Openings: 55,468
- ❋ Job Security: Least Secure
- ❋ Self-Employed: 5.7%
- ❋ Part-Time: 2.1%

Renewal Industries: Green Technologies; Infrastructure.

Industries with Greatest Employment: Specialty Trade Contractors (29.3%); Heavy and Civil Engineering

Construction (27.2%); Local Government (13.1%); Mining (Except Oil and Gas) (5.6%); Construction of Buildings (5.5%).

Highest-Growth Industries (Projected Growth for This Job): Professional, Scientific, and Technical Services (29.7%); Amusement, Gambling, and Recreation Industries (28.1%); Waste Management and Remediation Services (27.2%); Real Estate (22.5%); Administrative and Support Services (22.2%); Rental and Leasing Services (21.7%); Religious, Grantmaking, Civic, Professional, and Similar Organizations (16.0%); Management of Companies and Enterprises (15.3%).

Other Considerations for Job Outlook: Construction equipment operators who can use a large variety of equipment will have the best prospects. Operators with pipeline experience will have especially good opportunities.

Operate one or several types of power construction equipment, such as motor graders, bulldozers, scrapers, compressors, pumps, derricks, shovels, tractors, or front-end loaders, to excavate, move, and grade earth; erect structures; or pour concrete or other hard-surface pavement. May repair and maintain equipment in addition to other duties. Learn and follow safety regulations. Take actions to avoid potential hazards and obstructions such as utility lines, other equipment, other workers, and falling objects. Adjust handwheels and depress pedals to control attachments such as blades, buckets, scrapers, and swing booms. Start engines; move throttles, switches, and levers; and depress pedals to operate machines such as bulldozers, trench excavators, road graders, and backhoes. Locate underground services, such as pipes and wires, prior to beginning work. Monitor operations to ensure that health and safety standards are met. Align machines, cutterheads, or depth gauge makers with reference stakes and guidelines or ground or position equipment by following hand signals of other workers. Load and move dirt, rocks, equipment, and materials, using trucks, crawler tractors, power cranes, shovels, graders, and related equipment. Drive and maneuver equipment equipped with blades in successive passes over working areas to remove topsoil, vegetation, and rocks and to distribute and level earth or terrain. Coordinate machine actions with other activities, positioning or moving loads in response to hand or audio signals from crew members. Operate tractors and bulldozers to perform such tasks as clearing land, mixing sludge, trimming backfills, and building roadways and parking lots. Repair and maintain equipment, making emergency

adjustments or assisting with major repairs as necessary. Check fuel supplies at sites to ensure adequate availability. Connect hydraulic hoses, belts, mechanical linkages, or power takeoff shafts to tractors. Operate loaders to pull out stumps, rip asphalt or concrete, rough-grade properties, bury refuse, or perform general cleanup. Select and fasten bulldozer blades or other attachments to tractors, using hitches. Test atmosphere for adequate oxygen and explosive conditions when working in confined spaces. Operate compactors, scrapers, and rollers to level, compact, and cover refuse at disposal grounds. Talk to clients and study instructions, plans, and diagrams to establish work requirements.

Personality Type: Realistic-Conventional-Investigative.

Career Clusters: 02 Architecture and Construction; 16 Transportation, Distribution, and Logistics. **Career Pathways:** 02.2 Construction; 16.1 Transportation Operations.

Skills: Equipment Maintenance; Installation; Operation and Control; Operation Monitoring; Repairing; Equipment Selection.

Education and Training Programs: Construction/Heavy Equipment/Earthmoving Equipment Operation; Mobile Crane Operation/Operator. **Related Knowledge/Courses:** Building and Construction; Mechanical Devices; Engineering and Technology; Design; Production and Processing; Public Safety and Security.

Work Environment: Outdoors; noisy; very hot or cold; contaminants; whole-body vibration; using hands on objects, tools, or controls.

Optometrists

- ❋ Education/Training Required: First professional degree
- ❋ Annual Earnings: $93,800
- ❋ Beginning Wage: $47,980
- ❋ Earnings Growth Potential: High (48.8%)
- ❋ Growth: 11.3%
- ❋ Annual Job Openings: 1,789
- ❋ Job Security: Most Secure
- ❋ Self-Employed: 25.5%
- ❋ Part-Time: 20.8%

Renewal Industry: Health Care.

Industries with Greatest Employment: Ambulatory Health-Care Services (62.4%); Health and Personal Care Stores (7.8%).

Highest-Growth Industries (Projected Growth for This Job): Administrative and Support Services (23.6%); Ambulatory Health-Care Services (16.4%).

Other Considerations for Job Outlook: Job opportunities for optometrists should be very good over the next decade. Demand is expected to be much higher, and because there are only 16 schools of optometry, the number of students who can get a degree in optometry is limited. In addition to growth, the need to replace optometrists who retire or leave the occupation for other reasons will create more employment opportunities.

Diagnose, manage, and treat conditions and diseases of the human eye and visual system. Examine eyes and visual systems, diagnose problems or impairments, prescribe corrective lenses, and provide treatment. May prescribe therapeutic drugs to treat specific eye conditions. Examine eyes, using observation, instruments, and pharmaceutical agents, to determine visual acuity and perception, focus, and coordination and to diagnose diseases and other abnormalities such as glaucoma or color blindness. Prescribe medications to treat eye diseases if state laws permit. Analyze test results and develop treatment plans. Prescribe, supply, fit, and adjust eyeglasses, contact lenses, and other vision aids. Educate and counsel patients on contact lens care, visual hygiene, lighting arrangements, and safety factors. Remove foreign bodies from eyes. Consult with and refer patients to ophthalmologist or other health-care practitioners if additional medical treatment is determined necessary. Provide patients undergoing eye surgeries such as cataract and laser vision correction with pre- and post-operative care. Prescribe therapeutic procedures to correct or conserve vision. Provide vision therapy and low vision rehabilitation.

Personality Type: Investigative-Social-Realistic.

Career Cluster: 08 Health Science. **Career Pathway:** 08.1 Therapeutic Services.

Skills: No data available.

Education and Training Program: Optometry (OD). **Related Knowledge/Courses:** Medicine and Dentistry;

Biology; Therapy and Counseling; Physics; Sales and Marketing; Economics and Accounting.

Work Environment: Indoors; disease or infections; sitting; using hands on objects, tools, or controls.

Oral and Maxillofacial Surgeons

- ❋ Education/Training Required: First professional degree
- ❋ Annual Earnings: More than $145,600
- ❋ Beginning Wage: $63,850
- ❋ Earnings Growth Potential: Cannot be calculated
- ❋ Growth: 9.1%
- ❋ Annual Job Openings: 400
- ❋ Job Security: Less Secure than Most
- ❋ Self-Employed: 30.6%
- ❋ Part-Time: 25.9%

Renewal Industry: Health Care.

Industries with Greatest Employment: Ambulatory Health-Care Services (65.5%).

Highest-Growth Industries (Projected Growth for This Job): None met the criteria.

Other Considerations for Job Outlook: As an increasing number of dentists from the baby-boom generation reach retirement age, many of them will retire or work fewer hours. However, the number of applicants to, and graduates from, dental schools has increased in recent years. Therefore, younger dentists will be able to take over the work from older dentists who retire or cut back on hours, as well as provide dental services to accommodate the growing demand.

Perform surgery on mouth, jaws, and related head and neck structure to execute difficult and multiple extractions of teeth, to remove tumors and other abnormal growths, to correct abnormal jaw relations by mandibular or maxillary revision, to prepare mouth for insertion of dental prosthesis, or to treat fractured jaws. Administer general and local anesthetics. Remove impacted, damaged, and non-restorable teeth. Evaluate the position of the wisdom teeth in order to determine whether problems exist currently or might occur in the future. Collaborate with other professionals such as restorative dentists and orthodontists in order to plan treatment. Perform surgery to prepare the mouth for dental implants and to aid in the regeneration of deficient bone and gum tissues. Remove tumors and other abnormal growths of the oral and facial regions, using surgical instruments. Treat infections of the oral cavity, salivary glands, jaws, and neck. Treat problems affecting the oral mucosa such as mouth ulcers and infections. Provide emergency treatment of facial injuries, including facial lacerations, intra-oral lacerations, and fractured facial bones. Perform surgery on the mouth and jaws in order to treat conditions such as cleft lip and palate and jaw growth problems. Restore form and function by moving skin, bone, nerves, and other tissues from other parts of the body in order to reconstruct the jaws and face. Perform minor cosmetic procedures such as chin and cheekbone enhancements and minor facial rejuvenation procedures including the use of Botox and laser technology. Treat snoring problems, using laser surgery.

Personality Type: Realistic-Social-Investigative.

Career Cluster: 08 Health Science. **Career Pathway:** 08.1 Therapeutic Services.

Skills: Science; Management of Financial Resources; Equipment Selection; Service Orientation; Complex Problem Solving; Management of Personnel Resources.

Education and Training Programs: Oral/Maxillofacial Surgery (Cert, MS, PhD); Dental/Oral Surgery Specialty. **Related Knowledge/Courses:** Medicine and Dentistry; Biology; Therapy and Counseling; Chemistry; Psychology; Personnel and Human Resources.

Work Environment: Indoors; disease or infections; standing; using hands on objects, tools, or controls; bending or twisting the body; repetitive motions.

Orthodontists

- ✺ Education/Training Required: First professional degree
- ✺ Annual Earnings: More than $145,600
- ✺ Beginning Wage: $95,740
- ✺ Earnings Growth Potential: Cannot be calculated
- ✺ Growth: 9.2%
- ✺ Annual Job Openings: 479
- ✺ Job Security: Less Secure than Most
- ✺ Self-Employed: 43.3%
- ✺ Part-Time: 25.9%

Renewal Industry: Health Care.

Industries with Greatest Employment: Ambulatory Health-Care Services (55.5%).

Highest-Growth Industries (Projected Growth for This Job): None met the criteria.

Other Considerations for Job Outlook: As an increasing number of dentists from the baby-boom generation reach retirement age, many of them will retire or work fewer hours. However, the number of applicants to, and graduates from, dental schools has increased in recent years. Therefore, younger dentists will be able to take over the work from older dentists who retire or cut back on hours, as well as provide dental services to accommodate the growing demand.

Examine, diagnose, and treat dental malocclusions and oral cavity anomalies. Design and fabricate appliances to realign teeth and jaws to produce and maintain normal function and to improve appearance. Fit dental appliances in patients' mouths to alter the position and relationship of teeth and jaws and to realign teeth. Study diagnostic records such as medical/dental histories, plaster models of the teeth, photos of a patient's face and teeth, and X-rays to develop patient treatment plans. Diagnose teeth and jaw or other dental-facial abnormalities. Examine patients to assess abnormalities of jaw development, tooth position, and other dental-facial structures. Prepare diagnostic and treatment records. Adjust dental appliances periodically to produce and maintain normal function. Provide patients with proposed treatment plans and cost estimates. Instruct dental officers and technical assistants in orthodontic procedures and techniques. Coordinate orthodontic services with other dental and medical services. Design and fabricate appliances, such as space maintainers, retainers, and labial and lingual arch wires.

Personality Type: Investigative-Realistic-Social.

Career Cluster: 08 Health Science. **Career Pathway:** 08.1 Therapeutic Services.

Skills: Management of Financial Resources; Equipment Selection; Management of Personnel Resources; Management of Material Resources; Technology Design; Judgment and Decision Making.

Education and Training Programs: Orthodontics/ Orthodontology (Cert, MS, PhD); Orthodontics Specialty. **Related Knowledge/Courses:** Medicine and Dentistry; Biology; Sales and Marketing; Economics and Accounting; Personnel and Human Resources; Customer and Personal Service.

Work Environment: Indoors; disease or infections; sitting; using hands on objects, tools, or controls; bending or twisting the body; repetitive motions.

Orthotists and Prosthetists

- ❋ Education/Training Required: Bachelor's degree
- ❋ Annual Earnings: $60,520
- ❋ Beginning Wage: $31,670
- ❋ Earnings Growth Potential: High (47.7%)
- ❋ Growth: 11.8%
- ❋ Annual Job Openings: 295
- ❋ Job Security: More Secure than Most
- ❋ Self-Employed: 6.5%
- ❋ Part-Time: 15.4%

Renewal Industry: Health Care.

Industries with Greatest Employment: Miscellaneous Manufacturing (27.6%); Health and Personal Care Stores (24.8%); Hospitals, Public and Private (13.2%); Ambulatory Health-Care Services (11.4%); Federal Government (8.2%).

Highest-Growth Industries (Projected Growth for This Job): Ambulatory Health-Care Services (26.8%).

Other Considerations for Job Outlook: Job outlook information is limited, but prospects probably vary in different parts of the nation. In many areas, a shortage of trained prosthetists and orthotists has created a strong demand for these professionals.

Assist patients with disabling conditions of limbs and spine or with partial or total absence of limb by fitting and preparing orthopedic braces or prostheses. Examine, interview, and measure patients in order to determine their appliance needs and to identify factors that could affect appliance fit. Fit, test, and evaluate devices on patients and make adjustments for proper fit, function, and comfort. Instruct patients in the use and care of orthoses and prostheses. Design orthopedic and prosthetic devices based on physicians' prescriptions and examination and measurement of patients. Maintain patients' records. Make and modify plaster casts of areas that will be fitted with prostheses or orthoses for use in the device construction process. Select materials and components to be used, based on device design. Confer with physicians to formulate specifications and prescriptions for orthopedic or prosthetic devices. Repair, rebuild, and modify prosthetic and orthopedic appliances. Construct and fabricate appliances or supervise others who are constructing the appliances. Train and supervise orthopedic and prosthetic assistants and technicians and other support staff. Update skills and knowledge by attending conferences and seminars. Show and explain orthopedic and prosthetic appliances to health-care workers. Research new ways to construct and use orthopedic and prosthetic devices. Publish research findings and present them at conferences and seminars.

Personality Type: Social-Realistic-Investigative.

Career Cluster: 08 Health Science. **Career Pathway:** 08.3 Health Informatics.

Skills: Technology Design; Management of Financial Resources; Management of Material Resources; Operations Analysis; Service Orientation; Science.

Education and Training Programs: Orthotist/Prosthetist; Assistive/Augmentative Technology and Rehabiliation Engineering. **Related Knowledge/Courses:** Engineering and Technology; Medicine and Dentistry; Design; Therapy and Counseling; Psychology; Production and Processing.

Work Environment: Indoors; noisy; contaminants; disease or infections; hazardous equipment; using hands on objects, tools, or controls.

Painters, Construction and Maintenance

- ❋ Education/Training Required: Moderate-term on-the-job training
- ❋ Annual Earnings: $32,080
- ❋ Beginning Wage: $21,720
- ❋ Earnings Growth Potential: Low (32.3%)
- ❋ Growth: 11.8%
- ❋ Annual Job Openings: 101,140
- ❋ Job Security: Least Secure
- ❋ Self-Employed: 42.2%
- ❋ Part-Time: 9.8%

Renewal Industry: Infrastructure.

Industries with Greatest Employment: Specialty Trade Contractors (41.0%).

Highest-Growth Industries (Projected Growth for This Job): Nursing and Residential Care Facilities (34.7%); Museums, Historical Sites, and Similar Institutions (34.2%); Amusement, Gambling, and Recreation Industries (32.9%); Waste Management and Remediation Services (27.2%); Building Material and Garden Equipment and Supplies Dealers (25.6%); Administrative and Support Services (24.2%); Professional, Scientific, and Technical Services (23.4%); Performing Arts, Spectator Sports, and Related Industries (22.1%); Rental and Leasing Services (18.6%); Real Estate (17.5%); Support Activities for Transportation (16.7%); Accommodation, Including Hotels and Motels (15.0%).

Other Considerations for Job Outlook: Job prospects for painters should be excellent because of the need to replace workers who leave the occupation for other jobs. There are no strict training requirements for entry into these jobs, so many people with limited skills work as painters or helpers for a relatively short time and then move on to other types of work with higher pay or better working conditions.

Paint walls, equipment, buildings, bridges, and other structural surfaces with brushes, rollers, and spray guns. May remove old paint to prepare surfaces before painting. May mix colors or oils to obtain desired color or consistencies. Cover surfaces with dropcloths or masking tape and paper to protect surfaces during painting. Fill cracks, holes, and joints with caulk, putty, plaster, or other fillers, using caulking guns or putty knives. Apply primers or sealers to prepare new surfaces such as bare wood or metal for finish coats. Apply paint, stain, varnish, enamel, and other finishes to equipment, buildings, bridges, and/or other structures, using brushes, spray guns, or rollers. Calculate amounts of required materials and estimate costs, based on surface measurements and/or work orders. Read work orders or receive instructions from supervisors or homeowners to determine work requirements. Erect scaffolding and swing gates, or set up ladders, to work above ground level. Remove fixtures such as pictures, door knobs, lamps, and electric switch covers prior to painting. Wash and treat surfaces with oil, turpentine, mildew remover, or other preparations, and sand rough spots to ensure that finishes will adhere properly. Mix and match colors of paint, stain, or varnish with oil and thinning and drying additives to obtain desired colors and consistencies. Remove old finishes by stripping, sanding, wire brushing, burning, or using water and/or abrasive blasting. Select and purchase tools and finishes for surfaces to be covered, considering durability, ease of handling, methods of application, and customers' wishes. Smooth surfaces, using sandpaper, scrapers, brushes, steel wool, and/or sanding machines. Polish final coats to specified finishes. Use special finishing techniques such as sponging, ragging, layering, or faux finishing. Waterproof buildings, using waterproofers and caulking. Cut stencils, and brush and spray lettering and decorations on surfaces. Spray or brush hot plastics or pitch onto surfaces. Bake finishes on painted and enameled articles, using baking ovens.

Personality Type: Realistic-Conventional.

Career Cluster: 02 Architecture and Construction. **Career Pathway:** 02.2 Construction.

Skills: No data available.

Education and Training Program: Painting/Painter and Wall Coverer. **Related Knowledge/Courses:** Building and Construction; Design; Transportation; Customer and Personal Service; Production and Processing; Administration and Management.

Work Environment: Contaminants; standing; climbing ladders, scaffolds, or poles; using hands on objects, tools, or controls; bending or twisting the body; repetitive motions.

Painters, Transportation Equipment

❊ Education/Training Required: Long-term on-the-job training
❊ Annual Earnings: $36,000
❊ Beginning Wage: $22,560
❊ Earnings Growth Potential: Medium (37.3%)
❊ Growth: 8.4%
❊ Annual Job Openings: 3,268
❊ Job Security: More Secure than Most
❊ Self-Employed: 3.8%
❊ Part-Time: 3.7%

Renewal Industry: Advanced Manufacturing.

Industries with Greatest Employment: Repair and Maintenance (43.4%); Transportation Equipment Manufacturing (30.4%); Motor Vehicle and Parts Dealers (11.5%).

Highest-Growth Industries (Projected Growth for This Job): Administrative and Support Services (32.8%); Amusement, Gambling, and Recreation Industries (28.9%); Professional, Scientific, and Technical Services (28.8%); Rental and Leasing Services (18.6%); Support Activities for Transportation (18.2%); Repair and Maintenance (16.4%).

Other Considerations for Job Outlook: Opportunities should be good for those with painting experience. Excellent opportunities will exist for experienced painters in the oil and gas industry and the ship building industry over the next decade.

Operate or tend painting machines to paint surfaces of transportation equipment, such as automobiles, buses, trucks, trains, boats, and airplanes. Dispose of hazardous waste in an appropriate manner. Select paint according to company requirements and match colors of paint following specified color charts. Mix paints to match color specifications or vehicles' original colors; then stir and thin the paints, using spatulas or power mixing equipment. Remove grease, dirt, paint, and rust from vehicle surfaces in preparation for paint application, using abrasives, solvents, brushes, blowtorches, washing tanks, or sandblasters. Pour paint into spray guns and adjust nozzles and paint mixes to get the proper paint flow and coating thickness. Monitor painting operations to identify flaws such as blisters and streaks so that their causes can be corrected. Sand vehicle surfaces between coats of paint or primer to remove flaws and enhance adhesion for subsequent coats. Disassemble, clean, and reassemble sprayers and power equipment, using solvents, wire brushes, and cloths for cleaning duties. Remove accessories from vehicles, such as chrome or mirrors, and mask other surfaces with tape or paper to protect them from paint. Spray prepared surfaces with specified amounts of primers and decorative or finish coatings. Allow the sprayed product to dry and then touch up any spots that may have been missed. Apply rust-resistant undercoats and caulk and seal seams. Select the correct spray gun system for the material being applied. Apply primer over any repairs made to vehicle surfaces. Adjust controls on infrared ovens, heat lamps, portable ventilators, and exhaust units to speed the drying of vehicles between coats. Fill small dents and scratches with body fillers and smooth surfaces to prepare vehicles for painting. Apply designs, lettering, or other identifying or decorative items to finished products, using paint brushes or paint sprayers. Paint by hand areas that cannot be reached with a spray gun or those that need retouching, using brushes. Sand the final finish and apply sealer once a vehicle has dried properly. Buff and wax the finished paintwork. Lay out logos, symbols, or designs on painted surfaces according to blueprint specifications, using measuring instruments, stencils, and patterns.

Personality Type: Realistic-Conventional.

Career Cluster: 16 Transportation, Distribution, and Logistics. **Career Pathway:** 16.4 Facility and Mobile Equipment Maintenance.

Skills: Repairing; Equipment Maintenance; Monitoring; Operation and Control; Technology Design; Science.

Education and Training Program: Autobody/Collision and Repair Technology/Technician. **Related Knowledge/Courses:** Chemistry; Production and Processing; Mechanical Devices.

Work Environment: Noisy; contaminants; hazardous conditions; standing; using hands on objects, tools, or controls; repetitive motions.

Pediatricians, General

* Education/Training Required: First professional degree
* Annual Earnings: $140,690
* Beginning Wage: $67,430
* Earnings Growth Potential: Very high (52.1%)
* Growth: 14.2%
* Annual Job Openings: 38,027
* Job Security: Most Secure
* Self-Employed: 14.7%
* Part-Time: 8.1%

Our sources did not provide separate job openings data for this occupation. The job openings listed here are shared with Anesthesiologists; Family and General Practitioners; Internists, General; Obstetricians and Gynecologists; Psychiatrists; and Surgeons.

Renewal Industry: Health Care.

Industries with Greatest Employment: Ambulatory Health-Care Services (55.9%); Hospitals, Public and Private (17.8%).

Highest-Growth Industries (Projected Growth for This Job): Social Assistance (58.6%); Administrative and Support Services (26.8%); Professional, Scientific, and Technical Services (22.6%); Nursing and Residential Care Facilities (21.0%); Ambulatory Health-Care Services (19.4%); Religious, Grantmaking, Civic, Professional, and Similar Organizations (16.7%); Management of Companies and Enterprises (15.3%).

Other Considerations for Job Outlook: Opportunities for individuals interested in becoming physicians and surgeons are expected to be very good. Unlike their predecessors, new physicians are much less likely to enter solo practice and more likely to take salaried jobs in group medical practices, clinics, and health networks. Reports of shortages in some specialties, such as general or family practice, internal medicine, and OB/GYN, or in rural or low-income areas should attract new entrants, encouraging schools to expand programs and hospitals to increase available residency slots. However, because physician training is so lengthy, employment change happens gradually. Opportunities should be particularly good in rural and low-income areas, as some physicians find these areas unattractive because of less control over work hours, isolation from medical colleagues, or other reasons.

Diagnose, treat, and help prevent children's diseases and injuries. Examine patients or order, perform, and interpret diagnostic tests to obtain information on medical condition and determine diagnosis. Examine children regularly to assess their growth and development. Prescribe or administer treatment, therapy, medication, vaccination, and other specialized medical care to treat or prevent illness, disease, or injury in infants and children. Collect, record, and maintain patient information, such as medical history, reports, and examination results. Advise patients, parents or guardians, and community members concerning diet, activity, hygiene, and disease prevention. Treat children who have minor illnesses, acute and chronic health problems, and growth and development concerns. Explain procedures and discuss test results or prescribed treatments with patients and parents or guardians. Monitor patients' condition and progress and re-evaluate treatments as necessary. Plan and execute medical care programs to aid in the mental and physical growth and development of children and adolescents. Refer patient to medical specialist or other practitioner when necessary. Direct and coordinate activities of nurses, students, assistants, specialists, therapists, and other medical staff. Provide consulting services to other physicians. Plan, implement, or administer health programs or standards in hospital, business, or community for information, prevention, or treatment of injury or illness. Operate on patients to remove, repair, or improve functioning of diseased or injured body parts and systems. Conduct research to study anatomy and develop or test medications, treatments, or procedures to prevent or control disease or injury. Prepare reports for government or management of birth, death, and disease statistics; workforce evaluations; or medical status of individuals.

Personality Type: Investigative-Social.

Career Cluster: 08 Health Science. **Career Pathway:** 08.1 Therapeutic Services.

Skills: Science; Social Perceptiveness; Active Learning; Reading Comprehension; Persuasion; Critical Thinking.

Education and Training Programs: Child/Pediatric Neurology; Family Medicine; Neonatal-Perinatal Medicine; Pediatric Cardiology; Pediatric Endocrinology; Pediatric Hemato-Oncology; Pediatric Nephrology; Pediatric

Orthopedics; Pediatric Surgery; Pediatrics. **Related Knowledge/Courses:** Medicine and Dentistry; Therapy and Counseling; Biology; Psychology; Chemistry; Sociology and Anthropology.

Work Environment: Indoors; disease or infections; standing; using hands on objects, tools, or controls.

Petroleum Engineers

- ❋ Education/Training Required: Bachelor's degree
- ❋ Annual Earnings: $103,960
- ❋ Beginning Wage: $58,840
- ❋ Earnings Growth Potential: High (43.4%)
- ❋ Growth: 5.2%
- ❋ Annual Job Openings: 1,016
- ❋ Job Security: More Secure than Most
- ❋ Self-Employed: 9.2%
- ❋ Part-Time: 2.9%

Renewal Industry: Green Technologies.

Industries with Greatest Employment: Oil and Gas Extraction (42.7%); Support Activities for Mining (17.0%); Professional, Scientific, and Technical Services (6.8%); Petroleum and Coal Products Manufacturing (6.3%).

Highest-Growth Industries (Projected Growth for This Job): Professional, Scientific, and Technical Services (42.8%); Securities, Commodity Contracts, and Other Financial Investments and Related Activities (41.4%).

Other Considerations for Job Outlook: Favorable opportunities are expected for petroleum engineers because the number of job openings is likely to exceed the relatively small number of graduates. Petroleum engineers work around the world; in fact, the best employment opportunities may include some work in other countries.

Devise methods to improve oil and gas well production and determine the need for new or modified tool designs. Oversee drilling and offer technical advice to achieve economical and satisfactory progress. Assess costs and estimate the production capabilities and economic value of oil and gas wells to evaluate the economic viability of potential drilling sites. Monitor production rates and plan rework processes to improve production. Analyze data to recommend placement of wells and supplementary processes to enhance production. Specify and supervise well modification and stimulation programs to maximize oil and gas recovery. Direct and monitor the completion and evaluation of wells, well testing, or well surveys. Assist engineering and other personnel to solve operating problems. Develop plans for oil and gas field drilling and for product recovery and treatment. Maintain records of drilling and production operations. Confer with scientific, engineering, and technical personnel to resolve design, research, and testing problems. Write technical reports for engineering and management personnel. Evaluate findings to develop, design, or test equipment or processes. Assign work to staff to obtain maximum utilization of personnel. Interpret drilling and testing information for personnel. Design and implement environmental controls on oil and gas operations. Coordinate the installation, maintenance, and operation of mining and oilfield equipment. Supervise the removal of drilling equipment, the removal of any waste, and the safe return of land to structural stability when wells or pockets are exhausted. Inspect oil and gas wells to determine that installations are completed. Simulate reservoir performance for different recovery techniques, using computer models. Take samples to assess the amount and quality of oil, the depth at which resources lie, and the equipment needed to properly extract them. Coordinate activities of workers engaged in research, planning, and development. Design or modify mining and oilfield machinery and tools, applying engineering principles. Test machinery and equipment to ensure that it is safe and conforms to performance specifications. Conduct engineering research experiments to improve or modify mining and oil machinery and operations.

Personality Type: Investigative-Realistic-Conventional.

Career Cluster: 15 Science, Technology, Engineering, and Mathematics. **Career Pathway:** 15.1 Engineering and Technology.

Skills: Management of Financial Resources; Science; Operations Analysis; Troubleshooting; Mathematics; Technology Design.

Education and Training Program: Petroleum Engineering. **Related Knowledge/Courses:** Engineering and Technology; Physics; Geography; Chemistry; Design; Economics and Accounting.

Work Environment: Indoors; sitting.

Pharmacists

❋ Education/Training Required: First professional degree

❋ Annual Earnings: $100,480

❋ Beginning Wage: $73,010

❋ Earnings Growth Potential: Low (27.3%)

❋ Growth: 21.7%

❋ Annual Job Openings: 16,358

❋ Job Security: Most Secure

❋ Self-Employed: 0.5%

❋ Part-Time: 18.1%

Renewal Industry: Health Care.

Industries with Greatest Employment: Health and Personal Care Stores (44.1%); Hospitals, Public and Private (23.2%); General Merchandise Stores (9.6%); Food and Beverage Stores (8.3%).

Highest-Growth Industries (Projected Growth for This Job): Social Assistance (62.8%); Nonstore Retailers (50.1%); Professional, Scientific, and Technical Services (48.3%); Warehousing and Storage (33.7%); Ambulatory Health-Care Services (31.7%); Administrative and Support Services (27.8%); General Merchandise Stores (26.2%); Chemical Manufacturing (26.0%); Health and Personal Care Stores (22.1%); Hospitals, Public and Private (21.1%); Food and Beverage Stores (20.0%); Merchant Wholesalers, Nondurable Goods (18.9%); Religious, Grantmaking, Civic, Professional, and Similar Organizations (18.8%); Nursing and Residential Care Facilities (17.2%); Merchant Wholesalers, Durable Goods (16.6%); Management of Companies and Enterprises (15.2%).

Other Considerations for Job Outlook: Excellent opportunities are expected for pharmacists over the 2006 to 2016 period. Job openings will result from rapid employment growth, and from the need to replace workers who retire or leave the occupation for other reasons. As the use of prescription drugs increases, demand for pharmacists will grow in most practice settings, such as community pharmacies, hospital pharmacies, and mail-order pharmacies. As the population ages, assisted living facilities and home care organizations should see particularly rapid growth. Demand will also increase as cost conscious insurers, in an attempt to improve preventative care, use

pharmacists in areas such as patient education and vaccination administration.

Compound and dispense medications, following prescriptions issued by physicians, dentists, or other authorized medical practitioners. Review prescriptions to assure accuracy, to ascertain the needed ingredients, and to evaluate their suitability. Provide information and advice regarding drug interactions, side effects, dosage, and proper medication storage. Analyze prescribing trends to monitor patient compliance and to prevent excessive usage or harmful interactions. Order and purchase pharmaceutical supplies, medical supplies, and drugs, maintaining stock and storing and handling it properly. Maintain records, such as pharmacy files; patient profiles; charge system files; inventories; control records for radioactive nuclei; and registries of poisons, narcotics, and controlled drugs. Provide specialized services to help patients manage conditions such as diabetes, asthma, smoking cessation, or high blood pressure. Advise customers on the selection of medication brands, medical equipment, and health-care supplies. Collaborate with other health-care professionals to plan, monitor, review, and evaluate the quality and effectiveness of drugs and drug regimens, providing advice on drug applications and characteristics. Compound and dispense medications as prescribed by doctors and dentists by calculating, weighing, measuring, and mixing ingredients or oversee these activities. Offer health promotion and prevention activities—for example, training people to use devices such as blood-pressure or diabetes monitors. Refer patients to other health professionals and agencies when appropriate. Prepare sterile solutions and infusions for use in surgical procedures, emergency rooms, or patients' homes. Plan, implement, and maintain procedures for mixing, packaging, and labeling pharmaceuticals according to policy and legal requirements to ensure quality, security, and proper disposal. Assay radiopharmaceuticals, verify rates of disintegration, and calculate the volume required to produce the desired results to ensure proper dosages. Manage pharmacy operations, hiring and supervising staff, performing administrative duties, and buying and selling nonpharmaceutical merchandise. Work in hospitals, clinics, or for health maintenance organizations (HMOs), dispensing prescriptions, serving as a medical team consultant, or specializing in specific drug therapy areas such as oncology or nuclear pharmacotherapy.

Personality Type: Investigative-Conventional-Social.

Career Cluster: 08 Health Science. **Career Pathways:** 08.1 Therapeutic Services; 08.5 Biotechnology Research and Development.

Skills: Science; Reading Comprehension; Social Perceptiveness; Active Listening; Instructing; Mathematics.

Education and Training Programs: Pharmacy (PharmD [USA] PharmD, BS/BPharm [Canada]); Pharmacy Administration and Pharmacy Policy and Regulatory Affairs (MS, PhD); Pharmaceutics and Drug Design (MS, PhD); Medicinal and Pharmaceutical Chemistry (MS, PhD); Natural Products Chemistry and Pharmacognosy (MS, PhD); Clinical and Industrial Drug Development (MS, PhD); Pharmacoeconomics/Pharmaceutical Economics (MS, PhD); Clinical, Hospital, and Managed Care Pharmacy (MS, PhD); others. **Related Knowledge/Courses:** Medicine and Dentistry; Chemistry; Therapy and Counseling; Biology; Psychology; Mathematics.

Work Environment: Indoors; disease or infections; standing; repetitive motions.

Pharmacy Technicians

- ❋ Education/Training Required: Moderate-term on-the-job training
- ❋ Annual Earnings: $26,720
- ❋ Beginning Wage: $18,520
- ❋ Earnings Growth Potential: Low (30.7%)
- ❋ Growth: 32.0%
- ❋ Annual Job Openings: 54,453
- ❋ Job Security: Most Secure
- ❋ Self-Employed: 0.2%
- ❋ Part-Time: 20.8%

Renewal Industry: Health Care.

Industries with Greatest Employment: Hospitals, Public and Private (18.2%); General Merchandise Stores (9.3%); Food and Beverage Stores (6.7%).

Highest-Growth Industries (Projected Growth for This Job): Nonstore Retailers (50.1%); General Merchandise Stores (41.0%); Professional, Scientific, and Technical Services (39.4%); Warehousing and Storage (33.3%); Hospitals, Public and Private (31.9%); Ambulatory Health-Care Services (31.1%); Food and Beverage Stores (30.9%); Merchant Wholesalers, Nondurable Goods (18.9%); Nursing and Residential Care Facilities (17.3%); Merchant Wholesalers, Durable Goods (16.6%); Management of Companies and Enterprises (15.3%).

Other Considerations for Job Outlook: Good job opportunities are expected for full-time and part-time work, especially for technicians with formal training or previous experience. Job openings for pharmacy technicians will result from employment growth, and from the need to replace workers who transfer to other occupations or leave the labor force. Almost all states have legislated the maximum number of technicians who can safely work under a pharmacist at one time. Changes in these laws could directly affect employment.

Prepare medications under the direction of a pharmacist. May measure, mix, count out, label, and record amounts and dosages of medications. Receive written prescription or refill requests and verify that information is complete and accurate. Maintain proper storage and security conditions for drugs. Answer telephones, responding to questions or requests. Fill bottles with prescribed medications and type and affix labels. Assist customers by answering simple questions, locating items, or referring them to the pharmacist for medication information. Price and file prescriptions that have been filled. Clean and help maintain equipment and work areas and sterilize glassware according to prescribed methods. Establish and maintain patient profiles, including lists of medications taken by individual patients. Order, label, and count stock of medications, chemicals, and supplies and enter inventory data into computer. Receive and store incoming supplies, verify quantities against invoices, and inform supervisors of stock needs and shortages. Transfer medication from vials to the appropriate number of sterile disposable syringes, using aseptic techniques. Under pharmacist supervision, add measured drugs or nutrients to intravenous solutions under sterile conditions to prepare intravenous (IV) packs. Supply and monitor robotic machines that dispense medicine into containers and label the containers. Prepare and process medical insurance claim forms and records. Mix pharmaceutical preparations according to written prescriptions. Operate cash registers to accept payment from customers. Compute charges for medication and equipment dispensed to hospital patients and enter data in computer. Deliver medications and pharmaceutical supplies to patients, nursing stations, or surgery. Price stock and mark items for sale. Maintain and merchandise home health-care products and services.

Personality Type: Conventional-Realistic.

Career Cluster: 08 Health Science. **Career Pathway:** 08.1 Therapeutic Services.

Skills: No data available.

Education and Training Program: Pharmacy Technician/Assistant. **Related Knowledge/Courses:** Medicine and Dentistry; Chemistry; Customer and Personal Service; Mathematics; Clerical Practices.

Work Environment: Indoors; standing; using hands on objects, tools, or controls; repetitive motions.

Philosophy and Religion Teachers, Postsecondary

- ✸ Education/Training Required: Master's degree
- ✸ Annual Earnings: $56,380
- ✸ Beginning Wage: $32,640
- ✸ Earnings Growth Potential: High (42.1%)
- ✸ Growth: 22.9%
- ✸ Annual Job Openings: 3,120
- ✸ Job Security: Most Secure
- ✸ Self-Employed: 0.4%
- ✸ Part-Time: 27.8%

Renewal Industry: Education.

Industries with Greatest Employment: Educational Services, Public and Private (97.3%).

Highest-Growth Industries (Projected Growth for This Job): Administrative and Support Services (48.3%); Amusement, Gambling, and Recreation Industries (45.2%); Social Assistance (38.6%); Support Activities for Transportation (32.8%); Religious, Grantmaking, Civic, Professional, and Similar Organizations (29.9%); Professional, Scientific, and Technical Services (28.8%); Management of Companies and Enterprises (26.8%); Local Government (23.5%); Educational Services, Public and Private (22.8%); Hospitals, Public and Private (21.4%).

Other Considerations for Job Outlook: Retirements of current postsecondary teachers should create numerous openings for all types of postsecondary teachers, so job opportunities are generally expected to be very good.

However, one of the main reasons why students attend postsecondary institutions is to prepare themselves for careers, so the best job prospects for postsecondary teachers are likely to be in rapidly growing fields that offer many nonacademic career options, unlike philosophy and religious studies. Community colleges and other institutions offering career and technical education have been among the most rapidly growing, and these institutions are expected to offer some of the best opportunities for postsecondary teachers.

Teach courses in philosophy, religion, and theology. Evaluate and grade students' classwork, assignments, and papers. Initiate, facilitate, and moderate classroom discussions. Prepare and deliver lectures to undergraduate and graduate students on topics such as ethics, logic, and contemporary religious thought. Prepare course materials such as syllabi, homework assignments, and handouts. Compile, administer, and grade examinations or assign this work to others. Keep abreast of developments in their field by reading current literature, talking with colleagues, and participating in professional conferences. Maintain student attendance records, grades, and other required records. Plan, evaluate, and revise curricula, course content, and course materials and methods of instruction. Maintain regularly scheduled office hours to advise and assist students. Select and obtain materials and supplies such as textbooks. Advise students on academic and vocational curricula and on career issues. Conduct research in a particular field of knowledge and publish findings in professional journals, books, or electronic media. Perform administrative duties such as serving as department head. Serve on academic or administrative committees that deal with institutional policies, departmental matters, and academic issues. Collaborate with colleagues to address teaching and research issues. Participate in campus and community events. Participate in student recruitment, registration, and placement activities. Compile bibliographies of specialized materials for outside reading assignments. Supervise undergraduate and graduate teaching, internship, and research work. Act as advisers to student organizations. Write grant proposals to procure external research funding. Provide professional consulting services to government or industry.

Personality Type: Social-Artistic-Investigative.

Career Clusters: 10 Human Services; 15 Science, Technology, Engineering, and Mathematics. **Career Pathways:**

10.2 Counseling and Mental Health Services; 15.3 Science and Mathematics.

Skills: Writing; Instructing; Reading Comprehension; Critical Thinking; Speaking; Learning Strategies.

Education and Training Programs: Philosophy; Ethics; Philosophy, Other; Religion/Religious Studies; Buddhist Studies; Christian Studies; Hindu Studies; Philosophy and Religious Studies, Other; Bible/Biblical Studies; Missions/Missionary Studies and Missiology; Religious Education; Religious/Sacred Music; Theology/Theological Studies; Divinity/Ministry (BD, MDiv.); Pre-Theology/Pre-Ministerial Studies; others. **Related Knowledge/Courses:** Philosophy and Theology; History and Archeology; Sociology and Anthropology; Foreign Language; English Language; Education and Training.

Work Environment: Indoors; sitting.

Physical Therapist Aides

- ✳ Education/Training Required: Short-term on-the-job training
- ✳ Annual Earnings: $22,990
- ✳ Beginning Wage: $16,740
- ✳ Earnings Growth Potential: Low (27.2%)
- ✳ Growth: 24.4%
- ✳ Annual Job Openings: 4,092
- ✳ Job Security: Most Secure
- ✳ Self-Employed: 0.2%
- ✳ Part-Time: 27.1%

Renewal Industry: Health Care.

Industries with Greatest Employment: Ambulatory Health-Care Services (57.2%); Hospitals, Public and Private (27.1%); Nursing and Residential Care Facilities (10.0%).

Highest-Growth Industries (Projected Growth for This Job): Ambulatory Health-Care Services (32.5%); Social Assistance (28.8%).

Other Considerations for Job Outlook: Physical therapist aides may face keen competition from the large pool of qualified individuals. Physical therapist aides with prior experience working in a physical therapy office or other health care setting will have the best job opportunities. The

increasing number of people who need therapy reflects, in part, the increasing elderly population. The elderly population is particularly vulnerable to chronic and debilitating conditions that require therapeutic services. These patients often need additional assistance in their treatment, making the roles of assistants and aides vital. In addition, the large baby-boom generation is entering the prime age for heart attacks and strokes, further increasing the demand for cardiac and physical rehabilitation. Moreover, future medical developments should permit an increased percentage of trauma victims to survive, creating added demand for therapy services.

Under close supervision of physical therapists or physical therapy assistants, perform delegated, selected, or routine tasks in specific situations. These duties include preparing patients and treatment areas. Clean and organize work areas and disinfect equipment after treatment. Administer active and passive manual therapeutic exercises; therapeutic massages; and heat, light, sound, water, or electrical modality treatments such as ultrasound. Instruct, motivate, safeguard, and assist patients practicing exercises and functional activities under direction of medical staff. Record treatment given and equipment used. Confer with physical therapy staff or others to discuss and evaluate patient information for planning, modifying, and coordinating treatment. Observe patients during treatment to compile and evaluate data on patients' responses and progress and report to physical therapists. Secure patients into or onto therapy equipment. Change linens such as bed sheets and pillowcases. Transport patients to and from treatment areas, using wheelchairs or providing standing support. Arrange treatment supplies to keep them in order. Maintain equipment and furniture to keep it in good working condition, including performing the assembly and disassembly of equipment and accessories. Assist patients to dress, undress, and put on and remove supportive devices such as braces, splints, and slings. Perform clerical duties such as taking inventory, ordering supplies, answering telephones, taking messages, and filling out forms. Administer traction to relieve neck and back pain, using intermittent and static traction equipment. Schedule patient appointments with physical therapists and coordinate therapists' schedules. Train patients to use orthopedic braces, prostheses, or supportive devices. Measure patient's range-of-joint motion, body parts, and vital signs to determine effects of treatments or for patient evaluations. Participate in patient care tasks such as assisting with passing food trays, feeding residents, or bathing residents on bed rest. Fit patients for orthopedic braces, prostheses, or supportive devices, adjusting fit as needed.

Personality Type: Social-Realistic.

Career Cluster: 08 Health Science. **Career Pathway:** 08.1 Therapeutic Services.

Skills: No data available.

Education and Training Program: Physical Therapist Assistant. **Related Knowledge/Courses:** Medicine and Dentistry; Therapy and Counseling; Customer and Personal Service; Psychology; Public Safety and Security.

Work Environment: Indoors; disease or infections; standing; walking and running; using hands on objects, tools, or controls; bending or twisting the body.

Physical Therapist Assistants

- ❋ Education/Training Required: Associate degree
- ❋ Annual Earnings: $44,130
- ❋ Beginning Wage: $27,800
- ❋ Earnings Growth Potential: Medium (37.0%)
- ❋ Growth: 32.4%
- ❋ Annual Job Openings: 5,957
- ❋ Job Security: Most Secure
- ❋ Self-Employed: 0.2%
- ❋ Part-Time: 27.1%

Renewal Industry: Health Care.

Industries with Greatest Employment: Ambulatory Health-Care Services (48.6%); Hospitals, Public and Private (33.2%); Nursing and Residential Care Facilities (11.4%).

Highest-Growth Industries (Projected Growth for This Job): Ambulatory Health-Care Services (36.4%); Amusement, Gambling, and Recreation Industries (33.3%); Social Assistance (32.9%); Hospitals, Public and Private (32.1%); Administrative and Support Services (26.6%); Nursing and Residential Care Facilities (23.7%); Management of Companies and Enterprises (15.5%).

Other Considerations for Job Outlook: Opportunities are expected to be very good. Physical therapist aides

with prior experience working in a physical therapy office or other health care setting will have the best job opportunities. The increasing number of people who need therapy reflects, in part, the increasing elderly population.

Assist physical therapists in providing physical therapy treatments and procedures. May, in accordance with state laws, assist in the development of treatment plans, carry out routine functions, document the progress of treatment, and modify specific treatments in accordance with patient status and within the scope of treatment plans established by physical therapists. Generally requires formal training. Instruct, motivate, safeguard, and assist patients as they practice exercises and functional activities. Observe patients during treatments to compile and evaluate data on their responses and progress; provide results to physical therapists in person or through progress notes. Confer with physical therapy staffs or others to discuss and evaluate patient information for planning, modifying, and coordinating treatment. Transport patients to and from treatment areas, lifting and transferring them according to positioning requirements. Secure patients into or onto therapy equipment. Administer active and passive manual therapeutic exercises; therapeutic massages; aquatic physical therapy; and heat, light, sound, and electrical modality treatments such as ultrasound. Communicate with or instruct caregivers and family members on patient therapeutic activities and treatment plans. Measure patients' ranges-of-joint motion, body parts, and vital signs to determine effects of treatments or for patient evaluations. Monitor operation of equipment and record use of equipment and administration of treatment. Fit patients for orthopedic braces, prostheses, and supportive devices such as crutches. Train patients in the use of orthopedic braces, prostheses, or supportive devices. Clean work areas and check and store equipment after treatments. Assist patients to dress; undress; or put on and remove supportive devices such as braces, splints, and slings. Attend or conduct continuing education courses, seminars, or in-service activities. Perform clerical duties such as taking inventory, ordering supplies, answering telephones, taking messages, and filling out forms. Prepare treatment areas and electrotherapy equipment for use by physiotherapists. Administer traction to relieve neck and back pain, using intermittent and static traction equipment. Perform postural drainage, percussions, and vibrations and teach deep breathing exercises to treat respiratory conditions.

Personality Type: Social-Realistic-Investigative.

Career Cluster: 08 Health Science. **Career Pathway:** 08.1 Therapeutic Services.

Skills: No data available.

Education and Training Program: Physical Therapist Assistant. **Related Knowledge/Courses:** Therapy and Counseling; Medicine and Dentistry; Psychology; Biology; Customer and Personal Service; Education and Training.

Work Environment: Indoors; disease or infections; standing; walking and running.

Physical Therapists

- ❋ Education/Training Required: Master's degree
- ❋ Annual Earnings: $69,760
- ❋ Beginning Wage: $48,530
- ❋ Earnings Growth Potential: Low (30.4%)
- ❋ Growth: 27.1%
- ❋ Annual Job Openings: 12,072
- ❋ Job Security: Most Secure
- ❋ Self-Employed: 8.4%
- ❋ Part-Time: 22.7%

Renewal Industry: Health Care.

Industries with Greatest Employment: Ambulatory Health-Care Services (44.2%); Hospitals, Public and Private (30.5%); Nursing and Residential Care Facilities (6.9%).

Highest-Growth Industries (Projected Growth for This Job): Social Assistance (39.7%); Ambulatory Health-Care Services (37.2%); Amusement, Gambling, and Recreation Industries (33.0%); Administrative and Support Services (26.6%); Nursing and Residential Care Facilities (23.8%); Hospitals, Public and Private (22.1%); Management of Companies and Enterprises (15.2%).

Other Considerations for Job Outlook: Job opportunities will be good for licensed physical therapists in all settings. Job opportunities should be particularly good in acute hospital, rehabilitation, and orthopedic settings, where the elderly are most often treated. Physical therapists with specialized knowledge of particular types of treatment also will have excellent job prospects. The increasing

elderly population will drive growth in the demand for physical therapy services. The elderly population is particularly vulnerable to chronic and debilitating conditions that require therapeutic services. Also, the baby-boom generation is entering the prime age for heart attacks and strokes, increasing the demand for cardiac and physical rehabilitation. And increasing numbers of children will need physical therapy as technological advances save the lives of a larger proportion of newborns with severe birth defects.

Assess, plan, organize, and participate in rehabilitative programs that improve mobility, relieve pain, increase strength, and decrease or prevent deformity of patients suffering from disease or injury. Perform and document initial exams, evaluating data to identify problems and determine diagnoses prior to interventions. Plan, prepare, and carry out individually designed programs of physical treatment to maintain, improve, or restore physical functioning; alleviate pain; and prevent physical dysfunction in patients. Record prognoses, treatments, responses, and progresses in patients' charts or enter information into computers. Identify and document goals, anticipated progresses, and plans for reevaluation. Evaluate effects of treatments at various stages and adjust treatments to achieve maximum benefits. Administer manual exercises, massages, or traction to help relieve pain, increase patient strength, or decrease or prevent deformity or crippling. Test and measure patients' strength, motor development and function, sensory perception, functional capacity, and respiratory and circulatory efficiency and record data. Instruct patients and families in treatment procedures to be continued at home. Confer with patients, medical practitioners, and appropriate others to plan, implement, and assess intervention programs. Review physicians' referrals and patients' medical records to help determine diagnoses and physical therapy treatments required. Obtain patients' informed consent to proposed interventions. Discharge patients from physical therapy when goals or projected outcomes have been attained and provide for appropriate follow-up care or referrals. Provide information to patients about proposed interventions, material risks, and expected benefits and any reasonable alternatives. Inform patients when diagnoses reveal findings outside the scope of physical therapy to treat and refer to appropriate practitioners. Direct, supervise, assess, and communicate with supportive personnel. Provide educational information about physical therapy and physical therapists, injury prevention, ergonomics, and ways to promote health. Refer clients to community resources and services. Administer treatment involving application of physical agents, using equipment, moist packs, ultraviolet and infrared lamps, and ultrasound machines.

Personality Type: Social-Investigative-Realistic.

Career Cluster: 08 Health Science. **Career Pathway:** 08.3 Health Informatics.

Skills: No data available.

Education and Training Programs: Physical Therapy/Therapist; Kinesiotherapy/Kinesiotherapist. **Related Knowledge/Courses:** Therapy and Counseling; Medicine and Dentistry; Psychology; Education and Training; Biology; Customer and Personal Service.

Work Environment: Indoors; disease or infections; standing.

Physician Assistants

- ❋ Education/Training Required: Bachelor's degree
- ❋ Annual Earnings: $78,450
- ❋ Beginning Wage: $46,750
- ❋ Earnings Growth Potential: High (40.4%)
- ❋ Growth: 27.0%
- ❋ Annual Job Openings: 7,147
- ❋ Job Security: Most Secure
- ❋ Self-Employed: 1.8%
- ❋ Part-Time: 15.6%

Renewal Industry: Health Care.

Industries with Greatest Employment: Ambulatory Health-Care Services (64.0%); Hospitals, Public and Private (23.6%).

Highest-Growth Industries (Projected Growth for This Job): Ambulatory Health-Care Services (36.5%); Administrative and Support Services (26.9%); Management of Companies and Enterprises (15.2%).

Other Considerations for Job Outlook: Job opportunities for PAs should be good, particularly in rural and inner-city clinics because those settings have difficulty attracting physicians. In addition to job openings from employment growth, openings will result from the need to replace physician assistants who retire or leave the occupation permanently during the 2006–2016 decade. Opportunities will be best in states that allow PAs a wider scope of practice, such as allowing PAs to prescribe medications. Physicians and institutions are expected to employ more PAs to provide primary care and to assist with medical and surgical procedures because PAs are cost-effective and productive members of the health-care team. Physician assistants can relieve physicians of routine duties and procedures. Telemedicine—using technology to facilitate interactive consultations between physicians and physician assistants—also will expand the use of physician assistants.

Under the supervision of physicians, provide health-care services typically performed by a physician. Conduct complete physicals, provide treatment, and counsel patients. May, in some cases, prescribe medication. Must graduate from an accredited educational program for physician assistants. Examine patients to obtain information about their physical conditions. Obtain, compile, and record patient medical data, including health history, progress notes, and results of physical examinations. Interpret diagnostic test results for deviations from normal. Make tentative diagnoses and decisions about management and treatment of patients. Prescribe therapy or medication with physician approval. Administer or order diagnostic tests, such as X-ray, electrocardiogram, and laboratory tests. Instruct and counsel patients about prescribed therapeutic regimens, normal growth and development, family planning, emotional problems of daily living, and health maintenance. Perform therapeutic procedures such as injections, immunizations, suturing and wound care, and infection management. Provide physicians with assistance during surgery or complicated medical procedures. Visit and observe patients on hospital rounds or house calls, updating charts, ordering therapy, and reporting back to physicians. Supervise and coordinate activities of technicians and technical assistants. Order medical and laboratory supplies and equipment.

Personality Type: Social-Investigative-Realistic.

Career Cluster: 08 Health Science. **Career Pathway:** 08.2 Diagnostics Services.

Skills: Social Perceptiveness; Systems Analysis; Systems Evaluation; Persuasion; Complex Problem Solving; Reading Comprehension.

Education and Training Program: Physician Assistant. **Related Knowledge/Courses:** Medicine and Dentistry; Biology; Therapy and Counseling; Psychology; Chemistry; Sociology and Anthropology.

Work Environment: Indoors; disease or infections; standing; using hands on objects, tools, or controls.

Physicians and Surgeons

See *Anesthesiologists; Family and General Practitioners; Internists, General; Obstetricians and Gynecologists; Pediatricans, General; Psychiatrists; and Surgeons*, described separately.

Physics Teachers, Postsecondary

- ❇ Education/Training Required: Master's degree
- ❇ Annual Earnings: $70,090
- ❇ Beginning Wage: $40,580
- ❇ Earnings Growth Potential: High (42.1%)
- ❇ Growth: 22.9%
- ❇ Annual Job Openings: 2,155
- ❇ Job Security: Most Secure
- ❇ Self-Employed: 0.4%
- ❇ Part-Time: 27.8%

Renewal Industry: Education.

Industries with Greatest Employment: Educational Services, Public and Private (97.3%).

Highest-Growth Industries (Projected Growth for This Job): Administrative and Support Services (48.3%); Amusement, Gambling, and Recreation Industries (45.2%); Social Assistance (38.6%); Support Activities for Transportation (32.8%); Religious, Grantmaking, Civic, Professional, and Similar Organizations (29.9%); Professional, Scientific, and Technical Services (28.8%); Management of Companies and Enterprises (26.8%); Local Government (23.5%); Educational Services, Public and Private (22.8%); Hospitals, Public and Private (21.4%).

Other Considerations for Job Outlook: Retirements of current postsecondary teachers should create numerous openings for all types of postsecondary teachers, so job opportunities are generally expected to be very good.

One of the main reasons why students attend postsecondary institutions is to prepare themselves for careers, so the best job prospects for postsecondary teachers are likely to be in rapidly growing fields that offer many nonacademic career options. Physics is a key part of the curriculum for many technician majors and some health-care majors. Community colleges and other institutions offering career and technical education have been among the most rapidly growing, and these institutions are expected to offer some of the best opportunities for postsecondary teachers.

Teach courses pertaining to the laws of matter and energy. Includes both teachers primarily engaged in teaching and those who do a combination of both teaching and research. Evaluate and grade students' classwork, laboratory work, assignments, and papers. Prepare and deliver lectures to undergraduate and/or graduate students on topics such as quantum mechanics, particle physics, and optics. Compile, administer, and grade examinations or assign this work to others. Maintain student attendance records, grades, and other required records. Supervise students' laboratory work. Prepare course materials such as syllabi, homework assignments, and handouts. Maintain regularly scheduled office hours to advise and assist students. Supervise undergraduate and/or graduate teaching, internship, and research work. Keep abreast of developments in their field by reading current literature, talking with colleagues, and participating in professional conferences. Plan, evaluate, and revise curricula, course content, and course materials and methods of instruction. Initiate, facilitate, and moderate classroom discussions. Conduct research in a particular field of knowledge and publish findings in professional journals, books, and/or electronic media. Advise students on academic and vocational curricula and on career issues. Select and obtain materials and supplies such as textbooks and laboratory equipment. Collaborate with colleagues to address teaching and research issues. Participate in student recruitment, registration, and placement activities. Serve on academic or administrative committees that deal with institutional policies, departmental matters, and academic issues. Write grant proposals to procure external research funding. Perform administrative duties such as serving as department head. Act as advisers to student organizations. Provide professional consulting services to government and/or industry. Compile bibliographies of specialized materials for outside reading assignments. Participate in campus and community events.

Personality Type: Social-Investigative.

Career Cluster: 15 Science, Technology, Engineering, and Mathematics. **Career Pathway:** 15.3 Science and Mathematics.

Skills: Science; Programming; Mathematics; Instructing; Writing; Reading Comprehension.

Education and Training Programs: Physics, General; Atomic/Molecular Physics; Elementary Particle Physics; Plasma and High-Temperature Physics; Nuclear Physics; Optics/Optical Sciences; Solid State and Low-Temperature Physics; Acoustics; Theoretical and Mathematical Physics; Physics, Other. **Related Knowledge/Courses:** Physics; Mathematics; Chemistry; Engineering and Technology; Education and Training; Computers and Electronics.

Work Environment: Indoors; sitting.

Pipe Fitters and Steamfitters

- ❋ Education/Training Required: Long-term on-the-job training
- ❋ Annual Earnings: $44,090
- ❋ Beginning Wage: $26,550
- ❋ Earnings Growth Potential: Medium (39.8%)
- ❋ Growth: 10.6%
- ❋ Annual Job Openings: 68,643
- ❋ Job Security: Least Secure
- ❋ Self-Employed: 12.3%
- ❋ Part-Time: 3.4%

Our sources did not provide separate job openings data for this occupation. The job openings listed here are shared with Plumbers.

Renewal Industries: Green Technologies; Infrastructure.

Industries with Greatest Employment: Specialty Trade Contractors (64.3%).

Highest-Growth Industries (Projected Growth for This Job): Amusement, Gambling, and Recreation Industries (35.0%); Waste Management and Remediation Services (31.9%); Professional, Scientific, and Technical Services (28.9%); Administrative and Support Services (27.4%); Building Material and Garden Equipment and Supplies Dealers (27.0%); Real Estate (21.9%); Support Activities

for Transportation (18.5%); Accommodation, Including Hotels and Motels (16.8%); Management of Companies and Enterprises (15.3%); Food Services and Drinking Places (15.1%).

Other Considerations for Job Outlook: Job opportunities are expected to be very good, as demand for skilled pipefitters and steamfitters is expected to outpace the supply of workers well trained in this craft in some areas. Some employers report difficulty finding workers with the right qualifications. In addition, many people currently working in these trades are expected to retire over the next 10 years, which will create additional job openings. Workers with welding experience should have especially good opportunities.

Lay out, assemble, install, and maintain pipe systems, pipe supports, and related hydraulic and pneumatic equipment for steam, hot water, heating, cooling, lubricating, sprinkling, and industrial production and processing systems. Cut, thread, and hammer pipe to specifications, using tools such as saws, cutting torches, and pipe threaders and benders. Assemble and secure pipes, tubes, fittings, and related equipment according to specifications by welding, brazing, cementing, soldering, and threading joints. Attach pipes to walls, structures, and fixtures, such as radiators or tanks, using brackets, clamps, tools, or welding equipment. Inspect, examine, and test installed systems and pipelines, using pressure gauge, hydrostatic testing, observation, or other methods. Measure and mark pipes for cutting and threading. Lay out full scale drawings of pipe systems, supports, and related equipment, following blueprints. Plan pipe system layout, installation, or repair according to specifications. Select pipe sizes and types and related materials, such as supports, hangers, and hydraulic cylinders, according to specifications. Cut and bore holes in structures such as bulkheads, decks, walls, and mains prior to pipe installation, using hand and power tools. Modify, clean, and maintain pipe systems, units, fittings, and related machines and equipment, following specifications and using hand and power tools. Install automatic controls used to regulate pipe systems. Turn valves to shut off steam, water, or other gases or liquids from pipe sections, using valve keys or wrenches. Remove and replace worn components. Prepare cost estimates for clients. Inspect work sites for obstructions and to ensure that holes will not cause structural weakness. Operate motorized pumps to remove water from flooded manholes, basements, or facility floors.

Dip nonferrous piping materials in a mixture of molten tin and lead to obtain a coating that prevents erosion or galvanic and electrolytic action.

Personality Type: Realistic-Conventional.

Career Cluster: 02 Architecture and Construction. **Career Pathway:** 02.2 Construction.

Skills: Installation; Repairing; Systems Analysis; Management of Personnel Resources; Equipment Maintenance; Operation Monitoring.

Education and Training Program: Pipefitting/Pipefitter and Sprinkler Fitter. **Related Knowledge/Courses:** Building and Construction; Design; Mechanical Devices; Engineering and Technology; Economics and Accounting; Transportation.

Work Environment: Outdoors; hazardous equipment; minor burns, cuts, bites, or stings; standing; using hands on objects, tools, or controls; repetitive motions.

Pipelayers

- ❋ Education/Training Required: Moderate-term on-the-job training
- ❋ Annual Earnings: $31,280
- ❋ Beginning Wage: $21,270
- ❋ Earnings Growth Potential: Low (32.0%)
- ❋ Growth: 8.7%
- ❋ Annual Job Openings: 8,902
- ❋ Job Security: Least Secure
- ❋ Self-Employed: 11.6%
- ❋ Part-Time: 3.4%

Renewal Industry: Green Technologies.

Industries with Greatest Employment: Heavy and Civil Engineering Construction (44.4%); Specialty Trade Contractors (19.6%); Local Government (16.1%).

Highest-Growth Industries (Projected Growth for This Job): Professional, Scientific, and Technical Services (27.3%).

Other Considerations for Job Outlook: The jobs of pipelayers are generally less sensitive to changes in economic conditions than jobs in other construction trades. Even when construction activity declines, maintenance, rehabilitation, and replacement of existing piping systems provide many jobs.

Lay pipe for storm or sanitation sewers, drains, and water mains. Perform any combination of these tasks: grade trenches or culverts, position pipe, or seal joints. Check slopes for conformance to requirements, using levels or lasers. Cover pipes with earth or other materials. Cut pipes to required lengths. Connect pipe pieces and seal joints, using welding equipment, cement, or glue. Install and repair sanitary and stormwater sewer structures and pipe systems. Install and use instruments such as lasers, grade rods, and transit levels. Grade and level trench bases, using tamping machines and hand tools. Lay out pipe routes, following written instructions or blueprints and coordinating layouts with supervisors. Align and position pipes to prepare them for welding or sealing. Dig trenches to desired or required depths by hand or using trenching tools. Operate mechanized equipment such as pickup trucks, rollers, tandem dump trucks, front-end loaders, and backhoes. Train others in pipe-laying and provide supervision. Tap and drill holes into pipes to introduce auxiliary lines or devices. Locate existing pipes needing repair or replacement, using magnetic or radio indicators.

Personality Type: Realistic.

Career Cluster: 02 Architecture and Construction. **Career Pathway:** 02.2 Construction.

Skills: Installation; Quality Control Analysis; Operation and Control; Operation Monitoring; Equipment Maintenance; Equipment Selection.

Education and Training Program: Plumbing Technology/Plumber. **Related Knowledge/Courses:** Building and Construction; Mechanical Devices.

Work Environment: Outdoors; noisy; hazardous equipment; standing; using hands on objects, tools, or controls; repetitive motions.

Plumbers

- ✻ Education/Training Required: Long-term on-the-job training
- ✻ Annual Earnings: $44,090
- ✻ Beginning Wage: $26,550
- ✻ Earnings Growth Potential: Medium (39.8%)
- ✻ Growth: 10.6%
- ✻ Annual Job Openings: 68,643
- ✻ Job Security: Least Secure
- ✻ Self-Employed: 12.3%
- ✻ Part-Time: 3.4%

Our sources did not provide separate job openings data for this occupation. The job openings listed here are shared with Pipe Fitters and Steamfitters.

Renewal Industries: Green Technologies; Infrastructure.

Industries with Greatest Employment: Specialty Trade Contractors (64.3%).

Highest-Growth Industries (Projected Growth for This Job): Amusement, Gambling, and Recreation Industries (35.0%); Waste Management and Remediation Services (31.9%); Professional, Scientific, and Technical Services (28.9%); Administrative and Support Services (27.4%); Building Material and Garden Equipment and Supplies Dealers (27.0%); Real Estate (21.9%); Support Activities for Transportation (18.5%); Accommodation, Including Hotels and Motels (16.8%); Management of Companies and Enterprises (15.3%); Food Services and Drinking Places (15.1%).

Other Considerations for Job Outlook: Job opportunities are expected to be very good, as demand for skilled plumbers is expected to outpace the supply of workers well trained in this craft in some areas. Some employers report difficulty finding workers with the right qualifications. In addition, many people currently working in these trades are expected to retire over the next 10 years, which will create additional job openings. Workers with welding experience should have especially good opportunities.

Assemble, install, and repair pipes, fittings, and fixtures of heating, water, and drainage systems according to specifications and plumbing codes. Measure, cut, thread, and bend pipe to required angles, using hand and power tools or machines such as pipe cutters, pipe-threading machines, and pipe-bending machines. Study building plans and inspect structures to assess material and equipment needs to establish the sequence of pipe installations and to plan installation around obstructions such as electrical wiring. Locate and mark the position of pipe installations, connections, passage holes, and fixtures in structures, using measuring instruments such as rulers and levels. Assemble pipe sections, tubing, and fittings, using couplings, clamps, screws, bolts, cement, plastic solvent, caulking, or soldering, brazing, and welding equipment. Fill pipes or plumbing fixtures with water or air and observe pressure gauges to detect and locate leaks. Install pipe assemblies, fittings, valves, appliances such as dishwashers and water heaters, and fixtures such as sinks and toilets, using hand and power tools. Direct workers engaged in pipe cutting and preassembly and installation of plumbing systems and components. Cut openings in structures to accommodate pipes and pipe fittings, using hand and power tools. Review blueprints and building codes and specifications to determine work details and procedures. Install underground storm, sanitary, and water piping systems and extend piping to connect fixtures and plumbing to these systems. Repair and maintain plumbing, replacing defective washers, replacing or mending broken pipes, and opening clogged drains. Keep records of assignments and produce detailed work reports. Hang steel supports from ceiling joists to hold pipes in place. Perform complex calculations and planning for special or very large jobs. Clear away debris in renovations. Install oxygen and medical gas in hospitals. Prepare written work cost estimates and negotiate contracts. Use specialized techniques, equipment, or materials, such as performing computer-assisted welding of small pipes or working with the special piping used in microchip fabrication.

Personality Type: Realistic-Conventional-Investigative.

Career Cluster: 02 Architecture and Construction. **Career Pathway:** 02.2 Construction.

Skills: No data available.

Education and Training Programs: Pipefitting/Pipefitter and Sprinkler Fitter; Plumbing Technology/Plumber; Plumbing and Related Water Supply Services, Other. **Related Knowledge/Courses:** Building and Construction; Physics; Mechanical Devices; Design; Engineering and Technology; Customer and Personal Service.

Work Environment: Outdoors; noisy; very hot or cold; hazardous equipment; standing; using hands on objects, tools, or controls.

Plumbers, Pipefitters, and Steamfitters

See *Pipe Fitters and Steamfitters* and *Plumbers*, *described separately.*

Podiatrists

- ❋ Education/Training Required: First professional degree
- ❋ Annual Earnings: $110,510
- ❋ Beginning Wage: $45,260
- ❋ Earnings Growth Potential: Very high (59.0%)
- ❋ Growth: 9.5%
- ❋ Annual Job Openings: 648
- ❋ Job Security: Most Secure
- ❋ Self-Employed: 23.9%
- ❋ Part-Time: 23.6%

Renewal Industry: Health Care.

Industries with Greatest Employment: Ambulatory Health-Care Services (67.0%); Federal Government (5.0%).

Highest-Growth Industries (Projected Growth for This Job): None met the criteria.

Other Considerations for Job Outlook: Although the occupation is small and most podiatrists continue to practice until retirement, job opportunities should be good for entry-level graduates of accredited podiatric medicine programs. Job growth and replacement needs should create enough job openings for the supply of new podiatric medicine graduates. Opportunities will be better for board-certified podiatrists because many managed-care organizations require board certification. Newly trained podiatrists will find more opportunities in group medical practices, clinics, and health networks than in traditional solo practices. Establishing a practice will be most difficult in the areas surrounding colleges of podiatric medicine, where podiatrists concentrate.

Diagnose and treat diseases and deformities of the human foot. Treat bone, muscle, and joint disorders affecting the feet. Diagnose diseases and deformities of the foot, using medical histories, physical examinations, X-rays, and laboratory test results. Prescribe medications, corrective devices, physical therapy, or surgery. Treat conditions such as corns, calluses, ingrown nails, tumors, shortened tendons, bunions, cysts, and abscesses by surgical methods. Advise patients about treatments and foot care techniques necessary for prevention of future problems. Refer patients to physicians when symptoms indicative of systemic disorders, such as arthritis or diabetes, are observed in feet and legs. Correct deformities by means of plaster casts and strapping. Make and fit prosthetic appliances. Perform administrative duties such as hiring employees, ordering supplies, and keeping records. Educate the public about the benefits of foot care through techniques such as speaking engagements, advertising, and other forums. Treat deformities, using mechanical methods, such as whirlpool or paraffin baths, and electrical methods, such as shortwave and low-voltage currents.

Personality Type: Investigative-Social-Realistic.

Career Cluster: 08 Health Science. **Career Pathway:** 08.1 Therapeutic Services.

Skills: Science; Active Listening; Complex Problem Solving; Management of Financial Resources; Reading Comprehension; Equipment Selection.

Education and Training Program: Podiatric Medicine/Podiatry (DPM). **Related Knowledge/Courses:** Medicine and Dentistry; Biology; Therapy and Counseling; Sales and Marketing; Chemistry; Psychology.

Work Environment: Indoors; contaminants; disease or infections; sitting; using hands on objects, tools, or controls; repetitive motions.

Political Science Teachers, Postsecondary

- ❋ Education/Training Required: Master's degree
- ❋ Annual Earnings: $63,100
- ❋ Beginning Wage: $35,600
- ❋ Earnings Growth Potential: High (43.6%)
- ❋ Growth: 22.9%
- ❋ Annual Job Openings: 2,435
- ❋ Job Security: Most Secure
- ❋ Self-Employed: 0.4%
- ❋ Part-Time: 27.8%

Renewal Industry: Education.

Industries with Greatest Employment: Educational Services, Public and Private (97.3%).

Highest-Growth Industries (Projected Growth for This Job): Administrative and Support Services (48.3%); Amusement, Gambling, and Recreation Industries (45.2%); Social Assistance (38.6%); Support Activities for Transportation (32.8%); Religious, Grantmaking, Civic, Professional, and Similar Organizations (29.9%); Professional, Scientific, and Technical Services (28.8%); Management of Companies and Enterprises (26.8%); Local Government (23.5%); Educational Services, Public and Private (22.8%); Hospitals, Public and Private (21.4%).

Other Considerations for Job Outlook: Retirements of current postsecondary teachers should create numerous openings for all types of postsecondary teachers, so job opportunities are generally expected to be very good. However, one of the main reasons why students attend postsecondary institutions is to prepare themselves for careers, so the best job prospects for postsecondary teachers are likely to be in rapidly growing fields that offer many nonacademic career options—unlike political science. Community colleges and other institutions offering career and technical education have been among the most rapidly growing, and these institutions are expected to offer some of the best opportunities for postsecondary teachers.

Teach courses in political science, international affairs, and international relations. Initiate, facilitate, and moderate classroom discussions. Prepare and deliver lectures to undergraduate or graduate students on topics such as classical political thought, international relations, and democracy and citizenship. Evaluate and grade students' classwork, assignments, and papers. Compile, administer, and grade examinations or assign this work to others. Prepare course materials such as syllabi, homework assignments, and handouts. Keep abreast of developments in their field by reading current literature, talking with colleagues, and participating in professional conferences. Plan, evaluate, and revise curricula, course content, and course materials and methods of instruction. Maintain student attendance records, grades, and other required records. Maintain regularly scheduled office hours in order to advise and assist students. Advise students on academic and vocational curricula and on career issues. Select and obtain materials and supplies such as textbooks. Conduct research in a particular field of knowledge and publish findings in professional journals, books, and electronic media. Supervise undergraduate and graduate teaching, internship, and research work. Collaborate with colleagues to address teaching and research issues. Serve on academic or administrative committees that deal with institutional policies, departmental matters, and academic issues. Participate in student recruitment, registration, and placement activities. Participate in campus and community events. Compile bibliographies of specialized materials for outside reading assignments. Act as advisers to student organizations. Perform administrative duties such as serving as department head. Write grant proposals to procure external research funding. Provide professional consulting services to government and industry.

Personality Type: Social-Enterprising-Artistic.

Career Clusters: 07 Government and Public Administration; 15 Science, Technology, Engineering, and Mathematics. **Career Pathways:** 07.1 Governance; 07.4 Planning; 15.3 Science and Mathematics.

Skills: Writing; Instructing; Reading Comprehension; Learning Strategies; Persuasion; Critical Thinking.

Education and Training Programs: Social Science Teacher Education; Political Science and Government, General; American Government and Politics (United States); Political Science and Government, Other. **Related Knowledge/Courses:** History and Archeology; Philosophy and Theology; Sociology and Anthropology; Geography; Law and Government; English Language.

Work Environment: Indoors; sitting.

Preschool Teachers, Except Special Education

* ❀ Education/Training Required: Postsecondary vocational training
* ❀ Annual Earnings: $23,130
* ❀ Beginning Wage: $15,380
* ❀ Earnings Growth Potential: Low (33.5%)
* ❀ Growth: 26.3%
* ❀ Annual Job Openings: 78,172
* ❀ Job Security: Most Secure
* ❀ Self-Employed: 1.1%
* ❀ Part-Time: 25.1%

Renewal Industry: Education.

Industries with Greatest Employment: Social Assistance (63.0%); Religious, Grantmaking, Civic, Professional, and Similar Organizations (17.9%); Educational Services, Public and Private (15.9%).

Highest-Growth Industries (Projected Growth for This Job): Amusement, Gambling, and Recreation Industries (32.2%); Social Assistance (31.8%); Administrative and Support Services (26.8%); Professional, Scientific, and Technical Services (26.2%); Ambulatory Health-Care Services (26.2%); Nursing and Residential Care Facilities (19.6%); Religious, Grantmaking, Civic, Professional, and Similar Organizations (18.5%); Educational Services, Public and Private (16.0%); Management of Companies and Enterprises (15.2%).

Other Considerations for Job Outlook: Job prospects are expected to be favorable, with particularly good prospects for teachers in less desirable urban or rural school districts and for those with licensure in more than one subject. Fast-growing states in the South and West—led by Nevada, Arizona, Texas, and Georgia—will experience the largest enrollment increases. Enrollments in the Midwest are expected to hold relatively steady, while those in the Northeast are expected to decline. The number of teachers employed is dependent on state and local expenditures for education and on the enactment of legislation to increase the quality and scope of public education. At the federal level, there has been a large increase in funding for education, particularly for the hiring of qualified teachers in lower-income areas. Also, some states are instituting programs to improve early childhood education.

Instruct children (normally up to 5 years of age) in activities designed to promote social, physical, and intellectual growth needed for primary school in preschool, day care center, or other child development facility. May be required to hold state certification. Provide a variety of materials and resources for children to explore, manipulate, and use, both in learning activities and in imaginative play. Attend to children's basic needs by feeding them, dressing them, and changing their diapers. Establish and enforce rules for behavior and procedures for maintaining order. Read books to entire classes or to small groups. Teach basic skills such as color, shape, number, and letter recognition; personal hygiene; and social skills. Organize and lead activities designed to promote physical, mental, and social development, such as games, arts and crafts, music, storytelling, and field trips. Observe and evaluate children's performance, behavior, social development, and physical health. Meet with parents and guardians to discuss their children's progress and needs, determine their priorities for their children, and suggest ways that they can promote learning and development. Identify children showing signs of emotional, developmental, or health-related problems and discuss them with supervisors, parents or guardians, and child development specialists. Enforce all administration policies and rules governing students. Prepare materials and classrooms for class activities. Serve meals and snacks in accordance with nutritional guidelines. Teach proper eating habits and personal hygiene. Assimilate arriving children to the school environment by greeting them, helping them remove outerwear, and selecting activities of interest to them. Adapt teaching methods and instructional materials to meet students' varying needs and interests. Establish clear objectives for all lessons, units, and projects and communicate those objectives to children. Demonstrate activities to children. Arrange indoor and outdoor space to facilitate creative play, motor-skill activities, and safety. Plan and conduct activities for a balanced program of instruction, demonstration, and work time that provides students with opportunities to observe, question, and investigate. Maintain accurate and complete student records as required by laws, district policies, and administrative regulations.

Personality Type: Social-Artistic.

Career Clusters: 05 Education and Training; 10 Human Services. **Career Pathways:** 05.3 Teaching/Training; 10.1 Early Childhood Development and Services.

Skills: No data available.

Education and Training Programs: Montessori Teacher Education; Early Childhood Education and Teaching; Child Care and Support Services Management. **Related Knowledge/Courses:** Philosophy and Theology; Sociology and Anthropology; Psychology; Customer and Personal Service; Education and Training.

Work Environment: Indoors; standing; walking and running; bending or twisting the body.

Production, Planning, and Expediting Clerks

- ❋ Education/Training Required: Short-term on-the-job training
- ❋ Annual Earnings: $39,690
- ❋ Beginning Wage: $24,520
- ❋ Earnings Growth Potential: Medium (38.2%)
- ❋ Growth: 4.2%
- ❋ Annual Job Openings: 52,735
- ❋ Job Security: More Secure than Most
- ❋ Self-Employed: 1.4%
- ❋ Part-Time: 6.7%

Renewal Industry: Advanced Manufacturing.

Industries with Greatest Employment: Professional, Scientific, and Technical Services (7.3%); Transportation Equipment Manufacturing (6.8%); Merchant Wholesalers, Durable Goods (5.5%); Computer and Electronic Product Manufacturing (5.1%).

Highest-Growth Industries (Projected Growth for This Job): Securities, Commodity Contracts, and Other Financial Investments and Related Activities (43.6%); Internet Publishing and Broadcasting (40.4%); Social Assistance (34.2%); Professional, Scientific, and Technical Services (34.0%); Warehousing and Storage (33.6%); Funds, Trusts, and Other Financial Vehicles (33.3%); Ambulatory Health-Care Services (30.7%); Administrative and Support Services (29.0%); Waste Management and Remediation Services (27.3%); Building Material and Garden Equipment and Supplies Dealers (25.3%); Internet Service Providers, Web Search Portals, and Data Processing Services (25.0%); Water Transportation (23.2%); Real Estate (23.0%); Support Activities for Transportation (22.5%);

Performing Arts, Spectator Sports, and Related Industries (21.5%); Nursing and Residential Care Facilities (20.8%); Nonstore Retailers (17.1%); Religious, Grantmaking, Civic, Professional, and Similar Organizations (15.8%); Accommodation, Including Hotels and Motels (15.7%); Motion Picture, Video, and Sound Recording Industries (15.6%); Management of Companies and Enterprises (15.3%); Repair and Maintenance (15.3%).

Other Considerations for Job Outlook: Manufacturing firms and wholesale and retail trade establishments are the primary employers.

Coordinate and expedite the flow of work and materials within or between departments of an establishment according to production schedules.inventory levels, costs, and production problems. Examine documents, materials, and products, and monitor work processes to assess completeness, accuracy, and conformance to standards and specifications. Review documents such as production schedules, work orders, and staffing tables to determine personnel and materials requirements, and material priorities. Revise production schedules when required due to design changes, labor or material shortages, backlogs, or other interruptions, collaborating with management, marketing, sales, production, and engineering. Confer with department supervisors and other personnel to assess progress and discuss needed changes. Confer with establishment personnel, vendors, and customers to coordinate production and shipping activities, and to resolve complaints or eliminate delays. Record production data, including volume produced, consumption of raw materials, and quality control measures. Requisition and maintain inventories of materials and supplies necessary to meet production demands. Calculate figures such as required amounts of labor and materials, manufacturing costs, and wages, using pricing schedules, adding machines, calculators, or computers. Distribute production schedules and work orders to departments. Compile information such as production rates and progress, materials inventories, materials used, and customer information, so that status reports can be completed. Arrange for delivery, assembly, and distribution of supplies and parts to expedite flow of materials and meet production schedules. Contact suppliers to verify shipment details. Maintain files such as maintenance records, bills of lading, and cost reports. Plan production commitments and timetables for business units, specific programs, and/or jobs, using sales forecasts. Establish and prepare product construction directions and locations; information on required tools, materials, and equipment; numbers of workers needed; and cost projections. Compile and prepare documentation related to production sequences, transportation, personnel schedules, and purchase, maintenance, and repair orders. Provide documentation and information to account for delays, difficulties, and changes to cost estimates.

Personality Type: Conventional-Enterprising.

Career Cluster: 16 Transportation, Distribution, and Logistics. **Career Pathway:** 16.3 Warehousing and Distribution Center Operations.

Skills: Management of Material Resources; Operations Analysis; Management of Financial Resources; Systems Evaluation; Negotiation; Mathematics.

Education and Training Program: Parts, Warehousing, and Inventory Management Operations. **Related Knowledge/Courses:** Production and Processing; Clerical Practices; Computers and Electronics; Administration and Management; Mathematics; Customer and Personal Service.

Work Environment: Indoors; noisy; contaminants; sitting.

Prosthodontists

- ❇ Education/Training Required: First professional degree
- ❇ Annual Earnings: More than $145,600
- ❇ Beginning Wage: $75,450
- ❇ Earnings Growth Potential: Cannot be calculated
- ❇ Growth: 10.7%
- ❇ Annual Job Openings: 54
- ❇ Job Security: Less Secure than Most
- ❇ Self-Employed: 51.3%
- ❇ Part-Time: 25.9%

Renewal Industry: Health Care.

Industries with Greatest Employment: Ambulatory Health-Care Services (36.3%).

Highest-Growth Industries (Projected Growth for This Job): Ambulatory Health-Care Services (18.7%).

Other Considerations for Job Outlook: As an increasing number of dentists from the baby-boom generation reach retirement age, many of them will retire or work fewer hours. However, the number of applicants to, and graduates from, dental schools has increased in recent years. Therefore, younger dentists will be able to take over the work from older dentists who retire or cut back on hours, as well as provide dental services to accommodate the growing demand.

Construct oral prostheses to replace missing teeth and other oral structures to correct natural and acquired deformation of mouth and jaws; to restore and maintain oral function, such as chewing and speaking; and to improve appearance. Replace missing teeth and associated oral structures with permanent fixtures, such as crowns and bridges, or removable fixtures, such as dentures. Fit prostheses to patients, making any necessary adjustments and modifications. Design and fabricate dental prostheses or supervise dental technicians and laboratory bench workers who construct the devices. Measure and take impressions of patients' jaws and teeth to determine the shape and size of dental prostheses, using face bows, dental articulators, recording devices, and other materials. Collaborate with general dentists, specialists, and other health professionals to develop solutions to dental and oral health concerns. Repair, reline, and/or rebase dentures. Restore function and aesthetics to traumatic injury victims or to individuals with diseases or birth defects. Use bonding technology on the surface of the teeth to change tooth shape or to close gaps. Treat facial pain and jaw joint problems. Place veneers onto teeth to conceal defects. Bleach discolored teeth to brighten and whiten them.

Personality Type: Investigative-Realistic.

Career Cluster: 08 Health Science. **Career Pathway:** 08.1 Therapeutic Services.

Skills: Science; Management of Financial Resources; Social Perceptiveness; Equipment Selection; Reading Comprehension; Active Learning.

Education and Training Programs: Prosthodontics/Prosthodontology (Cert, MS, PhD); Prosthodontics Specialty. **Related Knowledge/Courses:** Medicine and Dentistry; Biology; Chemistry; Psychology; Engineering and Technology; Sales and Marketing.

P

Work Environment: Indoors; noisy; contaminants; disease or infections; hazardous equipment; using hands on objects, tools, or controls.

Psychiatrists

* ❋ Education/Training Required: First professional degree
* ❋ Annual Earnings: More than $145,600
* ❋ Beginning Wage: $59,090
* ❋ Earnings Growth Potential: Cannot be calculated
* ❋ Growth: 14.2%
* ❋ Annual Job Openings: 38,027
* ❋ Job Security: Most Secure
* ❋ Self-Employed: 14.7%
* ❋ Part-Time: 8.1%

Our sources did not provide separate job openings data for this occupation. The job openings listed here are shared with Anesthesiologists; Family and General Practitioners; Internists, General; Obstetricians and Gynecologists; Pediatricians, General; and Surgeons.

Renewal Industry: Health Care.

Industries with Greatest Employment: Ambulatory Health-Care Services (55.9%); Hospitals, Public and Private (17.8%).

Highest-Growth Industries (Projected Growth for This Job): Social Assistance (58.6%); Administrative and Support Services (26.8%); Professional, Scientific, and Technical Services (22.6%); Nursing and Residential Care Facilities (21.0%); Ambulatory Health-Care Services (19.4%); Religious, Grantmaking, Civic, Professional, and Similar Organizations (16.7%); Management of Companies and Enterprises (15.3%).

Other Considerations for Job Outlook: Opportunities for individuals interested in becoming physicians and surgeons are expected to be very good. Unlike their predecessors, new physicians are much less likely to enter solo practice and more likely to take salaried jobs in group medical practices, clinics, and health networks. Reports of shortages in some specialties, such as general or family practice, internal medicine, and OB/GYN, or in rural or low-income areas should attract new entrants, encouraging schools to expand

programs and hospitals to increase available residency slots. However, because physician training is so lengthy, employment change happens gradually. Opportunities should be particularly good in rural and low-income areas, as some physicians find these areas unattractive because of less control over work hours, isolation from medical colleagues, or other reasons.

Diagnose, treat, and help prevent disorders of the mind. Prescribe, direct, and administer psychotherapeutic treatments or medications to treat mental, emotional, or behavioral disorders. Analyze and evaluate patient data and test findings to diagnose nature and extent of mental disorders. Collaborate with physicians, psychologists, social workers, psychiatric nurses, or other professionals to discuss treatment plans and progress. Gather and maintain patient information and records, including social and medical histories obtained from patients, relatives, and other professionals. Design individualized care plans, using a variety of treatments. Counsel outpatients and other patients during office visits. Examine or conduct laboratory or diagnostic tests on patients to provide information on general physical conditions and mental disorders. Advise and inform guardians, relatives, and significant others of patients' conditions and treatments. Teach, take continuing education classes, attend conferences and seminars, and conduct research and publish findings to increase understanding of mental, emotional, and behavioral states and disorders. Review and evaluate treatment procedures and outcomes of other psychiatrists and medical professionals. Prepare and submit case reports and summaries to government and mental health agencies. Serve on committees to promote and maintain community mental health services and delivery systems.

Personality Type: Investigative-Social-Artistic.

Career Cluster: 08 Health Science. **Career Pathway:** 08.1 Therapeutic Services.

Skills: Social Perceptiveness; Systems Evaluation; Systems Analysis; Active Listening; Writing; Speaking.

Education and Training Programs: Child Psychiatry; Psychiatry; Physical Medical and Rehabilitation/Psychiatry. **Related Knowledge/Courses:** Therapy and Counseling; Medicine and Dentistry; Psychology; Biology; Sociology and Anthropology; Philosophy and Theology.

Work Environment: Indoors; disease or infections; sitting.

Psychology Teachers, Postsecondary

* Education/Training Required: Master's degree
* Annual Earnings: $60,610
* Beginning Wage: $34,030
* Earnings Growth Potential: High (43.9%)
* Growth: 22.9%
* Annual Job Openings: 5,261
* Job Security: Most Secure
* Self-Employed: 0.4%
* Part-Time: 27.8%

Renewal Industry: Education.

Industries with Greatest Employment: Educational Services, Public and Private (97.3%).

Highest-Growth Industries (Projected Growth for This Job): Administrative and Support Services (48.3%); Amusement, Gambling, and Recreation Industries (45.2%); Social Assistance (38.6%); Support Activities for Transportation (32.8%); Religious, Grantmaking, Civic, Professional, and Similar Organizations (29.9%); Professional, Scientific, and Technical Services (28.8%); Management of Companies and Enterprises (26.8%); Local Government (23.5%); Educational Services, Public and Private (22.8%); Hospitals, Public and Private (21.4%).

Other Considerations for Job Outlook: Retirements of current postsecondary teachers should create numerous openings for all types of postsecondary teachers, so job opportunities are generally expected to be very good. However, one of the main reasons why students attend postsecondary institutions is to prepare themselves for careers, so the best job prospects for postsecondary teachers are likely to be in rapidly growing fields that offer many nonacademic career options. Psychology is a course requirement in many health-care majors. Community colleges and other institutions offering career and technical education have been among the most rapidly growing, and these institutions are expected to offer some of the best opportunities for postsecondary teachers.

Teach courses in psychology, such as child, clinical, and developmental psychology, and psychological counseling. Prepare and deliver lectures to undergraduate and/or graduate students on topics such as abnormal psychology, cognitive processes, and work motivation. Evaluate and grade students' classwork, laboratory work, assignments, and papers. Initiate, facilitate, and moderate classroom discussions. Compile, administer, and grade examinations or assign this work to others. Keep abreast of developments in their field by reading current literature, talking with colleagues, and participating in professional conferences. Prepare course materials such as syllabi, homework assignments, and handouts. Plan, evaluate, and revise curricula, course content, and course materials and methods of instruction. Maintain student attendance records, grades, and other required records. Supervise undergraduate and/or graduate teaching, internship, and research work. Maintain regularly scheduled office hours to advise and assist students. Conduct research in a particular field of knowledge and publish findings in professional journals, books, and electronic media. Advise students on academic and vocational curricula and on career issues. Select and obtain materials and supplies such as textbooks. Collaborate with colleagues to address teaching and research issues. Serve on academic or administrative committees that deal with institutional policies, departmental matters, and academic issues. Compile bibliographies of specialized materials for outside reading assignments. Participate in student recruitment, registration, and placement activities. Supervise students' laboratory work. Perform administrative duties such as serving as department head. Act as advisers to student organizations. Write grant proposals to procure external research funding. Participate in campus and community events. Provide professional consulting services to government and industry.

Personality Type: Social-Investigative-Artistic.

Career Clusters: 05 Education and Training; 08 Health Science; 10 Human Services; 12 Law, Public Safety, Corrections, and Security. **Career Pathways:** 05.3 Teaching/Training; 08.1 Therapeutic Services; 10.2 Counseling and Mental Health Services; 12.1 Correction Services.

Skills: Science; Learning Strategies; Instructing; Social Perceptiveness; Writing; Reading Comprehension.

Education and Training Programs: Social Science Teacher Education; Psychology Teacher Education; Psychology, General; Clinical Psychology; Cognitive Psychology and Psycholinguistics; Community Psychology; Comparative Psychology; Counseling Psychology; Developmental and

Child Psychology; Experimental Psychology; Industrial and Organizational Psychology; Personality Psychology; Physiological Psychology/Psychobiology; others. **Related Knowledge/Courses:** Therapy and Counseling; Psychology; Sociology and Anthropology; Philosophy and Theology; Education and Training; English Language.

Work Environment: Indoors; sitting.

Purchasing Agents, Except Wholesale, Retail, and Farm Products

* Education/Training Required: Work experience in a related occupation
* Annual Earnings: $52,460
* Beginning Wage: $32,580
* Earnings Growth Potential: Medium (37.9%)
* Growth: 0.1%
* Annual Job Openings: 22,349
* Job Security: More Secure than Most
* Self-Employed: 1.6%
* Part-Time: 3.8%

Renewal Industry: Advanced Manufacturing.

Industries with Greatest Employment: Federal Government (10.6%); Professional, Scientific, and Technical Services (8.0%); Computer and Electronic Product Manufacturing (6.9%); Transportation Equipment Manufacturing (6.4%); Management of Companies and Enterprises (5.5%).

Highest-Growth Industries (Projected Growth for This Job): Securities, Commodity Contracts, and Other Financial Investments and Related Activities (44.8%); Amusement, Gambling, and Recreation Industries (41.0%); Museums, Historical Sites, and Similar Institutions (36.4%); Social Assistance (35.7%); Warehousing and Storage (33.6%); General Merchandise Stores (32.5%); Waste Management and Remediation Services (28.9%); Lessors of Nonfinancial Intangible Assets (Except Copyrighted Works) (27.6%); Ambulatory Health-Care Services (27.4%); Administrative and Support Services (26.7%); Building Material and Garden Equipment and Supplies Dealers (26.3%); Performing Arts, Spectator Sports, and Related Industries (22.9%); Real Estate (21.8%); Water

Transportation (21.0%); Professional, Scientific, and Technical Services (20.8%); Nursing and Residential Care Facilities (20.7%); Personal and Laundry Services (20.6%); Support Activities for Transportation (19.8%); Nonstore Retailers (18.3%); Religious, Grantmaking, Civic, Professional, and Similar Organizations (17.2%); Accommodation, Including Hotels and Motels (16.2%); Management of Companies and Enterprises (15.3%); Rental and Leasing Services (15.2%).

Other Considerations for Job Outlook: Some firms prefer to promote existing employees to these positions, while others recruit and train college graduates. Opportunities should be best for those with a college degree.

Purchase machinery, equipment, tools, parts, supplies, or services necessary for the operation of an establishment. Purchase raw or semi-finished materials for manufacturing. Purchase the highest-quality merchandise at the lowest possible price and in correct amounts. Prepare purchase orders, solicit bid proposals, and review requisitions for goods and services. Research and evaluate suppliers based on price, quality, selection, service, support, availability, reliability, production and distribution capabilities, and the supplier's reputation and history. Analyze price proposals, financial reports, and other data and information to determine reasonable prices. Monitor and follow applicable laws and regulations. Negotiate, or renegotiate, and administer contracts with suppliers, vendors, and other representatives. Monitor shipments to ensure that goods come in on time and trace shipments and follow up undelivered goods in the event of problems. Confer with staff, users, and vendors to discuss defective or unacceptable goods or services and determine corrective action. Evaluate and monitor contract performance to ensure compliance with contractual obligations and to determine need for changes. Maintain and review computerized or manual records of items purchased, costs, delivery, product performance, and inventories. Review catalogs, industry periodicals, directories, trade journals, and Internet sites and consult with other department personnel to locate necessary goods and services. Study sales records and inventory levels of current stock to develop strategic purchasing programs that facilitate employee access to supplies. Interview vendors and visit suppliers' plants and distribution centers to examine and learn about products, services, and prices. Arrange the payment of duty and freight charges. Hire, train, and/or supervise purchasing clerks, buyers, and expediters. Write and review product specifications, maintaining a working technical knowledge of the goods or services to be purchased. Monitor changes affecting supply and demand, tracking market conditions, price trends, or futures markets. Formulate policies and procedures for bid proposals and procurement of goods and services. Attend meetings, trade shows, conferences, conventions, and seminars to network with people in other purchasing departments.

Personality Type: Conventional-Enterprising.

Career Cluster: 14 Marketing, Sales, and Service. **Career Pathway:** 14.3 Buying and Merchandising.

Skills: Operations Analysis; Management of Financial Resources; Management of Material Resources; Mathematics; Writing; Management of Personnel Resources.

Education and Training Programs: Sales, Distribution, and Marketing Operations, General; Merchandising and Buying Operations. **Related Knowledge/Courses:** Clerical Practices; Economics and Accounting; Production and Processing; Administration and Management; Computers and Electronics; Communications and Media.

Work Environment: Indoors; sitting; using hands on objects, tools, or controls; repetitive motions.

Purchasing Managers

- ❋ Education/Training Required: Work experience plus degree
- ❋ Annual Earnings: $85,440
- ❋ Beginning Wage: $48,480
- ❋ Earnings Growth Potential: High (43.3%)
- ❋ Growth: 3.4%
- ❋ Annual Job Openings: 7,243
- ❋ Job Security: More Secure than Most
- ❋ Self-Employed: 2.7%
- ❋ Part-Time: 1.9%

Renewal Industry: Advanced Manufacturing.

Industries with Greatest Employment: Management of Companies and Enterprises (11.8%); Merchant Wholesalers, Durable Goods (7.4%); Computer and Electronic Product Manufacturing (6.7%); Professional, Scientific, and Technical Services (5.6%); Transportation Equipment Manufacturing (5.5%).

Highest-Growth Industries (Projected Growth for This Job): Amusement, Gambling, and Recreation Industries (51.6%); Warehousing and Storage (33.3%); Waste Management and Remediation Services (28.8%); Administrative and Support Services (28.8%); Lessors of Nonfinancial Intangible Assets (Except Copyrighted Works) (28.1%); Ambulatory Health-Care Services (25.2%); Professional, Scientific, and Technical Services (25.0%); Building Material and Garden Equipment and Supplies Dealers (23.7%); Internet Service Providers, Web Search Portals, and Data Processing Services (23.6%); Support Activities for Transportation (21.5%); Water Transportation (21.3%); Nonstore Retailers (19.7%); Real Estate (19.4%); Religious, Grantmaking, Civic, Professional, and Similar Organizations (18.6%); Accommodation, Including Hotels and Motels (16.4%); Management of Companies and Enterprises (15.3%); Rental and Leasing Services (15.2%).

Other Considerations for Job Outlook: Employment of purchasing managers is expected to grow more slowly than average. The use of the Internet to conduct electronic commerce has made information easier to obtain, thus increasing the productivity of purchasing managers. The Internet also allows both large and small companies to bid on contracts. Exclusive supply contracts and long-term contracting have allowed companies to negotiate with fewer suppliers less frequently.

Plan, direct, or coordinate the activities of buyers, purchasing officers, and related workers involved in purchasing materials, products, and services. Maintain records of goods ordered and received. Locate vendors of materials, equipment, or supplies and interview them to determine product availability and terms of sales. Prepare and process requisitions and purchase orders for supplies and equipment. Control purchasing department budgets. Interview and hire staff and oversee staff training. Review purchase order claims and contracts for conformance to company policy. Analyze market and delivery systems to assess present and future material availability. Develop and implement purchasing and contract management instructions, policies, and procedures. Participate in the development of specifications for equipment, products, or substitute materials. Resolve vendor or contractor grievances and claims against suppliers. Represent companies in negotiating contracts and formulating policies with suppliers. Review, evaluate, and approve specifications for issuing and awarding bids. Direct and coordinate activities of personnel engaged in buying, selling, and distributing materials, equipment, machinery, and supplies. Prepare bid awards requiring board approval. Prepare reports regarding market conditions and merchandise costs. Administer online purchasing systems. Arrange for disposal of surplus materials.

Personality Type: Enterprising-Conventional.

Career Cluster: 04 Business, Management, and Administration. **Career Pathway:** 04.1 Management.

Skills: Management of Material Resources; Management of Financial Resources; Negotiation; Operations Analysis; Mathematics; Systems Evaluation.

Education and Training Program: Purchasing, Procurement/Acquisitions and Contracts Management. **Related Knowledge/Courses:** Economics and Accounting; Personnel and Human Resources; Production and Processing; Administration and Management; Mathematics; Transportation.

Work Environment: Indoors; noisy; sitting.

Radiation Therapists

- ✲ Education/Training Required: Associate degree
- ✲ Annual Earnings: $70,010
- ✲ Beginning Wage: $46,580
- ✲ Earnings Growth Potential: Low (33.5%)
- ✲ Growth: 24.8%
- ✲ Annual Job Openings: 1,461
- ✲ Job Security: Most Secure
- ✲ Self-Employed: 0.0%
- ✲ Part-Time: 10.3%

Renewal Industry: Health Care.

Industries with Greatest Employment: Hospitals, Public and Private (73.0%); Ambulatory Health-Care Services (21.4%).

Highest-Growth Industries (Projected Growth for This Job): Ambulatory Health-Care Services (34.9%); Hospitals, Public and Private (22.1%).

Other Considerations for Job Outlook: Job prospects are expected to be good. Job openings will result from employment growth and from the need to replace workers who retire or leave the occupation for other reasons. Applicants who are certified should have the best opportunities. As the U.S. population grows and an increasing share of it is in the older age groups, the number of people needing treatment is expected to increase and to spur demand for radiation therapists. In addition, as radiation technology advances and is able to treat more types of cancer, radiation therapy will be prescribed more often.

Provide radiation therapy to patients as prescribed by radiologists according to established practices and standards. Duties may include reviewing prescriptions and diagnoses; acting as liaisons with physicians and supportive care personnel; preparing equipment such as immobilization, treatment, and protection devices; and maintaining records, reports, and files. May assist in dosimetry procedures and tumor localization. Position patients for treatment with accuracy according to prescription. Administer prescribed doses of radiation to specific body parts, using radiation therapy equipment according to established practices and standards. Check radiation therapy equipment to ensure proper operation. Review prescriptions, diagnoses, patient charts, and identification. Follow principles of radiation protection for patients, radiation therapists, and others. Maintain records, reports, and files as required, including such information as radiation dosages, equipment settings, and patients' reactions. Conduct most treatment sessions independently, in accordance with long-term treatment plans and under general direction of patients' physicians. Enter data into computers and set controls to operate and adjust equipment and regulate dosages. Observe and reassure patients during treatments and report unusual reactions to physicians or turn equipment off if unexpected adverse reactions occur. Calculate actual treatment dosages delivered during each session. Check for side effects such as skin irritation, nausea, and hair loss to assess patients' reaction to treatment. Prepare and construct equipment such as immobilization, treatment, and protection devices. Educate, prepare, and reassure patients and their families by answering questions, providing physical assistance, and reinforcing physicians' advice regarding treatment reactions and post-treatment care. Provide assistance to other health-care personnel during dosimetry procedures and tumor localization. Help physicians, radiation oncologists, and clinical physicists to prepare physical and technical aspects of radiation treatment plans, using information about patient conditions and anatomies. Photograph treated areas of patients and process film. Act as liaisons with medical physicists and supportive care personnel. Train and supervise student or subordinate radiotherapy technologists. Implement appropriate follow-up care plans. Assist in the preparation of sealed radioactive materials such as cobalt, radium, cesium, and isotopes for use in radiation treatments. Store, sterilize, or prepare the special applicators containing the radioactive substances implanted by physicians.

Personality Type: Social-Realistic-Conventional.

Career Cluster: 08 Health Science. **Career Pathway:** 08.2 Diagnostics Services.

Skills: No data available.

Education and Training Program: Medical Radiologic Technology/Science—Radiation Therapist. **Related Knowledge/Courses:** Medicine and Dentistry; Biology; Physics; Psychology; Philosophy and Theology; Therapy and Counseling.

Work Environment: Indoors; radiation; disease or infections; standing; walking and running; using hands on objects, tools, or controls.

Radiologic Technicians

- ❀ Education/Training Required: Associate degree
- ❀ Annual Earnings: $50,260
- ❀ Beginning Wage: $33,910
- ❀ Earnings Growth Potential: Low (32.5%)
- ❀ Growth: 15.1%
- ❀ Annual Job Openings: 12,836
- ❀ Job Security: Most Secure
- ❀ Self-Employed: 1.1%
- ❀ Part-Time: 17.3%

Our sources did not provide separate job openings data for this occupation. The job openings listed here are shared with Radiologic Technologists.

Renewal Industry: Health Care.

Industries with Greatest Employment: Hospitals, Public and Private (60.7%); Ambulatory Health-Care Services (32.9%).

Highest-Growth Industries (Projected Growth for This Job): Professional, Scientific, and Technical Services (37.7%); Administrative and Support Services (26.7%); Ambulatory Health-Care Services (23.7%); Management of Companies and Enterprises (15.2%).

Other Considerations for Job Outlook: In addition to job growth, job openings also will arise from the need to replace technologists who leave the occupation. Radiologic technologists are willing to relocate and who also are experienced in more than one diagnostic imaging procedure—such as CT, MR, and mammography—will have the best employment opportunities as employers seek to control costs by using multi-credentialed employees. CT is becoming a frontline diagnosis tool. Instead of taking X-rays to decide whether a CT is needed, as was the practice before, CT is often the first choice for imaging because of its accuracy. MR also is increasing in frequency of use. Technologists with credentialing in either of these specialties will be very marketable to employers.

Maintain and use equipment and supplies necessary to demonstrate portions of the human body on X-ray film or fluoroscopic screen for diagnostic purposes. Use beam-restrictive devices and patient-shielding techniques to minimize radiation exposure to patient and staff. Position X-ray equipment and adjust controls to set exposure factors, such as time and distance. Position patient on examining table and set up and adjust equipment to obtain optimum view of specific body area as requested by physician. Determine patients' X-ray needs by reading requests or instructions from physicians. Make exposures necessary for the requested procedures, rejecting and repeating work that does not meet established standards. Process exposed radiographs, using film processors or computer-generated methods. Explain procedures to patients to reduce anxieties and obtain cooperation. Perform procedures such as linear tomography; mammography; sonograms; joint and cyst aspirations; routine contrast studies; routine fluoroscopy; and examinations of the head, trunk, and extremities under supervision of physician. Prepare and set up X-ray room for patient. Assure that sterile supplies, contrast materials, catheters, and other required equipment are present and in working order, requisitioning materials as necessary. Maintain records of patients examined, examinations performed, views taken, and technical factors used. Provide assistance to physicians or other technologists in the performance of more complex procedures. Monitor equipment operation and report malfunctioning equipment to supervisor. Provide students and other technologists with suggestions of additional views, alternate positioning, or improved techniques to ensure the images produced are of the highest quality. Coordinate work of other technicians or technologists when procedures require more than one person. Assist with on-the-job training of new employees and students and provide input to supervisors regarding training performance. Maintain a current file of examination protocols. Operate mobile X-ray equipment in operating room, in emergency room, or at patient's bedside. Provide assistance in radiopharmaceutical administration, monitoring patients' vital signs and notifying the radiologist of any relevant changes.

Personality Type: Realistic-Conventional.

Career Cluster: 08 Health Science. **Career Pathways:** 08.1 Therapeutic Services; 08.2 Diagnostics Services.

Skills: Science; Operation Monitoring; Equipment Selection; Operation and Control; Service Orientation; Active Listening.

Education and Training Programs: Medical Radiologic Technology/Science—Radiation Therapist; Radiologic Technology/Science—Radiographer; Allied Health Diagnostic, Intervention, and Treatment Professions, Other. **Related Knowledge/Courses:** Medicine and Dentistry; Clerical Practices; Psychology; Physics; Biology; Chemistry.

Work Environment: Indoors; radiation; disease or infections; standing; walking and running; using hands on objects, tools, or controls.

Radiologic Technologists

* Education/Training Required: Associate degree
* Annual Earnings: $50,260
* Beginning Wage: $33,910
* Earnings Growth Potential: Low (32.5%)
* Growth: 15.1%
* Annual Job Openings: 12,836
* Job Security: Most Secure
* Self-Employed: 1.1%
* Part-Time: 17.3%

Our sources did not provide separate job openings data for this occupation. The job openings listed here are shared with Radiologic Technicians.

Renewal Industry: Health Care.

Industries with Greatest Employment: Hospitals, Public and Private (60.7%); Ambulatory Health-Care Services (32.9%).

Highest-Growth Industries (Projected Growth for This Job): Professional, Scientific, and Technical Services (37.7%); Administrative and Support Services (26.7%); Ambulatory Health-Care Services (23.7%); Management of Companies and Enterprises (15.2%).

Other Considerations for Job Outlook: In addition to job growth, job openings also will arise from the need to replace technologists who leave the occupation. Radiologic technologists are willing to relocate and who also are experienced in more than one diagnostic imaging procedure—such as CT, MR, and mammography—will have the best employment opportunities as employers seek to control costs by using multi-credentialed employees. CT is becoming a frontline diagnosis tool. Instead of taking X-rays to decide whether a CT is needed, as was the practice before, CT is often the first choice for imaging because of its accuracy. MR also is increasing in frequency of use. Technologists with credentialing in either of these specialties will be very marketable to employers.

Take X-rays and Computerized Axial Tomography (CAT or CT) scans or administer nonradioactive materials into patient's bloodstream for diagnostic purposes. Includes technologists who specialize in other

modalities such as computed tomography, ultrasound, and magnetic resonance. Use radiation safety measures and protection devices to comply with government regulations and to ensure safety of patients and staff. Review and evaluate developed X-rays, videotape, or computer-generated information to determine if images are satisfactory for diagnostic purposes. Position imaging equipment and adjust controls to set exposure times and distances, according to specification of examinations. Explain procedures and observe patients to ensure safety and comfort during scans. Key commands and data into computers to document and specify scan sequences, adjust transmitters and receivers, or photograph certain images. Operate or oversee operation of radiologic and magnetic imaging equipment to produce images of the body for diagnostic purposes. Position and immobilize patients on examining tables. Record, process, and maintain patient data and treatment records, and prepare reports. Take thorough and accurate patient medical histories. Remove and process film. Set up examination rooms, ensuring that all necessary equipment is ready. Monitor patients' conditions and reactions, reporting abnormal signs to physicians. Coordinate work with clerical personnel or other technologists. Provide assistance in dressing or changing seriously ill, injured, or disabled patients. Demonstrate new equipment, procedures, and techniques to staff and provide technical assistance. Collaborate with other medical team members such as physicians and nurses to conduct angiography or special vascular procedures. Prepare and administer oral or injected contrast media to patients. Monitor video displays of areas being scanned and adjust density or contrast to improve picture quality. Operate fluoroscope to aid physicians to view and guide wires or catheters through blood vessels to areas of interest. Assign duties to radiologic staffs to maintain patient flows and achieve production goals. Perform scheduled maintenance and minor emergency repairs on radiographic equipment. Perform administrative duties such as developing departmental operating budgets, coordinating purchases of supplies and equipment, and preparing work schedules.

Personality Type: Realistic-Social.

Career Cluster: 08 Health Science. **Career Pathways:** 08.1 Therapeutic Services; 08.2 Diagnostics Services.

Skills: No data available.

Education and Training Programs: Medical Radiologic Technology/Science—Radiation Therapist; Radiologic Technology/Science—Radiographer; Allied Health Diagnostic, Intervention, and Treatment Professions, Other. **Related Knowledge/Courses:** Medicine and Dentistry; Physics; Customer and Personal Service; Biology; Psychology; Chemistry.

Work Environment: Indoors; radiation; disease or infections; standing; using hands on objects, tools, or controls; repetitive motions.

Radiologic Technologists and Technicians

See *Radiologic Technicians* and *Radiologic Technologists*, *described separately.*

Recreation and Fitness Studies Teachers, Postsecondary

- ✹ Education/Training Required: Master's degree
- ✹ Annual Earnings: $52,170
- ✹ Beginning Wage: $26,790
- ✹ Earnings Growth Potential: High (48.6%)
- ✹ Growth: 22.9%
- ✹ Annual Job Openings: 3,010
- ✹ Job Security: Most Secure
- ✹ Self-Employed: 0.4%
- ✹ Part-Time: 27.8%

Renewal Industry: Education.

Industries with Greatest Employment: Educational Services, Public and Private (97.3%).

Highest-Growth Industries (Projected Growth for This Job): Administrative and Support Services (48.3%); Amusement, Gambling, and Recreation Industries (45.2%); Social Assistance (38.6%); Support Activities for Transportation (32.8%); Religious, Grantmaking, Civic, Professional, and Similar Organizations (29.9%); Professional, Scientific, and Technical Services (28.8%); Management of Companies and Enterprises (26.8%); Local Government (23.5%);

Educational Services, Public and Private (22.8%); Hospitals, Public and Private (21.4%).

Other Considerations for Job Outlook: Retirements of current postsecondary teachers should create numerous openings for all types of postsecondary teachers, so job opportunities are generally expected to be very good. However, one of the main reasons why students attend postsecondary institutions is to prepare themselves for careers, so the best job prospects for postsecondary teachers are likely to be in rapidly growing fields that offer many nonacademic career options, such as recreation and fitness studies. Community colleges and other institutions offering career and technical education have been among the most rapidly growing, and these institutions are expected to offer some of the best opportunities for postsecondary teachers.

Teach courses pertaining to recreation, leisure, and fitness studies, including exercise physiology and facilities management. Evaluate and grade students' classwork, assignments, and papers. Maintain student attendance records, grades, and other required records. Prepare and deliver lectures to undergraduate and graduate students on topics such as anatomy, therapeutic recreation, and conditioning theory. Prepare course materials such as syllabi, homework assignments, and handouts. Maintain regularly scheduled office hours to advise and assist students. Compile, administer, and grade examinations or assign this work to others. Plan, evaluate, and revise curricula, course content, and course materials and methods of instruction. Initiate, facilitate, and moderate classroom discussions. Keep abreast of developments in their field by reading current literature, talking with colleagues, and participating in professional conferences. Advise students on academic and vocational curricula and on career issues. Participate in student recruitment, registration, and placement activities. Collaborate with colleagues to address teaching and research issues. Select and obtain materials and supplies such as textbooks. Participate in campus and community events. Serve on academic or administrative committees that deal with institutional policies, departmental matters, and academic issues. Compile bibliographies of specialized materials for outside reading assignments. Supervise undergraduate or graduate teaching, internship, and research work. Perform administrative duties such as serving as department heads. Prepare students to act as sports coaches. Conduct research in a particular field of knowledge and publish findings in professional journals, books,

or electronic media. Act as advisers to student organizations. Write grant proposals to procure external research funding. Provide professional consulting services to government or industry.

Personality Type: Social.

Career Clusters: 01 Agriculture, Food, and Natural Resources; 05 Education and Training. **Career Pathways:** 01.5 Natural Resources Systems; 05.1 Administration and Administrative Support; 05.3 Teaching/Training.

Skills: Instructing; Learning Strategies; Science; Social Perceptiveness; Persuasion; Time Management.

Education and Training Programs: Parks, Recreation and Leisure Studies; Health and Physical Education, General; Sport and Fitness Administration/Management. **Related Knowledge/Courses:** Education and Training; Philosophy and Theology; Psychology; Therapy and Counseling; Medicine and Dentistry; Sociology and Anthropology.

Work Environment: More often indoors than outdoors; standing.

Refuse and Recyclable Material Collectors

- ❋ Education/Training Required: Short-term on-the-job training
- ❋ Annual Earnings: $29,420
- ❋ Beginning Wage: $17,070
- ❋ Earnings Growth Potential: High (42.0%)
- ❋ Growth: 7.4%
- ❋ Annual Job Openings: 37,785
- ❋ Job Security: Least Secure
- ❋ Self-Employed: 6.1%
- ❋ Part-Time: 13.4%

Renewal Industry: Green Technologies.

Industries with Greatest Employment: Waste Management and Remediation Services (49.9%); Local Government (35.6%).

Highest-Growth Industries (Projected Growth for This Job): Warehousing and Storage (19.7%).

Other Considerations for Job Outlook: Job opportunities are sensitive to economic downturns. A cooling off of business activity reduces the prices of recycled commodities, such as paper pulp and glass. That may cause layoffs in the recycling industry.

Collect and dump refuse or recyclable materials from containers into truck. May drive truck. Inspect trucks prior to beginning routes to ensure safe operating condition. Refuel trucks and add other necessary fluids, such as oil. Fill out any needed reports for defective equipment. Drive to disposal sites to empty trucks that have been filled. Drive trucks along established routes through residential streets and alleys or through business and industrial areas. Operate equipment that compresses the collected refuse. Operate automated or semi-automated hoisting devices that raise refuse bins and dump contents into openings in truck bodies. Dismount garbage trucks to collect garbage and remount trucks to ride to the next collection point. Communicate with dispatchers concerning delays, unsafe sites, accidents, equipment breakdowns, and other maintenance problems. Keep informed of road and weather conditions to determine how routes will be affected. Tag garbage or recycling containers to inform customers of problems such as excess garbage or inclusion of items that are not permitted. Clean trucks and compactor bodies after routes have been completed. Sort items set out for recycling and throw materials into designated truck compartments. Organize schedules for refuse collection. Provide quotes for refuse collection contracts.

Personality Type: Realistic-Conventional.

Career Cluster: 01 Agriculture, Food, and Natural Resources. **Career Pathway:** 01.5 Natural Resources Systems.

Skills: No data available.

Education and Training Program: No related CIP programs; this job is learned through informal short-term on-the-job training. **Related Knowledge/Courses:** Transportation; Customer and Personal Service.

Work Environment: Outdoors; noisy; contaminants; using hands on objects, tools, or controls; bending or twisting the body; repetitive motions.

Registered Nurses

* Education/Training Required: Associate degree
* Annual Earnings: $60,010
* Beginning Wage: $42,020
* Earnings Growth Potential: Low (30.0%)
* Growth: 23.5%
* Annual Job Openings: 233,499
* Job Security: Most Secure
* Self-Employed: 0.8%
* Part-Time: 21.8%

Renewal Industry: Health Care.

Industries with Greatest Employment: Hospitals, Public and Private (59.0%); Ambulatory Health-Care Services (17.3%); Nursing and Residential Care Facilities (6.5%).

Highest-Growth Industries (Projected Growth for This Job): Social Assistance (51.0%); Professional, Scientific, and Technical Services (44.8%); Ambulatory Health-Care Services (37.5%); Internet Service Providers, Web Search Portals, and Data Processing Services (34.3%); Amusement, Gambling, and Recreation Industries (32.5%); Administrative and Support Services (26.7%); Nursing and Residential Care Facilities (25.2%); Nonstore Retailers (25.0%); Funds, Trusts, and Other Financial Vehicles (23.6%); Performing Arts, Spectator Sports, and Related Industries (23.3%); Hospitals, Public and Private (21.6%); Religious, Grantmaking, Civic, Professional, and Similar Organizations (19.3%); Real Estate (18.8%); Merchant Wholesalers, Nondurable Goods (18.8%); Personal and Laundry Services (15.5%); Management of Companies and Enterprises (15.3%).

Other Considerations for Job Outlook: Overall job opportunities are expected to be excellent for registered nurses, but they can vary by employment setting. Generally, RNs with at least a bachelor's degree will have better job prospects than those without a bachelor's. In addition, all four advanced practice specialties—clinical nurse specialists, nurse practitioners, nurse-midwives, and nurse anesthetists—will be in high demand, particularly in medically underserved areas such as inner cities and rural areas. Relative to physicians, these RNs increasingly serve as lower-cost primary care providers.

Assess patient health problems and needs, develop and implement nursing care plans, and maintain medical records. Administer nursing care to ill, injured, convalescent, or disabled patients. May advise patients on health maintenance and disease prevention or provide case management. Licensing or registration required. Includes advance practice nurses such as nurse practitioners, clinical nurse specialists, certified nurse midwives, and certified registered nurse anesthetists. Advanced practice nursing is practiced by RNs who have specialized formal, post-basic education and who function in highly autonomous and specialized roles. Monitor, record, and report symptoms and changes in patients' conditions. Maintain accurate, detailed reports and records. Record patients' medical information and vital signs. Order, interpret, and evaluate diagnostic tests to identify and assess patients' conditions. Modify patient treatment plans as indicated by patients' responses and conditions. Direct and supervise less skilled nursing or health-care personnel or supervise particular units. Consult and coordinate with health-care team members to assess, plan, implement, and evaluate patient care plans. Monitor all aspects of patient care, including diet and physical activity. Instruct individuals, families, and other groups on topics such as health education, disease prevention, and childbirth and develop health improvement programs. Prepare patients for, and assist with, examinations and treatments. Assess the needs of individuals, families, or communities, including assessment of individuals' home or work environments to identify potential health or safety problems. Provide health care, first aid, immunizations, and assistance in convalescence and rehabilitation in locations such as schools, hospitals, and industry. Prepare rooms, sterile instruments, equipment, and supplies and ensure that stock of supplies is maintained. Inform physicians of patients' conditions during anesthesia. Administer local, inhalation, intravenous, and other anesthetics. Perform physical examinations, make tentative diagnoses, and treat patients en route to hospitals or at disaster site triage centers. Observe nurses and visit patients to ensure proper nursing care. Conduct specified laboratory tests. Direct and coordinate infection control programs, advising and consulting with specified personnel about necessary precautions. Prescribe or recommend drugs; medical devices; or other forms of treatment such as physical therapy, inhalation therapy, or related therapeutic procedures. Perform administrative and managerial functions such as taking

responsibility for a unit's staff, budget, planning, and long-range goals. Hand items to surgeons during operations.

Personality Type: Social-Investigative-Conventional.

Career Cluster: 08 Health Science. **Career Pathway:** 08.1 Therapeutic Services.

Skills: No data available.

Education and Training Programs: Nursing—Registered Nurse Training (RN, ASN, BSN, MSN); Adult Health Nurse/Nursing; Nurse Anesthetist; Family Practice Nurse/Nurse Practitioner; Maternal/Child Health and Neonatal Nurse/Nursing; Nurse Midwife/Nursing Midwifery; Nursing Science (MS, PhD); Pediatric Nurse/Nursing; Psychiatric/Mental Health Nurse/Nursing; Public Health/Community Nurse/Nursing; others. **Related Knowledge/Courses:** Medicine and Dentistry; Psychology; Therapy and Counseling; Biology; Philosophy and Theology; Sociology and Anthropology.

Work Environment: Indoors; disease or infections; standing; walking and running; using hands on objects, tools, or controls.

Rehabilitation Counselors

- ❋ Education/Training Required: Master's degree
- ❋ Annual Earnings: $29,630
- ❋ Beginning Wage: $19,610
- ❋ Earnings Growth Potential: Low (33.8%)
- ❋ Growth: 23.0%
- ❋ Annual Job Openings: 32,081
- ❋ Job Security: Most Secure
- ❋ Self-Employed: 5.9%
- ❋ Part-Time: 15.4%

Renewal Industry: Health Care.

Industries with Greatest Employment: Social Assistance (42.3%); Nursing and Residential Care Facilities (23.7%); State Government (13.0%).

Highest-Growth Industries (Projected Growth for This Job): Professional, Scientific, and Technical Services (55.6%); Social Assistance (34.6%); Administrative and Support Services (34.5%); Nursing and Residential

Care Facilities (26.8%); Ambulatory Health-Care Services (21.5%); Management of Companies and Enterprises (15.3%).

Other Considerations for Job Outlook: The number of people who will need rehabilitation counseling is expected to grow as advances in medical technology allow more people to survive injury or illness and live independently again. In addition, legislation requiring equal employment rights for people with disabilities will spur demand for counselors, who not only help these people make a transition to the workforce but also help companies to comply with the law. Prospects for rehabilitation counselors are excellent because many people are leaving the field or retiring.

Counsel individuals to maximize the independence and employability of persons coping with personal, social, and vocational difficulties that result from birth defects, illness, disease, accidents, or the stress of daily life. Coordinate activities for residents of care and treatment facilities. Assess client needs and design and implement rehabilitation programs that may include personal and vocational counseling, training, and job placement. Monitor and record clients' progress in order to ensure that goals and objectives are met. Confer with clients to discuss their options and goals so that rehabilitation programs and plans for accessing needed services can be developed. Prepare and maintain records and case files, including documentation such as clients' personal and eligibility information, services provided, narratives of client contacts, and relevant correspondence. Arrange for physical, mental, academic, vocational, and other evaluations to obtain information for assessing clients' needs and developing rehabilitation plans. Analyze information from interviews, educational and medical records, consultation with other professionals, and diagnostic evaluations to assess clients' abilities, needs, and eligibility for services. Develop rehabilitation plans that fit clients' aptitudes, education levels, physical abilities, and career goals. Maintain close contact with clients during job training and placements to resolve problems and evaluate placement adequacy. Locate barriers to client employment, such as inaccessible work sites, inflexible schedules, and transportation problems, and work with clients to develop strategies for overcoming these barriers. Develop and maintain relationships with community referral sources such as schools and community groups. Arrange for on-site job coaching or assistive devices such as specially equipped wheelchairs in order to help clients adapt to work or school environments. Confer with physicians, psychologists, occupational therapists, and other professionals to develop and implement client rehabilitation programs. Develop diagnostic procedures for determining clients' needs. Participate in job development and placement programs, contacting prospective employers, placing clients in jobs, and evaluating the success of placements. Collaborate with clients' families to implement rehabilitation plans that include behavioral, residential, social, and/or employment goals. Collaborate with community agencies to establish facilities and programs to assist persons with disabilities.

Personality Type: Social-Investigative.

Career Cluster: 08 Health Science. **Career Pathway:** 08.3 Health Informatics.

Skills: Management of Financial Resources; Social Perceptiveness; Writing; Service Orientation; Monitoring; Coordination.

Education and Training Programs: Vocational Rehabilitation Counseling/Counselor; Assistive/Augmentative Technology and Rehabiliation Engineering. **Related Knowledge/Courses:** Therapy and Counseling; Psychology; Philosophy and Theology; Education and Training; Personnel and Human Resources; Sociology and Anthropology.

Work Environment: More often indoors than outdoors; sitting; walking and running.

Respiratory Therapists

- ❋ Education/Training Required: Associate degree
- ❋ Annual Earnings: $50,070
- ❋ Beginning Wage: $36,650
- ❋ Earnings Growth Potential: Low (26.8%)
- ❋ Growth: 22.6%
- ❋ Annual Job Openings: 5,563
- ❋ Job Security: Most Secure
- ❋ Self-Employed: 1.1%
- ❋ Part-Time: 15.0%

Renewal Industry: Health Care.

Industries with Greatest Employment: Hospitals, Public and Private (78.0%); Ambulatory Health-Care Services (7.2%).

Highest-Growth Industries (Projected Growth for This Job): Professional, Scientific, and Technical Services (71.7%); Ambulatory Health-Care Services (32.5%); Rental and Leasing Services (29.9%); Hospitals, Public and Private (22.6%); Nursing and Residential Care Facilities (22.1%); Administrative and Support Services (19.5%); Merchant Wholesalers, Durable Goods (16.5%); Management of Companies and Enterprises (15.4%).

Other Considerations for Job Outlook: Job opportunities are expected to be very good. The vast majority of job openings will continue to be in hospitals. However, a growing number of openings are expected to be outside of hospitals, especially in home health care services, offices of physicians or other health practitioners, consumer-goods rental firms, or in the employment services industry as a temporary worker in various settings. The increasing demand will come from substantial growth in the middle-aged and elderly population—a development that will heighten the incidence of cardiopulmonary disease. Growth in demand also will result from the expanding role of respiratory therapists in case management, disease prevention, emergency care, and the early detection of pulmonary disorders.

Assess, treat, and care for patients with breathing disorders. Assume primary responsibility for all respiratory care modalities, including the supervision of respiratory therapy technicians. Initiate and conduct therapeutic procedures; maintain patient records; and select, assemble, check, and operate equipment. Set up and operate devices such as mechanical ventilators, therapeutic gas administration apparatus, environmental control systems, and aerosol generators, following specified parameters of treatment. Provide emergency care, including artificial respiration, external cardiac massage, and assistance with cardiopulmonary resuscitation. Determine requirements for treatment, such as type, method, and duration of therapy; precautions to be taken; and medication and dosages, compatible with physicians' orders. Monitor patient's physiological responses to therapy, such as vital signs, arterial blood gases, and blood chemistry changes, and consult with physician if adverse reactions occur. Read prescription, measure arterial blood gases, and review patient information to assess patient condition. Work as part of a team of physicians, nurses, and other health-care professionals to manage patient care. Enforce safety rules and ensure careful adherence to physicians' orders. Maintain charts that contain patients' pertinent identification and therapy information. Inspect, clean, test, and maintain respiratory therapy equipment to ensure equipment is functioning safely and efficiently, ordering repairs when necessary. Educate patients and their families about their conditions and teach appropriate disease management techniques, such as breathing exercises and the use of medications and respiratory equipment. Explain treatment procedures to patients to gain cooperation and allay fears. Relay blood analysis results to a physician. Perform pulmonary function and adjust equipment to obtain optimum results in therapy. Perform bronchopulmonary drainage and assist or instruct patients in performance of breathing exercises. Demonstrate respiratory care procedures to trainees and other health-care personnel. Teach, train, supervise, and utilize the assistance of students, respiratory therapy technicians, and assistants. Make emergency visits to resolve equipment problems. Use a variety of testing techniques to assist doctors in cardiac and pulmonary research and to diagnose disorders. Conduct tests, such as electrocardiograms (EKGs), stress testing, and lung capacity tests, to evaluate patients' cardiopulmonary functions.

Personality Type: Social-Investigative-Realistic.

Career Cluster: 08 Health Science. **Career Pathway:** 08.1 Therapeutic Services.

Skills: Science; Mathematics; Operation Monitoring; Reading Comprehension; Active Learning; Troubleshooting.

Education and Training Program: Respiratory Care Therapy/Therapist. **Related Knowledge/Courses:** Medicine and Dentistry; Biology; Psychology; Customer and Personal Service; Therapy and Counseling; Chemistry.

Work Environment: Indoors; disease or infections; standing.

Roofers

- ❋ Education/Training Required: Moderate-term on-the-job training
- ❋ Annual Earnings: $33,240
- ❋ Beginning Wage: $21,290
- ❋ Earnings Growth Potential: Medium (36.0%)
- ❋ Growth: 14.3%
- ❋ Annual Job Openings: 38,398
- ❋ Job Security: More Secure than Most
- ❋ Self-Employed: 20.1%
- ❋ Part-Time: 7.6%

Renewal Industries: Green Technologies; Infrastructure.

Industries with Greatest Employment: Specialty Trade Contractors (74.1%).

Highest-Growth Industries (Projected Growth for This Job): Administrative and Support Services (26.0%); Specialty Trade Contractors (16.5%).

Other Considerations for Job Outlook: Job opportunities for roofers will arise primarily because of the need to replace workers who leave the occupation. The proportion of roofers who leave the occupation each year is higher than in most construction trades—roofing work is hot, strenuous, and dirty, and a significant number of workers treat roofing as a temporary job until they find other work. Some roofers leave the occupation to go into other construction trades. Jobs should be easiest to find during spring and summer.

Cover roofs of structures with shingles, slate, asphalt, aluminum, wood, and related materials. May spray roofs, sidings, and walls with material to bind, seal, insulate, or soundproof sections of structures. Install, repair, or replace single-ply roofing systems, using waterproof sheet materials such as modified plastics, elastomeric coatings, or other asphaltic compositions. Apply alternate layers of hot asphalt or tar and roofing paper to roofs, according to specification. Apply gravel or pebbles over top layers of roofs, using rakes or stiff-bristled brooms. Cement or nail flashing strips of metal or shingle over joints to make them watertight. Punch holes in slate, tile, terra cotta, or wooden shingles, using punches and hammers. Hammer and chisel away rough spots or remove them with rubbing bricks to prepare surfaces for waterproofing. Align roofing materials with edges of roofs. Mop or pour hot asphalt or tar onto roof bases. Apply plastic coatings and membranes, fiberglass, or felt over sloped roofs before applying shingles. Install vapor barriers and/or layers of insulation on the roof decks of flat roofs and seal the seams. Install partially overlapping layers of material over roof insulation surfaces, determining distance of roofing material overlap using chalk lines, gauges on shingling hatchets, or lines on shingles. Inspect problem roofs to determine the best procedures for repairing them. Glaze top layers to make a smooth finish, or embed gravel in the bitumen for rough surfaces. Cut roofing paper to size, using knives, and nail or staple roofing paper to roofs in overlapping strips to form bases for other materials. Cut felt, shingles, and strips of flashing and fit them into angles formed by walls, vents, and intersecting roof surfaces. Cover roofs and exterior walls of structures with slate, asphalt, aluminum, wood, gravel, gypsum, and/or related materials, using brushes, knives, punches, hammers, and other tools. Clean and maintain equipment. Cover exposed nailheads with roofing cement or caulking to prevent water leakage and rust. Waterproof and damp-proof walls, floors, roofs, foundations, and basements by painting or spraying surfaces with waterproof coatings or by attaching waterproofing membranes to surfaces. Spray roofs, sidings, and walls with material to bind, seal, insulate, or soundproof sections of structures, using spray guns, air compressors, and heaters.

Personality Type: Realistic-Conventional.

Career Cluster: 02 Architecture and Construction. **Career Pathway:** 02.2 Construction.

Skills: Repairing; Installation; Equipment Maintenance; Operations Analysis; Technology Design; Mathematics.

Education and Training Program: Roofer. **Related Knowledge/Courses:** Building and Construction; Design; Engineering and Technology; Transportation.

Work Environment: Outdoors; very hot or cold; high places; standing; walking and running; using hands on objects, tools, or controls.

Rough Carpenters

* Education/Training Required: Long-term on-the-job training
* Annual Earnings: $37,660
* Beginning Wage: $23,370
* Earnings Growth Potential: Medium (37.9%)
* Growth: 10.3%
* Annual Job Openings: 223,225
* Job Security: Least Secure
* Self-Employed: 31.8%
* Part-Time: 6.1%

Our sources did not provide separate job openings data for this occupation. The job openings listed here are shared with Construction Carpenters.

Renewal Industries: Green Technologies; Infrastructure.

Industries with Greatest Employment: Construction of Buildings (31.8%); Specialty Trade Contractors (23.1%).

Highest-Growth Industries (Projected Growth for This Job): Securities, Commodity Contracts, and Other Financial Investments and Related Activities (41.0%); Museums, Historical Sites, and Similar Institutions (36.3%); Professional, Scientific, and Technical Services (35.7%); Nursing and Residential Care Facilities (33.3%); Warehousing and Storage (33.3%); Amusement, Gambling, and Recreation Industries (32.7%); Waste Management and Remediation Services (31.4%); Social Assistance (28.7%); Building Material and Garden Equipment and Supplies Dealers (27.7%); Administrative and Support Services (27.5%); Rental and Leasing Services (20.8%); Accommodation, Including Hotels and Motels (17.6%); Support Activities for Transportation (17.3%); Real Estate (17.3%); Religious, Grantmaking, Civic, Professional, and Similar Organizations (17.0%); Food Services and Drinking Places (15.6%); Management of Companies and Enterprises (15.3%).

Other Considerations for Job Outlook: Carpenters with all-around skills will have better opportunities for steady work than carpenters who can perform only a few relatively simple, routine tasks.

Build rough wooden structures, such as concrete forms, scaffolds, tunnel, bridge, or sewer supports, billboard signs, and temporary frame shelters, according to sketches, blueprints, or oral instructions. Study blueprints and diagrams to determine dimensions of structure or form to be constructed. Measure materials or distances, using square, measuring tape, or rule to lay out work. Cut or saw boards, timbers, or plywood to required size, using handsaw, power saw, or woodworking machine. Assemble and fasten material together to construct wood or metal framework of structure, using bolts, nails, or screws. Anchor and brace forms and other structures in place, using nails, bolts, anchor rods, steel cables, planks, wedges, and timbers. Mark cutting lines on materials, using pencil and scriber. Erect forms, framework, scaffolds, hoists, roof supports, or chutes, using hand tools, plumb rule, and level. Install rough door and window frames, subflooring, fixtures, or temporary supports in structures undergoing construction or repair. Examine structural timbers and supports to detect decay and replace timbers as required, using hand tools, nuts, and bolts. Bore boltholes in timber, masonry, or concrete walls, using power drill. Fabricate parts, using woodworking and metalworking machines. Dig or direct digging of post holes and set poles to support structures. Build sleds from logs and timbers for use in hauling camp buildings and machinery through wooded areas. Build chutes for pouring concrete.

Personality Type: Realistic-Conventional-Investigative.

Career Cluster: 02 Architecture and Construction. **Career Pathway:** 02.2 Construction.

Skills: No data available.

Education and Training Program: Carpentry/Carpenter. **Related Knowledge/Courses:** Building and Construction; Design; Engineering and Technology; Mechanical Devices; Production and Processing; Physics.

Work Environment: Outdoors; noisy; very hot or cold; contaminants; standing; using hands on objects, tools, or controls.

Sales Engineers

- ❋ Education/Training Required: Bachelor's degree
- ❋ Annual Earnings: $80,270
- ❋ Beginning Wage: $48,290
- ❋ Earnings Growth Potential: Medium (39.8%)
- ❋ Growth: 8.5%
- ❋ Annual Job Openings: 7,371
- ❋ Job Security: Least Secure
- ❋ Self-Employed: 0.0%
- ❋ Part-Time: 2.0%

Renewal Industries: Advanced Manufacturing; Information and Telecommunication Technologies.

Industries with Greatest Employment: Merchant Wholesalers, Durable Goods (27.9%); Professional, Scientific, and Technical Services (17.4%); Computer and Electronic Product Manufacturing (12.0%); Machinery Manufacturing (8.5%); Wholesale Electronic Markets and Agents and Brokers (8.4%); Telecommunications (6.9%).

Highest-Growth Industries (Projected Growth for This Job): Professional, Scientific, and Technical Services (37.8%); Administrative and Support Services (28.1%); Publishing Industries (Except Internet) (27.3%); Credit Intermediation and Related Activities (18.9%); Management of Companies and Enterprises (15.3%).

Other Considerations for Job Outlook: Employment opportunities may fluctuate from year to year because sales are affected by changing economic conditions, legislative issues, and consumer preferences. Prospects will be best for those with the appropriate knowledge or technical expertise, as well as the personal traits necessary for successful sales work. In addition to new positions created as companies expand their sales forces, some openings will arise each year from the need to replace sales engineers who transfer to other occupations or leave the labor force.

Sell business goods or services, the selling of which requires a technical background equivalent to a baccalaureate degree in engineering. Plan and modify product configurations to meet customer needs. Confer with customers and engineers to assess equipment needs and to determine system requirements. Collaborate with sales teams to understand customer requirements, to promote the sale of company products, and to provide sales support. Secure and renew orders and arrange delivery. Develop, present, or respond to proposals for specific customer requirements, including request for proposal responses and industry-specific solutions. Sell products requiring extensive technical expertise and support for installation and use, such as material handling equipment, numerical-control machinery, and computer systems. Diagnose problems with installed equipment. Prepare and deliver technical presentations that explain products or services to customers and prospective customers. Recommend improved materials or machinery to customers, documenting how such changes will lower costs or increase production. Provide technical and non-technical support and services to clients or other staff members regarding the use, operation, and maintenance of equipment. Research and identify potential customers for products or services. Visit prospective buyers at commercial, industrial, or other establishments to show samples or catalogs and to inform them about product pricing, availability, and advantages. Create sales or service contracts for products or services. Arrange for demonstrations or trial installations of equipment. Keep informed on industry news and trends; products; services; competitors; relevant information about legacy, existing, and emerging technologies; and the latest product-line developments. Attend company training seminars to become familiar with product lines. Provide information needed for the development of custom-made machinery. Develop sales plans to introduce products in new markets. Write technical documentation for products. Identify resale opportunities and support them to achieve sales plans. Document account activities, generate reports, and keep records of business transactions with customers and suppliers.

Personality Type: Enterprising-Realistic-Investigative.

Career Cluster: 14 Marketing, Sales, and Service. **Career Pathway:** 14.2 Professional Sales and Marketing.

Skills: Operations Analysis; Science; Systems Evaluation; Technology Design; Programming; Installation.

Education and Training Programs: Aerospace Engineering; Agricultural Engineering; Chemical Engineering; Computer Engineering; Construction Engineering; Electrical, Electronic, and Communications Engineering; Environmental Engineering; Forest Engineering; Industrial Engineering; Manufacturing Engineering; Materials Engineering; Mechanical Engineering; Metallurgical

Engineering; Mining and Mineral Engineering; Nuclear Engineering; Petroleum Engineering; Transportation and Highway Engineering; Water Resources Engineering; others. **Related Knowledge/Courses:** Sales and Marketing; Engineering and Technology; Design; Physics; Computers and Electronics; Customer and Personal Service.

Work Environment: Indoors; sitting; repetitive motions.

Sales Representatives, Wholesale and Manufacturing, Technical and Scientific Products

* Education/Training Required: Moderate-term on-the-job training
* Annual Earnings: $68,270
* Beginning Wage: $35,090
* Earnings Growth Potential: High (48.6%)
* Growth: 12.4%
* Annual Job Openings: 43,469
* Job Security: Least Secure
* Self-Employed: 4.2%
* Part-Time: 6.7%

Renewal Industry: Information and Telecommunication Technologies.

Industries with Greatest Employment: Merchant Wholesalers, Durable Goods (29.0%); Merchant Wholesalers, Nondurable Goods (15.5%); Wholesale Electronic Markets and Agents and Brokers (11.2%); Professional, Scientific, and Technical Services (9.3%).

Highest-Growth Industries (Projected Growth for This Job): Securities, Commodity Contracts, and Other Financial Investments and Related Activities (45.7%); Internet Publishing and Broadcasting (40.3%); Professional, Scientific, and Technical Services (34.1%); Ambulatory Health-Care Services (33.0%); Amusement, Gambling, and Recreation Industries (32.3%); Waste Management and Remediation Services (26.7%); Publishing Industries (Except Internet) (26.0%); Administrative and Support Services (25.2%); Support Activities for Transportation (22.0%); Building Material and Garden Equipment and Supplies Dealers (21.9%); Religious, Grantmaking, Civic, Professional, and Similar Organizations (20.6%); Nonstore Retailers (20.5%); Merchant Wholesalers, Nondurable Goods (15.3%); Management of Companies and Enterprises (15.3%); Broadcasting (Except Internet) (15.2%).

Other Considerations for Job Outlook: Employment opportunities will be best for those with a college degree, the appropriate knowledge or technical expertise, and the personal traits necessary for successful selling.

Sell goods for wholesalers or manufacturers where technical or scientific knowledge is required in such areas as biology, engineering, chemistry, and electronics that normally obtained from at least two years of postsecondary education. Contact new and existing customers to discuss their needs and to explain how these needs could be met by specific products and services. Answer customers' questions about products, prices, availability, product uses, and credit terms. Quote prices, credit terms, and other bid specifications. Emphasize product features based on analyses of customers' needs and on technical knowledge of product capabilities and limitations. Negotiate prices and terms of sales and service agreements. Maintain customer records, using automated systems. Identify prospective customers by using business directories, following leads from existing clients, participating in organizations and clubs, and attending trade shows and conferences. Prepare sales contracts for orders obtained and submit orders for processing. Select the correct products or assist customers in making product selections, based on customers' needs, product specifications, and applicable regulations. Collaborate with colleagues to exchange information such as selling strategies and marketing information. Prepare sales presentations and proposals that explain product specifications and applications. Provide customers with ongoing technical support. Demonstrate and explain the operation and use of products. Inform customers of estimated delivery schedules, service contracts, warranties, or other information pertaining to purchased products. Attend sales and trade meetings and read related publications in order to obtain information about market conditions, business trends, and industry developments. Visit establishments to evaluate needs and to promote product or service sales. Complete expense reports, sales reports, and other paperwork. Initiate sales campaigns and follow marketing plan guidelines in order to meet sales and production expectations. Recommend ways for customers to alter product usage in order to improve production. Complete product and development training as required. Provide feedback to company's product design teams so that products can be tailored to clients' needs. Arrange for installation and test-operation of machinery.

Personality Type: Enterprising-Conventional.

Career Cluster: 14 Marketing, Sales, and Service. **Career Pathway:** 14.2 Professional Sales and Marketing.

Skills: Persuasion; Negotiation; Science; Management of Financial Resources; Service Orientation; Coordination.

Education and Training Programs: Selling Skills and Sales Operations; Business, Management, Marketing, and Related Support Services. **Related Knowledge/Courses:** Sales and Marketing; Customer and Personal Service; Production and Processing; Administration and Management; Computers and Electronics; Transportation.

Work Environment: Indoors; sitting.

School Psychologists

- ❋ Education/Training Required: Doctoral degree
- ❋ Annual Earnings: $62,210
- ❋ Beginning Wage: $37,300
- ❋ Earnings Growth Potential: High (40.0%)
- ❋ Growth: 15.8%
- ❋ Annual Job Openings: 8,309
- ❋ Job Security: Most Secure
- ❋ Self-Employed: 34.2%
- ❋ Part-Time: 24.0%

Our sources did not provide separate job openings data for this occupation. The job openings listed here are shared with Clinical Psychologists and with Counseling Psychologists.

Renewal Industry: Education.

Industries with Greatest Employment: Educational Services, Public and Private (30.4%); Ambulatory Health-Care Services (13.2%); Hospitals, Public and Private (6.0%); Social Assistance (5.9%).

Highest-Growth Industries (Projected Growth for This Job): Social Assistance (56.2%); Professional, Scientific, and Technical Services (34.6%); Ambulatory Health-Care Services (26.8%); Nursing and Residential Care Facilities (24.8%); Funds, Trusts, and Other Financial Vehicles (23.3%); Religious, Grantmaking, Civic, Professional, and Similar Organizations (19.4%); Management of Companies and Enterprises (15.2%).

Other Considerations for Job Outlook: Growing awareness of how students' mental health and behavioral problems, such as bullying, affect learning will increase demand for school psychologists to offer student counseling and mental health services. Job prospects should be the best for people with a specialist or doctoral degree in school psychology. Opportunities directly related to psychology will be limited for bachelor's degree holders. Those who meet state certification requirements may become high school psychology teachers.

Investigate processes of learning and teaching and develop psychological principles and techniques applicable to educational problems. Compile and interpret students' test results, along with information from teachers and parents, to diagnose conditions and to help assess eligibility for special services. Report any pertinent information to the proper authorities in cases of child endangerment, neglect, or abuse. Assess an individual child's needs, limitations, and potential, using observation, review of school records, and consultation with parents and school personnel. Select, administer, and score psychological tests. Provide consultation to parents, teachers, administrators, and others on topics such as learning styles and behavior modification techniques. Promote an understanding of child development and its relationship to learning and behavior. Collaborate with other educational professionals to develop teaching strategies and school programs. Counsel children and families to help solve conflicts and problems in learning and adjustment. Develop individualized educational plans in collaboration with teachers and other staff members. Maintain student records, including special education reports, confidential records, records of services provided, and behavioral data. Serve as a resource to help families and schools deal with crises, such as separation and loss. Attend workshops, seminars, or professional meetings to remain informed of new developments in school psychology. Design classes and programs to meet the needs of special students. Refer students and their families to appropriate community agencies for medical, vocational, or social services. Initiate and direct efforts to foster tolerance, understanding, and appreciation of diversity in school communities. Collect and analyze data to evaluate the effectiveness of academic programs and other services, such as behavioral management systems. Provide educational programs on topics such as classroom management, teaching strategies, or parenting skills. Conduct research to generate new knowledge that can be used to address learning and behavior issues.

Personality Type: Investigative-Social.

Career Clusters: 08 Health Science; 10 Human Services.
Career Pathways: 08.1 Therapeutic Services; 10.2 Counseling and Mental Health Services.

Skills: Social Perceptiveness; Negotiation; Learning Strategies; Persuasion; Writing; Active Listening.

Education and Training Programs: Educational Assessment, Testing, and Measurement; Psychology, General; Clinical Psychology; Counseling Psychology; Developmental and Child Psychology; School Psychology; Psychoanalysis and Psychotherapy. **Related Knowledge/ Courses:** Therapy and Counseling; Psychology; Sociology and Anthropology; Philosophy and Theology; Education and Training; Medicine and Dentistry.

Work Environment: Indoors; sitting.

Self-Enrichment Education Teachers

- ❋ Education/Training Required: Work experience in a related occupation
- ❋ Annual Earnings: $34,580
- ❋ Beginning Wage: $18,530
- ❋ Earnings Growth Potential: High (46.4%)
- ❋ Growth: 23.1%
- ❋ Annual Job Openings: 64,449
- ❋ Job Security: Most Secure
- ❋ Self-Employed: 21.5%
- ❋ Part-Time: 41.3%

Renewal Industry: Education.

Industries with Greatest Employment: Educational Services, Public and Private (37.8%); Religious, Grantmaking, Civic, Professional, and Similar Organizations (25.5%).

Highest-Growth Industries (Projected Growth for This Job): Social Assistance (38.7%); Museums, Historical Sites, and Similar Institutions (36.2%); Amusement, Gambling, and Recreation Industries (31.0%); Scenic and Sightseeing Transportation (30.1%); Administrative and Support Services (28.3%); Professional, Scientific, and Technical Services (25.1%); Nursing and Residential Care Facilities (23.9%); Educational Services, Public and Private (23.1%); Ambulatory Health-Care Services (22.2%); Support Activities for Transportation (20.9%); Religious, Grantmaking, Civic, Professional, and Similar Organizations (19.0%); Management of Companies and Enterprises (15.3%).

Other Considerations for Job Outlook: Job prospects should be favorable as increasing demand and high turnover creates many opportunities, but opportunities may vary as some fields have more prospective teachers than others. Opportunities should be best for teachers of subjects that are not easily researched on the Internet and those that benefit from hands-on experiences, such as cooking, crafts, and the arts. Classes on self-improvement, personal finance, and computer and Internet-related subjects are also expected to be popular.

Teach or instruct courses other than those that normally lead to an occupational objective or degree. Courses may include self-improvement, nonvocational, and nonacademic subjects. Teaching may or may not take place in a traditional educational institution. Adapt teaching methods and instructional materials to meet students' varying needs and interests. Conduct classes, workshops, and demonstrations and provide individual instruction to teach topics and skills such as cooking, dancing, writing, physical fitness, photography, personal finance, and flying. Monitor students' performance to make suggestions for improvement and to ensure that they satisfy course standards, training requirements, and objectives. Observe students to determine qualifications, limitations, abilities, interests, and other individual characteristics. Instruct students individually and in groups, using various teaching methods such as lectures, discussions, and demonstrations. Establish clear objectives for all lessons, units, and projects and communicate those objectives to students. Instruct and monitor students in use and care of equipment and materials to prevent injury and damage. Prepare students for further development by encouraging them to explore learning opportunities and to persevere with challenging tasks. Prepare materials and classrooms for class activities. Enforce policies and rules governing students. Plan and conduct activities for a balanced program of instruction, demonstration, and work time that provides students with opportunities to observe, question, and investigate. Prepare instructional program objectives, outlines, and lesson plans. Maintain accurate and complete student records as required by administrative policy. Participate in publicity planning and student recruitment. Plan and supervise class projects, field trips, visits by guest speakers, contests, or other experiential activities and guide students in learning from those activities. Attend professional meetings, conferences, and workshops in order to maintain and improve professional competence. Meet with other instructors to discuss individual students and their progress. Confer with other teachers and professionals to plan and schedule lessons promoting learning and development. Attend staff meetings and serve on committees as required. Prepare and administer written, oral, and performance tests and issue grades in accordance with performance.

Personality Type: Social-Artistic-Enterprising.

Career Cluster: 05 Education and Training. **Career Pathway:** 05.3 Teaching/Training.

Skills: No data available.

Education and Training Program: Adult and Continuing Education and Teaching. **Related Knowledge/Courses:** Fine Arts; Education and Training; Psychology; Customer and Personal Service; Sales and Marketing; Administration and Management.

Work Environment: Indoors; standing.

Sheet Metal Workers

- ❋ Education/Training Required: Long-term on-the-job training
- ❋ Annual Earnings: $39,210
- ❋ Beginning Wage: $22,820
- ❋ Earnings Growth Potential: High (41.8%)
- ❋ Growth: 6.7%
- ❋ Annual Job Openings: 31,677
- ❋ Job Security: Least Secure
- ❋ Self-Employed: 4.7%
- ❋ Part-Time: 4.2%

Renewal Industries: Green Technologies; Infrastructure.

Industries with Greatest Employment: Specialty Trade Contractors (63.5%); Fabricated Metal Product Manufacturing (11.8%).

Highest-Growth Industries (Projected Growth for This Job): Professional, Scientific, and Technical Services (48.4%); Waste Management and Remediation Services (30.2%); Administrative and Support Services (25.0%); Support Activities for Transportation (16.6%).

Other Considerations for Job Outlook: Job opportunities are expected to be good for sheet metal workers in the construction industry, reflecting both employment growth and openings arising each year as experienced sheet metal workers leave the occupation. Opportunities should be particularly good for individuals who have apprenticeship training or who are certified welders. Applicants for jobs in manufacturing may experience competition because a number of manufacturing plants that employ sheet metal workers are moving to other countries and the plants that remain are becoming more productive.

Fabricate, assemble, install, and repair sheet metal products and equipment, such as ducts, control boxes, drainpipes, and furnace casings. Work may involve any of the following: setting up and operating fabricating machines to cut, bend, and straighten sheet metal; shaping metal over anvils, blocks, or forms, using hammer; operating soldering and welding equipment to join sheet metal parts; and inspecting, assembling, and smoothing seams and joints of burred surfaces. Determine project requirements, including scope, assembly sequences, and required methods and materials, according to blueprints, drawings, and written or verbal instructions. Lay out, measure, and mark dimensions and reference lines on material such as roofing panels according to drawings or templates, using calculators, scribes, dividers, squares, and rulers. Maneuver completed units into position for installation and anchor the units. Convert blueprints into shop drawings to be followed in the construction and assembly of sheet metal products. Install assemblies such as flashing, pipes, tubes, heating and air conditioning ducts, furnace casings, rain gutters, and downspouts in supportive frameworks. Select gauges and types of sheet metal or non-metallic material according to product specifications. Drill and punch holes in metal for screws, bolts, and rivets. Fasten seams and joints together with welds, bolts, cement, rivets, solder, caulks, metal drive clips, and bonds to assemble components into products or to repair sheet metal items. Fabricate or alter parts at construction sites, using shears, hammers, punches, and drills. Finish parts, using hacksaws and hand, rotary, or squaring shears. Trim, file, grind, deburr, buff, and smooth surfaces, seams, and joints of assembled parts, using hand tools and portable power tools. Maintain equipment, making repairs and modifications when necessary. Shape metal material over anvils, blocks, or other forms, using hand tools. Transport prefabricated parts to construction sites for assembly and installation. Develop and lay out patterns that use materials most efficiently, using computerized metalworking equipment to experiment with different layouts. Inspect individual parts, assemblies, and installations for conformance to specifications and building codes, using measuring instruments such as calipers, scales, and micrometers. Secure metal roof panels in place and interlock and fasten grooved panel edges. Fasten roof panel edges and machine-made molding to structures, nailing or welding pieces into place.

Personality Type: Realistic.

Career Cluster: 13 Manufacturing. **Career Pathway:** 13.1 Production.

Skills: Installation; Repairing; Equipment Maintenance; Mathematics; Technology Design; Equipment Selection.

Education and Training Program: Sheet Metal Technology/Sheetworking. **Related Knowledge/Courses:** Building and Construction; Mechanical Devices; Physics; Design; Production and Processing; Mathematics.

Work Environment: Noisy; contaminants; hazardous equipment; minor burns, cuts, bites, or stings; standing; using hands on objects, tools, or controls.

Shipping, Receiving, and Traffic Clerks

* Education/Training Required: Short-term on-the-job training
* Annual Earnings: $26,990
* Beginning Wage: $17,390
* Earnings Growth Potential: Medium (35.6%)
* Growth: 3.7%
* Annual Job Openings: 138,967
* Job Security: More Secure than Most
* Self-Employed: 0.2%
* Part-Time: 8.9%

Renewal Industry: Advanced Manufacturing.

Industries with Greatest Employment: Merchant Wholesalers, Durable Goods (12.7%); Merchant Wholesalers, Nondurable Goods (7.7%); Administrative and Support Services (7.0%); General Merchandise Stores (5.6%); Warehousing and Storage (5.1%).

Highest-Growth Industries (Projected Growth for This Job): Amusement, Gambling, and Recreation Industries (45.3%); Securities, Commodity Contracts, and Other Financial Investments and Related Activities (40.5%); Museums, Historical Sites, and Similar Institutions (31.3%); Professional, Scientific, and Technical Services (30.2%); Performing Arts, Spectator Sports, and Related Industries (28.6%); Warehousing and Storage (28.5%); Administrative and Support Services (23.8%); Internet Service Providers, Web Search Portals, and Data Processing Services (23.6%); Waste Management and Remediation Services (23.4%); Lessors of Nonfinancial Intangible Assets (Except Copyrighted Works) (22.9%); Building Material and Garden Equipment and Supplies Dealers (21.9%); Ambulatory Health-Care Services (20.2%); Nursing and Residential Care Facilities (19.6%); Support Activities for Transportation (18.9%); Social Assistance (18.8%); Nonstore Retailers (16.7%).

Other Considerations for Job Outlook: Employers prefer to hire those familiar with computers and other electronic office and business equipment.

Verify and keep records on incoming and outgoing shipments. Prepare items for shipment. Examine contents and compare with records such as manifests, invoices, or orders to verify accuracy of incoming or outgoing shipment. Prepare documents such as work orders, bills of lading, and shipping orders to route materials. Determine shipping method for materials, using knowledge of shipping procedures, routes, and rates. Record shipment data such as weight, charges, space availability, and damages and discrepancies for reporting, accounting, and recordkeeping purposes. Contact carrier representative to make arrangements and to issue instructions for shipping and delivery of materials. Confer and correspond with establishment representatives to rectify problems such as damages, shortages, and nonconformance to specifications. Requisition and store shipping materials and supplies to maintain inventory of stock. Deliver or route materials to departments, using work devices such as handtruck, conveyor, or sorting bins. Compute amounts such as space available and shipping, storage, and demurrage charges, using calculator or price list. Pack, seal, label, and affix postage to prepare materials for shipping, using work devices such as hand tools, power tools, and postage meter.

Personality Type: Conventional-Realistic-Enterprising.

Career Clusters: 04 Business, Management, and Administration; 16 Transportation, Distribution, and Logistics. **Career Pathways:** 04.6 Administrative and Information Support; 16.3 Warehousing and Distribution Center Operations.

Skills: No data available.

Education and Training Programs: General Office Occupations and Clerical Services; Traffic, Customs, and Transportation Clerk/Technician. **Related Knowledge/Courses:** Clerical Practices; Production and Processing; Transportation; Computers and Electronics; Education and Training; Public Safety and Security.

Work Environment: Indoors; noisy; contaminants; sitting; walking and running; using hands on objects, tools, or controls.

Social Work Teachers, Postsecondary

- ✸ Education/Training Required: Master's degree
- ✸ Annual Earnings: $56,240
- ✸ Beginning Wage: $33,840
- ✸ Earnings Growth Potential: Medium (39.8%)
- ✸ Growth: 22.9%
- ✸ Annual Job Openings: 1,292
- ✸ Job Security: Most Secure
- ✸ Self-Employed: 0.4%
- ✸ Part-Time: 27.8%

Renewal Industry: Education.

Industries with Greatest Employment: Educational Services, Public and Private (97.3%).

Highest-Growth Industries (Projected Growth for This Job): Administrative and Support Services (48.3%); Amusement, Gambling, and Recreation Industries (45.2%); Social Assistance (38.6%); Support Activities for Transportation (32.8%); Religious, Grantmaking, Civic, Professional, and Similar Organizations (29.9%); Professional, Scientific, and Technical Services (28.8%); Management of Companies and Enterprises (26.8%); Local Government (23.5%); Educational Services, Public and Private (22.8%); Hospitals, Public and Private (21.4%).

Other Considerations for Job Outlook: Retirements of current postsecondary teachers should create numerous openings for all types of postsecondary teachers, so job opportunities are generally expected to be very good. One of the main reasons why students attend postsecondary institutions is to prepare themselves for careers, so the best job prospects for postsecondary teachers are likely to be in rapidly growing fields that offer many nonacademic career options. Community colleges and other institutions offering career and technical education have been among the most rapidly growing, and these institutions are expected to offer some of the best opportunities for postsecondary teachers.

Teach courses in social work. Initiate, facilitate, and moderate classroom discussions. Evaluate and grade students' classwork, assignments, and papers. Prepare and deliver lectures to undergraduate or graduate students on topics such as family behavior, child and adolescent mental health, and social intervention evaluation. Keep abreast of developments in their field by reading current literature, talking with colleagues, and participating in professional conferences. Supervise students' laboratory work and fieldwork. Conduct research in a particular field of knowledge and publish findings in professional journals, books, or electronic media. Prepare course materials such as syllabi, homework assignments, and handouts. Maintain regularly scheduled office hours to advise and assist students. Supervise undergraduate or graduate teaching, internship, and research work. Plan, evaluate, and revise curricula, course content, and course materials and methods of instruction. Collaborate with colleagues and with community agencies to address teaching and research issues. Compile, administer, and grade examinations or assign this work to others. Advise students on academic and vocational curricula and on career issues. Maintain student attendance records, grades, and other required records. Write grant proposals to procure external research funding. Serve on academic or administrative committees that deal with institutional policies, departmental matters, and academic issues. Perform administrative duties such as serving as department head. Compile bibliographies of specialized materials for outside reading assignments. Select and obtain materials and supplies such as textbooks and laboratory equipment. Participate in student recruitment, registration, and placement activities. Participate in campus and community events. Provide professional consulting services to government and industry. Act as advisers to student organizations.

Personality Type: Social-Investigative.

Career Clusters: 05 Education and Training; 10 Human Services. **Career Pathways:** 05.3 Teaching/Training; 10.2 Counseling and Mental Health Services; 10.3 Family and Community Services.

Skills: Social Perceptiveness; Service Orientation; Instructing; Learning Strategies; Writing; Complex Problem Solving.

Education and Training Programs: Teacher Education and Professional Development, Specific Subject Areas, Other; Social Work; Clinical/Medical Social Work. **Related Knowledge/Courses:** Therapy and Counseling; Sociology and Anthropology; Psychology; Philosophy and Theology; Education and Training; English Language.

Work Environment: Indoors; sitting.

Sociology Teachers, Postsecondary

* Education/Training Required: Master's degree
* Annual Earnings: $58,160
* Beginning Wage: $31,310
* Earnings Growth Potential: High (46.2%)
* Growth: 22.9%
* Annual Job Openings: 2,774
* Job Security: Most Secure
* Self-Employed: 0.4%
* Part-Time: 27.8%

Renewal Industry: Education.

Industries with Greatest Employment: Educational Services, Public and Private (97.3%).

Highest-Growth Industries (Projected Growth for This Job): Administrative and Support Services (48.3%); Amusement, Gambling, and Recreation Industries (45.2%); Social Assistance (38.6%); Support Activities for Transportation (32.8%); Religious, Grantmaking, Civic, Professional, and Similar Organizations (29.9%); Professional, Scientific, and Technical Services (28.8%); Management of Companies and Enterprises (26.8%); Local Government (23.5%); Educational Services, Public and Private (22.8%); Hospitals, Public and Private (21.4%).

Other Considerations for Job Outlook: Retirements of current postsecondary teachers should create numerous openings for all types of postsecondary teachers. However, one of the main reasons why students attend postsecondary institutions is to prepare themselves for careers, so the best job prospects for postsecondary teachers are likely to be in rapidly growing fields that offer many nonacademic career options, unlike sociology. Community colleges and other institutions offering career and technical education have been among the most rapidly growing, and these institutions are expected to offer some of the best opportunities for postsecondary teachers.

Teach courses in sociology. Evaluate and grade students' classwork, assignments, and papers. Prepare and deliver lectures to undergraduate and graduate students on topics such as race and ethnic relations, measurement and data collection, and workplace social relations. Initiate, facilitate, and moderate classroom discussions. Prepare course materials such as syllabi, homework assignments, and handouts. Compile, administer, and grade examinations or assign this work to others. Keep abreast of developments in their field by reading current literature, talking with colleagues, and participating in professional conferences. Maintain student attendance records, grades, and other required records. Maintain regularly scheduled office hours in order to advise and assist students. Plan, evaluate, and revise curricula, course content, and course materials and methods of instruction. Advise students on academic and vocational curricula and on career issues. Collaborate with colleagues to address teaching and research issues. Conduct research in a particular field of knowledge and publish findings in professional journals, books, or electronic media. Select and obtain materials and supplies such as textbooks and laboratory equipment. Supervise undergraduate and graduate teaching, internship, and research work. Serve on academic or administrative committees that deal with institutional policies, departmental matters, and academic issues. Participate in student recruitment, registration, and placement activities. Perform administrative duties such as serving as department head. Supervise students' laboratory work and fieldwork. Write grant proposals to procure external research funding. Act as advisers to student organizations. Compile bibliographies of specialized materials for outside reading assignments. Participate in campus and community events. Provide professional consulting services to government and industry.

Personality Type: Social-Investigative-Artistic.

Career Cluster: 02 Architecture and Construction. **Career Pathway:** 02.2 Construction.

Skills: Science; Instructing; Writing; Learning Strategies; Social Perceptiveness; Critical Thinking.

Education and Training Programs: Social Science Teacher Education; Sociology. **Related Knowledge/ Courses:** Sociology and Anthropology; Philosophy and Theology; History and Archeology; Education and Training; English Language; Geography.

Work Environment: Indoors; sitting.

Software Quality Assurance Engineers and Testers

- ❋ Education/Training Required: No data available.
- ❋ Annual Earnings: $71,510
- ❋ Beginning Wage: $37,600
- ❋ Earnings Growth Potential: High (47.4%)
- ❋ Growth: 15.1%
- ❋ Annual Job Openings: 14,374
- ❋ Job Security: More Secure than Most
- ❋ Self-Employed: 6.6%
- ❋ Part-Time: 5.6%

Our sources did not provide separate job openings data for this occupation. The job openings listed here are shared with Computer Systems Engineers/Architects, Network Designers, Web Administrators, and Web Developers.

Renewal Industry: Information and Telecommunication Technologies.

Industries with Greatest Employment: Professional, Scientific, and Technical Services (22.9%); Educational Services, Public and Private (10.0%); Management of Companies and Enterprises (8.0%); State Government (5.5%).

Highest-Growth Industries (Projected Growth for This Job): Amusement, Gambling, and Recreation Industries (53.3%); Securities, Commodity Contracts, and Other Financial Investments and Related Activities (46.9%); Social Assistance (44.2%); Internet Publishing and Broadcasting (40.3%); Warehousing and Storage (33.3%); Professional, Scientific, and Technical Services (31.4%); Real Estate (25.8%); General Merchandise Stores (25.0%); Nursing and Residential Care Facilities (24.8%); Ambulatory Health-Care Services (24.7%); Building Material and Garden Equipment and Supplies Dealers (24.2%); Publishing Industries (Except Internet) (21.7%); Nonstore Retailers (21.4%); Religious, Grantmaking, Civic, Professional, and Similar Organizations (19.6%); Chemical Manufacturing (19.0%); Merchant Wholesalers, Durable Goods (15.9%); Management of Companies and Enterprises (15.3%).

Other Considerations for Job Outlook: Because employers continue to seek computer specialists who can combine strong technical skills with good business skills, individuals with a combination of experience inside and outside the IT arena will have the best job prospects.

Develop and execute software test plans in order to identify software problems and their causes. Design test plans, scenarios, scripts, or procedures. Test system modifications to prepare for implementation. Document software defects, using a bug tracking system, and report defects to software developers. Develop testing programs that address areas such as database impacts, software scenarios, regression testing, negative testing, error or bug retests, or usability. Identify, analyze, and document problems with program function, output, online screens, or content. Monitor bug resolution efforts and track successes. Create or maintain databases of known test defects. Plan test schedules or strategies in accordance with project scope or delivery dates. Participate in product design reviews to provide input on functional requirements, product designs, schedules, or potential problems. Review software documentation to ensure technical accuracy, compliance, or completeness or to mitigate risks. Document test procedures to ensure replicability and compliance with standards. Develop or specify standards, methods, or procedures to determine product quality or release readiness. Update automated test scripts to ensure currency. Investigate customer problems referred by technical support. Install, maintain, or use software testing programs. Provide feedback and recommendations to developers on software usability and functionality. Monitor program performance to ensure efficient and problem-free operations. Install and configure recreations of software production environments to allow testing of software performance. Collaborate with field staff or customers to evaluate or diagnose problems and recommend possible solutions. Conduct software compatibility tests with programs, hardware, operating systems, or network environments. Identify program deviance from standards and suggest modifications to ensure compliance. Design or develop automated testing tools. Coordinate user or third-party testing. Perform initial debugging procedures by reviewing configuration files, logs, or code pieces to determine breakdown sources. Visit beta testing sites to evaluate software performance. Evaluate or recommend software for testing or bug tracking.

Personality Type: Investigative-Conventional-Realistic.

Career Cluster: 11 Information Technology. **Career Pathway:** 11.2 Programming and Software Development.

Skills: Quality Control Analysis; Programming; Systems Analysis; Systems Evaluation; Troubleshooting; Technology Design.

Education and Training Programs: Computer and Information Sciences, General; Information Technology; Information Science/Studies; Computer Science; Computer and Information Sciences and Support Services, Other; Computer Engineering, General; Computer Software Engineering; Computer Engineering Technologies/Technicians, Other. **Related Knowledge/Courses:** Computers and Electronics; Engineering and Technology; Design; English Language; Mathematics; Clerical Practices.

Work Environment: Indoors; sitting; using hands on objects, tools, or controls; repetitive motions.

Solderers and Brazers

- ❋ Education/Training Required: Long-term on-the-job training
- ❋ Annual Earnings: $32,270
- ❋ Beginning Wage: $21,680
- ❋ Earnings Growth Potential: Low (32.8%)
- ❋ Growth: 5.1%
- ❋ Annual Job Openings: 61,125
- ❋ Job Security: More Secure than Most
- ❋ Self-Employed: 6.3%
- ❋ Part-Time: 1.9%

Our sources did not provide separate job openings data for this occupation. The job openings listed here are shared with Welders, Cutters, and Welder Fitters.

Renewal Industries: Advanced Manufacturing; Green Technologies.

Industries with Greatest Employment: Fabricated Metal Product Manufacturing (22.4%); Machinery Manufacturing (16.0%); Transportation Equipment Manufacturing (14.2%); Specialty Trade Contractors (5.7%).

Highest-Growth Industries (Projected Growth for This Job): Warehousing and Storage (42.2%); Amusement, Gambling, and Recreation Industries (38.5%); Building Material and Garden Equipment and Supplies Dealers (35.3%); Administrative and Support Services (34.9%); Waste Management and Remediation Services (34.2%);

Professional, Scientific, and Technical Services (33.7%); Rental and Leasing Services (26.0%); Management of Companies and Enterprises (22.6%); Support Activities for Transportation (22.0%); Water Transportation (21.5%); Wholesale Electronic Markets and Agents and Brokers (20.7%); Nonstore Retailers (20.7%); Truck Transportation (20.1%); Motor Vehicle and Parts Dealers (19.9%); Local Government (19.5%); Construction of Buildings (19.2%); Specialty Trade Contractors (18.7%); Merchant Wholesalers, Durable Goods (17.0%); Educational Services, Public and Private (16.0%).

Other Considerations for Job Outlook: Outlook information for solderers and welders is limited, but information about welders probably applies to a large extent. Despite overall employment declines in the manufacturing industry, the outlook for welders in manufacturing is far stronger than for other occupations. Welding schools report that graduates have little difficulty finding work, and some welding employers report difficulty finding trained welders.

Braze or solder together components to assemble fabricated metal parts with soldering iron, torch, or welding machine and flux. Melt and apply solder along adjoining edges of workpieces to solder joints, using soldering irons, gas torches, or ultrasonic equipment. Heat soldering irons or workpieces to specified temperatures for soldering, using gas flames or electrical current. Examine seams for defects and rework defective joints or broken parts. Melt and separate brazed or soldered joints to remove and straighten damaged or misaligned components, using hand torches, irons, or furnaces. Melt and apply solder to fill holes, indentations, and seams of fabricated metal products, using soldering equipment. Clean workpieces to remove dirt and excess acid, using chemical solutions, files, wire brushes, or grinders. Guide torches and rods along joints of workpieces to heat them to brazing temperature, melt braze alloys, and bond workpieces together. Adjust electrical current and timing cycles of resistance welding machines to heat metals to bonding temperature. Clean equipment parts such as tips of soldering irons, using chemical solutions or cleaning compounds. Turn valves to start flow of gases and light flames and adjust valves to obtain desired colors and sizes of flames. Brush flux onto joints of workpieces or dip braze rods into flux to prevent oxidation of metal. Remove workpieces from fixtures, using tongs, and cool workpieces, using air or water. Align and clamp workpieces together, using rules, squares, or hand tools, or position items in fixtures,

jigs, or vises. Sweat together workpieces coated with solder. Smooth soldered areas with alternate strokes of paddles and torches, leaving soldered sections slightly higher than surrounding areas for later filing. Remove workpieces from molten solder and hold parts together until color indicates that solder has set. Select torch tips, flux, and brazing alloys from data charts or work orders. Turn dials to set intensity and duration of ultrasonic impulses according to work order specifications. Dip workpieces into molten solder or place solder strips between seams and heat seams with irons to bond items together. Clean joints of workpieces with wire brushes or by dipping them into cleaning solutions.

Personality Type: Realistic.

Career Cluster: 13 Manufacturing. **Career Pathway:** 13.1 Production.

Skills: No data available.

Education and Training Program: Welding Technology/Welder. **Related Knowledge/Courses:** Production and Processing; Mechanical Devices; Engineering and Technology.

Work Environment: Indoors; noisy; contaminants; minor burns, cuts, bites, or stings; using hands on objects, tools, or controls; repetitive motions.

Special Education Teachers, Preschool, Kindergarten, and Elementary School

* Education/Training Required: Bachelor's degree
* Annual Earnings: $48,350
* Beginning Wage: $32,700
* Earnings Growth Potential: Low (32.4%)
* Growth: 19.6%
* Annual Job Openings: 20,049
* Job Security: More Secure than Most
* Self-Employed: 0.3%
* Part-Time: 9.6%

Renewal Industry: Education.

Industries with Greatest Employment: Educational Services, Public and Private (93.5%).

Highest-Growth Industries (Projected Growth for This Job): Social Assistance (37.1%); Ambulatory Health-Care Services (31.7%); Nursing and Residential Care Facilities (23.6%); Educational Services, Public and Private (18.9%); Religious, Grantmaking, Civic, Professional, and Similar Organizations (16.8%); Management of Companies and Enterprises (15.0%).

Other Considerations for Job Outlook: Excellent job prospects are expected because of rising enrollments of special education students and reported shortages of qualified teachers.

Teach elementary and preschool school subjects to educationally and physically handicapped students. Includes teachers who specialize and work with audibly and visually handicapped students and those who teach basic academic and life processes skills to the mentally impaired. Instruct students in academic subjects, using a variety of techniques such as phonetics, multisensory learning, and repetition to reinforce learning and to meet students' varying needs and interests. Employ special educational strategies and techniques during instruction to improve the development of sensory- and perceptual-motor skills, language, cognition, and memory. Teach socially acceptable behavior, employing techniques such as behavior modification and positive reinforcement. Modify the general education curriculum for special-needs students based upon a variety of instructional techniques and technologies. Meet with parents and guardians to discuss their children's progress and to determine their priorities for their children and their resource needs. Plan and conduct activities for a balanced program of instruction, demonstration, and work time that provides students with opportunities to observe, question, and investigate. Establish and enforce rules for behavior and policies and procedures to maintain order among the students for whom they are responsible. Confer with parents, administrators, testing specialists, social workers, and professionals to develop individual educational plans designed to promote students' educational, physical, and social development. Maintain accurate and complete student records and prepare reports on children and activities as required by laws, district policies, and administrative regulations. Establish clear objectives for all lessons, units, and projects and communicate those objectives to students. Develop and implement strategies to meet the needs of students with a variety of handicapping conditions. Prepare classrooms for class activities and provide a variety of materials and resources for children to explore, manipulate, and use, both in learning activities and imaginative play. Confer with parents or guardians, teachers, counselors, and administrators to resolve students' behavioral and academic problems. Observe and evaluate students' performance, behavior, social development, and physical health. Teach students personal development skills such as goal setting, independence, and self-advocacy.

Personality Type: Social-Artistic.

Career Cluster: 05 Education and Training. **Career Pathway:** 05.3 Teaching/Training.

Skills: Learning Strategies; Instructing; Social Perceptiveness; Monitoring; Negotiation; Time Management.

Education and Training Programs: Special Education and Teaching, General; Education/Teaching of Individuals with Hearing Impairments, Including Deafness; Education/Teaching of the Gifted and Talented; Education/Teaching of Individuals with Emotional Disturbances; Education/Teaching of Individuals with Mental Retardation; Education/Teaching of Individuals with Multiple Disabilities; Education/Teaching of Individuals with Orthopedic and Other Physical Health Impairments; others. **Related Knowledge/Courses:** Psychology; History and Archeology; Therapy and Counseling; Geography; Philosophy and Theology; Sociology and Anthropology.

Work Environment: Indoors; noisy; standing.

Speech-Language Pathologists

- ❋ Education/Training Required: Master's degree
- ❋ Annual Earnings: $60,690
- ❋ Beginning Wage: $40,200
- ❋ Earnings Growth Potential: Low (33.8%)
- ❋ Growth: 10.6%
- ❋ Annual Job Openings: 11,160
- ❋ Job Security: Most Secure
- ❋ Self-Employed: 8.8%
- ❋ Part-Time: 24.6%

Renewal Industries: Education; Health Care.

Industries with Greatest Employment: Educational Services, Public and Private (48.0%); Ambulatory Health-Care Services (18.1%); Hospitals, Public and Private (12.8%).

Highest-Growth Industries (Projected Growth for This Job): Social Assistance (40.5%); Administrative and Support Services (26.5%); Ambulatory Health-Care Services (16.2%); Nursing and Residential Care Facilities (15.5%); Management of Companies and Enterprises (15.2%); Religious, Grantmaking, Civic, Professional, and Similar Organizations (15.1%).

Other Considerations for Job Outlook: The combination of growth in the occupation and an expected increase in retirements over the coming years should create excellent job opportunities for speech-language pathologists. Opportunities should be particularly favorable for those with the ability to speak a second language, such as Spanish. Job prospects also are expected to be especially favorable for those who are willing to relocate, particularly to areas experiencing difficulty in attracting and hiring speech-language pathologists.

Assess and treat persons with speech, language, voice, and fluency disorders. May select alternative communication systems and teach their use. May perform research related to speech and language problems. Monitor patients' progress and adjust treatments accordingly. Evaluate hearing and speech/language test results and medical or background information to diagnose and plan treatment for speech, language, fluency, voice, and swallowing disorders. Administer hearing or speech and language evaluations, tests, or examinations to patients to collect information on type and degree of impairments, using written and oral tests and special instruments. Record information on the initial evaluation, treatment, progress, and discharge of clients. Develop and implement treatment plans for problems such as stuttering, delayed language, swallowing disorders, and inappropriate pitch or harsh voice problems, based on own assessments and recommendations of physicians, psychologists, or social workers. Develop individual or group programs in schools to deal with speech or language problems. Instruct clients in techniques for more effective communication, including sign language, lip reading, and voice improvement. Teach clients to control or strengthen tongue, jaw, face muscles, and breathing mechanisms. Develop speech exercise programs to reduce disabilities. Consult with and advise educators or medical staff on speech or hearing topics, such as communication strategies or speech and language stimulation. Instruct patients and family members in strategies to cope with or avoid communication-related misunderstandings. Design,

develop, and employ alternative diagnostic or communication devices and strategies. Conduct lessons and direct educational or therapeutic games to assist teachers dealing with speech problems. Refer clients to additional medical or educational services if needed. Participate in conferences or training, or publish research results, to share knowledge of new hearing or speech disorder treatment methods or technologies. Communicate with non-speaking students, using sign language or computer technology. Provide communication instruction to dialect speakers or students with limited English proficiency. Use computer applications to identify and assist with communication disabilities.

Personality Type: Social-Investigative-Artistic.

Career Cluster: 08 Health Science. **Career Pathway:** 08.1 Therapeutic Services.

Skills: Learning Strategies; Instructing; Social Perceptiveness; Speaking; Monitoring; Service Orientation.

Education and Training Programs: Communication Disorders, General; Speech-Language Pathology/Pathologist; Audiology/Audiologist and Speech-Language Pathology/Pathologist; Communication Disorders Sciences and Services, Other. **Related Knowledge/Courses:** Therapy and Counseling; Psychology; Sociology and Anthropology; Medicine and Dentistry; Education and Training; English Language.

Work Environment: Indoors; disease or infections; sitting.

Storage and Distribution Managers

- ❋ Education/Training Required: Work experience in a related occupation
- ❋ Annual Earnings: $76,310
- ❋ Beginning Wage: $44,900
- ❋ Earnings Growth Potential: High (41.2%)
- ❋ Growth: 8.3%
- ❋ Annual Job Openings: 6,994
- ❋ Job Security: More Secure than Most
- ❋ Self-Employed: 2.6%
- ❋ Part-Time: 2.3%

Our sources did not provide separate job openings data for this occupation. The job openings listed here are shared with Transportation Managers.

Renewal Industry: Advanced Manufacturing.

Industries with Greatest Employment: Truck Transportation (9.9%); Federal Government (9.3%); Merchant Wholesalers, Nondurable Goods (8.6%); Merchant Wholesalers, Durable Goods (7.2%); Warehousing and Storage (5.9%); Management of Companies and Enterprises (5.7%).

Highest-Growth Industries (Projected Growth for This Job): Professional, Scientific, and Technical Services (40.4%); Warehousing and Storage (33.6%); Social Assistance (32.8%); Amusement, Gambling, and Recreation Industries (32.1%); Administrative and Support Services (29.5%); Ambulatory Health-Care Services (27.3%); Waste Management and Remediation Services (26.9%); Scenic and Sightseeing Transportation (26.7%); Personal and Laundry Services (26.6%); Building Material and Garden Equipment and Supplies Dealers (25.4%); Support Activities for Transportation (23.9%); Water Transportation (20.7%); Accommodation, Including Hotels and Motels (18.0%); Motion Picture, Video, and Sound Recording Industries (15.9%); Management of Companies and Enterprises (15.3%).

Other Considerations for Job Outlook: Opportunities will continue to arise from the need to replace the managers who retire or leave the labor force for other reasons. Also, the continuing increase of Internet purchases will create a continuing need for shipping services and managers.

Plan, direct, and coordinate the storage and distribution operations within organizations or the activities of organizations that are engaged in storing and distributing materials and products. Prepare and manage departmental budgets. Supervise the activities of workers engaged in receiving, storing, testing, and shipping products or materials. Interview, select, and train warehouse and supervisory personnel. Plan, develop, and implement warehouse safety and security programs and activities. Prepare or direct preparation of correspondence; reports; and operations, maintenance, and safety manuals. Issue shipping instructions and provide routing information to ensure that delivery times and locations are coordinated. Review invoices, work orders, consumption reports, and demand forecasts to estimate peak delivery periods and to issue work assignments. Confer with department heads to coordinate warehouse activities such as production, sales, records control, and purchasing. Inspect physical conditions of warehouses, vehicle fleets, and equipment and order testing, maintenance, repair, or replacement as necessary. Schedule and monitor air or surface pickup, delivery, or distribution of products or materials. Respond to customers' or shippers' questions and complaints regarding storage and distribution services. Develop and document standard and emergency operating procedures for receiving, handling, storing, shipping, or salvaging products or materials. Develop and implement plans for facility modification or expansion such as equipment purchase or changes in space allocation or structural design. Track and trace goods while they are en route to their destinations, expediting orders when necessary. Negotiate with carriers, warehouse operators, and insurance company representatives for services and preferential rates. Arrange for necessary shipping documentation and contact customs officials to effect release of shipments. Evaluate freight costs and the inventory costs associated with transit times to ensure that costs are appropriate. Advise sales and billing departments of transportation charges for customers' accounts. Examine invoices and shipping manifests for conformity to tariff and customs regulations. Evaluate locations for new warehouses and distribution networks to determine their potential usefulness.

Personality Type: Enterprising-Conventional.

Career Clusters: 04 Business, Management, and Administration; 07 Government and Public Administration; 16 Transportation, Distribution, and Logistics. **Career Pathways:** 04.1 Management; 07.1 Governance; 16.1 Transportation Operations; 16.2 Logistics Planning and Management Services.

Skills: No data available.

Education and Training Programs: Public Administration; Aeronautics/Aviation/Aerospace Science and Technology, General; Aviation/Airway Management and Operations; Business Administration and Management, General; Logistics and Materials Management; Transportation/Transportation Management. **Related Knowledge/Courses:** Transportation; Personnel and Human Resources; Production and Processing; Administration and Management; Economics and Accounting; Psychology.

Work Environment: Indoors; standing.

Structural Iron and Steel Workers

- ❋ Education/Training Required: Long-term on-the-job training
- ❋ Annual Earnings: $42,130
- ❋ Beginning Wage: $24,180
- ❋ Earnings Growth Potential: High (42.6%)
- ❋ Growth: 6.0%
- ❋ Annual Job Openings: 6,969
- ❋ Job Security: Less Secure than Most
- ❋ Self-Employed: 5.3%
- ❋ Part-Time: 5.8%

Renewal Industry: Green Technologies.

Industries with Greatest Employment: Specialty Trade Contractors (54.3%); Construction of Buildings (21.2%); Heavy and Civil Engineering Construction (9.3%).

Highest-Growth Industries (Projected Growth for This Job): Professional, Scientific, and Technical Services (16.7%); Management of Companies and Enterprises (15.4%).

Other Considerations for Job Outlook: In addition to new jobs from employment growth, many job openings will result from the need to replace experienced ironworkers who leave the occupation or retire. In most areas, job opportunities should be excellent, although the number of job openings can fluctuate from year to year with economic conditions and the level of construction activity. Many workers prefer to enter other occupations with better working conditions, leading to opportunities for those who wish to become structural and reinforcing iron and metal workers.

Raise, place, and unite iron or steel girders, columns, and other structural members to form completed structures or structural frameworks. May erect metal storage tanks and assemble prefabricated metal buildings. Read specifications and blueprints to determine the locations, quantities, and sizes of materials required. Verify vertical and horizontal alignment of structural-steel members, using plumb bobs, laser equipment, transits, and/or levels. Connect columns, beams, and girders with bolts, following blueprints and instructions from supervisors. Hoist steel beams, girders, and columns into place, using cranes, or signal hoisting equipment operators to lift and position structural-steel members. Bolt aligned structural-steel members in position for permanent riveting, bolting, or welding into place. Ride on girders or other structural-steel members to position them or use rope to guide them into position. Fabricate metal parts, such as steel frames, columns, beams, and girders, according to blueprints or instructions from supervisors. Pull, push, or pry structural-steel members into approximate positions for bolting into place. Cut, bend, and weld steel pieces, using metal shears, torches, and welding equipment. Fasten structural-steel members to hoist cables, using chains, cables, or rope. Assemble hoisting equipment and rigging such as cables, pulleys, and hooks to move heavy equipment and materials. Force structural-steel members into final positions, using turnbuckles, crowbars, jacks, and hand tools. Erect metal and precast concrete components for structures such as buildings, bridges, dams, towers, storage tanks, fences, and highway guard rails. Unload and position prefabricated steel units for hoisting as needed. Drive drift pins through rivet holes to align rivet holes in structural-steel members with corresponding holes in previously placed members. Dismantle structures and equipment. Insert sealing strips, wiring, insulating material, ladders, flanges, gauges, and valves, depending on types of structures being assembled. Catch hot rivets in buckets and insert rivets in holes, using tongs. Place blocks under reinforcing bars used to reinforce floors. Hold rivets while riveters use air-hammers to form heads on rivets.

Personality Type: Realistic-Investigative-Conventional.

Career Cluster: 02 Architecture and Construction. **Career Pathway:** 02.2 Construction.

Skills: Equipment Maintenance; Installation; Troubleshooting; Equipment Selection; Coordination; Technology Design.

Education and Training Programs: Metal Building Assembly/Assembler; Construction Trades, Other. **Related Knowledge/Courses:** Building and Construction; Engineering and Technology; Mechanical Devices; Production and Processing; Design; Physics.

Work Environment: Outdoors; noisy; very hot or cold; high places; hazardous equipment; using hands on objects, tools, or controls.

Substance Abuse and Behavioral Disorder Counselors

- ❋ Education/Training Required: Master's degree
- ❋ Annual Earnings: $35,580
- ❋ Beginning Wage: $23,780
- ❋ Earnings Growth Potential: Low (33.2%)
- ❋ Growth: 34.3%
- ❋ Annual Job Openings: 20,821
- ❋ Job Security: Most Secure
- ❋ Self-Employed: 5.8%
- ❋ Part-Time: 15.4%

Renewal Industry: Health Care.

Industries with Greatest Employment: Ambulatory Health-Care Services (24.2%); Nursing and Residential Care Facilities (22.8%); Social Assistance (16.1%); Hospitals, Public and Private (11.0%); Local Government (7.6%).

Highest-Growth Industries (Projected Growth for This Job): Social Assistance (57.9%); Professional, Scientific, and Technical Services (56.6%); Ambulatory Health-Care Services (48.3%); Nursing and Residential Care Facilities (48.1%); Administrative and Support Services (37.7%); Religious, Grantmaking, Civic, Professional, and Similar Organizations (17.6%); Management of Companies and Enterprises (15.3%).

Other Considerations for Job Outlook: Employment of substance abuse and behavioral disorder counselors is expected to grow much faster than the average for all occupations. As society becomes more knowledgeable about addiction, it is increasingly common for people to seek treatment. Furthermore, drug offenders are increasingly being sent to treatment programs rather than jail. Job opportunities are very good because relatively low wages and long hours make recruiting new entrants difficult.

Counsel and advise individuals with alcohol; tobacco; drug; or other problems, such as gambling and eating disorders. May counsel individuals, families, or groups or engage in prevention programs. Counsel clients and patients individually and in group sessions to assist in overcoming dependencies, adjusting to life, and making changes. Complete and maintain accurate records and reports regarding the patients' histories and progress, services provided, and other required information. Develop client treatment plans based on research, clinical experience, and client histories. Review and evaluate clients' progress in relation to measurable goals described in treatment and care plans. Interview clients, review records, and confer with other professionals to evaluate individuals' mental and physical condition and to determine their suitability for participation in a specific program. Intervene as advocate for clients or patients to resolve emergency problems in crisis situations. Provide clients or family members with information about addiction issues and about available services and programs, making appropriate referrals when necessary. Modify treatment plans to comply with changes in client status. Coordinate counseling efforts with mental health professionals and other health professionals such as doctors, nurses, and social workers. Attend training sessions to increase knowledge and skills. Plan and implement follow-up and aftercare programs for clients to be discharged from treatment programs. Conduct chemical dependency program orientation sessions. Counsel family members to assist them in understanding, dealing with, and supporting clients or patients. Participate in case conferences and staff meetings. Act as liaisons between clients and medical staff. Coordinate activities with courts, probation officers, community services, and other post-treatment agencies. Confer with family members or others close to clients to keep them informed of treatment planning and progress. Instruct others in program methods, procedures, and functions. Follow progress of discharged patients to determine effectiveness of treatments. Develop, implement, and evaluate public education, prevention, and health promotion programs, working in collaboration with organizations, institutions, and communities.

Personality Type: Social-Artistic-Investigative.

Career Clusters: 08 Health Science; 10 Human Services. **Career Pathways:** 08.1 Therapeutic Services; 08.3 Health Informatics; 10.2 Counseling and Mental Health Services.

Skills: Social Perceptiveness; Persuasion; Service Orientation; Negotiation; Active Listening; Learning Strategies.

Education and Training Programs: Substance Abuse/ Addiction Counseling; Clinical/Medical Social Work; Mental and Social Health Services and Allied Professions, Other. **Related Knowledge/Courses:** Therapy and

Counseling; Psychology; Sociology and Anthropology; Philosophy and Theology; Customer and Personal Service; Education and Training.

Work Environment: Indoors; disease or infections; sitting.

Surgeons

- ❋ Education/Training Required: First professional degree
- ❋ Annual Earnings: More than $145,600
- ❋ Beginning Wage: $104,410
- ❋ Earnings Growth Potential: Cannot be calculated
- ❋ Growth: 14.2%
- ❋ Annual Job Openings: 38,027
- ❋ Job Security: Most Secure
- ❋ Self-Employed: 14.7%
- ❋ Part-Time: 8.1%

Our sources did not provide separate job openings data for this occupation. The job openings listed here are shared with Anesthesiologists; Family and General Practitioners; Internists, General; Obstetricians and Gynecologists; Pediatricians, General; and Psychiatrists.

Renewal Industry: Health Care.

Industries with Greatest Employment: Ambulatory Health-Care Services (55.9%); Hospitals, Public and Private (17.8%).

Highest-Growth Industries (Projected Growth for This Job): Social Assistance (58.6%); Administrative and Support Services (26.8%); Professional, Scientific, and Technical Services (22.6%); Nursing and Residential Care Facilities (21.0%); Ambulatory Health-Care Services (19.4%); Religious, Grantmaking, Civic, Professional, and Similar Organizations (16.7%); Management of Companies and Enterprises (15.3%).

Other Considerations for Job Outlook: Opportunities for individuals interested in becoming physicians and surgeons are expected to be very good. Unlike their predecessors, new physicians are much less likely to enter solo practice and more likely to take salaried jobs in group medical practices, clinics, and health networks. Reports of shortages in some specialties, such as general or family practice, internal medicine, and OB/GYN, or in rural or low-income areas should attract new entrants, encouraging schools to expand programs and hospitals to increase available residency slots. However, because physician training is so lengthy, employment change happens gradually. Opportunities should be particularly good in rural and low-income areas, as some physicians find these areas unattractive because of less control over work hours, isolation from medical colleagues, or other reasons.

Treat diseases, injuries, and deformities by invasive methods, such as manual manipulation, or by using instruments and appliances. Analyze patient's medical history, medication allergies, physical condition, and examination results to verify operation's necessity and to determine best procedure. Operate on patients to correct deformities, repair injuries, prevent and treat diseases, or improve or restore patients' functions. Follow established surgical techniques during the operation. Prescribe preoperative and postoperative treatments and procedures, such as sedatives, diets, antibiotics, and preparation and treatment of the patient's operative area. Examine patient to provide information on medical condition and surgical risk. Diagnose bodily disorders and orthopedic conditions and provide treatments, such as medicines and surgeries, in clinics, hospital wards, and operating rooms. Direct and coordinate activities of nurses, assistants, specialists, residents, and other medical staff. Provide consultation and surgical assistance to other physicians and surgeons. Refer patient to medical specialist or other practitioners when necessary. Examine instruments, equipment, and operating room to ensure sterility. Prepare case histories. Manage surgery services, including planning, scheduling and coordination, determination of procedures, and procurement of supplies and equipment. Conduct research to develop and test surgical techniques that can improve operating procedures and outcomes.

Personality Type: Investigative-Realistic-Social.

Career Cluster: 08 Health Science. **Career Pathway:** 08.1 Therapeutic Services.

Skills: Science; Reading Comprehension; Judgment and Decision Making; Complex Problem Solving; Management of Financial Resources; Critical Thinking.

Education and Training Programs: Colon and Rectal Surgery; Critical Care Surgery; General Surgery; Hand

Surgery; Neurological Surgery/Neurosurgery; Ortho-pedics/Orthopedic Surgery; Otolaryngology; Pediatric Orthopedics; Pediatric Surgery; Plastic Surgery; Sports Medicine; Thoracic Surgery; Urology; Vascular Surgery; Adult Reconstructive Orthopedics (Orthopedic Surgery); Orthopedic Surgery of the Spine. **Related Knowledge/ Courses:** Medicine and Dentistry; Biology; Therapy and Counseling; Psychology; Chemistry; Customer and Personal Service.

Work Environment: Indoors; contaminants; radiation; disease or infections; standing; using hands on objects, tools, or controls.

Surgical Technologists

- ✸ Education/Training Required: Postsecondary vocational training
- ✸ Annual Earnings: $37,540
- ✸ Beginning Wage: $26,650
- ✸ Earnings Growth Potential: Low (29.0%)
- ✸ Growth: 24.5%
- ✸ Annual Job Openings: 15,365
- ✸ Job Security: Most Secure
- ✸ Self-Employed: 0.2%
- ✸ Part-Time: 20.8%

Renewal Industry: Health Care.

Industries with Greatest Employment: Hospitals, Public and Private (71.8%).

Highest-Growth Industries (Projected Growth for This Job): Professional, Scientific, and Technical Services (43.5%); Administrative and Support Services (32.4%); Hospitals, Public and Private (21.9%).

Other Considerations for Job Outlook: Job opportunities will be best for technologists who are certified. The number of surgical procedures is expected to rise as the population grows and ages. Hospitals will continue to be the primary employer of surgical technologists, although much faster employment growth is expected in offices of physicians and in outpatient care centers, including ambulatory surgical centers.

Assist in operations under the supervision of surgeons, registered nurses, or other surgical personnel. May help set up operating rooms; prepare and transport patients for surgery; adjust lights and equipment; pass instruments and other supplies to surgeons and surgeons' assistants; hold retractors; cut sutures; and help count sponges, needles, supplies, and instruments. Count sponges, needles, and instruments before and after operations. Maintain a proper sterile field during surgical procedures. Hand instruments and supplies to surgeons and surgeons' assistants, hold retractors and cut sutures, and perform other tasks as directed by surgeons during operations. Prepare patients for surgery, including positioning patients on operating tables and covering them with sterile surgical drapes to prevent exposure. Scrub arms and hands and assist surgical teams to scrub and put on gloves, masks, and surgical clothing. Wash and sterilize equipment, using germicides and sterilizers. Monitor and continually assess operating room conditions, including needs of the patient and surgical team. Prepare dressings or bandages and apply or assist with their application following surgeries. Clean and restock operating rooms, gathering and placing equipment and supplies and arranging instruments according to instructions such as those found on a preference card. Operate, assemble, adjust, or monitor sterilizers, lights, suction machines, and diagnostic equipment to ensure proper operation. Prepare, care for, and dispose of tissue specimens taken for laboratory analysis. Provide technical assistance to surgeons, surgical nurses, and anesthesiologists. Maintain supply of fluids such as plasma, saline, blood, and glucose for use during operations. Maintain files and records of surgical procedures. Observe patients' vital signs to assess physical condition. Order surgical supplies.

Personality Type: Realistic-Social-Conventional.

Career Cluster: 08 Health Science. **Career Pathway:** 08.2 Diagnostics Services.

Skills: No data available.

Education and Training Programs: Pathology/Pathologist Assistant; Surgical Technology/Technologist. **Related Knowledge/Courses:** Medicine and Dentistry; Biology; Psychology; Chemistry; Therapy and Counseling; Customer and Personal Service.

Work Environment: Indoors; contaminants; radiation; disease or infections; standing; using hands on objects, tools, or controls.

Surveying and Mapping Technicians

See *Mapping Technicians* and *Surveying Technicians*, described separately.

Surveying Technicians

- ❋ Education/Training Required: Moderate-term on-the-job training
- ❋ Annual Earnings: $33,640
- ❋ Beginning Wage: $20,670
- ❋ Earnings Growth Potential: Medium (38.6%)
- ❋ Growth: 19.4%
- ❋ Annual Job Openings: 8,299
- ❋ Job Security: Less Secure than Most
- ❋ Self-Employed: 4.2%
- ❋ Part-Time: 4.5%

Our sources did not provide separate job openings data for this occupation. The job openings listed here are shared with Mapping Technicians.

Renewal Industries: Green Technologies; Infrastructure.

Industries with Greatest Employment: Professional, Scientific, and Technical Services (71.8%); Local Government (10.3%).

Highest-Growth Industries (Projected Growth for This Job): Real Estate (25.4%); Professional, Scientific, and Technical Services (24.7%); Management of Companies and Enterprises (15.3%).

Other Considerations for Job Outlook: Opportunities should be stronger for professional surveyors than for surveying technicians. Advancements in technology, such as total stations and GPS, have made surveying parties smaller than they once were.

Adjust and operate surveying instruments such as theodolite and electronic distance-measuring equipment and compile notes, make sketches, and enter data into computers. Perform calculations to determine Earth curvature corrections, atmospheric impacts on measurements, traverse closures and adjustments, azimuths, level runs, and placement of markers. Record survey measurements and descriptive data using notes, drawings, sketches, and inked tracings. Search for section corners, property irons, and survey points. Position and hold the vertical rods, or targets, that theodolite operators use for sighting to measure angles, distances, and elevations. Lay out grids and determine horizontal and vertical controls. Compare survey computations with applicable standards to determine adequacy of data. Set out and recover stakes, marks, and other monumentation. Conduct surveys to ascertain the locations of natural features and man-made structures on Earth's surface, underground, and underwater, using electronic distance-measuring equipment and other surveying instruments. Direct and supervise work of subordinate members of surveying parties. Compile information necessary to stake projects for construction, using engineering plans. Prepare topographic and contour maps of land surveyed, including site features and other relevant information, such as charts, drawings, and survey notes. Place and hold measuring tapes when electronic distance-measuring equipment is not used. Collect information needed to carry out new surveys using source maps, previous survey data, photographs, computer records, and other relevant information. Operate and manage land-information computer systems, performing tasks such as storing data, making inquiries, and producing plots and reports. Run rods for benches and cross-section elevations. Perform manual labor, such as cutting brush for lines, carrying stakes, rebar, and other heavy items, and stacking rods. Maintain equipment and vehicles used by surveying crews. Provide assistance in the development of methods and procedures for conducting field surveys.

Personality Type: Realistic-Conventional.

Career Clusters: 02 Architecture and Construction; 07 Government and Public Administration. **Career Pathways:** 02.1 Design/Pre-Construction; 07.1 Governance.

Skills: No data available.

Education and Training Programs: Surveying Technology/Surveying; Cartography. **Related Knowledge/Courses:** Geography; Design; Building and Construction; Mathematics; Law and Government; Engineering and Technology.

Work Environment: Outdoors; hazardous equipment; minor burns, cuts, bites, or stings; standing; walking and running; using hands on objects, tools, or controls.

Surveyors

- ✺ Education/Training Required: Bachelor's degree
- ✺ Annual Earnings: $51,630
- ✺ Beginning Wage: $28,590
- ✺ Earnings Growth Potential: High (44.6%)
- ✺ Growth: 23.7%
- ✺ Annual Job Openings: 14,305
- ✺ Job Security: Less Secure than Most
- ✺ Self-Employed: 3.7%
- ✺ Part-Time: 4.6%

Renewal Industry: Infrastructure.

Industries with Greatest Employment: Professional, Scientific, and Technical Services (77.1%); Local Government (5.4%).

Highest-Growth Industries (Projected Growth for This Job): Administrative and Support Services (32.5%); Professional, Scientific, and Technical Services (28.6%); Real Estate (26.5%); Management of Companies and Enterprises (15.5%).

Other Considerations for Job Outlook: Surveyors should have favorable job prospects. As technologies become more complex, opportunities will be best for surveyors who have a bachelor's degree and strong technical skills.

Make exact measurements and determine property boundaries. Provide data relevant to the shape, contour, gravitation, location, elevation, or dimension of land or land features on or near Earth's surface for engineering, mapmaking, mining, land evaluation, construction, and other purposes. Verify the accuracy of survey data, including measurements and calculations conducted at survey sites. Calculate heights, depths, relative positions, property lines, and other characteristics of terrain. Search legal records, survey records, and land titles to obtain information about property boundaries in areas to be surveyed. Prepare and maintain sketches, maps, reports, and legal descriptions of surveys to describe, certify, and assume liability for work performed. Direct or conduct surveys to establish legal boundaries for properties, based on legal deeds and titles. Prepare or supervise preparation of all data, charts, plots, maps, records, and documents related to surveys. Write descriptions of property boundary surveys for use in deeds, leases, or other legal documents. Compute geodetic measurements and interpret survey data to determine positions, shapes, and elevations of geomorphic and topographic features. Determine longitudes and latitudes of important features and boundaries in survey areas, using theodolites, transits, levels, and satellite-based global positioning systems (GPS). Record the results of surveys, including the shape, contour, location, elevation, and dimensions of land or land features. Coordinate findings with the work of engineering and architectural personnel, clients, and others concerned with projects. Establish fixed points for use in making maps, using geodetic and engineering instruments. Train assistants and helpers and direct their work in such activities as performing surveys or drafting maps. Plan and conduct ground surveys designed to establish baselines, elevations, and other geodetic measurements. Adjust surveying instruments to maintain their accuracy. Analyze survey objectives and specifications to prepare survey proposals or to direct others in survey proposal preparation. Develop criteria for survey methods and procedures. Survey bodies of water to determine navigable channels and to secure data for construction of breakwaters, piers, and other marine structures. Conduct research in surveying and mapping methods, using knowledge of techniques of photogrammetric map compilation and electronic data processing.

Personality Type: Realistic-Conventional-Investigative.

Career Cluster: 02 Architecture and Construction. **Career Pathway:** 02.1 Design/Pre-Construction.

Skills: No data available.

Education and Training Program: Surveying Technology/Surveying. **Related Knowledge/Courses:** Geography; Design; Building and Construction; History and Archeology; Engineering and Technology; Mathematics.

Work Environment: Outdoors; very hot or cold; hazardous equipment; minor burns, cuts, bites, or stings; standing; using hands on objects, tools, or controls.

Team Assemblers

- ❋ Education/Training Required: Moderate-term on-the-job training
- ❋ Annual Earnings: $24,630
- ❋ Beginning Wage: $16,450
- ❋ Earnings Growth Potential: Low (33.2%)
- ❋ Growth: 0.1%
- ❋ Annual Job Openings: 264,135
- ❋ Job Security: More Secure than Most
- ❋ Self-Employed: 1.7%
- ❋ Part-Time: 6.2%

Renewal Industry: Advanced Manufacturing.

Industries with Greatest Employment: Transportation Equipment Manufacturing (17.8%); Administrative and Support Services (16.6%); Machinery Manufacturing (9.4%); Fabricated Metal Product Manufacturing (7.6%); Electrical Equipment, Appliance, and Component Manufacturing (5.4%); Miscellaneous Manufacturing (5.4%).

Highest-Growth Industries (Projected Growth for This Job): Educational Services, Public and Private (36.6%); Warehousing and Storage (33.6%); Building Material and Garden Equipment and Supplies Dealers (27.4%); Administrative and Support Services (27.2%); Social Assistance (24.0%); Professional, Scientific, and Technical Services (21.1%); Nonstore Retailers (17.3%); Motor Vehicle and Parts Dealers (16.7%); Management of Companies and Enterprises (15.3%).

Other Considerations for Job Outlook: Job opportunities are expected to be good for qualified applicants in the manufacturing sector, particularly in jobs needing more training.

Work as part of a team having responsibility for assembling an entire product or component of a product. Team assemblers can perform all tasks conducted by the team in the assembly process and rotate through all or most of them rather than being assigned to a specific task on a permanent basis. May participate in making management decisions affecting the work. Team leaders who work as part of the team should be included. Rotate through all the tasks required in a particular production process. Determine work assignments and procedures. Shovel and sweep work areas. Operate heavy equipment such as forklifts. Provide assistance in the production of wiring assemblies.

Personality Type: Realistic-Conventional-Enterprising.

Career Cluster: 13 Manufacturing. **Career Pathway:** 13.1 Production.

Skills: No data available.

Education and Training Program: Precision Production, Other. **Related Knowledge/Courses:** Production and Processing; Mechanical Devices.

Work Environment: Indoors; noisy; contaminants; standing; using hands on objects, tools, or controls; repetitive motions.

Technical Writers

- ❋ Education/Training Required: Bachelor's degree
- ❋ Annual Earnings: $60,390
- ❋ Beginning Wage: $36,490
- ❋ Earnings Growth Potential: Medium (39.6%)
- ❋ Growth: 19.5%
- ❋ Annual Job Openings: 7,498
- ❋ Job Security: More Secure than Most
- ❋ Self-Employed: 6.0%
- ❋ Part-Time: 6.5%

Renewal Industries: Advanced Manufacturing; Information and Telecommunication Technologies; Infrastructure.

Industries with Greatest Employment: Professional, Scientific, and Technical Services (37.7%); Publishing Industries (Except Internet) (11.7%); Computer and Electronic Product Manufacturing (8.9%); Administrative and Support Services (5.1%).

Highest-Growth Industries (Projected Growth for This Job): Securities, Commodity Contracts, and Other Financial Investments and Related Activities (42.6%); Internet Publishing and Broadcasting (40.2%); Performing Arts, Spectator Sports, and Related Industries (38.6%); Social Assistance (36.0%); Professional, Scientific, and Technical Services (36.0%); Administrative and Support Services (28.0%); Waste Management and Remediation Services (26.6%); Ambulatory Health-Care Services (26.6%);

Chemical Manufacturing (23.4%); Support Activities for Transportation (21.0%); Religious, Grantmaking, Civic, Professional, and Similar Organizations (18.4%); Motion Picture, Video, and Sound Recording Industries (17.9%); Educational Services, Public and Private (16.2%); Merchant Wholesalers, Durable Goods (15.5%); Management of Companies and Enterprises (15.3%); Publishing Industries (Except Internet) (15.1%).

Other Considerations for Job Outlook: Demand for technical writers and writers with expertise in areas such as law, medicine, or economics is expected to increase because of the continuing expansion of scientific and technical information and the need to communicate it to others. Legal, scientific, and technological developments and discoveries generate demand for people to interpret technical information for a more general audience. Rapid growth and change in the high-technology and electronics industries result in a greater need for people to write users' guides, instruction manuals, and training materials. This work requires people who not only are technically skilled as writers, but also are familiar with the subject area.

Write technical materials, such as equipment manuals, appendices, or operating and maintenance instructions. May assist in layout work. Organize material and complete writing assignment according to set standards regarding order, clarity, conciseness, style, and terminology. Maintain records and files of work and revisions. Edit, standardize, or make changes to material prepared by other writers or establishment personnel. Confer with customer representatives, vendors, plant executives, or publisher to establish technical specifications and to determine subject material to be developed for publication. Review published materials and recommend revisions or changes in scope, format, content, and methods of reproduction and binding. Select photographs, drawings, sketches, diagrams, and charts to illustrate material. Study drawings, specifications, mockups, and product samples to integrate and delineate technology, operating procedure, and production sequence and detail. Interview production and engineering personnel and read journals and other material to become familiar with product technologies and production methods. Observe production, developmental, and experimental activities to determine operating procedure and detail. Arrange for typing, duplication, and distribution of material. Assist in laying out material for publication. Analyze developments in specific field to determine need

for revisions in previously published materials and development of new material. Review manufacturer's and trade catalogs, drawings, and other data relative to operation, maintenance, and service of equipment. Draw sketches to illustrate specified materials or assembly sequence.

Personality Type: Artistic-Investigative-Conventional.

Career Clusters: 03 Arts, Audio/Video Technology, and Communications; 04 Business, Management, and Administration. **Career Pathways:** 03.5 Journalism and Broadcasting; 04.5 Marketing.

Skills: Writing; Technology Design; Quality Control Analysis; Active Listening; Operations Analysis; Reading Comprehension.

Education and Training Programs: Communication Studies/Speech Communication and Rhetoric; Technical and Business Writing; Business/Corporate Communications. **Related Knowledge/Courses:** Communications and Media; Clerical Practices; English Language; Computers and Electronics; Education and Training; Engineering and Technology.

Work Environment: Indoors; sitting; using hands on objects, tools, or controls; repetitive motions.

Telecommunications Equipment Installers and Repairers, Except Line Installers

- ✳ Education/Training Required: Long-term on-the-job training
- ✳ Annual Earnings: $54,070
- ✳ Beginning Wage: $31,520
- ✳ Earnings Growth Potential: High (41.7%)
- ✳ Growth: 2.5%
- ✳ Annual Job Openings: 13,541
- ✳ Job Security: More Secure than Most
- ✳ Self-Employed: 4.1%
- ✳ Part-Time: 3.1%

Renewal Industry: Infrastructure.

Industries with Greatest Employment: Telecommunications (63.7%); Specialty Trade Contractors (12.0%).

Highest-Growth Industries (Projected Growth for This Job): Specialty Trade Contractors (40.5%); Professional, Scientific, and Technical Services (38.8%); Administrative and Support Services (26.5%); Ambulatory Health-Care Services (25.9%); Nonstore Retailers (22.2%); Merchant Wholesalers, Durable Goods (17.8%); Accommodation, Including Hotels and Motels (17.3%); Real Estate (17.2%); Management of Companies and Enterprises (15.3%).

Other Considerations for Job Outlook: Applicants with computer skills and postsecondary training in electronics should have the best opportunities for radio and telecommunications equipment installer and repairer jobs, but opportunities will vary by specialty. Good opportunities should be available for central office and PBX installers and repairers experienced in current technology. Station installers and repairers can expect keen competition. Radio mechanics should find good opportunities if they have a strong background in electronics and an ability to work independently.

Set up, rearrange, or remove switching and dialing equipment used in central offices. Service or repair telephones and other communication equipment on customers' properties. May install equipment in new locations or install wiring and telephone jacks in buildings under construction. Note differences in wire and cable colors so that work can be performed correctly. Test circuits and components of malfunctioning telecommunications equipment to isolate sources of malfunctions, using test meters, circuit diagrams, polarity probes, and other hand tools. Test repaired, newly installed, or updated equipment to ensure that it functions properly and conforms to specifications, using test equipment and observation. Drive crew trucks to and from work areas. Inspect equipment on a regular basis to ensure proper functioning. Repair or replace faulty equipment such as defective and damaged telephones, wires, switching system components, and associated equipment. Remove and remake connections to change circuit layouts, following work orders or diagrams. Demonstrate equipment to customers, explain how it is to be used, and respond to any inquiries or complaints. Analyze test readings, computer printouts, and trouble reports to determine equipment repair needs and required repair methods. Adjust or modify equipment to enhance equipment performance or to respond to customer requests. Remove loose wires and other debris after work is completed. Request support from technical service centers when on-site procedures fail to solve installation or maintenance problems. Communicate with bases, using telephones or two-way radios, to receive instructions or technical advice or to report equipment status. Assemble and install communication equipment such as data and telephone communication lines, wiring, switching equipment, wiring frames, power apparatus, computer systems, and networks. Collaborate with other workers to locate and correct malfunctions. Review manufacturers' instructions, manuals, technical specifications, building permits, and ordinances to determine communication equipment requirements and procedures. Test connections to ensure that power supplies are adequate and that communications links function. Refer to manufacturers' manuals to obtain maintenance instructions pertaining to specific malfunctions. Climb poles and ladders, use truck-mounted booms, and enter areas such as manholes and cable vaults to install, maintain, or inspect equipment.

Personality Type: Realistic-Investigative-Conventional.

Career Cluster: 03 Arts, Audio/Video Technology, and Communications. **Career Pathway:** 03.6 Telecommunications.

Skills: Installation; Repairing; Troubleshooting; Technology Design; Equipment Selection; Systems Analysis.

Education and Training Program: Communications Systems Installation and Repair Technology. **Related Knowledge/Courses:** Telecommunications; Mechanical Devices; Computers and Electronics; Engineering and Technology; Design; Public Safety and Security.

Work Environment: Outdoors; noisy; very hot or cold; contaminants; cramped work space, awkward positions; using hands on objects, tools, or controls.

Telecommunications Line Installers and Repairers

- ❋ Education/Training Required: Long-term on-the-job training
- ❋ Annual Earnings: $47,220
- ❋ Beginning Wage: $25,140
- ❋ Earnings Growth Potential: High (46.8%)
- ❋ Growth: 4.6%
- ❋ Annual Job Openings: 14,719
- ❋ Job Security: More Secure than Most
- ❋ Self-Employed: 3.3%
- ❋ Part-Time: 1.9%

Renewal Industry: Infrastructure.

Industries with Greatest Employment: Telecommunications (55.4%); Specialty Trade Contractors (15.5%); Heavy and Civil Engineering Construction (9.7%); Broadcasting (Except Internet) (8.5%).

Highest-Growth Industries (Projected Growth for This Job): Professional, Scientific, and Technical Services (43.0%); Administrative and Support Services (30.2%); Broadcasting (Except Internet) (20.3%); Merchant Wholesalers, Durable Goods (17.5%); Management of Companies and Enterprises (15.2%).

Other Considerations for Job Outlook: A growing number of retirements should create very good job opportunities, especially for electrical power-line installers and repairers.

String and repair telephone and television cable, including fiber optics and other equipment for transmitting messages or television programming. Travel to customers' premises to install, maintain, and repair audio and visual electronic reception equipment and accessories. Inspect and test lines and cables, recording and analyzing test results, to assess transmission characteristics and locate faults and malfunctions. Splice cables, using hand tools, epoxy, or mechanical equipment. Measure signal strength at utility poles, using electronic test equipment. Set up service for customers, installing, connecting, testing, and adjusting equipment. Place insulation over conductors and seal splices with moisture-proof covering. Access specific areas to string lines and install terminal boxes, auxiliary equipment, and appliances, using bucket trucks, or by climbing poles and ladders or entering tunnels, trenches, or crawl spaces. String cables between structures and lines from poles, towers, or trenches and pull lines to proper tension. Install equipment such as amplifiers and repeaters to maintain the strength of communications transmissions. Lay underground cable directly in trenches or string it through conduits running through trenches. Pull up cable by hand from large reels mounted on trucks; then pull lines through ducts by hand or with winches. Clean and maintain tools and test equipment. Explain cable service to subscribers after installation and collect any installation fees that are due. Compute impedance of wires from poles to houses to determine additional resistance needed for reducing signals to desired levels. Use a variety of construction equipment to complete installations, including digger derricks, trenchers, and cable plows. Dig trenches for underground wires and cables. Dig holes for power poles, using power augers or shovels, set poles in place with cranes, and hoist poles upright, using winches. Fill and tamp holes, using cement, earth, and tamping devices. Participate in the construction and removal of telecommunication towers and associated support structures.

Personality Type: Realistic-Enterprising.

Career Cluster: 13 Manufacturing. **Career Pathway:** 13.3 Maintenance, Installation, and Repair.

Skills: Installation; Troubleshooting; Repairing; Equipment Maintenance; Programming; Technology Design.

Education and Training Program: Communications Systems Installation and Repair Technology. **Related Knowledge/Courses:** Telecommunications; Engineering and Technology; Building and Construction; Customer and Personal Service; Design; Mechanical Devices.

Work Environment: Outdoors; very hot or cold; contaminants; cramped work space, awkward positions; hazardous equipment; using hands on objects, tools, or controls.

Transportation Managers

- ❀ Education/Training Required: Work experience in a related occupation
- ❀ Annual Earnings: $76,310
- ❀ Beginning Wage: $44,900
- ❀ Earnings Growth Potential: High (41.2%)
- ❀ Growth: 8.3%
- ❀ Annual Job Openings: 6,994
- ❀ Job Security: More Secure than Most
- ❀ Self-Employed: 2.6%
- ❀ Part-Time: 2.3%

Our sources did not provide separate job openings data for this occupation. The job openings listed here are shared with Storage and Distribution Managers.

Renewal Industry: Advanced Manufacturing.

Industries with Greatest Employment: Truck Transportation (9.9%); Federal Government (9.3%); Merchant Wholesalers, Nondurable Goods (8.6%); Merchant Wholesalers, Durable Goods (7.2%); Warehousing and Storage (5.9%); Management of Companies and Enterprises (5.7%).

Highest-Growth Industries (Projected Growth for This Job): Professional, Scientific, and Technical Services (40.4%); Warehousing and Storage (33.6%); Social Assistance (32.8%); Amusement, Gambling, and Recreation Industries (32.1%); Administrative and Support Services (29.5%); Ambulatory Health-Care Services (27.3%); Waste Management and Remediation Services (26.9%); Scenic and Sightseeing Transportation (26.7%); Personal and Laundry Services (26.6%); Building Material and Garden Equipment and Supplies Dealers (25.4%); Support Activities for Transportation (23.9%); Water Transportation (20.7%); Accommodation, Including Hotels and Motels (18.0%); Motion Picture, Video, and Sound Recording Industries (15.9%); Management of Companies and Enterprises (15.3%).

Other Considerations for Job Outlook: The fastest growth for managers will be with courier services, such as UPS and FedEx. As companies add additional services, they need more managers to run them efficiently. However, the use of computers to track the movement of freight may reduce the number of transportation managers needed.

Plan, direct, and coordinate the transportation operations within an organization or the activities of organizations that provide transportation services. Direct activities related to dispatching, routing, and tracking transportation vehicles such as aircraft and railroad cars. Plan, organize, and manage the work of subordinate staff to ensure that the work is accomplished in a manner consistent with organizational requirements. Direct investigations to verify and resolve customer or shipper complaints. Serve as contact persons for all workers within assigned territories. Implement schedule and policy changes. Collaborate with other managers and staff members to formulate and implement policies, procedures, goals, and objectives. Monitor operations to ensure that staff members comply with administrative policies and procedures, safety rules, union contracts, and government regulations. Promote safe work activities by conducting safety audits, attending company safety meetings, and meeting with individual staff members. Develop criteria, application instructions, procedural manuals, and contracts for federal and state public transportation programs. Monitor spending to ensure that expenses are consistent with approved budgets. Direct and coordinate, through subordinates, activities of operations department to obtain use of equipment, facilities, and human resources. Direct activities of staff performing repairs and maintenance to equipment, vehicles, and facilities. Conduct investigations in cooperation with government agencies to determine causes of transportation accidents and to improve safety procedures. Analyze expenditures and other financial information to develop plans, policies, and budgets for increasing profits and improving services. Negotiate and authorize contracts with equipment and materials suppliers and monitor contract fulfillment. Supervise workers assigning tariff classifications and preparing billing. Set operations policies and standards, including determination of safety procedures for the handling of dangerous goods. Recommend or authorize capital expenditures for acquisition of new equipment or property to increase efficiency and services of operations department. Prepare management recommendations, such as proposed fee and tariff increases or schedule changes.

Personality Type: Enterprising-Conventional.

Career Clusters: 04 Business, Management, and Administration; 07 Government and Public Administration; 16 Transportation, Distribution, and Logistics. **Career Pathways:** 04.1 Management; 07.1 Governance; 16.1

Transportation Operations; 16.2 Logistics Planning and Management Services.

Skills: Negotiation; Time Management; Coordination; Management of Financial Resources; Mathematics; Monitoring.

Education and Training Programs: Public Administration; Aeronautics/Aviation/Aerospace Science and Technology, General; Aviation/Airway Management and Operations; Business Administration and Management, General; Logistics and Materials Management; Transportation/Transportation Management. **Related Knowledge/ Courses:** Transportation; Clerical Practices; Customer and Personal Service; Sales and Marketing; Production and Processing; Psychology.

Work Environment: Indoors; noisy; sitting.

Transportation, Storage, and Distribution Managers

See *Storage and Distribution Managers* and *Transportation Managers, described separately.*

Truck Drivers, Heavy and Tractor-Trailer

- ❋ Education/Training Required: Moderate-term on-the-job training
- ❋ Annual Earnings: $36,220
- ❋ Beginning Wage: $23,380
- ❋ Earnings Growth Potential: Medium (35.5%)
- ❋ Growth: 10.4%
- ❋ Annual Job Openings: 279,032
- ❋ Job Security: Least Secure
- ❋ Self-Employed: 8.8%
- ❋ Part-Time: 7.2%

Renewal Industry: Infrastructure.

Industries with Greatest Employment: Truck Transportation (43.8%); Merchant Wholesalers, Nondurable Goods (7.1%).

Highest-Growth Industries (Projected Growth for This Job): Professional, Scientific, and Technical Services

(55.7%); Internet Service Providers, Web Search Portals, and Data Processing Services (35.4%); Warehousing and Storage (33.6%); Amusement, Gambling, and Recreation Industries (30.6%); Social Assistance (28.3%); Ambulatory Health-Care Services (27.0%); Waste Management and Remediation Services (26.7%); Administrative and Support Services (26.5%); General Merchandise Stores (25.2%); Building Material and Garden Equipment and Supplies Dealers (23.9%); Performing Arts, Spectator Sports, and Related Industries (22.4%); Religious, Grantmaking, Civic, Professional, and Similar Organizations (19.7%); Repair and Maintenance (17.8%); Rental and Leasing Services (17.2%); Transit and Ground Passenger Transportation (16.1%); Water Transportation (15.5%); Management of Companies and Enterprises (15.3%).

Other Considerations for Job Outlook: A commercial driver's license is required to operate most larger trucks.

Drive a tractor-trailer combination or a truck with a capacity of at least 26,000 GVW to transport and deliver goods, livestock, or materials in liquid, loose, or packaged form. May be required to unload truck. May require use of automated routing equipment. Requires commercial drivers' license. Follow appropriate safety procedures when transporting dangerous goods. Check vehicles before driving them to ensure that mechanical, safety, and emergency equipment is in good working order. Maintain logs of working hours and of vehicle service and repair status, following applicable state and federal regulations. Obtain receipts or signatures when loads are delivered and collect payment for services when required. Check all load-related documentation to ensure that it is complete and accurate. Maneuver trucks into loading or unloading positions, following signals from loading crew as needed; check that vehicle position is correct and any special loading equipment is properly positioned. Drive trucks with capacities greater than 3 tons, including tractor-trailer combinations, to transport and deliver products, livestock, or other materials. Secure cargo for transport, using ropes, blocks, chain, binders, or covers. Read bills of lading to determine assignment details. Report vehicle defects, accidents, traffic violations, or damage to the vehicles. Read and interpret maps to determine vehicle routes. Couple and uncouple trailers by changing trailer jack positions, connecting or disconnecting air and electrical lines, and manipulating fifth-wheel locks. Collect delivery instructions from appropriate sources, verifying instructions and routes. Drive trucks to weigh stations before and after loading and along routes to document weights and to comply with state regulations. Operate equipment such as truck cab computers, CB radios, and telephones to exchange necessary information with bases, supervisors, or other drivers. Check conditions of trailers after contents have been unloaded to ensure that there has been no damage. Crank trailer landing gear up and down to safely secure vehicles. Wrap goods, using pads, packing paper, and containers, and secure loads to trailer walls, using straps. Perform basic vehicle maintenance tasks such as adding oil, fuel, and radiator fluid or performing minor repairs. Load and unload trucks or help others with loading and unloading, operating any special loading-related equipment on vehicles and using other equipment as necessary.

Personality Type: Realistic-Conventional.

Career Cluster: 16 Transportation, Distribution, and Logistics. **Career Pathway:** 16.1 Transportation Operations.

Skills: No data available.

Education and Training Program: Truck and Bus Driver/Commercial Vehicle Operation. **Related Knowledge/Courses:** Transportation; Geography; Public Safety and Security; Law and Government; Mechanical Devices.

Work Environment: Outdoors; very hot or cold; contaminants; sitting; using hands on objects, tools, or controls; repetitive motions.

Truck Drivers, Light or Delivery Services

- ❋ Education/Training Required: Short-term on-the-job training
- ❋ Annual Earnings: $26,380
- ❋ Beginning Wage: $16,180
- ❋ Earnings Growth Potential: Medium (38.7%)
- ❋ Growth: 8.4%
- ❋ Annual Job Openings: 154,330
- ❋ Job Security: Least Secure
- ❋ Self-Employed: 9.3%
- ❋ Part-Time: 7.2%

Renewal Industry: Infrastructure.

Industries with Greatest Employment: Couriers and Messengers (15.8%); Merchant Wholesalers, Durable Goods (9.1%); Merchant Wholesalers, Nondurable Goods (8.4%); Truck Transportation (6.3%); Motor Vehicle and Parts Dealers (5.3%).

Highest-Growth Industries (Projected Growth for This Job): Securities, Commodity Contracts, and Other Financial Investments and Related Activities (42.6%); Ambulatory Health-Care Services (35.6%); Social Assistance (35.4%); Internet Service Providers, Web Search Portals, and Data Processing Services (35.2%); Warehousing and Storage (33.6%); Professional, Scientific, and Technical Services (31.6%); Amusement, Gambling, and Recreation Industries (29.9%); Waste Management and Remediation Services (29.4%); Administrative and Support Services (28.0%); Nursing and Residential Care Facilities (26.9%); Credit Intermediation and Related Activities (26.4%); General Merchandise Stores (25.4%); Building Material and Garden Equipment and Supplies Dealers (24.1%); Transit and Ground Passenger Transportation (17.7%); Support Activities for Transportation (17.1%); Accommodation, Including Hotels and Motels (16.1%); Performing Arts, Spectator Sports, and Related Industries (15.8%); Management of Companies and Enterprises (15.3%).

Other Considerations for Job Outlook: Competition is expected for jobs offering the highest earnings or most favorable work schedules.

Drive a truck or van with a capacity of under 26,000 GVW primarily to deliver or pick up merchandise or to deliver packages within a specified area. May require use of automatic routing or location software. May load and unload truck. Obey traffic laws and follow established traffic and transportation procedures. Inspect and maintain vehicle supplies and equipment such as gas, oil, water, tires, lights, and brakes to ensure that vehicles are in proper working condition. Report any mechanical problems encountered with vehicles. Present bills and receipts and collect payments for goods delivered or loaded. Load and unload trucks, vans, or automobiles. Turn in receipts and money received from deliveries. Verify the contents of inventory loads against shipping papers. Maintain records such as vehicle logs, records of cargo, or billing statements in accordance with regulations. Read maps and follow written and verbal geographic directions. Report delays, accidents, or other traffic and transportation situations to bases or other vehicles, using telephones or mobile two-way radios. Sell and keep records of sales for products from truck inventory. Drive vehicles with capacities under three tons to transport materials to and from specified destinations such as railroad stations, plants, residences, and offices or within industrial yards. Drive trucks equipped with public address systems through city streets to broadcast announcements for advertising or publicity purposes. Use and maintain the tools and equipment found on commercial vehicles, such as weighing and measuring devices. Perform emergency repairs such as changing tires or installing light bulbs, fuses, tire chains, and spark plugs.

Personality Type: Realistic-Conventional.

Career Cluster: 16 Transportation, Distribution, and Logistics. **Career Pathway:** 16.1 Transportation Operations.

Skills: No data available.

Education and Training Program: Truck and Bus Driver/Commercial Vehicle Operation. **Related Knowledge/Course:** Transportation.

Work Environment: Outdoors; very hot or cold; contaminants; cramped work space, awkward positions; minor burns, cuts, bites, or stings; using hands on objects, tools, or controls.

Urban and Regional Planners

- ❋ Education/Training Required: Master's degree
- ❋ Annual Earnings: $57,970
- ❋ Beginning Wage: $36,950
- ❋ Earnings Growth Potential: Medium (36.3%)
- ❋ Growth: 14.5%
- ❋ Annual Job Openings: 1,967
- ❋ Job Security: More Secure than Most
- ❋ Self-Employed: 0.2%
- ❋ Part-Time: 6.0%

Renewal Industries: Green Technologies; Infrastructure.

Industries with Greatest Employment: Local Government (67.8%); Professional, Scientific, and Technical Services (18.7%); State Government (8.9%).

Highest-Growth Industries (Projected Growth for This Job): Professional, Scientific, and Technical Services

(32.6%); Real Estate (21.3%); Religious, Grantmaking, Civic, Professional, and Similar Organizations (17.0%); Management of Companies and Enterprises (15.2%).

Other Considerations for Job Outlook: Most new jobs will be in affluent, rapidly expanding communities. Job prospects will be best for those with a master's degree and strong computer skills.

Develop comprehensive plans and programs for use of land and physical facilities of local jurisdictions such as towns, cities, counties, and metropolitan areas. Design, promote, and administer government plans and policies affecting land use, zoning, public utilities, community facilities, housing, and transportation. Hold public meetings and confer with government, social scientists, lawyers, developers, the public, and special interest groups to formulate and develop land use or community plans. Recommend approval, denial, or conditional approval of proposals. Determine the effects of regulatory limitations on projects. Assess the feasibility of proposals and identify necessary changes. Create, prepare, or requisition graphic and narrative reports on land use data, including land area maps overlaid with geographic variables such as population density. Conduct field investigations, surveys, impact studies, or other research to compile and analyze data on economic, social, regulatory, and physical factors affecting land use. Advise planning officials on project feasibility, cost-effectiveness, regulatory conformance, and possible alternatives. Discuss with planning officials the purpose of land use projects such as transportation, conservation, residential, commercial, industrial, and community use. Keep informed about economic and legal issues involved in zoning codes, building codes, and environmental regulations. Mediate community disputes and assist in developing alternative plans and recommendations for programs or projects. Coordinate work with economic consultants and architects during the formulation of plans and the design of large pieces of infrastructure. Review and evaluate environmental impact reports pertaining to private and public planning projects and programs. Supervise and coordinate the work of urban planning technicians and technologists. Investigate property availability.

Personality Type: Investigative-Enterprising-Artistic.

Career Cluster: 07 Government and Public Administration. **Career Pathway:** 07.4 Planning.

Skills: Complex Problem Solving; Persuasion; Writing; Coordination; Judgment and Decision Making; Service Orientation.

Education and Training Program: City/Urban, Community and Regional Planning. **Related Knowledge/ Courses:** Design; Building and Construction; Geography; History and Archeology; Law and Government; Customer and Personal Service.

Work Environment: Indoors; noisy; very bright or dim lighting; sitting; using hands on objects, tools, or controls; repetitive motions.

Vocational Education Teachers, Postsecondary

- ❋ Education/Training Required: Work experience in a related occupation
- ❋ Annual Earnings: $45,850
- ❋ Beginning Wage: $26,380
- ❋ Earnings Growth Potential: High (42.5%)
- ❋ Growth: 22.9%
- ❋ Annual Job Openings: 19,313
- ❋ Job Security: Most Secure
- ❋ Self-Employed: 0.4%
- ❋ Part-Time: 27.8%

Renewal Industry: Education.

Industries with Greatest Employment: Educational Services, Public and Private (97.3%).

Highest-Growth Industries (Projected Growth for This Job): Administrative and Support Services (48.3%); Amusement, Gambling, and Recreation Industries (45.2%); Social Assistance (38.6%); Support Activities for Transportation (32.8%); Religious, Grantmaking, Civic, Professional, and Similar Organizations (29.9%); Professional, Scientific, and Technical Services (28.8%); Management of Companies and Enterprises (26.8%); Local Government (23.5%); Educational Services, Public and Private (22.8%); Hospitals, Public and Private (21.4%).

Other Considerations for Job Outlook: Retirements of current postsecondary teachers should create numerous openings for all types of postsecondary teachers, so job opportunities are generally expected to be very good.

However, one of the main reasons why students attend postsecondary institutions is to prepare themselves for careers, so the best job prospects for postsecondary teachers are likely to be in rapidly growing fields that offer many nonacademic career options. Community colleges and other institutions offering career and technical education have been among the most rapidly growing, and these institutions are expected to offer some of the best opportunities for postsecondary teachers.

Teach or instruct vocational or occupational subjects at the postsecondary level (but at less than the baccalaureate) to students who have graduated or left high school. Includes correspondence school instructors; industrial, commercial, and government training instructors; and adult education teachers and instructors who prepare persons to operate industrial machinery and equipment and transportation and communications equipment. Teaching may take place in public or private schools whose primary business is education or in a school associated with an organization whose primary business is other than education. Supervise and monitor students' use of tools and equipment. Observe and evaluate students' work to determine progress, provide feedback, and make suggestions for improvement. Present lectures and conduct discussions to increase students' knowledge and competence, using visual aids such as graphs, charts, videotapes, and slides. Administer oral, written, or performance tests to measure progress and to evaluate training effectiveness. Prepare reports and maintain records such as student grades, attendance rolls, and training activity details. Supervise independent or group projects, field placements, laboratory work, or other training. Determine training needs of students or workers. Provide individualized instruction and tutorial or remedial instruction. Conduct on-the-job training, classes, or training sessions to teach and demonstrate principles, techniques, procedures, and methods of designated subjects. Develop curricula and plan course content and methods of instruction. Prepare outlines of instructional programs and training schedules and establish course goals. Integrate academic and vocational curricula so that students can obtain a variety of skills. Develop teaching aids such as instructional software, multimedia visual aids, or study materials. Select and assemble books, materials, supplies, and equipment for training, courses, or projects. Advise students on course selection, career decisions, and other academic and vocational concerns. Participate in conferences, seminars, and training sessions to keep abreast of developments in the field and integrate relevant information into training programs. Serve on faculty and school committees concerned with budgeting, curriculum revision, and course and diploma requirements. Review enrollment applications and correspond with applicants to obtain additional information. Arrange for lectures by experts in designated fields.

Personality Type: Social-Realistic.

Career Cluster: 05 Education and Training. **Career Pathway:** 05.3 Teaching/Training.

Skills: Instructing; Learning Strategies; Social Perceptiveness; Service Orientation; Speaking; Time Management.

Education and Training Programs: Agricultural Teacher Education; Business Teacher Education; Technology Teacher Education/Industrial Arts Teacher Education; Sales and Marketing Operations/Marketing and Distribution Teacher Education; Technical Teacher Education; Trade and Industrial Teacher Education; Health Occupations Teacher Education; Teacher Education and Professional Development, Specific Subject Areas, Other. **Related Knowledge/Courses:** Education and Training; Psychology; Therapy and Counseling; Computers and Electronics; Sales and Marketing; Design.

Work Environment: Indoors; standing; using hands on objects, tools, or controls.

Web Administrators

- ✳ Education/Training Required: No data available.
- ✳ Annual Earnings: $71,510
- ✳ Beginning Wage: $37,600
- ✳ Earnings Growth Potential: High (47.4%)
- ✳ Growth: 15.1%
- ✳ Annual Job Openings: 14,374
- ✳ Job Security: More Secure than Most
- ✳ Self-Employed: 6.6%
- ✳ Part-Time: 5.6%

Our sources did not provide separate job openings data for this occupation. The job openings listed here are shared with Computer Systems Engineers/Architects, Network

Designers, Software Quality Assurance Engineers and Testers, and Web Developers.

Renewal Industry: Information and Telecommunication Technologies.

Industries with Greatest Employment: Professional, Scientific, and Technical Services (22.9%); Educational Services, Public and Private (10.0%); Management of Companies and Enterprises (8.0%); State Government (5.5%).

Highest-Growth Industries (Projected Growth for This Job): Amusement, Gambling, and Recreation Industries (53.3%); Securities, Commodity Contracts, and Other Financial Investments and Related Activities (46.9%); Social Assistance (44.2%); Internet Publishing and Broadcasting (40.3%); Warehousing and Storage (33.3%); Professional, Scientific, and Technical Services (31.4%); Real Estate (25.8%); General Merchandise Stores (25.0%); Nursing and Residential Care Facilities (24.8%); Ambulatory Health-Care Services (24.7%); Building Material and Garden Equipment and Supplies Dealers (24.2%); Publishing Industries (Except Internet) (21.7%); Nonstore Retailers (21.4%); Religious, Grantmaking, Civic, Professional, and Similar Organizations (19.6%); Chemical Manufacturing (19.0%); Merchant Wholesalers, Durable Goods (15.9%); Management of Companies and Enterprises (15.3%).

Other Considerations for Job Outlook: College graduates with a bachelor's degree in computer science, computer engineering, information science, or MIS also should enjoy favorable prospects, particularly if they have supplemented their formal education with practical experience. Because employers continue to seek computer specialists who can combine strong technical skills with good business skills, individuals with a combination of experience inside and outside the IT arena will have the best job prospects.

Manage Web environment design, deployment, development, and maintenance activities. Perform testing and quality assurance of Web sites and Web applications. Back up or modify applications and related data to provide for disaster recovery. Determine sources of Web page or server problems and take action to correct such problems. Review or update Web page content or links in a timely manner, using appropriate tools. Monitor systems for intrusions or denial of service attacks and report security breaches to appropriate personnel. Implement Web site security measures, such as firewalls or message encryption. Administer Internet/intranet infrastructure, including components such as Web, file transfer protocol (FTP), news, and mail servers. Collaborate with development teams to discuss, analyze, or resolve usability issues. Test backup or recovery plans regularly and resolve any problems. Monitor Web developments through continuing education; reading; or participation in professional conferences, workshops, or groups. Implement updates, upgrades, and patches in a timely manner to limit loss of service. Identify or document backup or recovery plans. Collaborate with Web developers to create and operate internal and external Web sites or to manage projects such as e-marketing campaigns. Install or configure Web server software or hardware to ensure that directory structure is well-defined, logical, and secure and that files are named properly. Gather, analyze, or document user feedback to locate or resolve sources of problems. Develop Web site performance metrics. Identify or address interoperability requirements. Document installation or configuration procedures to allow maintenance and repetition. Identify, standardize, and communicate levels of access and security. Track, compile, and analyze Web site usage data. Test issues such as system integration, performance, and system security on a regular schedule or after any major program modifications. Recommend Web site improvements and develop budgets to support recommendations. Inform Web site users of problems, problem resolutions, or application changes and updates. Document application and Web site changes or change procedures. Develop or implement procedures for ongoing Web site revision.

Personality Type: Conventional-Enterprising-Investigative.

Career Cluster: 11 Information Technology. **Career Pathway:** 11.2 Programming and Software Development.

Skills: Programming; Systems Evaluation; Systems Analysis; Troubleshooting; Operations Analysis; Technology Design.

Education and Training Programs: Computer and Information Sciences, General; Information Technology; Information Science/Studies; Computer Science; Web Page, Digital/Multimedia and Information Resources Design; Computer Systems Networking and Telecommunications; System, Networking, and LAN/WAN Management/Manager; Web/Multimedia Management and Webmaster; Computer and Information Sciences and Support Services, Other; E-Commerce/Electronic Commerce. **Related**

Knowledge/Courses: Computers and Electronics; Telecommunications; Design; Communications and Media; Sales and Marketing; Engineering and Technology.

Work Environment: Indoors; sitting; using hands on objects, tools, or controls; repetitive motions.

Web Developers

- ❋ Education/Training Required: No data available.
- ❋ Annual Earnings: $71,510
- ❋ Beginning Wage: $37,600
- ❋ Earnings Growth Potential: High (47.4%)
- ❋ Growth: 15.1%
- ❋ Annual Job Openings: 14,374
- ❋ Job Security: More Secure than Most
- ❋ Self-Employed: 6.6%
- ❋ Part-Time: 5.6%

Our sources did not provide separate job openings data for this occupation. The job openings listed here are shared with Computer Systems Engineers/Architects, Network Designers, Software Quality Assurance Engineers and Testers, and Web Administrators.

Renewal Industry: Information and Telecommunication Technologies.

Industries with Greatest Employment: Professional, Scientific, and Technical Services (22.9%); Educational Services, Public and Private (10.0%); Management of Companies and Enterprises (8.0%); State Government (5.5%).

Highest-Growth Industries (Projected Growth for This Job): Amusement, Gambling, and Recreation Industries (53.3%); Securities, Commodity Contracts, and Other Financial Investments and Related Activities (46.9%); Social Assistance (44.2%); Internet Publishing and Broadcasting (40.3%); Warehousing and Storage (33.3%); Professional, Scientific, and Technical Services (31.4%); Real Estate (25.8%); General Merchandise Stores (25.0%); Nursing and Residential Care Facilities (24.8%); Ambulatory Health-Care Services (24.7%); Building Material and Garden Equipment and Supplies Dealers (24.2%); Publishing Industries (Except Internet) (21.7%); Nonstore Retailers (21.4%); Religious, Grantmaking, Civic, Professional, and

M

Similar Organizations (19.6%); Chemical Manufacturing (19.0%); Merchant Wholesalers, Durable Goods (15.9%); Management of Companies and Enterprises (15.3%).

Other Considerations for Job Outlook: Given the rate at which the computer systems design and related services industry is expected to grow, and the increasing complexity of technology, job opportunities should be favorable for most workers. The best opportunities will be in professional and related occupations, reflecting their growth and the continuing demand for higher level skills to keep up with changes in technology.

Develop and design Web applications and Web sites. Create and specify architectural and technical parameters. Direct Web site content creation, enhancement, and maintenance. Design, build, or maintain Web sites, using authoring or scripting languages, content creation tools, management tools, and digital media. Perform or direct Web site updates. Write, design, or edit Web page content or direct others producing content. Confer with management or development teams to prioritize needs, resolve conflicts, develop content criteria, or choose solutions. Back up files from Web sites to local directories for instant recovery in case of problems. Identify problems uncovered by testing or customer feedback and correct problems or refer problems to appropriate personnel for correction. Evaluate code to ensure that it is valid; is properly structured; meets industry standards; and is compatible with browsers, devices, or operating systems. Maintain understanding of current Web technologies or programming practices through continuing education; reading; or participation in professional conferences, workshops, or groups. Analyze user needs to determine technical requirements. Develop or validate test routines and schedules to ensure that test cases mimic external interfaces and address all browser and device types. Develop databases that support Web applications and Web sites. Renew domain name registrations. Collaborate with management or users to develop e-commerce strategies and to integrate these strategies with Web sites. Write supporting code for Web applications or Web sites. Communicate with network personnel or Web site hosting agencies to address hardware or software issues affecting Web sites. Design and implement Web site security measures such as firewalls or message encryption. Perform Web site tests according to planned schedules or after any Web site or product revisions. Select programming languages, design tools, or applications. Incorporate technical considerations into Web site design plans, such as budgets, equipment, performance requirements, or legal issues including accessibility and privacy. Respond to user e-mail inquiries or set up automated systems to send responses. Develop or implement procedures for ongoing Web site revision.

Personality Type: Conventional-Investigative-Realistic.

Career Cluster: 11 Information Technology. **Career Pathway:** 11.2 Programming and Software Development.

Skills: Programming; Troubleshooting; Operations Analysis; Technology Design; Systems Evaluation; Quality Control Analysis.

Education and Training Programs: Computer and Information Sciences, General; Information Technology; Information Science/Studies; Computer Science; Web Page, Digital/Multimedia and Information Resources Design; Computer Systems Networking and Telecommunications; System, Networking, and LAN/WAN Management/Manager; Web/Multimedia Management and Webmaster; Computer and Information Sciences and Support Services, Other; E-Commerce/Electronic Commerce. **Related Knowledge/Courses:** Computers and Electronics; Design; Sales and Marketing; Communications and Media; Telecommunications; Clerical Practices.

Work Environment: Indoors; sitting; using hands on objects, tools, or controls; repetitive motions.

Welders, Cutters, and Welder Fitters

- ❋ Education/Training Required: Long-term on-the-job training
- ❋ Annual Earnings: $32,270
- ❋ Beginning Wage: $21,680
- ❋ Earnings Growth Potential: Low (32.8%)
- ❋ Growth: 5.1%
- ❋ Annual Job Openings: 61,125
- ❋ Job Security: More Secure than Most
- ❋ Self-Employed: 6.3%
- ❋ Part-Time: 1.9%

Our sources did not provide separate job openings data for this occupation. The job openings listed here are shared with Solderers and Brazers.

Renewal Industries: Advanced Manufacturing; Green Technologies.

Industries with Greatest Employment: Fabricated Metal Product Manufacturing (22.4%); Machinery Manufacturing (16.0%); Transportation Equipment Manufacturing (14.2%); Specialty Trade Contractors (5.7%).

Highest-Growth Industries (Projected Growth for This Job): Warehousing and Storage (42.2%); Amusement, Gambling, and Recreation Industries (38.5%); Building Material and Garden Equipment and Supplies Dealers (35.3%); Administrative and Support Services (34.9%); Waste Management and Remediation Services (34.2%); Professional, Scientific, and Technical Services (33.7%); Rental and Leasing Services (26.0%); Management of Companies and Enterprises (22.6%); Support Activities for Transportation (22.0%); Water Transportation (21.5%); Wholesale Electronic Markets and Agents and Brokers (20.7%); Nonstore Retailers (20.7%); Truck Transportation (20.1%); Motor Vehicle and Parts Dealers (19.9%); Local Government (19.5%); Construction of Buildings (19.2%); Specialty Trade Contractors (18.7%); Merchant Wholesalers, Durable Goods (17.0%); Educational Services, Public and Private (16.0%).

Other Considerations for Job Outlook: Job prospects should be excellent, because employers report difficulty finding enough qualified people.

Use hand-welding or flame-cutting equipment to weld or join metal components or to fill holes, indentations, or seams of fabricated metal products. Operate safety equipment and use safe work habits. Weld components in flat, vertical, or overhead positions. Ignite torches or start power supplies and strike arcs by touching electrodes to metals being welded, completing electrical circuits. Clamp, hold, tack-weld, heat-bend, grind, or bolt component parts to obtain required configurations and positions for welding. Detect faulty operation of equipment or defective materials and notify supervisors. Operate manual or semi-automatic welding equipment to fuse metal segments, using processes such as gas tungsten arc, gas metal arc, flux-cored arc, plasma arc, shielded metal arc, resistance welding, and submerged arc welding. Monitor the fitting, burning, and welding processes to avoid overheating of parts or warping, shrinking, distortion, or expansion of material. Examine workpieces for defects and measure workpieces with straightedges or templates to ensure conformance with specifications. Recognize, set up, and operate hand and power tools common to the welding trade, such as shielded metal arc and gas metal arc welding equipment. Lay out, position, align, and secure parts and assemblies prior to assembly, using straightedges, combination squares, calipers, and rulers. Chip or grind off excess weld, slag, or spatter, using hand scrapers or power chippers, portable grinders, or arc-cutting equipment. Analyze engineering drawings, blueprints, specifications, sketches, work orders, and material safety data sheets to plan layout, assembly, and welding operations. Connect and turn regulator valves to activate and adjust gas flow and pressure so that desired flames are obtained. Weld separately or in combination, using aluminum, stainless steel, cast iron, and other alloys. Determine required equipment and welding methods, applying knowledge of metallurgy, geometry, and welding techniques. Mark or tag material with proper job number, piece marks, and other identifying marks as required. Prepare all material surfaces to be welded, ensuring that there is no loose or thick scale, slag, rust, moisture, grease, or other foreign matter.

Personality Type: Realistic-Conventional.

Career Cluster: 13 Manufacturing. **Career Pathway:** 13.1 Production.

Skills: No data available.

Education and Training Program: Welding Technology/Welder. **Related Knowledge/Courses:** Building and Construction; Mechanical Devices; Design; Engineering and Technology.

Work Environment: Noisy; contaminants; minor burns, cuts, bites, or stings; standing; using hands on objects, tools, or controls; repetitive motions.

Welders, Cutters, Solderers, and Brazers

See *Solderers and Brazers* and *Welders, Cutters, and Welder Fitters, described separately.*

APPENDIX A

Definitions of Skills Used in Job Descriptions

Following are the definitions of skills that appear in job descriptions in Part III.

Skill Name	Definition
Active Learning	Working with new material or information to grasp its implications.
Complex Problem Solving	Identifying complex problems, reviewing the options, and implementing solutions.
Coordination	Adjusting actions in relation to others' actions.
Critical Thinking	Using logic and analysis to identify the strengths and weaknesses of different approaches.
Equipment Maintenance	Performing routine maintenance and determining when and what kind of maintenance is needed.
Equipment Selection	Determining the kind of tools and equipment needed to do a job.
Installation	Installing equipment, machines, wiring, or programs to meet specifications.
Instructing	Teaching others how to do something.
Judgment and Decision Making	Weighing the relative costs and benefits of a potential action.
Learning Strategies	Using multiple approaches when learning or teaching new things.
Management of Financial Resources	Determining how money will be spent to get the work done and accounting for these expenditures.
Management of Material Resources	Obtaining and seeing to the appropriate use of equipment, facilities, and materials needed to do certain work.

(continued)

(continued)

Skill Name	Definition
Management of Personnel Resources	Motivating, developing, and directing people as they work; identifying the best people for the job.
Mathematics	Using mathematics to solve problems.
Monitoring	Assessing how well one is doing when learning or doing something.
Negotiation	Bringing others together and trying to reconcile differences.
Operation and Control	Controlling operations of equipment or systems.
Operation Monitoring	Watching gauges, dials, or other indicators to make sure a machine is working properly.
Operations Analysis	Analyzing needs and product requirements to create a design.
Persuasion	Persuading others to approach things differently.
Programming	Writing computer programs for various purposes.
Quality Control Analysis	Evaluating the quality or performance of products, services, or processes.
Reading Comprehension	Understanding written sentences and paragraphs in work-related documents.
Repairing	Repairing machines or systems, using the needed tools.
Science	Using scientific methods to solve problems.
Service Orientation	Actively looking for ways to help people.
Social Perceptiveness	Being aware of others' reactions and understanding why they react the way they do.
Speaking	Talking to others to effectively convey information.
Systems Analysis	Determining how a system should work and how changes will affect outcomes.
Systems Evaluation	Looking at many indicators of system performance and taking into account their accuracy.
Technology Design	Generating or adapting equipment and technology to serve user needs.
Time Management	Managing one's own time and the time of others.
Troubleshooting	Determining what is causing an operating error and deciding what to do about it.
Writing	Communicating effectively with others in writing as indicated by the needs of the audience.

Definitions of Knowledges/ Courses Used in Job Descriptions

Following are the definitions of knowledges/courses that appear in job descriptions in Part III:

Knowledge/Course Name	Definition
Administration and Management	Knowledge of principles and processes involved in business and organizational planning, coordination, and execution. This includes strategic planning, resource allocation, manpower modeling, leadership techniques, and production methods.
Biology	Knowledge of plant and animal living tissue, cells, organisms, and entities, including their functions, interdependencies, and interactions with each other and the environment.
Building and Construction	Knowledge of materials, methods, and the appropriate tools to construct objects, structures, and buildings.
Chemistry	Knowledge of the composition, structure, and properties of substances and of the chemical processes and transformations that they undergo. This includes uses of chemicals and their interactions, danger signs, production techniques, and disposal methods.

(continued)

(continued)

Knowledge/Course Name	Definition
Clerical Practices	Knowledge of administrative and clerical procedures and systems, such as word-processing systems, filing and records management systems, stenography and transcription, forms, design principles, and other office procedures and terminology.
Communications and Media	Knowledge of media production, communication, and dissemination techniques and methods, including alternative ways to inform and entertain via written, oral, and visual media.
Computers and Electronics	Knowledge of electric circuit boards; processors; chips; and computer hardware and software, including applications and programming.
Customer and Personal Service	Knowledge of principles and processes for providing customer and personal services, including needs assessment techniques, quality service standards, alternative delivery systems, and customer satisfaction evaluation techniques.
Design	Knowledge of design techniques, principles, tools, and instruments involved in the production and use of precision technical plans, blueprints, drawings, and models.
Economics and Accounting	Knowledge of economic and accounting principles and practices, the financial markets, banking, and the analysis and reporting of financial data.
Education and Training	Knowledge of instructional methods and training techniques, including curriculum design principles, learning theory, group and individual teaching techniques, design of individual development plans, and test design principles.
Engineering and Technology	Knowledge of equipment, tools, and mechanical devices and their uses to produce motion, light, power, technology, and other applications.
English Language	Knowledge of the structure and content of the English language, including the meaning and spelling of words, rules of composition, and grammar.
Fine Arts	Knowledge of theory and techniques required to produce, compose, and perform works of music, dance, visual arts, drama, and sculpture.
Food Production	Knowledge of techniques and equipment for planting, growing, and harvesting of food for consumption, including crop rotation methods, animal husbandry, and food storage/handling techniques.

Knowledge/Course Name	Definition
Foreign Language	Knowledge of the structure and content of a foreign (non-English) language, including the meaning and spelling of words, rules of composition and grammar, and pronunciation.
Geography	Knowledge of various methods for describing the location and distribution of land, sea, and air masses, including their physical locations, relationships, and characteristics.
History and Archeology	Knowledge of past historical events and their causes, indicators, and impact on particular civilizations and cultures.
Law and Government	Knowledge of laws, legal codes, court procedures, precedents, government regulations, executive orders, agency rules, and the democratic political process.
Mathematics	Knowledge of numbers and their operations and interrelationships, including arithmetic, algebra, geometry, calculus, and statistics and their applications.
Mechanical Devices	Knowledge of machines and tools, including their designs, uses, benefits, repair, and maintenance.
Medicine and Dentistry	Knowledge of the information and techniques needed to diagnose and treat injuries, diseases, and deformities. This includes symptoms, treatment alternatives, drug properties and interactions, and preventive health-care measures.
Personnel and Human Resources	Knowledge of policies and practices involved in personnel/human resource functions. This includes recruitment, selection, training, and promotion regulations and procedures; compensation and benefits packages; labor relations and negotiation strategies; and personnel information systems.
Philosophy and Theology	Knowledge of different philosophical systems and religions, including their basic principles, values, ethics, ways of thinking, customs, and practices and their impact on human culture.
Physics	Knowledge and prediction of physical principles, laws, and applications, including air, water, material dynamics, light, atomic principles, heat, electric theory, earth formations, and meteorological and related natural phenomena.
Production and Processing	Knowledge of inputs, outputs, raw materials, waste, quality control, costs, and techniques for maximizing the manufacture and distribution of goods.

(continued)

(continued)

Knowledge/Course Name	Definition
Psychology	Knowledge of human behavior and performance, mental processes, psychological research methods, and the assessment and treatment of behavioral and affective disorders.
Public Safety and Security	Knowledge of weaponry; public safety; security operations, rules, regulations, precautions, and prevention; and the protection of people, data, and property.
Sales and Marketing	Knowledge of principles and methods involved in showing, promoting, and selling products or services. This includes marketing strategies and tactics, product demonstration and sales techniques, and sales control systems.
Sociology and Anthropology	Knowledge of group behavior and dynamics; societal trends and influences; and cultures and their history, migrations, ethnicity, and origins.
Telecommunications	Knowledge of transmission, broadcasting, switching, control, and operation of telecommunications systems.
Therapy and Counseling	Knowledge of information and techniques needed to rehabilitate physical and mental ailments and to provide career guidance, including alternative treatments, rehabilitation equipment and its proper use, and methods to evaluate treatment effects.
Transportation	Knowledge of principles and methods for moving people or goods by air, rail, sea, or road, including their relative costs, advantages, and limitations.

APPENDIX C

Definitions of Career Clusters Used in Job Descriptions

Following are the definitions of the 16 career clusters that appear in job descriptions in Part III.

01. Agriculture, Food, and Natural Resources. **Work with plants, animals, forests, or mineral resources for agriculture, horticulture, conservation, extraction, and other purposes.** In this cluster, you can work in farming, landscaping, forestry, fishing, mining, and related fields. You may like doing physical work outdoors, such as on a farm or ranch, in a forest, or on a drilling rig. If you have a scientific curiosity, you could study plants and animals or analyze biological or rock samples in a lab. If you have management ability, you could own, operate, or manage a fish hatchery, a landscaping business, or a greenhouse.

02. Architecture and Construction. **Work designing, assembling, and maintaining components of buildings and other structures.** You may want to be part of the team of architects, drafters, and others who design buildings and render plans. If construction interests you, you might find fulfillment in the many building projects that are being undertaken at all times. If you like to organize and plan, you can find careers in managing these projects. Or you can play a more direct role in putting up and finishing buildings by doing jobs such as plumbing, carpentry, masonry, painting, or roofing, either as a skilled craftsworker or as a helper. You can prepare the building site by operating heavy equipment or installing, maintaining, and repairing vital building equipment and systems such as electricity and heating.

03. Arts, Audio/Video Technology, and Communications. **Work in creatively expressing feelings or ideas, in communicating news or information, or in performing.** This cluster involves creative, verbal, or performing activities. For example, if you enjoy literature, perhaps writing or editing would appeal to you. Journalism and public relations are other fields for people who like to use their writing

or speaking skills. Do you prefer to work in the performing arts? If so, you could direct or perform in drama, music, or dance. If you especially enjoy the visual arts, you could create paintings, sculpture, or ceramics or design products or visual displays. A flair for technology might lead you to specialize in photography, broadcast production, or dispatching.

04. Business, Management, and Administration. **Work that makes a business organization or function run smoothly.** In this cluster, you can work in a position of leadership or specialize in a function that contributes to the overall effort in a business, a nonprofit organization, or a government agency. If you especially enjoy working with people, you may find fulfillment from working in human resources. An interest in numbers may lead you to consider accounting, finance, budgeting, billing, or financial record-keeping. A job as an administrative assistant may interest you if you like a variety of tasks in a busy environment. If you are good with details and word processing, you may enjoy a job as an administrative assistant or data-entry clerk. Or perhaps you would do well as the manager of a business.

05. Education and Training. **Work that helps people learn.** In this cluster, your students may be preschoolers, retirees, or any age in between. You may specialize in a particular academic field or work with learners of a particular age, with a particular interest, or with a particular learning problem. Working in a library or museum may give you an opportunity to expand people's understanding of the world.

06. Finance. **Work that helps businesses and people be assured of a financially secure future.** This cluster involves work in a financial or insurance business in a leadership or support role. If you like gathering and analyzing information, you may find fulfillment as an insurance adjuster or financial analyst. Or you may deal with information at the clerical level as a banking or insurance clerk or in person-to-person situations providing customer service. Another way to interact with people is to sell financial or insurance services that will meet their needs.

07. Government and Public Administration. **Work that helps a government agency serve the needs of the public.** In this cluster, you can work in a position of leadership or specialize in a function that contributes to the role of government. You may help protect the public by working as an inspector or examiner to enforce standards. If you enjoy using clerical skills, you could work as a clerk in a law court or government office. Or perhaps you prefer the top-down perspective of a government executive or urban planner.

08. Health Science. **Work that helps people and animals be healthy.** This cluster involves working on a health-care team as a professional, therapist, or nurse. You might specialize in one of the many different parts of the body (such as the teeth or eyes) or in one of the many different types of care. Or you may want to be a generalist who deals with the whole patient. If you like technology, you might find satisfaction working with X-rays or new diagnostic methods. You might work with relatively healthy people, helping them to eat better. If you enjoy working with animals, you might care for them and keep them healthy.

09. Hospitality and Tourism. **Work that caters to the personal wishes and needs of others so that they can enjoy a clean environment, good food and drink, comfortable lodging away from home, and recreation.** You can work in this cluster by providing services for the convenience, care,

and pampering of others in hotels, restaurants, airplanes, beauty salons, and so on. You may want to use your love of cooking as a chef. If you like working with people, you may want to provide personal services by being a travel guide, a flight attendant, a concierge, a hairstylist, or a waiter. You may want to work in cleaning and building services if you like a clean environment. If you enjoy sports or games, you could work for an athletic team or casino.

10. Human Service. **Work that improves people's social, mental, emotional, or spiritual well-being.** Workers in this cluster include counselors, social workers, or religious workers who help people sort out their complicated lives or solve personal problems. You may work as a caretaker for very young people or the elderly. Or you may interview people to help identify the social services they need.

11. Information Technology. **Work that designs, develops, manages, and supports information systems.** This cluster involves working with hardware, software, multimedia, or integrated systems. If you like to use your organizational skills, you might work as a systems, database, or Web administrator. Or you can solve complex problems as a software engineer or systems analyst. If you enjoy getting your hands on hardware, you might find work servicing computers, peripherals, and information-intense machines such as cash registers and ATMs.

12. Law, Public Safety, Corrections, and Security. **Work that upholds people's rights or protects people and property by using authority, inspecting, or investigating.** In this cluster, you can work in law, law enforcement, fire fighting, the military, and related fields. For example, if you enjoy mental challenge and intrigue, you could investigate crimes or fires for a living. If you enjoy working with verbal skills and research skills, you may want to defend citizens in court or research deeds, wills, and other legal documents. If you want to help people in critical situations, you may want to fight fires, work as a police officer, or become a paramedic. Or, if you want more routine work in public safety, perhaps a job in guarding, patrolling, or inspecting would appeal to you. If you have management ability, you could seek a leadership position in law enforcement and the protective services. Work in the military gives you a chance to use technical and leadership skills while serving your country.

13. Manufacturing Career. **Work that processes materials into intermediate or final products or that maintains and repairs products by using machines or hand tools.** In this cluster, you can work in one of many industries that mass-produce goods or work for a utility that distributes electrical power or other resources. You might enjoy manual work, using your hands or hand tools in highly skilled jobs such as assembling engines or electronic equipment. If you enjoy making machines run efficiently or fixing them when they break down, you could seek a job installing or repairing such devices as copiers, aircraft engines, cars, or watches. Perhaps you prefer to set up or operate machines that are used to manufacture products made of food, glass, or paper. You could enjoy cutting and grinding metal and plastic parts to desired shapes and measurements. Or you may want to operate equipment in systems that provide water and process wastewater. You may like inspecting, sorting, counting, or weighing products. Another option is to work with your hands and machinery to move boxes and freight in a warehouse. If leadership appeals to you, you could manage people engaged in production and repair.

14. Marketing Sales and Service. **Work that anticipates the needs of people and organizations and communicates the benefits of products and services.** The jobs in this cluster involve understanding customer demand and using persuasion and selling. If you like using knowledge of science, you may enjoy selling pharmaceutical, medical, or electronic products or services. Real estate offers several kinds

of sales jobs as well. If you like speaking on the phone, you could work as a telemarketer. Or you may enjoy selling apparel and other merchandise in a retail setting. If you prefer to help people, you may want a job in customer service.

15. Science, Technology, Engineering, and Mathematics. **Work that discovers, collects, and analyzes information about the natural world; applies scientific research findings to problems in medicine, the life sciences, human behavior, and the natural sciences; imagines and manipulates quantitative data; and applies technology to manufacturing, transportation, and other economic activities.** In this cluster, you can work with the knowledge and processes of the sciences. You may enjoy researching and developing new knowledge in mathematics, or perhaps solving problems in the physical, life, or social sciences would appeal to you. You may want to study engineering and help create new machines, processes, and structures. If you want to work with scientific equipment and procedures, you could seek a job in a research or testing laboratory.

16. Transportation, Distribution, and Logistics. **Work in operations that move people or materials.** In this cluster, you can manage a transportation service, help vehicles keep on their assigned schedules and routes, or drive or pilot a vehicle. If you enjoy taking responsibility, perhaps managing a rail line would appeal to you. If you work well with details and can take pressure on the job, you might consider being an air traffic controller. Or would you rather get out on the highway, on the water, or up in the air? If so, you could drive a truck from state to state, be employed on a ship, or fly a crop duster over a cornfield. If you prefer to stay closer to home, you could drive a delivery van, taxi, or school bus. You can use your physical strength to load freight and arrange it so that it gets to its destination in one piece.

Index

The 20 Advanced Manufacturing Jobs with the Most Openings, 64–65

The 20 Best Information and Telecommunication Technologies Jobs, 53

The 20 Best-Paying Advanced Manufacturing Jobs, 55–56

The 20 Best-Paying Education Jobs, 56

The 20 Best-Paying Green Technologies Jobs, 57

The 20 Best-Paying Health-Care Jobs, 57–58

The 20 Best-Paying Information and Telecommunication Technologies Jobs, 58

The 20 Best-Paying Infrastructure Jobs, 59

The 20 Education Jobs with the Most Openings, 65

The 20 Fastest-Growing Advanced Manufacturing Jobs, 60

The 20 Fastest-Growing Education Jobs, 60–61

The 20 Fastest-Growing Green Technologies Jobs, 61

The 20 Fastest-Growing Health-Care Jobs, 62

The 20 Fastest-Growing Information and Telecommunication Technologies Jobs, 62–63

The 20 Fastest-Growing Infrastructure Jobs, 63

The 20 Green Technologies Jobs with the Most Openings, 65–66

The 20 Health-Care Jobs with the Most Openings, 66–67

The 20 Information and Telecommunication Technologies Jobs with the Most Openings, 67

The 20 Infrastructure Jobs with the Most Openings, 67–68

The 40 Best Advanced Manufacturing Jobs, 46–48

The 50 Best Education Jobs, 48–49

The 50 Best Green Technologies Jobs, 49–51

The 50 Best Health-Care Jobs, 51–52

The 50 Best Infrastructure Jobs, 53–55

The 50 Best Jobs Overall in All Renewal Industries, 162–163

The 50 Best-Paying Jobs in All Renewal Industries, 164–165

The 50 Fastest-Growing Jobs in All Renewal Industries, 165–166

The 50 Jobs with the Most Openings in All Renewal Industries, 167–168

A

Active Learning skill, 415

Administration and Management knowledge/course, 417

advanced manufacturing

    best jobs, 46–48

    best-paying jobs, 55–56

    current state of field, 37–40

    fastest-growing jobs, 60

    initiatives for renewal, 40

    jobs benefiting from renewal, 41–43

    jobs by demographic

        men, 103–104

        older workers, 78–80

        part-time workers, 89–90

        rural workers, 116–117

        self-employed workers, 97

        urban workers, 114–116

        younger workers, 69–71

    jobs by personality type

        Artistic, 156

        Conventional, 161

        Enterprising, 159

        Investigative, 153

        Realistic, 150

    jobs requiring

        associate degree, 135

        bachelor's degree, 135–136

        long-term on-the-job training, 134

        moderate-term on-the-job training, 134

        postsecondary vocational training, 135

        short-term on-the-job training, 134

        work experience in a related occupation, 135

        work experience plus degree, 136

    jobs with most openings, 64–65

Metropolitan Areas with the Highest Concentration of Workers in Advanced Manufacturing, 169–170

Advanced Manufacturing Jobs with the Highest Percentage of Men, 103

Advanced Manufacturing Jobs with the Highest Percentage of Part-Time Workers, 89

Advanced Manufacturing Jobs with the Highest Percentage of Rural Workers, 116

Advanced Manufacturing Jobs with the Highest Percentage of Self-Employed Workers, 97

Advanced Manufacturing Jobs with the Highest Percentage of Urban Workers, 114–115

Advanced Manufacturing Jobs with the Highest Percentage of Workers Age 16–24, 69–70

Advanced Manufacturing Jobs with the Highest Percentage of Workers Age 55 and Over, 78–79

Advanced Research Projects Agency-Energy (ARPA-E), 35

aerospace industry, 39, 42

Agricultural Equipment Operators, 36

Agricultural Sciences Teachers, Postsecondary, 48, 56, 60, 90, 91, 138, 157, 164, 166, 177–178

Agriculture, Food, and Natural Resources career cluster, 421

Aircraft Structure, Surfaces, Rigging, and Systems Assemblers, 47, 60, 103, 104, 134, 150, 178–179

Alaska "Bridge to Nowhere", 22

Albuquerque, NM metro area, 174

Alexandria, LA metro area, 172

Anderson, SC metro area, 171

Anesthesiologists, 179–180. *See also* Physicians and Surgeons

Anthropology and Archeology Teachers, Postsecondary, 49, 56, 60, 90, 92, 138, 157, 166, 180–181

apparel manufacturing, 40, 43

Architects, Except Landscape and Naval, 53, 59, 63, 87, 88, 101, 112, 113, 128, 129, 148, 156, 163, 181

Architectural and Civil Drafters, 51, 54, 66, 72, 73, 76, 77, 82, 83, 87, 106, 112, 119, 120, 128, 130, 140, 148, 151, 153. *See also* Architectural Drafters; Civil Drafters

Architectural Drafters, 182. *See also* Architectural and Civil Drafters

Architecture Teachers, Postsecondary, 48, 56, 60, 90, 92, 138, 157, 165, 166, 183–184

Architecture and Construction career cluster, 421

Area, Ethnic, and Cultural Studies Teachers, Postsecondary, 49, 60, 90, 138, 157, 166, 184–185

ARPA-E (Advanced Research Projects Agency-Energy), 35

Art, Drama, and Music Teachers, Postsecondary, 48, 60, 65, 90, 92, 138, 157, 163, 166, 185–186

Artistic personality type, 150

    advanced manufacturing jobs, 156

    information and telecommunication technologies jobs, 156

    infrastructure jobs, 156

Arts, Audio/Video Technology, and Communications career cluster, 421–422

associate degree, 132

    advanced manufacturing jobs, 135

    green technologies jobs, 141

    health-care jobs, 143

    information and telecommunication technologies jobs, 145

    infrastructure jobs, 148

Atmospheric, Earth, Marine, and Space Sciences Teachers, Postsecondary, 48, 56, 60, 90, 92, 138, 157, 164, 166, 186–187

Austin–Round Rock, TX metro area, 171, 172

automobile manufacturing, 38–39, 43

B

bachelor's degree, 133

    advanced manufacturing jobs, 135–136

    education jobs, 137

    green technologies jobs, 141

    health-care jobs, 143

    information and telecommunication technologies jobs, 145

    infrastructure jobs, 148

Baicker, Katherine, 27

Bakers, 41

Bakersfield, CA metro area, 171

Baltimore-Towson, MD metro area, 171

Baton Rouge, LA metro area, 171, 174

Beaumont–Port Arthur, TX metro area, 171

Best Advanced Manufacturing Jobs for People with a Conventional Personality Type, 161

Best Advanced Manufacturing Jobs for People with a Realistic Personality Type, 150

Best Advanced Manufacturing Jobs for People with an Artistic Personality Type, 156

Best Advanced Manufacturing Jobs for People with an Enterprising Personality Type, 159

Best Advanced Manufacturing Jobs for People with an Investigative Personality Type, 153

Best Advanced Manufacturing Jobs Overall Employing 8 Percent or More Workers Age 16–24, 70–71

Best Advanced Manufacturing Jobs Overall Employing 10 Percent or More Rural Workers, 117

Best Advanced Manufacturing Jobs Overall Employing 15 Percent or More Part-Time Workers, 90

Best Advanced Manufacturing Jobs Overall Employing 15 Percent or More Workers Age 55 and Over, 79–80

Best Advanced Manufacturing Jobs Overall Employing 50 Percent or More Urban Workers, 115–116

Best Advanced Manufacturing Jobs Overall Employing 70 Percent or More Men, 104

Best Advanced Manufacturing Jobs Overall with 8 Percent or More Self-Employed Workers, 97

Best Advanced Manufacturing Jobs Requiring a Bachelor's Degree, 135–136

Best Advanced Manufacturing Jobs Requiring an Associate Degree, 135

Best Advanced Manufacturing Jobs Requiring Long-Term On-the-Job Training, 134

Best Advanced Manufacturing Jobs Requiring Moderate-Term On-the-Job Training, 134

Best Advanced Manufacturing Jobs Requiring Postsecondary Vocational Training, 135

Best Advanced Manufacturing Jobs Requiring Short-Term On-the-Job Training, 134

Best Advanced Manufacturing Jobs Requiring Work Experience in a Related Occupation, 135

Best Advanced Manufacturing Jobs Requiring Work Experience Plus Degree, 136

Best Education Jobs for People with a Social Personality Type, 157–158

Best Education Jobs for People with an Enterprising Personality Type, 159

Best Education Jobs for People with an Investigative Personality Type, 154

Best Education Jobs Overall Employing 8 Percent or More Workers Age 16–24, 71

Best Education Jobs Overall Employing 10 Percent or More Rural Workers, 118–119

Best Education Jobs Overall Employing 15 Percent or More Part-Time Workers, 91–92

Best Education Jobs Overall Employing 15 Percent or More Workers Age 55 and Over, 81

Best Education Jobs Overall Employing 50 Percent or More Urban Workers, 118

Best Education Jobs Overall Employing 70 Percent or More Women, 105

Best Education Jobs Overall with 8 Percent or More Self-Employed Workers, 97

Best Education Jobs Requiring a Bachelor's Degree, 137

Best Education Jobs Requiring a Doctoral Degree, 137–138

Best Education Jobs Requiring a First Professional Degree, 139

Best Education Jobs Requiring a Master's Degree, 137

Best Education Jobs Requiring Postsecondary Vocational Training, 136

Best Education Jobs Requiring Work Experience in a Related Occupation, 136

Best Education Jobs Requiring Work Experience Plus Degree, 137

Best Green Technologies Jobs for People with a Conventional Personality Type, 161

Best Green Technologies Jobs for People with a Realistic Personality Type, 151

Best Green Technologies Jobs for People with an Enterprising Personality Type, 160

Best Green Technologies Jobs for People with an Investigative Personality Type, 154

Best Green Technologies Jobs Overall Employing 8 Percent or More Workers Age 16–24, 73

Best Green Technologies Jobs Overall Employing 10 Percent or More Rural Workers, 122

Best Green Technologies Jobs Overall Employing 15 Percent or More Part-Time Workers, 93

Best Green Technologies Jobs Overall Employing 15 Percent or More Workers Age 55 and Over, 82–83

Best Green Technologies Jobs Overall Employing 50 Percent or More Urban Workers, 120–121

Best Green Technologies Jobs Overall Employing 70 Percent or More Men, 107

Best Green Technologies Jobs Overall with 8 Percent or More Self-Employed Workers, 98

Best Green Technologies Jobs Requiring a Bachelor's Degree, 141

Best Green Technologies Jobs Requiring a Master's Degree, 141–142

Best Green Technologies Jobs Requiring an Associate Degree, 141

Best Green Technologies Jobs Requiring Long-Term On-the-Job Training, 139–140

Best Green Technologies Jobs Requiring Moderate-Term On-the-Job Training, 139

Best Green Technologies Jobs Requiring Postsecondary Vocational Training, 140

Best Green Technologies Jobs Requiring Short-Term On-the-Job Training, 139

Best Green Technologies Jobs Requiring Work Experience in a Related Occupation, 140

Best Green Technologies Jobs Requiring Work Experience Plus Degree, 141

Best Health-Care Jobs for People with a Conventional Personality Type, 161

Best Health-Care Jobs for People with a Realistic Personality Type, 152

Best Health-Care Jobs for People with a Social Personality Type, 158–159

Best Health-Care Jobs for People with an Enterprising Personality Type, 160

Best Health-Care Jobs for People with an Investigative Personality Type, 154–155

Best Health-Care Jobs Overall Employing 8 Percent or More Workers Age 16–24, 74–75

Best Health-Care Jobs Overall Employing 10 Percent or More Rural Workers, 125–126

Best Health-Care Jobs Overall Employing 15 Percent or More Part-Time Workers, 94–95

Best Health-Care Jobs Overall Employing 15 Percent or More Workers Age 55 and Over, 85

Best Health-Care Jobs Overall Employing 50 Percent or More Urban Workers, 123–124

Best Health-Care Jobs Overall Employing 70 Percent or More Men, 110

Best Health-Care Jobs Overall Employing 70 Percent or More Women, 108–109

Best Health-Care Jobs Overall with 8 Percent or More Self-Employed Workers, 99–100

Best Health-Care Jobs Requiring a Bachelor's Degree, 143

Best Health-Care Jobs Requiring a Doctoral Degree, 144

Best Health-Care Jobs Requiring a First Professional Degree, 144

Best Health-Care Jobs Requiring a Master's Degree, 144

Best Health-Care Jobs Requiring an Associate Degree, 143

Best Health-Care Jobs Requiring Moderate-Term On-the-Job Training, 142

Best Health-Care Jobs Requiring Postsecondary Vocational Training, 142

Best Health-Care Jobs Requiring Short-Term On-the-Job Training, 142

Best Health-Care Jobs Requiring Work Experience Plus Degree, 143

Best Information and Telecommunication Technologies Jobs for People with a Conventional Personality Type, 161

Best Information and Telecommunication Technologies Jobs for People with a Realistic Personality Type, 152

Best Information and Telecommunication Technologies Jobs for People with an Artistic Personality Type, 156

Best Information and Telecommunication Technologies Jobs for People with an Enterprising Personality Type, 160

Best Information and Telecommunication Technologies Jobs for People with an Investigative Personality Type, 155

Best Information and Telecommunication Technologies Jobs Overall Employing 8 Percent or More Workers Age 16–24, 75

Best Information and Telecommunication Technologies Jobs Overall Employing 10 Percent or More Rural Workers, 128

Best Information and Telecommunication Technologies Jobs Overall Employing 15 Percent or More Part-Time Workers, 95

Best Information and Telecommunication Technologies Jobs Overall Employing 15 Percent or More Workers Age 55 and Over, 86

Best Information and Telecommunication Technologies Jobs Overall Employing 50 Percent or More Urban Workers, 127

Best Information and Telecommunication Technologies Jobs Overall Employing 70 Percent or More Men, 110–111

Best Information and Telecommunication Technologies Jobs Overall with 8 Percent or More Self-Employed Workers, 100

Best Information and Telecommunication Technologies Jobs Requiring a Bachelor's Degree, 145

Best Information and Telecommunication Technologies Jobs Requiring a Doctoral Degree, 146

Best Information and Telecommunication Technologies Jobs Requiring an Associate Degree, 145

Best Information and Telecommunication Technologies Jobs Requiring Work Experience in a Related Occupation, 145

Best Information and Telecommunication Technologies Jobs Requiring Work Experience Plus Degree, 146

Best Infrastructure Jobs for People with a Conventional Personality Type, 162

Best Infrastructure Jobs for People with a Realistic Personality Type, 152–153

Best Infrastructure Jobs for People with an Artistic Personality Type, 156

Best Infrastructure Jobs for People with an Enterprising Personality Type, 160

Best Infrastructure Jobs for People with an Investigative Personality Type, 155–156

Best Infrastructure Jobs Overall Employing 8 Percent or More Workers Age 16–24, 76–77

Best Infrastructure Jobs Overall Employing 10 Percent or More Rural Workers, 131

Best Infrastructure Jobs Overall Employing 15 Percent or More Part-Time Workers, 96

Best Infrastructure Jobs Overall Employing 15 Percent or More Workers Age 55 and Over, 88

Best Infrastructure Jobs Overall Employing 50 Percent or More Urban Workers, 129–130

Best Infrastructure Jobs Overall Employing 70 Percent or More Men, 113

Best Infrastructure Jobs Overall with 8 Percent or More Self-Employed Workers, 101

Best Infrastructure Jobs Requiring a Bachelor's Degree, 148

Best Infrastructure Jobs Requiring a Master's Degree, 149

Best Infrastructure Jobs Requiring an Associate Degree, 148

Best Infrastructure Jobs Requiring Long-Term On-the-Job Training, 147

Best Infrastructure Jobs Requiring Moderate-Term On-the-Job Training, 146–147

Best Infrastructure Jobs Requiring Postsecondary Vocational Training, 148

Best Infrastructure Jobs Requiring Short-Term On-the-Job Training, 146

Best Infrastructure Jobs Requiring Work Experience in a Related Occupation, 147

Best Infrastructure Jobs Requiring Work Experience Plus Degree, 149

biofuels, 34

Biological Science Teachers, Postsecondary, 48, 56, 60, 65, 90, 91, 137, 157, 163, 165, 166, 187–188

Biological Technicians, 47, 52, 60, 64, 67, 70, 74, 75, 114, 115, 123, 124, 135, 143, 150, 152, 188–189

Biology knowledge/course, 417

Boise City–Nampa, ID metro area, 173

Bookkeeping and Accounting Clerks, 36

Boston-Cambridge-Quincy, MA-NH metro area, 172

Boulder, CO metro area, 172

Bremerton-Silverdale, WA metro area, 171

bridge collapse in Minnesota, 22

"Bridge to Nowhere" in Alaska, 22

Bridgeport-Stamford-Norwalk, CT metro area, 173

Brownsville-Harlingen, TX metro area, 170

Building and Construction knowledge/course, 417

Bus Drivers, Transit and Intercity, 50, 61, 66, 81, 83, 92, 93, 119, 120, 139, 151, 189–190

Bush, George W., 35

Business, Management, and Administration career cluster, 422

Business Operations Specialists, 36

Business Teachers, Postsecondary, 48, 56, 61, 65, 90, 91, 137, 157, 163, 166, 190–191

C

CalWORKS, 20

Cape Coral–Fort Myers, FL metro area, 173

Cardiovascular Technologists and Technicians, 52, 62, 94, 95, 108, 109, 143, 158, 166, 191–192

career clusters, list of, 421–424

Carpenters, 25, 50, 54, 61, 65, 68, 72, 73, 76, 77, 98, 100, 101, 106, 107, 111, 113, 120, 121, 122, 129, 130, 131, 139, 147, 151, 152, 167. *See also* Construction Carpenters; Rough Carpenters

Cartographers and Photogrammetrists, 54, 63, 87, 88, 112, 113, 148, 152, 192–193

Cedar Rapids, IA metro area, 173

Cement Masons and Concrete Finishers, 25, 54, 68, 76, 77, 111, 113, 130, 131, 146, 152, 168, 193–194

Chandra, Amitabb, 27

Charleston, WV metro area, 171, 173

charter schools, 19

Chemical Engineers, 47, 50, 55, 57, 60, 70, 72, 73, 78, 79, 81, 83, 103, 104, 106, 107, 115, 120, 136, 141, 153, 154, 164, 194–195

chemical manufacturing, 39, 42

Chemical Technicians, 36

Chemistry knowledge/course, 417

Chemistry Teachers, Postsecondary, 48, 56, 61, 90, 91, 138, 157, 166, 195–196

Chemists, 47, 56, 60, 114, 115, 136, 153, 196–197

Child, Family, and School Social Workers, 49, 65, 80, 81, 105, 118, 119, 137, 158, 168, 197–198

Chiropractors, 52, 58, 84, 85, 93, 95, 99, 109, 110, 144, 159, 198–199

Civil Drafters, 199–200. *See also* Architectural and Civil Drafters

Civil Engineering Technicians, 54, 76, 77, 87, 112, 130, 131, 148, 153, 200–201

Civil Engineers, 36, 53, 59, 63, 87, 88, 112, 113, 128, 129, 148, 152, 163, 165, 201–202

Clerical Practices knowledge/course, 418

climate change, 33

Clinical, Counseling, and School Psychologists, 49, 52, 56, 58, 80, 81, 83, 85, 91, 93, 95, 97, 99, 117, 118, 119, 123, 124, 125, 126, 138, 144, 154. *See also* Clinical Psychologists; Counseling Psychologists; School Psychologists

Clinical Psychologists, 202–203. *See also* Clinical, Counseling, and School Psychologists

college education, cost of, 19

College Station–Bryan, TX metro area, 170

Colorado Springs, CO metro area, 172

Columbia, MO metro area, 172

Columbus, IN metro area, 169

Commercial and Industrial Designers, 47, 56, 60, 70, 78, 80, 89, 90, 97, 114, 116, 136, 156, 203–204

Communications and Media knowledge/course, 418

Communications Teachers, Postsecondary, 49, 61, 90, 138, 157, 166, 204–205

Complex Problem Solving skill, 415

computer and electronic product manufacturing, 39, 43

Computer and Information Scientists, Research, 53, 58, 62, 67, 126, 127, 146, 155, 164, 205–206

Computer and Information Systems Managers, 53, 58, 62, 67, 110, 126, 127, 146, 160, 162, 164, 206–207

Computer Hardware Engineers, 47, 53, 55, 58, 63, 67, 70, 71, 75, 79, 86, 103, 104, 110, 111, 114, 115, 126, 127, 136, 145, 153, 155, 164, 207–208

Computer Programmers, 36

Computer Science Teachers, Postsecondary, 48, 56, 61, 90, 91, 138, 157, 166, 208–209

Computer Security Specialists, 210–211. *See also* Network and Computer Systems Administrators

Computer Software Engineers, 36

Computer Software Engineers, Applications, 53, 58, 62, 67, 110, 126, 127, 145, 155, 162, 164, 165, 167, 211–212

Computer Software Engineers, Systems Software, 53, 58, 62, 67, 110, 126, 127, 145, 155, 162, 164, 165, 168, 212–214

Computer Specialists, All Other, 53, 58, 63, 67, 110, 111, 126, 127, 145, 161, 163, 165. *See also* Computer Systems Engineers/Architects; Network Designers; Software Quality Assurance Engineers and Testers; Web Administrators; Web Developers

Computer Support Specialists, 53, 58, 63, 67, 75, 110, 111, 127, 145, 152, 167, 214–215

Computer Systems Analysts, 53, 58, 62, 67, 126, 127, 145, 161, 162, 164, 165, 167, 215–216

computer systems design industry, 30

Computer Systems Engineers/Architects, 216–218. *See also* Computer Specialists, All Other computer technology, role in renewal, 15–16

Computers and Electronics knowledge/course, 418

conservation, 24, 35

Construction and Building Inspectors, 50, 54, 61, 63, 81, 83, 87, 88, 98, 101, 106, 107, 112, 113, 119, 120, 128, 129, 140, 147, 151, 152, 218

Construction Carpenters, 219–220. *See also* Carpenters

construction industry, 25

Construction Laborers, 25, 50, 54, 61, 65, 67, 72, 73, 76, 77, 98, 101, 106, 107, 111, 113, 120, 121, 122, 128, 129, 130, 131, 139, 147, 151, 152, 167, 220–221

Construction Managers, 25, 49, 53, 57, 59, 61, 63, 66, 68, 82, 87, 88, 98, 100, 101, 106, 107, 112, 113, 119, 120, 128, 129, 141, 148, 160, 162, 164, 167, 221–222

Conventional personality type, 150

    advanced manufacturing jobs, 161

    green technologies jobs, 161

    health-care jobs, 161

    information and telecommunication technologies jobs, 161

    infrastructure jobs, 162

Coordination skill, 415

corn-based ethanol, 34

Corpus Christi, TX metro area, 171

Cost Estimators, 53, 59, 63, 68, 76, 87, 88, 112, 113, 128, 129, 148, 162, 163, 168, 222–223

Counseling Psychologists, 223–224. *See also* Clinical, Counseling, and School Psychologists

courses, list of, 417–420

creativity, role in renewal, 16

Criminal Justice and Law Enforcement Teachers, Postsecondary, 49, 61, 90, 138, 158, 166, 224–225

Critical Thinking skill, 415

Cumberland, MD-WV metro area, 172

Customer and Personal Service knowledge/course, 418

Customer Service Representatives, 31

D

Dalton, GA metro area, 169

data processing services, 30

Database Administrators, 53, 58, 62, 67, 86, 126, 127, 145, 161, 163, 165, 225–226

Decatur, AL metro area, 170, 171

Deitz, Richard, 38

demographics

    men, 103–113

    older workers, 78–88

    part-time workers, 89–96

    rural workers, 116–131

    self-employed workers, 97–101

    urban workers, 114–130

    women, 105, 108–109

    younger workers, 69–77

Dental Assistants, 51, 62, 66, 74, 93, 94, 108, 109, 123, 124, 125, 142, 161, 163, 165, 226–227

Dental Hygienists, 51, 58, 62, 93, 94, 108, 123, 125, 143, 158, 162, 165, 227–228

Dentists, General, 52, 57, 83, 85, 93, 95, 99, 109, 110, 123, 124, 144, 154, 164, 228–229

Denver-Aurora, CO metro area, 173

Design knowledge/course, 418

Diagnostic Medical Sonographers, 52, 94, 95, 108, 109, 123, 124, 143, 155, 229–230

Dietitians and Nutritionists, 52, 84, 93, 108, 121, 123, 124, 125, 143, 155, 230–231

doctoral degree, 133

    education jobs, 137–138

    health-care jobs, 144

    information and telecommunication technologies jobs, 146

Dodd, Christopher J., 23

Dothan, AL metro area, 172

Driver/Sales Workers and Truck Drivers, 41

Drywall and Ceiling Tile Installers, 55, 68, 76, 77, 101, 111, 128, 130, 147, 153, 168, 231–232

Drywall Installers, Ceiling Tile Installers, and Tapers, 25

Duluth, MN-WI metro area, 172

Durham, NC metro area, 172

E

Economics and Accounting knowledge/course, 418

Economics Teachers, Postsecondary, 48, 56, 61, 90, 91, 138, 157, 163, 164, 166, 232–233

education

    best jobs, 48–49

    best-paying jobs, 56

current state of field, 18–19

fastest-growing jobs, 60–61

initiatives for renewal, 19–20

jobs benefiting from renewal, 20–21

jobs by demographic

    older workers, 80–81

    part-time workers, 90–92

    rural workers, 118–119

    self-employed workers, 97

    urban workers, 117–118

    women, 105

    younger workers, 71

jobs by personality type

    Enterprising, 159

    Investigative, 154

    Social, 157–158

jobs requiring

    bachelor's degree, 137

    doctoral degree, 137–138

    first professional degree, 139

    master's degree, 137

    postsecondary vocational training, 136

    work experience in a related occupation, 136

    work experience plus degree, 137

jobs with most openings, 65

Metropolitan Areas with the Highest Concentration of Workers in Education, 170–171

role in renewal, 16–17

Education Administrators, 21

Education Administrators, Elementary and Secondary School, 48, 56, 65, 80, 81, 118, 119, 137, 159, 163, 164, 233–234

Education Administrators, Postsecondary, 49, 56, 65, 80, 81, 118, 119, 137, 159, 163, 164, 234–235

Education Administrators, Preschool and Child Care Center/Program, 49, 60, 80, 81, 117, 118, 137, 157, 166, 235–236

Education and Training career cluster, 422

Education and Training knowledge/course, 418

Education at a Glance 2007, 16

Education Jobs with the Highest Percentage of Part-Time Workers, 90–91

Education Jobs with the Highest Percentage of Rural Workers, 118

Education Jobs with the Highest Percentage of Self-Employed Workers, 97

Education Jobs with the Highest Percentage of Urban Workers, 117

Education Jobs with the Highest Percentage of Women, 105

Education Jobs with the Highest Percentage of Workers Age 16–24, 71

Education Jobs with the Highest Percentage of Workers Age 55 and Over, 80

education levels

    associate degree, 135, 141, 143, 145, 148

    bachelor's degree, 135–137, 141, 143, 145, 148

    doctoral degree, 137–138, 144, 146

    first professional degree, 139, 144

    list of, 132–133

    long-term on-the-job training, 134, 139–140, 147

    master's degree, 137, 141–142, 144, 149

    moderate-term on-the-job training, 134, 139, 142, 146–147

    postsecondary vocational training, 135–136, 140, 142, 148

    short-term on-the-job training, 134, 139, 142, 146

    work experience in a related occupation, 135–136, 140, 145, 147

    work experience plus degree, 136–137, 141, 143, 146, 149

Education Teachers, Postsecondary, 48, 61, 65, 90, 92, 138, 157, 163, 236–237

Educational, Vocational, and School Counselors, 49, 65, 71, 80, 81, 91, 118, 119, 137, 158, 167, 237–238

El Centro, CA metro area, 170

El Paso, TX metro area, 170

Electrical and Electronic Engineering Technicians, 47, 50, 55, 56, 57, 59, 64, 70, 72, 73, 76, 77, 78, 80, 82, 83, 87, 103, 104, 106, 112, 115, 120, 128, 135, 141, 148, 150, 151, 153. *See also* Electrical Engineering Technicians; Electronics Engineering Technicians

Electrical and Electronics Drafters, 47, 51, 56, 57, 70, 71, 72, 73, 79, 82, 103, 104, 106, 114, 116, 119, 121, 135, 140, 150, 151. *See also* Electrical Drafters; Electronic Drafters

Electrical and Electronics Repairers, Commercial and Industrial Equipment, 47, 51, 60, 70, 72, 73, 78, 80, 81, 103, 104, 106, 116, 117, 121, 122, 135, 140, 150, 151, 238–239

Electrical Drafters, 240. *See also* Electrical and Electronics Drafters

Electrical Engineering Technicians, 241–242. *See also* Electrical and Electronic Engineering Technicians

Electrical Engineers, 47, 50, 53, 54, 56, 57, 58, 59, 63, 67, 78, 79, 82, 83, 86, 87, 88, 103, 104, 106, 107, 110, 111, 112, 114, 115, 119, 120, 127, 128, 129, 136, 141, 145, 148, 153, 154, 155, 156, 164, 242–243

Electrical Power-Line Installers and Repairers, 51, 55, 57, 59, 105, 111, 121, 122, 130, 131, 140, 147, 151, 153, 243–244

electrical transmission grid, 24

Electricians, 25, 36, 47, 50, 54, 60, 64, 65, 68, 70, 72, 73, 76, 79, 82, 83, 87, 88, 97, 98, 101, 103, 104, 105, 107, 111, 113, 115, 116, 117, 120, 121, 122, 129, 130, 131, 134, 139, 147, 150, 151, 152, 167, 244–245

Electro-Mechanical Technicians, 42

Electronic Drafters, 245–246. *See also* Electrical and Electronics Drafters

Electronics Engineering Technicians, 246–247. *See also* Electrical and Electronic Engineering Technicians

Electronics Engineers, Except Computer, 47, 53, 55, 58, 63, 67, 78, 80, 86, 103, 104, 110, 111, 114, 115, 127, 136, 145, 153, 155, 164, 247–248

Elementary School Teachers, Except Special Education, 21, 49, 65, 80, 81, 105, 118, 119, 137, 158, 163, 167, 248–249

Elevator Installers and Repairers, 54, 59, 111, 129, 147, 152, 249–250

Elkhart-Goshen, IN metro area, 169, 171

Emergency Medical Technicians and Paramedics, 52, 66, 74, 75, 124, 126, 142, 159, 250–251

energy conservation, 24, 35

energy efficiency, 36

energy industry
   current state of field, 33–34
   initiatives for renewal, 34–35

Engineering and Technology knowledge/course, 418

Engineering Managers, 47, 50, 53, 54, 55, 57, 58, 59, 60, 63, 67, 78, 79, 81, 83, 86, 87, 88, 103, 104, 106, 107, 110, 111, 112, 113, 114, 115, 119, 120, 127, 128, 129, 136, 141, 146, 149, 159, 160, 164, 251–252

Engineering Teachers, Postsecondary, 48, 56, 61, 90, 91, 137, 157, 163, 164, 252–253

English Language and Literature Teachers, Postsecondary, 48, 61, 65, 90, 92, 118, 119, 138, 157, 163, 253–254

English Language knowledge/course, 418

Enterprising personality type, 150
   advanced manufacturing jobs, 159
   education jobs, 159
   green technologies jobs, 160
   health-care jobs, 160
   information and telecommunication technologies jobs, 160
   infrastructure jobs, 160

Environmental Engineering Technicians, 54, 63, 76, 77, 87, 88, 112, 148, 152, 166, 254–255

Environmental Engineers, 50, 53, 57, 59, 61, 63, 82, 83, 87, 88, 106, 107, 112, 113, 119, 120, 128, 129, 141, 148, 154, 155, 163, 165, 166, 255–256

Environmental Science and Protection Technicians, Including Health, 50, 54, 61, 63, 72, 73, 76, 77, 92, 93, 95, 96, 141, 148, 154, 155, 165, 257

Environmental Science Teachers, Postsecondary, 49, 56, 61, 90, 138, 157, 258

Environmental Scientists and Specialists, Including Health, 50, 54, 57, 59, 61, 63, 81, 83, 87, 88, 106, 107, 112, 113, 119, 120, 128, 129, 141, 149, 154, 156, 163, 166, 259–260

Equipment Maintenance skill, 415

Equipment Selection skill, 415

ethanol, 34

Evansville, IN-KY metro area, 170

F

Fairbanks, AK metro area, 173

Family and General Practitioners, 260–261. *See also* Physicians and Surgeons

Farmington, NM metro area, 171, 173

Fayetteville-Springdale-Rogers, AR-MO metro area, 173

Finance career cluster, 422

Fine Arts knowledge/course, 418

Finland, United States compared to, 16–17

Fire-Prevention and Protection Engineers, 261. *See also* Health and Safety Engineers, Except Mining Safety Engineers and Inspectors

First-Line Supervisors/Managers of Construction Trades and Extraction Workers, 25, 50, 53, 57, 59, 65, 68, 82, 87, 88, 98, 101, 106, 107, 111, 113, 121, 122, 130, 131, 140, 147, 160, 167, 262

First-Line Supervisors/Managers of Mechanics, Installers, and Repairers, 54, 59, 87, 88, 112, 113, 130, 131, 147, 160, 263–264

First-Line Supervisors/Managers of Production and Operating Workers, 41, 47, 56, 64, 103, 104, 116, 117, 135, 159, 167, 264–265

first professional degree, 133

    education jobs, 139

    health-care jobs, 144

Florence, SC metro area, 172

Florida, Richard, 30

Food Batchmakers, 41

food manufacturing, 38–39, 43

Food Production knowledge/course, 418

Foreign Language and Literature Teachers, Postsecondary, 49, 90, 138, 157, 265–266

Foreign Language knowledge/course, 419

Forestry and Conservation Science Teachers, Postsecondary, 49, 56, 90, 138, 157, 266–267

Fort Walton Beach–Crestview–Destin, FL metro area, 173

Friedman, Thomas, 30

fuel cells, 34

funding. *See* stimulus funding

G

Gainesville, FL metro area, 172

Gainesville, GA metro area, 170

Gamesa, 40–41

gasoline taxes, 22

Geography knowledge/course, 419

Geography Teachers, Postsecondary, 49, 56, 90, 138, 157, 267–268

Geological and Petroleum Technicians, 51, 57, 81, 141, 151. *See also* Geological Sample Test Technicians; Geophysical Data Technicians

Geological Sample Test Technicians, 268. *See also* Geological and Petroleum Technicians

Geophysical Data Technicians, 269. *See also* Geological and Petroleum Technicians

Geoscientists, Except Hydrologists and Geographers, 50, 57, 61, 81, 83, 106, 107, 141, 154, 164, 269–270

geothermal power, 35

Glaziers, 51, 55, 61, 63, 72, 73, 76, 77, 106, 112, 119, 120, 128, 140, 147, 151, 153, 271

global trade

    foundations of success in, 16–17

    role in renewal, 15–16

Government and Public Administration career cluster, 422

Graduate Teaching Assistants, 49, 65, 90, 92, 137, 157, 272

Graphic Designers, 47, 60, 64, 70, 78, 79, 89, 90, 97, 114, 115, 135, 156, 273–274

Greeley, CO metro area, 173

green technologies, 32

    best jobs, 49–51

    best-paying jobs, 57

    current state of field, 33–34

    fastest-growing jobs, 61

    initiatives for renewal, 34–35

    jobs benefiting from renewal, 35–37

    jobs by demographic

        men, 105–107

        older workers, 81–83

        part-time workers, 92–93

        rural workers, 121–122

        self-employed workers, 98

        urban workers, 119–121

        younger workers, 72–73

    jobs by personality type

        Conventional, 161

        Enterprising, 160

        Investigative, 154

        Realistic, 151

    jobs requiring

        associate degree, 141

        bachelor's degree, 141

        long-term on-the-job training, 139–140

master's degree, 141–142

moderate-term on-the-job training, 139

postsecondary vocational training, 140

short-term on-the-job training, 139

work experience in a related occupation, 140

work experience plus degree, 141

jobs with most openings, 65–66

Metropolitan Areas with the Highest Concentration of Workers in Green Technologies, 171

Green Technologies Jobs with the Highest Percentage of Men, 105–106

Green Technologies Jobs with the Highest Percentage of Part-Time Workers, 92

Green Technologies Jobs with the Highest Percentage of Rural Workers, 121

Green Technologies Jobs with the Highest Percentage of Self-Employed Workers, 98

Green Technologies Jobs with the Highest Percentage of Urban Workers, 119–120

Green Technologies Jobs with the Highest Percentage of Workers Age 16–24, 72

Green Technologies Jobs with the Highest Percentage of Workers Age 55 and Over, 81–82

Greenville, NC metro area, 170

Greenville, SC metro area, 170

H

Hagel, Chuck, 23

Hartford–West Hartford–East Hartford, CT metro area, 173

Hattiesburg, MS metro area, 172

Hazardous Materials Removal Workers, 51, 61, 72, 73, 82, 106, 119, 121, 139, 151, 274–275

Health and Safety Engineers, Except Mining Safety Engineers and Inspectors, 47, 54, 56, 59, 60, 78, 79, 87, 88, 103, 104, 112, 115, 128, 129, 136, 148, 156, 165. *See also* Fire-Prevention and Protection Engineers; Industrial Safety and Health Engineers

health care

best jobs, 51–52

best-paying jobs, 57–58

current state of field, 26–27

fastest-growing jobs, 62

initiatives for renewal, 27–28

jobs benefiting from renewal, 28–29

jobs by demographic

men, 109–110

older workers, 83–85

part-time workers, 93–95

rural workers, 124–126

self-employed workers, 99–100

urban workers, 123–124

women, 108–109

younger workers, 74–75

jobs by personality type

Conventional, 161

Enterprising, 160

Investigative, 154–155

Realistic, 152

Social, 158–159

jobs requiring

associate degree, 143

bachelor's degree, 143

doctoral degree, 144

first professional degree, 144

master's degree, 144

moderate-term on-the-job training, 142

postsecondary vocational training, 142

short-term on-the-job training, 142

work experience plus degree, 143

jobs with most openings, 66–67

Metropolitan Areas with the Highest Concentration of Workers in Health Care, 172

role in renewal, 16–17

Health-Care Jobs with the Highest Percentage of Men, 109

Health-Care Jobs with the Highest Percentage of Part-Time Workers, 93–94

Health-Care Jobs with the Highest Percentage of Rural Workers, 124–125

Health-Care Jobs with the Highest Percentage of Self-Employed Workers, 99

Health-Care Jobs with the Highest Percentage of Urban Workers, 123

Health-Care Jobs with the Highest Percentage of Women, 108

Health-Care Jobs with the Highest Percentage of Workers Age 16–24, 74

Health-Care Jobs with the Highest Percentage of Workers Age 55 and Over, 83–84

Health Educators, 52, 62, 67, 74, 84, 85, 108, 109, 123, 124, 143, 158, 166, 275–276

Health Science career cluster, 422

Health Specialties Teachers, Postsecondary, 48, 56, 65, 90, 91, 137, 157, 162, 164, 276–277

Heating, Air Conditioning, and Refrigeration Mechanics and Installers, 25, 50, 54, 66, 68, 72, 73, 76, 77, 98, 101, 106, 107, 111, 121, 122, 130, 131, 140, 147, 151, 153, 277–278

Helpers—Brickmasons, Blockmasons, Stonemasons, and Tile and Marble Setters, 55, 76, 77, 112, 146, 153, 278–279

Helpers—Carpenters, 54, 68, 76, 77, 112, 130, 131, 146, 153, 168, 279–280

Helpers—Construction Trades, 25

Helpers—Installation, Maintenance, and Repair Workers, 50, 54, 61, 66, 68, 72, 73, 76, 77, 92, 93, 95, 96, 106, 107, 112, 113, 121, 122, 130, 131, 139, 146, 151, 152, 167, 280–281

Helpers—Pipelayers, Plumbers, Pipefitters, and Steamfitters, 50, 54, 61, 63, 66, 68, 72, 73, 76, 77, 106, 107, 112, 139, 146, 151, 153, 281–282

Helpers—Production Workers, 41

Hickory-Lenoir-Morganton, NC metro area, 170

high-speed rail systems, 24

Highway Maintenance Workers, 55, 68, 76, 77, 87, 111, 130, 131, 147, 153, 282

Hinesville–Fort Stewart, GA metro area, 170

History and Archeology knowledge/course, 419

History Teachers, Postsecondary, 48, 90, 92, 138, 157, 283

Holland–Grand Haven, MI metro area, 170

Holland, John L., 149

Home Economics Teachers, Postsecondary, 49, 90, 138, 158, 284–285

Home Health Aides, 29

Hospitality and Tourism career cluster, 422–423

Hot Springs, AR metro area, 172

Houma–Bayou Cane–Thibodaux, LA metro area, 170, 171

Houston–Sugar Land–Baytown, TX metro area, 171

Human Service career cluster, 423

Huntington-Ashland, WV-KY-OH metro area, 172

Huntsville, AL metro area, 170, 172

Hurricane Katrina, 22

HVAC Mechanics and Installers, 36

Hydrologists, 50, 57, 61, 82, 83, 106, 107, 142, 154, 166, 285–286

I

Industrial Engineering Technicians, 47, 50, 60, 70, 72, 73, 78, 79, 82, 83, 103, 104, 106, 116, 117, 121, 122, 135, 141, 153, 154, 286–287

Industrial Engineers, 46, 49, 53, 56, 57, 58, 59, 60, 61, 62, 63, 65, 67, 78, 79, 82, 86, 87, 88, 103, 104, 106, 107, 110, 111, 112, 113, 116, 117, 121, 122, 128, 130, 131, 135, 141, 145, 148, 153, 154, 155, 163, 165, 287–288

Industrial Machinery Installation, Repair, and Maintenance Workers, 41

Industrial Machinery Mechanics, 47, 50, 54, 60, 64, 66, 78, 79, 82, 83, 87, 88, 103, 104, 106, 107, 111, 116, 117, 121, 122, 130, 131, 134, 140, 147, 150, 151, 152, 288–289

Industrial Production Managers, 47, 50, 55, 57, 64, 78, 79, 82, 83, 103, 104, 106, 107, 116, 117, 121, 122, 135, 140, 159, 160, 164, 289–290

Industrial Safety and Health Engineers, 290–291. *See also* Health and Safety Engineers, Except Mining Safety Engineers and Inspectors

Industrial Truck and Tractor Operators, 41, 48, 51, 64, 65, 70, 71, 72, 103, 104, 106, 116, 117, 121, 122, 134, 139, 150, 151, 167, 291–292

information and telecommunication technologies
    best jobs, 53
    best-paying jobs, 58
    current state of field, 29–31
    fastest-growing jobs, 62–63
    initiatives for renewal, 31
    jobs benefiting from renewal, 31–32
    jobs by demographic
        men, 110–111
        older workers, 86
        part-time workers, 95
        rural workers, 128

self-employed workers, 100

urban workers, 127

younger workers, 75

jobs by personality type

Artistic, 156

Conventional, 161

Enterprising, 160

Investigative, 155

Realistic, 152

jobs requiring

associate degree, 145

bachelor's degree, 145

doctoral degree, 146

work experience in a related occupation, 145

work experience plus degree, 146

jobs with most openings, 67

Metropolitan Areas with the Highest Concentration of Workers in Information and Telecommunication Technologies, 172–173

Information and Telecommunication Technologies Jobs with the Highest Percentage of Men, 110

Information and Telecommunication Technologies Jobs with the Highest Percentage of Part-Time Workers, 95

Information and Telecommunication Technologies Jobs with the Highest Percentage of Rural Workers, 128

Information and Telecommunication Technologies Jobs with the Highest Percentage of Self-Employed Workers, 100

Information and Telecommunication Technologies Jobs with the Highest Percentage of Urban Workers, 126–127

Information and Telecommunication Technologies Jobs with the Highest Percentage of Workers Age 16–24, 75

Information and Telecommunication Technologies Jobs with the Highest Percentage of Workers Age 55 and Over, 86

Information Technology career cluster, 423

infrastructure

best jobs, 53–55

best-paying jobs, 59

components of, 21

current state of field, 22–23

fastest-growing jobs, 63

initiatives for renewal, 23–24

jobs benefiting from renewal, 24–25

jobs by demographic

men, 111–113

older workers, 87–88

part-time workers, 95–96

rural workers, 130–131

self-employed workers, 100–101

urban workers, 128–130

younger workers, 76–77

jobs by personality type

Artistic, 156

Conventional, 162

Enterprising, 160

Investigative, 155–156

Realistic, 152–153

jobs requiring

associate degree, 148

bachelor's degree, 148

long-term on-the-job training, 147

master's degree, 149

moderate-term on-the-job training, 146–147

postsecondary vocational training, 148

short-term on-the-job training, 146

work experience in a related occupation, 147

work experience plus degree, 149

jobs with most openings, 67–68

Metropolitan Areas with the Highest Concentration of Workers in Infrastructure, 173–174

role in renewal, 16–17

Infrastructure Jobs with the Highest Percentage of Men, 111–112

Infrastructure Jobs with the Highest Percentage of Part-Time Workers, 95

Infrastructure Jobs with the Highest Percentage of Rural Workers, 130

Infrastructure Jobs with the Highest Percentage of Self-Employed Workers, 100–101

Infrastructure Jobs with the Highest Percentage of Urban Workers, 128–129

Infrastructure Jobs with the Highest Percentage of Workers Age 16–24, 76

Infrastructure Jobs with the Highest Percentage of Workers Age 55 and Over, 87 innovation, role in renewal, 16

Inspectors, Testers, and Sorters, 36

Inspectors, Testers, Sorters, Samplers, and Weighers, 51, 66, 72, 82, 121, 122, 139, 161, 167, 292–293

Installation skill, 415

Instructing skill, 415

Instructional Coordinators, 49, 65, 80, 81, 91, 105, 118, 137, 158, 163, 293–294

Insulation Workers, Mechanical, 51, 72, 106, 139, 151, 294–295

Internet service providers, 30

Internists, General, 295–296. *See also* Physicians and Surgeons

Investigative personality type, 150

    advanced manufacturing jobs, 153

    education jobs, 154

    green technologies jobs, 154

    health-care jobs, 154–155

    information and telecommunication technologies jobs, 155

    infrastructure jobs, 155–156

J–K

Jackson, TN metro area, 172

Janitors and Cleaners, 36

Janitors and Cleaners, Except Maids and Housekeeping Cleaners, 21

Johnson City, TN metro area, 172

Johnstown, PA metro area, 172

Judgment and Decision Making skill, 415

Kennewick-Richland-Pasco, WA metro area, 171, 173

Killeen–Temple–Fort Hood, TX metro area, 170

Kindergarten Teachers, Except Special Education, 49, 65, 71, 91, 105, 118, 119, 137, 158, 296–297

knowledges, list of, 417–420

Kokomo, IN metro area, 171

L

Laborers and Freight, Stock, and Material Movers, Hand, 41, 47, 64, 69, 71, 89, 90, 103, 104, 115, 116, 117, 134, 150, 167, 297–298

Laborers and Material Movers, Hand, 41

Lake Charles, LA metro area, 171, 173

Law and Government knowledge/course, 419

Law, Public Safety, Corrections, and Security career cluster, 423

Law Teachers, Postsecondary, 48, 56, 91, 139, 157, 163, 164, 298–299

Learning Strategies skill, 415

Library Science Teachers, Postsecondary, 49, 91, 138, 158, 299–300

Licensed Practical and Licensed Vocational Nurses, 29, 52, 66, 84, 85, 93, 94, 108, 109, 124, 126, 142, 158, 167, 300–301

Lima, OH metro area, 172

lists

    The 20 Advanced Manufacturing Jobs with the Most Openings, 64–65

    The 20 Best Information and Telecommunication Technologies Jobs, 53

    The 20 Best-Paying Advanced Manufacturing Jobs, 55–56

    The 20 Best-Paying Education Jobs, 56

    The 20 Best-Paying Green Technologies Jobs, 57

    The 20 Best-Paying Health-Care Jobs, 57–58

    The 20 Best-Paying Information and Telecommunication Technologies Jobs, 58

    The 20 Best-Paying Infrastructure Jobs, 59

    The 20 Education Jobs with the Most Openings, 65

    The 20 Fastest-Growing Advanced Manufacturing Jobs, 60

    The 20 Fastest-Growing Education Jobs, 60–61

    The 20 Fastest-Growing Green Technologies Jobs, 61

    The 20 Fastest-Growing Health-Care Jobs, 62

    The 20 Fastest-Growing Information and Telecommunication Technologies Jobs, 62–63

    The 20 Fastest-Growing Infrastructure Jobs, 63

    The 20 Green Technologies Jobs with the Most Openings, 65–66

    The 20 Health-Care Jobs with the Most Openings, 66–67

    The 20 Information and Telecommunication Technologies Jobs with the Most Openings, 67

    The 20 Infrastructure Jobs with the Most Openings, 67–68

The 40 Best Advanced Manufacturing Jobs, 46–48

The 50 Best Education Jobs, 48–49

The 50 Best Green Technologies Jobs, 49–51

The 50 Best Health-Care Jobs, 51–52

The 50 Best Infrastructure Jobs, 53–55

The 50 Best Jobs Overall in All Renewal Industries, 162–163

The 50 Best-Paying Jobs in All Renewal Industries, 164–165

The 50 Fastest-Growing Jobs in All Renewal Industries, 165–166

The 50 Jobs with the Most Openings in All Renewal Industries, 167–168

Advanced Manufacturing Jobs with the Highest Percentage of Men, 103

Advanced Manufacturing Jobs with the Highest Percentage of Part-Time Workers, 89

Advanced Manufacturing Jobs with the Highest Percentage of Rural Workers, 116

Advanced Manufacturing Jobs with the Highest Percentage of Self-Employed Workers, 97

Advanced Manufacturing Jobs with the Highest Percentage of Urban Workers, 114–115

Advanced Manufacturing Jobs with the Highest Percentage of Workers Age 16–24, 69–70

Advanced Manufacturing Jobs with the Highest Percentage of Workers Age 55 and Over, 78–79

Best Advanced Manufacturing Jobs for People with a Conventional Personality Type, 161

Best Advanced Manufacturing Jobs for People with a Realistic Personality Type, 150

Best Advanced Manufacturing Jobs for People with an Artistic Personality Type, 156

Best Advanced Manufacturing Jobs for People with an Enterprising Personality Type, 159

Best Advanced Manufacturing Jobs for People with an Investigative Personality Type, 153

Best Advanced Manufacturing Jobs Overall Employing 8 Percent or More Workers Age 16–24, 70–71

Best Advanced Manufacturing Jobs Overall Employing 10 Percent or More Rural Workers, 117

Best Advanced Manufacturing Jobs Overall Employing 15 Percent or More Part-Time Workers, 90

Best Advanced Manufacturing Jobs Overall Employing 15 Percent or More Workers Age 55 and Over, 79–80

Best Advanced Manufacturing Jobs Overall Employing 50 Percent or More Urban Workers, 115–116

Best Advanced Manufacturing Jobs Overall Employing 70 Percent or More Men, 104

Best Advanced Manufacturing Jobs Overall with 8 Percent or More Self-Employed Workers, 97

Best Advanced Manufacturing Jobs Requiring a Bachelor's Degree, 135–136

Best Advanced Manufacturing Jobs Requiring an Associate Degree, 135

Best Advanced Manufacturing Jobs Requiring Long-Term On-the-Job Training, 134

Best Advanced Manufacturing Jobs Requiring Moderate-Term On-the-Job Training, 134

Best Advanced Manufacturing Jobs Requiring Postsecondary Vocational Training, 135

Best Advanced Manufacturing Jobs Requiring Short-Term On-the-Job Training, 134

Best Advanced Manufacturing Jobs Requiring Work Experience in a Related Occupation, 135

Best Advanced Manufacturing Jobs Requiring Work Experience Plus Degree, 136

Best Education Jobs for People with a Social Personality Type, 157–158

Best Education Jobs for People with an Enterprising Personality Type, 159

Best Education Jobs for People with an Investigative Personality Type, 154

Best Education Jobs Overall Employing 8 Percent or More Workers Age 16–24, 71

Best Education Jobs Overall Employing 10 Percent or More Rural Workers, 118–119

Best Education Jobs Overall Employing 15 Percent or More Part-Time Workers, 91–92

Best Education Jobs Overall Employing 15 Percent or More Workers Age 55 and Over, 81

Best Education Jobs Overall Employing 50 Percent or More Urban Workers, 118

Best Education Jobs Overall Employing 70 Percent or More Women, 105

Best Education Jobs Overall with 8 Percent or More Self-Employed Workers, 97

Best Education Jobs Requiring a Bachelor's Degree, 137

Best Education Jobs Requiring a Doctoral Degree, 137–138

Best Education Jobs Requiring a First Professional Degree, 139

Best Education Jobs Requiring a Master's Degree, 137

Best Education Jobs Requiring Postsecondary Vocational Training, 136

Best Education Jobs Requiring Work Experience in a Related Occupation, 136

Best Education Jobs Requiring Work Experience Plus Degree, 137

Best Green Technologies Jobs for People with a Conventional Personality Type, 161

Best Green Technologies Jobs for People with a Realistic Personality Type, 151

Best Green Technologies Jobs for People with an Enterprising Personality Type, 160

Best Green Technologies Jobs for People with an Investigative Personality Type, 154

Best Green Technologies Jobs Overall Employing 8 Percent or More Workers Age 16–24, 73

Best Green Technologies Jobs Overall Employing 10 Percent or More Rural Workers, 122

Best Green Technologies Jobs Overall Employing 15 Percent or More Part-Time Workers, 93

Best Green Technologies Jobs Overall Employing 15 Percent or More Workers Age 55 and Over, 82–83

Best Green Technologies Jobs Overall Employing 50 Percent or More Urban Workers, 120–121

Best Green Technologies Jobs Overall Employing 70 Percent or More Men, 107

Best Green Technologies Jobs Overall with 8 Percent or More Self-Employed Workers, 98

Best Green Technologies Jobs Requiring a Bachelor's Degree, 141

Best Green Technologies Jobs Requiring a Master's Degree, 141–142

Best Green Technologies Jobs Requiring an Associate Degree, 141

Best Green Technologies Jobs Requiring Long-Term On-the-Job Training, 139–140

Best Green Technologies Jobs Requiring Moderate-Term On-the-Job Training, 139

Best Green Technologies Jobs Requiring Postsecondary Vocational Training, 140

Best Green Technologies Jobs Requiring Short-Term On-the-Job Training, 139

Best Green Technologies Jobs Requiring Work Experience in a Related Occupation, 140

Best Green Technologies Jobs Requiring Work Experience Plus Degree, 141

Best Health-Care Jobs for People with a Conventional Personality Type, 161

Best Health-Care Jobs for People with a Realistic Personality Type, 152

Best Health-Care Jobs for People with a Social Personality Type, 158–159

Best Health-Care Jobs for People with an Enterprising Personality Type, 160

Best Health-Care Jobs for People with an Investigative Personality Type, 154–155

Best Health-Care Jobs Overall Employing 8 Percent or More Workers Age 16–24, 74–75

Best Health-Care Jobs Overall Employing 10 Percent or More Rural Workers, 125–126

Best Health-Care Jobs Overall Employing 15 Percent or More Part-Time Workers, 94–95

Best Health-Care Jobs Overall Employing 15 Percent or More Workers Age 55 and Over, 85

Best Health-Care Jobs Overall Employing 50 Percent or More Urban Workers, 123–124

Best Health-Care Jobs Overall Employing 70 Percent or More Men, 110

Best Health-Care Jobs Overall Employing 70 Percent or More Women, 108–109

Best Health-Care Jobs Overall with 8 Percent or More Self-Employed Workers, 99–100

Best Health-Care Jobs Requiring a Bachelor's Degree, 143

Best Health-Care Jobs Requiring a Doctoral Degree, 144

Best Health-Care Jobs Requiring a First Professional Degree, 144

Best Health-Care Jobs Requiring a Master's Degree, 144

Best Health-Care Jobs Requiring an Associate Degree, 143

Best Health-Care Jobs Requiring Moderate-Term On-the-Job Training, 142

Best Health-Care Jobs Requiring Postsecondary Vocational Training, 142

Best Health-Care Jobs Requiring Short-Term On-the-Job Training, 142

Best Health-Care Jobs Requiring Work Experience Plus Degree, 143

Best Information and Telecommunication Technologies Jobs for People with a Conventional Personality Type, 161

Best Information and Telecommunication Technologies Jobs for People with a Realistic Personality Type, 152

Best Information and Telecommunication Technologies Jobs for People with an Artistic Personality Type, 156

Best Information and Telecommunication Technologies Jobs for People with an Enterprising Personality Type, 160

Best Information and Telecommunication Technologies Jobs for People with an Investigative Personality Type, 155

Best Information and Telecommunication Technologies Jobs Overall Employing 8 Percent or More Workers Age 16–24, 75

Best Information and Telecommunication Technologies Jobs Overall Employing 10 Percent or More Rural Workers, 128

Best Information and Telecommunication Technologies Jobs Overall Employing 15 Percent or More Part-Time Workers, 95

Best Information and Telecommunication Technologies Jobs Overall Employing 15 Percent or More Workers Age 55 and Over, 86

Best Information and Telecommunication Technologies Jobs Overall Employing 50 Percent or More Urban Workers, 127

Best Information and Telecommunication Technologies Jobs Overall Employing 70 Percent or More Men, 110–111

Best Information and Telecommunication Technologies Jobs Overall with 8 Percent or More Self-Employed Workers, 100

Best Information and Telecommunication Technologies Jobs Requiring a Bachelor's Degree, 145

Best Information and Telecommunication Technologies Jobs Requiring a Doctoral Degree, 146

Best Information and Telecommunication Technologies Jobs Requiring an Associate Degree, 145

Best Information and Telecommunication Technologies Jobs Requiring Work Experience in a Related Occupation, 145

Best Information and Telecommunication Technologies Jobs Requiring Work Experience Plus Degree, 146

Best Infrastructure Jobs for People with a Conventional Personality Type, 162

Best Infrastructure Jobs for People with a Realistic Personality Type, 152–153

Best Infrastructure Jobs for People with an Artistic Personality Type, 156

Best Infrastructure Jobs for People with an Enterprising Personality Type, 160

Best Infrastructure Jobs for People with an Investigative Personality Type, 155–156

Best Infrastructure Jobs Overall Employing 8 Percent or More Workers Age 16–24, 76–77

Best Infrastructure Jobs Overall Employing 10 Percent or More Rural Workers, 131

Best Infrastructure Jobs Overall Employing 15 Percent or More Part-Time Workers, 96

Best Infrastructure Jobs Overall Employing 15 Percent or More Workers Age 55 and Over, 88

Best Infrastructure Jobs Overall Employing 50 Percent or More Urban Workers, 129–130

Best Infrastructure Jobs Overall Employing 70 Percent or More Men, 113

Best Infrastructure Jobs Overall with 8 Percent or More Self-Employed Workers, 101

Best Infrastructure Jobs Requiring a Bachelor's Degree, 148

Best Infrastructure Jobs Requiring a Master's Degree, 149

Best Infrastructure Jobs Requiring an Associate Degree, 148

Best Infrastructure Jobs Requiring Long-Term On-the-Job Training, 147

Best Infrastructure Jobs Requiring Moderate-Term On-the-Job Training, 146–147

Best Infrastructure Jobs Requiring Postsecondary Vocational Training, 148

Best Infrastructure Jobs Requiring Short-Term On-the-Job Training, 146

Best Infrastructure Jobs Requiring Work Experience in a Related Occupation, 147

Best Infrastructure Jobs Requiring Work Experience Plus Degree, 149

Education Jobs with the Highest Percentage of Part-Time Workers, 90–91

Education Jobs with the Highest Percentage of Rural Workers, 118

Education Jobs with the Highest Percentage of Self-Employed Workers, 97

Education Jobs with the Highest Percentage of Urban Workers, 117

Education Jobs with the Highest Percentage of Women, 105

Education Jobs with the Highest Percentage of Workers Age 16–24, 71

Education Jobs with the Highest Percentage of Workers Age 55 and Over, 80

Green Technologies Jobs with the Highest Percentage of Men, 105–106

Green Technologies Jobs with the Highest Percentage of Part-Time Workers, 92

Green Technologies Jobs with the Highest Percentage of Rural Workers, 121

Green Technologies Jobs with the Highest Percentage of Self-Employed Workers, 98

Green Technologies Jobs with the Highest Percentage of Urban Workers, 119–120

Green Technologies Jobs with the Highest Percentage of Workers Age 16–24, 72

Green Technologies Jobs with the Highest Percentage of Workers Age 55 and Over, 81–82

Health-Care Jobs with the Highest Percentage of Men, 109

Health-Care Jobs with the Highest Percentage of Part-Time Workers, 93–94

Health-Care Jobs with the Highest Percentage of Rural Workers, 124–125

Health-Care Jobs with the Highest Percentage of Self-Employed Workers, 99

Health-Care Jobs with the Highest Percentage of Urban Workers, 123

Health-Care Jobs with the Highest Percentage of Women, 108

Health-Care Jobs with the Highest Percentage of Workers Age 16–24, 74

Health-Care Jobs with the Highest Percentage of Workers Age 55 and Over, 83–84

Information and Telecommunication Technologies Jobs with the Highest Percentage of Men, 110

Information and Telecommunication Technologies Jobs with the Highest Percentage of Part-Time Workers, 95

Information and Telecommunication Technologies Jobs with the Highest Percentage of Rural Workers, 128

Information and Telecommunication Technologies Jobs with the Highest Percentage of Self-Employed Workers, 100

Information and Telecommunication Technologies Jobs with the Highest Percentage of Urban Workers, 126–127

Information and Telecommunication Technologies Jobs with the Highest Percentage of Workers Age 16–24, 75

Information and Telecommunication Technologies Jobs with the Highest Percentage of Workers Age 55 and Over, 86

Infrastructure Jobs with the Highest Percentage of Men, 111–112

Infrastructure Jobs with the Highest Percentage of Part-Time Workers, 95

Infrastructure Jobs with the Highest Percentage of Rural Workers, 130

Infrastructure Jobs with the Highest Percentage of Self-Employed Workers, 100–101

Infrastructure Jobs with the Highest Percentage of Urban Workers, 128–129

Infrastructure Jobs with the Highest Percentage of Workers Age 16–24, 76

Infrastructure Jobs with the Highest Percentage of Workers Age 55 and Over, 87

Metropolitan Areas with the Highest Concentration of Workers in Advanced Manufacturing, 169–170

Metropolitan Areas with the Highest Concentration of Workers in Education, 170–171

Metropolitan Areas with the Highest Concentration of Workers in Green Technologies, 171

Metropolitan Areas with the Highest Concentration of Workers in Health Care, 172

Metropolitan Areas with the Highest Concentration of Workers in Information and Telecommunication Technologies, 172–173

Metropolitan Areas with the Highest Concentration of Workers in Infrastructure, 173–174

Logisticians, 46, 53, 56, 59, 60, 63, 79, 87, 88, 115, 128, 129, 135, 148, 159, 160, 301–302

long-term on-the-job training, 132

advanced manufacturing jobs, 134

green technologies jobs, 139–140

infrastructure jobs, 147

Longview, TX metro area, 171

M

machinery manufacturing, 39, 43

Machinists, 36, 48, 51, 64, 66, 78, 82, 103, 106, 116, 117, 121, 122, 134, 140, 150, 151, 167, 302–303

Madera, CA metro area, 170

Maintenance and Repair Workers, General, 41, 46, 60, 64, 78, 79, 103, 104, 116, 117, 134, 150, 167, 304–305

Maintenance Workers, Machinery, 48, 64, 70, 71, 78, 103, 116, 117, 134, 150, 305–306

Management of Financial Resources skill, 415

Management of Material Resources skill, 415

Management of Personnel Resources skill, 416

manufacturing. *See* advanced manufacturing

Manufacturing career cluster, 423

Manufacturing Extension Partnership (MEP), 40

Mapping Technicians, 306–307. *See also* Surveying and Mapping Technicians

Marketing Sales and Service career cluster, 423–424

Marriage and Family Therapists, 52, 62, 74, 84, 85, 94, 123, 124, 144, 158, 165, 307–308

Massage Therapists, 52, 74, 75, 93, 99, 108, 109, 123, 124, 142, 159, 308–309

master's degree, 133

education jobs, 137

green technologies jobs, 141–142

health-care jobs, 144

infrastructure jobs, 149

Mathematical Science Teachers, Postsecondary, 48, 91, 118, 119, 138, 157, 163, 309–310

Mathematics knowledge/course, 419

Mathematics skill, 416

McAllen-Edinburg-Mission, TX metro area, 170

McCain, John, 17

Meat, Poultry, and Fish Cutters and Trimmers, 41

Mechanical Devices knowledge/course, 419

Mechanical Drafters, 47, 55, 65, 70, 71, 76, 77, 79, 80, 87, 103, 104, 112, 116, 117, 130, 131, 135, 148, 150, 153, 310–311

Mechanical Engineering Technicians, 47, 51, 60, 70, 71, 72, 73, 78, 82, 103, 104, 106, 115, 116, 120, 135, 141, 153, 154, 311–312

Mechanical Engineers, 36, 47, 50, 53, 56, 57, 58, 63, 64, 67, 103, 104, 106, 110, 111, 136, 141, 145, 153, 154, 155, 165, 312–313

Medicaid, 26

Medical and Clinical Laboratory Technicians, 52, 84, 108, 123, 124, 125, 126, 143, 155, 313–314

Medical and Clinical Laboratory Technologists, 52, 84, 85, 108, 109, 123, 124, 125, 126, 143, 155, 314–315

Medical and Health Services Managers, 51, 57, 66, 84, 85, 99, 123, 124, 125, 143, 160, 162, 164, 168, 315–316

Medical and Public Health Social Workers, 52, 62, 66, 84, 85, 108, 109, 123, 124, 125, 143, 158, 163, 166, 316–317

Medical Assistants, 29, 51, 62, 66, 74, 93, 94, 108, 123, 125, 142, 158, 163, 165, 167, 317–318

Medical Records and Health Information Technicians, 52, 66, 74, 75, 84, 85, 108, 109, 124, 126, 143, 161, 168, 318–319

Medical Scientists, Except Epidemiologists, 52, 58, 123, 124, 144, 154, 319–320

Medical Transcriptionists, 52, 66, 74, 75, 93, 99, 108, 109, 124, 126, 142, 161, 320–321

Medicare, 26

Medicine and Dentistry knowledge/course, 419

men, jobs for

advanced manufacturing, 103–104

green technologies, 105–107

health care, 109–110

information and telecommunication technologies, 110–111

infrastructure, 111–113

Mental Health and Substance Abuse Social Workers, 51, 62, 66, 84, 85, 108, 109, 125, 144, 158, 163, 165, 321–322

Mental Health Counselors, 51, 62, 66, 74, 84, 85, 94, 123, 124, 144, 158, 163, 165, 322–323

MEP (Manufacturing Extension Partnership), 40

Merced, CA metro area, 170

Metropolitan Areas with the Highest Concentration of Workers in Advanced Manufacturing, 169–170

Metropolitan Areas with the Highest Concentration of Workers in Education, 170–171

Metropolitan Areas with the Highest Concentration of Workers in Green Technologies, 171

Metropolitan Areas with the Highest Concentration of Workers in Health Care, 172

Metropolitan Areas with the Highest Concentration of Workers in Information and Telecommunication Technologies, 172–173

Metropolitan Areas with the Highest Concentration of Workers in Infrastructure, 173–174

Middle School Teachers, Except Special and Vocational Education, 21, 49, 65, 80, 81, 105, 118, 119, 137, 158, 167, 323–324

Millwrights, 47, 78, 103, 116, 117, 134, 150, 324–325

Mining and Geological Engineers, Including Mining Safety Engineers, 50, 57, 106, 121, 122, 141, 154, 164, 325–326

Minneapolis–St. Paul–Bloomington, MN-WI metro area, 173

Minnesota bridge collapse, 22

Miscellaneous Food Processing Workers, 41

Miscellaneous Production Workers, 41

Mobile, AL metro area, 171, 173

Mobile Heavy Equipment Mechanics, Except Engines, 50, 54, 61, 63, 82, 83, 87, 105, 107, 111, 113, 121, 122, 130, 131, 140, 147, 151, 152, 326–327

moderate-term on-the-job training, 132

   advanced manufacturing jobs, 134

   green technologies jobs, 139

   health-care jobs, 142

   infrastructure jobs, 146–147

Monitoring skill, 416

Monroe, LA metro area, 172

Morristown, TN metro area, 169

Multi-Media Artists and Animators, 53, 58, 62, 67, 86, 95, 100, 126, 127, 145, 156, 163, 166, 327–328

N

Naples–Marco Island, FL metro area, 173

National Infrastructure Bank legislation, 23

National Scorecard on U.S. Health System Performance, 26

Negotiation skill, 416

Network and Computer Systems Administrators, 53, 58, 62, 67, 110, 111, 126, 127, 145, 155, 162, 166, 168, 329–330. *See also* Computer Security Specialists

Network Designers, 330–331. *See also* Computer Specialists, All Other

Network Systems and Data Communications Analysts, 53, 58, 62, 67, 75, 100, 110, 111, 126, 127, 145, 155, 162, 165, 168, 331–333

New Bedford, MA metro area, 170

New Orleans damage from Hurricane Katrina, 22

Niles–Benton Harbor, MI metro area, 170

No Child Left Behind, 19

Nuclear Engineers, 50, 57, 81, 83, 141, 154, 164, 333–334

Nuclear Medicine Technologists, 52, 58, 94, 108, 109, 123, 124, 143, 155, 334–335

nuclear power, 34

Nursing Aides, Orderlies, and Attendants, 29, 52, 66, 74, 75, 84, 85, 93, 95, 108, 109, 124, 126, 142, 159, 167, 335–336

Nursing Instructors and Teachers, Postsecondary, 48, 91, 92, 138, 157, 336–337

O

Obama, Barack, 17–19, 23, 27, 35

Obstetricians and Gynecologists, 337–338. *See also* Physicians and Surgeons

Occupational Health and Safety Specialists, 52, 84, 125, 126, 143, 153, 155, 338–339

Occupational Therapist Assistants, 52, 62, 84, 85, 94, 95, 108, 109, 143, 159, 166, 339–340

Occupational Therapists, 52, 58, 62, 93, 94, 99, 108, 109, 123, 124, 144, 158, 163, 166, 340–341

Odessa, TX metro area, 171, 174

Office Clerks, General, 21, 25

Ogden-Clearfield, UT metro area, 171, 173

oil production/consumption, 33

older workers, jobs for
  advanced manufacturing, 78–80
  education, 80–81
  green technologies, 81–83
  health care, 83–85
  information and telecommunication technologies, 86
  infrastructure, 87–88

Olympia, WA metro area, 173

Operating Engineers and Other Construction Equipment Operators, 25, 50, 54, 66, 68, 72, 73, 76, 77, 82, 83, 87, 88, 105, 107, 111, 113, 121, 122, 130, 131, 139, 146, 151, 152, 167, 341–342

Operation and Control skill, 416

Operation Monitoring skill, 416

Operations Analysis skill, 416

Optometrists, 52, 57, 84, 85, 93, 99, 144, 155, 164, 342–343

Oral and Maxillofacial Surgeons, 52, 57, 84, 85, 93, 99, 100, 109, 110, 144, 152, 164, 343–344

organic food, 35

Orr, James, 38

Orthodontists, 52, 57, 84, 85, 93, 99, 109, 110, 144, 155, 164, 344–345

Orthotists and Prosthetists, 52, 58, 143, 159, 345

Osstem, 41

P

Packaging and Filling Machine Operators and Tender, 41

Packers and Packagers, Hand, 41

Painters and Paperhangers, 25

Painters, Construction and Maintenance, 25, 54, 68, 100, 101, 112, 113, 128, 129, 146, 152, 167, 346

Painters, Transportation Equipment, 48, 60, 69, 71, 103, 134, 150, 347

Palm Bay–Melbourne–Titusville, FL metro area, 173

part-time workers, jobs for
  advanced manufacturing, 89–90
  education, 90–92
  green technologies, 92–93

health care, 93–95
  information and telecommunication technologies, 95
  infrastructure, 95–96

Pediatricians, General, 348–349. *See also* Physicians and Surgeons

Personal and Home Care Aides, 29

personality types
  Artistic personality type, 156
  Conventional personality type, 161–162
  Enterprising personality type, 159–160
  Investigative personality type, 153–156
  list of, 149–150
  Realistic personality type, 150–153
  Social personality type, 157–159

Personnel and Human Resources knowledge/course, 419

Persuasion skill, 416

Petroleum Engineers, 51, 57, 81, 83, 98, 106, 141, 154, 164, 349

Pharmacists, 51, 57, 66, 84, 85, 94, 123, 124, 125, 144, 154, 162, 164, 350–351

Pharmacy Technicians, 51, 62, 66, 74, 93, 94, 108, 109, 124, 125, 142, 161, 163, 165, 167, 351–352

Philosophy and Religion Teachers, Postsecondary, 49, 91, 138, 157, 352–353

Philosophy and Theology knowledge/course, 419

Physical Therapist Aides, 52, 62, 74, 75, 93, 108, 125, 142, 159, 166, 353–354

Physical Therapist Assistants, 52, 62, 74, 93, 94, 108, 109, 124, 125, 143, 158, 165, 354–355

Physical Therapists, 51, 57, 62, 93, 94, 99, 123, 125, 144, 158, 162, 165, 355–356

Physician Assistants, 51, 57, 62, 94, 108, 144, 154, 162, 164, 166, 356–357

Physicians and Surgeons, 29, 51, 57, 66, 84, 85, 99, 144, 154, 162, 164, 168. *See also* Anesthesiologists; Family and General Practitioners; Internists, General; Obstetricians and Gynecologists; Pediatricians, General; Psychiatrists; Surgeons

Physics knowledge/course, 419

Physics Teachers, Postsecondary, 48, 56, 91, 92, 138, 157, 165, 357–358

Pipe Fitters and Steamfitters, 358–359. *See also* Plumbers, Pipefitters, and Steamfitters

Pipelayers, 51, 72, 73, 98, 105, 121, 122, 139, 151, 359

Plumbers, 360–361. *See also* Plumbers, Pipefitters, and Steamfitters

Plumbers, Pipefitters, and Steamfitters, 25, 36, 50, 54, 61, 66, 68, 72, 73, 76, 98, 101, 105, 107, 111, 113, 120, 121, 122, 129, 130, 131, 139, 147, 151, 152, 167. *See also* Pipe Fitters and Steamfitters; Plumbers

Podiatrists, 52, 57, 93, 99, 100, 144, 155, 164, 361

Political Science Teachers, Postsecondary, 48, 56, 91, 92, 138, 157, 362

Ponce, PR metro area, 170

Postsecondary Teachers, 21

postsecondary vocational training, 132

    advanced manufacturing jobs, 135

    education jobs, 136

    green technologies jobs, 140

    health-care jobs, 142

    infrastructure jobs, 148

Preschool Teachers, Except Special Education, 48, 60, 65, 71, 91, 92, 105, 117, 118, 136, 157, 163, 166, 167, 363–364

Prescott, AZ metro area, 174

printing industry, 39, 43

Production and Processing knowledge/course, 419

Production, Planning, and Expediting Clerks, 47, 64, 78, 80, 115, 116, 117, 134, 161, 167, 364–365

Programming skill, 416

Prosthodontists, 52, 57, 84, 85, 93, 99, 109, 110, 144, 155, 164, 365–366

Psychiatrists, 366. *See also* Physicians and Surgeons

Psychology knowledge/course, 420

Psychology Teachers, Postsecondary, 48, 91, 92, 138, 157, 367–368

Public Safety and Security knowledge/course, 420

Punta Gorda, FL metro area, 172

Purchasing Agents, Except Wholesale, Retail, and Farm Products, 47, 56, 64, 78, 80, 114, 116, 117, 134, 161, 368–369

Purchasing Managers, 47, 55, 78, 79, 114, 115, 136, 159, 164, 369–370

Q–R

Quality Control Analysis skill, 416

Radiation Therapists, 52, 57, 62, 108, 109, 143, 158, 165, 166, 370–371

Radiologic Technicians, 371–372. *See also* Radiologic Technologists and Technicians

Radiologic Technologists, 372–373. *See also* Radiologic Technologists and Technicians

Radiologic Technologists and Technicians, 52, 94, 95, 108, 109, 124, 126, 143, 152. *See also* Radiologic Technicians; Radiologic Technologists

Raleigh-Cary, NC metro area, 173

Reading Comprehension skill, 416

Realistic personality type, 149–150

    advanced manufacturing jobs, 150

    green technologies jobs, 151

    health-care jobs, 152

    information and telecommunication technologies jobs, 152

    infrastructure jobs, 152–153

Receptionists and Information Clerks, 29

Recreation and Fitness Studies Teachers, Postsecondary, 49, 91, 138, 158, 373–374

recycling programs, 35

Refuse and Recyclable Material Collectors, 51, 66, 72, 73, 82, 83, 106, 121, 122, 139, 151, 168, 374–375

Registered Nurses, 29, 51, 62, 66, 84, 85, 93, 94, 108, 123, 125, 143, 158, 162, 166, 167, 375–376

Rehabilitation Counselors, 52, 66, 74, 84, 85, 94, 95, 124, 126, 144, 159, 166, 168, 376–377

renewable energy. *See* green technologies

renewal

    advanced manufacturing initiatives, 40

    advanced manufacturing jobs benefiting from, 41–43

    education initiatives, 19–20

    education jobs benefiting from, 20–21

    foundations of success in, 16–17

    green technologies initiatives, 34–35

    green technologies jobs benefiting from, 35–37

    health-care initiatives, 27–28

    health-care jobs benefiting from, 28–29

    information and telecommunication initiatives, 31

    information and telecommunication jobs benefiting from, 31–32

    infrastructure initiatives, 23–24

    infrastructure jobs benefiting from, 24–25

    necessity of, 15–16

    in United States, signs of, 17–18

Reno-Sparks, NV metro area, 174

Repairing skill, 416

Respiratory Therapists, 52, 84, 85, 125, 126, 143, 159, 377–378

Retail Salespersons, 31

Rockford, IL metro area, 169, 171

Rocky Mount, NC metro area, 170

Roofers, 50, 54, 61, 63, 66, 68, 72, 73, 76, 77, 98, 101, 105, 107, 111, 113, 120, 129, 139, 146, 151, 152, 168, 379

Rough Carpenters, 380. *See also* Carpenters

rural workers, jobs for
    advanced manufacturing, 116–117
    education, 118–119
    green technologies, 121–122
    health care, 124–126
    information and telecommunication technologies, 128
    infrastructure, 130–131

S

Sales and Marketing knowledge/course, 420

Sales Engineers, 47, 53, 55, 58, 60, 63, 67, 78, 79, 86, 103, 104, 110, 111, 114, 115, 126, 127, 136, 145, 159, 160, 164, 381–382

Sales Representatives, 36

Sales Representatives, Services, All Other, 31

Sales Representatives, Wholesale and Manufacturing, Technical and Scientific Products, 53, 58, 63, 67, 86, 110, 111, 127, 145, 160, 163, 165, 167, 382–383

San Francisco–Oakland–Fremont, CA metro area, 173

San German–Cabo Rojo, PR metro area, 170, 173

San Jose–Sunnyvale–Santa Clara, CA metro area, 172

SCHIP (State Children's Health Insurance Program), 26–27

school choice, 19

School Psychologists, 383–384. *See also* Clinical, Counseling, and School Psychologists

Science skill, 416

Science, Technology, Engineering, and Mathematics career cluster, 424

SDS (Self-Directed Search), 149

Seattle-Tacoma-Bellevue, WA metro area, 172

Secondary School Teachers, 21

Secondary School Teachers, Except Special and Vocational Education, 21

Secretaries, Except Legal, Medical, and Executive, 21

Self-Directed Search (SDS), 149

self-employed workers, jobs for
    advanced manufacturing, 97
    education, 97
    green technologies, 98
    health care, 99–100
    information and telecommunication technologies, 100
    infrastructure, 100–101, 101

Self-Enrichment Education Teachers, 48, 60, 65, 71, 80, 81, 90, 92, 97, 117, 118, 136, 157, 163, 166, 167, 384–385

Service Orientation skill, 416

Sheet Metal Workers, 50, 54, 66, 68, 72, 73, 76, 77, 106, 111, 140, 147, 151, 153, 168, 385–386

Shipping and Receiving Clerks, 36

Shipping, Receiving, and Traffic Clerks, 47, 64, 70, 71, 79, 80, 114, 116, 117, 134, 161, 167, 386–387

short-term on-the-job training, 132
    advanced manufacturing jobs, 134
    green technologies jobs, 139
    health-care jobs, 142
    infrastructure jobs, 146

skills, list of, 415–416

Slaughterers and Meat Packers, 41

Social Perceptiveness skill, 416

Social personality type, 150
    education jobs, 157–158
    health-care jobs, 158–159

Social Work Teachers, Postsecondary, 49, 91, 138, 158, 387–388

Sociology and Anthropology knowledge/course, 420

Sociology Teachers, Postsecondary, 49, 91, 138, 157, 388–389

software publishing industry, 30

Software Quality Assurance Engineers and Testers, 389–390. *See also* Computer Specialists, All Other

solar power, 34

Solderers and Brazers, 390–391. *See also* Welders, Cutters, Solderers, and Brazers

Spartanburg, SC metro area, 169

Speaking skill, 416

Special Education Teachers, 21

Special Education Teachers, Preschool, Kindergarten, and Elementary School, 49, 65, 80, 81, 105, 118, 119, 137, 158, 391–392

Speech-Language Pathologists, 49, 52, 58, 65, 80, 81, 84, 85, 91, 93, 95, 97, 99, 100, 105, 108, 109, 117, 118, 119, 123, 124, 126, 137, 144, 158, 159, 392–393

Springfield, MA-CT metro area, 170

St. George, UT metro area, 173

State Children's Health Insurance Program (SCHIP), 26–27

steel manufacturing, 40, 43

Stevens, Ted, 22

stimulus funding
    for education, 19–20
    for health care, 27–28
    for infrastructure, 23–24

Storage and Distribution Managers, 393–394. *See also* Transportation, Storage, and Distribution Managers

Structural Iron and Steel Workers, 51, 72, 73, 105, 120, 121, 140, 151, 395

Substance Abuse and Behavioral Disorder Counselors, 51, 62, 66, 74, 84, 85, 94, 125, 143, 158, 163, 165, 396–397

Sumter, SC metro area, 169

Surgeons, 397–398. *See also* Physicians and Surgeons

Surgical Technologists, 52, 62, 67, 74, 93, 94, 108, 109, 142, 152, 166, 398

Surveying and Mapping Technicians, 50, 54, 61, 63, 72, 73, 76, 77, 82, 83, 87, 88, 106, 107, 112, 121, 122, 130, 131, 139, 147, 161, 162. *See also* Mapping Technicians; Surveying Technicians

Surveying Technicians, 399. *See also* Surveying and Mapping Technicians

Surveyors, 53, 59, 63, 87, 88, 112, 113, 130, 131, 148, 152, 163, 166, 400

Systems Analysis skill, 416

Systems Evaluation skill, 416

T

Teacher Assistants, 21

Teachers and Instructors, All Other, 21

Team Assemblers, 48, 64, 70, 71, 79, 116, 117, 134, 150, 167, 401

Technical Writers, 47, 53, 54, 56, 58, 59, 60, 62, 63, 67, 78, 79, 86, 87, 88, 114, 115, 126, 127, 128, 129, 136, 145, 148, 156, 401–402

Technology Design skill, 416

Technology Innovation Program (TIP), 40

Telecommunications Equipment Installers and Repairers, Except Line Installers, 31, 55, 59, 76, 77, 87, 112, 128, 130, 148, 153, 402–403

telecommunications industry, 31

Telecommunications knowledge/course, 420

Telecommunications Line Installers and Repairers, 31, 55, 112, 128, 130, 131, 147, 153, 404

textile manufacturing, 40, 43

Therapy and Counseling knowledge/course, 420

Time Management skill, 416

TIP (Technology Innovation Program), 40

Toledo, OH metro area, 172

Transportation, Distribution, and Logistics career cluster, 424

Transportation knowledge/course, 420

Transportation Managers, 405–406. *See also* Transportation, Storage, and Distribution Managers

Transportation, Storage, and Distribution Managers, 47, 56, 60, 78, 79, 103, 104, 115, 135, 159, 164. *See also* Storage and Distribution Managers; Transportation Managers

Troubleshooting skill, 416

Truck Drivers, 36

Truck Drivers, Heavy and Tractor-Trailer, 54, 67, 87, 88, 101, 111, 113, 130, 131, 146, 152, 167, 406–407

Truck Drivers, Light or Delivery Services, 55, 68, 87, 88, 101, 112, 129, 130, 131, 146, 153, 167, 407–408

Tyler, TX metro area, 172

U

United States
    Finland compared to, 16–17
    signs of renewal in, 17–18

Urban and Regional Planners, 50, 54, 57, 59, 61, 63, 82, 83, 87, 88, 106, 107, 112, 113, 119, 120, 128, 129, 142, 149, 154, 156, 408–409

urban workers, jobs for
   advanced manufacturing, 114–116
   education, 117–118
   green technologies, 119–121
   health care, 123–124
   information and telecommunication technologies, 127
   infrastructure, 128–130
Utica-Rome, NY metro area, 171, 172

V

Vestas Wind Systems, 40
Victoria, TX metro area, 171, 173
Vineland-Millville-Bridgeton, NJ metro area, 170
Visalia-Porterville, CA metro area, 171
Vocational Education Teachers, Postsecondary, 48, 65, 91, 92, 118, 119, 136, 157, 163, 409–410

W

Warner Robins, GA metro area, 173
Washington-Arlington-Alexandria, DC-VA-MD-WV metro area, 172
water conservation, 35
Wausau, WI metro area, 170
Web Administrators, 410–411. *See also* Computer Specialists, All Other
Web Developers, 411–412. *See also* Computer Specialists, All Other
Web search portals, 30
Welders, Cutters, and Welder Fitters, 412–413. *See also* Welders, Cutters, Solderers, and Brazers
Welders, Cutters, Solderers, and Brazers, 47, 51, 64, 66, 70, 71, 72, 73, 103, 104, 106, 116, 117, 121, 122, 135, 140, 150, 151, 167. *See also* Solderers and Brazers; Welders, Cutters, and Welder Fitters

wind power, 34, 40
women, jobs for
   education, 105
   health care, 108–109
Worcester, MA-CT metro area, 170, 172
work experience in a related occupation, 132
   advanced manufacturing jobs, 135
   education jobs, 136
   green technologies jobs, 140
   information and telecommunication technologies jobs, 145
   infrastructure jobs, 147
work experience plus degree, 133
   advanced manufacturing jobs, 136
   education jobs, 137
   green technologies jobs, 141
   health-care jobs, 143
   information and telecommunication technologies jobs, 146
   infrastructure jobs, 149
world trade. *See* global trade
Writing skill, 416

X–Z

younger workers, jobs for
   advanced manufacturing, 69–71
   education, 71
   green technologies, 72–73
   health care, 74–75
   information and telecommunication technologies, 75
   infrastructure, 76–77
Yuba City, CA metro area, 170